W9-CNY-862

Methodologies for Intelligent Systems

The Second International Symposium on Methodologies for Intelligent Systems was sponsored by:

University of North Carolina at Charlotte

The Data Systems Research and Development Program of Martin Marrietta Energy Systems, and the Oak Ridge National Laboratory

Microelectronics Center of North Carolina

Vanderbilt University

University of Tennessee, Knoxville

IBM – Charlotte

Methodologies for Intelligent Systems

Proceedings of the Second International Symposium, held October 14-17, 1987, in Charlotte, North Carolina

Editors:

Zbigniew W. Ras, Ph.D.
Department of Computer Science
University of North Carolina at Charlotte

and

Maria Zemankova, Ph.D.
Department of Computer Science
University of Tennessee, Knoxville

North-Holland
New York • Amsterdam • London

Elsevier Science Publishing Co., Inc.
52 Vanderbilt Avenue, New York, New York 10017

Distributors outside the United States and Canada:

Elsevier Science Publishers B.V.
P.O. Box 211, 1000 AE Amsterdam, The Netherlands

Library of Congress Cataloging in Publication Data

International Symposium on Methodologies for Intelligent
Systems (2nd : 1987 : Charlotte, N.C.)
Methodologies for intelligent systems.

"The proceedings of the Second International Symposium
on Methodologies for Intelligent Systems were sponsored
by the University of North Carolina at Charlotte. . .[et al.]."

Includes index.

1. Artificial intelligence—Congresses. 2. Expert
systems (Computer science)—Congresses. I. Ras,
Zbigniew. II. Zemankova, Maria. III. University of
North Carolina at Charlotte. IV. Title.
Q334.I576 1987 006.3 87-24032
ISBN 0-444-01295-8

Current printing (last digit):
10 9 8 7 6 5 4 3 2 1

Manufactured in the United States of America

TABLE OF CONTENTS

FOREWORD

This volume contains papers which were selected for presentation at the Second International Symposium on Methodologies for Intelligent Systems - ISMIS'87, held in Charlotte, North Carolina at the University Place, October 14-17, 1987. The Symposium was hosted by the University of North Carolina at Charlotte and sponsored by The Data Systems Research and Development Program of Martin Marrietta Energy Systems, The Oak Ridge National Laboratory, Microelectronics Center of North Carolina, IBM-Charlotte, Vanderbilt University, University of Tennessee and University of North Carolina at Charlotte.

The ISMIS symposia are expected to be held every year in October. ISMIS'86 was hosted by the University of Tennessee at Knoxville. ISMIS'88 will be hosted by the University of Torino, Italy.

The Organizing Committee has decided to select the following seven major areas for ISMIS'87:

* Approximate Reasoning
* Expert Systems
* Intelligent Databases
* Knowledge Representation
* Learning and Adaptive Systems
* Logic for Artificial Intelligence
* Man-Machine Interaction

The contributed papers have been selected from about 115 full draft papers by the following Program Committee: R.B. Banerji (St. Joseph's), A.G. Barto (UM-Amherst), J. Bezdek (USC-Columbia), J.R. Bourne (Vanderbilt), J. Carbonell (Carnegie-Mellon), B. Chandrasekaran (Ohio State), M. Fitting (CUNY), B.R. Gaines (Calgary, Canada), J. Gruska (Bratislava, Czechoslovakia), M. Karpinski (Bonn, West Germany and UNC-C), E. Knuth (Budapest, Hungary), V. Lifschitz (Stanford), D. Loveland (Duke), W. Marek (Kentucky), R. Michalski (Illinois-Urbana), J. Minker (Maryland), M. Nagao (Kyoto, Japan), S. Navathe (UF-Gainesville), R. Nelson (Case Western Reserve and UNC-C), J. Nievergelt (UNC-Chapel Hill), E. Nissan (Ben Gurion, Israel), D. Plaisted (UNC-Chapel Hill), L. Saitta (Torino, Italy), E. Sandewall (Linkoping, Sweden), R.R. Yager (Iona College), L.A. Zadeh (UC-Berkeley). The activity of this Committee and of the cooperating referees was a great help in completing the final program. This help is highly appreciated by the organizers.

The Symposium has been organized by the Department of Computer Science of the University of North Carolina at Charlotte with the following Organizing Committee: K. Chen (UNC-C), S.S. Chen (Program Chairman, UNC-C), M. Emrich (ORNL), G. Epstein (UNC-C), A. Jankowski (UNC-C and Warsaw, Poland), K. Kawamura (Vanderbilt), S. Kundu (LSU), A. Pettorossi (Roma, Italy), Z.W. Ras (Symposium Chairman, UNC-C), G.D. Rohrer (IBM-Charlotte), M. Togai (Rockwell International), M. Zemankova (UT-Knoxville).

The Organizers wish to express their thanks to The Data Systems Research and Development Program of Martin Marrietta Energy Systems, The Oak Ridge National Laboratory, Microelectronics Center of North Carolina, IBM-Charlotte, Vanderbilt University, University of Tennessee and University of North Carolina at Charlotte for the sponsorship of ISMIS'87. We would like to express our appreciation to all who submitted papers for presentation at ISMIS'87 and publication in these proceedings, to all of those who contributed to the symposium program, and to Elsevier without whose help the present volume could not be completed.

Zbigniew W. Ras
Maria Zemankova

Charlotte, July 1987

Methodologies for Intelligent Systems

MIDST: AN EXPERT SYSTEM SHELL FOR MIXED INITIATIVE REASONING

Gautam Biswas and *Tejwansh S. Anand*

Department of Computer Science
University of South Carolina
Columbia, S.C. 29208.

ABSTRACT

This paper describes a rule-based expert system shell for mixed-initiative reasoning. Inexact reasoning mechanisms based on the Dempster Shafer evidence combination scheme are incorporated into a combined forward-backward inferencing mechanism. Domain knowledge is stored as rules with associated belief functions. A graphic rule editor facilitates knowledge base construction.

1. INTRODUCTION

The development of a knowledge-based system, involves two main processes: (i) knowledge acquisition and representation, and (ii) the design of appropriate and efficient knowledge manipulation procedures. Earlier expert systems, such as MYCIN and PROSPECTOR for the most part were developed from scratch using dialects of Lisp. Since then it has been realized that the inferencing and knowledge representation components can be separated from the domain-specific knowledge base of one application and applied to a completely different task. These tools or shells as they are sometimes called, facilitate rapid development of the initial prototype of a knowledge based system. In addition, they provide a convenient debugging tool for both knowledge engineers and domain experts. Knowledge base construction aids make it easier for system designers (experts or knowledge engineers) to enter domain specific knowledge in a manner that can be directly interpreted by the built in inferencing mechanism. A number of tools are currently available to aid the knowledge engineering process and the development of prototype systems. They fall into two categories: (i) skeletals systems extracted from previously built expert systems, and (ii) general-purpose languages developed specifically to simplify the knowledge engineering task. Examples of skeletal systems are EMYCIN, KAS and EXPERT [1]. ROSIE, OPS5, RLL and HEARSAY-III [2] are examples of general-purpose programming languages.

This paper discusses **MIDST**, a **M**ixed **I**nferencing expert system shell that incorporates the **D**empster **S**hafer evidence combination scheme for inexact reasoning. The shell was extracted from OASES, an expert system developed for trouble-shooting production processes [3]. Domain-specific knowledge is encoded as premise-conclusion rules. The system designer is also provided with facilities for partitioning the rule base. This paper specifically discusses two aspects of the shell: the control structures of the inferencing mechanism, and the rule editor for constructing the knowledge base. The inferencing mechanism uses a combined forward and backward chaining procedure to guide a mixed-initiative dialogue with the system user. Other features that we are developing for this shell, such as debugging aids, etc., are not discussed in this paper.

Section 2 presents a brief overview of the Dempster Shafer framework. Section 3 discusses the structure of the knowledge base. Section 4 discusses the inferencing and control mechanism. Section 5 discusses the rule editor and simple techniques for checking rule consistency. Section 6 contains the conclusions and directions for future work.

2. THE DEMPSTER SHAFER APPROACH TO INEXACT REASONING

The following discussion follows the notation used in Shafer [4] and Gordon & Shortliffe [5]. The Dempster Shafer formulation is based on a frame of discernment, Θ a set of propositions or hypotheses about the exclusive and exhaustive possibilities in the domain under consideration. The notation 2^{Θ} is used to denote the set of all subsets of Θ. Further discussion is based on two concepts that are adopted for representing the impact of evidence on judgemental conclusions: the *measure of belief* committed exactly to a subset A of Θ (i.e., $A \in 2^{\Theta}$) and the *total belief* committed to A. Exact belief represented by a function, m called the basic probability assignment, relates to the situation where an observed evidence implies the subset of hypotheses, A, but this evidence does not provide any further discriminating evidence between individual hypotheses in A. The measure of **total** belief committed to a subset A ($A \subseteq \Theta$) is defined as:

$$Bel(A) = \sum_{B \subseteq A} m(B), \qquad (1)$$

Methodologies for Intelligent Systems
Z. W. Ras and M. Zemankova, Editors

where the summation is conducted over all B that are subsets of A. For a bpa function m, if $\sum_{A \subset \Theta} m(A) < 1$ then $(1 - \sum_{A \subset \Theta} m(A))$ defines a measure of ignorance, denoted by $m(\Theta)$. In other words, $m(\Theta)$ is the extent to which the observations provide no discriminating evidence among the hypothesis in the frame of discernment Θ.

Judgemental rules provided by experts basically represent patterns of evidence that imply subsets of hypothesis from Θ with weights that correspond to measures of exact belief (details of rule structure are given in section 3). Corresponding to two different pieces of evidence, e_1 and e_2, with bpa's m_1 and m_2, respectively, over the same frame of discernment, Dempster's rule of orthogonal products is applied to combine the effects of observing the two evidence patterns and compute a new bpa, m, that is given by

$$m(C_k) = \frac{\sum_{A_i \cap B_j = C_k} m_1(A_i)\, m_2(B_j)}{1 - \sum_{A_i \cap B_j = \varnothing} m_1(A_i)\, m_2(B_j)} \tag{2}$$

A_i represents hypotheses subsets that are supported by e_1, B_j represents hypotheses subsets supported by e_2, and C_k represents the hypotheses subsets that are supported by the observation of both e_1 and e_2. More detailed discussions on the Dempster Shafer theory of evidence combination appear in [4].

3. KNOWLEDGE BASE STRUCTURE

The knowledge base of MIDST is formulated as a partitioned rule base. The structure of the rules (i.e., the rule language) as well as the partitions are designed to facilitate domain knowledge representation and incorporate uncertainty in terms of belief functions in the Dempster Shafer framework.

The basic rule format is shown in Figure 1. A rule links a pattern on its left hand side (LHS) to one or more conclusions and/or a sequence of actions on its right hand side (RHS). The LHS pattern represents relevant evidence for the conclusions on the RHS. Single pieces of evidence are represented as attribute-value pairs, and, in general, a LHS pattern is a conjunction of pieces of evidence, (e.g., *[(<process-type> <continuous flow>) & (<problem occurrence> <continual>) & (<insufficient capacity> <late in process flow>)]*). Actually, evidence in the LHS pattern of a rule can be one of two types:

(i) **askable**, corresponding to evidence that can be obtained by directly querying the user (therefore, they have expert supplied queries associated with them), or

(ii) **verifiable**, corresponding to evidence obtained from rule firings. (They probably correspond to intermediate conclusions in the chaining process).

Each conclusion on the RHS is a disjunctive set of hypotheses, where an individual hypothesis is represented as an attribute-value pair. In addition to conclusions, the system designer may also specify a sequence of forward-chaining actions on the RHS of a rule. These actions are usually Lisp functions which permit the system designer to perform additional computations, or incorporate overriding control constraints.

To accommodate uncertainty in the rule structure, the shell associates an expert supplied belief value with every conclusion on the RHS. Belief values are modelled as a bpa (basic probability assignment) function in the Dempster-Shafer framework. Note that belief values may also be associated with individual pieces of evidence in the LHS pattern. They may be derived from user input for askable patterns or computed values for verifiable patterns. *BF* is a Lisp function that computes the overall belief value for the LHS pattern of a rule. If multiple pieces of evidence are involved the belief value associated with the LHS pattern is the *minimum* of the belief values of each piece of evidence on the LHS of the rule.

A rule from the OASES [3] system illustrates the rule structure described above:

[(<process-type> <continuous flow>) bf_a and
(<insufficient capacity> <late in process flow>) bf_b] $\rightarrow$
{*[(<cause> <process design>) 0.5]*
[(<cause> <(raw materials, technology, maintenance)> 0.3]}.

The expert may also supply evidence that negates the belief in a conclusion. Such heuristic rules enable the expert to apply the process of elimination in the diagnostic process. In the D-S framework, evidence against a hypothesis is treated as evidence in favor of the negation of the hypothesis in the set theoretic sense.

The knowledge base may be partitioned into separate chunks or units to facilitate the modeling of the expert's reasoning process. Conceptually, partitions represent the breakdown of a complex problem solving process into a sequence of component subproblems. This step-by-step process makes problem solving manageable. OASES, a system for trouble shooting production processes [3], first identifies specific characteristics of the product and process, and uses this information and general symptoms to establish a **general cause** category such as *raw material sourcing, process design*, or *bottlenecks* for the observed problem. Using the general cause as a frame of reference, it obtains detailed information about the process and product, and observed deviations in performance of process components to derive a **specific cause**. For example, starting with *raw material sourcing* as the general cause, the system may establish *inconsistency in raw materials* or *post scale contamination* to be the specific cause for the observed problems in a fiberglass manufacturing continuous flow process. These partitions are sequential in nature in that the problem solving process moves from one partition to another in succession till a problem solution is obtained. The division of the knowledge base into partitions is an attempt to streamline and make efficient the inferencing mechanism by imposing a structure on the problem solving process.

In summary, the partitioning approach provides an efficient way to model the expert's reasoning process. As a result, the knowledge acquisition process can be made more structured, thus, making a little simpler an otherwise difficult task. Another benefit of partitioning that we discuss later is that it makes the Dempster Shafer scheme easier to implement and computationally more efficient.

4. INFERENCING/CONTROL STRUCTURES

The overall inferencing mechanism in MIDST has four main components: the evidence combination scheme, the procedure for selecting the top ranked hypothesis, the query selection mechanism that directs the user-system dialogue, and a top level controller that guides the selection of partitions within the rule base. The overall flow of control for the inferencing mechanism is shown in Figure 2. The system adopts a mixed-initiative form of control. ASKQ queries the user and directs the user-system dialogue. In the initial step, users may be asked to provide facts and evidence that they consider relevant to the problem. DEDUCE forward chains on this evidence, establishes intermediate conclusions, and then GETMAXH ranks the goal hypotheses based on some criteria, such as the belief values associated with each goal hypothesis. The Dempster combining formula (Equation (2)) is used to update belief values of the hypotheses depending on assertions made by the user and previously derived evidence. After the forward chaining process is complete, and a top ranked hypothesis is identified, the shell goes into the backward chaining mode, and CHOOSEQ identifies the best question to ask the user so that the resulting evidence provided might result in a maximum increase in belief in the top ranked hypothesis. At any step in the query answering process, the user may provide more information than the query requires, or the user may consider the current query to be irrelevant, and provide other facts and evidence. This switches the system back into the forward chaining mode, and illustrates the mixed initiative nature of the reasoning mechanism. At each step, before querying the user for more information the exit condition is checked by EXITCHK. The basic function of EXITCHK is to determine if current belief values imply that the system has come to a definite conclusion. Instead of having a fixed EXITCHK function for all partitions, MIDST allows the system designer to define individual EXITCHK routines for individual partitions. For example, a conjunction of the following conditions: (i) ignorance factor $m(\Theta)$ below a certain threshold, (ii) belief value committed to the top ranked hypothesis greater than a second threshold, and (iii) difference in belief values between the two top hypotheses greater than a third threshold defines the EXITCHK function for lower level partitions in OASES [3].

The query selection mechanism implemented in the CHOOSEQ routine makes extensive use of a rule network for efficient processing. Given the leading hypothesis which the system is trying to establish, CHOOSEQ examines the rule network for the current partition to determine which rule can provide the maximum increase in belief in the leading hypothesis. The rule network basically represents a compilation of individual rules, and links conclusions to relevant evidence. For example, Figure 3(b) shows a portion of the rule network corresponding to rules in XX (a system being developed at the University of South Carolina to aid geologists during oil exploration [6]), which deal

-Each partition in the rule base has a separate rule network.

with the identification of the site of a hydrocarbon play. The rules are listed in Figure 3(a). As discussed earlier, both conclusions and evidence are represented in the same conceptual framework: attribute-value pairs. They form the nodes of the network. Rules relate evidence patterns to conclusions, and appear as links in the network. Links have weights associated with them. These weights are directly dependent on the amount of belief that the evidence pattern provides for the particular conclusion it is linked to. Final conclusions represent the top layer of nodes in the rule network. Other nodes correspond to evidence patterns. In Figure 3(b) the top layer of the network represent the plausible values of the site of a hydrocarbon play: within the craton, within the continental shelf along the oceanic margin, and on seaward edge of the continent. In addition there are two other kinds of *dummy* nodes. The first is an *AND* node: a conclusion that depends on a conjunction of evidences is linked to the evidence nodes through this kind of node. The second is a *level* node: nodes corresponding to verifiable evidence patterns are linked to this node. Evidence nodes corresponding to the same attribute converge onto the same level node. For example, in Figure 3(b) the <slope of the play> is a verifiable attribute, and therefore, the nodes corresponding to pieces of evidence (<slope of the play> <landward>) and (<slope of the play> <seaward>) are linked to the same level node. Level nodes link two hypotheses spaces. Conceptually, a hypothesis space is a set of rules that verify the same attribute. In the rule network a hypothesis space will contain nodes that represent pieces of evidence on the LHS of the associated rules, conclusions on the RHS of the rules, and any dummy nodes that are associated in the links between these nodes. It should be noted that the conclusions in a hypothesis space may be final conclusions or intermediate conclusions for the partition and evidence may be either askable or verifiable. In Figure 3(b), the nodes enclosed in the dashed box represent a hypothesis space. Thus, the overall structure of the rule network is that of hypotheses spaces linked to each other through level nodes. To select the most relevant query, CHOOSEQ examines the evidence node linked to the leading hypothesis with the maximum weight. In case this piece of evidence is askable and the user was not asked about it previously, CHOOSEQ returns the corresponding query to ASKQ. On the other hand if the evidence is verifiable, CHOOSEQ calls itself recursively, setting this pattern as the leading hypothesis and descending to the hypothesis space linked to the verifiable attribute. In inferencing terminology, verifiable pieces of evidence represent intermediate conclusions and their presence leads to chaining, or reasoning at multiple levels. To handle chaining in the Dempster Shafer framework each hypothesis space defines a separate frame of discernment (Θ). This approach closely mirrors the method suggested by Gordon and Shortliffe for implementing MYCIN in this framework [5]. The conceptual structures in the knowledge base are the attribute-value pairs and each verifiable attribute defines a frame of discernment extending over the possible values of that attribute. The main reason for such a implementation is to maintain mutual exclusiveness of hypotheses and independence of evidence in the Dempster Shafer framework. Consider an example from XX, with *play slopes landward* as the leading hypothesis. The network in Figure 3(b) identifies *sedimentary facies show evidence of deepening landward* as the most relevant evidence. As this pattern is verifiable, the system invokes the corresponding hypothesis space (i.e., level number 2). Now the leading hypothesis is *sedimentary facies show evidence of deepening landward.* The evidence node linked to this hypothesis is askable and the system asks the associated query:
Do the fauna deepen seaward or landward ?
landward (user response)

The corresponding rule [Figure 3(a)] provides a belief of 0.8 for
sedimentary facies show evidence of deepening landward which is returned as evidence to the next higher level to determine the belief value for *play slopes landward.* For a more detailed description of the network and the propagation of belief values see [7].

5. THE RULE EDITOR

The principal task of an expert system designer is to create, test and debug the knowledge base, and make it consistent with the expert's problem solving process. This section briefly summarizes mechanisms developed for MIDST to facilitate this task. We discuss functions for structuring the overall knowledge base as sequential partitions, entering and editing rules, and obtaining queries for askable evidence. The rules in each sequential partition are compiled into a rule network, which links hypotheses to corresponding evidence patterns. It is assumed that the system designer by prior interactions with the domain expert, has already designed the overall knowledge base partitions, formulated evidence and hypotheses in the problem-solving domain as attribute-value pairs, and formed rules in the format described in Section 3.

The rule editor is implemented on an APOLLO DN3000 workstation with a graphics terminal, and runs under CommonLisp. This programming environment provides support for the display and use of multiple windows on the screen. The salient characteristics of the rule editor are: (i) a multiple window display, (ii) the use of special templates to facilitate rule entry, and (iii) simple mouse-controlled operations that allow the user to interact with the system in multiple windows simultaneously.

The entry of domain knowledge is divided into two distinct phases. In the first phase, the rule editor captures the overall problem solving methodology of the expert, i.e., it makes the system designer specify sequential partitions for each subtask of the problem solving process. The aim is to obtain the sequential partitions (if any), and the hierarchical relationship between them. The skeletal structure of the knowledge base is displayed in the *Structure Window.*

MIDST begins by explaining to the system designer the purposes and benefits of partitions, and then interacts with the system designer to obtain partitions and the relationships between partitions. As an example, consider the system designer entering the domain knowledge base for the OASES system [3]. The rule editor prompts are depicted in bold font and the system designer's input is in italics.

Would you like to enter a new knowledge base?
yes
Enter a name for your knowledge base
OASES
Would you like to partition the knowledge base?
yes
How many steps have you divided your problem-solving process into?
3
How many partitions do you need at step 1?
1
Enter a name for the partition.
process type
How many partitions do you need at step 2?
5
Enter names for the 5 partitions. Separate the names by commas.
continuous flow, batch flow, worker paced, machine paced, job shop
To which partitions in step2 is the partition process type in step1 connected?
all

This information is displayed to the system designer in a separate window (the Structure Window). Window management is done from CommonLisp routines using underlying operating system calls. After relationships between partitions in steps 2 and 3 have been obtained, the rule editor enters the rule entry phase to allow the system designer to enter rules for each partition. The designer is required to input the LHS pattern of a rule, and then the RHS conclusions, and the rule editor converts the rule into the internal Lisp format. When the system designer supplies rules which negate a hypothesis, the appropriate conversion is done automatically. For example, consider the system designer entering an OASES rule:

Enter the attributes and values of the LHS pattern:
(separate attributes and values by a comma; one attribute-value pair per line)
machinery speed and size, good balance

Enter the attributes and values of the RHS conclusions
(one conclusion per line; an attribute followed by a set of values separated by commas)
cause, materials management, workforce
cause, capacity planning, process design

In order to extract the expert's belief in the RHS conclusions given the LHS evidence, the rule editor prompts the system designer to rank the RHS conclusions on a scale of 1-10. Note here that the expert is not supplying an absolute support or belief value for the conclusion, but is merely providing a relative ranking based on his judgement.

Enter the relative ranking for the conclusion on a scale 1-10.
9 3

A very desirable feature of the D-S framework in representing knowledge in uncertain domains is the explicit definition and representation of ignorance. Therefore, in formulating the rule, the editor specifically queries the expert (system designer) as to his belief in the relevance of the LHS evidence, i.e., given that the system designer will be examining other evidence for making conclusions in this frame of discernment, on a scale of 1-10 to what extent does this contribute to making a final conclusion.

On a scale of 1-10 what is the relevance of this evidence in the overall reasoning process?
8

From this the system computes $m(\Theta)$ for the belief function corresponding to this rule to be 0.2 (i.e., 1 - 8/10). The relative ranking supplied by the expert is then normalized to yield the belief values (the m function) for the rule according to the equation:

$$(bf)_{new} = (bf)_{old} \times \frac{1-m(\Theta)}{\sum (bf)_{old}} \tag{3}$$

Using $m(\Theta) = 0.2$, rule editor formulates the following rule:

[(<machinery_speed_and_size> <good_balance>) BF] →
{[(<cause> <materials_management> <cause> <work_force>) 0.6]
[(<cause> <capacity_planning> <cause> <process_design>) 0.2]}

The $m(\Theta)$ value along with the above values represents the measure of exact belief function for this rule.

For the current partition in which rules are being entered, a *Partition Window* displays the partition id, the goals for that partition, and the Lisp form of the last rule that was entered. For every individual piece of evidence, the rule editor prompts the system designer for an associated query. This appears as a separate template within the *Interaction Window*. The list of queries entered for the current partition are stored in the *Query Window*. If a LHS evidence is to be linked to a query that has already been entered, the system designer can place the mouse on the particular query and click a button. This saves him the trouble of having to retype a query. In addition, the system designer can open up the *Query Window* to independently edit the queries.

When the system designer indicates that he has finished entering rules within a partition the rule editor asks him to specify the ASKFIRST queries, if any, for that partition. Finally, rules relating to the transfer of control from the current partition to the partitions it is linked at the next step are obtained from the system designer.

Once the system designer has entered all the rules and the associated queries, the rule editor separates the patterns into askable and verifiable patterns. The verifiable evidence patterns do not have queries associated with them, and thereby need to be derived by firing rules. For each verifiable pattern there must be a set of rules whose RHS contains this pattern. If no rule is found, the system designer is informed, and he either converts the evidence pattern to the askable type by providing a query, or enters rules that could be used to derive the pattern.

The rules are compiled into a rule network by the rule editor and this is displayed in the *Network Window*. The network, discussed in the last section, links the hypotheses to the relevant evidence patterns based on the expert-supplied rules. RHS conclusions of rules correspond to hypothesis nodes, and LHS evidence patterns make up the evidence nodes. Askable evidence nodes contain pointers to associated queries, and verifiable evidence nodes are linked to level nodes as explained earlier. A level node contains the frame of discernment, corresponding to the plausible values of the verifiable attribute it is linked to. The rule editor examines the network to check for incomplete Θ and missing rules. The patterns representing Θ make up the top layer of the network. The lowest layer nodes in the network represent askable patterns and in case there are verifiable patterns not connected to any nodes in the lowest layer, the rule editor prompts the system designer for missing rules. These capabilites are as yet very simplistic but will be further enhanced as the rule editor is redesigned.

In summary, the knowledge acquisition process follows a top down approach. First the system designer specifies the knowledge base framework in terms of sequential partitions linked together in a hierarchical structure. Then the system designer fills in the expert supplied rules into each partition, and the rule editor provides mechanisms for specifying the frames of discernment in each partition, and at different levels within each partition. Special attention is paid to explicitly acquire the measure of ignorance [$m(\Theta)$], corresponding to evidence patterns for each rule. The advantage of having information distributed over several windows are two fold: (i) the system designer can directly go into different windows and modify previously specified information, and (ii) it aids in interactive debugging by making it very easy to browse through the knowledge base

6. SUMMARY

In this paper we have discussed the design and implementation of a rule-based expert system shell that incorporates a partitioned knowledge base structure, a combined forward-backward control structure to provide mixed-initiative interaction, and inexact reasoning mechanisms based on the Dempster Shafer framework. A rule editor is provided to help the system designer construct the knowledge base. Templates are used to facilitate rule entry, and the system designer is engaged in a dialogue to construct the knowledge base partitions. Information is stored in specialized windows such as the Structure Window, Partition Window and the Query Window to allow the system designer to interact with the system in multiple windows. The system also compiles rules into a network to provide a computationally efficient means for implementing the mixed-initiative control structure.

At present, we are developing mechanisms for debugging the knowledge base. These include "HOW" and "WHY" type explanation facilities, and mechanisms for single-stepping through a case. Efforts are also being made to improve the capabilities of the rule editor, and incorporate more efficient schemes for computing the Dempster Shafer belief functions [8].

REFERENCES

[1] D.A. Waterman and F. Hayes-Roth, "An Investigation of Tools for Building Expert Systems", from **Building Expert Systems**, F. Hayes-Roth, D.A. Waterman, and D.B. Lenat, eds., pp. 169-215, Addison-Weseley, Reading, MA, 1983.

[2] S.M. Weiss and C.A. Kulikowski, **A Practical Guide to Designing Expert Systems**, Rowman and Allenheld, Totowa, NJ, 1984.

[3] G. Biswas, R. Abramczyk and M. Oliff, "OASES: An Expert System for Operations Analysis - The System for General Cause Analysis", *IEEE Trans. on Systems, Man, and Cybernetics*, vol. SMC-17, pp. 133-145, 1987.

[4] G. Shafer, **A Mathematical Theory of Evidence**, Princeton Univ. Press, NJ, 1976.

[5] J. Gordon and E.H. Shortliffe, "A Method for Managing Evidential Reasoning in a Hierarchical Hypothesis Space", *Artificial Intelligence*, vol. 26, pp. 323-357, 1985.

[6] C.G.C. Kendall, J.C. Bezdek, and G. Biswas, "XX: Expert Explorer; An Expert Database System of "Electronic Case Histories of Oil Fields", *Tech. Report*, Depts. of Geology and Computer Science, Univ. of South Carolina, May 1986.

[7] T.S. Anand, **MIDST: An Expert System Shell for Mixed-Initiative Reasoning**, M.S. Thesis, Department of Computer Science, University of South Carolina, Columbia, July 1987.

[8] P.P. Shenoy and G. Shafer, "Propagating Belief Functions with Local Computations", *IEEE Computer*, vol. 1, pp. 43-51, 1986.

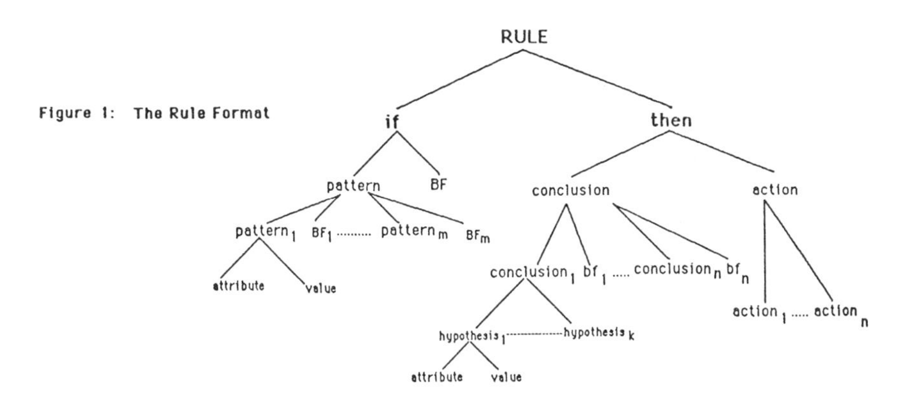

Figure 1: The Rule Format

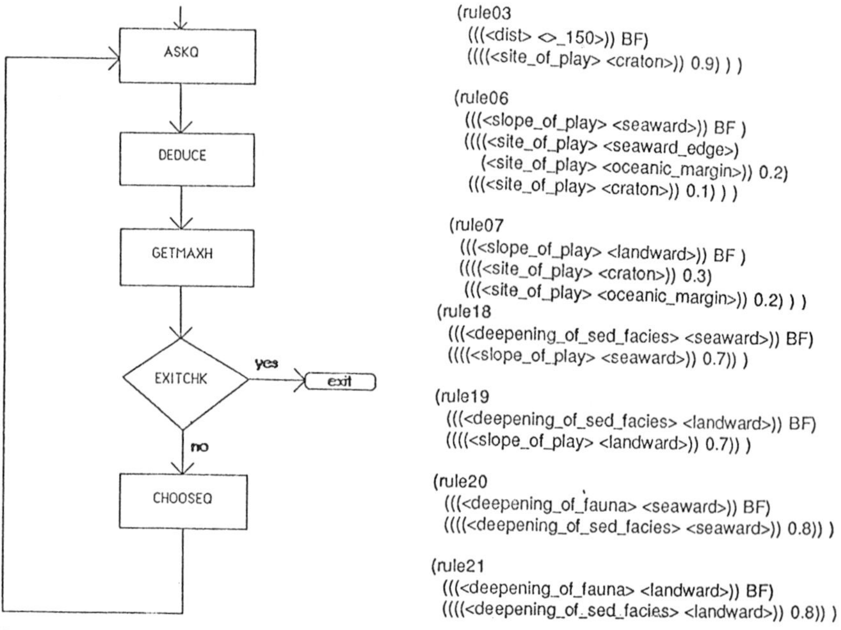


```
(rule03
  (((<dist> <>_150>)) BF)
  ((((<site_of_play> <craton>)) 0.9) ) )

(rule06
  (((<slope_of_play> <seaward>)) BF )
  ((((<site_of_play> <seaward_edge>)
     (<site_of_play> <oceanic_margin>)) 0.2)
  (((<site_of_play> <craton>)) 0.1) ) )

(rule07
  (((<slope_of_play> <landward>)) BF )
  ((((<site_of_play> <craton>)) 0.3)
  (((<site_of_play> <oceanic_margin>)) 0.2) ) )
(rule18
  (((<deepening_of_sed_facies> <seaward>)) BF)
  ((((<slope_of_play> <seaward>)) 0.7)) )

(rule19
  (((<deepening_of_sed_facies> <landward>)) BF)
  ((((<slope_of_play> <landward>)) 0.7)) )

(rule20
  (((<deepening_of_fauna> <seaward>)) BF)
  ((((<deepening_of_sed_facies> <seaward>)) 0.8)) )

(rule21
  (((<deepening_of_fauna> <landward>)) BF)
  ((((<deepening_of_sed_facies> <landward>)) 0.8)) )
```

Figure 2: The Inference Control Structure

Figure 3(a): Some of the XX rules

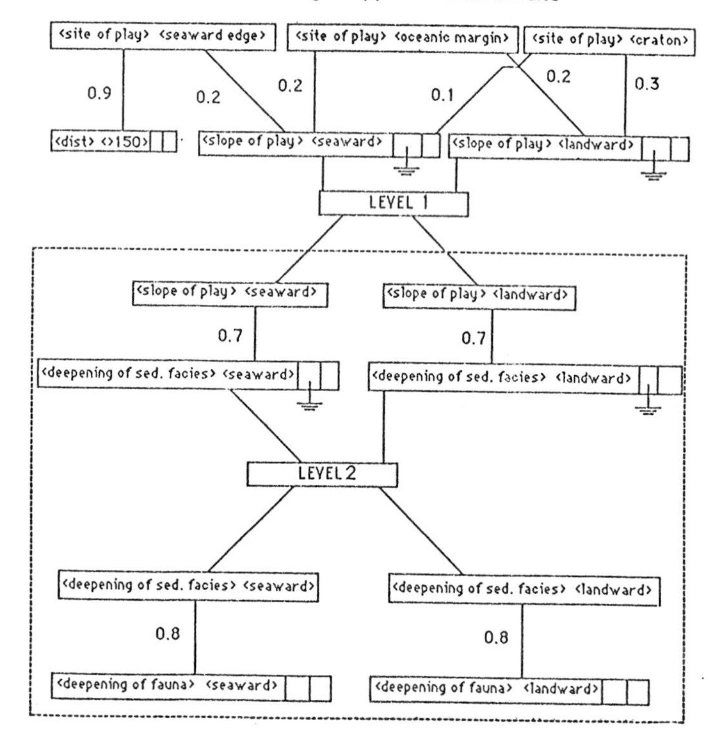

Figure 3(b): A Section of the Rule Network for XX

A SPATIAL REASONING AND DECISION SUPPORT SYSTEM

S. Chen*, M. Zhang and W. Zhang
Department of Computer Science
University of North Carolina
Charlotte, NC 28223

ABSTRACT

A spatial reasoning and decision support (SRDS) system is developed for military battlefield management and target tracking, environmental planning, land development decision support, and industrial robotics and automation. This system consists of several components: (1) a human-machine interface module, (2) a 2-D and 3-D spatial database management system, (3) an image processing and understanding module, (4) a spatial and application domain knowledge base, and (5) a LISP-based approximate reasoning and decision support system. In order to illustrate the ideas, we shall present an airport-site planning system.

1. INTRODUCTION

A spatial information system with reasoning and decision support capabilities are useful to military, industrial and environmental applications. There have been a large number of expert and decision support systems concerning non-spatial information and knowledge. On the contrary, systems which are concerned with additional spatial information are only in the research stage. In dealing with spatial (2-D or 3-D) data and knowledge, some new techniques are required. The complexity of systems is also much greater than ordinary expert and decision support systems.

There are several different kinds of spatial reasoning. One kind is rule-based image understanding and computer vision. The goal is to understand sensory data (or image). The second kind is robotic control and manipulation in industrial and military automation which requires reasoning about the geometry of the work space. The third kind is concerned with general spatial information with reasoning and decision support capabilities. Such systems are used for decision support of various application domains involving spatial information. Moreover, the first two kinds may be contained in the last kind as subsystems. Incrementally, we are expanding the system to an intelligent workstation, and further to a distributed environment of intelligent workstations.

A basic system characteristics is uncertainty and approximate reasoning [1]-[10]. In computer vision and spatial reasoning, sensory data are usually partial and uncertain. Some requirements of these areas are beyond the scope of the current state-of-the-art of uncertainty and approximate reasoning. In this paper, spatial features are extracted and sent, together with linguistic and numerical features, to an uncertainty and approximate reasoning scheme which provides decision support outputs. Another characteristic is the capability of fuzzy linguistic variables for human-machine interface. For instance, we may reason with ratings of {not important, important, very important, extremely important}.

---

*Research has been partially supported by NSF.

Methodologies for Intelligent Systems
Z. W. Ras and M. Zemankova, Editors

2. SYSTEM DESCRIPTION

The SRDS system has several components: (1) a human-machine interface module, (2) a 2-D or 3-D spatial semantic database management system, (3) an image processing module, (4) a spatial and application knowledge base, and (5) a reasoning and decision support system. A decision maker has a visual/literal interface with the main system. The visual interface deals with 2-D or 3-D images and data. Preprocessed or on-line sensed data and images may be input into the main system. The output of the system is displayed to the decision maker. The literal interface is an OPS5 and LISP based system with natural language capability. The spatial semantic database is composed of spatial data, such as geographical data and maps, (2) binary preprocessed data, such as freeways, rivers and specific area boundaries, (3) semantic information of spatial data, such as population, weather, and description of a scenic site. The image processing module operates on the spatial database under the OPS5 control system. Some common operations of the image processing module are intersection, union, thinning, complementation, and display commands. Although we have a few hundreds of image processing commands, only a few of them will be used in the airport-site planning system. Spatial information and data output of the image processing module are represented by features which are sent to the reasoning and decision support system.

The knowledge base encodes spatial knowledge and application for reasoning and decision support. Adopted in this system is a structured combination of two main knowledge representation schemes - production rules and fuzzy relations. In addition, semantics of linguistic terms are represented by fuzzy sets in the three categories: rating, weighting and certainty [9],[10]. The advantage of this system is a combination of numerical computation and linguistic representation. The reasoning system employes both exact and approximate reasoning.

This system is developed on a MICROVAX GPX Workstation under VMS operating system with a VAX 11/780 host. It is suitable for a distributed environment of workstations communicating among themselves or through a host computer. The SRDS system architecture is described in Figure 1. The human-machine interface is depicted in Figure 2.

3. SPATIAL DATABASE

The spatial database is composed of spatial data, such as geographical data and maps, binary preprocessed data, such as freeways, rivers, airport runways and specific area boundaries, and semantic information of spatial data, such as population, weather, and description of a specific area (Figure 3). The first kind of data are symbolic and gray-scale images. The second kind of data are binary templates and images. The third kind of data are numerical and linguistic attributes of the first two kinds of images. Geographical data, such as elevation of a region, may be represented by 2-D histogram in the 3-D space.

Spatial data types of the database is quite complex. Moreover, spatial data constraints are different from ordinary data constraints. Geometric and topological relations among spatial data entities are considered. Database query involves with pictorial display of spatial information. This is the visual interface mentioned in the introduction. Associated with each spatial data entity, there are several numerical and linguistic attributes. In the reasoning and decision support system, additional attributes and features may be derived and used for reaching decisions. In order to aid extraction of additional attributes and features, an image processing module is used to manipulate geographical data and preprocessed binary data.

This relational database system is constructed from pictorial and image data. Extracted descriptions and inherent registrations of images are integrated in the relational database. We want to retrieve not only image contents, but also image registrations. Through the interface between our database system and the image processing support system, query may be translated to primitive image operations.

4. THE IMAGE PROCESSING MODULE

A set of primitive operations on images (written in Fortran) are defined in the following :

(1) Belt Given a line image and a width parameter, a belted area is returned.
(2) Circle Given some point image and a radius, a circled area is returned.
(3) Complement Given an area image, the complement image is returned.
(4) Threshold Given an image, a higher and a lower thresholds, an image is returned that is between the thresholds.
(5) Mask Any region is masked out by a certain mask.
(6) Label An image is labelled by a numerical or linguistic label.
(7) Union The union of two regions is returned.
(8) Intersection The intersection of two regions is returned.
(9) Getattribute(i) For any region, attribute(i) of that region is returned. Examples include area, population, weather, elevation, and etc.

The above mentioned operations will be used commonly in the system. Other image operations may be used whenever necessary [15],[16].

5. AN AIRPORT-SITE PLANNING SYSTEM

This system will be useful to select optimal sites for a proposed airport and to evaluate impacts of an existing or a planned airport. There are three major impact kinds: economic, social and environmental impacts. The selection of an optimal site is to optimize the overall impact. Some impacts have numerical measurements, such as dollars in economic impacts. Others can not be measured numerically. The aesthetic impact of airport visibility to residents of community and physical and logical impacts to terrestrial and aquatic ecosystems are better described by linguistic impacts.

The phase 1 of our airport optimization procedure is to derive a set of feasible sites from many possible locations. A list of constraints making an location of the airport infeasible is represented by LISP functions which deal with a set of primitive image operations. There are three types of contraints: (1) topographical constraints, (2) legal constraints and (3) locational constraints. Topographical constraints may be that the terrain is too variable in elevation; and rivers and streams are perpendicular to runways. Legal constraints may be national historic landmarks, and national wilderness areas. Locational constraints include major highways, railroads, high-voltage power corridors, urban areas, major recreational areas and existing airports.

In phase 1, some rules in the knowledge base are given:
(1) The proposed airport should be more than 3 miles from major highways and railroads.
(2) It should be more than 5 miles from urban and residential areas, parks and recreational areas.
(3) It should be more than 5 miles from the high voltage power corridors, and more than 50 miles from existing airports.
(4) Standard deviation of elevation within selected airport area should be less than 6 feet.
(5) It should not be located at unpermissible areas, e.g. national wilderness areas and national wildlife refuges.

These rules are domain dependent and are contained in the application knowledge base. The list of spatial data collected for our spatial information system includes: 1) elevation, 2) slope, 3) aspect, 4) utilities, 5) topographical shape, 6) streams and rivers, 7) urban density, 8) marshes and wetlands, 9) general land use, 10) roads, 11) soils, 12) powerlines, 13) political boundaries, 14) lakes, 15) recreational sites, 16) climate, 17) watershed boundaries, 18) registered historic sites, 19) national wilderness areas.

Phase 2 of the optimization procedure involves with approximate reasoning and decision support. We use the framework of linguistic fuzzy relation, linguistic similarity relation and linguistic transitive closure [9],[10] which are generalizations of numerical fuzzy relation, numerical similarity relation and the extension principle [7],[8]. The relation matrix of a linguistic fuzzy relation has elements which are linguistic terms instead of numbers as in conventional binary relations and fuzzy relations. Each linguistic term has one predefined fuzzy subset as a prototype membership function. The terms may be subjectively entered to the matrix in a database or derived from linguistic approximation. Two algorithms developed in [7], [8] will be used to obtain linguistic transitive closures.

In [7], Zadeh generalized the notion of binary relation to fuzzy binary relation which is defined as a fuzzy collection of ordered pairs. The membership function which associates with each pair is the strength of the relation. There is a matrix, called the relation matrix, associated with each fuzzy relation. In [8], Zadeh generalized the notion of equivalence relation to similarity relation which is defined as a fuzzy relation on the product of a set with reflexive, symmetric and max-min transitive relations. Since Zadeh's fuzzy relations and similarity relations are expressed numerically, they are called numerical fuzzy and similarity relations here. In [8], Zadeh defined and proved that, if R is a numerical fuzzy relation matrix of order n, then the transitive closure of R is the sum of n powers of R.

Since spatial information and knowledge are often uncertain and incomplete, we use fuzzy relations for spatial knowledge representation. This is a good choice, because fuzzy knowledge-based systems have been widely employed in knowledge-based information retrieval, decision support and management systems. A general point of view of this representation scheme is the fuzzy relational database. We illustrate the basic idea by a simple example: Let X be a set of objects, C be a set of concepts and R_1, R_2, R_3 be relationship functions. R_1 indicates that a given object is related to a concept with a weight in the interval [0,1]. R_2 and R_3 indicate strengths of relations in [0,1] that can be assigned to each pair of objects and concepts. In the spatial information system, a fuzzy relational database has advantages over ordinary relational database in the following aspects: (1) imprecise and uncertain knowledge representation, (2) relationships can be propagated through transitive closure computation or fuzzy rules so that new relationships can be inferred by approximate reasoning, (3) This database supports the aggregation of subjective opinions of multiple experts so that knowledge acquisition is made easier. In Figure 4, our approximate reasoning scheme is illustrated by an example.

6. CONCLUSION

A spatial information system with approximate reasoning is proposed. The development of this system involves with integration of several systems - the image processing system, the fuzzy knowledge representation system, the fuzzy and ordinary inference engine, the spatial database management system and the human-machine interface. Our approach is evolutive and incremental with the goal of developing an intelligent system.

REFERENCES

1. F. Hayes-Roth, D. A. Waterman and D. B. Lenat, Building Expert Systems, Addison-Wesley, 1983.
2. E. H. Shortliffe and B. G. Buchanan, A model of inexact reasoning in medicine, Mathematical Biosciences, 23 (1975), 351-379.
3. A. P. Dempster, Upper and lower probabilities induced by multivalued mappings, Annals of Math. Statistics, 38 (1967), 325-339.
4. G. Shafer, A Mathematical Theory of Evidence, Princeton University Press, 1976.
5. D. Dubois and H. Prade, Combination and propagation of uncertainty with belief functions, Proc. IJCAI, 1985, 111-113.
6. P. P. Bonissone and K. S. Decker, Selecting uncertainty calculi and granularity: A experiment in trading-off precision and complexity, GE Technical Report, 1985.
7. L. A. Zadeh, Fuzzy sets, Information and Control, 8 (1965), 338-353.
8. L. A. Zadeh, Similarity relations and fuzzy ordering, Information Sciences, 3 (1971), 177-200.
9. J. C. Bezdek, R. O. Pettus, L. M. Stephens and W. R. Zhang, Knowledge representation using linguistic fuzzy similarity relations, International Journal of Man-Machine Studies, 1986.
10. W. R. Zhang, J. C. Bezdek, R. O. Pettus and L. M. Stephens, Linguistic fuzzy relations in knowledge-based systems, Proc. Third Annual Computer Science Symposium, Columbia, SC, 1986.
11. S. Chen, A data flow computer architecture for Markov image models, IEEE Computer Society Workshop on Computer Architecture for Pattern Analysis and Image Database Management, 1985, 75-79.
12. R. O. Duda and P. E. Hart, Pattern Classification and Scene Analysis, John Wiley & Sons, 1973, pp. 405-424.
13. K. S. Fu and A. Rosenfeld, Pattern recognition and image processing, IEEE Trans. on Computer, Vol. C-25, Dec. 1976, 1336-1346.
14. M. Zhang and S. Chen, Evidential reasoning in image understanding, AAAI Workshop on Uncertainty in AI, Seattle, Washington, July 1987.
15. M. Zhang and J. B. Campbell, Automatic delineation of drainage basins within digital elevation data using the topographic primal sketch and facet model, Journal of the International Association for Math. Geology, 1987.
16. M. Zhang and J. B. Campbell, A geographic information system within the GYPSY environment, American Congress on Surveying and Mapping and American Society for photogrammetry and Remote Sensing Convention, Washington, DC, March 1986.

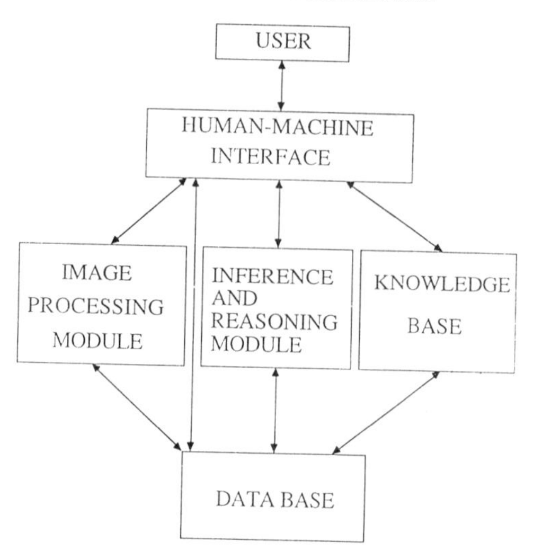

Figure 1. SRDS System Architecture

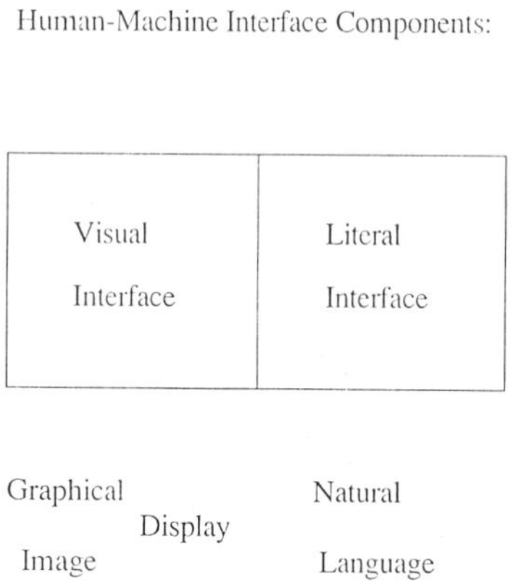

Human-Machine Interface Components:

Visual Interface

Literal Interface

Graphical Image

Display

Natural Language

Figure 2. Human-Machine Interface Components

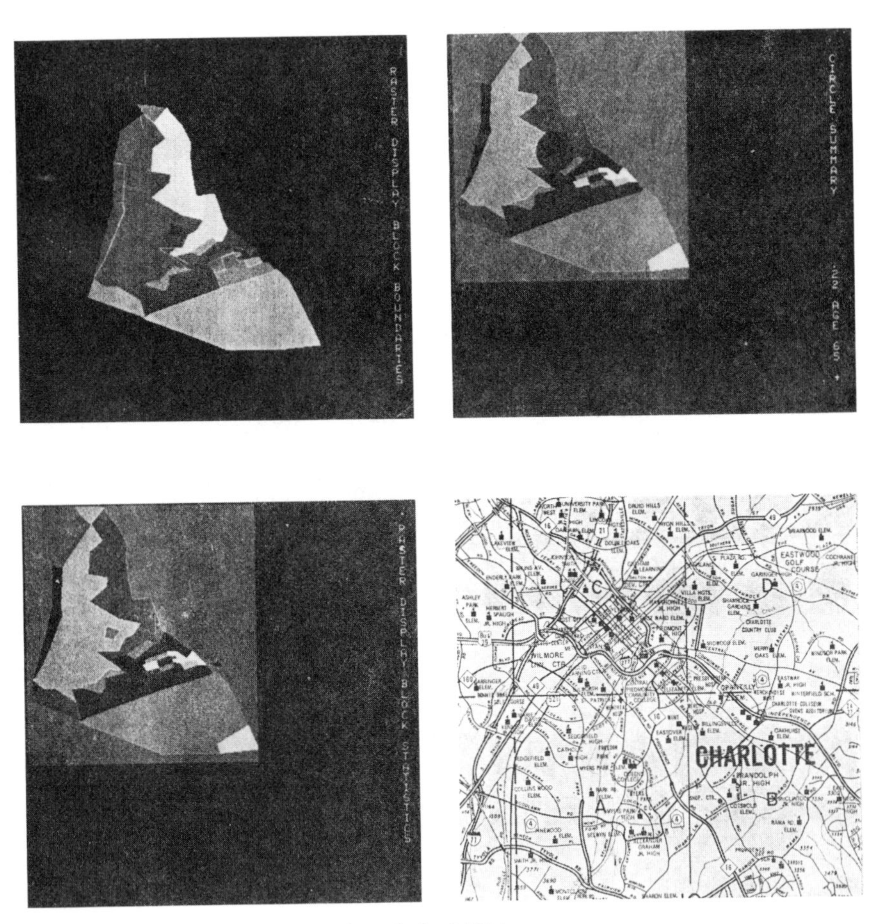

Figure 3. Spatial Data

INPUT

1. FEATURE SPACE:

f1: Environmental impact (noise, pollution) L
f2: Construction cost (cut and fill) N
f3: Construction cost (transpotation) N
f4: Availability of prime agricultural land L
f5: Human travel cost N
f6: Economic impact L
f7: Social impact L
f8: Aesthetic impact L

Feature Space: F = {F1, F2}
Numerical Subspace: F1 = {f1, f4, f6, f7, f8}
Linguisic Subspace: F2 = {f2, f3, f5}

2. CANDIDATE SPACE (AREAS):

A = {a1, a2, a3, a4, a5}

3. RATING MATRIX: [R]

	f1	f2	f3	f4	f5	f6	f7	f8
a1	v-g	0.8	0.5	mol-b	0.9	g	f	b
a2	f	0.3	0.8	mol-g	0.5	f	b	v-g
a3	b	0.7	0.9	v-g	0.6	g	f	mol-b
a4	g	0.9	0.3	f	0.4	b	v-g	v-g
a5	v-g	0.4	0.9	mol-g	0.9	g	f	b

4. WEIGHTING MATRIX: [W]

	f1	f2	f3	f4	f5	f6	f7	f8
[W] = [	v-i	i	i	m-i	m-i	i	mol-i	u]^T

5. TERM SET DEFINITION: Define the linguistic terms using fuzzy numbers according to expert knowledge

OUTPUT

1. SUITABILITY COMPUTATION:

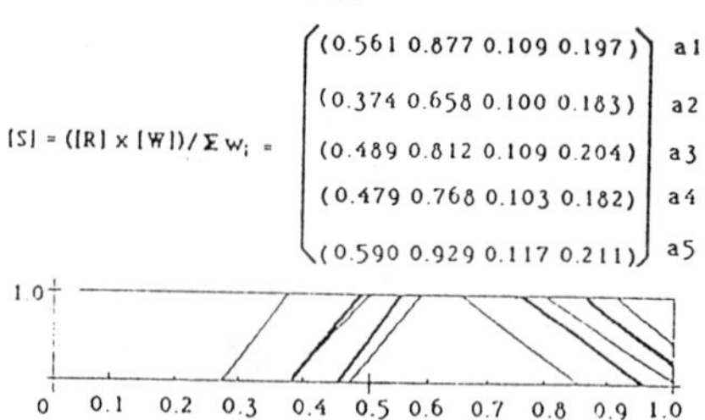

2. LINGUISIC APPROXIMATION: fuzzy numbers are transformed to linguistic terms

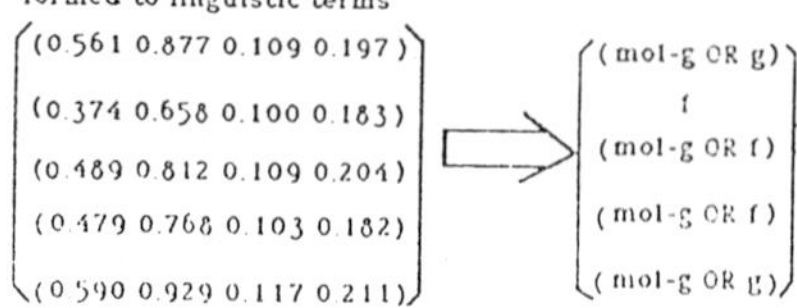

3. RANKING:

a5	0.735	(mol-g OR g)	best
a1:	0.702	(mol-g OR g)	⋮
a3:	0.642	(mol-g OR f)	⋮
a4:	0.619	(mol-g OR f)	↓
a2:	0.525	f	worst

PHASE2: APPROXIMATE REASONING AND DECISION SUPPORT

Figure 4. Approximate Reasoning and Decision Support

Real-Time Fuzzy Control: From Linguistic Rules to Implementation on a Chip†

Stephen Chiu and Masaki Togai
Rockwell International Science Center
Thousand Oaks, CA 91360

ABSTRACT

Application of knowledge-based systems to the control of complex processes is often appropriate, but impracticable. The control problem poses stringent demands on processing speed. Knowledge-based systems are inference intensive and often cannot provide the speed required for the application of interest.

Our work is concerned with the implementation of real-time control systems based on fuzzy logic inferencing. We have designed the architecture of a VLSI chip that can perform an entire inference process required for a fuzzy control system. The chip is capable of processing 16 control rules in parallel, producing 250,000 inferences per second at 16 MHz clock. A programming environment is also being developed to translate linguistically expressed rules into this hardware implementation. In this environment, a set of rules can be easily described, modified, and tested through simulation. The rules are translated into discretized numerical distributions which can be written directly into the chip memory.

1. INTRODUCTION

As systems become more complex and mathematically intractable, the application of conventional methods of control becomes increasingly difficult. The use of knowledge-based techniques that simulates the action of a human expert is well suited for such systems. However, the control problem poses stringent demands on processing speed. The response time of the controller determines the stability and the achievable performance of the overall system. In real-world siutations where conflicting information and conflicting objectives must be considered, the computation time required for most applicable knowledge-based techniques becomes prohibitive.

Fuzzy logic is a method of approximate reasoning that provides a means for resolving the effects of conflicting factors. The reasoning process is computationally efficient because fuzzy logic utilizes approximation rather than formal mathematical aggregation of probabilities or beliefs (e.g. Dempster-Shafer method [1]). The cost of using approximations is that the resultant decisions may be sub-optimal. However, since real-world situations tend to be non-deterministic, there is no assurance that any decision will be optimal in its outcome. An optimal decision only exists in the sense of maximizing the probability of a successful outcome. The use of approximations is appropriate whenever the cost of detailed analysis outweighs the possible increase in performance.

Another important aspect of fuzzy logic is its ability to represent vague, linguistically expressed knowledge. Several successful industrial applications of fuzzy logic to process control have been demonstrated [2]. The acquired experiences of human operators are naturally captured as fuzzy control rules. This may be attributable to the fact that human reasoning under time constraints is by nature approximate.

Although the fuzzy inference process is computationally efficient, the stringent time constraints of many systems still preclude the application of fuzzy control. Our work is focused on the implementation of fuzzy control in hardware to achieve the required real-time performance. We are designing a VLSI chip that can perform an entire inference process required for a fuzzy logic control system. The developed chip will be capable of processing 16 fuzzy control rules in

† This work was supported by the Independent Research and Development Program of Rockwell International Corporation.

Methodologies for Intelligent Systems
Z. W. Ras and M. Zemankova, Editors

parallel, producing 250,000 inferences per second at 16 MHz clock. Large rule sets can be handled by cascading chips in parallel.

A fuzzy logic programming environment is also being developed in conjunction with the chip. The environment allows a human expert to easily describe a set of rules, modify them, and verify the rules through simulation. In an actual control system, the rules will reside in and be processed by a fuzzy inference chip. To reflect this hardware architecture, each set of rules is associated with a chip object simulated in software. The content of the chip object is changed as the rules are modified. When the simulation results are satisfactory, the content of the simulated chip will represent the state to be duplicated in the hardware chip. Hence, this environment enables the direct translation of linguistically expressed rules into real-time hardware implementations.

In this paper, we describe the fuzzy inference chip and its programming environment. The chip is highly self-sufficient; both the rule memory and the inference processor are contained in the chip. It is currently being designed using 2μ CMOS technology. The programming environment is implemented on a Xerox 1186 Lisp workstation.

2. FUZZY CONTROL

Motivated by Zadeh's [3] work on linguistic decision rules, Mamdani and Assilian [4] first utilized fuzzy set theory to translate verbal statements of control strategies into a set of fuzzy decision rules. They discovered that system performance under fuzzy control was comparable to that obtained from optimally tuned proportional-integral-derivative (PID) control. The discovery that control rules derived from vague, linguistic expressions was highly effective has lead to a slew of applications of fuzzy control to complex, mathematically ill-understood processes that defied the tools of system theory. A comprehensive survey of fuzzy control is given in [5].

2.1 Representing Control Knowledge

The fuzzy controller developed by Mamdani and Assilian encoded human strategies for controlling a steam engine. The rules were expressed in the following form:

IF the pressure error is negative small and
the change in pressure error is positive big
THEN make the heat change positive big.

This rule can be written more concisely as

IF X_1 is NS and X_2 is PB
THEN Y is PB

where X_1 and X_2 are the inputs to the controller (pressure error and change in pressure error), Y is the output of the controller (heat change), and NS and PB are *fuzzy variables* defining what is meant by negative small and positive big. A fuzzy variable, say A, is represented by a distribution function $A(x)$, called the membership function. The NS membership function, for example, determines the level of truth that a given pressure error is negative small. The membership functions are usually chosen to be either normal or triangular distributions, as shown in Fig. 1. The range of possible values for the argument, e.g. from -1 to +1, is called the *universe of discourse* of the fuzzy variable.

2.2 Fuzzy Reasoning

The fuzzy inference chip uses the compositional rule of inference, or maximum operation, to combine control rules. Suppose we have the following two rules:

Rule 1: IF X_1 is A_{11} and X_2 is A_{12}
THEN Y is B_1

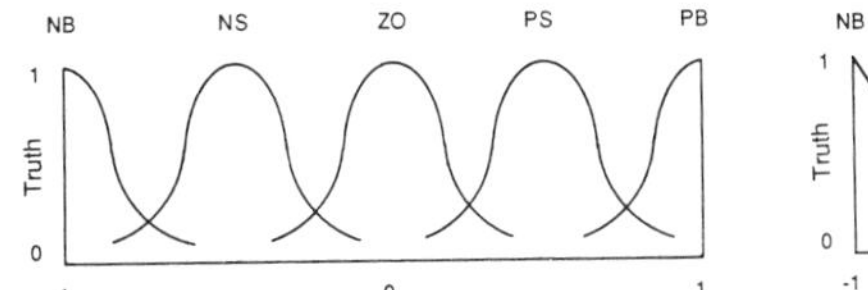

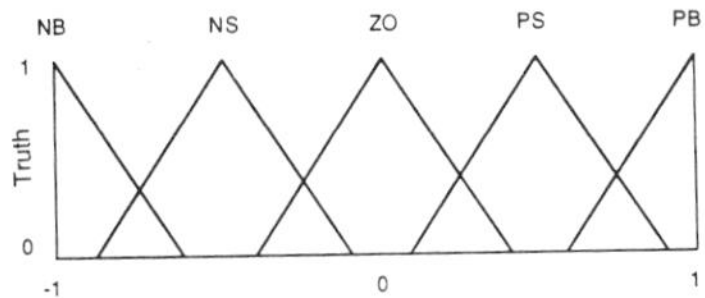

FIG. 1. Normal and triangular membership functions.

Rule2: IF X_1 is A_{21} and X_2 is A_{22}
THEN Y is B_2 .

Given inputs x_1 and x_2, the truth values α_1 and α_2 of the propositions are given by

$$\alpha_1 = A_{11}(x_1) \wedge A_{12}(x_2)$$

$$\alpha_2 = A_{21}(x_1) \wedge A_{22}(x_2)$$

where $\wedge$ denotes the minimum operator.

We form an output membership function B(y) as

$$B(y) = (\alpha_1 \wedge B_1(y)) \vee (\alpha_2 \wedge B_2(y)) \tag{1}$$

where V denotes the maximum operator. Often the output membership function is computed as

$$B(y) = (\alpha_1 \times B_1(y)) \vee (\alpha_2 \times B_2(y)) \,. \tag{2}$$

However, the form given by Eq. 1 is more efficient and suited for VLSI implementation. Hence, it is the method used in the chip.

The output Y is inferred from the centroid of the output membership function:

$$Y = \frac{\int B(y)\, y\, dy}{\int B(y)\, dy}$$

The inference process is illustrated in Fig. 2.

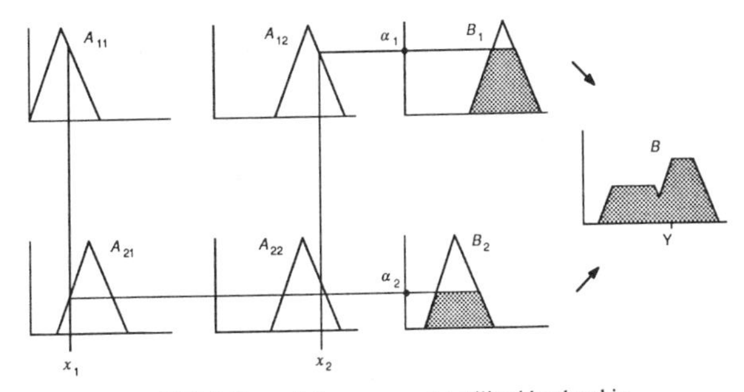

FIG. 2. Fuzzy inference process utilized by the chip.

3. CHIP ARCHITECTURE

The present chip design is based on the approach used in a previous single-input/single-output prototype [6]. The approach is extended to handle rules of the more general form:

$$\text{IF } X_1 \text{ is } A_1 \text{ and } X_2 \text{ is } A_2 \text{ and } X_3 \text{ is } A_3 \text{ and } X_4 \text{ is } A_4$$
$$\text{THEN } Y_1 \text{ is } B_1 \text{ and } Y_2 \text{ is } B_2 \ .$$

3.1 Rule Storage

The rule set is stored in RAM to enable an adaptive control system to dynamically adjust the membership functions to continually optimize performance. The universe of discourse of a membership function is discretized into 16 levels of resolution, and the truth value of a membership function is also discretized into 16 levels. Hence, a fuzzy variable can be stored as a 16 element vector, where each element is a 4 bit truth value. A single variable is then digitized by 64 bits. Because of die size limitation, we estimated that sixteen is the maximum number of rules that can be stored on the chip. Thus, the size of the rule memory unit on the chip is 6K. Two memory modules are used to store the antecedent variables (A_1, A_2, A_3, A_4) and conclusion variables (B_1 , B_2), respectively.

3.2 Inference Processor

In implementing the inference scheme, the memory and inference units are coupled tightly. The system architecture of the chip is shown in Fig. 3. The inference unit consists of two basic logical circuits: minimum and maximum operators. The inference cycle begins with fetching the proper four 4-bit truth values per rule from the antecedent memory unit. The four truth values of a rule are compared in a minimum operator. The minimum truth value is then compared in another minimum operator with the value fetched from the conclusion memory unit. The resultant values from all the rules are then compared in a maximum operator to obtain the final output membership function. Registers are inserted between the logical circuits to pipeline the process. By using a parallel architecture with pipelined data flow, an inference can be performed every 64 clock cycles. Hence, we anticipate the performance of 250,000 inferences per second at 16 MHz clock.

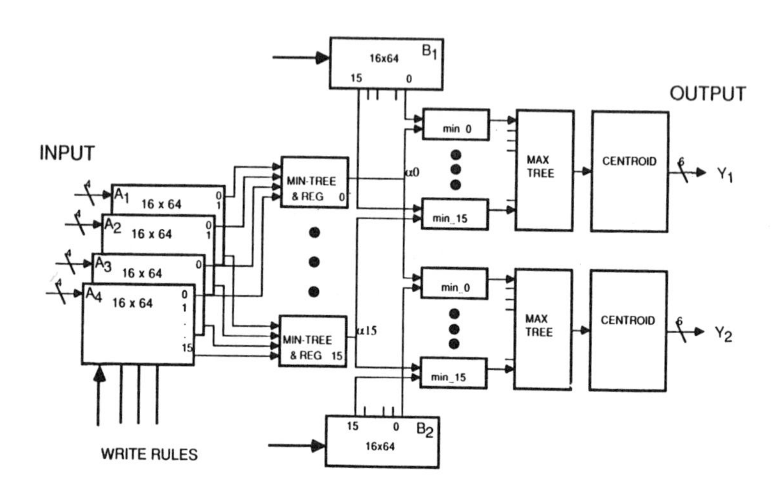

FIG. 3. Architecture of fuzzy inference chip.

4. PROGRAMMING ENVIRONMENT

The programming environment for the chip is implemented on a Xerox workstation using the Interlisp language. In this environment, each set of rules is associated with a chip object. A set of rules is tested by applying inputs to the corresponding chip object. The rules may be interactively modified based on the observed outputs.

4.1 Rule Syntax

The rules are defined in text files by using a standard text editor. A simple rule file is shown in Fig. 4. In this example, TEMPERATURE and PRESSURE are the inputs to the chip; HEATER.POWER and VALVE.OPENING are the outputs. The numerical expressions, e.g. (0 200), define the universe of discourse for each input and output. The universe of discourse is actually represented in the chip as an integer between 0 and 15; these expressions are used to scale the input and output values accordingly. Adjectives such as HIGH.TEMP and LOW.PRESS are fuzzy variables that are each associated with a membership function. The adverbs ABOVE and VERY modify the membership functions, as will be described later.

Because the hardware chip is designed to process conjunctive rules, i.e. those consisting exclusively of AND logic, the rule file is currently restricted to contain only conjunctive rules. However, a disjunctive rule can always be formulated in terms of a set of conjunctive rules. For example, the rule

IF (X_1 is NS and X_2 is PB) or (X_1 is NB)
THEN Y is PB

is equivalent to the two conjunctive rules:

Rule 1: IF X_1 is NS and X_2 is PB
THEN Y is PB

Rule 2: IF X_1 is NB
THEN Y is PB

It is possible to write a rule compiler that will translate disjunctive rules into equivalent conjunctive rules.

```
(* Rules for Boiler Control)

(INPUT TEMPERATURE (0 200) PRESSURE (0 500))
(OUTPUT HEATER.POWER (0 10) VALVE.OPENING (0 10))

(IF TEMPERATURE IS HIGH.TEMP AND
    PRESSURE IS LOW.PRESS
THEN
    HEATER.POWER IS LOW AND
    VALVE.OPENING IS SMALL)

(IF TEMPERATURE IS ABOVE AVERAGE.TEMP AND
    PRESSURE IS VERY HIGH.PRESS
THEN
    HEATER.POWER IS LOW AND
    VALVE.OPENING IS VERY LARGE)
```

FIG. 4. Rule file format

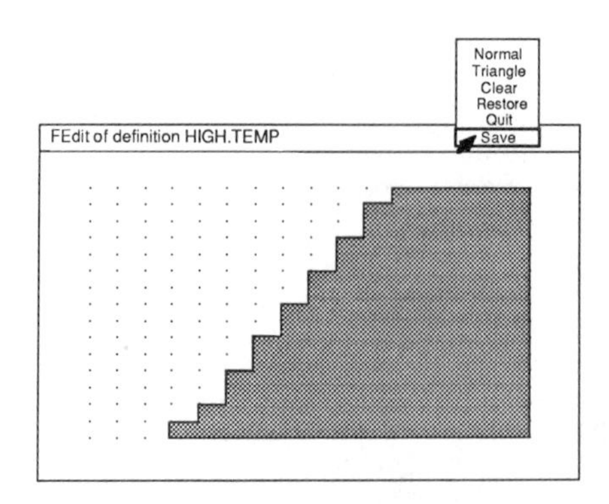

FIG. 5. A fuzzy definition editor window.

4.2 Defining Fuzzy Variables

The fuzzy variables are defined by using a graphic editor (Fig. 5). The discretized membership function corresponds to the representation in the chip. The discretization can be easily changed to adapt the environment to new types of chips.

Definition editing is performed via the mouse. A user can define normal or triangular distributions by selecting from an options menu. After selecting either the "Normal" or the "Triangle" option, the first mouse click on the grid marks the center of the distribution and the second click marks the tail of the distribution. Arbitrary distributions can also be defined by simply drawing with the mouse. By selecting the "Save" option from the menu, the definition is saved in a dictionary of fuzzy variables.

Adverbs are used to modify the definition of a fuzzy variable. Some adverbs, such as "above" and "below," are used to indicate a relation with a definition. Others, such as "very" and "somewhat," are used to narrow or relax a definition. The effects of some adverbs are shown in Fig. 6.

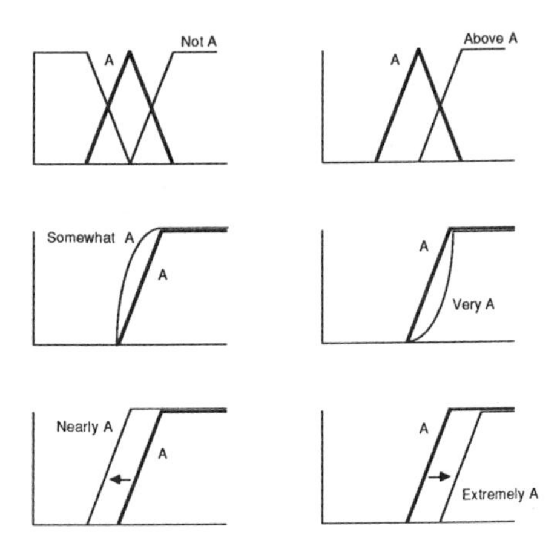

FIG. 6. Some adverb modifiers.

```
(SETQ MYCHIP (CREATE-OBJECT CHIP :TYPE MINMAX) ) -----> sets MYCHIP to
                                                        be a chip object

(READRULE 'MYCHIP.RULE MYCHIP) -----> reads a rule file into MYCHIP

(ASSERT-INPUT '(150 200) MYCHIP) => (4.35 2.82)

(ASSERT-INPUT '(150 400) MYCHIP) => (2.91 8.87)

(DISPLAY-OUTPUT MYCHIP) -----> displays the output membership functions
```

FIG. 7. Sequence of user commands for testing the rules.
The symbol "=>" indicates the value returned by a function.

4.3 The Chip Object

To verify the action of the rules, a user needs to create a chip object and read the rules into the chip object. The rules are tested by applying inputs to the chip object. Figure 7 shows the sequence of user commands necessary to accomplish this. The input/output behavior of the chip object will be identical to that of an actual controller based on the chip. The output is returned as the result of applying input. The output membership functions may also be examined graphically (Fig. 8). If the output is not satisfactory, the definition editor can be used to adjust the definition of the fuzzy variables. The content of the chip object is automatically updated to reflect any change in definitions. When the simulation results are satisfactory, the content of the chip object then represent the state to be duplicated in the hardware chip.

Although the developed chip utilizes the min-max operation to combine rules (Eq. 1), other methods of fuzzy reasoning can also be simulated in this environment. Currently two methods of fuzzy reasoning may be applied. The second method utilizes the max-product operation (Eq. 2) to combine rules. The method of reasoning to be used is specified by creating chip objects of the corresponding type. Chip objects of the "Minmax" type utilize the first method of fuzzy reasoning; chip objects of the "Multiplicative" type utilize the second method. This capability allows comparison of controllers utilizing different methods of reasoning. This also provides a framework for extending the environment to incorporate new types of chips.

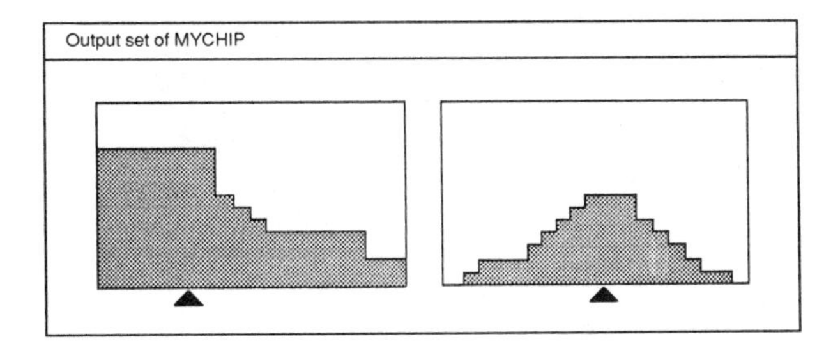

FIG. 8. Graphical display of output membership function.

By using a CONNECT function, the chip objects may be interconnected in such a way that the output of a chip becomes the input to any number of other chips. When an input is asserted on a chip, its output is propagated to all its "downstream" chips. Hence, a circuit of cascaded chips may be easily simulated. This capability facilitates the construction of complex controllers from simple, modular components. In particular, a complex controller that involves multiple domains of expertise may be developed by first focusing on component chip objects and then interconnecting the components.

5. CONCLUSION

Fuzzy logic provides a means for capturing the approximate, qualitative aspect of human decision-making. It is suited for applications in which an accurate model of the environment cannot be obtained or in which the objective cannot be precisely defined. The success of fuzzy logic in the control of industrial processes portends its use in high-performance control systems. Applications to problems such as aircraft flight control [7] and object tracking for Shuttle rendezvous [8] have been studied. The fuzzy inference chip is designed to provide the processing speed necessary for such applications. Combined with the programming environment, linguistic rules derived from an expert can be directly translated into an implementation on a chip. Control systems incorporating multiple chips, each representing a specific expertise, can also be easily developed within the object-oriented programming environment.

REFERENCES

1. G. Shafer, *A Mathematical Theory of Evidence* (Princeton University Press, Princeton, NJ 1976).

2. M. Sugeno (editor), *Industrial Applications of Fuzzy Control* (North-Holland, Amsterdam 1985).

3. L.A. Zadeh, Outline of a new approach to the analysis of complex systems and decision processes, *IEEE Trans. Syst., Man, and Cybern.*, SMC-3-1:28-44 (1973).

4. E.H. Mamdani and S. Assilian, A case study on the application of fuzzy set theory to automatic control, *Proc. IFAC Stochastic Control Symposium*, Budapest (1974).

5. M. Sugeno, "An introductory survey of fuzzy control," *Information Sciences,* Vol. 36, pp. 59-83 (1985).

6. M. Togai and H. Watanabe, A VLSI Implementation of a Fuzzy-Inference Engine: Toward an Expert System on a Chip, *Information Sciences* 38:147-163 (1986).

7. L.I. Larkin, A Fuzzy Logic Controller for Aircraft Flight Control, *Proc. 23rd IEEE Conf. on Decision and Control,* Las Vegas, NV (1984).

8. R.N. Lea and J. Giarratano, An Expert System Program Using Fuzzy Logic for Shuttle Rendezvous Sensor Control, ISA Paper # 86-0644 (1986).

A MANY-VALUED LOGIC FOR BELIEF/DISBELIEF PAIRS

DIMITER DRIANKOV
University of Linköping
Department of information and Computer Science
S-581 83 Linköping, Sweden

ABSTRACT

A many-valued variant of *relevance logic* is proposed. Furthermore, using the notion of an *epistemic state* some non-truthfunctional aspects of knowledge about beliefs are considered.

INTRODUCTION

The type of logic we have in mind is shaped after the circumstances under which a hypothetical reasoning machine obtains its input-data. In the first place, we consider the case when the input-data on which its inferences are based come from multiple sources all considered to be equally trustworthy on the whole, but none being assumed to be a ultimate truth-teller. In this context a situation emerges in which contradictions threaten. Thus, one major motive for the logic proposed is, that it should not lead to irrelevant conclusions which infect the whole system.

In the second place, instead of being only *true* or *false* the input-data may carry some credentials regarding their validity, i.e., there is uncertainty as to whether the input-data are definitely *true* or *false* - they are only believed, up to a certain degree, to be *true* or *false*. Furthermore, since we want to be able to represent situations in which contradictory beliefs are hold, these credentials should allow for an integrated *quantification* of the amount of belief and disbelief hold in the validity of data in question.

In the third place, we want to allow the reasoning machine to receive inputs not only in the form of atomic formulas but also complexes such as A *or* B. In this case, only a belief with respect to the validity of the whole formula is supplied while nothing is said as to the individual beliefs in the validity of A and B. If we represent such an *epistemic* state with a single *set-up* in which A *or* B is marked as *believed*, this will be a *set-up* in which either A or B is marked as *believed*. Any such *set-up* would make the reasoning machine either to tell us that A is *believed*, if asked about the belief-state of A, or to tell us that B is *believed*, if asked about the belief-state of B. And it should not be able to answer either of these questions, since it has been told only to believe that A *or* B is the case.

THE CONCEPT OF A BELIEF/DISBELIEF PAIR

A *belief/disbelief pair* is a summary of two items of information: a report on how strongly the validity of a proposition is believed and a report on how strongly its validity is disbelieved, i.e, how strongly the validity of the negation of this same proposition is believed. Furthermore, a proposition is said to be viewed as *plausible* in the light of the evidence available to the extent that parts of this evidence do not support a belief in the validity of its negation. Thus, the degree to which the *plausibility* of a proposition is believed, can be interpreted as the degree to which it is believed that the negative evidence available fails to refute the validity of this particular proposition, i.e., $plausibility(A) = 1 - belief(\neg A)$.

An integrated quantified representation of these two items of information can be introduced as an ordered pair $[s(A), p(A)]$ consisting of a crisp number s(A) indicating the *degree of belief* in the validity of A, and of a crisp number p(A) indicating its *degree of plausibility*, and representing implicitly the degree to which the validity of A is disbelieved. Furthermore, we require that s(A) and $s(\neg A)$ are bound by the following relationship: $s(A) + s(\neg A) \in [0,2]$ Taking into account the relationship between s(A) and p(A) we then obtain that: $p(A) + p(\neg A) \in [0,2]$. Thus, our notions of graded *belief* and *plausibility* obey neither the relationship existing between the *probabilistic measures* of *support* and *plausibility*

Methodologies for Intelligent Systems
Z. W. Ras and M. Zemankova, Editors

proposed by G.Shafer in [2], nor the relationship between their counterparts in the face of the ***necessity*** and ***possibility fuzzy set-theoretic*** measures introduced by L.Zadeh in [3]. On the other hand, the fact that these measures of belief and disbelief were defined as crisp numbers, is a problem inherent to all approaches for numerical representations of uncertainty: they all tend to represent it as a precise quantity on a given scale. Such a single value tells nothing about its precision, which may be very low when the value is derived from uncertain evidence. All this raises the question of ***uncertainty granularity***, i.e. the finest level of distinction among different quantifications of uncertainty that adequately represent the expert's discriminating perceptions. In [1] P.Bonissone has proposed an approach for dealing with the ***granularity*** of representation: a verbal scale of qualitative linguistic estimates E_i , for the ***likelihood*** of the validity of a proposition is proposed. The semantics of each linguistic estimate E_i is provided by a ***fuzzy number*** N_i on the interval [0,1]. In our further considerations we employ a verbal scale, called L (see [1] for details), consisting of nine linguistic estimates for the ***likelihood*** of the validity of a proposition:

Linguistic estimate	*Fuzzy number*
E_1 = impossible	$N_1 = (0,0,0,0)$
E_2 = extremely unlikely	$N_2 = (0,.02,0,.05)$
E_3 = very low chance	$N_3 = (.1,.18,.06,.05)$
E_4 = small chance	$N_4 = (.22,.36,.05,.06)$
E_5 = it may	$N_5 = (.41,.58,.09,.07)$
E_6 = meaningful	$N_6 = (.63,.80,.05,.06)$
E_7 = most likely	$N_7 = (.78,.92,.06,.05)$
E_8 = extremely likely	$N_8 = (.98,1,.05,0)$
E_9 = certain	$N_9 = (1,1,0,0)$

A very important feature of the linguistic estimates proposed is, that each one of them ,say E_i , has its ***mirror-image*** E_{n+1-i} (n is the index of the ***linguistic estimate*** of maximum ***likelihood***) about E_5.

BELIEF/DISBELIEF PAIRS AND BELIEF STATES

A verbally defined ***belief/disbelief pair***, /A/, is an ordered pair [s(A), p(A)] with s(A), p(A) $\in$ L, and where: (i) s(A) indicates how likely it is that A may turn out as ***true***, and (ii) p(A) indicates how likely it is to fail to refute the validity of A; p(A) is determined from the knowledge about the how likely it is that the negation of A may turn out ***true*** in the following way: $p(A) = E_9 - s(\neg A)$. To make s(A) and $s(\neg A)$ take their values in L would mean that we interpret the ***likelihood*** of A to turn out as ***true*** as a measure of the ***degree of belief*** in the validity of A. Similarly, $s(\neg A)$, is interpreted as a measure of the ***degree of disbelief*** in the validity of A. Since, $p(A) = E_9 - s(\neg A)$ gives how likely it is to fail to refute the validity of A given $s(\neg A)$, p(A) can be interpreted as the degree to which the ***plausibility*** of A being valid is believed.

Now a ***contradictory*** (*C*) belief-state indicates that there is a ***meaningful*** belief in the validity of A as well as in the validity of its negation. Then, in terms of the ***degrees of belief*** in the validity of A and $\neg A$, a ***contradictory*** belief-state is encountered whenever the ***degree of belief*** in the validity of A and the ***degree of belief*** in the validity of $\neg A$ are both at least ***meaningful*** i.e. $E_6 \leq s(A) \leq E_9$ and $E_6 \leq s(\neg A) \leq E_9$. The latter implies, according to the relationship between $s(\neg A)$ and p(A) and the ***mirror-image*** property of the E_i 's, that $E_1 \leq p(A) \leq E_4$. Then a ***contradictory*** belief-state is expressed by any ***belief/disbelief pair*** of the form,

$$/A/ = [E_6 \leq s(A) \leq E_9 , E_1 \leq p(A) \leq E_4]$$

A belief-state in which the validity of a proposition is ***believed to a degree*** (*B*) would mean that we hold some ***meaningful*** belief in the validity of A while there is no belief at all in its falsity (or in the validity of $\neg$A). Thus, in terms of the *degrees of belief* in the validity of A and $\neg$A, such a belief-state can be expressed by any *belief/disbelief pair* of the form:

$$/A/ = [\, E_6 \leq s(A) \leq E_9 \, , E_9 \,]$$

Another type of a belief state is the one where there is not only a *meaningful* belief in the validity of A, but its falsity is also believed, though to a much lesser degree. In other words we have a belief-state in which the validity of A is *rather believed than disbelieved (RB)*, and it is represented by any *belief/disbelief pair* given as:

$$/A/ = [E_6 \leq s(A) \leq E_9 \, , E_5 \leq p(A) \leq E_8 \,]$$

The belief-state in which there is no belief at all in the validity of A while there is a *meaningful* belief in its falsity represents the case when the validity of A is *disbelieved to a degree (D)*. In terms of the *degrees of belief* in A and $\neg$A, such a belief-state is provided by any *belief/disbelief pair* that has the form:

$$/A/ = [\, E_1 \, , E_1 \leq p(A) \leq E_4 \,]$$

Another category of a belief-state corresponds to the case when there is not only a *meaningful* belief in the falsity of A, but its validity is also believed, though to a much lesser degree. Thus we have a case when the validity of A is *rather disbelieved than believed (RD)*, this being expressed by any *belief/disbelief pair* of the type:

$$/A/ = [E_2 \leq s(A) \leq E_5 \, , E_1 \leq p(A) \leq E_4 \,]$$

Finally, we have a belief-state which will allow for explicit representation of *ignorance* i.e. the case when there is *meaningful* belief neither in the validity of A nor in its falsity. In terms of the *degrees of belief* in the validity of A and $\neg$A this means that they are of such a dimension so that very little is known to allow us to be more or less definite with respect to both belief and disbelief in the validity of A. We call this belief-state the *unknown (U)*, and it is represented by any *belief/disbelief pair* of the type:

$$/A/ = [\, E_1 \leq s(A) \leq E_5 \, , E_5 \leq p(A) \leq E_9 \,]$$

Now, the notion of a *set-up* [6], is to be maintained in terms of a table assigning a particular *belief-disbelief pair* to each atomic formula. Such a *set-up* is denoted by *s* and it is in fact a mapping from atomic formulas into the set, *I*, of all *belief/disbelief pairs* that form the six belief-states from above.

THE LOGIC OF A SET-UP

Let us define a partial order $\preceq$ (less-or-equally believed to be true than) on *belief/disbelief pairs* such that, for every /A/ and /B/ we have:

$$/A/ \preceq /B/ \text{ iff } s(A) \leq s(B) \text{ and } p(A) \leq p(B)$$

Pr 1. The set *I* of all *belief/disbelief pairs* is a *partially ordered set* with respect to $\preceq$.

Let us define *meet*, denoted by $\wedge$, and *join*, denoted by $\vee$, as:

$$/A/ \wedge /B/ = [\min(s(A),s(B)), \min(p(A),p(B))]$$

$$/A/ \vee /B/ = [\max(s(A),s(B)), \max(p(A),p(B))]$$

Pr 2. $\wedge$ and $\vee$ are the greatest-lower-bound (g.l.b.) and the least-upper-bound operations for the partial order $\preceq$.

As to the properties of the *meet* and *join* operations defined above it can be shown that they are: *idempotent*, *commutative*, *associative*, *distributive*, *continuous* and *strictly increasing* in both arguments. We can now use the operations on our *logical lattice* to induce a semantics for a language involving *and* and *or*. Given an arbitrary set-up *s*, that is, a mapping of atomic formulas into *I*, we can extend *s* to a mapping of all formulas into *I* in the standard inductive way. Furthermore, following the definition of a *belief/disbelief pair*, a *negation* operator can be naturally introduced as:

$$NOT(/A/) = [E_9 - p(A), E_9 - s(A)] = /not\ A/$$

The so-defined *negation* has a number of properties, namely it is *involutive*, *continuous*, *strictly monotonic decreasing*, and finally, it is such that ∧ and ∨ are duals in the sense of the De Morgan's laws. Furthermore, the results produced by the *negation* operator when the latter is applied to an arbitrary *belief/disbelief pair* belonging to one of the six belief-states can be summarized as,

/A/	*B*	*RB*	*U*	*C*	*RD*	*D*
/¬A/	*D*	*RD*	*U*	*C*	*RB*	*B*

As to the behavior of the other two logical operators when applied to any pair of *belief/disbelief pairs*, where each of the constituents of the pair belongs to one the six truth-categories is given by the following propositions:

Pr 3. ∧ produces a "truth-table" as:

∧	*B*	*RB*	*U*	*C*	*RD*	*D*
B	*B*	*RB*	*U*	*C*	*RD*	*D*
RB	*RB*	*RB*	*U*	*C*	*RD*	*D*
U	*U*	*U*	*U*	*RD or D*	*RD or D*	*D*
C	*C*	*C*	*RD or D*	*C*	*RD*	*D*
RD	*RD*	*RD*	*RD or D*	*RD*	*RD*	*D*
D	*D*	*D*	*D*	*D*	*D*	*D*

Pr 4. ∨ produces a "truth-table" as:

∨	*B*	*RB*	*U*	*C*	*RD*	*D*
B	*B*	*B*	*B*	*B*	*B*	*B*
RB	*B*	*RB*	*RB or B*	*RB*	*RB*	*RB*
U	*B*	*RB or B*	*U*	*RB or B*	*U*	*U*
C	*B*	*RB*	*RB or B*	*C*	*C*	*C*
RD	*B*	*RB*	*U*	*C*	*RD*	*RD*
D	*B*	*RB*	*U*	*C*	*RD*	*D*

However, we still do not have a logic i.e. rules for generating and evaluating inferences. Our inference rule relies on the *logical lattice* we have just developed. In this lattice *entailment* goes up hill. Thus, given any formulas A and B that might be compounded by the use of our logical connectives, we will say that A *entails* B or A *implies* B in any one of the following three cases:

(I) The case when $/A/ \preceq /B/$;
(II) The case when $/B/ \preceq /A/$, but/A/ and /B/ belong to the same belief-state.
(III) The case when /A/ and /B/ can not be ordered with respect to $\preceq$, but /A/ and /B/ either belong to the same belief-state, or the belief-state of /B/ is *above* the belief-state of /A/.

Here we say that a belief-state Y is *above* another belief-state X, iff for at least one $/A_j/ \in Y$ there is at least one $/B_j/ \in X$ such that $/B_j/ \preceq /A_i/$, and for any other $/B_k/ \in X$ $(k \neq j)$ and any $/A_i/ \in Y$, $/A_i/$and $/B_k/$ can not be ordered. We say also that X and Y can not be ordered, or stay at the same level, if and only if for any $/A/ \in Y$ and any $/B/ \in X$ they can not be ordered. Than it can be shown that with respect to $\preceq$ the belief-state *believed to a degree* is *above* any other belief-state; *rather believed than disbelieved* stays under *believed to a degree* but *above* the remaining belief-states; *contradictory* and *unknown* are on the same level, but below *rather believed than disbelieved* and *above rather disbelieved* and *disbelieved to a degree; rather disbelieved than believed* is below *contradictory* and *unknown*, but *above disbelieved* which itself is at the bottom of all belief-states.

In [5] the authors establish a group of principles, called *tautological entailments*, for making inferences; these principles are semantically valid, and taken together semantically complete. Let A, B, C, etc. be formulas in $\vee$, $\wedge$, and $\neg$ and /A/, /B/, /C/, etc. be their corresponding *belief/disbelief pairs*. Let $/A/\rightarrow/B/$ signify that the inference from A to B is valid as defined by (I), (II), and (III) from above. Also let $/A/\leftrightarrow/B/$ signify that A and B are semantically equivalent. This according to our definition of *implication* means that either /A/ = /B/, or that /A/ and /B/ belong to the same belief-state. Then the following propositions provide us with the set of principles from [5]:

Pr 5. $/A_1/\wedge/A_2/\wedge...\wedge/A_m/ \rightarrow /B_1/\vee/B_2/\vee...\vee/B_n/$, provided some $/A_i/$ is some $/B_j/$, and $/A_i/$ and $/B_j/$ are atomic formulas or negated atomic formulas.

Pr 6. $/A\vee B/\rightarrow/C/$ iff $/A/\rightarrow/C/$ and $/B/\rightarrow/C/$.

Pr 7. $/A/\rightarrow/B\wedge C/$ iff $/A/\rightarrow/B/$ and $/A/\rightarrow/C/$.

Pr 8. $/A/\rightarrow/B/$ iff $/\neg B/\rightarrow/\neg A/$.

Pr 9. $/A\vee B/\leftrightarrow/B\vee A/$, $/A\wedge B/\leftrightarrow/B\wedge A/$.

Pr 10. $/A/\vee/B\vee C/\leftrightarrow/A\vee B/\vee/C/$, $/A/\wedge/B\wedge C/\leftrightarrow/A\wedge B/\wedge/C/$.

Pr 11. $\neg/\neg A/\leftrightarrow/A/$, $\neg/A\vee B/\leftrightarrow/\neg A/\wedge/\neg B/$, $\neg/A\wedge B/\leftrightarrow/\neg A/\vee/\neg B/$.

Pr 12. If $/A/\rightarrow/B/$ and $/B/\rightarrow/C/$ then $/A/\rightarrow/C/$, If $/A/\leftrightarrow/B/$ and $/B/\leftrightarrow/C/$ then $/A/\leftrightarrow/C/$.

Pr 13. $/A/\rightarrow/B/$ iff $/A/\leftrightarrow/A\wedge B/$ iff $/A\vee B/\leftrightarrow/B/$.

Pr 14. $/A/\wedge/B\vee C/\leftrightarrow/A\wedge B/\vee/A\wedge C/$, $/A/\vee/B\wedge C/\leftrightarrow/A\vee B/\wedge/A\vee C/$.

Some important observations are to be made here with respect to certain special features of the logic of a *set-up*. First, not derivable from our set of principles and not semantically valid, are the paradoxes of *implication*: $/A\wedge\neg A/\rightarrow/B/$ and $/A/\rightarrow/B\vee\neg B/$. The failure of the first of them means that just because we believe in the validity of A and we also do believe in the validity of its negation, we cannot conclude that we believe in the validity of everything else. Indeed we may be ignorant as to the validity of B, or just we may not believe it. The failure of the second paradox is equally evident: From the fact that we believe in the validity of A , we can not conclude that we know something about our belief or disbelief in the validity of B. For $/B\vee\neg B/$ to belong to the truth-category, say *B*, is either /B/ to belong to *B* or /B/ to belong to *D*; and it may be neither of the two. Or for a different way of counterexampling $/A/\rightarrow/B\vee\neg B/$, /A/ may just belong to *B* while $/B \vee \neg B/$ belongs to *C* because /B/ does. The second thing to be stressed here is, that the truth-values from the set *I* are proposed only in connection with *inferences*, and are not supposed to be used for determining which formulas in our language based on $\wedge$, $\vee$ and $\neg$, count as the so-called *logical truths* or *tautologies*. No formula belongs always to the truth-category *B* or *RB* so, this property will not do as a semantic account of *logical truth*.

THE INFORMATION LATTICE

Let us define the partial order $\sqsubseteq$ (conveys less-than-or-equal amount of information) on *belief/disbelief pairs* so, that

$$/A/\sqsubseteq/B/ \text{ iff } s(A)\leq s(B) \text{ and } p(A)\geq p(B)$$

Pr 15. The set I of all *belief/disbelief pairs* is a *partially ordered set* with respect to $\sqsubseteq$.

Let us define *meet*, denoted by $\sqcap$, and *join*, denoted by $\sqcup$, as

$$/A/ \sqcap /B/ = [\min(s(A),s(B)),\ \max(p(A),p(B))]$$

$$/A/ \sqcup /B/ = [\max(s(A),s(B)),\ \min(p(A),p(B))]$$

Pr 16. $\sqcap$ and $\sqcup$ are the *greatest-lower-bound* (g.l.b.) and the least-upper-bound operations for the partial order $\sqsubseteq$.

As to the properties of the *meet* and *join* operations defined above it can be shown that they are: *idempotent, commutative associative, distributive, monotone,* and *strictly increasing* in both arguments. Furthermore, the results produced by $\sqcap$ and $\sqcup$ in terms of the six truth categories are established by the following propositions:

Pr 17. $\sqcup$ produces a "truth-table" as

$\sqcup$	*B*	*RB*	*U*	*C*	*RD*	*D*
B	*B*	*RB*	*B or RB*	*C*	*C*	*C*
RB	*RB*	*RB*	*RB*	*C*	*C*	*C*
U	*B or RB*	*RB*	*U*	*C*	*RD*	*D or RD*
C	*C*	*C*	*C*	*C*	*C*	*C*
RD	*C*	*C*	*RD*	*C*	*RD*	*RD*
D	*C*	*C*	*D or RD*	*C*	*RD*	*D*

Pr 18. $\sqcap$ produces a "truth-table" as

$\sqcap$	*B*	*RB*	*U*	*C*	*RD*	*D*
B	*B*	*B*	*U*	*B*	*U*	*U*
RB	*B*	*RB*	*U*	*RB*	*U*	*U*
U	*U*	*U*	*U*	*U*	*U*	*U*
C	*B*	*RB*	*U*	*C*	*RD*	*D*
RD	*U*	*U*	*U*	*RD*	*RD*	*D*
D	*U*	*U*	*U*	*D*	*D*	*D*

REPRESENTING BELIEFS ABOUT COMPLEX FORMULAS

Suppose we are told that *Taxes will be raised or deficit will be high.* Let this complex formula $\mathcal{F}$ be assigned a *belief/disbelief pair* belonging to *B*, but no *belief/disbelief pairs* are assigned to the atomic formulas A = *Taxes will be raised* and B = *Deficit will be high.* In this case a single *set-up* can not represent the *epistemic state* in which we should be if told that $/\mathcal{F}/ \in B$, but are told nothing about /A/ and /B/. For any single *set-up* in which A *or* B is assigned a *belief/disbelief pair* belonging to *B* is, a *set-up* in which either A or B is assigned a *belief/disbelief pair* belonging to *B* and therefore has too much information. Such a *set-up* would cause an affirmative answer either to the question *Will taxes be raised?* or to the question *Will deficit be high?* We should not be able to answer either questions since we have been told only that $/\mathcal{F}/ \in B$, but not that either /A/ or /B/ belong to the same belief-state.

The solution to this problem is to use a *collection of set-ups* to represent this *epistemic state* [6]. When we are told that $/\mathcal{F}/ \in B$, we will represent this information by building two *set-ups*: one in which $/A/ \in B$ and $/B/ \in U$, and the other in which $/A/ \in U$ and $/B/ \in B$. Later, when asked *Will taxes be raised?* we will answer that we do not know, i.e., a *belief/disbelief pair* belonging to *U* will be assigned to A since this atomic formula does not have a *belief/disbelief pair* belonging to *B* in every *set-up.* We will also give the same answer to the question *Will deficit be high?*. But when asked *Will taxes be raised or deficit will be high?* we will produce an affirmative answer, i.e., $/\mathcal{F}/$ will belong to *B*, since in both *set-ups* $/\mathcal{F}/ = /A$ *or* $B/ \in B$.

Let us then define the *epistemic state* of the reasoning machine as a *collection of set-ups*, that is a subset of $\mathcal{S}$, the latter being the set of all possible *set-ups*. Let E be an *epistemic state*. In the context of E, the *beief/disbelief pair* of the complex formula $\mathcal{F}$, is denoted by E(/A/), and is determined by taking the *meet* of all *belief/disbelief pairs* that can be assigned to $\mathcal{F}$ in the separate *set-ups* of E:

$$E(/\mathcal{F}/) = \sqcap\{\ s(/\mathcal{F}/):\ s \in E\ \}$$

Why this particular definition for the value of $\mathcal{F}$ in E ? It was already noted that *set-ups*, when considered separately, tend to convey more information than there actually is about a formula. This in terms of the *information lattice*, would mean that:

$$E(/\mathcal{F}/) \sqsubseteq s\ (/\mathcal{F}/) \quad \text{for each } s \in E$$

So, it seems natural to define E(/$\mathcal{F}$/) as maximal while retaining the relationship from above. In other words, the *belief/disbelief pair* to be assigned to the complex formula $\mathcal{F}$ in the *epistemic state* E, that is E(/$\mathcal{F}$/), is to be defined as the g.l.b of all $s(/\mathcal{F}/)$ for $s \in E$.

To sum up, we will stress upon the following two cases: First, let the *epistemic state* E be given as a *collection of set-ups* $\{\ s_i\ \}$ i=1,...,n , and each *set-up* consist of a number of atomic formulas A_j , j = 1,...,m with $s_i\ (/A_j\ /)$ being the *belief/disbelief pair* assigned to A_j in the *set-up* s_i . Now one is ready to answer questions concerning the *belief/disbelief pair* to be assigned to an arbitrary complex formula $\mathcal{F}$ ($\mathcal{F}$ being a logical combination of particular A_j 's) in the *epistemic state* E. Using our logical operators we can determine the *belief/disbelief pair* of $\mathcal{F}$ in each of the *set-ups* s_i , that is $s_i\ (/\mathcal{F}/)$. Then to determine the *belief/disbelief pair* of $\mathcal{F}$ in E we have to find the g.l.b. of all $s_i\ (/\mathcal{F}/)$, i = 1,...,n which could be done by using $\sqcap$.

Secondly, let a complex formula $\mathcal{F}$ together with its *belief-interval* /$\mathcal{F}$/ be supplied to us. The question here is, how do we represent this complex formula so, that we can not only answer questions regarding the belief in the validity of $\mathcal{F}$, but also questions concerning the belief in the validity of the atomic formulas that constitute $\mathcal{F}$. The solution is as follows: Represent $\mathcal{F}$ as an *epistemic state* E that is, a *collection of set-ups* s_i , each *set-up* consisting of the atomic formulas A_j that are in $\mathcal{F}$. Then to each A_j in a *set-up* s_i assign a *belief-interval* $s_i\ (/A_j\ /)$ such that the g.l.b. of all $s_i\ (/A_j\ /)$, i =1,2,... is equal to /$\mathcal{F}$/.

FORMULAS AS INPUTS

Now let us turn to the *join*-operation between *set-ups*. Let us first introduce the notion of a partial ordering $\subseteq$ (contains less-or-equal amount of information) between *set-ups*:

> $s \subseteq s^*$ iff for each atomic formula A_i either $s(/A_i\ /) \sqsubseteq s^*(/A_i\ /)$, or they can not be ordered but $s^*(/A_i\ /)$ belongs to a belief state that is *above* the belief-state of s(/A/) while all other $s(/A_k\ /)$ and $s^*(/A_k\ /)$ (k≠i) belong to the same truth category and can not be ordered.

Here a belief-state Y is *above* another belief-state X, if and only if there is at least one $/B_i\ / \in Y$ and at least one $/A_j\ / \in X$ such that $/A_j\ / \sqsubseteq /B_i\ /$, and for any other $/A_k\ / \in X$ (k≠j), and any $/\ B_i\ / \in Y$, $/B_i\ /$ and $/A_k\ /$ can not be ordered. We also say that X and Y can not be ordered, or are at the same level, if an only if for any $/B/ \in Y$ and any $/A/ \in Y$ they can not be ordered. Then it can be shown that with respect to $\sqsubseteq$ the belief-state *contradictory* stays is *above* any other belief-state; *rather believed than disbelieved* and *rather disbelieved than believed* stay under *contradictory*, but are on the same level - the first one being *above believed to a degree and unknown*, and the second one being *above disbelieved to a degree* and *unknownn*; *believed to a degree* and *disbelieved to a degree* stay on the same level under *rather believed than disbelieved* and *rather disbelieved than believed* respectively, but both are *above unknown*, which in turn is at the bottom of all belief-states. It can be easily shown that $\mathcal{S}$ constitutes a lattice with respect to $\subseteq$, with $\sqcup$ and $\sqcap$ being a l.u.b. and g.l.b. operations. Moving to *epistemic states* we can also talk about one *epistemic state* containing less-or-equal amount of information than another one. Formally speaking,

$$E \subseteq E^* \quad \text{iff} \quad \forall\, s^* \in E^*, \exists\, s \in E \text{ such that } s \subseteq s^*$$

It should be stressed here that the ordering $\subseteq$ on *epistemic states* that are *collections of set-ups* does not yield a lattice because *anti-symmetry* fails. Now let us turn our attention to atomic formulas only and try to answer the following question: What we are to do with the present *epistemic state* E when an atomic formula A, already represented in E by a certain *belief/disbelief pair* /A/, is at some new point in time affirmed or denied ? We say that A is affirmed if /A/ belongs to either *B* or *RB*, and denied if /A/ belongs to either *D* or *RD*. Furthermore, we represent the affirmation of A by generating a *set-up* A_t in which /A/ $\in$ *B* or *RB* and all other atomic formulas belong *U*. In a similar way, denying A generates a *set-up* A_f in which /A/ $\in$ *D* or *RD* and all other atomic formulas belong to *U*. Let us also associate with A two functions: a function f^+ (E) representing the transformation of the present *epistemic state* E into some new *epistemic state* E* when A is affirmed, and f^- (E) representing the transformation of E when A is denied. To define what we want E* to be, we assume here that we always use an input to increase the information about the beliefs in the validity of the formulas, or at least we never use input to throw away information. In terms of the partial ordering between *epistemic states* this condition can be expressed as follows:

$$E \sqsubseteq f^+ (E)$$

Secondly, we assume that f^+ (E) should say no less than the affirmation of A, this being expressed as:

$$A_t \sqsubseteq f^+ (E)$$

Lastly, we want f^+ (E) to be the minimum mutilation of E which renders the *belief-interval* of A to belong at least to either *B* or *RB*, namely we want the least of those *epistemic states* satisfying the above two requirements. This means that we should define f^+ (E) in the following way:

$$f^+ (E) = \{\, s \sqcup A_t : s \in E \,\}$$

and in a similar way,

$$f^- (E) = \{\, s \sqcup A_f : s \in E \,\}$$

Thus when A is affirmed, say /A/ $\in$ *B*, we make a run through each *set-up* of E and perform $\sqcup$: this will make /A/ $\in$ *B* if /A/ belonged to *U* before, it will leave /A/ the same if it already belonged to *B* or *C*, and will make it belong to *C* if it already belonged to *D*. The case of a complex formula being an input and the corresponding transformation of the present *epistemic state* into a new one, are considered in a similar way (for details see [4]).

References

1. P. Bonissone, Selecting uncertainty calculi and granularity: An experiment in trading-off precision and complexity, KBS Working Paper (General Electric Research and Development Center, Schenectady, New York 1985).
2. G. Shafer, A Mathematical Theory of Evidence (NJ:Princeton University Press 1976)
3. L.A. Zadeh, Fuzzy sets as a basis for a theory of possibility, Fuzzy Sets and Systems, 1, No. 1, pp. 3-28 (1978).
4. Driankov, D. (1986). Many-valued-logic of belief: The information lattice, Research Report (University of Linköping, Linköping 1987)
5. A.R. Anderson and N.D. Belnap, Jr., Entailment: The Logic of Relevance and Necessity, vol. I. (NJ: Princeton University Press 1975).
6. N.D. Belnap, Jr., How a computer should think, in: Contemporary Aspects of Philosophy G. Ryle (ed.) (Oriel Press Limited 1976) pp. 30-55.

APPROXIMATION REASONING AND SCOTT'S INFORMATION SYSTEMS

HELENA RASIOWA,* GEORGE EPSTEIN**
*Institute of Mathematics, University of Warsaw, PKiN, 00-901 Warsaw, Poland, **Department of Computer Science, University of North Carolina at Charlotte, Charlotte, NC 28223, USA

ABSTRACT

An algebraic approach to approximation reasoning over modified Scott's information systems is proposed. Semi-Post algebras investigated in [1], [2] are a tool for this approach. A method of approximation reasoning is formulated which for finitistic cases enables us to give an algorithm.

INTRODUCTION

Approximation reasoning is a topic of a great interest now because of its importance in certain branches of computer science such as machine learning, pattern recognition, automatic classification, knowledge representation, data bases, in AI and expert systems. Our approach is based on an observation that approximation reasoning may be considered as a gradual approximating of a set of objects to be recognized, by a family of sets covering this set, and their intersection. This point of view has been presented in [7]. It is close to that of approximating by descending sequences of sets as in [6], or by equivalence classes of equivalence relations - connected with rough sets due to Pawlak [5] and represented e.g. in [4] - but much more general. The algebraic approach proposed in this paper is based on basic semi-Post algebras. For our purpose these algebras are constructed over modified Scott's information systems. In such a system a set Con of consistent finite subsets of its domain is considered as a set of queries and on another hand a poset (Con, $\subset$) is taken as a type of corresponding basic semi-Post algebra $\underline{\text{LCon}}$. Ideals over (Con, $\subset$) and the empty set $\emptyset$ are elements of this algebra. It is a complete distributive set lattice (and a Heyting algebra) equipped with Boolean operations d_t for $t \in \text{Con}$ into the two element Boolean algebra formed of the empty set $\emptyset$ and Con. A very important role is played by information functions with values in $\underline{\text{LCon}}$ and their approximations being functions with values in $\{\emptyset, \text{Con}\}$. They are treated as characteristic functions of sets approximating a set to be recognized.

A theory to be proposed in this paper leads to a method of approximation reasoning over information systems and giving for finitistic cases an algorithm.

This approach gives a link between logic for approximation reasoning as presented in paper [7], prepared for ISMVL'87, and approximation reasoning over Scott's information systems.

1. Examples of Approximation Reasoning

Example 1. Consider a game of two players: a questioner Q and a responder R. The task of Q is to guess in a given number of questions what R is thinking about. Assume R is

Methodologies for Intelligent Systems
Z. W. Ras and M. Zemankova, Editors

thinking about Kurt Gödel. The following dialogue leads to the win of Q.

Q: Is this a human being?

R: Yes.

Q: Is this a man?

R: Yes.

Q: Is he famous?

R: Yes.

Q: Is he a scientist?

R: Yes.

Q: Is he a specialist in philology?

R: No.

Q: Is he a mathematician?

R: Yes.

Q: Is his field mathematical logic?

R: Yes.

Q: Is he alive?

R: No.

Q: Was his 80th anniversary celebrated in 1986?

R: Yes.

Q: Is he Kurt Gödel?

R: Yes.

Observe that answers to any questions define sets approximating a set to be recognized and the intersection of these sets led to a solution.

Example 2. Another example is connected with reasoning of detectives who look for a perpetrator of a crime. Imagine that Sherlock Holmes looks for killers of a person X. Clearly he is interested to obtain answers to the following queries:

q_1: Y was near the place of a crime and at time of a crime.

q_2: Y doesn't have a alibi.

q_3: Y has been interested in the death of X.

q_4: Y is a man (if it is known that a woman was not a killer).

q_5: Y looks like a murderer of X according to a description of witnesses.

Assume that U is a set of inhabitants of a town in which the crime was committed and that the following information was obtained by Sherlock Holmes.

$U_1,\dots,U_{10}$ satisfy q_1;

$U_3,\dots,U_{10}$ satisfy q_2;

U_1, U_2, $U_3,\dots,U_7$ satisfy q_3;

U_1, U_6, U_7 satisfy q_4;

U_1, U_7 satisfy q_5.

Then sets $\{U_1,\dots, U_{10}\} = Sq_1$, $\{U_3,\dots, U_{10}\} = Sq_2$,

$\{U_1, U_2, U_3,\dots, U_7\} = Sq_3$, $\{U_1, U_6, U_7\} = Sq_4$ and $\{U_1, U_7\} = Sq_5$ approximate a set of killers. The intersection $Sq_1 \cap Sq_2 \cap Sq_3 \cap Sq_4 \cap Sq_5 = \{U_7\}$. Of those who are suspect, U_7 is most likely to be a killer.

2. Basic semi-Post algebras. Semi-Post algebras (briefly sP-algebras) have been introduced and investigated in [1] and [2]. In this section preliminary concepts and properties concerning sP-algebras will be shortly summarized in a scope necessary to constitute a tool to formulate and examine problems to be discussed.

Let $\underline{T} = (T,\leq)$ be an arbitrary poset (partially ordered set). A subset I of T is said to be an ideal in $\underline{T}$ if $I \neq \emptyset$ and for every $s \in I$, $t \leq s$ implies $t \in I$. For any $t \in I$ we shall denote by $I(t)$ the ideal generated by t, i.e. the set of all $s \in T$, such that $s \leq t$. The set consisting of $\emptyset$ and of all ideals in $\underline{T}$ will be denoted by LT. It is easy to see that LT is closed with respect to all unions and intersections and constitutes a complete set lattice determined uniquely by $\underline{T}$. The greatest element in LT which exists always and is equal to T will be denoted by $\bigvee$ and the least element equal to $\emptyset$ will be denoted by $\bigwedge$. Clearly $\bigwedge \notin T$ and $\bigwedge \notin I$ for each ideal I. Notice that every ideal I in LT is represented as a union in LT of all ideals in $\underline{T}$ generated by elements $t \in I$, i.e.

$$(1)\quad I = \bigcup^{LT}\{I(t): I(t) \subset I\}.$$

Let us introduce on LT new operations d_t for $t \in T$, as follows.

$$(2)\ d_t \bigwedge = \bigwedge \qquad (3)\ d_t I = \begin{cases} \bigvee \text{if } t \in I, \text{ i.e. if } I(t) \subset I \\ \bigwedge \text{otherwise.} \end{cases}$$

Then

$$(4)\quad \underline{LT} = (LT, \cup, \cap, (d_t)_{t \in T}, (I)_{I \in LT})$$

is said to be a basic sP-algebra of type $\underline{T} = (T,\leq)$. Notice that by (1), (2) (3) every element a of $\underline{LT}$ has the following representation.

$$(5)\quad a = \bigcup_{t \in T} (d_t a \cap I(t))$$

and

$$(6)\quad t_1 \leq t_2 \text{ implies } d_{t_2} a \leq d_{t_1} a.$$

Example 1.

Let $T = \{t_1, t_2\}$ and assume $t_i \leq t_i$ for $i = 1, 2$, define a partial ordering on T. Then LT consists of $\emptyset$, $\{t_1\}$, $\{t_2\}$, $\{t_1, t_2\}$. Thus LT is a four element Boolean algebra. We have $\emptyset = \wedge$, $\{t_1, t_2\} = \vee$ and two operations d_{t_1}, d_{t_2} defined as follows:

$d_{t_1}\wedge = \wedge$, $d_{t_1}\{t_1\} = \vee$, $d_{t_1}\{t_2\} = \wedge$, $d_{t_1}\{t_1, t_2\} = \vee$

$d_{t_2}\wedge = \wedge$, $d_{t_2}\{t_1\} = \wedge$, $d_{t_2}\{t_2\} = \vee$, $d_{t_2}\{t_1, t_2\} = \vee$

$\{t_1, t_2\} = \vee$; $\{t_1\}$, $\{t_2\}$; $\emptyset = \wedge$

Basic sP-algebras of a given type $\underline{T} = (T, \leq)$ are special examples of the more general concept of sP-algebras of a given type. The class of all sP-algebras of a given type has been defined by a system of axioms in [1].

For an exposition the reader is referred to [1] and [2].

Example 2.

Let $T = \{t_1, t_2, t_3\}$, where $t_1 \leq t_3$, $t_2 \leq t_3$ and $t_i \leq t_i$ for $i = 1, 2, 3$ determine a partial ordering. Then LT consists of 0, T, and $\{t_1\}$, $\{t_2\}$, $\{t_1, t_2\}$. LT is a five element distributive lattice. The operations d_t for $t \in T$ are defined thus:

$d_{t_1}\wedge = d_{t_2}\wedge = d_{t_3}\wedge = \wedge$

$d_{t_1}\{t_1\} = d_{t_1}\{t_1, t_2\} = d_{t_1}\{t_1, t_2, t_3\} = \vee$, $d_{t_1}\{t_2\} = \wedge$

$d_{t_2}\{t_2\} = d_{t_2}\{t_1, t_2\} = d_{t_2}\{t_1, t_2, t_3\} = \vee$, $d_{t_2}\{t_1\} = \wedge$

$d_{t_3}\{t_1\} = d_{t_3}\{t_2\} = d_{t_3}\{t_1, t_2\} = \wedge$, $d_{t_3}\{t_1, t_2, t_3\} = \vee$

$\{t_1, t_2, t_3\} = \vee$; $\{t_1, t_2\}$; $\{t_1\}$, $\{t_2\}$; $\emptyset = \wedge$

3. Ideal valued sP-functions. Let $\underline{T} = (T, \leq)$ be any established poset and consider the basic sP-algebra $\underline{LT} = (LT, \cup, \cap, (d_t)_{t \in T}, (I)_{I \in LT})$. Thus LT consists of $\emptyset$ and of all ideals in $\underline{T}$. Let $U \neq \emptyset$ be an arbitrary nonempty set. Any function $f: U \to LT$ has as values $\emptyset$ or ideals in $\underline{T}$ and is said to be an ideal valued sP-function of type $\underline{T}$.

The set $(LT)^U$ is the set of all such functions. With every $f \in (LT)^U$ there are associated Boolean functions $d_t f$, for $t \in T$, where according to (2), (3) in Sec. 2

$$d_t f(u) = \begin{cases} \vee = T \text{ if } t \in f(u) \\ \wedge = 0 \text{ if } t \notin f(u). \end{cases}$$

Thus for $u \in U$, $d_t f(u)$ tells whether t belongs to f(u) or not.

By (5) in Sec. 2, we have the following representation of f(u),

$$(2)\quad f(u) = \cup_{t \in T} (d_t f(u) \cap I(t)).$$

Notice that

(3) $f(u) = \vee$ if for every $t \in T$, $t \in f(u)$.

Let us set for each $t \in T$

$$(4)\ S(d_t f) = \{u \in U : d_t f(u) = \vee\} = \{u \in U : t \in f(u)\}.$$

Thus $S(d_t f)$ is a subset of U, such that its characteristic function is $d_t f$. Observe that by (6) in Section 2 it follows that for any $t_1, t_2 \in T$

$$(5)\ t_1 \leq t_2 \text{ implies } S(d_{t_2} f) \subset S(d_{t_1} f).$$

We say that the family of sets $(S(d_t f))_{t \in T}$ is a descending set sequence of type $\underline{T}$.

Let us set

$$(6)\ Sf = \{u \in U : f(u) = \vee\}.$$

It follows from (3), (4), and (6) that

$$(7)\ Sf \subset S(d_t f) \text{ for every } t \in T$$

$$(8)\ Sf = \bigcap_{t \in T} S(d_t f).$$

4. Basic semi-Post algebras over Scott's information systems. Let us start this section by reminding the reader of a concept of an information system in the sense of Scott [8]. An information system is a system

$$(1)\ \mathcal{A} = (D, \Delta, Con, \vdash),$$

where D is a set of data or propositions, $\Delta \in D$ is the least informative member of D, Con is a family of finite subsets of D (consistent sets of objects or propositions) and $\vdash$ is an entailment relation $\vdash \subset (Con \times D)$, characterized by the following axioms.

(i) if $t \subset s$ and $s \in Con$, then $t \in Con$,

(ii) if $A \in D$, then $\{A\} \in Con$,

(iii) if $t \vdash A$, then $t \cup \{A\} \in Con$,

(iv) $t \vdash \Delta$ for every $t \in Con$,

(v) if $A \in t$, then $t \vdash A$,

(vi) if $s \vdash B$ for all $B \in t$ and $t \vdash A$, then $s \vdash A$.

Elements of the information system $\mathcal{A}$ are subsets $z \subset D$ such that

(2) if $t \subset z$ and t is finite, then $t \in Con$,

(3) if $t \subset z$ and $t \vdash A$, then $A \in z$.

We write $z \in |\mathcal{A}|$ to mean that z is an element of the system $\mathcal{A}$. For every element $z \in |\mathcal{A}|$ we have the following representation.

$$(4) \quad z = \bigcup \{\bar{t} : t \in Con \text{ and } t \subset z\},$$

where for each $t \in Con$, $\bar{t} = \{A \in D: t \vdash A\}$.

For our purpose information systems to be considered in this paper will be constructed as follows.

Let U be a fixed universe, $U \neq \emptyset$, and let L be a first order predicate lanquaqe of formulas without quanitfers interpreted in a model M in U, i.e. M assigns to predicates $q_1, .., q_n$ in L $m(i)$ - ary relations over U, where $m(i)$ is the arity of q_i for $i = 1, ..., m$ and M is extended on the set of all formulas as usual. Assume that for every $u \in U$ there is an individual constant $\underline{u}$ in L. We shall write for any formula $A(x_1, ..., x_n)$ with individual variables $x_1, ..., x_n$, $u \models A_M$ iff $u = (u_1, ..., u_n)$ and $(u_1, ..., u_n)$ bears the relation A_M being the interpretation of A in M. Let D be a subset of the set of all formulas in L such that for every formula A there is u such that $u \models A_M$ and there is an effective method of checking whether this holds or not, and among formulas in D there is a formula Δ valid in M. In particular D can be taken as a set of atomic formulas. For the sake of simplilcity we shall assume in the sequel that in formulas in D only one individual variable occurs, but it is easy to see that this assumption is not essential and that in all considerations can be omitted. For any set s of formulas in D we shall write

$$(5) \quad u \models s_M \text{ iff for every } A \in s, u \models A_M.$$

A subset $s \subset D$ is consistent if there is $u \in U$ such that $u \models s_M$. We shall write $s \vdash A$ iff for every $u \in U$, $u \models s_M$ implies $u \models A_M$. Now we adopt as Con and as an entailment relation $\vdash \subset (Con \times D)$, respectively, any family of finite consistent subsets of D such that the conditions (i) - (vi) are satisfied.

Now, corresponding to an information system $\mathcal{A} = (D, \Delta, Con, \vdash)$ there is a universe $U \neq \emptyset$ and a model M.

Applying our method of defining Scott's information systems, Example 1 in [8] can be presented as follows.

Let $U = \{0, 1, 2, ...\}$ and let one binary predicate $\leq$ occur in L. Then $\{\underline{0}, \underline{1}, \underline{2}, ...\}$ is the set of all individual constants in L. M assigns to any $\underline{n}$ the integer n and to $\leq$ the relation $\leq$. Let $D = \{\underline{0} \leq x, \underline{1} \leq x, ...\}$. Adopt as Δ formula $\underline{0} \leq x$ and as Con the family of all finite subsets of D. Moreover $\{\underline{n_1} \leq x, ..., \underline{n_K} \leq x\} \vdash \underline{m} \leq x$ holds iff $\underline{m} = \underline{0}$ or $m \leq n_i$ for some $i \leq k$.

Now we shall consider a poset $\underline{Con} = (Con, \subset)$, with $\subset$ being the inclusion relation, and $\underline{LCon} = (LCon, \cup, \cap, (d_t)_{t \in Con}, (I)_{I \in LCon})$ is a basic sP-algebra of type $\underline{Con}$. An ideal I in $\underline{Con}$ is said to be consistent if for any $t_1, t_2 \in Con$, the condition $t_1, t_2 \in I$ implies $t_1 \cup t_2 \in Con$ and $t_1 \cup t_2 \in I$.

4.1. Every element $s \in |\mathcal{A}|$ determines a consistent ideal in Con. More exactly if $s = \bigcup \{\bar{t} : t \in Con \text{ and } t \subset s\}$, then

$$(6) \quad I_s = \{t \in Con : t \subset s\} \text{ is a consistent ideal.}$$

Proof. If $s \in |\mathfrak{A}|$ then by (4), $s = \bigcup\{\bar{t}: t \in Con$ and $t \subset s\}$. Suppose $t_1, t_2 \in I_s$. Then $t_1, t_2 \in Con$ and $t_1, t_2 \subset s$. Hence $t_1 \cup t_2 \subset s$ and $t_1 \cup t_2$ is a finite subset of s. By (2), $t_1 \cup t_2 \in Con$. This yields $t_1 \cup t_2 \in I_s$. Thus I_s is consistent.

Notice that if $s, z \in |\mathfrak{A}|$ and $s \neq z$, then $I_s \neq I_z$. In fact if $s \not\subset z$ then there is $A \in s$ and $A \notin z$. Hence $\{A\} \in I_s$ and $\{A\} \notin I_z$.

4.2 If I is a consistent ideal, then I determines an element $s \in |\mathfrak{A}|$. More exactly

(7) $s = \bigcup\{\bar{t}: t \in Con$ and $t \in I\}$.

Moreover every element $s \in |\mathfrak{A}|$ is an image of a conistent ideal.

Proof. Let $\{A_1,\ldots,A_n\} \subset s$. Then there are $t_1,\ldots,t_n \in I$ such that $A_i \in \bar{t}_i$, $i \leq n$. Hence $t_i \vdash A_i$, $i \leq n$. Since I is consistent, $t_1 \cup \ldots \cup t_n \in I$. Moreover $t_1 \cup \ldots \cup t_n \vdash A_i$ for $i \leq n$. By (iii) $t_1 \cup \ldots \cup t_n \cup \{A_1,\ldots,A_n\} \in Con$ and hence by (i), $\{A_1,\ldots,A_n\} \in Con$. Thus every finite subset of s is in Con.

Now suppose that $t \subset s$ and $t \vdash A$. We claim that $A \in s$. Since $t \vdash A$, $t \in Con$, thus t is finite. Assume $t = \{A_1,\ldots,A_n\} \in Con$. Then $\{A_1,\ldots A_n\} \vdash A$. Moreover there are $t_1,\ldots,t_n \in I$ such that $t_i \vdash A_i$, $i \leq n$. Since I is consistent, $t_1 \cup \ldots \cup t_n \in I$. This yields $t_1 \cup \ldots \cup t_n \in Con$ and $t_1 \cup \ldots \cup t_n \vdash A_i$ for $i \leq n$. Since $\{A_1,\ldots, A_n\} \vdash A$, on applying (vi) we obtain $t_1 \cup \ldots \cup t_n \vdash A$. Thus $A \in s$. To prove the second part of 4.2 assume $s \in |\mathfrak{A}|$. Let $I_s = \{t \in Con: t \subset s\}$. By 4.1 I_s is a consistent ideal. Then $z = \bigcup\{\bar{t}: t \in I\} = \bigcup\{\bar{t}: t \in Con$ and $t \subset s\} = s$.

4.3 For any element $s \in |\mathfrak{A}|$, and $u \in U$

(8) $u \models s_M$ iff for every $t \in I_s$, $u \models t_M$.

Assume $s = \bigcup\{\bar{t}: t \in Con$ and $t \subset s\}$. Then $u \models s_M$ iff $u \models \bar{t}_M$ for $t \subset s$. This holds iff $u \models t_M$ for $t \subset s$. Since $I_s = \{t \in Con: t \subset s\}$, (8) follows.

If follows from 4.3 that the set of $u \in U$ satisfying the set s_M assigned by M to an element $s \in |\mathfrak{A}|$ coincides with the set of $u \in U$ such that for every t in the ideal I_s, $u \models t_M$.

5. <u>Information functions over information systems.</u> Let $\mathfrak{A} = (D, \Delta, Con, \vdash)$ be an information system over a universe $U \neq \emptyset$ with a model M. Consider the basic sP-algebra <u>LCon</u> = $(LCon, \cup, \cap, (d_t)_{t \in Con}, (I)_{I \in LCon})$ over $\mathfrak{A}$.

By an information function we shall mean any function $f: U \to LCon$ such that for any $u \in U$, f(u) is a consistent ideal or Con or $\emptyset$. The functions $d_t f$, for $t \in Con$, defined by (1) in Sec. 3, are said to be approximation functions for f.

It follows from (1), (2) in Sec. 3 that any information function f has a representation

(1) $f(u) = \bigcup_{t \in Con} (d_t f(u) \cap I(t))$, where $d_t f(u) = \begin{cases} \vee & \text{if } t \in f(u) \\ \wedge & \text{otherwise.} \end{cases}$

5.1 If $f: u \to LCon$ is an information function, then for every $u \in U$

(2) if $t_1 \subset t_2$, then $d_{t_2} f(u) \subset d_{t_1} f(u)$, $t_1, t_2 \in Con$

(3) if $t \cup z \notin Con$ or $d_{t \cup z}\, f(u) = \Lambda$, and $f(u) \neq Con$, then either $d_t f(u) = \Lambda$ or $d_z f(u) = \Lambda$.

Conversely if functions $d_t f: U \to \{V, \Lambda\}$ satisfy conditions (2) and (3), then they are approximation functions for an information function f defined by (1).

Proof. The first part follows from (1) in Sec. 3. If $t \cup z \notin Con$ or $d_{t \cup z} f(u) = \Lambda$ and $f(u) \neq Con$, moreover $d_t f(u) = V$ and $d_z f(u) = V$, then $t \in f(u)$ and $z \in f(u)$. This contradicts with the assumption that $f(u)$ is a consistent ideal or Con. Now assume that $d_t f$ are defined in a way that (2), (3) are satisfied. For a given $u \in U$, let $I_u = \{t \in Con: d_t f(u) = V\}$. Then I_u is equal either to $\emptyset$ or Con or a consistent ideal. Assume $z \in I_u$ and $t \subset z$. Then $d_z f(u) = V$. By (2) $d_t f(u) = V$, i.e. $t \in I_u$. Thus I_u is an ideal. Suppose $t, z \in I_u$. Then $d_t f(u) = d_z f(u) = V$. By (3), $t \cup z \in Con$ and $d_{t \cup z} f(u) = V$. Hence $t \cup z \in I_u$.

5.2 For every element $\in |\mathcal{U}|$ there is an information function $g: U \to LCon$ defining s_M, i.e. $\{u \in U: u \models s_M\}$, satisfying the following conditions.

$$(4)\ Sg = \{u \in U: g(u) = Con\} = \{u \in U: u \models s_M\},$$

$$(5)\ Sd_t g = \{u \in U: u \models t_M\} \text{ for all } t \in I_s,$$

$$(6)\ Sd_t g = \{u \in U: \text{for every } z \in I_s,\ u \models z_M\} \text{ for } t \notin I_s.$$

Proof.

Let us set

$$(7)\ d_t g(u) = \begin{cases} V \text{ if } u \models t_M \\ \Lambda \quad \text{otherwise} \end{cases} \quad \text{for every } t \in I_s$$

$$(8)\ d_t g(u) = \begin{cases} V \text{ if } u \models z_M \text{ for all } z \in I_s \\ \Lambda \quad \text{otherwise} \end{cases} \quad \text{for every } t \notin I_s$$

$$(9)\ g(u) = \bigcup_{t \in Con}^{LCon} (d_t g(u) \cap I(t)) \text{ for } u \in U.$$

Proof. We claim that conditions (2), (3) are satisfied. To prove (2) assume $t \subset z$, $d_z g(u) = V$. If $t, z \in I_s$, then by (7), $u \models z_M$. Hence $u \models t_M$ and by (7) $d_t g(u) = V$. If $t \in I_s$ and $z \notin I_s$, by (8) $u = w_M$ for every $w \in I_s$, hence also for t. By (7) $d_t g(u) = V$. If $t \notin I_s$ and $z \notin I_s$ then $u \models w_M$ for all $w \in I_s$. Hence by (8) $d_t g(u) = V$.

To prove (3) assume $d_t g(u) = V$ and $d_z g(u) = V$. If $t, z \in I_s$, then - since I_s is consistent - it follows that $t \cup z \in I_s$. By (7) $u \models t_M$ and $u \models z_M$. Hence $u \models (t \cup z)_M$ and by (7) $d_{t \cup z} g(u) = V$. If $t \notin I_s$ or $z \notin I_s$, then by (8) $u \models w_M$ for every $w \in I_s$. Hence $d_w g(u) = V$ for $w \in I_s$ by (7).

On the other hand $d_w g(u) = V$ for all $w \notin I_s$ by (8). Thus by (9) $g(u) = Con$. We just proved that g is an information function and that $d_t g$ are its approximation functions. Conditions (7) and (8) yield (5) and (6). Moreover (4) follows from 4.3, (1) and (5).

Notice that by (4), (5), (6)

$$(10)\ Sg \subset Sd_t g \text{ for } t \in Con$$

$$(11)\ Sg = \bigcap_{t \in Con} Sd_t g = \bigcap_{t \in I_s} Sd_t g.$$

6. Approximation reasoning over an information system. Let $\mathcal{J} = (D, \Delta, Con, \vdash)$ be an information system over a universe U with a model M and assume that formulas in D are from a language L.

Suppose that p(x) is a propositional function over U, not belonging to L, e.g. "x is a killer of John Smith" and let X = $\{u \in U: p(x)$ is true about $u\}$. By an approximation reasoning to recognize X we shall mean a process of defining approximation functions of an information function $g: U \to LCon$, such that the set $Sg = \{u \in U: g(u) = \vee\}$ would be equal to X. If $X = s_M$ for some element $s \in |\mathcal{J}|$, then by 5.2 such a function g exists and there is given a method of defining its approximation functions. Otherwise X would be a subset of Sg.

Two tasks have to be achieved in a process of reasoning. The first task is to establish dependencies of queries $t \in Con$ with respect to p(x). We assume that there is an oracle mapping $o: \{(p(x), t\}_{t \in Con} \to \{\vee, \wedge\}$ which to ordered pairs (p(x), t) for $t \in Con$ assigns $\vee$ or $\wedge$, i.e. gives an answer "yes" or "no". The intuitive meaning of $o(p(x),t) = \vee$ is that for every $u \in U$ if p(x) is true about u, then $u \models t_M$. It is easy to prove that $I = \{t \in Con: o(p(x),t) = \vee\}$ is a consistent ideal. Thus by 4.2 this ideal determines an element $s \in |\mathcal{J}|$. The second task is to define $d_t g$ for $t \in Con$. If $t \in I$, then $d_t g(u)$ are defined by applying (7) in Sec 5. For $t \notin I$, $d_t g(u)$ are defined according to (8) in Sec. 5. If U and Con are finite sets, then it is easy to formulate an algorithm for approximation reasoning to recognize a set X if $X = s_M$ for some $s \in |\mathcal{J}|$, determined by I.

7. Conclusion. It is possible to generalise our considerations to approximating arbitrary propositional functions corresponding to formulas of first order predicate languages. Logic dealing with such formulas --in which also approximation connectives d_t, $t \in Con$ and modal connectives C_t, $t \in Con$, determined by equivalence relations with respect to t, occur--with semantics connected with basic semi-Post algebras will be the subject of further investigations. This will present a special case of a more general logic for approximation reasoning as formulated in [7].

References

[1] N. Cat Ho and H. Rasiowa, Semi-Post algebras, Studia Logica, to appear.

[2] N. Cat Ho and H. Rasiowa, Subalgebras and homomorphisms of semi-Post algebras, Studia Logica, to appear.

[3] Y. Halpern, Reasoning about Knowledge, Ed. Y. Halpern, Morgan Kaufmann, 1986.

[4] W. Marek and H. Rasiowa, Approximating Sets With Equivalence Relations, Theoretical Computer Science, to appear.

[5] Z. Pawlak, Rough Sets, Int. Journal of Computer and Information Science 11(5), 1982, 341-356.

[6] H. Rasiowa, Logic Approximating Sequences of Sets, Invited Lecture, Proc. Int. Advanced School and Symp. on Mathematical Logic and its Applications, Drushba, Bulgaria 1986, Plenum Press.

[7] H. Rasiowa, An Algebraic Approach to Some Approximate Reasonings, Invited lecture, Proceedings ISMVL'87, Computer Society Press, 342-347.

[8] D. Scott, Domains for Denotational Semantics. A Corrected and Expanded Version of a Paper Prepared for ICALP 1982 Aarhus, Denmark 1982.

[9] R. Turner, Logic for Artificial Intelligence, Ellis Horwood Limited, Holsted Press, 1984.

Research reported here has been supported by Polish Government Grant CPBP08.15.

What Kind of Information Processing is Intelligence? A Perspective on AI Paradigms and A Proposal [1]

B. Chandrasekaran
Laboratory for AI Research
The Ohio State University
Department of Computer & Information Science
Columbus, OH 43210

Summary

The only truly universally shared paradigm among AI workers (and its friends in other disciplines) is: "Significant aspects of cognition and perception are usefully understood as *information processing activities on representations.*" While this characterization rules out needing to worry about chemistry and holograms for capturing the essence of information processing (IP) in intelligence, it does not characterize the nature of intelligent IP sufficiently within the class of all information processing activities. What is the *essential* nature of intelligence as information processing that can be used to characterize all its manifestations: human, alpha-centaurian and artificial?

In this talk we will trace the historical currents in AI with a view to giving a sense for various answers to this question, and concentrate, for convenience, on cognition , though we think appropriate extensions can be made for perception. Even within representational theories, there are two streams. The so-called symbolic paradigm, the traditional one in AI, works on the hypothesis that the representations are discrete symbol systems, which are processed by algorithmic interpretations. More recently, the connectionist school has suggested that the representations are non-symbolic, and proposed an alternative representation in the forms of weights of connections in a network.

I will discuss the connectionist-symbolic debate briefly, but concentrate mostly on the major symbolic paradigms. Most of the early work in AI within the symbolic IP framework merely served to show that many mental functions were *computable*, and created, in the form of programs, "realities in the field" that performed versions of tasks that in humans clearly require intelligence. The net effect of this was to make the idea of AI more plausible. However, with additional work in the following decade, three broad kinds of theories about intelligence constituting different answers to the question about the nature of underlying IP:

1. Architectural theories, which sought or proposed a level of abstraction and a corresponding IP architecture at which intel-

[1]Research supported by DARPA/RADC Contract F30602-85-C-0010, NSF grant MCS-8305032 and AFOSR grant 82-0255. Earlier versions of this talk have been presented at the AAAI Workshops on Foundations of Artificial Intelligence, February 6-7, 1986, Las Cruces, NM and on Theoretical Issues in Conceptual Information Processing, Philadelphia, PA. 1986, and Washington, D. C., 1987.

Methodologies for Intelligent Systems
Z. W. Ras and M. Zemankova, Editors

ligence *qua* intelligence emerges. Above this level are lots of particulars of an agent, and below is implementation.

2. Logical theories which describe an intelligent agent abstractly as a knower of propositions (a significant part of these propositions would deal with common sense knowledge of the world) and which typically propose the use of *deductive inference* as the IP mechanism to produce intelligence. Actual intelligent agents that exist, e.g., human beings, capture and implement this abstract design more or less well by using *heuristics.*

3. Functional theories of AI that embody one or more generic, functional properties of intelligence to solve a "natural kind" of a cognitive problem. These theories typically emphasize generic *organizational* aspects, which facilitate particular *classes of inference* in a *computationally efficient* way.

We will briefly outline our reasons for believing that types 1 and 2 above do not provide a satisfactory answer to the question about the nature of intelligence, and cast our sympathies with theories of type 3. We will point out that GPS, frames, some of Schank's theories and our own theories of knowledge-based problem solving are examples of type 3 theories. We will use *classification* as an example of an IP strategy to both illustrate a theory of this type and as a means to introduce and motivate our proposal about the essential nature of the IP operations that constitute intelligence:

The basic constraint to which intelligence as IP is a response
is one of *computational complexity* of the input/output problem
faced by the agent. Intelligence is a coherent
repertoire of generic information-processing
strategies, each of which solves an information processing problem
in a computationally efficient way, using knowledge of a certain
type, organized in a particular way, and using a particular
control regime.

Strategies of this type are what unite Einstein and the "man on the street" (and alpha-centaurians). While theories of type III do not by themselves constitute psychological theories, they nevertheless *provide the formalisms for couching cognitive theories.* They characterize intelligence abstractly to the extent that they define IP tasks, and propose knowledge forms and processing mechanisms to match the needs of the task. It also seems to us that the union of knowledge representation primitives for these tasks together constitute a good part of *mentalese.* Finally, the proposed view is consistent with the multiplicity of structures and mechanisms that one would expect of *intelligence as a biological phenomenon*, evolved to solve real problems of agents in real time.

On the Mechanization of Programmer's Knowledge

HENRYK JAN KOMOROWSKI
ARTIFICIAL INTELLIGENCE LABORATORY
MASSACHUSETTS INSTITUTE OF TECHNOLOGY
CAMBRIDGE, MA 02139

ABSTRACT

What do programmers with experience in writing programs know and how can this knowledge be mechanized so it can be used by a computer? This paper presents an informal overview of the foundations of mechanical support for declarative diagnosing of specifications. The goal of the mechanization is to provide an intelligent assistant for the programmer that can uncover flaws in the design rather than automatically generate programs.

What a programmer knows can be divided into knowledge of data structures, recursive schemata, assimilation rules, and the process of designing a program which is similar to extension of a theory. A prototype system now implemented provides salient advice, despite its limited knowledge-base.

1. INTRODUCTION

For the past three years I have investigated what the experienced programmers seem to know about writing programs, with the purpose of mechanizing this knowledge so it can be used by a mechanical process in a computer which supports the process of developing a program. The approach is to divide the work between the cooperating programmer and the computer letting each one do its best work. The initiative, and, at least in the beginning, the most of the decisions were expected to be handled by the programmer, but as the computer gains knowledge it may take over many of these activities. Mechanization can provide a basis for an intelligent assistant that can recognize ill-formed designs and suggest possible corrections. This situation is the opposite of the goal of a knowledge-based automatic synthesis of programs.

This work addresses a missing link: the support for the programmer at the most crucial and creative part of programming, that is the moment of formalizing a description of the problem while its method of solution is developed with and for the computer. The long range results of this research will lead to a software designer laboratory which provides a knowledge-based environment for the early, creative phases of programming, from conception to validation of a specification. In contrast, traditional software engineering tools usually deal with the later stages of program development such as the transformation of a specification into another representation, maintenance, and other bookkeeping chores. Similarly, knowledge-based automatic programming is concerned with generating correct programs from very high-level specifications by making appropriate selections of data-structure and using suitable methods of problem-solving.

The mechanized programming knowledge developed so far covers a portion of commonly used data structures and recursive schemata. The knowledge is based on an empirical study of how novice and advanced programmers write code. A prototype support system for a language of executable specifications has been implemented, which, in spite of its small knowledge of programming, provides useful assistance to the programmer.

The goals of the project call for application of various techniques, including Artificial Intelligence (AI), Software Engineering (SE), Databases (DB), and logic. We use AI methods, because no systematic, direct algorithm for program writing exists. Next, the domain of the discourse is the subject of SE: data structures, procedures, recursion, etc. DB's provide a conceptual framework for assimilating new knowledge while preserving (a degree of) consistency of the program database. Finally, logic supplies a convenient paradigm for writing specifications and interpreting their development as a formation of a theory.

Methodologies for Intelligent Systems
Z. W. Ras and M. Zemankova, Editors

Although the results of the research presented here seem general and may apply to a variety of programming paradigms, in order to be concrete the results are discussed in the context of executable specifications exhibited by the "pure" Prolog programs [1]. Therefore the terms a specification and a program will be used synonymously in this paper.

2. THE PROCESS OF PROGRAMMING

Program writing is a skill that requires experience, a substantial knowledge of both the domain and related areas and, if a computerized skill, nontrivial computational resources. The task of writing program involves establishment of a discourse domain, extensive planning and formulation of hypotheses, and a framework to explain the computer's decisions. Initially, the computer has some low-level knowledge of design issues, (e.g., knowledge of the syntax of the language) but needs to be told about the particular problem and its solution. A true knowledge-based approach would be characterized by the system's ability to complete the design from an outline or review the design to uncover mistakes, or both. The entire process is probably best described as an incremental transfer from the programmer to the computer of the specific knowledge about the problem to be solved. The partnership makes programming similar to traditional engineering in that the computerized apprentice fulfills roles of a team working for the chief engineer. Consequently, the computer needs to know about the process of designing a program, the domain of the discourse, the properties of the building blocks and methods of putting them together, and about possible solutions to easier and recurring subproblems. It also should be knowledgeable about finding errors and missing details i.e. able to diagnose the programs. Finally, since the knowledge of programming is highly subjective, the computer's decisions or suggestions must be accountable through a mechanism of explanations.

The various aspects of the programming process do not have to be established fully and a priori. The domain of the discourse, the plan, and the hypotheses of the design of a program, which can be partial and changed during the design as new evidence and new knowledge become available, might be completed only when the design of the program is finished. After all, only trivial programs are written in one attempt, while all others undergo several changes before reaching a satisfactory form, which affect the programmer's intuitions and understanding of the problem. The entire body of programming knowledge is not likely to be made available to the computer all at once, so the assistant must be able to deal with incomplete descriptions and acquire new skills.

3. PROGRAMMER'S KNOWLEDGE

A programmer has two sources of knowledge: programming knowledge and problem-specific knowledge. The latter is pertinent to the problem domain, e.g., knowledge of diseases and diagnoses, or of syntax-editing, (and which varies from domain to domain), and usually, is acquired from another expert. Programming knowledge is more generic and does not vary between task domains. (Although problem-specific knowledge is important to the success of programming, a separate study beyond the scope of this paper would be required for each application; for example, some aspects of domain knowledge were emphasized in the context of automatic program synthesis.) Specifically, a programmer will also know about the consequences of adding, modifying, or removing a part of the specification, i.e., about assimilating knowledge.

3.1. Programming Knowledge

The starting point for development of a program is an intuition of the problem to be solved. Usually, a collection of objects and relations between these objects are considered, and the program to be developed has to compute these relations. One programming tasks, then, is to represent these objects and define the relations in some formal way. The executable specification should be validated by checking its properties and executing it.

Conceptually, the process of design a program consists of the following iterative steps:

1. Intuitive description of the problem
2. Formal specification of the object domains
3. Formal specification of the relations on the object domains
4. Validation

Correspondingly, standard programming knowledge is concerned with data structures, relation schemata, and validation, in which the steps just given, outline a plan for designing a program. At each iteration a part of the specification may be extended, updated, or deleted.

In the programming process the selection of data structures and the choice of the recursive schema are often hypothetical. The programmer makes a hypothesis and then tries to verify its assumptions. A computer that can help make and verify hypotheses as well as indicate consequences of the choices will greatly enhance this process.

The standard knowledge is essential in the design of programs but another, and often overlooked aspect of programming is distinguishing between, when an addition or a modification might introduce redundancy or a contradiction, and when an addition supplies new and independent information. This distinction is characteristic of the *assimilation* knowledge and is treated in section 3.1.3.

3.1.1 Knowledge of Data Structures

The knowledge of data structures and the knowledge of recursive schemata are closely related and sometimes difficult to separate, but for the sake of discussion separating the sources seems useful.

Elementary data structures are assumed to be atoms, numbers, lists, and trees. Purpose-oriented, complex data structures such as stacks, queues, records, and sets, are built from the elementary structures. Empirical study of the knowledge applied by the experienced programmer confirms that in addition to such obvious properties as termination, the well-written specifications that use these data structures very often are mutually exclusive, exhaustive, and, in the case of sequential implementations, can have consistent annotations. (An annotation, roughly, is a declaration concerning the input and output arguments of the relation)

Redundancy and incompleteness in coverage of the domains of the data structures can often be a problem for both beginners and moderately experienced programmers. The study showed that at times even experienced programmers will overlook the multitude of choices, as simple but typical instance below illustrates. (For reasons of space a larger example cannot be included here) Consider the following attempt to define the `factorial`:

```
factorial( 0, 1)
factorial( N, R) ←                % for all N
      sub1( N, N1) ∧ factorial( N1, R1) ∧ times( R1, N, R)
```

More than 60% of the students interviewed in the group of novice programmers and about 10% of those in the experienced group did not notice that this definition is incorrect; the reader may try to solve the problem before proceeding further.

First, since the specification of the first argument in the second clause says "for all N's" and since the range of N is not qualified then, in particular, N could be equal to 0. This interpretation is contrary to the meaning intended by, say, the inexperienced or inattentive Prolog programmer, who often assumes the **if-then-else** meaning of these clauses. Second, although such a redundancy might not be discovered immediately, sooner or later it will create a problem (an infinite recursion upon negative input or upon backtracking). The unexpected meaning of the factorial program is due to nondeterminism, rather than to the execution mechanism. As soon as nondeterminism is allowed, execution forms other than backtracking will exhibit analogous problem.

Similarly, because the development of a specification is open-ended, safeguards must be provided in the cases when knowing all the input data *a priori* is not possible. Consider, for instance, the definition of an input command handler taken from a structure editor (unimportant details are omitted for clarity): the first line is a comment which says that `exeCommand` is a relation of three arguments and that the first argument can be one of the four explicitly mentioned or an unknown one:

```
% exeCommand :  {back, down, next, up} ∪ Unknown × ... × ...
exeCommand( back, _, _) ←
            back( _, _)
exeCommand( down, _, _) ←
            down( _, _)
exeCommand( next, _, _) ←
            next( _, _)
exeCommand( up, _, _) ←
            up( _, _)
```

This example illustrates incompleteness in a definition. Namely, the specification does not state explicitly what would happen in the case of an "unknown" value. A safeguard would be an explicit completion of the domain with the "catch-all" clause:

```
exeCommand( Otherwise, _, _) ←
            not_a_member( Otherwise, [back, down, next, up]) ∧
            message( error, 'Undefined command')
```

Such additions significantly ease validation of larger software. In order that the computer could support them it needs to understand which situations are open-ended and handle them correctly, an approach better than defaulting to one standard behavior. For instance, many Lisps would not inform the user if none of the conditions of a COND statement were satisfied.

In conclusion, programming knowledge of data structures suggests that a specification should be checked for redundancy and incompleteness in coverage of the domain of the data structures.

3.1.2 Knowledge of Recursive Schemata

Recursive relations are intimately connected with (recursive) data structures, the analysis of the recursive schemata being performed simultaneously with the analysis of the data structures used by the clauses. Several programming principles can easily be identified, including knowledge of arithmetic and boolean operators, list and binary tree manipulation, naming and using convention (i.e. an object named should be used within the scope), and basic heuristics about termination. The definition of `factorial` used above lends itself very well to an illustration of the reasoning mechanism used by the system to diagnose recursive specifications.

The necessary information deduced from the provided knowledge of the arithmetic operators and boolean comparison relations and from the (polymorphic) type-consistency hypothesis allows the conclusion that N is an integer. From the dataflow information and functional dependencies the use of parameters is inferred and N and 0 are discovered not to be mutually exclusive; hence, N can be zero. Explicit checking shows that no constraint such as $N > 0$, $N \neq 0$, or $N < 0$ is present in the body of the second clause. Consequently, the programmer is appropriately warned.

The underlying principles can be briefly described as follows. In an inductive definition with the termination condition $N = C$ (where C is a constant) a descent function, say σ, is such that

$$(\forall N)\,(\exists i)\,\sigma^i(N) = C.$$

Hence, during analysis of the definition the descent function and the constant must be found, as well as whether getting "below the floor" is possible. This fairly simplified picture accounts for only one induction schema. Consider, for example, another definition like the factorial but with an additional clause: `factorial( -17, 55)`. Of course, it is hard to suggest any rule, other than *a priori* specification of the domain , that could reject this clause. Such problems become even worse when double recursion, or more complicated descent functions are considered. A better definition of `factorial` in a nondeterministic language would be:

```
factorial( 0, 1)
factorial( N , R) ←
      N > 0 ∧ subtract( N, 1, N1) ∧ factorial( N1, R1) ∧ times( N, R1, R)
```

An even better result and somewhat more elegant solution could be obtained by selecting another data structure. Let `s` be the conventional successor functor, then the following definition of `factorial` is correct.

```
factorial( 0, s(0))
factorial( s( N), R) ←
      factorial( N, R1) ∧ times( R1, s( N), R)
```

This definition is satisfactory, because `0` and `s( N)` are known to be mutually exclusive. Further, by subtracting one (i.e., by going from `s( N)` to `N` in the recursive call to `factorial`) "the floor will be hit" without getting below it. The computer will eventually be able to comment on the choice of data structures and on the choice of recursive schemata.

The diagnosis can currently point to the mistake of redundancy, but knowledge of the descent/ascent functions also is applied. Similarly, there is knowledge of simpler non-termination cases, like a missing case for the empty list or for a list with a finite number of elements for recursive procedures operating on lists and binary trees.

3.1.3 Rules of Knowledge Assimilation

The programming process described in section 3.1 is concerned with the properties of new data in relation to the existing database of specifications. For example, new data can be provable from the existing specification, they can contradict it, be more general than a part of the specification, or be independent of the specification. Assimilation is a process in which these properties are verified.

In logic, each property can be expressed by the relation of provability. Recall that program P implies an atom G if and only if (iff) P ⊢ G, that is, iff G is provable from P. The provability relation ⊢ can be expressed in the specification language itself; using ⊢, the assimilation properties can be informally described as:

1. If P ⊢ G then G is provable from P

2. If P ⊢ ¬G, that is not G is provable from P, then G is contradictory with P

3. Let C be a new clause. If for some G ∈ P, (P - {G}) ∪ C ⊢ G, that is, P without G but augmented with C can prove G, then C is a generalization of G

4. If neither G nor ¬G is provable from P then G is independent

For lack of space only a simple example of the assimilation is considered. This program defines the `ancestor` relation.

```
ancestor( X, Y) ←
      parent( X, Y)
ancestor( X, Z) ←
      parent( X, Y), ancestor( Y, Z)
parent( A, B) ←
      mother( A, B) or father( A, B)
mother( violette, jan)
mother( violette, stanislaw)
father( jerzy, henryk)
father( henryk, jan)
father( henryk, stanislaw)
...
father( stanislaw, carol)
```

If the user wants to add:

```
ancestor( jerzy, jan)
```

then the addition is redundant, and if a redundancy-free program is required, the second clause of `ancestor` could be modified:

```
ancestor( X, Z) ←
      parent( X, Y) ∧ ancestor( Y, Z) ∧ not( X = jerzy ∧ Z = jan)
```

The order of the subgoals is to emphasize that general programming with specifications is considered rather than a particular case of, for instance, sequential Prolog.

3.2. Formation of Hypothesis

Currently, the knowledge-base is used only for diagnosing code, but the same knowledge could be used to generate hypotheses about the possible completion of partially specified programs. The underlying principle is that specifications are usually symmetrical: if a ≥ check is in one clause, then the other will probably have a < check. Since the programmer provides the idea for an implementation by supplying a clause, the search space for possible completion is dramatically smaller than in the case of automatic programming. The alternatives can be presented to the user who, if none is correct, will write an option.

4. INTEGRITY CONSTRAINTS AND EXTENSION OF THEORY

Knowledge of programming is expressed in the form of integrity constraints, similar to those of databases, which express general knowledge of programming and serve as a mechanism for expressing valid extensions of the theory described by the program. To this end, integrity constraints are verified when a clause is added to the program. If an integrity constraint is violated, the message associated with the constraint is displayed and the addition blocked.

5. TESTING

An approach to testing based on automatic test generation was outlined in [2]. Briefly, the domain D of an argument of a relation is defined by grammatical rules of the form

$$D ::= E_1 \mid \ldots \mid E_n$$

which can be used to construct the test data. Each rule describes the structure of the data and a partitioning of the data domain into disjoint sets. For a systematic test an element is heuristically selected from each of the sets. If more exhaustive testing is required, a subpartition of the partition can be constructed by applying grammatical rules to sentential forms. Since test elements selected in the previous step will fall into some of the new subdomains, new test elements should be selected from the other subdomains. In this way, test sets satisfy the asymptotic reliability and the validity criteria of [3]. In contrast to the declarative debugging of [4] selective tests are guided, on one hand, by the domain specification and, on the other hand, by the knowledge of heuristics encoding of programmer selecting the granularity of a partition and the elements of the subdomains.

6. ARCHITECTURE OF THE IMPLEMENTATION

The advice provided by the computer, based on both heuristics and, often, on resources of rather complex knowledge results in implementation of an expert system, so explanations of its decisions are possible, in particular, positive and negative explanations. The system is implemented in Prolog.

7. CONCLUSIONS AND FUTURE RESEARCH

The approach to knowledge-based software engineering outlined here is rather promising. Although the prototype implementation encodes only a minimal subset of programmer's knowledge, the support of the system is salient. Mechanization of the programmer's knowledge provides a framework for writing and validating programs. Encoding assimilation knowledge allows new, learning-oriented approaches to program design. Strictly speaking the system only supports addition without dependency maintenance, and the user is responsible for the consequences of removing clauses. Limited support can be obtained, because incomplete definitions can be analyzed and some consequences of clause removal thus assessed.

The approach is viable, but further theoretical results are needed, especially in the domain of the assimilation techniques. The knowledge base is still small; extending it and providing explicit coding of the design plans should be the primary goals of current research. Later, experiments in encoding task domain knowledge are planned.

Prolog provided a good framework for expressing the basic ideas, but it lacks many techniques of modern programming. More research in the logic programming languages is required.

8. RELATED RESEARCH

The first outline of the new approach to incremental programming was given in [5], and continuation of that research reported in [2] and [6], to which the reader interested in further details is referred. Research on automatic programming and intelligent software assistants offers a fruitful ground for a comparison. In the past it was especially common to consider a programming language of a much lower level than executable specifications. The choices ranged from Lisp [7], to Lisp and Ada [8], to Pascal [9].

Barstow provides an excellent argument for the task domain knowledge essential for a successful automatic programming system [10].

Results on the amalgamation of meta-level with the object level [11] served as the starting point for the formalization of the assimilation knowledge.

The best known approach to diagnosing programs is [12] which could be called a "model-theoretic debugging". In this approach the oracle, that is usually the programmer, is presented with an instantiated axiom and needs to decide whether it belongs to the intended model. For example,

```
Axiom: append( nil, 2.nil, nil).
Oracle's Diagnosis: not true in the intended model.
```

The approach is very elegant but requires the user to have a complete knowledge of the program being developed. In the declarative diagnosing approach, also called the "extension-of-theory diagnosing", the computer uses its sources of programming knowledge. Hence, the programmer needn't have a complete knowledge of programming. For instance, the declarative diagnosing approach seems more suitable for teaching specification programming to the beginners. For a sample of an "extension-of-theory diagnosis" see Appendix 2.

Appendix 1

The samples of declarative diagnostics included here have been edited for better legibility; in particular, internal variable names have been replaced by names used in the definitions. **Bold face** is user's input, `plain text` is diagnoser's findings, and the *italic font* denotes author's comments.

There are self-explanatory declarations of the types and modes which are used to diagnose the code.

SAMPLE 1

```
>> declare
...  goal_schemata(remove/3,  (list,  atom,  list),  (+,  +,  -)).
>> add  remove(nil,  Elt,  nil).
>> diagnose.
       - variable Elt used once.
>> delete  remove/3
>> add
      remove(nil,   _,   nil).
      remove(X.Xs,   Elt,   Zs)  <-
            X=Elt,    remove(Xs,  Elt,  Zs).
>> diagnose.
    - complementary case(s) to X=Elt missing.
    - dangling argument -- output argument not modified in recursive calls.
>> add
      remove(X.Xs,     Elt,  Zs)  <-
            not(X=Elt),  remove(Xs,     Elt,  Zs).
```

```
>> diagnose.
    - clauses 2:remove/3 and 3:remove/3 have equal heads.
>> delete 3:remove/3      % delete third clause of remove.
>> add
      remove(X.Xs,    Elt,  X.Zs)  <-
            not(X=Elt),  remove(Xs,    Elt,  Zs).
>> diagnose.
      None.
```

SAMPLE 2

```
>> declare
...  goal_schemata(replace/4,  (list,atom,atom,list),(+,  +,  +,  -)).
>> add
      replace(nil,  _,  _,  nil).
      replace(X.Xs,  Old,  New,  Zs)  <-
            X=Old,  replace(New.Xs,  Old,  New,  Zs).
      replace(X.Xs,  Old,  New,  Zs)  <-
            not(X=Old),  replace(Xs,  Old,  New,  Zs).
>> diagnose.
    - equal heads in 2:replace/3 and 3:replace/3.
    - possibly ill-formed recursive case in 3:replace/4 the input list not
      decreasing on recursion.
    - dangling 4th argument,  output argument not modified in recursive
      calls.
>> run  goal(replace(for.every.x.x.equals.x.nil,  x,y,Result)).
Result = for.every.y.y.equals.y.nil
```

SAMPLE 3

```
>> declare
...  goal_schemata(  reverse/2,  (+,  -),  (list,  list)).
>> add
      append(nil,  L,  L).
      append(X.Xs,  Ys,  X.Zs)  <-
            append(Xs,   Ys,   Zs).
      reverse(nil,  nil).
      reverse(X.Xs,    Rev)  <-
            reverse(Xs,  NR),
            append(X,  NR,  Rev).
>> diagnose.
      in 2:reverse/3 call to append: first argument not a list.
>> run  goal(  reverse(  p.a.l.nil,  Result  )).
Result = l.a.p.nil
```

SAMPLE 4

The fact that a relation is reflexive often escapes programmer's attention. A heuristic helps discover the problem.

```
>> declare
...  goal_schemata(sibling/2,  (+,  -);(-,  -);(-,  +),  (atom,  atom)).
      % alternative modes are declared.
>> add
      sibling(S1,  S2)  <-
            parent(P,  S1),  parent(P,  S2).
>> diagnose.
      warning: sibling/2 is reflexive
```

However, if the above schemata is replaced by a new schema then sibling/2 is not diagnosed as reflexive. Similarly, the addition of the inequality check in the body of sibling/2 (with the first set of mode declarations) alleviates the problem.

```
>> declare
... goal_schemata(sibling/2, (+, +), (atom, atom)).
>> diagnose.
      None.
>> add
      sibling(S1, S2) <-
            parent(P, S1), parent(P, S2), not S1 = S2.
>> diagnose.
      None.
```

SAMPLE 5

```
>> declare
... goal_schemata(frev/2, (list, list), (+, -)).
>> add
      frev(List, Rev) <-
            rev1(List, nil, Rev).
      rev1(nil, Stack, Stack).
      rev1(X.Xs, X.Collect, Reved) <-
            rev1(Xs, Collect, Reved).
>> diagnose.
    - second argument in call to rev1/3 in frev is nil; execution will never
      use the recursive clause 2:rev/3.
          or
    - call to rev1/3 in frev/2 will fail if List does not equal nil.
```

SAMPLE 6

In this sample the user might be interested in obtaining a more efficient version of the standard append/3 by adding a special case for the empty second argument. However, he misses the fact that this will introduce undesirable redundancy. The system suggests a method of overcoming the problem without giving up on the efficiency .

```
>> declare
... goal_schemata(append/3, (list, list, list), (+, +, -)).
>> add
      append(nil, L, L).
      append(Xs, nil, Xs).
      append(X.Xs, Ys, X.Zs) <-
            append(Xs, Ys, Zs).
>> diagnose.
      - clause 1.append/3 and clause 2.append/3 redundant when the arguments
      are nil.
      - clause 2.append/3 and clause 3.append/3 redundant when the second
      argument is nil.
```

SAMPLE 7

```
>> declare
... goal_schemata(merge/3, (list, list, list), (+, +, -)).
>> add
      merge(X.Xs, Y.Ys, X.Zs) <-
            X<Y, merge(Xs, Y.Ys, Zs).
      merge(X.Xs, Y.Ys, Y.Zs) <-
            X>Y, merge(X.Xs, Ys, Zs).
>> diagnose.
      - missing a case(s) for the empty list(s).
      - missing a case for equality.
```

```
>> add
      merge(nil,  nil,  nil).
>> diagnose.
      - missing case for equality.
>> add
      merge(X.Xs,  Y.Ys,  X.Zs)  <-
            X=Y,  merge(Xs,  Y.Ys,  Zs).
>> diagnose.
      None.
>> run  goal( merge( 1.3.5.nil,  2.4.5.6.nil,  Result)).
Result = 1.3.5._1085
```

Currently the reasoning mechanism is too weak to conclude that the lists need not be simultaneously empty, that is, it does not discover that one of the input lists can be empty while the other one could still contain some input. The correct definition is to replace the empty list case by two cases.

Appendix 2

As a matter of comparison with Shapiro's model theoretic approach to diagnosing his Shapiro's "buggy" quick-sort program was diagnosed declaratively in our previously reported work [6].

```
qsort([X|Xs], Sorted) <-
      partition( Xs, X, Smaller, Larger),
      qsort( Smaller, SS), qsort( Larger, LS),
      append( [X|SS], LS, Sorted).

partition( [A|As], Key, Smaller, [A|Larger]) <-
      partition( As, Key, Smaller, Larger).
partition( [A|As], Key, [A|Smaller], Larger) <-
      Key =< A, partition( As, Key, Smaller, Larger).

append( [X|Xs], Ys, [X|Zs]) <-
      append( Xs, Ys, Ys)
append( [], L, []).
```

"Buggy" quick-sort program

```
qsort/2: list cases incomplete for arg #1
qsort/2: no termination case.

partition/4: list cases incomplete for arg #1.
partition/4: no termination case.
partition/4: =< check not accompanied by complementary case(s).

append/3: variable(s) Zs used only once.
append/3: variable(s) L used only once.
```

Summary of the declarative diagnosis

Five out of the six bugs are diagnosed prior to executing the program. The only bug which is not discovered is the incorrectly placed X in the call to `append` in the body of `qsort`. This last bug is located through a convenient explanation mechanism.

REFERENCES

[1] J. W. Lloyd, "Foundations of Logic Programming", (Springer Verlag, Berlin, 1984).
[2] H. J. Komorowski and J. Maluszynski, "Logic Programming and Rapid Prototyping", to appear in the Science of Computer Programming journal.
[3] L. Bouge, N. Choquet, L. Fribourg and M.C. Gaudel, "Application of Prolog to test set generation from algebraic specifications", in: H. Ehrig, C. Floyd, M. Nivat and J. Thatcher, Eds., "Formal Methods and Software Development" TAPSOFT, Vol. 2, LNCS 186, Springer Verlag, Berlin 1985, pp. 261-275.
[4] R. Kowalski, Logic programming, in: R.E.A. Mason, Ed., Information Processing 83 (North Holland, 1983) 133-145.
[5] H. J. Komorowski, "Past, Present and Future of Programming Environments", invited talk, in: "Proceedings of the Programming Environments Colloquium Series", (J. Heering and J Klint, eds.), Matematisch Centrum, Amsterdam, The Netherlands, 1982.
[6] H. J. Komorowski, "A Declarative Logic Programming Environment", to appear in the Journal of Systems and Software.
[7] D. Barstow, "An Experiment in Knowledge-Based Automatic Programming", in: C. Rich and R. C. Waters, (Eds.) "Readings in Artificial Intelligence and Software Engineering", Morgan Kaufman Publishers, Inc., 1986.
[8] R. C. Waters, "The Programmer's Apprentice: A Session with KBEMacs", in: C. Rich and R. C. Waters, (Eds.) "Readings in Artificial Intelligence and Software Engineering", Morgan Kaufman Publishers, Inc., 1986.
[9] W. Johnson, E. Soloway, "PROUST: Knowledge-Based Software Understanding", in: C. Rich and R. C. Waters, (Eds.) "Readings in Artificial Intelligence and Software Engineering", Morgan Kaufman Publishers, Inc., 1986.
[10] D. Barstow, "A Perspective on Automatic Programming", in: in: C. Rich and R. C. Waters, (Eds.) "Readings in Artificial Intelligence and Software Engineering", Morgan Kaufman Publishers, Inc., 1986.
[11] K.A. Bowen and R.A. Kowalski, "Amalgamating Language and Meta-language in Logic Programming", in: *Logic Programming*, (K. Clark and S.-Å. Tärnlund, eds), Academic Press, 1982.
[12] E.Y. Shapiro, "Algorithmic Debugging of Programs", MIT Press, Cambridge, 1983.

A KNOWLEDGE BASE FOR AN INFORMATION SYSTEM DESIGN TOOL

C. CAUVET C.PROIX C.ROLLAND
University of Paris 1,
12 Place du Pantheon, 75231 PARIS Cedex 05
FRANCE

ABSTRACT

We present in this paper some aspects of an expert design tool so-called OICSI. The scope of OICSI is to generate the IS conceptual schema from a description of the application domain given with a subset of the french natural language.

The tool starts, in a first step with an interpretation of natural language descriptions leading to a first version of the conceptual schema. Then in the second step, OICSI uses design rules in order to complete and transform this first version into a normalized network which describes all the elements of the final conceptual schema.

The paper focusses on the second step. It presents the representation and rules included in the OICSI knowledge based as a formalization of design rules issued from our own practice and experience of Information System design.

1. INTRODUCTION

An Information System (IS) design methodology is a consistent set of models (concepts and rules to manipulate them), languages (constructions to describe the design product), methods (operating processes) and software tools.

The oldest methodologies focus on methods SSA[1], SADT[2], AXIAL[3]; today's methodologies ACM/PCM[4], TAXIS[5], REMORA[6] IDA[7] emphasize the use of models; the most recent ones combine semantically powerfull models and intelligent design tools. This attitude is justified by the nature of the design task; models help the designer to analyse the real world, to describe its pertinent aspects and to represent them by data structures and associated constraints and rules; but the main part of the design task is a creative one which depends on the designer's experience and expertise. Thus, to be really useful a tool must have some intelligence in order to have a behaviour similar to the human expert behaviour.

Assuming that it is possible to formalize the designer's experimental knowledge, we have chosen to develop an expert design tool in order to support the design of large and semantically complex information systems.

The operational prototype of the tool so-called OICSI [8] (french acronym for intelligent tool for IS design) generates the IS conceptual schema from a description of the application domain. This description is given in a sub-set of the French natural language.

In a first step (descriptive step), the tool interpretes the application domain description given by the OICSI's user [8]. The result of this interpretation is a semantic network corresponding to a first draft of the conceptual schema. This semantic network shows the Real World pertinent classes of facts and the relationships between them that must be represented in the IS.

Methodologies for Intelligent Systems
Z. W. Ras and M. Zemankova, Editors

Then the tool transforms the semantic network with some conceptualization rules in order to choose a consistent , non redundant and complete representation of classes of facts and classes of relationships (conceptualization step).

This paper is concerned with the conceptualization step. It focusses rather on the representation of the knowledge used during the conceptualization process more than on the process itself. The paper is organized as follows: section 2 brievly introduces the semantic network, section 3 presents the knowledge base used by OICSI to perform the transformation.

2. PRESENTATION OF THE SEMANTIC NETWORK

The model underlying the semantic network is object-oriented and belong to the family of data semantic models like SHM [4], TAXIS [5] and CIAM [9]. It has the particularity to allow the description and representation of both IS structural (static) and behavioural (dynamic) aspects.The description of dynamic aspects is based on a causal approach of the behaviour of a real system : events trigger actions which modify the state of entities. These state changes can be events that in turn, and so on.

The model is normative. It implies constraints of representation that make conceptual schema non redundant, complete and consistent . These norms are presented in [10].

It includes five object types so-called ENTITY, ACTION, EVENT, DOMAIN and CONDITION. A type of node is associated to each of these types.

The **Entity** type node modelizes classes of either concrete or abstract real world entities (such as Accounts, Orders, Clients). Notation: ▭

The **Action** type node modelizes classes of actions which are regularly executed within the real world (such as an order analysis, a payroll, a reorder, a delivery of products). Notation: ⬭

The **Event** type node describes classes of similar state changes of the real world that trigger the effective executions of similar actions (such as an order arrival, a stock-breacking, a hiring of an employee). Notation: ▱

The **Domain** type represents properties characterizing entities (such as the number order, the name of the client). Notation ▨

The **Condition** type node has a different nature. It is a predicate declaration that completes the description either of an Action or an Event or an Entity: for instance, the "delivery of an order" is possible only if the stock is sufficient. Notation: ⬡

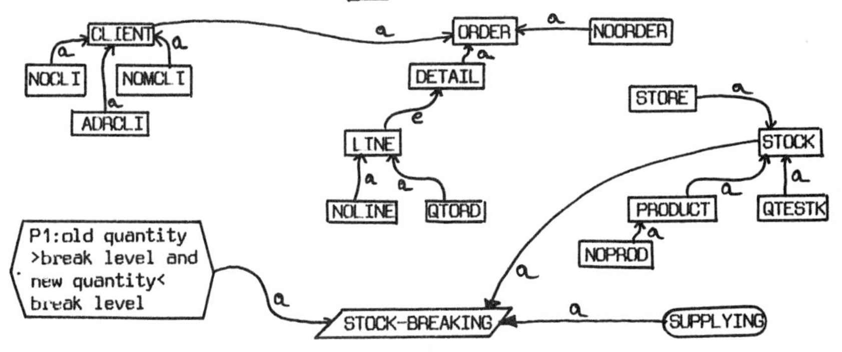

Figure 1: Example of semantic network

The model uses usual abstraction forms: classification, generalization [11], aggregation [12] and association [13]. These abstraction forms allow to construct objects of any types. The aggregation, association and generalization forms are respectively represented by the "a", "e" and "g" arcs of the semantic network (figure 1).

3. THE CONCEPTUALIZATION PROCESS AND ASSOCIATED KNOWLEDGE BASE

3.1 OBJECTIVE

The first draft of the conceptual schema is generally incomplete and partially wrong. The role of conceptualization process is to define in all details the representation finally chosen as a compromise. This representation must be complete (complete does not mean exhaustive), not redundant and consistent.

Then the conceptualization process leading to the final version of the schema must satisfy three main objectives:

- To raise up questions that will be help the designer to make the most adequate and pertinent modelling choices.

- To assist him in his choices by proposing solutions.

- To check the consistency, completness and non redundancy of elaborated solutions.

In order to satisfy these objectives OICSI uses a conceptualization policy which reproduces as closely as possible the experimental policy of design experts.

3.2 NATURE OF THE KNOWLEDGE USED BY DESIGNERS

Representation is the main task of the design process. It consists of using the description of the application domain to find the object structures the most adapted to the representation of the real phenomea and relationships. Starting from our design practice we reach the two following conclusions:

-It is when the designer tries to apply norms of representation to the perceived reality that he can detect lacks and errors; and then get complementary information to progressively lead to a satisfactory solution. Therefore the conceptualization process is an interactive one, requiring a permanent dialogue between the designer and the application domain specialists.

A pertinent representation of real facts must take temporal aspects into account. Indeed, the designer has different possibilities to represent evolutionary phenomena. He can decide to limit representation to snapshot descriptions of the real world but also choose historics on the evolution of such descriptions over time.

Thus, we have formalized the knowledge of designers in the representation area with "representation patterns" mainly based on these two aspects: **respect of norms and temporal aspects.**

3.3 REPRESENTATION PATTERNS

We have defined more than thirty representation patterns grouped in three classes:

(1) object representation patterns
(2) structural relationships representation patterns
(3) behavioural relationships representation patterns.

Each pattern associates to an initial situation (which is part of the semantic network) a target situation more precise, more complete and more consistent with the norms.

Each pattern is expressed by the set of rules of three types:

. **mapping** rules which maps the initial situation onto one or several alternative object structure(s).

. **dialogue** rules between OICSI and the designer.

. **diagnosis** rules to detect abnormal situations.

Each pattern uses one or both of the two representation criteria we have pointed out: respect of norms and temporal aspects.

For instance the representation of an entity by an aggregate object implies the choice of an identifier (norm) whose life-cycle is identical to the life-cycle of the aggregate object (temporal aspect).

3.4 EXAMPLES OF REPRESENTATION PATTERNS

3.4.1 Representation patterns of entities nodes

These patterns classify entity nodes of the first version of the semantic network into complex nodes and basic nodes.

R1: Any entity type node is a basic node if it is not origin of arcs and is a complex node if not.

For example in figure-1 NOCLI and NOMCLI are basic nodes; CLIENT is a complex node.
The basic nodes correspond to domain type nodes.
The research of the complex node identifiers leads to choose the right type of the node. A complex node without identifier is a domain type node. The others are entity type nodes.
In order to get these identifiers, OICSI uses dialogue rules.

3.4.2 Representation patterns of structural relationships between entities

In the first version of the semantic network, the arcs describe relationships between entities.
The meaning of these relationships must be precised. This leads to map these arcs into "a", "e", "g" arcs or into a combination of them. This mapping may involve the creation of new nodes which are not yet in the semantic network.

The transformation of these arcs is a complex task.
We have defined twelve patterns which follow the same principle. We illustrate them by three examples.

PRINCIPLE

The representation of an arc requires to specify the nature of the relationship expressed by this arc. In order to help the designer in this task, we have:

(1) defined a taxonomy of the relationships between entities which is similar to the cardinality concept but takes into account the temporal aspects. This taxonomy leads to valuate relationships between entities of the real world.

(2) ordered the different rules of the pattern such as the designer starts giving information of the type of the arc as they are in the real world and then has to consider alternative choices for their representation.

Thus, all the patterns are interactive and generally executed in three steps:

- get type of the arc.
- proposing the more complete representation.
- adapt it according to the designer decision.

We present the taxonomy and examples of patterns in turn.

THE TAXONOMY

The taxonomy of the arcs is based on three criteria so-called: totalness valuation and permanency.

totalness

A relation f between two entities A and B is total, if and only if each instance of A is associated with at least one instance of B, at any point of time, f is partial if not.
more formally:

f is total (t) $\longleftrightarrow \forall t \in T\ \forall a \in A\ \exists\ g \in Gt(f): \Pi 1(g)=a.$

f is partial (pa) $\longleftrightarrow \exists\, t \in T\ \exists\, a \in A\ \nexists\ g \in Gt(f): \Pi 1(g)=a.$

where T=[points of time which are ordered]
Gt(f)=$\{(a,b) \in A \times B\ /\ f(a)=b \text{ at } t\}$
$\Pi 1(a,b)$: first component projection.

valuation

A relation f between two entities A and B is simple if and only if each instance of A is associated with at most one instance of B at any point of time, else f is multiple.
more formally:

f is simple (s) $\longleftrightarrow \forall t \in T\ \forall a \in A\ \exists\ g,g' \in Gt(f)\ \Pi 1(g)=a\ \Pi 1(g')=a \longrightarrow g=g'$

f is multiple (m) $\longleftrightarrow \exists t \in T\ \exists\, a \in A\ \exists\, g,g' \in Gt(f):\ g \neq g'\ \Pi 1(g)=a \wedge \Pi 1(g')=a$

permanency

A relation f between two entities A and B is <u>permanent</u> if and only if the set of the images of an instance of A at t is included in the set of the images of this instance at t' (t'>t), if not, f is <u>changeable</u>.
more formally:

f is permanent (p) $\Longleftrightarrow \forall t,t' \in T \; t<t' \; \forall a \in A$ we have:
$$\{g \in Gt(f), \Pi 1(g)=a\} \subset \{g \in Gt'(f), \Pi 1(g)=a\}$$

f is strongly permanent (sp) $\Longleftrightarrow \forall t,t' \in T \; t<t' \; \forall a \in A$ we have:
$$\{g \in Gt(f), \Pi 1(g)=a\} = \{g \in Gt'(f), \Pi 1(g)=a\}$$

f is changeable (v) $\Longleftrightarrow \exists t,t' \in T \; t<t' \; \exists a \in A$ we have:
$$\{g \in Gt(f), \Pi 1(g)=a\} \neq \{g \in Gt'(f), \Pi 1(g)=a\}$$

EXAMPLES OF PATTERNS

EXAMPLE 1: construction of an aggregate object

R2: For each total-simple-changeable relationship between two entities A and B , if the opposite relationship is total-multiple-changeable, then propose an aggregate object which is necessary composed with A,B and an object C. C is a set of dates where relationships between instances of A and B were born.

The application of R2 to the (a) situation leads to the (b) situation. This representation is an historic description of the entity OWNERSHIP which represents the car ownerships.

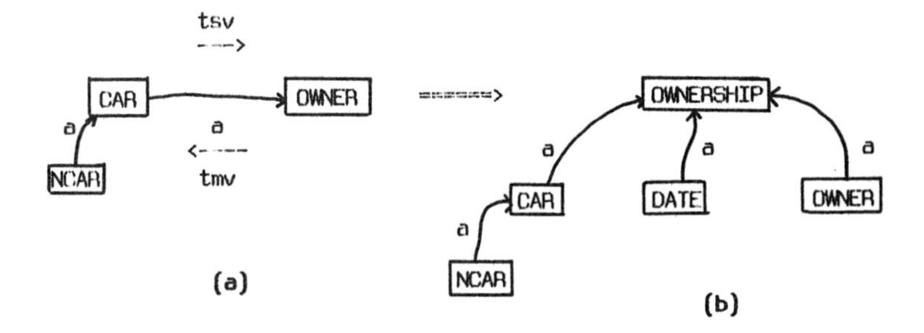

(a) (b)

The user may confirm this representation choice (which is justified by the nature of the "a" arc) but he can invalidate it. Then an alternative solution is proposed by OICSI ((c) situation).

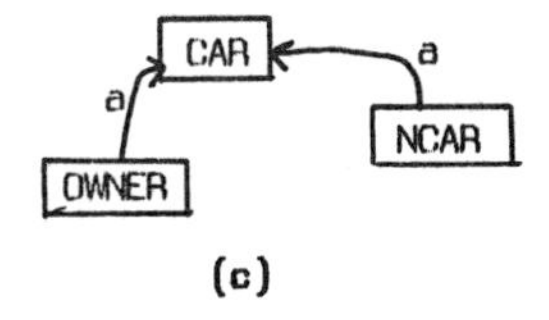

(c)

In this solution, the representation of ownerships is instantaneous. The IS would be only able to tell who is actually the owner of a car.

EXAMPLE 2: construction of a set object

R3: For each total-multiple-permanent relationship between two entities A and B, if the opposite relationship is total-simple-permanent then represent the arc by an "e" arc from A to B.

The application of R3 to the (a) situation leads to (b) situation.

EXAMPLE 3: construction of a generic object

R4: For each partial-simple-changeable relationship between two entities A and B, if the opposite relationship is total-simple-permanent then propose an object A' which is a specialization of the entity A. The arc between A and B is switched to A' and B. The relationship which it expresses becomes total.

The application of R4 to the (a) situation leads to (b) situation.

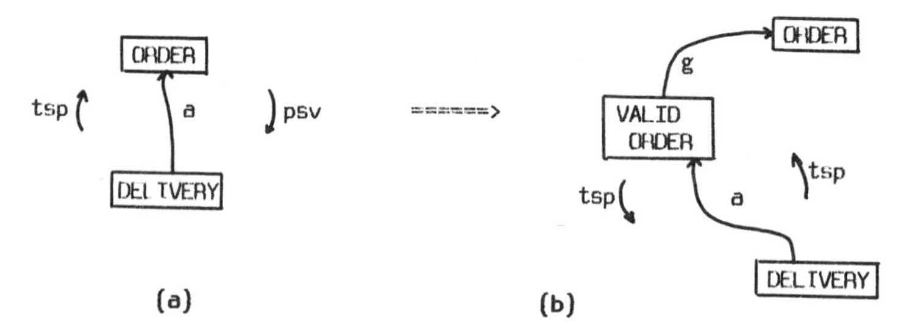

4. CONCLUSION

From the three years of OICSI development, we can raise up the following comments:

. The formalization of practical design rules is an instructive and intellectually exciting effort. The design process is the part which is less formalized in methodologies. These methodologies focus on models and formal languages. But they generally limit the support to the design process itself to a proposal decomposition into several steps and sub-steps. The expert design approach implies an innovative effort to formalize the human behaviour in processing IS design.

. The flexibility of the system expert approach is really an advantage. It allows to build a software which enables both to integrate new concepts in the network and new rules in the OICSI's knowledge base.

Prolog is a suitable tool for software development. In our case it is very well fitted to the natural language processing [8].
It allows an easy and powerfull description of the different components of the two networks. It is totally adapted to an incremental description of patterns and validation rules.

Unfortunately, the performances of the actual prototype are insufficient for a real use in concrete projects. In order to improve performance we needed to try to do some "intelligent strategies of resolution" both for the natural language interpretation and for patterns execution.

REFERENCES

[1] C. Gael T. Sarson: Structured systems analysis Prentice Hall 1979
[2] Dt. Ross, Kl Schaum: Structured systems analysis for requirements definition IEEE Transaction on software engineering 1977
[3] AXIAL in IFIP Open CRIS (comparative review on information system) conference 1984
[4] M.L. Brodie, E. Silva: Active and Passive Component Modeling: ACM/PCM in IFIP WG8.1 working conference on "Information systems design methodologies: a comparative review" 1982.
[5] J. Mylopoulos,H. Wong: Some features of the TAXIS model Proc. 6th Int conf. on VLDB 1980.
[6] C. Rolland, C. Richard: The Remora methodology fo information systems design and management in IFIP WG8.1 working conference on "Information systems design methodologies: a comparative review" 1982
[7] Bodart, Pigneur: Conception assistées des applications informatiques Masson 1983.
[8] C. Rolland, C. Proix: An expert system approach to information system design in Proc. IFIP Congress 86 North Holland 1986.
[9] J.A. Bubenko, M.R. Gustafsson, T. Karlsson: "A Declarative Approach to Conceptual Information Processing" in IFIP WG8.1 Working Conference on "Information Systems Design Methodologies: a comparative review" 1982.
[10] C. Cauvet, C. PROIX, D. Trecourt: Une base de connaissance pour la conception des systèmes d'information. INFORSID (Lyon) 1987.
[11] J.M Smith, C.P. Smith: Database Abstractions : Aggregation. Communications of ACM. June 1977.
[12] J.M. Smith, C.P. Smith: Database Abstractions : Aggregation and Generalization. ACM TRANSACTIONS on Database Systems. June 1977.
[13] M.L. Brodie: Fundamental Concepts for Semantic Modelling of Objects. Computer Corporation of America. October 1984.

A MODEL-BASED FRAMEWORK FOR CHARACTERIZATION OF APPLICATION DOMAINS FOR THE EXPERT SYSTEM TECHNOLOGY

Mirsad Hadzikadic, David Y. Y. Yun, and William P. -C. Ho
Department of Computer Science and Engineering
Southern Methodist University
Dallas, Texas 75275

ABSTRACT

Application domains potentially suitable for development using the expert system technology vary widely in terms of requirements, features, and utility. Heuristic classifications of application domains have been attempted with limited success. Yet, the need for better characterization of these domains increases with the popularity of the expert system technology. The need arises both from fitting the domains with appropriate representations and from matching applications with proper development tools. This paper endeavors to establish a set of primitives and compound processes that comprise a framework usable for describing a wide class of application domains. It differs from previous attempts of classification in that the primitives encompass more fundamental concepts, while the framework allows the capture of high-level abstractions and concrete representations of application domains.

INTRODUCTION

As the Expert System (ES) technology becomes increasingly popular for (yet) untested applications, a serious gap in knowledge has become correspondingly prominent - the question of determining the appropriateness of the match between a prospective application domain and the technology and tools of ES. Can a prospective developer of an ES discern whether his particular problem is a candidate for using the ES technology, or can he simply use a traditional programming methodology? If so, is it appropriate to use a development tool, often called a Knowledge-Base Development Environment (KBDE), or would it be necessary to develop new knowledge representation schemes and to design a different inference mechanism? And, if so, which of the available KBDEs has strengths in the features most vital to his problem?

The standard development procedure of an application ES today is for the knowledge engineer (who is chosen and sponsored by a project manager) to select what he feels is the most appropriate KBDE as the system skeleton and then to incorporate application knowledge and requirements into the provided knowledge representation formats of the chosen KBDE. However, matching application domains to ES technology is not yet a well defined process. Mistakes are often easy to make, difficult to detect, and extremely costly in misdirected time, effort, and money. In essence, a body of knowledge is lacking to guide the ES design team in selecting the appropriate tool(s) based on the specific characteristics of their target application domain. Apriori determination of appropriateness for a problem to be solved by the ES technology is even more an art.

The need to fill in this knowledge gap has been alluded to indirectly, "The next generation of knowledge representation tools may even help users to select appropriate methodologies for each particular class of knowledge, and then automatically integrate the various methodologies so selected into a consistent framework for knowledge" [1]. The AI literature has also mentioned this need directly: "In addition, continued research studies should help us classify problem types and indicate which representational frameworks are more appropriate for a given problem class" [2]; "The selection of the domain is a critical task in an expert system development. ... They (the knowledge engineering project team) must decide whether the selected application(s) are best suited to solution by present expert system technology, or if there might be a better way (or, possibly, no way) to attack the problems." [3]; and "In short, attempts

Methodologies for Intelligent Systems
Z. W. Ras and M. Zemankova, Editors

to describe a mapping between 'kinds of problems' and programming languages have not been satisfactory because they don't describe what a given program 'knows': Applications-oriented descriptions like 'diagnosis' are too general ... , and technological terms like 'rule-based' do not describe what kind of problem is being solved. We need a better description of what heuristic programs do and know - a computational characterization of their competence - independent of task and independent of programming language implementation." [4].

Chandrasekaran [7] has pointed out the importance of making a distinction between the information processing level and the implementation level:

> " ... the field of expert systems is stuck in a level of abstraction that obscures the essential nature of the information processing tasks that current systems perform. The available paradigms often force us to fit the problem to the tools rather than fashion the tools to reflect the structure of the problem. ... Most available languages, be they rule-, frame-, or logic-based, are more like the assembly languages of the field than programming languages with constructs essential for capturing the essence of the information processing phenomena."

Also, Clancey [4] has argued that:

> " ... attempts to describe a mapping between *kinds of problems* and programming languages have not been satisfactory because they don't describe what a given program *knows*: Applications-oriented descriptions like 'diagnosis' are too general ... , and technological terms like 'rule-based' do not describe what kind of problem is being solved. ... We need a better description of what heuristic programs do and know - a computational characterization of their competence - independent of task and independent of programming language implementation."

RELATED WORK

Chandrasekaran and his associates have found six generic tasks that are useful as building blocks for the construction (and understanding) of knowledge-based systems: hierarchical classification, hypothesis matching, knowledge-directed information passing, object synthesis by plan selection and refinement, state abstraction, and abductive assembly of hypotheses. Chandrasekaran [7] suggested that what we need is knowledge representation languages that will enable us to directly encode knowledge at the appropriate level by using primitives that naturally describe the domain knowledge for a given generic task. The problem-solving behavior for the task can then be automatically controlled by regimes appropriate for the task.

Clancey has described [4] [9] the *heuristic classification* model that characterizes *a form of knowledge and reasoning*-patterns of familiar problem situations and solutions, heuristically related. In capturing problem situations that tend to occur and solutions that tend to work, this knowledge is essentially *experiential*, with an overall form that is problem-area-independent. Heuristic classification is a method of computation, not a kind of problem to be solved. Thus, Clancey refers to 'the heuristic classification method', not 'classification problem'."

As Clancey pointed out, the heuristic classification model gives us two new angles for comparing problem-solving methods and kinds of problems. It suggests that we characterize programs by whether solutions are selected or constructed, as well as that different 'kinds of things' might be selected or constructed. Clancey has revised the *generic categories of knowledge engineering applications*, defined in [6], by organizing descriptions of problems around the concept of a system instead of an object. As an answer to the question: *What can we do to or with a system?*, Clancey has come up with the *generic operations for synthesizing and analyzing a system.*

However, being a 'method' rather than a 'problem', heuristic classification doesn't help us in our attempt to characterize application domains for the expert system technology. At the same time, the generic operations for synthesizing and analyzing a system can be used to characterize (describe) a specific application domain. However, the problem here lies in the fact that it is hard to establish the appropriate level of abstraction that would be useful across different domains. What aspects of a system are relevant to the problem-solving process? How does the goal of the problem-solving process relate to the complexity of the system? What level of abstraction is sufficient to capture this relationship in a useful manner?

Chandrasekaran has argued that there are six generic tasks useful as building blocks for the construction of knowledge-based systems, thus, in fact, characterizing problems within application domains as well. But, the author himself has recognized that this list of generic tasks is not exhaustive. Now, this fact gives a rise to new questions. What are the criteria of "admitting" a task into the set of the tasks already recognized as the generic ones? How do we define the appropriate level of abstraction for a candidate task? Without the proper answers to these questions it is hard to avoid the ad-hoc nature of any approach to the problem of characterization of either application domains or knowledge-based systems.

To avoid the problems encountered by the approaches described above, our approach relies on the notions of: (a) *mental model* and (b) *mental-model state* [8]. To reduce the complexity of the real world and selectively attend only the relevant aspects of problems, we organize descriptions of problems around the concept of a mental model instead of a system. A model-construction process, that maps objects and relationships from the outside world into the mental structure, by its nature reduces the level of detail used to describe a system, thus characterizing effectively the application domain itself. The question is now: What can we do to or with a mental model? The answer is: We can *change its state.* We translate a mental model from the current state to the next one by applying one of the applicable *operators.* At what level of abstraction is an operator defined? At the level of abstraction used to describe a mental-model state, which is captured by the model-construction process. The more specific the descriptions of model states, the lower a level of abstraction used to define the operators. And vice versa, the more general the descriptions of model states, the more abstract the operators. In the former case, the operators essentially characterize the problem-solving process employed by the mental model. In the latter case, however, the operators effectively characterize the application domain itself. Based on this analysis, we have set the goal of deriving a set of primitives (operators) representing the answer to the question: *What can we do to or with a mental model?*, given a description of a model state as general as possible. But, before we proceed, it is in place to define the terminology used in the rest of the paper.

TERMINOLOGY

The following basic notation will help us to describe the proposed primitives and compound processes that encompass a broad spectrum of application domains.

world

Refers to a domain at hand. It is the world where the objects of interest to us exist and the relationships between them hold. Because of the complexity of the world, we are interested in a subset of overall objects and relationships, specifically the ones related to our application. A degree of regularities we discover among the concepts in the chosen subset, gives us a measure of completeness of a representation of the world in a computer.

model

A representation of the world. A model captures the relationships and objects of interest for an application at hand. The model is "complete" if we have captured all of the concepts and respective relationships (of interest to us) which exist in the real world.

world state

Current state of the world. A good analogy is that of a snap shot of the world. A world state by nature is incomplete.

model state

A full description of a particular state of the model. Once the underlying model is considered to be complete, a resulting model state is also complete.

model parameters

Incomplete set of concepts (existing in the outside world) which act as the agents as well as the objects of the relationships which hold in the world (and are described by the model). These parameters are considered to be abstractions of the world. The modeler continues to abstract until there is enough information represented about the world to construct a model.

FRAMEWORK

We have adopted 12 distinct primitives as the basic constituents of the framework.

Primitives

The primitives should be thought of as transitions that mimic the changes in the outside world by "moving" the system from one state to another, according to the regularities caught by the underlying model.

1.	Recognize	2.	Classify
3.	Compare1, Compare2	4.	Specify1, Specify2
5.	Simulate1, Simulate2	6.	Analyze
7.	Infer	8.	Refine
9.	Construct1, Construct2	10.	Explain
11.	Execute1, Execute2	12.	Prescribe

Some of the primitives, as can be easily noticed, exist in two versions (Compare1 and Compare2, Specify1 and Specify2, etc.). The two versions of the same primitive differ only in the type of input they expect, and not in the nature of the primitive itself. We now continue with a description of each of these primitives.

Recognize

In: a sequence of world states (a sequence explicates a role of *time*).

Out: a set of model parameters.

A model builder observes some aspects of the world and creates a set of model parameters. This is the initial process of both model building and modification. In order to extract the model parameters a model builder needs to consider a sequence of discrete world states. He tries to "capture" the regularities between the concepts, paying a special attention to the order of occurrence of the specific events. A set of concepts, which describes a domain at hand as close as possible, is called *model parameters.*

Classify

In: model parameters, model classes.

Out: a model.

We are given a set of possible classes of a model. Based on the parameters of the model, extracted from the real world, we may decide on the model which best fits a set of input model parameters. Of course, the more complete our set of model parameters gets the better a chosen model fit to the particular application (a subset of problems to be handled by the system). A well defined model represents a basic precondition for a successful system.

Compare

Compare 1

In: a model state, a referent model state, a tolerance, a model.

Out: a model state.

Compare 2

In: a world state, a referent model state, a tolerance, a model.

Out: a model state.

By comparing a referent model state with the input model state(s), a discrimination is made among model states (one is chosen) according to a tolerance defined by the underlied model. Depending on type of input state, model state or world state, we may invoke Compare1 or Compare2, respectively. Both, a referent model state and a tolerance, are given (determined) by the model and its current state. Referent model state represents an "ideal" state of the system. A tolerance gives us a limit of how much an input state may differ from the ideal one to be still acceptable. An output model state represents the first input state which satisfies a predefined tolerance.

Specify

Specify 1

In: a sequence of world states, a model.

Out: an initial model state, a final model state.

Specify 2

In: a set of constraints, a model.

Out: an initial model state, a final model state.

Given a model, we can specify the constraints explicitly or "describe" them through a sequence of world states. In both cases, the output contains both an initial and a final state. Very often, we have a need to specify characteristics of the system (process, object) by listing a set of constraints which the system should satisfy. "Planing" and "Design" are certainly processes which implicitly include a constraint specification. But, sometimes we are unable to extract those constraints explicitly. Instead, we may sample the world states during the prespecified period, and supply discrete (ordered) world states to the system. The more the sequence resembles a behavior of the target process, the better the process is modeled by the system. In either case, however, an output of the specification process gives us both an initial model state and a final model state.

Simulate

Simulate 1

In: a world state, a model, time info.

Out: a model state.

Simulate 2

In: an initial model state, a model, time info.

Out: a model state.

Given a model, an input state, and a duration of a period of simulation, we simulate a behavior of the controlled (monitored) outside world (device, process, etc.) according to a predefined model, thus reaching a resulting model state. When the input state represents a world state, we actually create, after a prespecified time period, a snap shot of the world according to the model. The next sample of the world state, received after an elapsed time period, will allow us to derive a distance between simulated and actual state of the world. The distance may be used (if necessary) for corrective action on the model of the world, or the world itself. The situation is similar with an input state representing a model state. The only difference is caused by a lack of immediate feedback from the outside world.

Analyze

In: a world state, a model.

Out: an (incomplete) model state.

Given both a model and a current state of the world, we perform predefined tests to reveal regularities in the behavior of the world. If all of the tests are "negative", we are done. Otherwise, we proceed with a set of general tests whose results are regarded as a starting point for subsequent deductive processes. An output state is incomplete if any of the performed tests had a "positive" result. Since it indicates the existence of some irregularities, we can not be sure whether the revealed irregularities are the only ones or there are some more. The only way to find that out is to discover a cause of the observed irregularities, thus making an output model state complete.

Infer

In: an (incomplete) model state, a model.

Out: (the most likely) model state.

Given both, a model which deals with uncertainty aspects of the relationships between the objects in the world and an incomplete model state, we are looking for the cause of the model state incompleteness. Once the most likely cause of the model state incompleteness was found (which depends on the current state of the knowledge), the state becomes complete. This is a logical continuation of the situation we had with the *Analyze* primitive. We need feedback from the outside world in order to validate the hypothesis.

Refine

In: a world state, (the most likely) model state, a model.

Out: a model state.

During the deduction process, we may end up with a need to perform more tests on the world's counterparts of the specific constituents of a model state, in order to justify (or abandon) a current line of reasoning. Once we have decided on a specific strategy (line of reasoning), we need to set the subgoals in terms of different aspects of a domain at hand (detailed snap shots). Additional tests would allow us to discriminate among different hypotheses, thus guiding a process of refinement.

Construct

Construct 1

In: an initial model state, a final model state, a model.

Out: a sequence of model states.

Construct 2

In: a sequence of model states, a model.

Out: a final model state.

Given both, an initial model state and a final model state (along with a model), we construct a sequence of model states which reflects the transition from the prespecified initial to final state. On the other side, if we are given a sequence of model states as a pattern of behavior of some process (concept) existing in the world, we construct a final model state of the underlying model, where a model state stands, in fact, for a model itself of the "product" we want to design. The difference between the two aspects of the *Construct* primitive is obvious when thinking in terms of planning and actual design processes.

Explain

In: a sequence of model states, a user model.

Out: a sequence of world states.

Based on both a given sequence of model states and a model of a user, we are able to offer an explanation (to the user) of the operations performed by the system. A model of a user should contain description of needs and expectations of the average user. On the other side, instead of defining a user model, we may allow a user to specify directly the characteristics of an explanation process.

Execute

Execute 1

In: a sequence of model states.

Out: a sequence of world states.

Execute 2

In: a model state.

Out: a world state.

The *Execute* translates a model state(s) into a set of actions necessary to be performed in order to bring the changes described by the model state(s) to the world.

Prescribe

In: a model state, a model.

Out: a sequence of model states.

Given both a model and the most likely cause of the irregularities discovered in the world, we propose a sequence of model states (and accordingly the transitions to be taken) which describes the actions to be performed in the world, in order to get it back to the "normal" (tolerable) state.

Compound Processes

A term *compound processes* was employed to stress a fact that these processes are defined in terms of derived primitives. The way the primitives are listed impose a (left to right) ordering on them. Some definitions assume the existence of cycles (like an *Infer - Refine* part of the definition for *Diagnose*), which was not stated explicitly for the sake of simplicity.

Definitions:

Interpret ->	Recognize , Classify
Predict ->	(Specify1 , Specify2) , Simulate2 , Compare1
Plan ->	[(Specify1 , Specify2)] , Construct1
Design ->	(Specify1 , Specify2) , Plan , Construct2
Diagnose ->	Analyze , Infer , [Refine]
Monitor ->	Simulate1 , Compare2
Debug ->	Diagnose , Prescribe
Control ->	Predict, Execute2
Instruct ->	Debug , Explain
Repair ->	Debug , Execute1

Note:

X1 , X2	=>	X1 and X2
(X1 , X2)	=>	X1 or X2
[...]	=>	optional

Instead of describing the definitions one by one (mostly by repeating given definitions for the primitives, it may be useful to give an example of a graphical representation for one of the compound processes. Let's consider a *Repair* as an example (figure 1).

A process begins with sampling of the world states, one at a time. Upon discovering irregular behavior in the world, the *Analyze* builds an incomplete model state describing discovered irregularities. This is the starting point for the *Infer*-ence process, which deduces the most likely cause of nontolerable behavior. But, sometimes, we may not have all necessary data for a confident decision and, consequently, we go through additional testing and the *Refine*-ment process. Once we feel confident with our decision, we are ready to *Prescribe* the recovering procedure as well as to *Execute* it.

FIG. 1.

```
   world
   state

--+-------------------------------+
  |                               |
  | Analyze         Infer         |      Refine        Prescribe  Execute1
  |     ||            ||          +------->||            ||          ||
 --->|| (incomp.)     || (the most        || model       || seq.of   || seq.of
     ||------------->||--------------->||------------->||-------->||-------->
 --->||  model    +->||  likely)    +->|| state     +->|| model    || world
  |  ||  state    |   ||  model      |   ||          |   || states   || states
  |               |       state      |               |
  |               |                  |               |
--+---------------+------------------+---------------+

   model
```

SAMPLE APPLICATIONS

We have applied our framework to several "real-life" expert systems (described in [5]), thus effectively verifying the applicability of the suggested hierarchy. Among them are:

SACON	(diagnosis),
DIPMETER ADVISOR	(interpretation),
ABSTRIPS	(planning),
NOAH	(planning),
XCON/R1	(design and planning),
MIFASS	(planning),
SOPHIE	(diagnosis, debugging, and instruction),
PTRANS	(prediction, diagnosis, planning, monitoring, debugging, repair, and control).

Each of these application domains has been successfully mapped to the framework, using the appropriate primitives and compound processes. However, because of the space limitations, it is not possible to provide their models.

CONCLUSION

A framework to describe application domains has been established. It dissects the processes into finer grained primitives, which can be used to construct other compound processes. The list of compound processes, given in the paper, is certainly not exhaustive. In fact, that is the power of this approach - the set of defined primitives can be used in describing different activities (processes) characterizing different domains. Let's take, as an example, the *Redesign* and *Tutor* compound processes. They can readily be defined as:

Redesign -> Interpret, Design

Tutor -> Interpret, Instruct.

Our framework also allows for a more direct translation from requirements, features, and utilities of an application domain to the abstract model and concrete representation necessary in the process of developing an expert system.

The primitives seem to be so fundamental that not only the expert system technology should support, but also should be supported by any KBDE. For this reason, the primitives provide us with the basis to study the requirements, features, and utilities of KBDEs. Only when a similar characterization of KBDEs based on similar primitives is achieved can a mapping between the application domains and tools be attempted. Our research aims to culminate at the matching and mapping of features of domains with those of KBDEs. Whatever gaps exist in KBDEs or the technology itself to support the increasing demand from applications should also be identifiable through this research.

ACKNOWLEDGMENT

We would like to thank Ronlon Tsai and Shyh Chang Adam Su for their suggestions, as well as application of suggested framework to a number of existing expert systems and their respective domains.

REFERENCES

1. P. Friedland, "Special Section on Architectures for Knowledge-based Systems", Communications of the ACM, 28 (1985) 902-903.

2. M. H. Richer, "Evaluating the Existing Tools for Developing Knowledge-Based Systems," Technical Report, Stanford Knowledge Systems Laboratory.

3. D. S. Prerau, "Selection of an Appropriate Domain for an Expert System," The AI Magazine, Summer 1985, pp 26-30.

4. W. J. Clancey, "Heuristic Classification," Artificial Intelligence, 27 (1985) 289-350.

5. D. Waterman, "A Guide to Expert Systems", Addison-Wesley 1986.

6. F. Hayes-Roth, D. Waterman, D. Lenat (Eds.), "Building Expert Systems," Addison-Wesley, 1983.

7. B. Chandrasekaran, "Generic Tasks in Knowledge-Based Reasoning: High-Level Building Blocks for Expert System Design," in Proceedings of the Workshop on High Level Tools for Knowledge-Based Systems, Shawnee State Park, OH, October 6-8, 1986.

8. M. Hadzikadic, D. Y. Y. Yun, and W. P. -C. Ho, "Characterization of Application Domains for the Expert System Technology," in Proceedings of the Workshop on High Level Tools for Knowledge-Based Systems, Shawnee State Park, OH, October 6-8, 1986.

9. W. J. Clancey, "Representing Control Knowledge as Abstract Tasks and Metarules," in Proceedings of the Workshop on High Level Tools for Knowledge-Based Systems, Shawnee State Park, OH, October 6-8, 1986.

MODULE: A MODULAR PROGRAMMING ENVIRONMENT IN PROLOG

MARTIN HOFMANN,* ANNE USHA,* SOURI DAS,* KAZUHIKO KAWAMURA,* ATSUSHI KARA,** AND RAVI RASTOGI***
*Center for Intelligent Systems, Vanderbilt University, Nashville, TN 37235; **Software Development Dept., NEC Corporation, Kawasaki, Japan; ***Intellitek, Inc., Rockville, MD 20852

ABSTRACT

Knowledge-based programming requires specialized tools to represent and manipulate knowledge to solve the complex problems encountered in the real world. In this paper we introduce MODULE, a MODUlar Programming Environment in PROLOG. MODULE contains KRISP [1], a knowledge programming and inference system in PROLOG, a modular programming and a planning module. We chose PROLOG [2] as the basic implementation language because PROLOG combines the declarative style of predicate calculus with a simple but powerful inference mechanism based on resolution theorem proving and variable unification. KRISP is a tool which supports various structured forms of knowledge representation and provides the inference engine kernel. The modular programming module supports the package and multiple data base facilities and the planning module supports an experimental planning environment based on the AO* search algorithm. MODULE's support environment provides facilities for explanations, debugging, and the user interface. In short, MODULE provides not only a powerful environment for building expert systems, but also a rich educational environment for exploring AI techniques for those not familiar with knowledge engineering tools and techniques.

INTRODUCTION

We propose that no single form of knowledge representation can cope with the complexity of real world problems. Hence, MODULE should contain a sufficient set of representation methods to give the programmer the freedom to choose the methods which suit his or her application best and help build more understandable programs more quickly and economically.

Most of the available expert system shells are LISP-based, e.g., ART [3] and LOOPS [4]. The most complete environment for building expert systems in PROLOG is P-Shell [5]. P-Shell covers most aspects of the traditional expert system building environments with its numerous knowledge representation schemes and control strategies. An object-oriented programming facility in PROLOG was presented by Zaniolo [6] which contains a simple implementation of inheritance from multiple ancestors and a special syntax for passing messages to objects. MODULE complements these efforts and introduces a modular programming environment and a set of tools for planning in PROLOG. The modular environment allows the user to separate PROLOG clauses into individual packages. The encapsulation of clauses can serve both to increase the maintainability of the code of large programs and to create independent environments for the PROLOG goal satisfaction process. Planning is an integral part of the control layer of many expert systems. MODULE supports the implementation of a planning layer by supplying a set of search algorithms.

Methodologies for Intelligent Systems
Z. W. Ras and M. Zemankova, Editors

MODULE is an experimental system with primarily two objectives: 1) to study the various knowledge representation and manipulation techniques and to implement them in PROLOG and 2) to develop a knowledge programming environment for building expert systems and also for educating those uninitiated in AI techniques. MODULE is an enhancement to the existing system, KRISP, which provides the inference engine kernel and the knowledge representation framework.

THE KRISP ENVIRONMENT

KRISP supports structured knowledge representations, such as rules and frames, and provides an inference engine. KRISP can execute rules in both forward and backward chaining mode and distinguishes a global and a short-term memory. The rule format is independent of the inference modes which separates logic from control in KRISP. The inference kernel also supports a certainty factor mechanism. The matching process supplies the relevant probabilities for the rule antecedents and the inference engine takes care of the consistency and updating of the probabilities based on the current beliefs. Figure 1 shows the important constituents of the KRISP system.

Inference Engine Kernel
- Forward Chaining Subsystem
- Backward Chaining Subsystem
- Certainty Factor Mechanism

Knowledge Base
- Rule Base
- Fact Base
- Global Memory
- Short-Term Memory

Knowledge Representation Support System
- Object-PROLOG Representation
- Semantic Network Representation
- Frame Representation

FIG. 1. KRISP system constituents.

Knowledge Base

The knowledge base consists of rules and facts currently known to the system. Each rule in the rule base has the representational form

```
goal(Identifier,Predicate) :  provable(Predicate-1),
                              provable(Predicate-2),
                                  .
                                  .
                              provable(Predicate-n).
```

The body of the rule may contain any PROLOG predicates as well as the KRISP specific predicate "provable(P)." The special predicate "provable(P)" invokes the KRISP inference engine.

The fact base consists of the world knowledge represented as assertions (PROLOG clauses) and comprises two parts: the global memory and short-term memory. The global memory consists of all the facts inserted in the PROLOG data base explicitly by the user. The short-term memory stores all the facts inferred by the system during the inferencing process and also the user's answers to queries in the interactive mode. Keeping the newly inferred or elicited facts separate in the short-term memory makes it possible to easily retract assumptions and to undo the effects of reasoning steps which did not lead to the desired results. The user has the option of selecting either an open world or a closed world assumption (see Figure 2 for a list of the KRISP top level menu options). In the closed world mode, the system assumes that whatever fact is not stated explicitly is false. In the open world mode, the system queries the user for additional information whenever it cannot conclude a goal from the available information.

```
%%%%%%%%%%%%%%%%%%%%%%%%%%%%%%%%%%%%%%%%%%%%%%%%%%%%%%%%%%%%
% K R I S P                                                %
% Knowledge Representation and Inference System in PROLOG %
% Copyright 1986, Center for Intelligent Systems           %
% Vanderbilt University                                    %
%%%%%%%%%%%%%%%%%%%%%%%%%%%%%%%%%%%%%%%%%%%%%%%%%%%%%%%%%%%%
- init_krisp.              : initialize KRISP
- load(file).              : load file
- forward.                 : start forward chain
- backward(Hypo).          : start backward chain
- remember(Id,P,True).     : remember in short_term_memory
- forget(Id,P,True).       : forget from short_term_memory
- footprint/nofootprint.: trace
- how(Fact).               : how explanation
- why(Fact).               : why explanation
- world(open/closed)       : open/closed world assumption
- ls.                      : list short_term_memory
- cs.                      : clear short_term_memory
- ll.                      : list long_term_memory
- lr(Id).                  : list rules
- help.                    : display menu
- quit.                    : quit
```

FIG. 2. KRISP top level menu.

Inference Engine Kernel

The menu selections "forward" and "backward(Hypothesis)" (see Figure 2) invoke the KRISP inference engine. In forward chaining mode all rules in the KRISP rule base are inspected to see whether their antecedent predicates can be proven from facts in short-term or global memory. If so, the rule consequents are asserted into the short-term memory and the process continues to loop until no more rules fire. No KRISP rules are invoked to try to prove the antecedent predicates in forward chaining mode.

In backward chaining mode a goal predicate (the hypothesis) is stated in the call to the inference engine. First, the rules which can prove this hypothesis are retrieved from the rule base, then their antecedents are tested. Again, short-term and global memory are searched for the antecedent predicates. If this does not succeed and the antecedent is of the special predicate form "provable(P)," then the inference engine looks for KRISP rules whose goal matches the predicate "P." If all else fails and the world is assumed to be open, KRISP asks the user whether the predicate "P" is true.

Certainty Factor Mechanism

A great deal of uncertainty is associated with real world factual and inferential knowledge. In order to take these uncertainties into consideration MODULE provides a certainty factor mechanism which closely follows the PROSPECTOR model as described by Bratko [7, Chapter 14.6]. The certainty factor of each fact is a real number between 0 and 1 and is called the 'measure of belief.' A fact in this representation has the form:

```
fact(<prolog_form_fact>, probability).
```

The likelihood of a hypothesis is inferred by propagating the certainty factors from the supporting facts or events to this hypothesis in the belief tree. The belief tree is defined by the rule chains which have fired in the course of proving a hypothesis. The leaf nodes of the belief tree are simple facts with given prior probability. Each rule represents the arcs from the antecedent facts to the consequent fact in the belief tree which show how the certainty of an event E affects our belief in the dependent hypothesis H. The strength with which the likelihood of E influences the belief in H is modelled by two parameters: the necessity factor N and sufficiency factor S, as in the PROSPECTOR model. A prior probability is associated not only with the independent facts (the leaf nodes) but also with each dependent hypothesis in the belief tree. In order to find the resulting measure of belief in a hypothesis, the certainty calculation starts with the prior probability associated with the hypothesis and adjusts it according to the evidence accumulated from the antecedent events. This way the actual calculated certainties propagate through the rule network and result in an accumulated measure of belief in the original hypothesis H.

Figure 3 shows an example rule in the syntax which supports this method of certainty propagation. In this example, Prob01 and Prob02 are the prior probabilities of the antecedents "the animal flies" and "the animal lays eggs" and Prob1 and Prob2 are their actually calculated probabilities. 0.84 is the prior probability of the goal "the animal is a bird," 0.1 is the necessity factor, 1000 is the sufficiency factor, and the variable Ovprob will be bound to the calculated overall probability of the goal. The additional predicate "calcovall" triggers the certainty calculations.

```
goal(4,bird(X)) :
        provable(flies(X),Prob01,Prob1),
        provable(lays_eggs(X),Prob02,Prob2),
        calcovall(4,bird(X),0.84,[Prob01,Prob02],
                  [Prob1,Prob2],0.1,1000,Ovprob).
```

FIG. 3. Rule format for certainty factor propagation.

Knowledge Representation Support System

There are three forms of structured knowledge representations available to the user: semantic nets, objects and frames. These representations are supported by KRISP and their structures closely follow the most common format used in the literature.

Semantic network representation. In a semantic net, information is represented as a set of nodes connected to each other by a set of labeled arcs representing the relationships among the nodes. KRISP allows two types of nodes, namely concept nodes and instance nodes. The concept nodes can represent classes of objects while the instance nodes represent specific instances of the objects. This distinction is not enforced or checked by KRISP, however. Links between concept nodes usually describe the properties of all instances of the concept. The links from the instance nodes describe properties of individual instances. IS-A links are used to connect the concept nodes while INSTANCE-OF links connect a concept node to a specific instance. This semantic net structure in KRISP builds a hierarchy of nodes which supports multiple inheritance in the network based on the concept of specialization. KRISP provides the corresponding procedures for manipulating and reasoning with this network.

Frame representation. KRISP frames implement a "slot and filler"-type of representational object. Frames are generally used to represent stereotypical objects, concepts, or situations. They support a stricter organization of knowledge than semantic networks. The greater representational specificity of frames allowed us to supply a larger number of general support primitives. Frames can be built using the frame_append predicate, a value can be inserted into a slot by calling the frame_put predicate or removed by calling the frame_remove predicate. Demons can be attached to frame slots which are called when values are added or removed.

Object-PROLOG representation. In order to implement the object-oriented programming paradigm three main features must be provided: data abstraction and encapsulation, a communication protocol, and an inheritance mechanism.

Data abstraction can be implemented in a straightforward way in PROLOG. To the PROLOG interpreter it does not matter whether a variable is stored directly as a fact (the equivalent of an instance variable) or has to be calculated from other facts by applying a rule (the equivalent of a method). Consequently, instance variables have to be accessed via the normal message protocol. A universal "set_inst_var" predicate changes the value of an instance variable by replacing the complete object definition.

The message protocol is implemented by the infix operator ":" which links messages to objects. Messages in KRISP have the format "Object : Message." As explained above, the instance variables can be accessed in the same way. KRISP provides the infix operator "with" as a means to define the collection of variables and methods of an object, similar to [6]. An object definition looks like

ObjectName with Variable-and-Method-List.

Currently no support is provided for dynamically changing a single method. It is interesting to note that any specific method could theoretically be implemented as a plain PROLOG procedure, which means that whether a message is handled by a method or a procedure is transparent to the user as proposed, for example, by Bobrow et al. [8].

A multiple inheritance mechanism is provided which will redirect messages to ancestor objects if no method is found in the addressed object. This mechanism works naturally for both variables and methods. The inheritance links are set up via

Object is_a SuperObject

statements. The order of inheritance is defined by the order in which these statements are inserted into the PROLOG data base and a depth-first top-down precedence ordering. The inherited instance variables will be initialized to the values found in the ancestor object. Methods for the same message defined in an inheritance chain can be combined by forcing each method to fail after execution. In order to invoke the method of an ancestor object from inside a method, the object has to identify the ancestor explicitly by following the "is_a" link and then send it the identical message.

The Object-PROLOG representation does not provide any means to enforce a difference between classes and instances. Similar to ObjectLISP [9], there is only one basic representational entity, namely the object, and the concepts of class and instance are a matter of convention only.

MODULAR PROGRAMMING ENVIRONMENT

This environment consists of two facilities, i.e., the package facility and the multiple data base facility. Both partition the clause space of the PROLOG goal satisfaction process and eliminate unexpected interactions between independent parts of the PROLOG program. Parts of programs can be coded and tested separately and are guaranteed to preserve their function when put together as a collection of modules. Standard modules can contain libraries of useful common functions.

Package Facility

A package in MODULE establishes a mapping from print names to predicate names. The main purpose of this module is to facilitate modular programming and avoid naming conflicts between modules. The implementation loosely follows the definition of the package facility for Common Lisp [10]. Each package declares only a subset of its predicates as being externally accessible and hides the locally used auxiliary predicates from the environment.

If desired, the external predicates of a package can be made accessible without the package qualifier by making the package "internal" with a call to "use_package(<name>)." This can be reversed by the call "unuse_package(<name>)." In order to make the internal predicates of a package accessible, the package has to be made the "current_package" with "set_current_package(<name>)." Only one package can be current at any time. This allows the user to work with the procedures in a package without bothering about the package facility.

Great effort has been made to keep the package environment as transparent as possible. Files which contain packages need only contain the appropriate external declarations and it is recommended to include a "provide(<packagename>)" statement at the beginning so that the name of the package is known at load time. This can also be achieved by loading the package with a "require(<packagename>)" statement since the package "name" is always searched for in the file "name.pck." MODULE's package facility makes no distinction between packages and modules for reasons of simplicity. Each package corresponds to a module which in turn corresponds to a file.

It is possible to require and use packages from other packages. If a package being loaded contains a "require" or "use_package" statement, the current loading operation is suspended, the requested package is loaded (if necessary) and the external predicates of the requested package are inherited by the package being loaded. They do not automatically become visible to the user, however, but only to the requesting package. This allows two packages to request two different versions of another package without interference. This form of inheritance is direct: i.e., the inherited predicates are treated as if they had been declared in the requesting package itself.

(1) require(p): load package p
    external names become visible as "ppackage name"
    (internal names as "p_has_internal name," but
    they can never be made internal to another package)
(2) provide(p): directive for the loader: name of package
(3) external([name1, name2, ...]): directive: declares the
    external names
(4) use_package(p): makes the external predicates of p
    internal to the current package. If the predicate
    already exists this is equivalent to adding another

clause for the same predicate.
(5) unuse_package(p): reverse the effect of use_package
(6) set_current_package(p): makes all the predicates in p visible and reverses this for the previous current package

FIG. 4. Package facility predicates.

Figure 4 gives a concise description of the predicates necessary for the use of the package facility.

Multiple Data Base Facility

The purpose of this facility is to structure the available knowledge represented as PROLOG clauses into easily accessible individual knowledge bases. The data bases are organized into a tree structure similar to the directory trees in UNIX. In further analogy the data bases are called "directories" and the predicates defined to manipulate them are named according to the corresponding UNIX commands (see Figure 5 which displays the list of commands available in this facility as it is displayed in response to the "help." command). This facility is not transparent to the user since procedures even in the current directory have to be called through the special access predicate "calld(Procedure)." However, dividing the knowledge base into smaller units makes the accessing of facts or rules much faster and also makes it easier for the user to build large data bases systematically and unambiguously.

```
                    Multiple Data Base System
           Copyright 1986, C.I.S. Vanderbilt University

Commands :

  - is_directory(Abs_Path). : Returns Directories through Backtracking.
  - pwd.                    : Display the Current Directory.
  - ls.                     : List Sub_Directories/Clauses in Current Directory.
  - mkdir(Rel_Path).        : Make a new Directory.
  - rmdir(Rel_Path).        : Remove a Directory.
  - cd.                     : Return to the Top_Directory.
  - cd(..).                 : Move to the Parent Directory.
  - cd(Abs_Path).           : Change Directory.
  - cd(Rel_Path).           : Change Directory.
  - assertad(Clause).       : Asserta Clause into the Current Directory.
  - assertd(Clause).        : Assertz Clause into the Current Directory.
  - calld(Predicate).       : Call Predicate in the Current Directory.
  - retractd(Clause).       : Retract Clause from the Current Directory.
  - show.                   : Show all Directories/Clauses.
  - example(dir).           : Example

Note: Top_Directory=[/]
      Abs_Path=[/,a,bb,ccc] etc.
      Rel_Path=[bb,ccc] etc.
```

FIG. 5. Multiple data base help screen.

PLANNING ENVIRONMENT

The planning environment in MODULE is still in a primitive stage and supports only search algorithms useful for planning applications. It provides the AO* [7, Chapter 13.4] algorithm and breadth-first as well as best-first search procedures. However, the major burden of designing the actual planning process is still left to the user. This part of MODULE has been built mainly to acquaint the user with search mechanisms and their application to planning.

SUPPORT ENVIRONMENT

MODULE is equipped to provide the user with all the usual support tools for knowledge programming. It is capable of explaining its behavior by stating the rules and facts that lead to any conclusion. Thus it can answer the how and why type of questions. The user interface also supports an on-line help facility which recognizes and tolerates spelling mistakes and displays full screen help information when needed.

CONCLUSION

The MODULE project shows that it is possible to provide a rich knowledge-based programming environment in PROLOG. MODULE is an experimental system, however, and the individual facilities have not been fully coordinated or integrated. Nevertheless most of the mainstream features, such as modular and object-oriented programming and frame representations, are provided and have been applied to several smaller problems. MODULE is currently being developed at the Center for Intelligent Systems at Vanderbilt University. It is implemented in C-PROLOG [11] and runs on a VAX 11/785. Several extensions to this system are currently being implemented, a major part of which is the planning environment. This paper gives an outline of the system as it currently exists.

ACKNOWLEDGEMENTS

We wish to thank all the students in the MT391 class who contributed to this ongoing and continuously evolving project, without whom we could not have written this paper.

REFERENCES

1. A. Usha, "KRISP: Knowledge Representation and Inference System in PROLOG," unpublished project report, Vanderbilt University, Nashville, TN, 1986.
2. W.F. Clocksin, C.S. Mellish, Programming in PROLOG (Springer-Verlag, New York 1984).
3. G.D. Clayton, ART Programming Tutorial (Inference Corporation, California 1985).
4. D.G. Bobrow, M. Stefik, The LOOPS Manual (Xerox Corporation, California 1983).
5. N.S. Lee, "Programming with P-Shell," IEEE Expert, 1, No. 2, 50-62 (1986).
6. C. Zaniolo, "Object-Oriented Programming in PROLOG," Proc. IEEE 1984 International Symposium on Logic Programming, 265-270 (1984).
7. I. Bratko, PROLOG Programming for Artificial Intelligence (Addison-Wesley, Reading, Massachusetts 1986).
8. D.G. Bobrow, K. Kalm, G. Kiczales, L. Masinter, M. Stefik, F. Zdybel, "COMMONLOOPS," Intelligent Systems Laboratory Series, ISL-85-8, (Xerox Palo Alto Research Center, August 1985).
9. G.L. Drescher, ObjectLISP (LMI, Cambridge, Massachusetts 1985).
10. G.L Steele, Common LISP (Digital Press, Massachusetts 1984).
11. F. Pereira, C-PROLOG User's Manual, Version 1.5 (University of Edinburgh, February 1984).

USING AI IN THE PREPARATION OF BUDGET SUBMISSIONS

Ho-Ling Hwang, M. L. Emrich, and John Morris
Oak Ridge National Laboratory
P.O. Box X, 4500N, MS-179
Oak Ridge, Tennessee 37831-6179

ABSTRACT

This paper describes an automated budget preparation system that was developed using an expert system shell. Capabilities and operating environment of the tool are discussed. Specific features of the budget preparation system are covered.

INTRODUCTION

The preparation of annual budget proposals has historically been a labor-intensive, time-sensitive, and error-prone process for any organization. Rules, guidelines, and regulations for completing page-after-page of budget submission forms are often hard to understand, interpret, and implement. The turnaround time for completing such forms may be relatively short. Staff rotations often mean a loss of skilled, knowledgeable personnel. Consequently, resulting proposals may contain inaccurate, inconsistent, and incomplete data.

The Naval Sea Systems Command (NAVSEA) Inactive Ship Maintenance Facilities (ISMF) has four field activities. The field sites are located in Portsmouth, Virginia; Philadelphia, Pennsylvania; Bremerton, Washington; and Pearl Harbor, Hawaii. The Headquarters, NAVSEA DETACHMENT (NAVSEADET 07A6) is located in Norfolk, Virginia. The ISMFs are responsible for the maintenance, repair, and inactivation of Navy equipment, including ships and craft. They also oversee and monitor the activities of the private contractors who operate the sites. In fulfilling their responsibilities, the ISMFs must prepare a variety of budget submissions throughout the year.

The application of decision support methodologies, in particular expert systems, to aid Navy analysts with the budget preparation process has been explored. An automated support system (BUDPREP) has been designed, constructed, and pilot tested for the Naval Sea Systems Command. The system is tailored to assist with the preparation of Base Operating Support (BOS) budget submissions. The BOS budget requires that a large amount of budget data be gathered and detailed on forms. The data reflects the estimated requirements of all field activities. The final budget proposal represents the estimate of what a field activity will need to support its programs for maintaining buildings, providing utilities, managing waste disposal, etc. Prior to an automated aid, field activities prepared budgets manually.

BOS BUDGETING PROCESS WITHIN NAVSEADET

The BOS budget is one of nine separate budgeting processes in which NAVSEADET must participate on a continuing basis. BOS includes costs of services and materials incident to shore-based support functions. Also included under BOS are costs for maintenance and repair of real property, minor construction, utility operations, and other engineering support [1].

Methodologies for Intelligent Systems
Z. W. Ras and M. Zemankova, Editors

The BOS budget process under this study is initiated via a budget call memorandum from NAVSEA 07F2 (NAVSEA, Washington, D. C.) to NAVSEADET 07A6 [7,9]. The memorandum specifies the periods of data to be submitted. It provides general guidance and/or instructions for the budget submission.

While there are volumes of manuals citing Navy regulations regarding budgeting procedures, easy to understand, detailed, line-by-line descriptions and explanations are lacking. Therefore, each site and individuals at those sites have differing opinions about what data is requested, how and from where to gather data, and how to interpret that data once it is obtained. This has caused inconsistency among various forms and creates problems for NAVSEADET during the aggregation of ISMF submissions.

After NAVSEADET 07A6 receives a call, a cover letter is attached to the NAVSEA 07F2 budget call package and sent to each of the field sites. The cover letter states a request for information about the call. The ISMFs must respond with the required information before the due date indicated in the cover letter. All data provided from the four ISMF field activities are aggregated at the NAVSEADET 07A6 level. Headquarters adds its own budget requirements to the submissions. Justifications and explanations of the spending levels are assembled. Deficiencies, if any, are identified and classified. The total package is then submitted to NAVSEA 07F2, the next budget processing level.

Figure 1 presents a typical BOS budget call issued in December of any given fiscal year. Four programs are included in each of the calls: PY-1 actual, PY revised, CY apportionment, and BY initial. The abbreviation "PY" stands for prior year, "CY" stands for current year, and "BY" stands for the budgeted year. A separate BOS budget program call is initiated in November of each year. This call requests the mid-year review for the prior year and the apportionment for the current year (Figure 2).

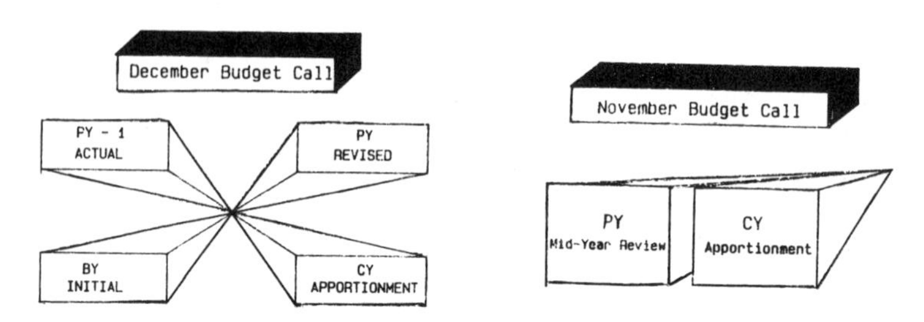

Figure 1. December Budget Call

Figure 2. November Budget Call

Note: All years are fiscal years.

KNOWLEDGE ACQUISITION PROCESS

Since the choice of the domain expert was critical to the construction of the system, a budget analyst was chosen who not only possessed special budgeting knowledge and experience, but also had developed heuristics involving the BOS budget preparation and submission process. Initial and follow-on interviews were conducted with the budget analyst. The results were used to aid the system designers in determining the financial concepts and their that needed to be attained by the support system. To gain general background and procedural information, auxiliary interviews were conducted with the expert's current and previous supervisors. Verbatim transcripts were processed after the initial interview sessions. Rules, facts, data points, and decision paths that were later encoded into the support system were identified. Follow-up questions were designed to cover deficiencies in the initial interviews. Follow-on interview sessions were recorded, but only new or modified information was transcribed.

A liaison who was familiar with the NAVSEA internal organization was identified prior to the initial interviews. That person, a retired Navy officer, helped the system designers understand the organization's internal politics and procedures. He was very knowledgeable about the operation of NAVSEA as a whole, and NAVSEADET in particular. The liaison provided assistance in obtaining access to information, people, reports, etc. and for gauging in-house acceptance of the project in general. Although retired, the liaison possessed the political savvy and connections, as well as financial expertise, to be extremely valuable to the project.

PROTOTYPE SYSTEM

The expert system shell, Guru, was used to prototype the Budget Preparation Systems (BUDPREP). Guru was selected because of its capability of integrating business-oriented applications with a knowledge-based system [2,8]. The package is marketed by Micro Data Base Systems (MDBS) Inc. [6, 10, 11, 12, 13, 14]. Its features include a spreadsheet with forms generation, expert system shell, data base management system with SQL data base manager and natural language interface, text editor, procedural language, business graphics facilities, and remote communications. The software is menu driven for ease of use, however, the system designer can use the command language provided by Guru [3,4]. The package is an application development tool; it is not end-user oriented [5].

BUDPREP is a microcomputer-based intelligent decision support system. It enables budget analysts to systematically maintain and update BOS budget information as well as automatically generate all budget forms. BUDPREP includes a series of menus for user selection and fill-in-the-blank questions for user input on specific information. No Guru or other programming knowledge is required to use the system. The budget analyst's input causes background programs (i.e., Guru procedures) to activate the appropriate module which either displays another menu or the desired output. The execution of Guru procedures is transparent to the budget analysts at all times.

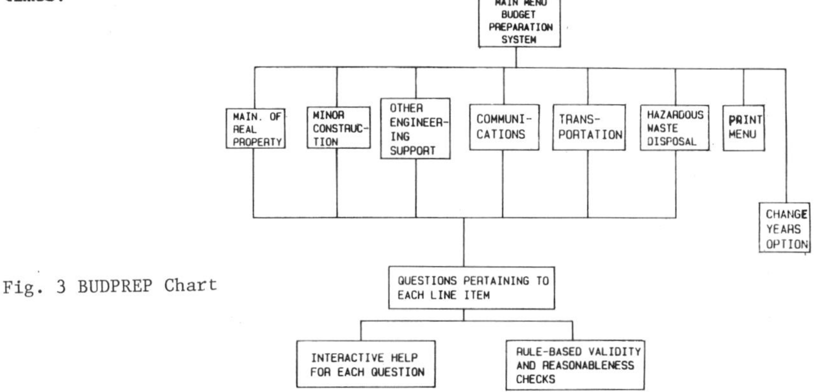

Fig. 3 BUDPREP Chart

Budget analysts select one option from the main menu, "BOS BUDGET PREPARATION," to access the next level menu (Figure 3). From the selection of each secondary menu and answers to a series of questions, the system gathers relevant information. This information is used to produce the budget submission for each AG/SAG (activity group/sub-activity group).

The spreadsheet cells in BUDPREP can be easily addressed from other applications including forms management. BUDPREP allows the budget analyst to input and output data via the forms, thereby, avoiding the interactive spreadsheet mode. The forms management capability is used to generate screen menus. Such menus allow the analyst to select a budget activity group or line item.

Once the analyst answers all relevant questions, the data is automatically stored in the spreadsheet. When the analyst chooses the print option from the main menu, the forms generator extracts information from the spreadsheet and prints a customized Navy budget form.

To develop the expert system features of BUDPREP, heuristics and procedures used by budget analysts during budget preparation were captured (previous section). This expertise is represented in the system by rules controlled by a forward-chaining strategy.

The expert system shell within Guru is not used to control the entire system. It is used to define those unknowns that have several factors contributing to their results. For instance, an experienced analyst might require only one question to be answered for obtaining the correct information for a line item. On the other hand, the inexperienced analyst may need to have additional questions answered to complete that same line item. This would be the case for an expert system routine.

Some rules are used to perform validity checks upon data entered by the analyst. For example, when the system asks for information regarding the amount of floor space, it will check the validity of the input. If the analyst tries to enter maintenance costs but fails to enter the amount of floor space, the system will inform the user of the error and offer a choice of remedies.

In addition to validity checking, tests for reasonableness are performed by the knowledge base. When analysts enter costs for a line item that exceeds 30% of the amount that was funded last fiscal year, BUDPREP will prompt the analyst to provide a justification for the increase. If the amount is reduced by 30%, BUDPREP will prompt the analyst to recheck the entry.

Context sensitive help screens were also developed using Guru's procedural language. The screens increase the accuracy of budget preparation and add user friendliness to the BUDPREP system. When "?" is entered in place of the number needed for a particular line item, pertinent on-line assistance is displayed. Budget analysts receive advice on where to find information for that line item, a description and definition of the line item, and/or examples of appropriate and inappropriate charges.

During system development, it was determined that analysts were likely to make certain errors in preparing the budget. These included entering a request for funds under a line item when it should have appeared elsewhere. To avoid the tendency to make such errors, a category headed "NOTE," provides instructions regarding where such costs should be entered. For example, under the "Maintenance of Real Property," when asked for the costs of grounds maintenance, the user is cautioned not to include chemical controls.

Instead, the BUDPREP system refers the user to the appropriate line item for entry of such costs. After help has been given for a specific question, the system again prompts the user for the answer to the original question.

SYSTEM STATUS

Initial pilot tests for the prototype were conducted with budget analysts from NAVSEADET 07A6 and ISMF-Portsmouth during February, 1987.

One purpose for individual pilot testing was to gather information needs germane to a specific site. It was found that services included under the host-tenant agreement at one site differed from those included at other sites. For example, basic phone costs are not included in Bremerton's Interservice Agreement (ISA), while such costs are supplied to Portsmouth via the shipyard ISA.

The user views, feedback, suggestions, and criticisms from the initial pilot tests were openly solicited. Because of the immediacy of feedback from end-users, the initial approximation could be evaluated and deficiencies identified. System modifications were designed to both eliminate errors and to more accurately approximate desired performance. A final pilot test at ISMF-Philadelphia is scheduled for early July, 1987.

An initial system review by NAVSEA 07F2 was held in early April, 1987. The results of the initial pilot tests and review were reflected in the modified system which was then tested at two other field sites (i.e., ISMF-Bremerton and ISMF-Pearl Harbor) in April and May, 1987. A system review by NAVSEADET was conducted in late June, 1987. The enhanced version, incorporating the capabilities required by field sites and Headquarters, will be deployed to all ISMF field sites for testing during the upcoming budget cycle.

DISCUSSION

The system discussed within this paper is intended to be used by the budget preparation analyst at the activity and field activity levels, particularly the Inactive Ship Maintenance Facilities. With little or no modification, the system could be tailored to handle budget preparation for other NAVSEA activities (i.e., public sector shipyards and supervisors of shipbuilding who manage private sector shipbuilding and repair facilities).

By automating the budget preparation process, the experienced budget analyst is available to perform other, more productive tasks. While less experienced personnel prepares the budget submission, the budget analyst could use the system to review historical data, to forecast budgets for incoming years, and to provide accurate and justified budget plans. Quality of the budget submissions and the consistency among various forms could be improved via the use of the automated system.

Due to the uniqueness of the budget preparation procedures within NAVSEADET, the budget analyst required extra support capabilities. Therefore, features such as electronically receiving budget submissions from the ISMF field activities, aggregating incoming data with the in-house budget of Headquarters into a single report, and electronically transferring the total NAVSEADET 07A6 budget submission to the 07F2 level are scheduled as future system enhancements.

REFERENCES

1. AMS, Silver Spring, Maryland, NAVSEA 076 Inactive Ship Maintenance Budget Analysis and Planning System: Requirements Document, prepared for the Naval Sea Systems Command Detachment, Department of the Navy, St. Juliens Creek Annex, Portsmouth, Virginia, 1983.

2. Barnes, R. W., M. L. Emrich, and Kumar, S., "A Comparison of Expert System Tools for Microcomputers," Joint National Meeting of TIMS/ORSA, May 4-6, 1987, New Orleans, Louisiana, The Institute of Management Sciences/Operation Research Society of America, Baltimore, Maryland, 1987.

3. GURU English Version Reference Manual: 1, Version 1.00, Micro Data Base Systems, Inc., Lafayette, Indiana, October, 1985a.

4. GURU English Version Reference Manual: 2, Version 1.00, Micro Data Base Systems, Inc., Lafayette, Indiana, October, 1985b.

5. Helliwell, J., "GURU: Brave New Expert System?" PC Magazine, 5(10), 151-163 (1986).

6. Holsapple, C. W., and A. B. Whinston, Manager's Guide to Expert Systems Using Guru, Dow Jones-Irwin, Homewood, Illinois, 1986.

7. Novak, W., Personal Interviews, ROH, Inc., Norfolk, Virginia, Fall/Winter, 1986-87.

8. Schwartz, T., "Guru: A Good First Effort for Integrated Shell," Applied Artificial Intelligence Reporter, 3(7), 3/6 (1986).

9. Shea, C., Personal Interviews, Naval Sea Systems Command Detachment 07A6, Norfolk, Virginia, Fall/Winter, 1986-87.

10. Tello, E. R., "GURU, A Complete, Integrated Software Package that Includes an Expert System Shell," Byte, 11(8), 281-285 (1986).

11. Williamson, M., "In GURU, the Business World Finally has Its First, True AI-Based Micro Package," PC Week, 3(11), 87, 92, 97 (1986a).

12. Williamson, M., "GURU's AI-Based Integrated Capabilities Allow Last-Minute Spreadsheet Updates," PC Week, 3(12), 107, 109, 114 (1986b).

13. Williamson, M., "GURU's Large Storage Capacity Provides for Impressive Database Capabilities," PC Week, 3(13), 73, 75, 77 (1986c).

14. Williamson, M., "GURU Boasts Versatile Natural-Language Function," PC Week, 3(14), 99, 103-104 (1986d).

Erasmus: Reconfigurable Object Oriented Blackboard System

V. Jagannathan, L. S. Baum, R. T. Dodhiawala
Boeing Advanced Technology Center
P.O. Box 24346, M. S. 7L-64
Seattle, Washington 98124-0346

ABSTRACT

There has been a proliferation of blackboard systems, each designed with a particular application in mind. Most of the decisions that go into building these systems are based on performance and problem-solving characteristics of the application. We investigate the issues involved in building a blackboard tool and discuss some of the implementation tradeoffs. We make an attempt to define some metrics by which to examine blackboard implementations. We then discuss how these are factored into our own blackboard system called Erasmus.

Introduction

Most artificial intelligence programming tools provide a general framework for problem-solving for a class of domains. This is certainly true for commercial tools such as KEE, Knowledge Craft, and ART which are meant to be general enough to be applicable to many classes of problem domains. One major drawback of this generality is that an application built using the tool may incur a performance penalty due to all the features the tool provides. For example, if a tool provides a sophisticated Truth Maintenance facility that facility may make all applications run slower, even those which do not need it.

The blackboard model of problem solving has been around for over a decade [1]. It is only recently, however, that flexible tools which incorporate this paradigm have become available to the practitioners of AI. Though the blackboard framework is not general enough to be placed in the class of tools mentioned above, blackboard tools certainly provide fairly complex problem-solving environments. In this paper we discuss the issues involved in designing a blackboard system tool and the tradeoffs that need to be explored in terms of performance and problem solving characteristics. The paper then discusses the Erasmus blackboard system being implemented at Boeing. Erasmus embodies the primary notion that an application should pay no performance penalty for problem solving features it does not use, and to pay minimum overhead for any feature that is indeed used. We conclude with a discussion of the current state of the Erasmus system and our planned future directions.

1.0 Blackboard System Design Issues

A blackboard system essentially comprises of a shared repository for (partial) solutions called the blackboard, and a set of knowledge sources which use this repository to communicate solutions. There has been a proliferation of blackboard systems using a variety of techniques guided by the application that it is no longer clear what a "blackboard system" means. For our discussion, we will use the definition of the blackboard system given below as our working definition.

> *A blackboard system is one which has an explicit representation for communication (the blackboard) between a set of independent, instantiable*

Methodologies for Intelligent Systems
Z. W. Ras and M. Zemankova, Editors

knowledge sources (processes) and supports some mechanism to control the invocation and execution of knowledge sources.

Given this definition, there is a set of decisions to be made in designing a blackboard system. These decisions include: the blackboard data structures and their access mechanisms, the structure and capabilities of the knowledge sources, and the mechanism used to control the problem-solving activity. These decisions affect the problem-solving capabilities and the performance of a system. With the proliferation of multiprocessor computer systems, another related issue in designing a blackboard system is how to exploit parallelism available in the underlying hardware. Along the same line, large networks of heterogeneous systems allow for distributed execution of knowledge sources. In what follows, we consider the implementation choices within a Lisp environment. Most of the discussion, however, is applicable to conventional programming environments also. Most of the issues and justifications are mentioned in [2].

1.1 Blackboard Data Structures

The data structures used for the blackboard will be influenced by the application. Some of the requirements of these data structures include:

1. *Communication efficiency:* The blackboard is primarily used as a communication mechanism and should allow for efficient posting and retrieval of information. Information is transmitted between knowledge sources only through the blackboard structures.

2. *Representational adequacy:* The blackboard should allow adequate encoding of the information of the problem domain. Since there is probably no one representation scheme which is well suited for all problems, the blackboard should support different representation schemes.

3. *Organizational efficacy:* The blackboard reflects the decomposition of the problem into meaningful chunks. This is really a software engineering issue. To achieve this objective, the system must support the efficient partitioning of the blackboard into discrete levels. These levels will usually reflect the increasingly abstract levels of the solution space.

Several candidate structures exists which may be able to achieve the desired functionality. In order to evaluate these structures, we consider four parameters, three related to the above mentioned functionalities and one related to the implementation price incurred.

1. *Message Volume:* This is a measure of the number of messages to the blackboard per unit time. The number of messages will establish the communication load that the blackboard has to handle.

2. *Message Complexity:* This is a qualitative measure of the complexity of the message. The capabilities of the data structure has direct bearing on this.

3. *Message Diversity:* This is a measure of the number of different types of messages which are posted to the blackboard. As above, the capabilities of the data structure has a direct bearing on the types of messages that it can handle.

4. *Memory Requirements:* The amount of memory that will be required to implement the data structure may influence the choice of the data structure. This is more of an implementation issue for the data structures, but is important when considering the different computing environments and languages.

The candidate structures for the blackboard can now be examined with respect to the functionality and assumptions regarding message volume, complexity, diversity, and memory requirements.

1. *Lists:* Lists may represent a reasonable way to implement the blackboard structures when message volume is low, messages are simple and message diversity is low. If any of these assumptions is violated the access functions tend to become inefficient. Memory overhead is higher than named structures, discussed below.

2. *Named structures:* Named structures (example, defstructs) provide a good way to implement blackboard structures. Most blackboard systems use this approach [3, 4]. The memory overhead is the overhead in setting up array structures, usually, and is minimal. The accessing may be a little more efficient than in lists because it involves array indexing compared to list searching. Auxiliary hashing structures to store instances of structures help to make accessing instances and posting and retrieval of information faster. The GBB system utilizes this scheme [5].

3. *Frames:* Frames as blackboard structures provide powerful ways of representing information. Memory overhead is higher, as the structures used need to handle inheritance. The Boeing Blackboard System [6] uses a frame system (KEE or Knowledge Craft) and the Poligon uses some form of a frame system [7].

4. *Objects:* Objects are similar in complexity to frames. While frames are more declarative in nature, objects represent capabilities. They are equally flexible in message volume, message complexity and message diversity. Examples of using objects in a blackboard include ABE [8] from Teknowledge, Inc. and the AGORA [9] system from Carnegie-Mellon University. KIT [10] from Advanced Decision System has a primitive blackboard system capability as one of its component systems and is implemented as an object system.

1.2. Structure and granularity of knowledge sources:

The functionality that needs to be represented in the knowledge sources are the following:

1. *Task invocation knowledge:* The knowledge source needs to specify what changes on the blackboard will cause its invocation. These changes trigger the knowledge source to potentially contribute towards the problem-solving. This information may be declarative or embedded in procedures.

2. *State knowledge:* After the knowledge source has been invoked, it may be necessary to wait for an appropriate state before the knowledge source executes. Also, the knowledge source may capture some of the state in its local environment.

3. *Task specific knowledge:* The knowledge source has encoded in it procedural knowledge to solve some aspect of the domain problem. This task specific knowledge may be represented as declarative rules or procedures.

In order to evaluate the implementation alternatives available to structure a knowledge source, we define some criteria for judging the same.

1. *Granularity:* This is a measure of the computation that a knowledge source must perform in order to accomplish its task. This is influenced by the division of the overall problem into subproblems.

2. *Overhead:* This is a measure of the overhead associated with the implementation, either in the form of memory requirements or in the form of process setup time. Since the desire is to build a fairly flexible tool, the representation chosen to implement the capabilities of a knowledge source may translate into overhead, particularly, when some aspect of the representation is not needed in an application.

The implementation choices we consider for encoding knowledge sources are the following:

1. *Functions:* This is a very flexible way of implementing knowledge sources. Task invocation knowledge is usually specified outside of the functional definition of knowledge source. The current state or context may be captured in the function's local memory. The task specific function can be repeatedly invoked, with multiple copies running in parallel if needed, and has no permanent local memory. It can be implemented efficiently. However, from the system point of view, the generality offered by implementing task specific knowledge as functions is harder to "comprehend" and may have to do more work to interpret the actions that the function implements. Coarse grained knowledge sources make this task even harder. Knowledge sources implemented as functions may be run in compiled mode. GBB implements knowledge sources as functions.

2. *Independent Processes:* A process maintains its own environment and hence has memory which lasts the life of the process. There is overhead in setting up the process and overhead in terms of maintaining the process when it has nothing to do. Depending upon the implementation, system resources may be wasted in the busy wait mode. But a process knowledge source on an independent processor can exploit parallelism if the granularity is optimal. This granularity should neither be too small nor too large. If small the overhead of setting up the process will make it expensive, and if it is too large one may miss potential parallelism in the knowledge source itself. The knowledge sources here are usually run in compiled mode. Examples of a system which implement knowledge sources as independent processes are the Flying Eye [11] and the Erasmus systems.

3. *Object Oriented Systems and Closures:* These provide mechanisms to invoke a function in a specific environment. This is an efficient way to maintain the local environment. The knowledge sources can be repeatedly invoked, in parallel if needed. There is no concern on the granularity of the knowledge sources, but some consideration has to be given if they are to be run in parallel. The knowledge sources here are usually run in compiled mode. Examples of this form of implementation are the Erasmus, CAGE and Poligon systems.

1.3. Control in blackboard system

The functionality which control should provide is the following:

1. *Focus of Attention:* Control should help focus problem-solving activity in the most fruitful areas; the notion is "work smarter but not harder". One advantage of flexible control especially at the development stage is the ability to experiment with knowledge source execution by varying control and fine tuning the application to achieve better performance.

2. *Utilization of Computing Resources:* Control should provide a way of using the available computing resources optimally. This is specially true in a multiprocessor environment where the control mechanism should be able to match the number of outstanding tasks to the number of available processors.

In a uniprocessor environment, the major concern is to direct the problem-solving activity to more promising areas.

The implementation choices for implementing control are by their very nature algorithmic. To evaluate various algorithmic approaches is practically impossible at this point. However one can identify several research themes. These are:

1. *Organization Issues:* Organization of the knowledge sources and blackboard structures is a source of controlling the problem-solving process. One may want to a have a hierarchically structured set of blackboard systems or a network of cooperating systems. To achieve desired performance, it may be necessary to implement varying organizational characteristics, either static or dynamic, so as to utilize knowledge inherent in these organizational structures [12].

2. *Distributed versus Centralized Control:* Issues here span from loosely coupled to tightly coupled problem-solving capability. Establishing coherence in a distributed system may be harder to accomplish. However, the control issues in a distributed system are pushed to the individual nodes who are most capable of controlling the local problem-solving activity. In a multiprocessor implementation, it is uncertain whether distributed control is desirable.

3. *Communication Computation Tradeoff:* Compared to a distributed environment, communication is relatively inexpensive in a multiprocessor environment. Communication and computation costs may be comparable. In a distributed environment, the emphasis is on computation rather than communication. Too much control may not be desirable in a distributed system if it leads to extensive communication between nodes.

4. *Explicitness:* Control may be explicitly specified, possibly using control blackboard and control knowledge sources. Sometimes, control may be embedded in domain knowledge sources in which case the flexibility that explicit control offers to guide problem-solving is lost. Implicit control is harder to maintain and change. A framework that treats uniformly both domain knowledge and control knowledge is attractive from the standpoint of exploring multiple control strategies simultaneously.

The various implementations of blackboard systems use an array of control mechanisms. We make an attempt to discuss research and performance issues related to control mechanism in a few blackboard systems we are familiar with. The systems we will consider are: Flying Eye, BBB, Distributed Vehicle Monitoring Testbed (DVMT), CAGE, and Poligon.

1. *Flying Eye:* The control here is essentially distributed in the sense that knowledge sources decide what they have to do. In some cases, there are master-slave relations setup so that one knowledge source can serve the needs of another. Control is not explicit. This system makes the assumption that there are no resource bottlenecks, and every knowledge source runs as a process on a dedicated processor.

2. *BBB:* The control in this system is centralized. The control blackboard has control information which has been created by control knowledge sources. The scheduler uses information on the control blackboard to decide which task needs to be done next. Control can be made as explicit as necessary.

3. *DVMT:* The control here is distributed. The knowledge sources (agents) are organized into a multilevel hierarchy. Control is explicit. There is the notion of an overall plan for obtaining coherence in problem-solving.

4. *CAGE:* Control is implicit, and is implemented within the knowledge sources. AGE scheduler is a queue. Concurrent AGE (CAGE) has switches to

exploit parallelism. There are switches to execute knowledge sources in parallel, execute rules in parallel, or check conditions in parallel [13]. The notion here is the user has control over what parallelism to exploit. A knowledge source can be invoked multiply in different contexts in parallel. CAGE system is under development at Stanford.

5. *Poligon:* The notion here is knowledge sources (demons) are attached to blackboard nodes (levels). All triggered knowledge sources are executed immediately in parallel. There is no notion of control. It tries to execute everything that has potential for execution. A knowledge source can be invoked multiply in different contexts in parallel. Poligon system is under development at Stanford.

2.0 Erasmus System Design

Up to this point we examined the factors that need to be taken into account in designing a blackboard system. Now we will present a particular design of a blackboard system, called Erasmus, being implemented at Boeing. The philosophy behind the system is captured in Figure 1. The object oriented design allows us to take a least commitment approach to blackboard system design. It allows us to tailor the blackboard framework, the knowledge source representation and the control specification to match the application needs. The details of the system are examined in [14].

An Erasmus application consists of a knowledge base specification and a configuration declaration. The knowledge base specification contains the definitions of knowledge sources and the blackboard structure. The configuration specification defines the functionality the user wants in the blackboard system itself. Configurations are specified by the **defconfiguration** declaration.The syntax for the configuration declaration is as follows:

(**defconfiguration** *configuration-name &key blackboard-framework control-option ks-structure-options run-time-options instance-variables make-instance init-plist multiple-erasmus*)

This creates an Erasmus configuration called *configuration-name*. Every configuration must have an underlying *blackboard-framework* or representation scheme for the blackboard. The *control-option* determines the control methodology used by the scheduler. The *ks-structure-options* specify the attributes of the application knowledge sources. The *run-time-options* determine the user interface features provided by the system. The *multiple-erasmus* option allows the user to create an application in which more than one Erasmus instance cooperates to solve the problem.

The actual blackboard application consists of three types of definition. These are: **defapplication, deflevel** and **defks**. The **defapplication** form sets several parameters needed by the system.

(**defapplication** *application-name &key first-function termination-condition post-processing-function phase-alist aux-file*)

This defines an application called *application-name* to the system. The *first-function* determines how to start the problem solving, the *termination-condition* determines how to end it, the *post-processing-function* determines what to do at the end of a given run, *phase-alist* provides a declarative representation of the problem solving phases in a given run, and *aux-file* has auxiliary lisp functions which needs to be loaded in a given run of Erasmus.

The blackboard levels are the templates for the data that will be instantiated on the blackboard. Levels are created by the **deflevel** form:

(**deflevel** *level-name application-name &key class-parents instance-parents*
class-slot-list instance-slot-list comment)

The *level-name* is a symbol which names the level. The *application-name* is the name of application from the **defapplication** form. The *class-parents* and *instance-parents* keywords allow one to establish a hierarchical relationship between levels. In both cases these should be lists of parent levels. The two types of parents differ in how slots are inherited. There are two types of slots, class slots and instance slots. Instance slots are never inherited by child levels. Class slots are inherited. If two levels are linked by the *class-parents* relationship, then the class slots remain class slots in the child level. If the link is an *instance-parents* link, then the class slot becomes an instance slot in the child.

Erasmus knowledge sources are specified by the **defks** form.

(**defks** *knowledge-source-name application-name ks-type*
&key trigger-conditions ksar-contexts preconditions obviation-conditions
knowledge-source-vars rules phases from-levels to-levels cost
reliability description)

The *knowledge-source-name* is a symbolic name for the knowledge source and *application-name* is as specified in the **defapplication** form. The *ks-type* specifies the knowledge source to be either **domain** or **control**. The *trigger-conditions* are a list of predicates that specify when this knowledge source should be triggered. The *ksar-contexts* allows the instantiation of multiple knowledge source activation records (KSARs) from a single event. The *preconditions* specify the condition under which the knowledge source can be executed. The *obviation-conditions* spell out the conditions which can obviate a triggered or executable activation of a given knowledge source. The *knowledge-source-vars* capture the local context in which the knowledge source will be executed. The *rules* specify the body of the knowledge source which may produce changes on the blackboard. The *phases* specify the problem solving phases in which the knowledge source can execute. *From-levels* and *to-levels* are a declarative specification of the levels from which a particular knowledge source reads information in and posts information out. *Cost* and *reliability* are provided by the user and can be used by the user in controlling the execution of a knowledge source.

The implementation strategy chosen is to use an object oriented approach. The system is implemented in Symbolics Common Lisp. It uses the capabilities of the flavor system and pure common lisp. It was felt that in order to meet the objectives of the design, an object oriented facility was imperative. Current common lisp standards does not include this aspect. However, both Flavors and Common Loops share some important characteristics. Only features of flavors, which can be easily reimplemented in Common Loops were used in the implementation of the Erasmus system.

3.0 Conclusion

We have discussed the design consideration in developing a blackboard system and provided a particular design and implementation for the Erasmus blackboard system. The design we have proposed offers the following:

1. *Reconfigurable:* This is the primary motivation, and the system design reflects this consideration.

2. *Performance evaluation:* The different ways in which an application may be configured will allow us to experiment with different implements of the application and evaluate the performance characteristics of the application.

3. *Self Contained:* The design essentially permits the creation of a blackboard run as a self contained entity. This allows multiple Erasmus instances to coexist in a given environment. Hence, it should be possible to put together a larger system which invokes several Erasmus runs in parallel [15].

We are in the process of evaluating the system with all the applications developed earlier with BBB. We are also developing some new applications. These applications will finally be the judge of how well the blackboard system performs. Preliminary indications are that the Erasmus system is twice as fast as the BBB system, even with a configuration which uses every feature available in Erasmus! We are compiling the results of our experiments.

4.0 References

1. Nii, H. P., "Blackboard Systems," AI Magazine, vol. 7, number 2, pp 39-53 and number 3, pp 82-106.

2. Benda, M., Baum, L.S., Dodhiawala, R.T., Jagannathan, V., "Boeing Blackboard System", presentation at the AAAI sponsored workshop on High Level Tools, October 1986.

3. Hayes-Roth, B., "A Blackboard Architecture for Control," Artificial Intelligence, Vol 26, No. 3., pp251-321, July 1985.

4. Nii, H. P., "CAGE and POLIGON: Two frameworks for Blackboard-based Concurrent Problem Solving," Proceedings of DARPA Workshop on Expert Systems, Report#SAIC-86/1701, pp. 142-145, April 1986.

5. Corkill, D. D., Gallagher, K. Q., Murray, K. E., "GBB:A generic blackboard development environment," AAAI-86,Philadelphia, August 1986.

6. Baum, L. S., Dodhiawala, R. T., Jagannathan, V., "BBB Manual," Boeing Technical Report # BCS-G2010-31.

7. Rice, J. P., "Poligon, A system for parallel problem-solving," Proceedings of DARPA Workshop on Expert Systems, Report# SAIC-86/1701, pp. 152-159, April 1986.

8. Erman, L. D., Lark, J. S., Hayes-Roth, F., "Engineering Intelligent Systems: Progress Report on ABE," Proceedings of DARPA Workshop on Expert Systems, Report#SAIC-86/1701, pp. 89-100, April 1986.

9. Bisiani, R., F. Alleva, F. Correrini, A. Forin, F. Lecouat, R. Lerner, "The AGORA Programming Environment," CMU-CS-87-113, March 1987.

10. Advanced Decision Systems, "Knowledge Integration Toolkit 3.0," Mountain View, CA, January 1987.

11. Skillman, T. "Distributed Cooperating Processes in a Mobil Robot System," Workshop on Blackboard System for Perception and Control, Carnegie-Mellon University, Pittsburg, PA, June 1986.

12. Benda, M., Jagannathan, V., Dodhiawala, R. T., "On Optimal Cooperation of Knowledge Sources" presented at the Distributed Artificial Intelligence Workshop, Gloucester, MA, October 1986.

13. Aiello, N., "User-Directed Control of Parallelism: The CAGE System," Proceedings of DARPA Workshop on Expert Systems, Report#SAIC-86/1701, pp. 146-151, April 1986.

14. Baum, L. S., Dodhiawala, R. T., Jagannathan, V., "Erasmus System" Boeing Technical Report, working draft.

15. Jagannathan, V., Baum, L. S., Dodhiawala, R. T., "Designing distributed blackboard system with Erasmus" Boeing Technical Report, working draft.

Investigating logical properties of the rule-based expert systems using combinatorial and geometrical techniques I

J.W. Jaromczyk* and W. Marek**
Department of Computer Science
University of Kentucky
Lexington, KY 40506-0027, USA

Abstract:
In this paper we address two issues pertaining to rule-based expert systems; consistency and completeness. These notions, as we shall see below, are closely connected with the analogous notions in logic. Some efficient algorithms solving these problems will be given as well as new ideas going in the direction of the improvement of their performance and generalization will be proposed.

Keywords: Rule-based expert systems, consistency, completeness, computational geometry.

1.Introduction.

An expert system is a computer program intended to serve as a consultant for decision making process, thus mimicking the reasoning process of one or several experts.

Such program is called "expert" system because it addresses problems usually thought to require human expertise for their solution, in particular incorporating expert's knowledge.

Building a good expert system is not an easy task and needs a good specification of the form in which the knowledge will be represented; in general a precise model of this system should be provided.

As pointed in the abstract, in this paper we intend to study the algorithmic aspects of the completeness and consistency concepts. These notions are fundamental for any type of logic-based system. During the crucial phase of the building of expert system, i.e. during the acquisition and organization of knowledge the knowledge engineer has to be able to realize the logical properties of the system he/she is building.

Completeness of the system means that, given the opportunity, system would be able to provide an answer to the query. To be a bit more precise, it means that if the user provides all the data the system requires, the system should be able to come with the answer to the query. Such a vague concept clearly generalizes the notion of the completeness as used by logicians ([CK]). Indeed, imagine a system ("black box", determined by a first order theory T) which accepts as an input formulas of the underlying first order language and provides the following answer: if the input formula ϕ is a consequence of T then the possible output is 1. If the negation of the input formula ϕ, $\neg\phi$ is a consequence of T then the output is 0. It is quite obvious to see that such system is complete if and only if the theory T is complete. Such system is usually quite complicated; testing the completeness of the system is a Π_2 problem (in arithmetical hierarchy). Even in case of a propositional calculus the problem is complex.

Consistency is, essentially, the problem of unique answer. Indeed, we can look at the consistency as follows: The system acts, in general, in a non-deterministic

(*) On leave from Institute of Informatics, Warsaw University, Warszawa, Poland

(**) Partially supported by USDA grant USDA/CSRS/84-CSRS-2-2524 and funds from NSF RII 8610671 grant and Commonwealth of Kentucky through Kentucky EPSCoR program.

Methodologies for Intelligent Systems
Z. W. Ras and M. Zemankova, Editors

way. Given a input (i.e. the data required by the system to provide the advice) is the answer unique? (we assume that every legal answer can be generated). Hence the consistency means that whichever path the system uses to generate the answer, the achieved result is always the same. Again a slightly modified example used in the discussion of the completeness property shows how this notion generalizes the concept of consistency as considered by logicians. Let us look at the same system as above, except that now it provides the output 2 if neither the formula ϕ nor its negation are consequences of T. Again it is quite obvious that this system is consistent precisely in the case the theory T is consistent (in sense of first order logic). Actually, let us notice that if this system answers 2 for the query ϕ it must be consistent. If the theory T is complete and consistent then the system would generate exactly one of the values $\{0, 1\}$ to any query.

During recent years expert systems are being produced in an ever increasing numbers. The reader is referred to [HLW] and [KW] for numerous examples. The present generation of expert systems is usually based on the knowledge bases formed of *rules*. Several interesting expert system "shells" are based on this concepts (for the discussion of this software see various issues of [ES]). The need for the investigation of logical concepts and in particular of consistency and completeness was realized early (see [SSS]). In [M] the concept of rule based system and of its logical properties were studied and some algorithms for testing those properties were introduced. This study intends to look at these concepts in a more detailed way.

One can also argue that the investigations of completeness and consistency are closely connected with the software organization and testing. Completeness is the most natural constraint on the software; when legal data are provided the system should react. Completeness is, consequently enforced by means of various devices, principally the so called default rules (this is the way PROLOG deals with this problem). Yet one should point that such methods may result in serious side effects.

Consistency is enforced usually by extralogical means (PROLOG uses for this purpose the order in which rules are listed). Yet there are at least two reason why the consistency of the rule-based system should be tested. The first is related to updates of the rule base. If the usual protocol of updates is accepted (that is if the rule is modified then it is retracted from its original place and the substitute rule (or rules) are asserted at the end) then inconsistency of the rule base may lead to uncontrolled behavior of the system. The second issue is related to the mode of execution of the system. If the system is consistent then it is possible to use its parts in parallel; it will not result in an error. Of course the whole idea of the abstract representation of the rule bases is that we do not want to deal with the question of the execution of the system (notice the analogy with Codd's approach to databases). Hence it is the logic of the system (and not the behavior of a particular representation) that we want to investigate.

In the present paper we propose a reasonably general model for knowledge representation. This model is a generalization of the model considered in [M] and conceptually resembles the transformation of variables to the case when all variables range over a parallelepiped. Dealing with such objects provides a natural connection with the techniques of computational geometry and this idea will be easily detectable in our work.

Let us state here that the model of expert systems treated in this paper, namely that of pairwise incompatible conclusions and the absence of imprecise information (like probabilities, confidence factors etc.) is restrictive but important for the current class of applications. In the ongoing research we shall address the above mentioned issues as well.

Due to space limitations we discuss in detail the concept of consistency only. There are several reasons for this choice. One of those is that the notion of consistency is important in the studies of the redundancy of attributes in rule-based systems ([MT]). One also notices that the question of the consistency checking becomes crucial when the knowledge comes from several sources and so the natural assumption (expert works in a consistent fashion) fails.

The paper is organized as follows. Next section includes basic notions and definitions relevant to the topic of the paper. Specifically a model of expert system and precise definitions of the completeness and consistency in this case will be given. In Section 3 we present some algorithms solving the consistency problem. Finally, last section gives concluding remarks and open problems related to the topics and solutions discussed in the paper.

2. Notions and notations.

In this section we discuss a model of rule-based system. This model is a generalization of the one discussed in [M], it seems to be reasonably general and covers several current applications of expert systems.

A rule-based system is a triple $<\mathbf{P}, \mathbf{A}, \mathbf{R}>$, where $\mathbf{P}$ is the set of *parameters* of the system, $\mathbf{A}$ is the set of *attributes* of the system and $\mathbf{R}$ is the set of the *rules* of the system.

To each of the parameters $P_i \in \mathbf{P}$ and attributes $A_j \in \mathbf{A}$ we associate its *domain*; for simplicity we identify the domain with the parameter or the attribute itself. In general, domains of parameters and attributes are different. Among the attributes in the collection $\mathbf{A}$ one plays a special role, different from all the others. It is the *action* attribute and it is denoted by A.

We are ready to introduce now the notion of a *rule*. Formally, a rule is a tuple $<<\Phi_1,B_1>, \ldots, <\Phi_n,B_n>,a>$ where:

$$\Phi_i : P_1 \times \cdots \times P_k \rightarrow A_i$$

is the procedure to compute the value of the ith attribute, $B_i \subseteq A_i$,

$$a : P_1 \times \cdots \times P_k \rightarrow A$$

is a function to compute the action to be taken.

Such a rule $\mathbf{r}$ is interpreted for $\bar{p} \in P_1 \times \cdots \times P_k$ by the following program:

(*) **if** $\Phi_1(\bar{p}) \in B_1$
and $\Phi_2(\bar{p}) \in B_2$
....
and $\Phi_n(\bar{p}) \in B_n$
then perform the action a($\bar{p}$)

At a time we may allow nonmembership relation $\notin$ in place of $\in$. In the general case this does not lead to the increased expressive power of the system, as the formula $\Phi_i(\bar{p}) \notin B_i$ is, of course equivalent to $\Phi_i(\bar{p}) \in -B_i$. If however, precisely as we are going to do below, the class of admissible ranges of attributes in the rules is restricted to segments, a considerable improvement of the expressive power is achieved.

The notion of rule, as considered in this paper is a very general one. We do not claim that is the best notion. Yet it allows us to provide a good formalization of the intuitive notions discussed in the introduction. In this fashion intuitive notions of completeness and consistency (as introduced above) are transformed to fully formal (and hence amenable to mathematical investigations) concepts. Let us point in this place that only a fully formal theory of rule based systems allows for the development of such programmer tools as debuggers. Moreover the refinement of the knowledge base may be done without referring to intuition.

The simplest case of the rules is considered in [M], where all the parameters are simply the attributes, functions Φ_i are projections, and the action function of each rule is constant. In this case rules take form $<B_1, \ldots, B_n, a>$ and are interpreted as follows:

(**) **If** $p_1 \in B_1$
and $p_2 \in B_2$
.....
and $p_n \in B_n$
then perform the action a

A simple example pertaining to pest management for alfalfa plant (taken from [BMYMFB]) of the rule of type (**) is the following:
Example:

If 525 $\leq$ Heat_unit
and First_harvest = True
and Post_harvest_epizootic = False
and 2$\leq$ Weevils/stem $<$ 4
then "Resample in two days"

Representing this rule in the format (*) we notice that:

$B_1 = [525, \infty)$
$B_2 = \{ \textit{True} \}$
$B_3 = \{ \textit{False} \}$
$B_4 = [2, 4)$
and a = "Resample in two days".

The case we investigate in this paper is that of *linear collections of rules.* A collection of rules $\mathbf{R}$ is called *linear*, if for every attribute A_i there exists a linear ordering $<_i$ such that for every rule $\mathbf{r}_i \in \mathbf{R}$ the corresponding range of the ith attribute is a *segment* in the ordering $<_i$ Let us recall that a (closed) segment $[a,b]$ is defined as follows:

$$[a,b]=\{x \in A_i\colon a<_i x<_i b\} \bigcup \{a,b\}.$$

Both a,b are called the endpoints of $[a,b]$. Half-closed and open segments are also considered.
The rule given in our example is obviously a linear one. In the current applications the collections of rules under consideration are usually linear, although a superficial nonlinear family of rules can easily be constructed. Generally, the attributes are either finite (and then usually small) or possess the linear structure (of integers, rationals or reals or their segments). The fact that we are considering linear collections of rules should not be surprising. As mentioned above expert rules are usually linear. In rare cases when they are not it is possible to find an equivalent linear family of rules (this problem is discussed in [M]).

To every rule we can assign its *type*, i.e. the collection of attributes appearing in the premises of that rule. If $\mathbf{R}$ is a collection of rules then $\mathbf{R}$ is partitioned naturally according to the type of rules involved. In particular any collection of rules of the same type is called *homogeneous.* One can think that a homogeneous collection of rules deals with situations of uniform type.

We introduce presently the notion of completeness and consistency of homogeneous collections of rules. To this end we say that a tuple (situation)

$<b_1, \ldots, b_n>$ *matches* a rule $\mathbf{r} = <B_1, \ldots, B_n, a>$ if and only if $b_1 \in B_1, \ldots, b_n \in B_n$. In this case we say that the rule $\mathbf{r}$ assigns to $<b_1, \ldots, b_n>$ the conclusion a. Analogously, $\bar{p} = <p_1, \ldots, p_k>$ matches the rule $\mathbf{r}$ of type (*), if and only if $\Phi_1(\bar{p}) \in B_1, \ldots, \Phi_n(\bar{p}) \in B_n$.

We say that the collection of rules **R** is *complete* if every valid situation matches some rule in **R**. We say that the collection **R** of rules is *consistent* iff for every situation b $= <b_1, \ldots, b_n>$ and every pair of rules $\mathbf{r}_1$ and $\mathbf{r}_2$ from **R**, if b matches both $\mathbf{r}_1$ and $\mathbf{r}_2$ then $\mathbf{r}_1$ and $\mathbf{r}_2$ offer the same conclusion.

These notions formalize, in the case of rule-based systems, the intuitive notions of completeness and consistency as introduced in Section 1.

Observe that the notions of completeness and consistency may be characterized in set-theoretic terms (see for instance [M]). In particular the characterizations presented below generalize their counterparts formulated in [M].

We say that the collection **R** of rules of type (*) is *uniform* iff for every i, the procedure to calculate the value of ith attribute is the same in all rules. Notice that the definition (*) does not require this. Yet we are able to prove some results for the uniform families of rules only.

Proposition 2.1 (a) A homogeneous uniform collection of rules of type (*) is complete if and only if:

$$\bigcup_{i=1}^{m}(Rng(\Phi_1)) \cap B_{1,i} \times \cdots \times (Rng(\Phi_n)) \cap B_{n,i} = (Rng(\Phi_1)) \cap A_1 \times \cdots \times (Rng(\Phi_n)) \cap A_n$$

where Rng(Φ) is the range, i.e. collection of values of Φ.
(b) A homogeneous collection of rules of type (**) is complete if and only if:

$$\bigcup_{i=1}^{m} B_{1,i} \times \cdots \times B_{n,i} = A_1 \times \cdots \times A_n$$

(recall that m is the number of rules).

The notion of consistency is characterized in the following fashion:

Proposition 2.2. (a) A homogeneous uniform collection of rules of type (*) is consistent if and only if for every choice of $\bar{p} \in P_1 \times \cdots \times P_k$ the following implication holds:

$$\Phi_1(\bar{p}) \in B_1 \wedge \Phi_1(\bar{p}) \in C_1 \wedge \cdots \Phi_n(\bar{p}) \in B_n \wedge \Phi_n(\bar{p}) \in C_n$$

implies that: $a(\bar{p}) = b(\bar{p})$.
(b) A homogeneous collection of rules **R** of type (**) is consistent if and only if for every choice of rules $\mathbf{r} = <B_1, \ldots, B_n, a>$ and $\mathbf{s} = <C_1, \ldots, C_n, b>$ in **R**, the following implication holds:

$$\text{if } B_1 \times \cdots \times B_n \cap C_1 \times \cdots \times C_n \neq \emptyset \text{ then a = b.}$$

Proofs of the above propositions follow directly from the definitions.

Knowing if the system is consistent and complete is vital during the designing process. When the knowledge has been collected we need to be able to see if this knowledge, specially if it comes from various sources, is consistent and complete. In the case of large systems, ones with thousands of rules, this task may be complicated. We studied some relevant algorithms in [M]. One notices, though, that the algorithms given below are simpler and more amenable to good programming. In fact in the next section, using ideas coming from computational geometry, we will present some efficient algorithms for checking the consistency property.

3. Algorithms for Consistency.

This section presents new algorithms for consistency testing in expert systems with linear rules (i.e., rules of the type (**)).
Let us recall that a rule-based system is consistent if for any choice of two rules $\mathbf{r}_1, \mathbf{r}_2$ if both $\mathbf{r}_1, \mathbf{r}_2$ are matched by a same situation then they advice to perform the same action.

Essentially two algorithms based on different approaches will be presented. The first is established on a concept of connected components and is of special interest if one is concerned with a refinement of the knowledge base. In turn the second algorithm (based on multidimensional divide-and-conquer paradigm) seems to be more general since it admits several interesting variations.

3.1. Consistency checking based on connected components

Let ES be a linear homogeneous rule-based system with m rules of type (**) and n attributes and let C stand for a collection of all the rules in ES.

We say that rules $\mathbf{r}_1$ and $\mathbf{r}_2$ in C are *(directly) connected* if there exists a situation $\mathbf{q}$ such that both $\mathbf{r}_1$ and $\mathbf{r}_2$ match $\mathbf{q}$.

The transitive, symmetric and reflexive closure of the above defined connectivity relation induces a partition of C into disjoint groups of the rules called *connected components* of the collection C.
It happens that the connected components are strictly related to the consistency of the expert system as explained in the following theorem.

Theorem 3.1. System ES is consistent iff all rules in each connected component of C have the same conclusion (action).
Proof: ☞ Assume that ES is consistent and there is a connected component and two rules $\mathbf{r}_1$ and $\mathbf{r}_2$ in this component with different actions.
Since $\mathbf{r}_1$ and $\mathbf{r}_2$ belong to the same component, there exists a path induced by the connectivity relation from $\mathbf{r}_1$ to $\mathbf{r}_2$. Consider now this path. As the labels of $\mathbf{r}_1$ and $\mathbf{r}_2$ are different, there are two directly connected rules on this path with different actions. This implies the inconsistency of ES. Contradiction.
☜ : Every pair of rules directly connected belongs to the same connected component so both the rules in this pair have the same action. It implies that ES is consistent.
□

Now we are ready to present our first algorithm. It consists of two main phases.

Consistency1
Input: A collection C of the rules in the rule-based system ES.
Output: Decision whether ES is consistent.
Phase 1: Find connected components of the set C
Phase 2: For each connected component check whether all member rules have the same conclusion (action).
Decision: If all actions in each connected component are the same then report "*system is consistent*" otherwise report "*system is inconsistent*".

Correctness of the above algorithm follows directly from theorem 1.

Phase 2 can be easily carried out in time proportional to the number of rules. The cost of the algorithm depends on an implementation of phase 1.

At this point we can gain the profit from computational geometry.

Theorem 3.2. There exists an implementation of Consistency1 algorithm (for $n \geq 2$) in $O(m \log^{n-1} m)$ time and $O(m)$ storage.
Proof: Observe that each rule in linear expert system can be viewed as a geometrical object, specifically n-dimensional rectangle. Now the claimed complexities follow from time and storage complexity of an algorithm for computing connected components of a set of m n-dimensional rectangles, see [ChI], also [EO]. □

Let us notice that a slight modification of the above algorithm can provide us with a list of all pairs of rules generating inconsistency. This information may be helpful at the time of designing an expert system.

Beyond the immediate application to the consistency checking connected components can be used also to debug and refine a knowledge base. Indeed, one observes that two rules not necessarily directly connected can belong to the same connected component. Consequently in a (consistent) expert system rules not directly dependent are forced (at least sometime) to advise the same action. This implies that the knowledge engineer should take a deep look at all the rules clustered in a connected component in order to see if these rules can be grouped into a single rule or rather should be separated with new actions assigned.

3.2. Consistency checking based on multidimensional divide-and-conquer.

In this subsection we will present another consistency checking algorithm. In the general case it works in time $O(m^2)$. Nevertheless the simple structure of the algorithm admits several modifications giving a better performance for various classes of linear rule-based systems. In fact some variants of the basic algorithm will be discussed.

In order to define the algorithm we introduce the notion of the median of a set of segments (for the definition of segment see section 2).

Let S be a set of segments (we assume that the segment endpoints are pairwise disjoint).
Definition: The *median* of S is a point splitting a set of all endpoints of S into two equal (w.r.t. cardinality) groups; endpoints less than the median and endpoints greater than the median.

Observe that a median of S divides the collection S into three groups called blocks: G_l - segments lying to the left of the median, G_m - segments containing the median, G_r - segments lying to the right of the median.

Assume now that we are given a collection of n-attribute rules. By j-median we mean the median of the set of segments corresponding to the j-th attribute, i.e., we consider the family of segments appearing as the values of the j-th attribute.

The following observation is crucial for further considerations: the median of a set of segments can be found in time proportional to the number of segments in this set.

Now we are ready for the algorithm (the algorithm uses a powerful multidimensional divide-and-conquer paradigm, see [B]).

Consistency2
Input: A collection C of m n-attribute rules
corresponding to an expert system ES.
Output: List of all pairs of inconsistent rules.

```
1.  begin
2.     j:=0;
3.     while there is block G with different actions do
4.   {i.e., for all non one-action (conclusion) blocks}
5.        begin
6.            find j- median;
7.            split block G into Gl,Gm,Gr
8.            report inconsistency if Gm is middle for the n-th round
9.            and is not one-action (scan Gm to detect different actions);
10.           check consistency by naive algorithm (i.e. by direct comparison)
11.           between groups Gl, Gm and Gr,Gm ;
12.           report all inconsistent pairs;
13.            j:= (j+1) mod n;
14.  end
   end ;
```

Observe that although the above algorithm uses a pretty standard technique of dividing with respect to changing coordinates (in our case changing attributes) it has an interesting feature inherent in the consistency notion.

To be more specific the instruction "report inconsistency if G_m is middle for the n-th round and is not one-action;" enables us to eliminate arbitrarily big blocks if they were not divided in the last n rounds. In other words block is either divided (divide-and-conquer paradigm) or will be "eliminated" after at most n rounds.

In this sense the multidimensional divide-and-conquer is well suited for the consistency checking problem. This feature is explained by Fact 3.3.1. Before presenting this fact some useful notation will be introduced.
Let G_α, where the index α is a string over alphabet {l,m,r}, denote a block obtained while running the algorithm. Then left, middle and right blocks obtained from G_α as an effect of splitting with respect to a current j-median will be denoted by $G_{\alpha l}$, $G_{\alpha m}$, $G_{\alpha r}$ respectively. Observe that the index α (empty at the beginning of the process) describes uniquely a way of creating the block G_α. It is convenient to think that the algorithm constructs a ternary tree with nodes corresponding to the blocks created at the process .

Let $\alpha=\beta m^n$, i.e., α ends with at least n m's where m stands for a middle.

Fact 3.3.1 If there are two rules in G_α with different actions (conclusions) then the expert system ES is inconsistent.
Proof: Inspecting the algorithm Consistency2 and using the form of α we find that all the rules in G_α match an n-tuple consisting of n j-medians recently used by the algorithm in the dividing process. Therefore if some rules in this block have different conclusions then the system ES is inconsistent. □

Now we can prove the following
Theorem 3.3.: The algorithm Consistency2 is correct, i.e., it reports all pairs of inconsistent rules.
Proof: It is not necessary to compare rules between groups $G_{\alpha l}$,$G_{\alpha r}$. All other

comparisons are tested. Additionally all "middle" blocks are handled properly by virtue of fact 3.3.1. □

In the general case the performance of the algorithm is $O(n*m^2)$ but still some fraction of comparisons out of $n*m^2$ for a naive algorithm can be avoided (actually depending on the size of blocks G_m).
This observation gives rise to consideration of some special subclasses of rule-based systems. The idea here is to study an important parameter of the system, namely its density. Let E(A_i) denote the family of segments which correspond to the attribute A_i of the family E of the rules.

We introduce the following definition:

Definition: Let d be a fixed natural number.
(a) For F a family of segments the size of the maximal subfamily with non-empty intersection is called its density and is denoted by d(F).
(b) An attribute A_i of the expert system ES is d-dense if $d(ES(A_i)) \leq d$.
(c) An expert system ES is d-dense, if for all i, $d(ES(A_i)) \leq d$.

Intuitively, the density of an expert system is small if the "nesting" of attribute values from different rules is small. It will become apparent at the end of this section that in fact it is important that at least some of attributes are of the small density.

The following theorem holds.

Theorem 3.4.: For expert systems with density d, COST(Consistency2) is $O(d*m*n*\log(m))$ comparisons plus number of reported inconsistent pairs of rules.
Proof: The number of algorithm rounds is $const*log(m)$. It is a simple observation that $card(G_l)=card(G_r)$ and $card(G_m)\leq d$. In each round we are looking for j-medians (total cost per round $O(m)$), and subsequently no more than d*n*m comparisons is performed (between groups and the middle group). For all the groups indexed by α as in fact 3.3.1. a simple scan is needed to detect different actions, so the global cost for all such blocks is not greater than m. It gives altogether $const*d*m*n*log(m)$ comparisons. □

We notice that the algorithm Consistency2 works faster than Consistency1 for d-dense expert systems and is based on a simple divide-and-conquer paradigm. In addition we find that, in the case of d-dense systems, the restriction to disjoint sets of endpoints is immaterial.

Let us observe that the algorithm Consistency2 can be modified further to handle efficiently expert systems with one (or few) d-dense attribute only (let us call such an attribute a *handle*). To this end it is enough to keep splitting the rules with respect to the median corresponding to the handle attribute only. So the divide process is based merely on one attribute with low density still giving a complexity $o(m^2)$ (in fact of the same order as stated in theorem 3.4.).
Because of its usefulness a corresponding algorithm is given below.
We start with an algorithm to determine the density of the attribute (see definition of d-dense attribute).

Algorithm d-density_check
Input: A set of segments corresponding to i-th attribute A_i.
Output: value of the variable *dens* equal to the density d(A_i).

phase1: Sort all endpoints of the segments in S in the list $\{e_1, \ldots, e_{2m}\}$.
phase2: dens:=0 ; tem:= 0;
for i:=1 **to** m **do**

```
begin
   if e_i is a left endpoint then
         begin
               tem:= tem+1;
               dens:= max(den, tem)
         end
         else  tem:= tem -1
 end;
```

Fact 3.3.2. Cost of the algorithm d-density_check is $O(m\log m)$.
Proof: Cost of the algorithm is dominated by phase1 which can be carried out in $O(m\ logm)$ steps, cost of the phase2 is $O(m)$. □

Now we are ready for a modification of the Consistency2 algorithm.

Consistency3
Input: A collection C of m n-attribute rules
corresponding to an expert system ES.
Output: List of all pairs of inconsistent rules.

phase1: Find density of each attribute using the algorithm d-dense_check.
Let j be the number of the attribute with the smallest
density d (i.e., j corresponds to the handle)
phase2:

```
  begin
     while there is a block G_α of size > d do
          begin
               find j- median of G_α;
               split block into G_αl,G_αm,G_αr
               { card(G_αm)≤d };
               check consistency by naive algorithm (i.e. by direct comparison)
               between groups G_αl, G_αm and G_αr,G_αm ;
               report all inconsistent pairs;
     end
  end ;
```

The price to pay for dividing with respect to one attribute only is that the fact 3.3.1 no longer works. Therefore the lines 8-9 from the algorithm Consistency2 had to be removed. In the effect, instead of spending a time m for dealing with "middle" groups as in original algorithm sometimes $d*m$ steps to accomplish this task might be needed.

Another modification can be suggested for expert systems with rules containing attributes with few discrete values (e.g. boolean values). It this case one should split the set of rules with respect to those attributes. This results in clustering potentially inconsistent rules at the very beginning of the process. In effect some unnecessary comparisons can be avoided.

Finally let us notice that the idea used in algorithm Consistency2 leads to an attractive data structure supporting efficient answering of partially specified queries. We intend to report on this application elsewhere.

4.Conclusions.

In this paper we have proposed the general model for rule-based action oriented expert systems. Strict and convenient structure of the model enabled us to give the precise definitions of the completness and consistency notions which happen to correspond to their pure logic counterparts.
For some restricted versions of this model set theoretical characterizations have been given. This results in new efficient algorithms checking consistency for the class of linear expert systems.

These algorithms have been developed using techniques and solutions of computational geometry. It demonstrates that certain general methods of that field can be successfully employed to specific problems stemming from knowledge engineering.

We believe that both the model and the algorithms can serve as a guidance for knowledge engineers interested in building expert systems and tools to develop them.

Finally let us notice that some important problems remain open. It would be interesting to find good characterizations and efficient algorithms for the general (as opposed to linear) models of action-oriented systems. In particular systems with incompletely specified attribute values (confidence levels, probabilities etc) should be considered.

Acknowledgements: We wish to thank Mirek Truszczynski for his comments on earlier versions of this paper. Also several remarks from anonymous referees are greatly appreciated.

References:

[B] Bentley,J.L., Multidimensional binary search trees used for associative searching, Communications of the ACM 18,509-517(1975).
[BMYMFB] Brown, G.C., Marek, W., Yeh, V., Mehs, S., Freedman, N., Bowen, E., Expert Systems in Agricultural Pest Management: An Implementation Example, NCCI Software Journal 1(2).
[ChI] Chazelle, B. , Incerpi,J., Computing the connected components of d-ranges, (1984), manuscript.
[CK] Chang, C.C., Keisler, H.J., Model Theory, North-Holland 1973.
[EO] Edelsbrunner,H., Overmars,M., Batched dynamic solutions to decomposable searching problems, (March 1983), technical report RUU-CS-83-8, Dep. Com.Sci. University of Utrecht.
[ES] Expert Systems, Int'l Journal of Knowledge Engineering, Learned Information.
[HLW] Hayes-Roth, F., Lenat, D., Waterman, D.A., Building Expert Systems, Addison-Wesley, 1983.
[KL] Klahr, P., Waterman, D.A.,(eds), Expert Systems, Techniques, Tools and Applications, Addison-Wesley, 1986.
[M] Marek, W., Consistency and Completeness of Rule-based Systems, In: Knowledge Frontier, essays in knowledge representation, Cercone N. and McCalla eds.
[MT] Marek, W., Truszczynski, M., Incompleteness of information in rule-based systems: role of minimal sets. TR no. 87-87, Department of Computer Science, University of Kentucky, 1987.
[PS] Preparata, F.P., Shamos M.I. Computational Geometry ,An Introduction, Springer-Verlag, 1985.
[SSS] Suwa M., Scott A.C., Shortliffe E.H.; Completeness and Consistency in Rule-based Systems, Chapter 9 in: Rule-based Expert Systems, Buchanan B.G. and Shortliffe E.H. Eds., Addison-Wesley 1985.

A MODEL-BASED INTELLIGENT TUTORING SYSTEM FOR POWER DISTRIBUTION SYSTEMS[1]

XIAOFENG LI,* JEFFREY R. CANTWELL,* JOHN R. BOURNE,* KAZUHIKO KAWAMURA,* CHARLES K. KINZER,* AND NOBUJI MIYASAKA**
*Center for Intelligent Systems, Vanderbilt University, Nashville, TN 37235; **Osaka Gas Co., Ltd., Osaka, Japan

ABSTRACT

This paper describes an architecture of a model-based Intelligent Tutoring System (ITS) in the domain of Power Distribution Systems (PDSs). The ITS utilizes a graphics-based qualitative modelling module for representing a PDS and simulating 'hands-on' operating methodologies. A Student Model is used to capture the on-going tutoring process. Planning techniques are employed to dynamically adjust tutoring and remediation strategies. This research is part of a project to develop a Generic Tutoring System (GTS) in the area of physical systems. The use of graphics-based qualitative modelling techniques potentially offers an ideal laboratory learning environment. The purpose of the GTS is to discover generic tutoring methodologies, and thereby develop a generic courseware tool, which will assist human instructors in organizing their knowledge and rapidly developing ITSs for specific domains.

INTRODUCTION

Research on Intelligent Computer-Aided Instruction (ICAI) (a.k.a., ITS, Intelligent Tutorial System) has been popular for almost two decades [1-2], and several systems have been created in example domains including games, computer languages, and mathematics [1-4]. However, few examples in engineering domains are found in the literature. Recently, the importance of such systems in industrial environments has become more apparent, largely because of increasing recognition of the complexity of physical systems and the mental models of system operations to be mastered by employees. These factors necessitate the use of increasingly effective employee training methods. In our view, model-based ITSs have the potential of significantly reducing the cost of employee training and can provide consistent training at a level that cannot be matched by traditional techniques. Although there are a few implementations of such systems (for example, STEAMER [5] and RBT [6]), most current systems stress domain-dependent simulations and explanation generation without considering deeply either individualized tutoring strategies or Student Models -- basic requirements for an ITS [2, 7].

During the last two years, a model-based Generic Tutoring System (GTS) [8] has been developed at Vanderbilt University for tutoring physical systems. One prominent feature of the GTS is the integration of the more standard Text-Based Tutor (TBT) with the Model-Based Tutor (MBT), where a robust graphics-based qualitative modelling module is employed to represent the physical systems being taught, and schedule their operating methodologies. There are two important goals for the GTS. First, to understand methodologies for incorporating qualitative modelling techniques in

[1] This research was supported, in part, by Osaka Gas Co., Ltd., Osaka, Japan.

Methodologies for Intelligent Systems
Z. W. Ras and M. Zemankova, Editors

laboratory learning environments for engineering domains. Second, to discover generic engineering training methodologies and, thereby, develop a generic courseware tool that will help human instructors in organizing their knowledge and enhancing their ability to rapidly develop ITSs for specific domains.

We have implemented an example in the domain of a Power Distribution System (PDS) as a prototype GTS, which basically fulfills the first task. In terms of general utility, our system allows a human instructor, who does not know any computer languages, to easily make substantive instructional modifications and to configure new PDS simulators.

Operators of PDSs need extensive training prior to being allowed to operate a physical PDS. Traditional training methodologies employ both classroom instruction and simulation using rigid and relatively inflexible physical models of simple PDSs. This type of training is expensive and does not offer a flexible means of providing training over a wide range of possible distribution systems. Our hypothesis is that an ITS can provide a viable substitute for the traditional training program and overcome traditional limitations. Further, it is also hypothesized that a model-based ITS that incorporates graphics-based qualitative simulation as an integral feature will have significant advantages over systems without a dynamic visual model. In our system a trainee is provided with a vivid graphic description of the internal functionality and behavior of a PDS in terms of physical connectivity, voltage propagation, current flow, and operation logic. This enhancement of the level of reality of the course material should improve students' comprehension of the material.

EXAMPLE DOMAIN: A POWER DISTRIBUTION SYSTEM

A PDS, as shown in Figure 1, typically consists of power sources (#1 and #2), consumers (sinks), transformers (#1Tr, #2Tr, and #3Tr) and several types of switches such as Disconnecting Switches (DS, e.g., 189rp) and Circuit Breakers (CB, e.g., 152r). Each switch type has its own rules of operation. For example, a CB can functionally be operated (on/off) without any constraints. On the other hand, a DS cannot be turned off while there is current flowing through it. In a PDS, all DSs are physically protected by built-in "interlock" facilities. Globally, any operation of these switches effects the entire distribution network. Therefore, it is imperative that operators learn to be sufficiently skillful in manipulating the various switches, especially in emergency situations.

A number of concepts and principles need to be taught in the PDS training program. These include concepts revolving around system component (e.g., DS, CB) and system behavior (interlock, synchronization), along with general operating principles, such as procedural knowledge about connecting and disconnecting paths. The most important skill is to be able to understand the global state of the PDS at any time.

PDS INTELLIGENT TUTORING SYSTEM

Figure 2 shows the overview of the ITS and the overall communication scheme. The ITS consists of the following five main modules: the Strategist, the TBT, the MBT, the Bug Detector (BD), and the Student Model (SM). These modules work together to form a highly interactive and flexible tutoring system for the PDS.

Strategist

The Strategist is an opportunistic planner capable of making instructional decisions dynamically in an event-driven manner. The Strategist is

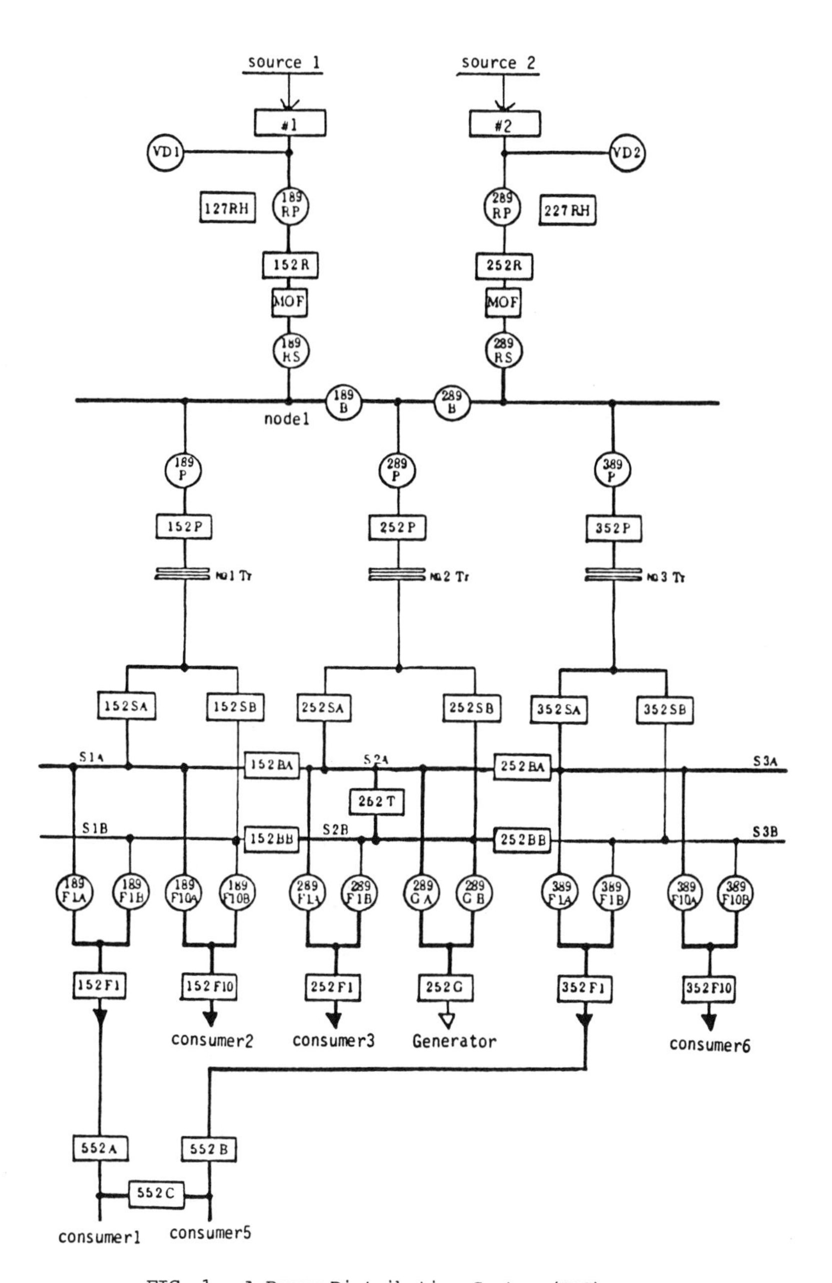

FIG. 1. A Power Distribution System (PDS).

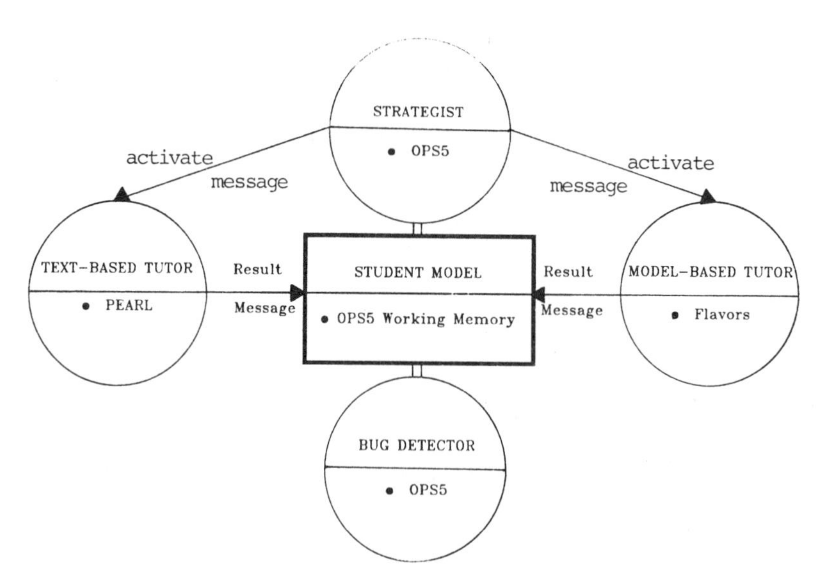

FIG. 2. An architectural overview of the ITS.

the top level in the system. It controls invocation and behavior of other system modules, and monitors the student's interactions with the system.

The Strategist was implemented in OPS5 [9] as a set of declarative rules containing generic (domain-independent) teaching knowledge and a minimum of domain-specific knowledge. This implementation allows the Strategist to be quite flexible. Instructional decision-making styles can be implemented or revised by adding or deleting rules. Many of the kinds of decisions that the Strategist can make are related to educational theory and principles of instructional design. For example, the Strategist may select one or more possible methods of gaining the learner's attention, such as the "nine events of instruction" addressed by Gagne and Briggs [10]. The nine points of the Gagne and Briggs model have been incorporated into our ITS-PDS, as have the levels of questioning presented by Barrett [11], based on Bloom's Taxonomy of Education Objectives [12].

The working memory (WM) of OPS5 serves as a blackboard, which is the only communication medium among the TBT, the MBT, the BD, and the Strategist. All modules can post messages on the blackboard, but only the BD and the Strategist can read from it. The Strategist reads the messages on the blackboard and uses the information to make control decisions. Usually, the Strategist, after reasoning about the knowledge in the WM, activates either the MBT or the TBT, and waits for new data to be inserted into the WM, at which time control will return to the Strategist. Depending on the student's performance, the Strategist might shift the control back and forth between the TBT and the MBT several times, until the training course is completed.

Two general strategic rules are:

```
rule1:  IF      the student failed to pass a TBT test,
        THEN    give the student hints and retest.
rule2:  IF      the student failed the retest,
        THEN    return the student to a previous lesson.
```

These simple rules exemplify the kind of generic rules the Strategist contains. Considerable effort was made to include only general teaching knowledge, which can be rather complex, for example, whether to provide only hints or in-depth tutoring when an error occurs. Specific knowledge, such as (1) the criteria for passing a test, or (2) the kind of hints and retesting which should be given, may be thought of as instantiations of the general rules. A human instructor-expert must provide such information to the system before the tutoring is started.

Text-Based Tutor (TBT)

The TBT performs fundamental textual teaching tasks. It is capable of delivering instruction, testing and locally evaluating the student, and providing help to a student who is having difficulty reaching mastery criteria. The TBT operates in three modes, instruct, test, and tutor, corresponding to the types of teaching activities which the TBT is capable of conducting.

The instruct mode provides the student with text-based instruction, supplemented with graphics displays and simple simulations as appropriate. Each initial presentation of a lesson is followed by a test of the knowledge presented.

The test mode presents the student with test questions. It locally evaluates the student's answer to each question and gives immediate feedback. After the entire question set is given, the test is scored and the results are posted on the blackboard. The Strategist then makes the decision about whether or not the student should advance to another lesson or if further tutoring is necessary.

The tutor mode is activated when the student does not meet mastery criteria in the test. The tutor mode is divided into two levels: hints and remediation. Hints are provided when an error is determined to be of relatively low importance, perhaps based on misreading the lesson. Remediation is provided when an error is judged to be of relatively high importance, and takes the form of additional lessons on terminology, general knowledge, and a presentation of the content in a less difficult manner than in the original lesson. Remediation is followed by new questions on the to-be-learned content.

The TBT was written in PEARL [13]. Domain-specific knowledge about lessons, questions, hints and retests are stored in PEARL associative data bases, where information can be easily retrieved.

Model-Based Tutor (MBT)

The MBT, like the TBT, also operates in three modes. Both the instruct and the tutor modes work in the same way as those in the TBT, except that more graphics presentations are possible. However, the MBT test environment is a graphics-based qualitative simulator, and the local evaluation of the student's performance is accomplished by the BD.

The PDS qualitative modelling was implemented in an object-oriented programming style (Flavors [14]) as a collection of components (objects) with qualitative states [15] and their topological connections. The well-known advantages of object-oriented programming such as modularity, data abstraction, and method inheritance are fully exploited. The behavioral descriptions of the objects follow the no-function-in-structure principle [13]. The object hierarchy was designed by specifically utilizing the concept of a Device-Centered Ontology (DCO) [15]. All "methods" for the control of constraint propagation are embedded in the object descriptions, and, therefore are system-independent. PDSs of any complexity can be simulated by only defining the topological connections among the components. The implementation strategy, features and other details are well summarized in [16].

During an MBT test, a student can readily observe in detail the effects of any switch manipulation, i.e., the internal functionality and the behavior of the PDS in terms of voltage propagation, current flow, and operation logic. The student's performance is recorded as a set of switch operations in the SM. An example in OPS5 is shown below:

```
(operation
        topic    test-1          ;name of topic
        action   1               ;operation sequence number
        object   o-289rp)        ;object name
```

In this example, the student is attempting test-1, and his first 'successful' operation is on switch '289rp.'

Not all operations will be 'successful' because some erroneous actions will not be accepted by the PDS. An action such as attempting turning a DS off while current is flowing through it will directly violate the interlock protection facilities. These errors are classified as local errors. The student is informed in real-time and this information is recorded in the SM as error information. Some erroneous actions concerned with global PDS situations, such as the violation of the procedural operation principle, cannot be detected by looking at only a single switch operation. Rather, this must be accomplished by evaluating a set of operations. The Bug Detector (BD) was created for this purpose.

<u>Bug Detector (BD)</u>

Critical to the intelligence of any tutoring system is not only what student information is recorded, but what is done with the recorded information. By using a complex group of rules, each of which may specify a pattern of interaction with either or both the TBT and the MBT, the system can perform a careful analysis of student behavior and reason about the misconceptions or bugs reflected in a particular student's performance. Identification of bugs allows the system to take intelligent action specifically related to the type of problem a certain student may be experiencing.

The BD was implemented in OPS5 as a set of declarative rules that contain the human instructor's diagnostic knowledge. The BD is activated whenever an MBT test begins. It observes every operation as it happens, but does not necessarily interrupt the student every time a bug is detected. Rather, it considers the priority of the bug. For example, when a power failure occurs, which is the most severe error (highest priority), the student will be interrupted immediately. On the other hand, the student may sometimes activate some redundant operations, or may not make the optimal choice. In such situations, the student may find the mistake and correct it without prompting. As long as the student does not stray too far or does not make any high priority mistakes, the BD will not interrupt him.

Once the student finishes an MBT test, the BD analyzes the student's behavior by: (1) selecting all bugs recorded in the SM, and classifying them into the prespecified bug categories and (2) reasoning about these categorized bugs, diagnosing the underlying possible misconceptions or missing conceptions that the errors reflect, and posting the results on the blackboard.

The Strategist reads the information posted by the BD, and creates an individualized tutoring strategy. Although the bug types may be made increasingly generic by including more variables, the BD may need to be capable of controlling domain-specific remediation, in order to keep the Strategist as free as possible of domain knowledge. Note that only with a very robust implementation of the BD, can the system appropriately infer what the student does not know, and therefore be able to perform individualized tutoring.

Student Model

The Student Model (SM) is the representation of what the student does and does not know [1, 2]. It consists of a record of the student's interaction with the system, along with inferences made by the BD based on these interactions. Existing primarily in the WM of OPS5, the SM is built from assertions made by the Strategist, the TBT, the MBT, and the BD, but is referenced only by the Strategist to make instructional decisions.

The purpose of the SM is to represent and use data on each student's interaction with the system and therefore, to achieve a better educational result. It is constructed so that inferences made about student knowledge can lead to valid instructional decision-making. At the lowest level, the SM is simply a record of the student's interaction with the system. For instance, it may be recorded that a student passed the level 1 test with a grade of 85%. At higher levels, the SM consists of inferences made by intelligent components of the system, such as the BD. For example, the BD may be able to determine one or more incorrect assumptions that the student has made, then recommend a highly efficient procedure to the Strategist for correcting these false assumptions. The tutoring strategy is individualized based on the "bug" information about a student. Therefore, the SM is basically a buggy model. Note that the SM is not a model in the same sense as the qualitative model used by the MBT. The SM represents the knowledge of the student, but does not actually simulate the student.

PDS Training

A training session on the PDS consists of the following activities. The student's level of knowledge is determined via a pretest to decide which lesson the student should be given first. The TBT's instruct mode will first present the student with a small self-contained unit of textual information, supplemented by graphics as appropriate. Following the instruct mode, the test mode begins by asking the student questions pertaining to the just-presented information (some simple simulations concerning parts of the PDS are also possible). The student's responses to the questions are evaluated. Depending on whether or not mastery is achieved, the student may proceed to the next level of instruction or receive remedial training (shift to tutor mode) on critical concepts with which the student had difficulty. After completing the textual units in the TBT, the student normally proceeds to the MBT where 'hands-on' exercises on the PDS Simulator are presented. These laboratory exercises check his understanding of the entire system operation as well as system components. After a student successfully completes interaction at all difficult levels with the MBT, the training course terminates.

Our current system runs on a MicroVAX II with a VSV21 color display. The software support is FRANZ LISP with AI tools (such as OPS5, Flavors, and PEARL) and a graphics editor [17].

CONCLUSIONS

We have demonstrated the feasibility of constructing a powerful tutoring system for a complex engineering domain through the use of AI techniques. We made use of qualitative simulation, student modelling, planning, knowledge-based and object-oriented programming, high resolution color graphics, and other methods to develop a unified tutoring system for the PDS. In this ITS, the general teaching knowledge (in the Strategist) is relatively well separated from domain-specific knowledge, including both operational knowledge (in the MBT) and diagnostic knowledge (in the BD).

In order to make the system truly generic, thus allowing it to be applied to other domains, and to make it powerful enough to be used by industrial training personnel in the development of new instructional modules, considerable system enhancement will be necessary. As our work continues, we expect to create an increasingly powerful and flexible GTS. Future research, based on our experience with the PDS ITS, will include expanding the system with several builder modules, including a general purpose simulation builder for constructing new simulations and simulation-based lessons. We are beginning to construct a rule base which contains operational knowledge not available at the level of the simulation of the physical system. This knowledge will improve bug detection and, therefore, the individualization of instruction. This rule base will also be closely interfaced with the simulation model.

REFERENCES

1. P. Cohen and E. Feigenbaum, The Handbook of Artificial Intelligence, Vol. 2 (William Kaufmann 1982).
2. D. Sleeman and B. Brown, ed., Intelligent Tutoring Systems (Academic Press 1982).
3. J. Anderson and B. Reiser, "The LISP Tutor," Byte Magazine (1985).
4. J. Anderson et al., "The Geometry Tutor," Proc. Ninth IJCAI, 1-7 (August 1985).
5. J. Hollan et al., "STEAMER: An Interactive Inspectable Simulation-Based Training System," The AI Magazine, 15-27 (Summer 1984).
6. B. Woolf et al., "Teaching A Complex Industrial Process," Proc. AAAI-86, 722-728 (1986).
7. R. Freedman, "Expert Systems that Teach," IEEE Expert Magazine, 13 (Summer 1987).
8. K. Kawamura et al., "Development of an Intelligent Tutoring System," Proc. IEEE International Conf. on Systems, Man, & Cybernetics, 1205-1209 (October 1986).
9. L. Brownston et al., Programming Expert Systems in OPS5 (Addison Wesley 1985).
10. R.M. Gagne and L.J. Briggs, Principles of Instructional Design (Holt, Rinehart, & Winston, New York 1979).
11. T. Barrett, "A Taxonomy of Reading Comprehension," in: Teaching in the Middle Grades, T. Barrett, ed. (Addison Wesley, Reading, MA 1974).
12. B. Bloom et al., "Taxonomy of Educational Objectives: The Classification of Educational Goals," in: Handbook I: Cognitive Domain (Longmans Green, New York 1956).
13. M. Deering et al., "Using the PEARL AI Package," Dept. of EECS. University of California, Berkeley, (February 1982).
14. D. Weinreb and D. Moon, "FLAVORS: Message Passing in the LISP Machine," MIT Press, Memo #602 (November 1980).
15. D. Bobrow, ed., Qualitative Reasoning about Physical Systems, (MIT Press 1985).
16. X. Li et al., "Qualitative Simulation of a Power Distribution System," Proc. of IEEE Systems, Man and Cybernetics (in press October, 1987).
17. DV-Draw/DV-Tools Reference Manual (V.I. Corporation, Mass. 1986).

A Uniform Architecture for Rule-based Meta Reasoning and Representation

Anthony S. Maida

Department of Computer Science
333 Whitmore Laboratory
Pennsylvania State University
University Park, PA 16802

Abstract

This paper describes the QPC system, an elegant rule-based architecture, based on quoted predicate calculus, and designed for meta reasoning and representation. The QPC system uses the same inference engine both for reasoning and meta reasoning. We discuss the theoretical considerations motivating the architecture and underlying the implementation. We also give examples of meta level knowledge which can be represented and used in the system. The QPC system is implemented in Zeta Lisp on a Symbolics Lisp Machine.

Introduction.

This paper describes the QPC system, an elegant rule-based architecture designed for meta reasoning and representation. The QPC system uses the same inference engine both for reasoning and meta reasoning. We discuss the theoretical considerations motivating the architecture and underlying the implementation. We also give examples of meta level knowledge which can be represented and used in the system. The QPC system is implemented in Zeta Lisp on a Symbolics Lisp Machine.

Relation to Other Work. There have been several programming languages with a meta reasoning facility. These include the procedural 3-Lisp [13, 14], the meta level object-oriented language of Maes [9], the logic programming language N-PROLOG [6], and the FOL theorem prover [17]. Meta reasoning is widely useful as documented in Haas [7], Maida [10], Perlis [11], and Smith [15]. Within the rule-based paradigm, meta reasoning has been used in expert systems such as TEIRESIAS [5] and MOLGEN [16]. It also occurs in planning [8, 18]. Although, meta reasoning has been done within the rule-based paradigm, the architecture in which it occurs is often unmotivated -- as explained in the next section.

Background.

In this section, we explain theoretically how rule-based systems reason about some application domain. Then we show how to build an elegant meta reasoning architecture based on analogy with these already-established principles.

The Representation Hypothesis. Nearly all knowledge-based systems are constructed in a manner that is consistent with what Brachman & Levesque [2], Smith [13], and others have called the Knowledge Representation Hypothesis. With respect to rule-based (RB) systems, Figure 1 depicts the hypothesis.

Methodologies for Intelligent Systems
Z. W. Ras and M. Zemankova, Editors

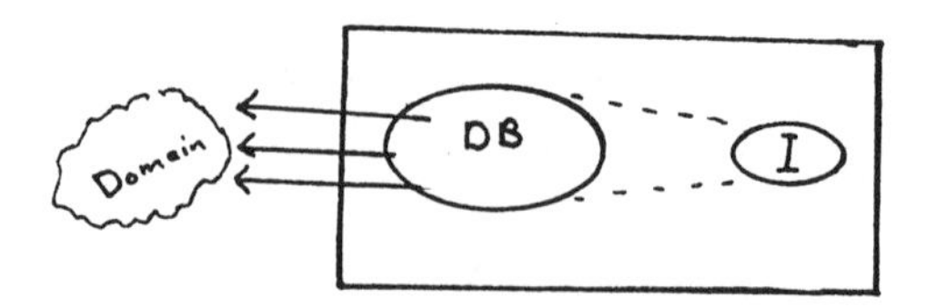

Figure 1. A Rule-based Architecture.

We have an RB system which can be partitioned in to two components -- a knowledge-base (KB) and a rule interpreter (I). The KB describes the application domain. Since the application domain is outside of the system, the system reasons about a domain which is external to it by manipulation of data structures which are internal to it.

Meta Reasoning and Representation. With these observations in mind, we can concisely characterize meta reasoning and representation. Here the application domain is some part of the system itself. The knowledge in the KB must describe the system -- this is *meta representation*. If an interpreter manipulates this meta KB to derive new facts, then it is doing *meta reasoning*. This trend can be continued arbitrarily for *n* levels of introspection to create a tower of interpreters. Existing RB systems that exhibit meta reasoning tend to be examples of this architecture. There are separate rule bases to hold meta rules and often a separate meta rule interpreter because the meta rules are in a different format than the "ordinary" rules.

The Reflection Hypothesis. There is a way to greatly condense this architecture by use of what Smith [13] has called the Reflection Hypothesis. The idea is this. We ensure that the representations at all meta levels use the same representational format and designation conventions as the object level representation (lowest level). This way we can use the same interpreter for each of the knowledge bases. If we wish to do meta reasoning, we simply tell the interpreter to switch to the meta knowledge base. The architecture is illustrated in Figure 2.

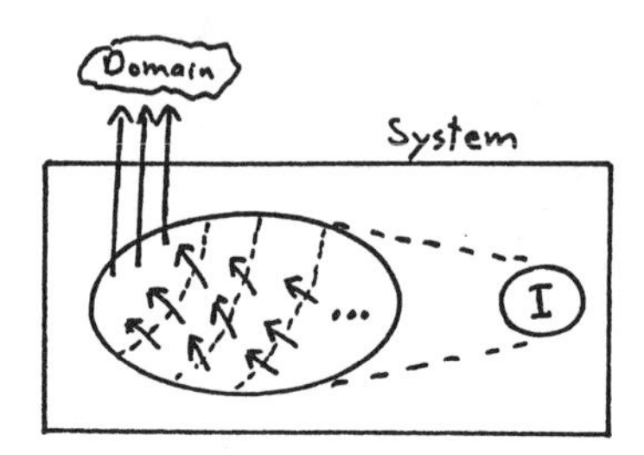

Figure 2. A Compact Meta-level Architecture.

Implementation Considerations.

This section describes how to implement an RB meta reasoner whose architecture is consistent with the reflection hypothesis.

Uniformity Between Representation and Meta Representation. As alluded to in the previous section, the key to constructing this architecture is to use a knowledge representation (KR) language which represents meta knowledge using the same format and designation conventions as for "ordinary" knowledge.

The KR language we have chosen is *quoted predicate calculus (QPC).* This is first-order logic augmented with a quotation device (cf., [7, 11]). The grammar appears below.

proposition	:==	"(" predicate-sym arg* ")"
proposition	:==	"(" quantifier var-list proposition ")"
var-list	:==	"(" variable* ")"
arg	:==	basic-constant | variable | function-term | quoted-term
function-term	:==	"(" function-sym arg* ")"
quoted-term	:==	"(" "quote" any-expression-generated-by-the-grammar ")"
quantifier	:==	"forall"
variable	:==	"$x" \| "$y" | "$z" | etc.
function-sym	:==	"father-of" | "sum-of" | "successor-of" | etc.
predicate-sym	:==	"likes" | "loves" | "between" | "is-grass" | etc.
basic-constant	:==	"john-1" | "bill-2" | "fido-3" | "banana-17"

This device allows us to refer to any expression in the language, simply and uniformly, by prefixing a single quote mark to it.[1] Examples are shown below. Expression {1} refers to expression {2} and expression {3} refers to expression {4}.

{1} 'John
{2} John
{3} '(is-taller-than John Bill)
{4} (is-taller-than John Bill)

In QPC, there is no need to give connectives special syntactic status. They are just predicates which take quoted propositions as arguments. We can write expressions such as:

'(not '(is-taller-than John Bill))
'(not '(and '(is-taller-than John Bill) '(is-taller-than Bill John)))

Meta statements simply involve the use of appropriate predicates. Below we assert that the constant "John" is a proper name, that the expression "(is-taller-than John Bill)" is a propositional sentence, and that the constant "John" denotes John.

'(is-p-name 'John)
'(is-proposition '(is-taller-than John Bill))
'(denote 'John John)

The predicate *denote* is significant. It enables the QPC-system to do full-fledged knowledge-based reasoning about designators. An example will be given in the section titled "Examples of Meta Reasoning."

Using Consistent Designation Conventions. In order to base a meta reasoning architecture on the reflection hypothesis, it is crucial to be meticulously uniform in the conventions by which symbols refer to, or designate, objects. Here is an example of a pitfall. A user of an RB system might type in the expression below:

{5} (assert (is-taller-than John Bill))

Here we intend the user to be adding the fact to the DB that John is taller than Bill. This means that the symbols "John" and "Bill" must be refering to something other than themselves (i.e., they are not refering to strings, but people); they are refering to entities in the application domain. This is standard denotational semantics where we use symbols to refer to what they denote. However, if we used the string "(is-taller-than John Bill)" to refer to what it denoted, we would either be referring to truth or falsity. Since, given such

[1] There is one exception. This is concerned with variables. A variable in a quoted context is unquoted so that its value can be substituted. Variables are prefixed by dollar signs.

a circumstance, we would never be able to encode more than two distinct things in the data base -- truth and falsity -- we must surely be using this string in a different way.

For the purposes of this paper, we take the position that when a user adds a propositional sentence to a data base, s/he is making the statement that *the particular sentence* denotes truth, rather than simply refering to truth. This means that there is an inconsistency in the designation conventions *within* expression {5}. We use the string "(is-taller-than John Bill)" to denote itself, but we use the string "John" do denote something which is not itself. This difference in usage conventions is subtle but is sufficient to render an object-level interpreter inoperative if it were switched to a meta-level data base. We can fix this by using expression {6} below in place of expression {5}. If we want to refer to an expression in the language, we quote it.

{6} (assert '(is-taller-than John Bill))

Changes to the Overall Architecture. The architecture of the QPC system is shown in Figure 3. It could characterize any RB system. At the lowest level, Level I, we have some set of data base manipulation primitives. In our particular system, they are based on Shapiro's [12] SNePS semantic network primitives, but the choice is neutral with respect to introspective architectures. Many sets of data base primitives will be sufficient.

Generic Rule Based Architecture		
Level IV	User Interface	
Level III	Inference Engine	Unification
Level II	Encoding Logic to and from DB	
Level I	Semantic Net or DB Primitives	

Figure 3. The Layed QPC System.

At Level II, we have procedures which map between the knowledge representation language -- QPC in our case -- and the data base primitives. It is here that the modifications from standard systems are needed to make a meta reasoner. At Level III would be any unification-based inference engine. There are no changes needed at Level III. Level IV involves the user interface. At Level IV, slight changes are recommended. These are because the uniform denotation conventions required of Level II are counter-intuitive to a programmer. In particular it is hard for a programmer to tell when quote marks are needed and to read expressions which have excessive numbers of quote marks. These can be mechanically inserted and removed by the user interface.

Implementation at Level II. The cardinal rule that must be obeyed when implementing Level II is to always refer to entities by the same denotation conventions. We will illustrate the conventions for mapping of QPC expressions into the data base (DB) by use of the function ENCODE-ARG. This function accepts a QPC expression that can be an argument to a predicate and returns a DB object. This function corresponds to the category ARG in the grammar of Appendix A. The QPC expression that is the argument to the function denotes what is to be encoded in the data base. The DB object returned denotes the data structure that encodes the entity under consideration. For instance, in the first function call illustrated below, "John" denotes some person. The returned value "JOHN" is a DB object that denotes some internal data base entity, perhaps "OBJECT-251." "OBJECT-251" is the data structure that the data base system uses to model the person John. Similarly, in the second function call below, the quoted term

Function Call		Returned Value
(ENCODE-ARG John)	=>	JOHN
(ENCODE-ARG '(is-taller-than John Bill))	=>	OBJECT-873

"*'(is-taller-than John Bill)*" denotes the expression "*(is-taller-than John Bill).*" The returned value, "OBJECT-873," is a DB object that denotes some other DB entity, perhaps "PROPOSITION-73." "PROPOSITION-73" is the data structure the data base system uses to model the propositional sentence.[2]

In the implementation, there is an ENCODE function for every syntactic category in the grammar of QPC. The designation conventions described so far represent what is called "transparent processing." We will have to add a second parameter to the ENCODE family of functions to indicate whether the processing mode is TRANSPARENT (as already described) or OPAQUE (to be described presently). When the processing mode is OPAQUE, the ENCODE functions still accept an expression and return a DB object. However, now the expression does not *denote* the expression to be encoded; it *is* the expression to be encoded. Analogously, the returned DB object does not *denote* the entity that models the expression; it *is* the entity that models the expression. There is only one point in which OPAQUE processing is invoked. This is in the function ENCODE-QUOTE, which encodes quoted expressions. ENCODE-QUOTE in turn calls ENCODE-QPC -- which accepts any expression from QPC -- on the argument of the quoted expression, but with OPAQUE processing turned on.

There is one other modification needed at Level II. This is concerned with wiring into the data base the knowledge that quoted expressions denote their arguments. This modification occurs, just as the first one did, in ENCODE-QUOTE. We simply construct a DB encoding of a QPC assertion expressing that the quoted expression denotes its argument. This is equivalent to explicitly asserting something like:

```
(assert '(denote 'John John))
```

The effect of this is that if the user ever references the expression 'A, then the system will dynamically construct the assertion *(denote 'A A)* as a side effect of the programmer's reference to "A."

The Payoff.

The implementor can now build an inference engine at Level III using standard methods (cf., [1, 4, 19]). The implementor need have no concern whatever for meta level knowledge. Suppose the implementor constructed an inference engine to process forward-chaining rules of the kind given in the next section. Then the inference engine will also be able to support meta reasoning.

An Inference Rule. Below we have a data base. The assertions are expressed in QPC but they do not express any sort of meta knowledge. The DB encodes the information that *John is sick,* that *John plays tennis with Bill,* and that *Bill is a good player.* Furthermore,

[2] These designation conventions are influenced by Smith's [13] 2-Lisp.

it encodes the inference rule that, *If John is sick, plays tennis with Bill, and Bill is a good player, then John is tired.* This is an example of information that any standard inference engine can encode.

```
'(is-sick John)
'(plays-tennis John Bill)
'(is-good-player Bill)

'(→ '(and
      '(is-sick John) '(plays-tennis John Bill) '(is-good-player Bill))
    '(is-tired John))
```

Examples of Meta Reasoning.

This section illustrates how standard kinds of meta reasoning can be encoded in the QPC system.

Knowledge-Based Reasoning About Designators. If the implementor builds an inference engine that can handle the above data base, then the inference engine, without modification will handle the data base below.[3] This data base says that *John equals the-butler.* It also says that *"John" is a proper name, "the-butler" is a definite description,* and *there is a goal to refer to the butler.* Finally, it says that *if you want to refer to the-butler, "John" denotes the butler, and "John" is a proper name, then say "John".*

```
'(equal John the-butler)
'(is-p-name 'John)
'(is-definite-description 'the-butler)
'(refer-goal the-butler)

'(→ '(and
      '(refer-goal the-butler) '(denote 'John the-butler) '(is-p-name 'John))
    '(say 'John))
```

This rule encodes information that cannot be easily encoded in a standard inference engine, because it makes use of meta knowledge. However, the QPC inference engine can handle this knowledge without modification because the method for representing meta knowledge is exactly uniform to the method for representing "ordinary" knowledge. In fact, except for the equality expression, both the data base in the previous section and this data base are syntactically isomorphic; the inference engine cannot tell the difference.

To make the above rule practically useful, we would have to quantify it as shown below. Now the rule says, *if you want to refer to some entity, then find a proper name for it and say the proper name.*

```
'(forall ($x $y)
  '(→
      '(and '(refer-goal $x) '(denote $y $x) '(is-p-name $y))
      '(say $y))
```

Reasons for Belief. Often it is important to keep track of one's reasons for drawing certain conclusions. A well-known method of implementing this is by use of data dependencies [3] which are a kind of pointer structure linking conclusions to their premises. Since this kind of information is actually meta knowledge, there should be natural

[3] There is one hedge: The unifier will have to allow matching of equal constants. For instance, unification of "John" with "the-butler" will succeed if John equals the butler.

approaches to managing it within the paradigm of meta reasoning. This next rule sketches an approach to implementing data dependencies. It says, *if "John is sick," and "If John is sick, then John is sleepy," then conclude that "John is sleepy."* It also says to record that the reason you believe John is sleepy, is because the rule fired. The predicate "dd-note" is based on Chapter 8 of [3].

```
'(→ '(and
        '(is-sick John)
        '(→ '(is-sick John) '(is-sleepy John)))
    '(and
        '(is-sleepy John)
        '(dd-note
            '(is-sick John)
            '(→ '(is-sick John) '(is-sleepy John))
            '(is-sleepy John))))
```

Reasoning about Control. Often meta reasoning is used to reason about control of an inference or problem solving process. In the QPC system, it is possible to make assertions of the sort that some rule is useful in some domain and should be invoked often, or that the rule should be used as a backward-chaining rule. The rule below describes backward-chaining.

```
'(forall ($p $q)
   (→
     '(and
          '(prove-goal $q)
          '(→ $p $q)
          '(is-back-chaining-rule '(→ $p $q))
          $p)
     '(and $q '(is-satisfied '(prove-goal $q)))))
```

It says *If there is a goal to prove an expression, and there is a rule whose consequent matches the expression to be proven, and the rule is a backward-chaining rule, and the antecedent of the rule is true, then assert the expression as true, and assert that the goal is satisfied.*

Concluding Remarks.

To reiterate, if the inference engine works on the first non-meta DB mentioned in this paper, then it will also work -- without modification -- on the other DB's, all of which involve meta reasoning. The system is based on quoted predicate calculus and achieves a remarkable abount of expressive power and uniformity for a remarkably small amount of implementation effort. Using a QPC data base does not inherently incure more overhead than a first-order DB, except when a meta level rule is used to interpret an object level rule. However, this sort of process is not even expressible in a first-order system.

---

[3] The rule *(-> '(is-sick John) '(is-sleepy John))* is syntactically acceptable to the inference engine and, hence, could independently fire. If this happened, the assertion *(is-sleepy John)* would be redundantly added to the data base, but no harm would be done.

References.

1. Abelson, H. & Sussman, G. (1985) *The structure and interpretation of computer programs.* Cambridge, MA: MIT Press.
2. Brachman, R. & Levesque, H. (1985) *Readings in knowledge representation.* Los Altos, CA: Morgan Kaufman.
3. Charniak, E. & McDermott, D. (1985) *Introduction to artificial intelligence.* Reading, MA: Addison-Wesley.
4. Charniak, E., Reisbeck, C., & McDermott, D. *Artificial intelligence programming.* Hillsdale, NJ: Erlbaum.
5. Davis, R. & Buchanan, B. (1977) Meta-level Knowledge: Overview and applications. *Proc. IJCAI, 5,* 920-927.
6. Gabbay, D.M. & Reyle, U. (1984) N-PROLOG: An extension of PROLOG with hypothetical implications. *Journal of Logic Programming,* 4.
7. Hass, A. R. (1986) A syntactic theory of belief and action. *Artificial Intelligence,* 28 (3), 245-292.
8. Laird, J. (1984) *Universal subgoaling.* Doctoral dissertation, Computer Science Department, Carnegie-Mellon University, Pittsburgh, PA.
9. Maes, P. Introspection in knowledge representation. *The 7th European Conference on Artificial Intelligence.* Brighton, U.K. July, 1986.
10. Maida, A. S. (1986) Introspection and reasoning about the beliefs of other agents. *Proc. Cognitive Science,* August, Amherst, MA, 187-195.
11. Perlis, D. (1985) Languages with self-reference I: Foundations (or We can have everything in first-order logic!). *Artificial Intelligence,* 25 (3), 301-322.
12. Shapiro, S. C. (1979) The SNePS semantic network processing system. In N. V. Findler (Ed.), *Associative networks: The representation and use of knowledge by computers* (pp. 179-203). New York: Academic Press.
13. Smith, B. C. (1982) Reflection and semantics in a procedural language. Ph. D. Thesis and Tech. Report MIT/LCS/TR-272, MIT, Cambridge, MA, 1982.
14. Smith, B. C. (1984) Reflection and semantics in LISP. Tech. Report CLSI-84-8. Center for the Study of Language and Information, Stanford University, 1984.
15. Smith, B. C. (1986) Varieties of self-reference. In J. Halpern (Ed.) *Theoretical aspects of reasoning about knowledge* (pp. 19-43). Los Altos, CA: Morgan Kaufmann.
16. Stefik, M. (1980) Planning with constraints. Report STAN-CS-80-784, Stanford University Computer Science Department.
17. Weyrauch, R. (1980) Prolegomena to a theory of mechanized formal reasoning. *Artificial Intelligence, 13,* 133-170.
18. Wilensky, R. (1983) *Planning and understanding.* Reading, MA: Addison-Wesley.
19. Wilensky, R. (1984) *LISPcraft.* New York, NY: Norton.

ABSTRACT INFERENCE STRUCTURES TO SUPPORT VARIABLE RULE STRUCTURES FOR EXPERT SYSTEMS

LAWRENCE J. MAZLACK
University of Cincinnati
Post Office Box 21048
Cincinnati, Ohio 45221

ABSTRACT

Knowledge-based systems have been successfully utilized in the prototype development of complex systems. In many cases, these prototype systems have emphasized the need for techniques to integrate knowledge-based processing with mehods for managing large amounts of data and knowledge. However, many potential applications for expert systems are precluded by limitations in the ability of conventional expert system technology to function in conjuntion with data systems without manual intervention.

Using a database to provide inference structures that support an expert system is the thrust of this report. In particular, the focus is the integration of knowledge-baseds and databases to provide expert systems with the capability to:
- *store and context select between parallel, competing expert system rule structures,*
- *cascade variable rule structures for expert systems,*
- *allow an expert system to be interppupted and subsequently restarted by storing the state of the inference engine, and*
- *handle simple data storage and retrieval.*

INTRODUCTION

A full understanding of the mutually reinforcing roles that data and knowledge-based systems *can* play in each others domains is still in the early stages. *Knowledge-bases* are used in expert systems to support complex decision processes. Conventional *databases* are used for the storage and retrieval of simple, discrete data. Databases are just beginning to emerge as useful tools in the expert system domain, either in: the production of knowledge, the integration of stored data into the decision making process, or the formation of information that would help in transforming available data into decisions. One possible goal of integration is so the expert system ability to retrieve/store both factual data and inference structures.

Using a database to provide inference structures that support an expert system is the thrust of this report. In particular, the focus is the integration of knowledge-bases and databases to provide expert systems with the capability to:
- store and context select between parallel, competing expert system rule structures,
- cascade variable rule structure for expert systems,
- allow an expert system to be interrupted and subsequently restarted by storing the state of the inference engine, and
- handle simple data storage and retrieval.

This requires the integration of two significantly different information sources, databases and knowledge-bases. Current practice is to use knowledge-bases whose elements are tightly coupled. In contrast, in a conventional database, the stored elements are taken to be independent with only loose coupling between the different elements (internal members of an element are tightly coupled). Conventional databases store data using methods that remove data coupling through techniques such as normalization. (In database terminology, an *element* is

Methodologies for Intelligent Systems
Z. W. Ras and M. Zemankova, Editors

known as a *record,* internal *members* are *items* or *fields,* and collections of records with the same internal typing are known as *files.*)

SOME BACKGROUND

The inherent nature of expert systems sets them apart from conventional data processing systems, and also call for a more engineering approach than much of the rest of artificial intelligence (AI). Expert systems have distinct characteristics that call for special tools and strategies. They often involve highly domain specific systems and have capabilities that go beyond the use of a database to support data processing's task of straight forward digestion of facts.

The functional distinction between databases and knowledge-bases is that database systems allow users to think in terms of *specific* data items instead of the files that are the whole of the collected data in while a knowledge-base consists of *collections* of facts, inferences, and procedures (Barr, 1982, p35). Databases are focused on delivering specific data values. In contrast, the knowledge in an expert system is placed into a contextual structure for the purpose of making or supporting decisions. None-the-less, the central concern of both knowledge and databases is stored information, albeit of different kinds and of differing levels of digestion.

Databases have highly formatted organizations to: store data, share data between multiple users for different purposes, allow flexible access, and avoid data redundancy. In contrast, knowledge-based systems tend to support a single task or user, require a relatively consistent approach as to how to use the stored knowledge, and the value of redundancy is unclear.

It is clear that as databases become larger, they have an increasing need to be able to do some of the things that AI systems do; such as deal with uncertainty, accommodate conflicting data, heuristically optimize search (Tou, 1982), and reduce the database imposed constraints (Ballard, 1984). At the same time, knowledge-based systems need to have some of the capabilities of a database; such as organizing information (Hayes-Roth, 1983), acquiring large amounts of data (Kellog, 1982), and representing data at a higher level of abstraction (Brachman, Levesque, 1984).

Strategies for integrating an expert system with a database can vary with the implementing language and the specific data requirements. Important to doing this are the questions (Jarke,Vassilou,1984) of

- allowing an expert system to access data from a database and
- enhancing databases with information provided by the expert system.

If this can be done, they may be able to contribute and enhance each other in the following ways:

- the database can act as a front end to the knowledge acquisition process,
- AI techniques can be applied to the development of database query tools, and
- the database can be used to contain specific knowledge-based rules.

It is this last case that this report is directed.

A database can be viewed as a form of a knowledge-base (Brachman, Levesque, 1984). Arguments against this idea are based mostly on the structural aspects of current knowledge-bases that place an emphasis on the combinatorics of the domain as a whole. Alternately, the structure of a database can be thought to be a surface representation of a knowledge-base (Chandrasekaran, Mittal, 1982). There are several advantages to viewing a knowledge-base at the more abstract level that a database might provide. They include:

- better semantic or conceptual models free of inadvertent domain derived biases,
- a good vantage point to consider potential generalizations to database query languages,
- easier comparisons of knowledge-bases to other representation schemes in terms of the range of knowledge that can be represented.

Of conceptual interest to this project are the tools of database abstraction, in particular abstract data types (ADTs). The concept of using the knowledge-base equivalent of ADTs and ADT instantiation is useful.

EXPERT SYSTEM USE OF A DATABASE

There are two major reasons for an expert system to access a database:

- access/store data from a traditional database to:
  + use the data directly to help make the decision
  + modify the data as a result of the decision of the associated expert system
- access a database for context sensitive rules whose use is dependent on the situation

A less important, but an operationally desirable potential use of database and knowledge-base integration is to

- provide an interruption/restart capability.

Using Simple Data Items

The straight forward situation where we might wish to access a traditional database can be discussed fairly quickly as the concerns are implementational than conceptual. For example, in the case of using stored data to help make a decision, the decision might be based on simple facts such as distances, depth of rivers, prevailing winds, etc. Before the committing any of the assets that are candidates for deployment, there is a need to query the database to discover the extent and nature of the deployable assets. Beyond simple availability, the desire to deploy an asset might also be a function of the inventory levels; i.e. there might be a greater relative desire to use assets that are in large supply over those that are in short supply.

Data that can be modified as the result of earlier decisions can be necessary to subsequent decisions. For example, take the case when a decision must be made to deploy assets. Once a decision has been made to deploy specific assets, the database must be updated to reflect the intended deployment. Both the quantity of asset deployed and the desire to deploy assets may be affected.

Normally, simple factual data (such as asset inventory levels) are kept in a conventional, general purpose database as this eases the data maintenance and acquisition problems as well as allows the data to be used for multiple purposes. Consequently, when an expert system needs to make use of information in a database (such as inventory levels), the expert system must have the capability to query the database.

Cascading

While simple data retrieval might serve some purposes, it is often necessary to combine knowledge sources that are context dependent. When these information sources are serially applied this can be thought of as a process of *cascading* knowledge source information. This is of interest because the cascaded information may be dynamically aquired from different knowledge sources. For example, in our inventory deployment illustration, after identifying those assets that might be useful, choosing those that are actually to deployed is often a combination of inventory levels of those assets (as in Figure 1) and the general desirability of deploying those assets (as in Figure 2). The desirability of deploying specific assets, when separated from issues of availability, may be either a simple preference or a second order combination of simple facts and tactical/strategic considerations involving many possible factors including political, economic, and asset effectiveness.

As this type of multiple-source rule combination requires context sensitivity between the knowledge sources, using cascaded knowledge that has been acquired from external sources requires inference structure capabilities beyond those supplied by simple rule representations.

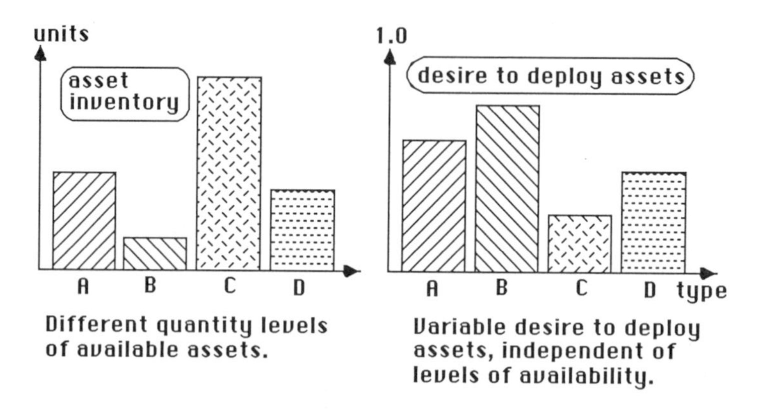

Figure 1. Levels of available assets. *Figure 2. Desire to deploy assets.*

Context Sensitive Rule Structures

For representational ease and to supply a methodology for describing the rule structures in an expert system's knowledge-base, rules will be represented as directed graphs and sub-graphs. The nodes of the graphs represent facts/inferences and the arcs of the graphs represent the implication paths that yield inferences.

Another possible use for the integration of a database with an expert system is the modification of the rule structure itself. Clearly, some decisions are context sensitive. For example, Figure 3 illustrates some context sub-trees that might be used in planning for a guest's refreshment; i.e., using the heuristic of a guest's nationality to determine whether a guest would want some beer.

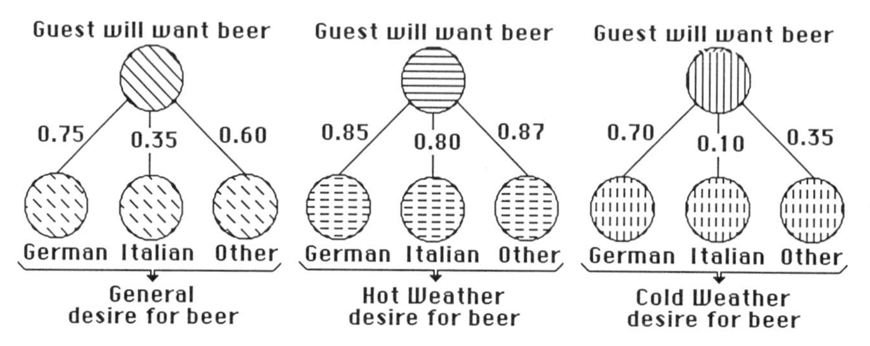

Figure 3. Parallel, competing, context sensitive rule subsets.

The problem with incorporating all possible context sensitive rule structures in the expert system at the same time is that of combinatorial explosion. Things can get overly complex in a hurry. In the case of the context variable implication values of Figure 3 (the numbers on the arcs of the graphs), retrieval of different implication values based on context would solve the context sensitivity requirements. However, it is also possible that different contexts could also require different graph structures for the different rule subsets.

Figure 4 illustrates the conceptual possibility of using a context selection mechanism to choose between competing context sensitive rule structures. It is clear that context sensitive rule structures that offer competing, parallel rules can rapidly become complex, irregardless of how context sensitivity is controlled if all of the sensitive structures remain invariently in the rule set. This is particularly the case when the competing rule structures are imbedded within a larger rule structure. In the worst case, the of complexity of a rule set that contains all of the parallel, competing context sensitive rules is geometrically increased. [This type of context sensitivity is different than that of Truth Maintenance Systems (Doyle, 1979) in that our context sensitivity is one of identifying proper rule chunks to be applied in a given problem context and TMS keeps models consistent with new information.]

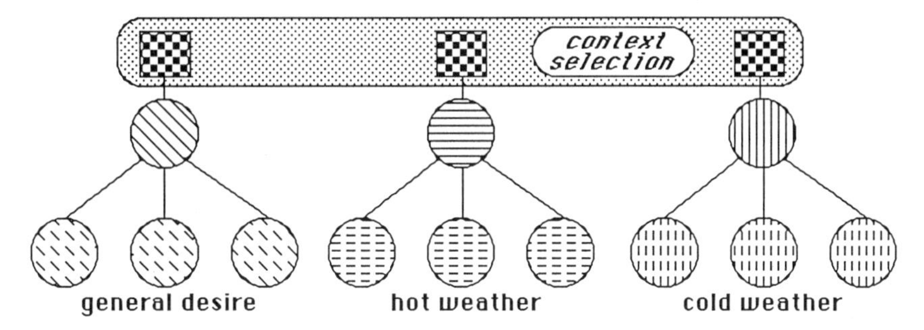

Figure 4. Using a context selection mechanism to choose between competing rule structures that are context sensitive.

Similarly, there can be a need to vary both tactical and strategic structures. A mini-case for this need can be found in the game of football. A highly simplified football decision structure is illustrated in Figure 5. Decisions in football usually initially follow a general plan that is comprised of both strategy and tactics. In this discussion, the inclination to punt, pass, or run will be considered to be strategic. Factors such as specific down and yards to go for a first down are tactical considerations that modify the desirability of selecting a particular type of play. [Obviously, the simple example of Figure 5 excludes other important considerations such as field position, weather, etc.] It is pretty clear that incorporating all of the possible relevant tactical and strategic decision structures into a single rule set faces a *severe combinatorial problem* because the combination of these rules may form many distinct chains.

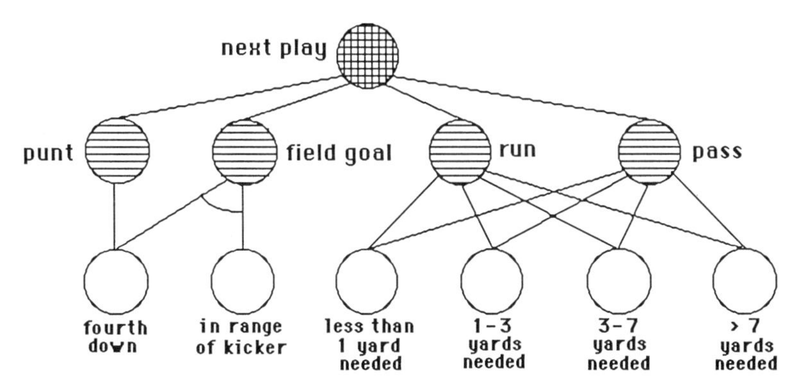

Figure 5. Simple abstract rule structure for choosing next football play. Context strategy rules to be supplied by database. Strategy rules are illustrated in Figure 6.

Changes to the game plan of Figure 5 can be at two levels, tactical or strategic, and can involve implication values and/or graph structure. (In Figure 5, strategic implication values are established between the "**next play**" node and its children.) Changes can reflect either experience or altered planning. Tactically for example, has our quarterback been able to pass successfully, or is he getting sacked more than expected? Changes in the environment can also alter strategic needs. For example, Figure 6 shows both a general strategy for a football game and the radically different strategic preferences if the team is seriously behind with less than two minutes to play.

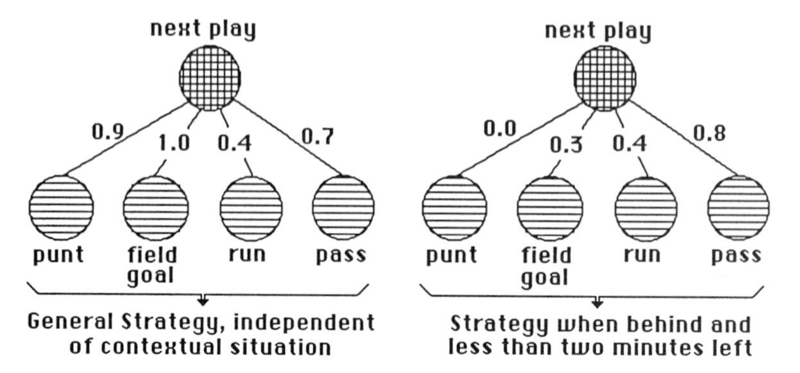

Figure 6. *Context strategy rules for the abstract rule structure of Figure 5. Selection of a particular strategy is context sensitive. Identification of an activity (punt, ...) depends on the tactical information shown in Figure 5 (down, yards needed,...).*

Time Sequences

Past history can affect current choices. This is obviously true for the feedback dependencies of process control problems, but it is also true for situations where it is necessary to have sequentially recorded information. These are the occasions where knowledge of the collection of past discrete actions affects the next decision. In these cases, data must be available indicating when and what was done. Conventional databases offer this capability to expert systems.

For example, the element of variety and/or relative surprize is often important. A commander must consider whether to repetitively use the same tactics. Likewise, a football coach may not want to repetitively run the same type of play, even if attractive, ten times in an unbroken sequence. In order to do this, it is clearly necessary to record a history and use that history to make decisions.

CURRENT RESEARCH CONCERNS

In the context of the preceding discussion, we are investigating the following topics:

- Integration with traditional databases to provide data storage/retrieval capabilities for expert systems.

- Strategies to consider two different decision structures [i.e., rule sets] to resolve the same issue. For example, in the football game mini-case, the issue could be how to combine the general game plan with the plan dictated by local, empirical experience.

- How to use a database to provide context sensitive decision structures to an abstract expert system. In particular,
  + development of abstract expert systems, and
  + control of the insertion of rule sets into abstract expert systems.

The last topic is the focus of our proposed investigation.

The particular actualization strategy applies the integrated database/expert system under development to support decision making in an inter-institution sports program. The basic structure uses a previously developed inference engine (Mazlack, 1986) to access an external, commercial, relational database. This engine stores rule sub-graphs and their attendant information as flat record elements (Samardar, Mazlack, Nevin, 1985). These can be readily stored, retrieved, indexed by a traditional relational database. Figure 7 illustrates our working environment. Figure 8 illustrates the elements of the inference engine and the database.

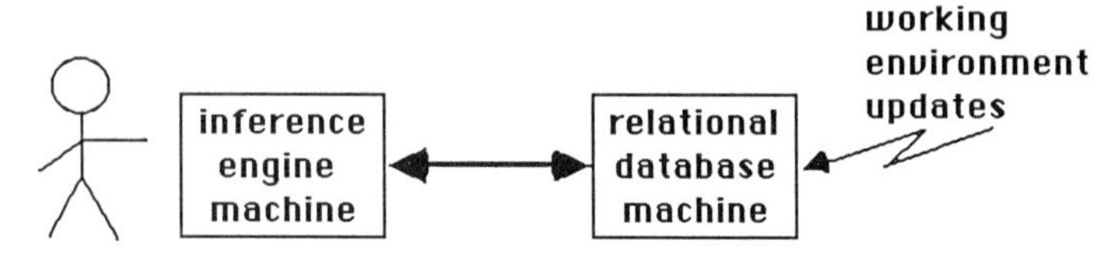

Figure 7. Working environment.

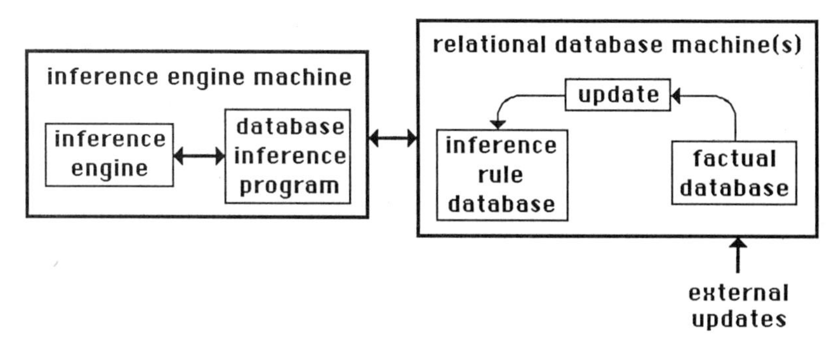

Figure 8. Tasks of each class of machine in the expert system/data base integration scheme.

Our procedure has been to precede as follows:

- develop an abstract knowledge-base structure representation
- develop an inference engine that can invoke, instantiate, and resolve abstract knowledge-base rules
- provide a stop/restart capability through the use of a database to store the interrupted state of the inference engine in a external, traditional database
- provide the capability to access external, traditional databases to provide on demand information to the expert system

- provide the capability to provide alternate, competing, parallel rule structures that have the same abstract rule structure; i.e., vary arc implication values, but not arc paths between nodes or the set of nodes

- vary the graph structure of the knowledge-base according to context requirements of the problem solution as it transpires.

This order was chosen as it reflects the order of increasing difficulty of the problem. It also reflects our understanding of the problem and our progress in its solution. The question of access is resolved. So is the rule structure representation and its storage format. Imperfectly understood are the control strategies to select between the competing rule structures. However, this last problem is really an extension of our original concern; i.e., supply a mechanism to integrate a database with an knowledge-base for the purpose of supplying context sensitive rule structures.

REFERENCES

Ballard,B.W., Lusth,J.C. (1984) *The design of DOMINO: A Knowledge-Based Retrieval Module for Transportable Natural Language Access to Personal Databases,* Proceedings First International Workshop on Expert Database Systems, October 24-27, p19-29

Barr, Avron, Feigenbaum, eds (1982) The Handbook of Artificial Intelligence, HeurisTech Press

Brachman,R.J., Levesque,H.J. (1984) *What Makes A Knowledge-base Knowledgeable? A View Of Databases From The Knowledge Level,* Proceedings First International Workshop on Expert Database Systems, October 24-27, p320-39

Chandrasekaran,B., Mittal,S. (1982) *Deep Versus Compiled Knowledge Approaches To Diagnostic Problem Solving,* AAAI-82 Proceedings, August 18-20, p349-354

Doyle,J. (1979) *A Truth Maintenance System*, Artificial Intelligence **12**(3)(1979), p231-272

Hayes-Roth,F. et.al. (1983) Building Expert Systems, Addison-Wesley

Jarke,M., Vassilou,Y. (1984) *Coupling Expert Systems WIth Database Systems,* Artificial Intelligence Applications for Business, Winston,P. (ed), Ablex, p65-85

Kellog,C.H. (1982) *Knowledge Management: A Practical Amalgam of Knowledge and Data Base Technology,* Proceedings AAAI-82, p306-309

Kellog,C.H. (1983) *Intelligent Assistants For Knowledge And Information Resources Management,* IJCAI-83 Proceedings, p170-173

Mazlack,L.J. (1986) *A Multi-threshold, Internal Rule Representation Form Used To Support User Modifiable Knowledge–based Systems,* Data and Knowledge Engineering Journal

Samardar,M., Mazlack,L.J., Nevin,J. (1985) *An Exercise In Engineering Circuit Design Using An Expert System,* Proceedings Of The Second IEEE Conference on Artificial Intelligence Applications

Tou,F.N. et.al. (1982) *RABBIT: An Intelligent Database Assistant,* Proceedings AAAI-82, p314-318

Domain Independent Support Propagation Architectures

Thomas Sudkamp
Department of Computer Science
Wright State University
Dayton, Ohio 45435

Abstract

Techniques for combining evidential support impose restrictions on the evidence that may be effectively processed. In this paper, we contrast the applicability of reasoning system architectures that employ fixed versus definable support propagation functions. Bayesian probability and the Dempster-Shafer theory are examples of reasoning systems with domain independent combination rules. Inference networks and endorsement based systems provide domain specific architectures for support propagation.

1. Introduction

Classification systems process information to determine the identity of an object from a set of possibilities. A reasoning system may be characterized by three components; the *evidential structure*, the *configuration* and the *support combining function.* The evidential structure encodes the information in a format suitable for the combining function. A configuration consists of an assessment of the total support for every possibility. The input to the support combining function is a configuration and evidence, the result is an updated configuration.

The domain is defined by two sets; the set **C** of characteristics and **P** of possibilities. The characteristics are the basic, indecomposable elements of the domain. An element of **P** is a subset of **C**. We refer to a domain defined by set inclusion as a hierarchy. The representation of the problem domain as characteristics and possibilities provides a general framework for support propagation. For example, a medical diagnosis system has a natural interpretation in these terms; the symptoms are the characteristics and a disease is completely characterized by its set of symptoms.

In this paper, inference systems are classified by their evaluation configuration and combining functions. The capabilities and limitations of several reasoning systems are compared by examining the restrictions placed on the domain and the evidence.

2. Hierarchies and evidence

Information is obtained concerning the presence of absence of characteristics. The first action of a reasoning system is to translate the information into a format suitable for the combination functions. The result of this transformation is referred to as evidence. Evidence supporting or refuting the presence of characteristics is used to generate support for the possibilities. For simplicity, our examples process evidence that asserts or denies to the presence of a single characteristic.

The hierarchy **H** defined in *Figure 1* and information below are used in the examples throughout this paper.

e_1 : supports with 50% likelihood the presence of characteristic **b**
e_2 : supports with certainty the presence of characteristic **a**
e_3 : supports with certainty the proposition that characteristic **d** is not present
e_4 : supports with certainty the presence of characteristic **c**
e_5 : supports with certainty the proposition that characteristic **b** is not present

Methodologies for Intelligent Systems
Z. W. Ras and M. Zemankova, Editors

The preceding statements attempt to express the information in a manner that is neutral with respect to the evidential structures of the various reasoning systems. The use of the numeric value in e_1, however, is readily translated to probabilistic systems but may require an interpretation for symbolic reasoning systems.

The flexibility of a reasoning system is measured by the types of evidence that can be processed and by the assumptions that are imposed on the domain. The combination of evidence may produce ambiguity or inconsistency. The combination $\{ e_2, e_3 \}$ in the hierarchy **H** is ambiguous since possibilities p_1 and p_3 are both consistent. Evidence $\{ e_2, e_3, e_4, e_5 \}$ is inconsistent; there are no possibilities that are consistent with this evidence.

3. Fixed propagation reasoning systems

An inference system is called a *fixed propagation reasoning system* if the support combining rule is domain independent. Probabilistic representation with Bayesian updating, the certainty factor representation introduced by the Mycin family of expert systems and the Dempster-Shafer theory are examples of such systems. One drawback of fixed propagation systems is that all the domain dependent information must be encoded in the evidential structures. These structures often consist of one ortwo numeric values. Consequently, the knowledge engineer assumes the difficult task transforming domain specific information into numeric representations.

The theory of evidential reasoning [6] is used to demonstrate the features of fixed propagation systems. Evidence supports set of possibilities and is represented by a basic probability assignment. A *basic probability assignment* is a function satisfying

i) $m(\emptyset) = 0$ ii) $\sum_{A \subseteq P(\mathbf{P})} m(A) = 1$

where $P(\mathbf{P})$ is the power set of **P**. The value $m(A)$ represents the support committed to the proposition that the object being identified is a member of A that cannot be distributed to individual members of A.

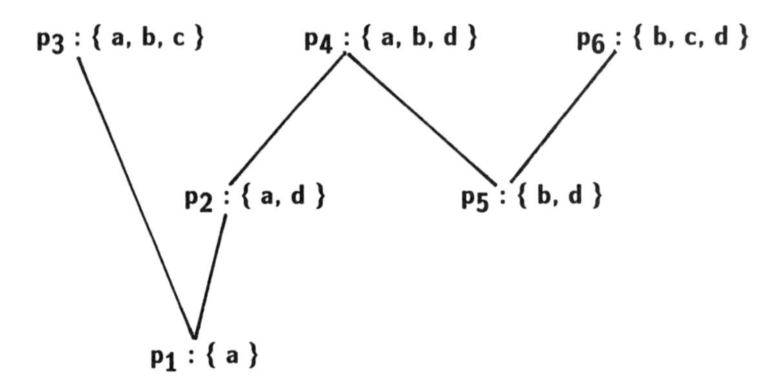

C = { a, b,c, d }
P = { { a }, { a, d }, { a, b, c }, { a, b, d }, { b, d }, { b, c, d } }

Figure 1. Sample hierarchy **H**

The probability assignment generated by e_1 assigns .5 to { p_3, p_4, p_5, p_6 }. Since the evidence does not favor any other possibilities, the remainder of the support is assigned to **P**. Evidence asserting the presence of a characteristic assigns its support to the set consisting of all possibilities that contain the characteristic. Thus, e_2 generates the basic probability assignment that assigns one to the set { p_1, p_2, p_3, p_4 }.

Basic probability assignments are positive support representations, information that denies a possibility is transformed into support for the alternatives. Evidence e_3 denies the presence of characteristic **d**. Interpreting this as a basic probability assignment generates the function that assigns one to { p_1, p_3 }.

The measure of support in an evidential reasoning environment is a two valued system known as an evidential interval. The evidential interval is defined in terms of a belief function *BEL* which is constructed from a basic probability assignment *m*. *BEL* is a function with domain *P*(**P**) defined by

$$BEL(A) = \sum_{B \subseteq A} m(B)$$

The value *BEL*(A) represents the total support for all the members of the set A. *PLS*(A), defined by 1 - *BEL*($\bar{A}$) where $\bar{A}$ is the complement of A in *P*(**P**), is the plausibility of A. *PLS*(A) represents the total measure of the evidence of *m* that does not support the refutation of A. The evidential interval, the measure by which the alternatives are evaluated in a evidential reasoning system, is defined as [*BEL*(A), *PLS*(A)]. The configuration consists of an evidential interval for each subset of *P*(**P**).

Dempster's rule combines basic probability assignments and updates configurations. Let m_1 and m_2 be two basic probability assignments over *P*(**P**). A basic probability assignment *m*, the orthogonal sum of m_1 and m_2 is defined as follows:

i) $m(\emptyset) = 0$

ii) $m(A) = \sum_{A_i \cap B_j = A} (m_1(A_i) m_2(B_j)) / (1-k)$

where k is the total support given to incompatible possibilities (disjoint sets) by m_1 and m_2. The multiplication of support for sets implicitly assumes the independence of evidential support. Evidence is inconsistent if the sum of the support for incompatible sets totals one. When this occurs, Dempster's rule does not provide a method for analyzing the information. The computation of the orthogonal sum also requires the set of possibilities to be mutually exclusive and exhaustive.

The configurations generated by the Dempster-Shafer theory are traced for a indentification using the hierarchy **H** and evidence e_1 - e_5.

evidence	configuration
e_1	.5 { p_3, p_4, p_5, p_6 } .5 **P**
e_1, e_2	.5 { p_3, p_4 } .5 { p_1, p_2, p_3, p_4 }
e_1, e_2, e_3	.5 { p_3 } .5 { p_1, p_3 }
e_1, e_2, e_3, e_4	1 { p_3 }
e_1, e_2, e_3, e_4, e_5	-

The restrictions for the Dempster-Shafer theory are also present in the probabilistic fixed propagation systems. The use of Baye's rule for evidence combination requires an exhaustive and mutually exclusive set of possibilities. The assumption of the independence of evidential support is frequently utilized by probabilistic systems to avoid the combinatorial problems associated with the prior probabilities required by a computation using Baye's rule.

4. Inference networks

Inference networks, also known as dependency graphs, are used to represent hierarchical relationships as a directed graph [2]. Quinlan [5], [6] and Pearl [3], [4] have developed architectures for defining the propagation of support through a network. A network contains two types of nodes; nodes corresponding to elements of the domain and nodes whose sole purpose is to assist in the propagation of support. Like the fixed propagation systems, most networks represent support numerically. The propagation techniques, however, are explicitly defined by the arcs of the graph. The *minimal assumption* inference network of Quinlan [5] is used to illustrate the propagation of support in a hierarchy. The flexibility of this system results from the variety of relationships that are specifiable. Each relationship has an associated set of propagation rules. Evidential independence and the mutually exclusive and exhaustive nature of **P** can be incorporated into the graph if desired but are not required.

Each node has a measure that indicates the support accumulated by the node. The measure of support in this system is an evidential interval. The interval for a node A is defined by two values, t(A) and f(A). The accumulated support for A is denoted t(A) while f(A) is the measure of evidence refuting A. Initially, both t(A) and f(A) are zero. The propagation of support can increase, but never decrease, these values. The evidential interval is defined as $[t(A), 1-f(A)]$. The evidence indicates an inconsistency whenever $f(A) + t(A) > 1$ for any node A in the graph.

The t and f values are increased as support is propagated through the network. If node A is related to nodes B_1 and B_2 the propagation rules have the form

$$t(A) \leftarrow \text{maximum} \{ t(A), F_1(t(B_1), f(B_1), t(B_2), f(B_2)) \}$$
$$f(A) \leftarrow \text{maximum} \{ f(A), F_2(t(B_1), f(B_1), t(B_2), f(B_2)) \}$$

where F_1 and F_2 are functions defined to numerically represent the relationship among A, B_1 and B_2. The operator <- may be read "is replaced by". Whenever one of the values in the function on the right-hand side is changed, that function is evaluated. The support for A, t(A), is then assigned the maximum of its current value and the value computed by F_1. Similarly, a new f value is assigned if F_2 is greater f(A). The choice of the maximum in the propagation rules enforces the increasing nature of support in the network. The set of relations and corresponding numeric propagation functions used in the propagation of support in a hierarchy can be found in [7].

Since evidence directly supports characteristics, the network relationships in the network propagate support to the possibilities. A network representing the hierarchy **H** is given in *Figure 2.* Nodes labelled **a**, **b**, **c** and **d** represent the total support for the presence of the corresponding characteristic. The interpretations of evidence e_1, e_2 and e_3 produce the evidential representations $t(\mathbf{b}) = .5$, $t(\mathbf{a}) = 1$ and $f(\mathbf{d}) = 1$, respectively.

A possibility is identified when its t value is one. The network in *Figure 2* makes tentative identifications and updates them as additional evidence is processed. Processing evidence identifies a possibility as soon as the presence of every chararcteristic is established. For example, evidence supporting **a** and **d** identifies possibility p_2 although additional information may ultimately indicate p_4. Identification is not mutually exclusive in a network that makes tentative identifications. If $t(p_i) = 1$, the t value of any possibility whose elements are contained in p_i will also be one. The inference system in *Figure 2* does not require **P** to be exhaustive. Evidence supporting the presence of characteristics **a**, **c** and **d** identifies possibilities p_1 and p_2 without indicating an inconsistency.

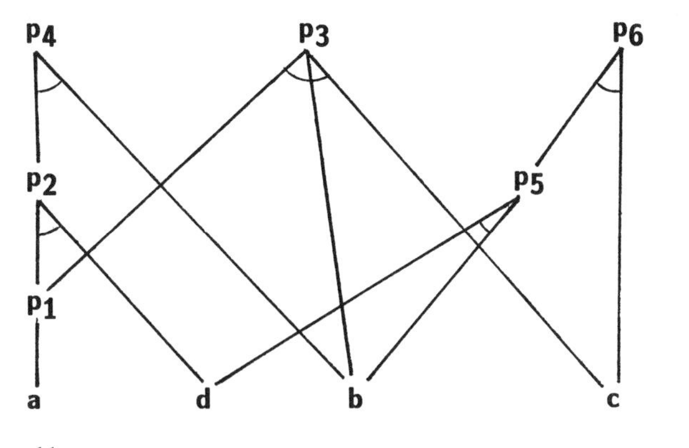

a enables p_1
p_2 conjoins { p_1, **d** }
p_4 conjoins { p_2, **b** }

p_3 conjoins { p_1, **b**, **c** }
p_5 conjoins { **b**, **d** }
p_6 conjoins { p_5, **c** }

Figure 2. Inference network for tentative identification.

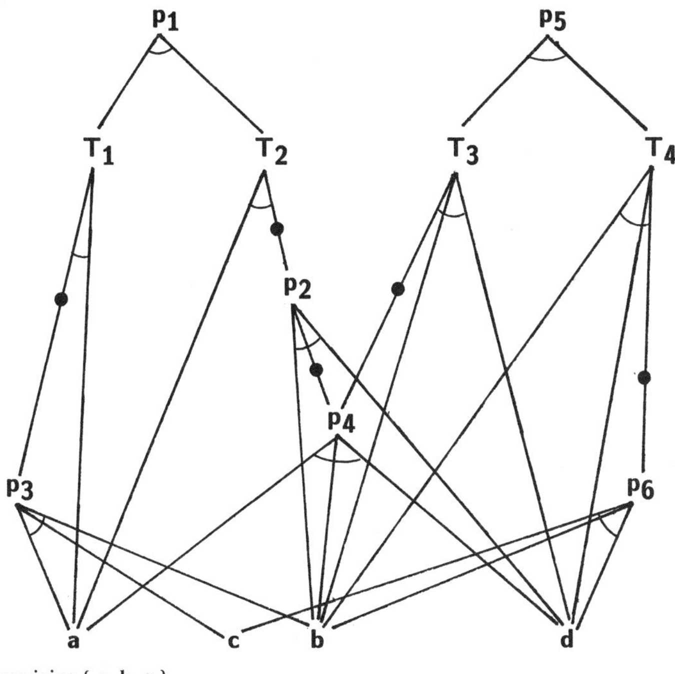

p_3 conjoins { **a**, **b**, **c** }
p_4 conjoins { **a**, **b**, **d** }
p_6 conjoins { **b**, **c**, **d** }
p_2 conjoins { **a**, **d**, not p_4 }
p_1 disjoins { T_1, T_2 }
p_2 disjoins { T_3, T_4 }

T_1 conjoins { **a**, not p_3 }
T_2 conjoins { **a**, not p_2 }
T_3 conjoins { **b**, **d**, not p_4 }
T_4 conjoins { **b**, **d**, not p_6 }

Figure 3. Inference network for deterministic identification.

The flexibility of the network architecture is illustrated by constructing an alternative network for the hierarchy **H**. The propagation of support in the network in *Figure 3* makes unique identifications. If $p_i \subseteq p_j$, then $t(p_i)$ is assigned one only if it has been established that all the characteristics of p_i are present and that a characteristic of p_j is absent.

This network does not assume **P** to be exhaustive but identification is exclusive for elements of **P**. Evidence supporting a set of characteristics X that is not in **P** is assigned to the maximal possibilities p_i that are contained in X. Support for **a** and **b** is attributed to p_1. Similary, evidence that establishes the presence of all the characteristics yields $t(p_3) = t(p_4) = t(p_6) = 1$.

5. Endorsement based reasoning

Cohen [1] introduced endorsement based reasoning as an alternative to the standard numeric approaches. Rather than representing information by a single number or a pair of numbers, evidence is interpreted and manipulated symbolically. This symbolic representation permits the use of information itself, rather than a numeric value, when combining evidence. Endorsements are propositions that offer support, either positive or negative, for a possibility. *Table 1* gives endorsements for reasoning in the hierarchical domain **H** defined in *Figure 1.* The total support for a possibility is determined by the endorsements assigned to the possibility.

A configuration in an endorsement based system consists of a set of endorsements for every possibility. The combining function is defined by a set of rules for updating endorsements. The symbol -> specifies replacement, the set of endorsements on the lefthand side is replaced by the righthand side. The rule

$$P(x,p_j),\ M(x,p_j) \rightarrow M(x,p_j)$$

indicates that there is no need to retain an endorsement when a stronger one has been asserted.

S, C, O and I are derived endorsements. They are not generated by evidence but rather by combinations of existing endorsements. The endorsement S(X) is generated when X is consistent with the acquired information and the endorsements assigned to each of the other possibilities indicate an inconsistency. The generation of derived endorsements is defined by rules of the form

condition => endorsement.

When the condition on the left-hand side is satisfied, the endorsement on the right-hand side is generated. Like the rules in an inference network, the generation rules must be evaluated whenever a value on the left-hand side is altered. The configuration produced by processing e_1 - e_4 is given below. The only consistent possibility is p_3. Processing e_5 results in all of the possibilities receiving the inconsistent endorsement.

evidence: e_1, e_2, e_3, e_4

p_1 : I, M(a), N(c)
p_2 : I, D(d), N(c)
p_3 : S, P(b), M(a), M(c)
p_4 : I, P(b), M(a), D(d), N(c)
p_5 : I, P(b), N(a), D(d), N(c)
p_6 : I, P(b), N(a), D(d), N(c)

evidence: e_1, e_2, e_3, e_4, e_5

p_1 : I, M(a), N(c)
p_2 : I, D(d), N(c)
p_3 : I, P(b), M(a), M(c), D(b)
p_4 : I, P(b), M(a), D(d), N(c), D(b)
p_5 : I, P(b), N(a), D(d), N(c), D(b)
p_6 : I, P(b), N(a), D(d), N(c), D(b)

Although inconsistent, p_3 is still a likely candidate. It has only one negative compared to three positive endorsements. On the other hand, p_6 is highly unlikely with four negative endorsements.

The assignment of endorsements makes no assumptions concerning the evidence or the set of possibilities. Support for a set of characteristics X that is not in the set ofpossibilities generates positive endorsements for possibilities containing X. Processing evidence that establishes the presence of all four characteristics assigns one negative and three positive endorsements of each system p_3, p_4 and p_6. Inconsistent evidence simultaneously supports and refutes the possibilties to varying degrees. This permits the reasoning system to draw conclusions with data that appears contradictory.

Endorsements	Interpretation
S(X)	X is the sole consistent possibility
C(X)	X is consistent
M(**a**,X)	**a**, whose presence is asserted, is a member of X
P(**a**,X)	**a**, whose presence is supported, is a member X
D(**a**,X)	**a**, whose presence is denied, is a member of X
N(**a**,X)	**a**, whose presence is established, is not in X
O(X)	other consistent possibilities
I(X)	X is not consistent with the evidence

Generation Rules

D(**a**,X) => I(X)
N(**a**,X) => I(X)
$C(X) \ \& \ \forall_{i \neq j} (X) \sim C(X) \Rightarrow S(X)$
$C(X) \ \& \ \forall_{i \neq j} (X)\ C(X) \Rightarrow O(X)$

Replacement Rules

S(X), C(X) -> C(X)
P(X), M(X) -> M(X)
C(X), I(X) -> I(X)
S(X), I(X) -> I(X)

Table 1. Endorsement system for hierarchy **H**.

6. Conclusions

The use of numeric values to indicate support provides a simple, understandable evidential representation. Combining rules are easily calculable domain independent arithmetic formulas. There are two major difficulties that limit the applicability of both the standard Bayesian probabilistic techniques and the Dempster-Shafer theory. The first is the knowledge engineering problem of translating domain specific experience and intuition into probability distributions. This is not the milieu in which the experts work and reason. They are often uncomfortable in representing their opinions in this manner.

Another objection relates to the assumptions required to make the combination techniques computationally tractable. Both Bayesian updating and the orthogonal sum of the Dempster-Shafer theory assume that evidential observations are independent. In many domains, this assumption is unwarranted. The algebraic combination rules also require that the set of possibilities be exhaustive and mutually exclusive. This requires extensive knowledge of the possibilities that may not be known in a rapidly changing environment. Finally, neither of these techniques are applicable in problem domains in which contradictory evidence may be acquired. Obtaining contradictary evidence, however, is not unlikely when evidence is acquired from disparate sources over a period of time. It is even more likely when the object being identified is not passive and has the ability to alter its characteristics in an attempt to hinder the identification.

The symbolic representation allows domain specific evidential representations (endorsements) and combination rules. This avoids the knowledge engineering problem since the expert may formulate combining rules in familiar terms, the domain specific information itself. The processing of contradictory information causes no difficulties for endorsement based systems. Each of the possibilities may be assigned both positive and some negative endorsements. Conclusions are made based on the accumulated evidence. A possibility with many strong positive endorsements and several negative ones may be a likely candidate even though the combination of endorsements themselves is inconsistent.

These capabilities are not gained without additional cost. Ranking the likelihood of the possibilities in a numeric system simply utilizes the numeric ordering. A symbolic system requires another reasoning component that analyzes the totality of the endorsements assigned to each possibility to obtain an estimate of its likelihood. It is this latter feature that provides the flexibility that allows an endorsement based system to compare the strengths of inconsistent information and draw conclusions.

REFERENCES

1. Cohen, P. R., Heuristic Reasoning about Uncertainty: An Artificial Intelligence Approach, (Pitman Publishing Co., Boston MA 1985).
2. Lowrance, J. D., Dependency-Graph Models of Evidential Support, Ph. D. Dissertation, Department of Computer Science, University of Massachusetts at Amherst(1982).
3. Pearl, J., Distributed Bayesian Processing for Belief Maintenance in Hierarchical Inference Systems, Cognitive Systems Laboratory, UCLA, Technical Report ENG-CSL-81-11 (1982).
4. Pearl, J., A Constraint-Propagation Approach to Probablisitic Reasoning, Computer Science Department, UCLA Technical Report, CSD-85002 (1985).
5. Quinlan, J. R., *INFERNO: A cautious approach to uncertain inference*, The Computer Journal 26, No. 3, pp. 255-269 (1983).
6. Shafer, G., A Mathematical Theory of Evidence, (Princeton University Press, Princeton 1976)
7. Sudkamp, T. A., Representation and Propagation in Hierarchical Systems, Wright State Univeristy Technical Report WSU-CS-87-13 (1987).

Tactical Manager in a Simulated Environment

Jan M. Żytkow and Michael D. Erickson
Computer Science Department, Wichita State University, Wichita, KS 67208

ABSTRACT

Cooperative, real-time action derived from a complex system of plans and goals in a dynamically changing environment is required from an aircraft pilot. We describe a prototype of a tactical manager expert system directed at meeting these requirements. It emphasizes quick selection of a plan and flexible execution that may be terminated when the plan becomes counterproductive. It performs in real time in a simulated combat environment, allows for cooperative tactics, and can be applied to a variety of air missions.

INTRODUCTION

A reliable automated pilot has become one of the focal points of applied artificial intelligence. The advantages are obvious, especially for dangerous airplane missions. But the knowledge requirements and decision making ability required of an automated pilot are tremendous, and certainly some time will pass before a solid, trustworthy automated pilot will seize the cockpit. An intermediate form of automated control, the so called "Pilot's Associate", is currently being investigated. The most sophisticated, central module of a Pilot's Associate, aiding the pilot in his decision making process, is called the "Tactical Manager" [2].

A tactical manager expert system is the subject of this paper. We describe the skeleton of an autonomous pilot system and reconstruct the basics of a pilot's decision making process. We start with an analysis of requirements, then describe the design and implementation of the system as well as its performance in tests. Finally, a learning mechanism is proposed that will enhance the performance of the tactical manager.

Our Tactical Manager is oriented towards an automated pilot rather than a pilot's associate, even if a pilot's associate is more feasible. In this way we can abstract from the issue of interaction between the system and pilot. The decision process is also simplified, since for any situation an automated pilot needs only a single good decision, while to be useful, the pilot's associate should provide several choices to the pilot, who then may select one using his own judgement.

The construction of a <u>reliable</u> automated pilot is far more difficult than construction of a <u>useful</u> pilot's associate. The pilot's associate is as strong as its strongest applications because the pilot may decide to follow only the suggestions that are particularly appealing. Conversely, an autonomous pilot is as weak as its weakest applications because there is no pilot who may disregard or modify an erroneous decision.

REQUIREMENTS: TASK PERSPECTIVE

A variety of operational requirements must be satisfied. They may be divided into several broad categories. An autonomous pilot must:

Methodologies for Intelligent Systems
Z. W. Ras and M. Zemankova, Editors

1. Work in real time. It should frequently update its view of the external situation and respond before the next input of data. The frequency of the recognition-action cycle may be on the order of one second, although it should eventually be shorter for real-life implementation.

2. Perform a broad variety of tasks. This requires utilizing large quantities of knowledge. The system needs to understand its top level mission goals in the context of various positional situations, available weapons, maneuvering capability, etc. and then proceed to choose an appropriate response. The response should not be schematic, because predictable tactics may be defeated. The system's knowledge should be easy to understand and structured in a way compatible with human knowledge, since it may then be evaluated more easily, and may be augmented with additional tactical knowledge of human pilots.

3. Apply cooperative tactics. It should be able to cooperate with a similar system or with a human pilot. Common knowledge says that "Under most combat conditions the advantages of mutual support will outweigh the advantages of single fighters." [7]. A tactical manager system should provide for and utilize such tactics.

4. Act reliably. This requires extensive testing under a broad range of situations.

5. Choose solutions that defeat the enemy. This requires some knowledge about enemy tactics and weapons, and may require an ability to learn.

REQUIREMENTS ANALYSIS: AI PERSPECTIVE

To meet the requirement of a real-time system our tactical manager operates in a one second recognition-action cycle which includes its decision making process, and must therefore avoid the combinatorial explosion in the application of knowledge. This suggests two design solutions.

First, the system should use preprogrammed plans, as opposed to doing its own planning, whenever possible. Autonomous planning, or plan generation, involves extensive search, while selection of an existing plan may be much quicker if the knowledge base is appropriately organized. Findings of knowledge engineering sessions with pilots further support this solution. Most pilots' knowledge is organized in plans that have operational conditions of application and a clear sequencing of execution. Modern day combat pilots are subject to extensive training which provides them with a large number of clearly defined procedures and a deep conviction that the procedures should be followed because they are more effective than ad hoc solutions. This is especially true in emergency situations or in cooperative tactics which require mutual understanding between allies, since any deviation from accepted plans may be counterproductive.

Second, the knowledge base should be distributed in a context-dependent manner rather than being stored in a single large database operating under a production system inference engine. The final system may utilize hundreds of plans, each of them with a variety of potential versions valid under different circumstances. The distributed solution was successfully used in MYCIN [1], and our system follows that example.

Cooperative tactics involve making a choice between conflicting decisions. A wingman, for instance, has to prioritize among a response to a direct threat, a new decision of his leader, an old decision, and his own judgement about satisfying the mission goals. The system should provide a capability for making such a choice at any cycle, even if the actual conflicts are rather infrequent.

Testing and development can best be conducted in a simulated combat environment. This allows the Tactical Manager to function in a mode close to its destination, and the consequences of a decision can be traced and thorougly evaluated. This also provides the opportunity to confront the tactical manager with a variety of possible enemy tactics.

IMPLEMENTATION METHODOLOGY

A symbol oriented language such as LISP appears to be the best programming tool for the development of the tactical manager. Symbol processing is vital for complex decision making, and numerical calculations can be also efficiently executed in LISP. Sophisticated programming environments are available on artificial intelligence workstations which utilize LISP and which provide numerous advantages for program development. We have been using a Symbolics 3670 Lisp Machine and ZetaLisp in our implementation.

The use of a standard production system such as OPS5 may have the disadvantage of violating real-time processing requirements. A production system with a response time of one second would be very limited in the number of rules and amount of knowledge it would allow in working memory.

Even if we do not use a production system approach, the notion of a rule is methodologically important, and representing certain types of knowledge as rules is very useful. For this reason we have implemented a plan selection mechanism in the form of condition-action rules, which are coded in LISP.

For a project of this size and complexity there is virtually no choice other than to concentrate on a single tactical mission and to develop an initial prototype that handles this limited scope. Working on particular examples enabled us to create a preliminary simulation and representation for a fighter sweep mission. This initial prototype was then tested, revised, and augmented, resulting in a second prototype which is described in this paper.

The possibility of choosing a plan at every cycle, coupled with prompt recognition of the consequences, enables decisions and actions to be computed more quickly at the cost of being somewhat less precise. A corrective action performed in one or a few seconds may correct a deviation from the desired trajectory. The same approach is useful in cases of limited prediction capability. Instead of trying to precisely predict, the system extrapolates quickly and corrects its predictions as soon as new facts are available.

Many goals need not and should not be meticulously exact either. To promote (and enable) the use of more flexible goals, the system uses approximate predicates. Since the system works in discrete cycles, an exact test that tells, for instance, best firing distance, may not yet be satisfied at one cycle, and no longer satisfied at the next cycle.

EXAMPLE OF A MISSION: FIGHTER SWEEP

Consider a simple mission to maintain control of an airspace. A patrol of two friendly aircraft fly a prescribed pattern while attempting to locate enemy aircraft. Any enemy aircraft located is then attacked.

A minimal scenario for this mission includes three aircraft: an allied patrol that consists of a leader and a wingman and an enemy plane entering the patrolled area. To execute a simulation for such a scenario requires three versions of the tactical manager, one for each plane. All three can, in our simulation, use the same network of plans, thus saving on memory.

The enemy plane is approached at a certain distance and attacked by firing a missile towards it. The firing distance is chosen so that the target plane is within the missile launch envelope of the firing plane, while keeping the firing plane out of the enemy's missile launch envelope, if possible. The second allied plane then 'illuminates' the target with a radar signal, thus guiding the missile. This allows the first allied plane to escape to safety, while the second may illuminate from a safe distance.

SIMULATION CYCLE

At the top level the system executes in a continuous simulation cycle, each cycle being composed of three steps:

1. Recognition-action cycle for each plane, which provides decisions concerning new velocities, missile firing, etc.
2. Updating of positions and velocities with their newly computed values (for each plane and missile),
3. Display of new positions of planes and missiles on the screen.

Calculations done in step 2 model the physical movement which modifies the world situation and provides fresh data for the next recognition-action cycle for each plane. In our simulation, each plane can read the position and velocity of every other plane. The system can handle any number of planes and missiles.

RECOGNITION-ACTION CYCLE

The tactical planning and decision making for each plane takes place in the recognition-action cycle. The cycle for each plane includes:

1. Recognition of the external situation within the context of the aircraft's goals,
2. Decision making and selection of an appropriate plan,
3. Execution of that plan, which may result in velocity and heading changes, missiles being fired, etc.

If the current plan has not yet been completed and is still suitable at the next cycle it will be continued from its current point in execution.

Knowledge of the aircraft's long-range (mission) goals, as well as short-term goals as they apply to the current world situation is critical in the choice of a plan. This requires a variety of situation recognition functions. Consider the situation in which a formation of enemy planes flies at a large distance from the formation of allied planes, so that it does not pose a direct threat. According to different mission goals, the enemy formation may or may not be of interest to the allied formation. If an allied fighter is on an escort task it may select enemy planes that are threatening the bomber formation it escorts. If its task is a fighter sweep, a different criterion for target selection will be used. Thus, the same physical situation may be treated differently depending upon an aircraft's goals. The application of rules allow an aircraft's goals to directly affect the selection of plans, for instance:

```
If the goal is fighter-sweep
   and there is a single enemy plane within the range
then enter cooperative attack with a missile.
```

KNOWLEDGE REPRESENTATION

The tactical manager's knowledge is organized primarily within plans. They are executable and provide action for every cycle until their goal, either long- or short-term is reached, or a termination condition is met. After a plan is selected, its parameters are instantiated in response to the detailed situation at each cycle. A particular plan may be 'Evade', but it is not enough to simply select this plan and hope for a swift turn. The direction of the turn must be specified, its allowable acceleration, and possibly its duration.

In addition to plans several layers of knowledge are implemented as procedures, including computational geometry, kinematics, tests for goal satisfaction, etc.

Parts of knowledge take the form of data structures, such as aircraft types and missile types. They are used by tactical managers for individual planes and by the module which updates the positions and velocities for all flying objects. That latter module, for instance, makes sure that no planned maneuver exceeds capabilities of a flying object of given type. Knowledge about missile type is divided into propulsion, control, and guidance. This knowledge is useful for tactical manager decisions about firing or evading a missile. This knowledge is also used by the missile driver for a missile of this type.

Instances of data in the categories of airplane types and missile types store knowledge that is permanent, while data instances in the categories of airplanes and missiles store information related to particular scenarios and varying during simulation. This information, referred to as data, is described in the next section. Airplane and missile types describe physical capabilities and limitations of aircraft and missiles, and therefore rarely, if ever, change. They form the knowledge base of possible types of aircraft which may be simulated and missiles that can be applied as weapons.

DATA REPRESENTATION

Data consist of information specific to a particular simulation. They can be divided into two categories, based upon the permanence of their values in relation to a particular scenario.

Part of data describe information which is mission dependent, but which remains constant throughout the mission. These include structures to describe a formation, attack information (friends, foes, etc.), as well as instances of these structures which are created for each aircraft in the scenario. By defining and giving initial values to this set of data structures, a scenario is created and can be executed in the simulation.

Some data items will change constantly throughout the simulation of a particular scenario. These include the values within each aircraft's data structure, the values within each missile's data structure, as well as the instantiation of the missile data structures themselves. Examples are such data as velocities, headings, current targets, known enemies within range, etc. By viewing their values at any instant during the simulation we may obtain a snapshot of the simulation at that time.

PLAN INTERPRETER AND PLAN EXECUTION

The Plan Interpreter can be seen as a level of program abstraction. It functions as a translator for plans, executing plans and maintaining a stack of plans for each aircraft. The current mission status for each airplane can be represented by a number of plans arranged in a stack. The plan on the top of the stack is currently being executed, while other plans in the stack are suspended in various stages of their execution.

Some plans are performed within one cycle, while others last for many cycles. At the end of each cycle the current stack of plans is converted into an instantaneous description that remembers the stage of execution of each plan in the stack. At the beginning of the next cycle the stack is retrieved by the Plan Interpreter, and after the initial priorities are checked, execution of the top level plan is continued. The plan is then advanced one cycle, packed again, and so on. There are several reasons for utilizing such an interpreter:

1. Plans are of a simple yet uniform format emphasizing ease of creation and coding.
2. The stack is directly accessible to the actions included in plans and can be easily modified. Any stack maintained by the machine would not be so flexible.
3. Flexibility is important when dealing with situations which may require stack manipulations. In real-life situations, some dangers may initiate a complete turnabout in plans, therefore a computer model must also have this capability.
4. Simulation includes action of several tactical managers, each having its own stack of plans. Instantaneous description of the stack for a given plane is put into storage when the system executes the cycle for the other planes. Then, at the next cycle it is 'unpacked' again.

Invocation of a plan may occur at nearly any time during either the decision or action phases. However, the plans are usually action-oriented in their scope. A plan may halt its execution after performing its task, or it may be exited earlier if it is no longer appropriate or if its continuation may be counterproductive. When a plan is halted, the next plan on the stack, usually corresponding to a higher level goal which had been suspended, is continued.

SEQUENTIAL AND RECURSIVE CALLS TO PLANS

Plans are callable either sequentially or recursively. A plan called sequentially replaces its calling plans on the stack and thereby prevents returning to the calling plan. Recursively called plans are placed on top of their calling plans in the stack, causing the calling plan to continue when the called plan has finished execution.

When execution simply requires making a decision, performing the action based on the decision, and proceeding to the next decision, sequential invocations of plans is appropriate. However, for some decision to be made or some action to be carried out, a sequence of decisions and actions must be made first, then control returned to the original decision or action to be completed. This is the format for recursively invoked plans. For instance, if the sequence of actions includes:

(1) Approach attack point,
(2) Fire a missile
(3) Guide the missile / Evade

then the plans for a wingman who fires a missile and leaves its illumination to his leader may be executed in such a manner:

```
Follow-leader
  Co-op-attack-with-missiles       (called recursively
    Check-and-choose-role                  recursively
    Approach-attack-point                  sequentially
    Fire-missile                           sequentially
    Disengage                              sequentially )
  (End Co-op-attack)
(Resume Follow-leader)
```

Recursive invocation of a plan may be also necessary when something of higher priority arises that requires an emergency plan and the original plan should be resumed when the priority action is completed. The principles for the priority actions are described in the next section.

PRIORITIES AND COOPERATIVE TACTICS

At the beginning of a cycle for any aircraft the current plan may be dropped and an emergency plan invoked. A check to see if such action is necessary is done once every cycle so that an immediate response to any danger is possible. It need not be done more frequently, because new data is available only once every cycle.

Thus far we have considered the influence of changes in the external situation on the performance of an aircraft during the next cycle. Cooperative tactics emphasize and depend upon communications that a given plane may receive. This creates a complex situation in which decisions must be based upon multiple factors:

(1) New commands (from the leader aircraft);
(2) Old commands;
(3) Threats;
(4) Default procedures.

A priority level may be given to each of these factors, causing the tactical manager to follow orders, continue carrying out old orders, autonomously react to threats, or proceed according to a default procedure. Each item is tested in the priority order to see if any action is required. If so, an appropriate action is selected and carried out by executing the appropriate plan(s). If no action is needed, the next item is checked, and so on. Default procedures are explicitly specified.

TESTING AND DEVELOPMENT THROUGH SIMULATION

In order to execute a simulation, it is necessary only to define the scenario, including the initial conditions and the mission (goals) for each aircraft. Defining a scenario simply requires creating several instances of data structures:

1. one for each aircraft in the simulation, specifying the initial location, velocity, flight role, etc.,
2. one for each formation in the simulation, specifying each plane in the formation and its relative location to the leader,
3. describing the attack information for each side, specifying friends, foes, firing-range, etc.
4. describing the mission for each aircraft by specifying priorities, goals and default actions to be taken. Mission will generally differ for different aircraft taking part in a scenario.

The creation of these structures and their values completely describes a scenario and enables its execution. In order to make creation of a scenario easier, various formations and attack information structures, as well as default actions, have been predefined. It is sufficient to specify a configuration of such data structures in order to create a new scenario.

PERFORMANCE

Our Tactical Management System has been successfully implementated. It performs in real time, and has the ability to react to various threats in a cooperative manner. Thus far we are focused on simulations consisting of up to four allied and two enemy aircraft, each utilizing a Tactical Manager. In such simulations, the Tactical Manager has been shown to select a good plan of action for allied aircraft in a variety of situations. In summary, our implementation:

1. Covers the most characteristic aspects of an autonomous pilot;
2. Simulates a real-time system and performs in real time;
3. Allows for varied responses of the system, depending on commands received, external situation recognition, and default plans;
4. Allows for switching from normal plans to emergency plans at any time;
5. Allows for simple and natural implementation of goals and plans.

The nature of the tactical manager system implies that it will not be supported by a clear and decidable underlying theory. But then, no existing approach to tactics generation throughout history has been, nor has any major engineering achievement been proven to work before it was demonstrated. Still, the tactics generated by and performance of the tactical manager may be subject to evaluation by comparison with human pilot performance or with another tactical manager.

FUTURE: LEARNING MECHANISM

Suppose that a satisfactory tactical manager expert system is completed and successfully tested. Despite the fact that such a development is unlikely in the near future, its consideration is worthwhile, because such an expert system must still contend with two problems. First, tactics that do not change are predictable, and predictable tactics are easily defeated. Existing systems, therefore, will initially provide expert advice, but such advice must necessarily deteriorate with time due to the systems' static level of performance. Second, even the best tactical knowledge today may not be effective in future combat scenarios. Transfer of existing expert knowledge to new weapons and new enemy tactics will create weak, inconsistent results. This effect refers as much to expert systems as to human experts. Since changes in equipment may require significant changes in tactics and expertise is usually gained by experience, nobody can be an expert on future combat.

Learning is therefore required to overcome the static performance of expert systems relative to time, and to generate tactics applicable in future situations. What type of learning can accomplish these goals? For expert system application, experience can be replaced by simulation of potential combat situations that we call scenarios. Each scenario, even if very simple, contains a number of independent parameters. A search can then be performed to locate a winning region in the problem space of parameter values. In addition, the time in which a win may be achieved may also be important for learning. Simulation can provide the answer in the form of win/tie/lose, as well as elapsed time for each state in that problem space.

How can the results of a large number of simulations be stored? Scientific experimentation faces a similar problem, and the scientific domain solves it by searching for regularities that summarize large bodies of data. We can also utilize this solution, especially when automated discovery systems such as BACON, ABACUS, and FAHRENHEIT may be applied to perform the task [3,4,5,6]. The summarized results can then be used to enhance the expert system.

This learning mechanism concentrates on the evaluation of the tactical knowledge-base and on improvements based on regularities found in results. This is long term learning based on a very large number of simulated tactical situations. Such a learning mechanism, based on this idea, is currently being implemented by the authors of this paper and their collaborators.

ACKNOWLEDGEMENTS

We would like to thank Esmond DeVun and Alan MacLean who participated in early stages of development of this project. This work was supported partially by the Boeing Military Aircraft Company under contract #644-727, and by the Army Research Office under grant #DAAL 03-87-G-0003.

REFERENCES

1. Buchanan, B.G., and Shortliffe, E.H. (1984), Rule-Based Expert Systems: The MYCIN Experiment of the Stanford Heuristic Programming Project. Reading, MA: Addison-Wesley Publ.
2. Eisenhardt, R.G. (1985), "Pilot's Associate Definition Study", Final Report for Period 7/84 - 5/85. Perceptronics, Inc., Ann Arbor, Michigan.
3. Falkenhainer, B.C., and Michalski, R.S. (1986), "Integrating Quantitative and Qualitative Discovery: The ABACUS System", Machine Learning, Vol 1.
4. Koehn, B.W. and J.M. Żytkow, (1986), "Experimenting and Theorizing in Theory Formation", Proceedings of the ACM SIGART International Symposium on Methodologies for Intelligent Systems. Knoxville, TN.
5. Langley, P.W.(1981), Data-driven discovery of physical laws, Cognitive Science, Vol 5.
6. Langley, P.W., Simon, H.A., Bradshaw, G., and Zytkow, J.M. (1987), Scientific Discovery: an Account of the Creative Processes. MIT Press.
7. Shaw, R.L. (1985), Fighter Combat: Tactics and Maneuvering. Naval Institute Press, Annapolis, MD.

Deductive Databases: An Overview of Some Alternative Theories

Jack Minker
University of Maryland
Department of Computer Science and
Institute for Advanced Computer Studies
College Park, Maryland 20742

Abstract

Alternative theories of a deductive database are described. These theories differ in the set of axioms and meta-rules used. The particular theories discussed are: open and closed worlds, completed databases, incomplete information and null values, non-Horn databases, protected databases, PROLOG as a query evaluator and extended Horn axioms, and stratified databases. We discuss some of the computational issues with respect to each theory.

1 Introduction

Although work in deductive databases extends back to approximately 1960 [Min87b], the start of the field of research called deductive databases may be attributed to the work of Cordell Green and Bertram Raphael [GR68]. Many theoretical developments have taken place in deductive databases that provide a firm theoretical basis for the field of databases. A historical perspective of deductive databases may be found in [Min87b]. A survey of the field of deductive databases as of 1984 may be found in [GMN84].

In this paper I will briefly describe some of the theoretical developments that have taken place, primarily since the late 1970's. These developments are important as they provide a firm basis to discuss databases and address fundamental issues that are not adequately handled in the relational theory of databases. Indeed, deductive databases encompass relational databases. It has also become clear that there may be alternative theories that describe the same set of data. Each theory may return a different answer to a query. Hence, it is important that when an organization obtains a database that they understand its limitations.

It would be well to define, first, what we mean by a deductive database.

Definition 1 *A* **deductive database** *is defined by a triple,* **D = (Th, IC, D0)** *, where,*

1. **D0** *is a finite set of constants over which the theory is defined.*
2. **Th** *is a theory that consists of a finite set of axioms written in logic, and possibly meta-rules that describe how one operate with the particular theory.*
3. **IC** *is a finite set of integrity constraints that must be satisfied by a database and consist of a finite set of well-formed formulae in the predicate calculus.*

The theory, **Th**, and the integrity constraints, **IC**, must satisfy the condition that **Th** ∪ **IC** is consistent. Furthermore, a wff **W** is derivable from a theory **Th** iff **W** is derivable from **Th** ∪ **IC**.

In the development of alternative theories of a database, what changes is the set of axioms or the meta-rules used in the system.

Methodologies for Intelligent Systems
Z. W. Ras and M. Zemankova, Editors

2 Some Alternative Database Theories

It is important that in developing a system to meet the needs of a user, that the developers understand the database that the organization has and the assumptions that the organization makes about the particular database. In a relational database the user data must comply with certain restrictions. Typically, the data in a tuple must be known completely. That is, no null values are allowed. In addition, in a relational database there is no ability to represent negative data, but yet the answers to queries about negative data may be found. The user, however, may wish to place negative data in his database rather than use the assumptions in the database. The user may also have to deal with indefinite data, where one has data of the form $\{p \vee q\}$ and the user cannot specify whether p is true, q is true or both are true. It is not up to the designer to state that a database must be of a particular type. Rather it is up to the user to specify his problem and it is then the responsibility of the developers to specify what they can or cannot do to meet the needs of the user. It is also the responsibility of the developer to inform the user of the consequences of his requirements. For example, it is, in general, unrealistic to place negative data in a database since the database could become immense. It may also be computationally complex to answer queries in some databases specified by the user. But, having failed to convince the user that this is what he wants, the designer must then comply with the needs of the user or not accept the challenge. However, in accepting the challenge, the developer must inform the user as to whether or not he will be able to answer all queries posed to the system and, if he is guaranteed to obtain only correct answers and all correct answers to arbitrary queries.

In the following I will discuss a number of approaches that have been taken to develop theories of deductive databases and what these theories entail with respect to the user.

2.1 Open and Closed Worlds

Reiter [GM78] was one of the first individuals to recognize that there were alternative theories of databases. In [Rei78b], he discusses two kinds of theories. One is a theory based on first-order logic. The user must specify both positive and negative data to the system. The user may also specify axioms. Answers to queries in this case are theorems that can be proven from the first-order theory. Reiter termed such a database an Open World Assumption (OWA). It is clear that an OWA does not model relational databases. In addition, if one is forced to use a theorem prover to answer queries, computation may be costly. However, this is a penalty that the user must pay to meet his needs. In such a database, the axioms are universally quantified and hence, null values cannot appear in the database.

The second class of database that one may have is one in which there are only positive relations and Horn axioms as part of the theory. Integrity constraints may exist, but are outside of the theory. Reiter has shown [Rei78a] that it is not necessary to use integrity constraints in such databases to answer questions. That is, answers to questions are the same whether or not the integrity constraints are made part of the theory. This database generalizes relational databases. If one only has relational tables and no Horn axioms, then one is back to the case of relational databases. Reiter defines a query to be an arbitrary well-formed formula of the predicate calculus. To answer a query, one must now be able to handle negative queries in addition to existential and universally quantified queries. To answer negative queries, Reiter makes the assumption that all of the information is known. In this case it can then be assumed that if one cannot prove a positive atom, then the positive atom is false. Hence, the first-order theory that consists of the relations and the Horn axioms is augmented by a rule that is outside of the first-order theory, namely that if one cannot prove the atom then it is false. With this assumption, Reiter then shows how to compute alternative types of queries. Although integrity constraints need not participate in the database search for an answer to a query, it has been shown by Chakravarthy [CGM86b,CGM86a] and his co-workers how one can semantically optimize queries in relational and deductive databases. In a companion paper, [Rei78a], Reiter has shown how one can compile non-recursive axioms so as to separate out the deductive search process from the relational retrieval to achieve a more efficient implementation of queries in deductive databases. In the event there are recursive axioms as part of the Horn theory, Reiter [Rei78c] had proposed that one avoids dealing with them by breaking cycles that are in the axioms. Extensive work has been done with regard to handling recursive axioms. See, for example the work of Bancilhon and Ramakrishnan [BR86b,BR86a], who both survey and provide performance evaluation of a large number of methods for handling recursion.

2.2 Completed Database

At about the same time as Reiter, Clark [Cla78] was giving consideration to the problem of negation in deductive databases and logic programming. He took a somewhat different approach than Reiter. He observed that in Horn deductive databases one is dealing only with "if" statements. What the user probably had in mind in defining his problem is an "if and only if" statement. Such statements provide the definitions of a predicate. The user, however, has not placed such statements in the database. Thus, to compute answers relative to the intended meaning of a database, one should add "only if" statements to effectively complete the database and to capture the intended meaning of the user. Clark refers to the "only if" axioms added for each predicate as the *completion of P* , written as *comp(P)*. Clark also notes that in addition to adding the only if part, one also has to add axioms to handle equality. One can, therefore compute answers to queries since now one has an open world assumption. However, as this is expensive (as a theorem prover is needed), one wants to answer queries without these added axioms. In particular, one wants to answer queries that contain negated atoms. If we are dealing with a Horn clause program P, then from P one can deduce only positive facts. An interpreter that uses SLD-resolution [Hil74,AvE82], (complete and sound for Horn clauses) can attempt to prove a ground atom and show if it is a logical consequence of the program P. However, it cannot be proved if a query $\neg Q$ is a logical consequence of P since the union of P with the negation of $\neg Q$, that is, Q, is easily shown to be satisfiable. Clark introduced the rule, *negation as finite failure* to avoid this problem. The rule states that if Q is ground and is in the finite failure set of P, then $\neg Q$ holds. That is, if the attempt to prove Q from P fails at a finite distance along every possible path, then $\neg Q$ can be assumed to be true. The significance of Clark's [Cla78] result is that he proved that if Q is in the finite failure set of P, then $\neg Q$ is a logical consequence of *comp(P)*. This provides a soundness for the negation as finite failure rule. However, negation as finite failure is, in general, not complete. Thus, approximating the "if and only if" theory augmented by equality axioms with negation as finite failure does not obtain all answers to a query. However, it is more efficient than computing answers in the first-order theory and in the CWA.

The approach by Reiter and by Clark were to compute answers to queries with negation by slightly different techniques. The answers that one obtains in each case is different. For a comprehensive discussion of the differences in the approaches see the papers by Shepherdson [She84,She87].

2.3 Deductive Databases and Logic Programming

One cannot divorce deductive databases from logic programming, as they are intimately related. In the area of logic programming, van Emden and Kowalski [vEK76] wrote a classic paper in which they outlined fixed point and operational semantics of Horn clause logic as a programming language. Their use of the least model and least fixed point constructions, as well as the procedural interpretation, have become standard tools in Logic Programming theory. They were the first to provide a clearly defined formal declarative semantics, which was shown to be compatible with a fixed point semantics and a procedural interpretation of a logic formula, viewed as a program. Their ideas also led to the concept of negation. If one takes the Herbrand Base and subtracts out the minimal model, then one can say that the atoms that remain are those that can be assumed to be false. This provides a model theoretic view of negation. Thus, the paper, written from the viewpoint of logic programming, had immediate consequences for databases.

Apt and van Emden [AvE82] in an elegant paper built upon the work of van Emden and Kowalski [vEK76]. To appreciate their contribution it is necessary to provide the following background. If P is a Horn clause logic program, the Herbrand base of P is denoted by $B(P)$. One can identify Herbrand interpretations for P as subsets of $B(P)$. The corresponding subset of the Herbrand base is the set of all ground atoms which are true in the interpretation. The set of all Herbrand interpretations of P is a complete lattice under the partial order of set inclusion. The mapping T_P, defined in [vEK76], from the lattice of Herbrand interpretations to itself is given as:

$$T_P(I) = \{ A \in B(P) : A \leftarrow B_1, B_2, \ldots, B_n \text{ is a ground instance of a clause in P and } B_1, B_2, \ldots, B_n \in I \}$$

The operator T_P is monotonic , and $T_P \downarrow \omega$ is defined as $\bigcap_{n=1}^{n=\omega} T_P^n(B(P))$

With the above as background, one of the results of Apt and van Emden is that A is in the SLD finite failure set if and only if $A \notin T_P \downarrow \omega$. Lassez and Maher [LM84] show that the finite failure set is characterized by $FF = B(P) \backslash T_P \downarrow \omega$, and thus the result of Apt and van Emden is essentially a weak soundness and completeness result of finite failure. It only guarantees the existence of one finitely failed SLD tree and others may be infinite. Using the concept of fairness they identified those computation rules which guarantee finitely failed SLD trees, leading to a strong soundness and completeness result of finite failure.

Jaffar, Lassez and Lloyd [JLL83] then showed that the inference system, SLDNF, selective linear resolution for definite clauses with negation as failure, was complete for ground negated atoms in the case of positive programs. Clark [Cla78] had shown the soundness of the negation as finite failure rule for Horn logic programs P, augmented by *comp(P)* and equality axioms. Jaffar, Lassez and Lloyd's contribution was to show that if $\neg Q$ is a logical consequence of *comp(P)*, then Q is in the finite failure set of the program P, which is the completeness result. Hence, a firm theoretical foundation was given to negation for logic programming and deductive databases.

2.4 Incomplete Information and Null Values

Reiter [Rei84], in addition to his work on the OWA and CWA, provided some fundamental insights into database theory. He was the first to propose formal theories of deductive databases that encompassed and generalized the work of Codd. Reiter reinterpreted the conventional model theoretic perspective on databases in purely proof theoretic terms. He demonstrated how relational databases can be seen as special theories of first-order logic, where the theories incorporated the following assumptions:

1. *The domain closure assumption. The individuals occurring in the database are all and only the existing individuals.*
2. *The unique name assumption. Individuals with distinct names are distinct.*
3. *The closed world assumption. The only possible instances of a relation are those implied by the database.*
4. *The equality axioms.*

The use of a proof theoretic approach permitted Reiter to provide a correct treatment of query evaluation for databases that have incomplete information and a class of null values; integrity constraints and their enforcement; and the extension of the relational model to incorporate more real world semantics such as the representation of events and hierarchies. The significance of Reiter's work is that he focused on the proof theoretic approach rather than the model theoretic approach, he gave precise definitions of a number of central issues and he clarified and extended relational databases to include deductive databases.

In another paper Reiter [Rei86] treated the problem of indexed null values when it is known that there is a value and that it may not be among the given constants in the domain. He shows how one may incorporate the indexed null values into the theories that he described in [Rei84] In this case he showed that one could compute answers in a reasonable way using the Horn formulation of the theory; however, in certain cases one obtains correct answers, but not necessarily all the answers. Hence, he has a sound, but not necessarily complete, theory. Of course, one can obtain all answers and only correct answers by going back to the first-order theory. However, in this case, again, the alternative is to use a theorem prover to obtain answers to queries.

2.5 Non-Horn Databases

In the presence of Non-Horn clauses, neither the CWA nor negation as finite failure handle negation correctly. As noted by Reiter, given the elementary database, $\{ p \vee q \}$, one can prove neither p nor q. If one were then to conclude $\neg p$ and $\neg q$, the conjunction of these two with the database is inconsistent. Hence, in a non-Horn database neither of these two approaches can be used to compute negated atoms.

Unlike Horn databases in which van Emden and Kowalski [vEK76] demonstrated that there is a unique minimal model, in the presence of non-Horn clauses, Minker [Min82] demonstrated that there is no unique minimal model, rather there are a set of minimal models. In the model theoretic approach, an atom that does not appear in any minimal model can be assumed to have its negation true. Thus, in the database that consists of the non-Horn clause, $\{p \vee q \}$, there are three models, $\{ p \}$, $\{ q \}$, and $\{ p, q \}$. Of these, two are minimal, $\{ p \}$ and $\{ q \}$, and neither are contained in the other. Hence, neither p nor q can be assumed to be false as each appears in a minimal model. Minker [Min82] also developed a proof theoretic approach to non-Horn databases and demonstrated that if one cannot prove $P(a) \vee K$, where K is an arbitrary ground positive clause (posibly null) and one cannot prove K, for all such possible K, then one can assume not $P(a)$. The method is termed the generalized closed world assumption (GCWA), [Min82]. Minker further demonstrated that for function-free clauses that the same responses to queries were obtained in the model theoretic and the proof theoretic definitions of the GCWA. Grant and Minker [MG86] have developed a method to compute answers to queries in the ground non-Horn case where all clauses (disjuncts of literals) are restricted to consist only of positive atoms. Henschen and his students [HP86,YH85] have also attempted to develop methods to answer queries in databases that comply with the GCWA. Gelfond, Przymusinska and Przymusinski [GPP86] used the concept of the GCWA to develop an extended closed world assumption (ECWA). Przymusinski [Prz86c,Prz86b] has also shown how one can utilize SL resolution to be able to answer queries in non-Horn databases subject to the GCWA. He terms the modified inference system SLSNF (linear resolution with subsumption based on negation as failure). The basic idea is to use SL resolution on the negation of some positive atom, say $P(a)$, selecting first, only negated atoms in a resolvent clause. Resolving away all negative literals leaves at most positive literals. One then uses SL resolution to determine if, starting with a clause containing the negation of the positive atoms one can find a proof. If one cannot find a proof, then one can assume the negation of the original atom, $P(a)$. For additional work on non-Horn clauses see Bossu and Siegel [BS85], and Bidoit and Hull [BH86].

Recent work has been reported by Ross and Topor [RT87] and by Minker and Rajasekar [MR] concerning fixed point theories for non-Horn databases that extend the fixed point theories for Horn clauses that was obtained by van Emden and Kowalski [vEK76]. The fixed point theories that have been developed by them are different and reflect different assumptions that can be made about a non-Horn database.

2.6 Protected Databases

In a so-called protected database, one is interested in answering queries in databases where it is known that it is unknown whether or not a particular fact is true. That is, we may know $P(a)$ is true and we may also know that we do not know whether or not $P(b)$ is true. This situation is not handled in relational databases. Minker and Perlis [MP84a,MP84b,MP85], were able to show that a slightly different "only if" statement than that specified by Clark could handle the situation and furthermore that one could modify the database to achieve a Horn theory that could be used to compute answers. The Horn theory is sound, but does not give all answers in a limited number of cases. An interesting aspect of the work was the applicability of circumscription, a concept introduced by McCarthy [McC80] to handle situations in artificial intelligence, to a problem in databases. Reiter also recognized the possibility of applying circumscription to databases. In [Rei82] he shows how Clark's negation as failure is a consequence of circumscription for Horn clauses and in [Rei84] he emphasizes the importance of circumscription for database theory.

2.7 PROLOG as a Query Evaluator and Extended Horn Axioms

Lloyd and Topor [LT84,LT85,LT86] in a series of three papers developed a theoretical basis for deductive database systems which are implemented using a PROLOG system as the query evaluator. They use a typed first-order logic to express data, queries and integrity constraints. They introduced extended programs and extended goals for logic programming. In contrast to Horn clause logic, a clause in extended programs can have an arbitrary first-order formula as its body, and similarly for an extended goal. They have provided a definition of an answer to a query being correct with respect to a database and also presented a definition of an integrity constraint being satisfied by a database. In addition they have developed two query evaluation processes and have proved that both are sound and, for definite and hierarchical databases, complete. A database is *hierarchical* if the predicates in the program P can be partitioned into levels so that the definition of level 0 predicates consist solely of unit clauses and the bodies of the clauses in the definition of level j predicates ($j > 0$) contain only level i predicates, where ($i < j$).

The work of Lloyd and Topor demonstrates that a formalism based on first-order logic provides an expressive environment for modeling databases; that a single formalism may be used, namely first-order logic; and that logic provides a theoretical foundation required for databases.

2.8 Stratified Databases

Negation in logic programming has been troublesome even with the developments that have been cited above. To handle these problems, the concept of stratified databases was introduced by a number of different researchers [ABW87,Naq86,Gel87]. A stratified database is one in which one deals with extended or general clauses that have negated atoms in the antecedent of a clause. The consequent of a clause is a single atom. Hence, we are referring to extended Horn clauses (since the antecedent of a Horn clause cannot contain a negated atom). A database is *stratified* if the clauses can be ordered such that if a negated atom appears in the body of a clause, then the definition of the atom (the consequent of a clause) precedes the clause in which the negated atom appears in the body of the clause. A stratified database is said to be "free from recursive negation" since stratification prevents recursion on negation. Theoretical results in this area were obtained by Apt, Blair and Walker [ABW87] and Van Gelder [Gel87]. Apt et al. develop a fixed point theory of non-monotonic operators and apply it to provide a declarative meaning of a general program. They also prove the consistency of Clark's completed model database for stratified programs and clarify some previously reported problems with negation in logic programming. Van Gelder showed that general logic programs with the so-called bounded term size property and freedom from recursive negation are "completely classified" by what he refers to as tight tree semantics in which every atom in the Herbrand Base of the program either succeeds or fails. As all programs terminate on every input, Van Gelder deals only with a strict subset of what is computable as opposed to Horn clauses. Shamim Naqvi [Naq86] also recognized the importance of stratified databases. The importance of stratification in databases, in a slightly different context, was noted by Chandra and Harel [CH85] who defined the class of stratified queries (which they referred to as Class C). They showed that stratified queries are identical with fixed point queries defined by Chandra and Harel [CH82] Lifschitz [Lif86a] used McCarthy's [McC84,McC86] concept of prioritized circumscription to obtain results with respect to the semantics and minimal model of stratified programs. For additional work on circumscription see [Lif85a,Lif85b,Lif86b] Przymusinski [Prz86a], using a model theoretic approach initiated in [Min82], extended the notion of stratified logic programs to deductive databases which allow negative premises and disjunctive consequents. He introduced the concept of a *perfect model* of a database and shows that the set of perfect models provides a correct semantics for such a database. He extends and strengthens the results of Apt et al., Van Gelder and Lifschitz. A paper by Shepherdson [She87] provides a comprehensive, excellent survey on negation in deductive databases and logic programming. The book, entitled **Foundations of Deductive Databases and Logic Programming** [Min87a] contains a number of papers that deal with theoretical issues in deductive databases and logic programming.

3 Summary

There now exist formal theories in both deductive databases and logic programming. Unified results now exist in databases rather than fragmented results on various topics. The book by Lloyd [Llo84] on foundations of logic programming contains the details of many of the results described in sections 2.3, 2.7 and 2.8, above.

The theories outlined above are important not only for the fields of databases and logic programming, but also for expert systems and artificial intelligence. Most expert systems will consist of a large deductive database augmented by other capabilities such as that of providing the proof tree to the user and augmenting the system with the ability to obtain fuzzy answers. To achieve such capabilities for expert systems, see the papers by [Ste84,SL85,Ste86] or by [CM82] for different approaches as to how to accomplish these objectives. The ability to work with large masses of extensional and intensional axioms will require interfacing logic programs with database technology. An effective amalgamation has not yet been achieved. However, it is clear that this can be accomplished, as may be seen in papers by [LM87,TNR86].

There remains a great deal that still has to be clarified about databases themselves. Handling updates and deletions efficiently and intelligently has yet to be achieved. Effective computation methods are required for alternative database classes, such as databases that are non-Horn , contain null values or are not function-free. Indeed, neither the theory nor the implementation of deductive databases have been described adequately.

I have described a number of theoretical developments that have taken place in the field of deductive databases. It is important to build upon theories. However, theories without consideration for implementation are sterile. Fortunately, in the theories that have been described in this paper, considerations have been given to practice. Many more developments are required both in the theory and practice of deductive databases. It is clear that deductive databases provide a theoretical framework for the field of databases in general. With the increased attention being given to this subject, such systems will also be more practical.

Acknowledgements

The following grants supported this work, AFOSR 82-0303, ARO DAAG-29-85-K-0177, and NSF IRI-8609170. I would like to express my appreciation to Mark Giuliano, Jorge Lobo and Arcot Rajasekar for their suggestions regarding the paper.

References

[ABW87] K.R. Apt, H.A. Blair, and A. Walker. Towards a theory of declarative knowledge. In J. Minker, editor, *Foundations of Deductive Databases and Logic Programming*, Morgan-Kaufmann Pub., Washington, D.C., 1987.

[AvE82] K.R. Apt and M.H. vanẼmden. Contributions to the theory of logic programming. *J.ACM*, 29:841–862, 1982.

[BH86] N. Bidoit and R. Hull. Positivism vs. minimalism in deductive databases. *Proc. ACM SIGACT-SIGMOD Symposium on the Principles of Database Systems*, 123–132, 1986.

[BR86a] F. Bancilhon and R. Ramakrishnan. An amateur's introduction to recursive query processing strategies. *Proc. of ACM SIGMOD '86*, 16–52, May 28-30, 1986.

[BR86b] F. Bancilhon and R. Ramakrishnan. Performance evaluation of data intensive logic programs. In J. Minker, editor, *Proc. Workshop on Foundation of Deductive Databases and Logic Programming*, pages 284–314, Washington, D.C., 1986 August 18-22, 1986.

[BS85] G. Bossu and P. Siegel. Saturation, nonmonotonic reasoning and the closed-world assumption. *Artificial Intelligence*, 25(1):13–63, 1985 January 1985.

[CGM86a] U.S. Chakravarthy, J. Grant, and J. Minker. Foundations of semantic query optimization for deductive databases. In J. Minker, editor, *Proc. Workshop on Foundations of Deductive Databases and Logic Programming*, pages 67–101, Washington, D.C., August 18-22, 1986.

[CGM86b] U.S. Chakravarthy, J. Grant, and J. Minker. Semantic query optimization: additional constraints and control strategies. In L. Kerschberg, editor, *Proc. Expert Database Systems*, pages 259–269, Charleston, April 1986.

[CH82] A. Chandra and D. Harel. Structure and complexity of relational queries. *Journal of Computer System Sciences*, 25:99–128, 1982.

[CH85] A. Chandra and D. Harel. Horn clause queries and generalizations. *Journal of Logic Programming*, 2(1):1–15, April 1985.

[Cla78] K. L. Clark. Negation as failure. In H. Gallaire J. Minker, editor, *Logic and Data Bases*, pages 293–322, Plenum Press, New York, 1978.

[CM82] K.L. Clark and F.G. McCabe. *A Language for Implementing Expert Systems*, pages 455–470. Ellis Horwood, 1982.

[Gel87] A. Van Gelder. Negation as failure using tight derivations for general logic programs. In J. Minker, editor, *Foundations of Deductive Databases and Logic Programming*, Morgan-Kaufmann, 1987.

[GM78] H. Gallaire and J. Minker, editors. *Logic and Databases*. Plenum Press, New York, April 1978.

[GMN84] H. Gallaire, J. Minker, and J-M. Nicolas. Logic and databases: a deductive ap proach. *ACM Computing Surveys*, 16(2):153–185, June 1984.

[GPP86] M. Gelfond, H. Przymusinska, and T. Przymusinski. The extended closed world assumption and its relation to parallel circumscription. *Proc. Fifth ACM SIGACT-SIGMOD Symposium on Principle of Database Systems*, 133–139, 1986.

[GR68] C.C. Green and B. Raphael. Research in intelligent question answering systems. *Proc. ACM 23rd National Conference*, 169–181, 1968.

[Hil74] R. Hill. *LUSH Resolution and its Completeness.* Technical Report, University of Edinburgh School of Artificial Intelligence, August 1974.

[HP86] L.J. Henschen and H. Park. Compiling the gcwa and indefinite databases. In J. Minker, editor, *Workshop on Foundations of Deductive Databases and Logic Programming*, August 22-28, 1986.

[JLL83] J. Jaffar, J.-L. Lassez, and J.W. Lloyd. Completeness of the negation as failure rule. In *Proceedings Eighth International Joint Conference on Artificial Intelligence*, pages 500–506, Karlsruhe, West Germany, 8-12 August 1983.

[Lif85a] V. Lifschitz. Closed world databases and circumscription. *Artificial Intelligence*, 27(2):229–235, 1985 November 1985.

[Lif85b] V. Lifschitz. Computing circumscription. *Proc. Ninth International Joint Conference on Artificial Intelligence*, Morgan Kaufman Publishers, Inc. 121–127, 1985.

[Lif86a] V. Lifschitz. On the declarative semantics of logic programs with negation. *Proc. Foundations of Deductive Databases and Logic Programming*, 420–432, August 18-22, 1986.

[Lif86b] V. Lifschitz. On the satisfiability of circumscription. *Artificial Intelligence*, 28(1):17–27, 1986.

[Llo84] J.W. Lloyd. *Foundations of Logic Programming.* Springer-Verlag Pub., Germany, 1984.

[LM84] J.-L. Lassez and M.J. Maher. Closure and fairness in the semantics of programming logic. *Theoretical Computer Science*, 29:167–184, 1984.

[LM87] J. Lobo and J. Minker. *A Metainterpreter to Semantically Optimize Queries in Deductive Databases.* Technical Report, Department of Computer Science University of Maryland, College Park, Maryland, June 1987.

[LT84] J.W. Lloyd and R.W. Topor. Making prolog more expressive. *Journal of Logic Programming*, 1(3):225–240, 1984 October 1984.

[LT85] J.W. Lloyd and R.W. Topor. A basis for deductive databases systems. *Journal of Logic Programming*, 2(2):93–109, July 1985.

[LT86] J.W. Lloyd and R.W. Topor. A basis for deductive database systems ii. *Journal of Logic Programming*, 3(1):55–67, 1986 April 1986.

[McC80] J. McCarthy. Circumscription - a form of non-monotonic reasoning. *Artificial Intelligence*, 13(1 and 2):27–39, 1980.

[McC84] J. McCarthy. Applications of circumscription to formalizing common sense knowledge. *Proc. AAAI Workshop on Non-Monotonic Reasoning*, 295–323, 1984.

[McC86] J. McCarthy. Applications of circumscription to formalizing commonsense knowledge. *Artificial Intelligence*, 28(1):89–116, 1986.

[MG86] J. Minker and J. Grant. *Answering Queries in Indefinite Databases and the Null Value Problem*, pages 247–267. 1986.

[Min82] J. Minker. *On Indefinite Databases and the Closed World Assumption*. Springer-Verlag, 1982.

[Min87a] J. Minker, editor. *Foundations of Deductive Databases and Logic Programming*. Morgan-kaufmann Pub., 1987.

[Min87b] J. Minker. *Perspectives in Deductive Databases*. Technical Report 1799, Department of Computer Science University of Maryland, College Park, Maryland, March 1987. to appear in J. Logic Programming.

[MP84a] J. Minker and D. Perlis. Applications of protected circumscription. *Proc. Conference on Automated Deduction*, May 1984.

[MP84b] J. Minker and D. Perlis. Protected circumscription. *Proc. Workshop on Non-Monotonic Reasoning*, 337–343, October 17-19, 1984.

[MP85] J. Minker and D. Perlis. Computing protected circumscription. *Journal of Logic Programming*, 2(4):235–249, December 1985.

[MR] J. Minker and A. Rajasekar. *A Fixpoint Semantics for Non-Horn Logic Programs*. Technical Report, Department of Computer Science University of Maryland, College Park, Maryland. In Preparation.

[Naq86] S.A. Naqvi. A logic for negation in database systems. In J. Minker, editor, *Proc. Workshop on Foundations of Deductive Databases and Logic Programming*, Washington, D.C., August 18-22, 1986.

[Prz86a] T. Przymusinski. On the semantics of stratified deductive databases. In J. Minker, editor, *Proc. Workshop on Foundations of Deductive Databases and Logic Programming*, pages 433–443, Washington, D.C., August 18-22, 1986.

[Prz86b] T. Przymusinski. A query answering algorithm for circumscriptive theories. *Proc. of the ACM SIGART International Symposium on Methodologies for Intelligent Systems*, 85–93, October 1986.

[Prz86c] T. Przymusinski. Query answering in circumscriptive and closed world theories. *Proc. Amer. Assoc. for Artificial Intelligence '86*, 186–190, August 1986.

[Rei78a] R. Reiter. Deductive question-answering on relational data bases. In H. Gallaire J. Minker, editor, *Logic and Data Bases*, pages 149–177, Plenum Press, New York, 1978.

[Rei78b] R. Reiter. On closed world data bases. In H. Gallaire J. Minker, editor, *Logic and Data Bases*, pages 55–76, Plenum Press, New York, 1978.

[Rei78c] R. Reiter. On structuring a first-order database. *Proc. of the Second Canadian Society for Computer Science National Conference*, July 1978.

[Rei82] R. Reiter. Circumscription implies predicate completion (sometimes). *Proc. Amer. Assoc. for Art. Intell. National Conference*, 418–420, 1982.

[Rei84] R. Reiter. *Towards a Logical Reconstruction of Relational Database Theory*. Springer-Verlag Pub., New York, 1984.

[Rei86] R. Reiter. A sound and sometimes complete query evaluation algorithm for relational databases with null values. *J.ACM*, 33(2):349–370, April 1986.

[RT87] K. A. Ross and R. W. Topor. *Inferring Negative Information from Disjunctive Databases.* Technical Report, University of Melbourne, Parkville, Australia, April, 1987.

[She84] J.C. Shepherdson. Negation as finite failure: a comparison of clark's completed data base and reiter's closed world assumption. *J. Logic Programming*, 1(15):51–79, 1984 June 1984.

[She87] J.C. Shepherdson. Negation in logic programming. In J. Minker, editor, *Foundations of Deductive Databases and Logic Programming*, Morgan-Kaufman Pub., 1987.

[SL85] L. Sterling and M. Latle. *An Explanation Shell for Expert Systems.* Technical Report, Center for Automation and Intelligent Systems Research, Cleveland, 1985.

[Ste84] L. Sterling. Technical Report, Rehovot Israel, 1984.

[Ste86] L. Sterling. Meta-interpreters: the flavors of logic programming. In J. Minker, editor, *Proc. Workshop on Foundations of Deductive Databases and Logic Programming*, pages 163–175, Washington, D.C., 1986 August 18-22, 1986.

[TNR86] J.A. Thom, L. Naish, and K. Ramamohanarao. A superjoin algorithm for deductive databases. In J. Minker, editor, *Proc. Workshop on Foundations of Deductive Databases and Logic Programming*, pages 118–135, Washington, D.C., August 18-22, 1986.

[vEK76] M.H. vanẼmden and R.A. Kowalski. The semantics of predicate logic as a programming language. *J.ACM*, 23(4):733–742, 1976.

[YH85] A. Yahya and L.J. Henschen. Deduction in non-horn databases. *J. Automated Reasoning*, 1(2):141–160, 1985.

DEDUCTIVE HETEROGENEOUS DATABASES

JOHN GRANT* AND TIMOS K. SELLIS**
*Department of Computer and Information Sciences, Towson State University, Towson, MD 21204 **Department of Computer Science, University of Maryland, College Park, MD 20742

ABSTRACT

The past decade has seen a great deal of interest in applications of logic to databases, particularly for deductive databases. In a different direction, database logic was proposed as an extension of first-order logic in order to deal in a uniform manner with heterogeneous (relational, hierarchic, and network) databases. The purpose of this paper is to tie together concepts involving deductive databases, complex objects, logic programming, and database logic to obtain deductive heterogeneous databases.

1. INTRODUCTION

The past decade has seen a great deal of interest in applications of logic to databases, particularly for deductive databases [4]. In contrast with conventional databases, deductive databases do not require the storage of all of the facts in the database. Instead, a deductive database consists of facts and rules, where the rules allow for the derivation of additional facts. First-order logic provides a convenient formalism for the definition of deductive databases (as well as conventional relational databases as a special case). In this formalism predicate symbols represent the relations of a database. Because of the prominence of the relational database model and the identification of relations with predicates, the treatment of deductive databases assumes the relational model.

In the late 1970's an extension of first-order logic, called database logic, was proposed to deal in a uniform manner with heterogeneous (relational, hierarchic, and network) databases. By the mid 1980's several important issues have been investigated using database logic [5]. Database logic allows for relations to be nested within relations; this way hierarchic and network structures can be formalized and manipulated directly within database logic. In particular, non-procedural user-oriented languages, such as SQL, can be extended to hierarchic databases.

Although the relational model provides a suitable framework for traditional data processing applications, several researchers have found the need for complex objects in newer applications such as engineering databases as well as advantages in using complex objects, for some aspects of standard database processing, such as report writers [1,2,3,10]. Complex objects are closely related to hierarchies; however, they allow for more complicated structures than standard hierarchic databases.

Logic programming is closely related to deductive databases, since typical deductive databases can be directly implemented (not necessarily efficiently) in a logic programming language, such as Prolog. The connection between logic programming and complex objects was discussed in [11], where it was shown that functions in a logic programming language (not used for relational databases) can be applied to represent complex objects. The purpose of this paper is to show that database logic can be extended to deal with complex objects and to

Methodologies for Intelligent Systems
Z. W. Ras and M. Zemankova, Editors

have deductive capabilities. We wish to tie together concepts involving deductive databases, complex objects, logic programming, and database logic to obtain deductive heterogeneous databases.

The organization of this paper is as follows. In Section 2 we review the connections between deductive databases and logic programming by showing how such deductive databases are represented in logic programming. We introduce database logic for heterogeneous databases in Section 3. Then, in Section 4 we explain the notion of complex objects and show how such objects can be represented within a logic programming language. In Section 5 we show how to extend database logic to complex objects and how deductive capabilities may be expressed within database logic. We discuss implementation aspects in Section 6 and end the paper with a summary in Section 7.

2. LOGIC PROGRAMMING AND DEDUCTIVE RELATIONAL DATABASES

Logic programming involves the use of logical formulas, basically clauses, as the building blocks of a computer program. The most prominent logic programming language is Prolog, which provides a restricted set of clauses, the Horn clauses, for writing programs. A fundamental concept in logic programming is the dual declarative and procedural interpretation of clauses. Thus, a clause $A \leftarrow B_1, B_2, \ldots, B_k$ (terms omitted) may be understood declaratively as indicating that if B_1, $B_2, \ldots, B_k$ are all true then A is true, as well as procedurally solving for A requires solving for B_1, $B_2, \ldots$, B_k. In the database context non-Horn clauses express indefinite information. We will restrict our consideration to Horn clauses and thus will deal only with definite information.

A deductive relational database, DB, consists of two parts, a theory T and a set of integrity constraints IC. Such a theory has three groups of axioms. The first group consists of standard axioms: the <u>domain closure</u> axiom, the <u>unique name</u> axiom and the <u>equality</u> axioms. The second group consists of atomic formulas which stand for facts: tuples in relations. This is called the <u>extensional database</u>. The third group represents the deductive rules; this comprises the <u>intensional database</u>. Additionally, a meta-rule is added to deal with negative information; we may choose the so-called <u>Closed World Assumption</u> for this purpose. The set of integrity constraints must be satisfied by the database; hence, T∪IC must be consistent. Additionally, it is assumed that the axioms do not contain function symbols.

Suppose that the database consists of two extensional relations EMPLOYEE(ENAME,DNAME,AGE,SALARY), DEPARTMENT(DNAME,MANAGER,PHONE) and one intensional relation SUPERVISOR(DNAME,MANAGER) defined as follows

```
∀ ENAME ∀ DNAME ∀ AGE ∀ SALARY ∀ MANAGER ∀ PHONE
(EMPLOYEE(ENAME,DNAME,AGE,SALARY) & DEPARTMENT(DNAME,MANAGER,PHONE)
 → SUPERVISOR(ENAME,MANAGER))
```

In logic, queries are written in the relational calculus; for example

1) Find the name, age, and manager of every employee whose salary is greater than 25000

```
{<ENAME,AGE,MANAGER> | ∃ DNAME ∃ SALARY ∃ PHONE
 ( EMPLOYEE(ENAME,DNAME,AGE,SALARY) & DEPARTMENT(DNAME,MANAGER,PHONE)
 & SALARY > 25000)}
```

A deductive relational database is represented in Prolog by writing the second and third groups of axioms of T as Prolog clauses. The Prolog interpreter takes care of aspects of the first group in T as well as the meta-rule for negative information. The formulas in IC are handled separately. To give an example, the following shows the definition of the "supervisor" predicate and the above query in Prolog

```
supervisor(Ename,Manager) :- employee(Ename,D,_,_),department(D,Manager,_)
```

```
1) answer1(Ename,Age,Manager):- employee(Ename,Dname,Age,Salary),
                                department(Dname,Manager,Phone), Salary>25000.
   ?- answer1(Ename,Age,Manager).
```

3. DATABASE LOGIC FOR HETEROGENEOUS DATABASES

Database logic was developed as an extension to first-order logic that could be applied in a uniform manner to heterogeneous (relational, hierarchic, or network) databases. In particular, database logic provides a uniform non-procedural language for expressing queries in a any database whose model is one of the tree standard models. The fundamental idea in database logic is to allow relations within relations, that is, a column of a table may itself be a table.

We illustrate database logic on a hierarchical database obtained from the relational database portion of the deductive database presented in the previous section. This database has the following data structure diagram

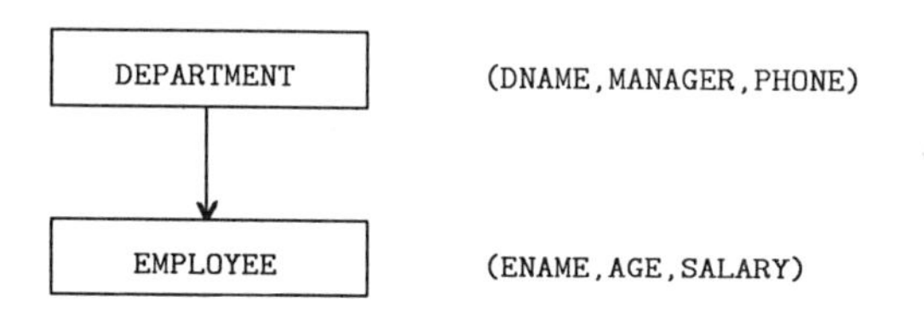

The schema and extensional database for such a database in database logic is

```
SCHEMA       DEPTEMP
TABLE        ATTRIBUTES
  DEPARTMENT   DNAME,MANAGER,PHONE,EMPLOYEE
  EMPLOYEE     ENAME,AGE,SALARY
```

DEPARTMENT					
DNAME	MANAGER	PHONE	EMPLOYEE		
			ENAME	AGE	SALARY
Sales	Samuels	555-1113	Jones	33	28500
			Moore	61	42300
Accounting	Lever	434-2219	Baker	25	22400
			Wilson	42	35000
Service	Simmons	913-2425	Adams	50	27000
			Rogers	47	26000

There are three rows in the DEPARTMENT table; the fourth column is itself the EMPLOYEE table that corresponds to a particular department. A predicate may have a predicate nested within it; it is also convenient to use so-called <u>cluster</u> predicates which are predicate combinations, as we will soon demonstrate. We rewrite now the query from the previous section in database logic. We give two versions, the first one uses database logic predicates, the second one uses a cluster predicate.

1) Find the name, age, and manager of every employee whose salary is greater than 25000

(a) {<ENAME,AGE,MANAGER> | ∃ DNAME ∃ PHONE ∃ EMPLOYEE ∃ SALARY
(DEPARTMENT(DNAME,MANAGER,PHONE,EMPLOYEE) & EMPLOYEE(ENAME,AGE,SALARY)
& SALARY > 25000)}

```
(b) {<ENAME,AGE,MANAGER> | ∃ DNAME ∃ PHONE ∃ EMPLOYEE ∃ SALARY
     ( DEPARTMENT-EMPLOYEE(DNAME,MANAGER,PHONE,EMPLOYEE(ENAME,AGE,SALARY))
     & SALARY > 25000)}
```

4. COMPLEX OBJECTS IN LOGIC PROGRAMMING

In modeling some newer applications, such as engineering databases, the notion of complex objects has been found useful [1,2]. It turns out that complex objects are actually useful in many applications, including standard data processing databases. In this section we illustrate the notion of a complex object and show how complex objects can be represented in a natural way within the framework of logic programming.

A complex object may involve hierarchies in several different ways. In a traditional hierarchic database the purpose of the hierarchy is to represent a one-to-many relationship. Thus, the example of the previous section illustrates the use of a hierarchy to represent the one-to-many relationship between a department and its employees. In a complex object a hierarchy may also be used in other ways. We deal with two typical cases. One application is for breaking up an object into several parts (or grouping several objects together). For example, it may be convenient to divide a name into first name and last name, while allowing for the possibility of treating a name as a single object. Another application allows for different alternatives, as in our example later in this section, where different data is stored about an employee's education depending on the employee's degree.

Complex objects may be represented in Prolog by using functions in predicates; however, functions are not needed for deductive (relational) databases. For example, the hierarchic DEPARTMENT database of the previous section can be represented in Prolog as a predicate

```
department(Dname,Manager,Phone,employee(Ename,Age,Salary))
```

Next we show how to write queries in Prolog using the hierarchic representation.

1) Find the name,age,and manager of employees with salary greater than 25000

```
answer1(Ename,Age,Manager):- department(Dname,Manager,Phone,
                             employee(Ename,Age,Salary)), Salary>25000.
?- answer1(Ename,Age,Manager).
```

2) Find the name and salary of every employee who works for a manager younger than him/her

```
answer2(Ename,Salary):- department(Dname,Manager,Phone,employee(Ename,
            Age1,Salary)), managers(Manager,Age2), Age1>Age2.
?- answer2(Ename,Salary).
```

Question 2 assumes the existence of the "managers" predicate.

Our next example illustrates all three uses of hierarchies, that we discussed earlier, in Prolog. This example is based on, but is not identical to, an example in [11]. Essentially we use the EMPLOYEE relation given in Section 2 but break up the ENAME attribute, change DNAME to JOBCLASS, and add an attribute for DEGREE. The Prolog program is as follows:

```
employee(name(jones,mary),sales,33,28500,degree(hs,1972)).
employee(name(moore,pat),sales,61,42300,degree(hs,1944)).
employee(name(baker,john),accounting,25,22400,degree(hs,1971)).
employee(name(wilson,david),accounting,42,35000,
                          degree(bs,1970,accounting,school(nyu,ny))).
employee(name(adams,john),service,50,27000).
```

```
employee(name(rogers,susan),service,47,26000,
                              degree(bs,1980,business,school(gwu,dc))).
employee(name(rogers,susan),service,47,26000,
                              degree(ms,1982,business,school(ub,md))).
```

Note that in this example all college degrees (if any) of an individual are listed, with year and school information; otherwise the high school degree is listed with the year value only. "degree" under "employee" represents the traditional one-to-many relationship. "name" is a grouping of first and last names, while "school" is a grouping of name and state. "degree" by itself illustrates the application of alternatives, as a high-school degree is treated differently than a university degree.

We now write a few queries for this database.

3) Find the name and salary of all employees who are only high school graduates

```
?- employee(Name,_,_,Salary,degree(hs,_)).
```

4) Find the last name, job classification, and major of employees who obtained a B.S. after 1970

```
answer4(Last,Jobclass,Major) :- employee(name(Last,First),Jobclass,Age,
                  Salary,degree(bs,Year,Major,School))), Year > 1970.
?- answer4(Last,Jobclass,Major).
```

We end this section by showing how to write the definition of an intensional predicate for a complex object in Prolog. In fact, the definition for answer4 can be thought of as the definition of an intensional predicate. Another example is the following, where "collegegrad" is a predicate containing information about college graduates

```
collegegrad(Name,Salary,Sname) :- employee(Name,Jobclass,Age,Salary,
                     degree(Type,Year,Major,school(Sname,State))).
```

5. EXTENDING DATABASE LOGIC TO COMPLEX OBJECTS AND WITH DEDUCTIVE CAPABILITIES

As we pointed out in Section 3, database logic was developed as an extension to first-order logic to provide the standard hierarchic and network models with the capabilities that first-order logic provides for the relational model: a non-procedural query language with precise semantics and the expression of queries and constraints in one language.

We illustrate what needs to be done for complex objects by showing how database logic can be extended to deal with the second example of the previous section, i.e. the employees and their degrees. The schema will be

SCHEMA	EMPED
TABLE	ATTRIBUTES
EMPLOYEE	NAME,JOBCLASS,AGE,SALARY,DEGREE
NAME	LAST,FIRST
DEGREE	TYPE,YEAR [TYPE $\neq$ hs $\rightarrow$,MAJOR,SCHOOL]
SCHOOL	SNAME,STATE

Note how the case of alternatives is handled by writing the condition and additional attributes in brackets. Let's see now how the instance of this schema given in the previous section would be represented as a database logic table.

EMPLOYEE									
NAME		JOBCLASS	AGE	SALARY	DEGREE				
LAST	FIRST				TYPE	YEAR	MAJOR	SCHOOL	
								SNAME	STATE
Jones	Mary	Sales	33	28500	HS	1972			
Moore	Pat	Sales	61	42300	HS	1944			
Baker	John	Accounting	25	22400	HS	1971			
Wilson	David	Accounting	42	35000	BS	1970	Accounting	NYU	NY
Adams	John	Service	50	27000					
Rogers	Susan	Service	47	26000	BS	1980	Business	GWU	DC
					MS	1982	Business	UB	MD

Now we write in database logic the queries for this database that we wrote in Prolog in the previous section.

3) Find the name and salary of all employees who are only high school graduates

{<NAME,SALARY> | ∃ JOBCLASS ∃ AGE ∃ DEGREE ∃ YEAR
(EMPLOYEE-DEGREE(NAME,JOBCLASS,AGE,SALARY,DEGREE("HS",YEAR))}

4) Find the last name, job classification, and major of employees who obtained a B.S. after 1970

{<LAST,JOBCLASS,MAJOR> | ∃ NAME ∃ FIRST ∃ AGE ∃ SALARY ∃ DEGREE ∃ YEAR ∃ SCHOOL
(EMPLOYEE-NAME-DEGREE(NAME(LAST,FIRST),JOBCLASS,AGE,SALARY,
DEGREE("BS",YEAR,MAJOR,SCHOOL)) & YEAR > 1970)}

Finally, we show how deductive capabilities may be added to database logic by writing the definition of the intensional predicate given at the end of Section 4 in database logic.

∀ NAME ∀ JOBCLASS ∀ AGE ∀ SALARY ∀ DEGREE ∀ TYPE ∀ YEAR ∀ MAJOR
∀ SCHOOL ∀ SNAME ∀ STATE
(EMPLOYEE-DEGREE-SCHOOL (NAME,JOBCLASS,AGE,SALARY,DEGREE(TYPE,YEAR,MAJOR,
SCHOOL(SNAME,STATE))) → COLLEGEGRAD(NAME,SALARY,SNAME)

In general, a deductive heterogeneous database may be defined by a theory T and a set of integrity constraints IC, where both T and IC are formulas in database logic. The Closed World Assumption can be extended to this case to take care of negative information. Such a deductive heterogeneous database may represent standard hierarchies or complex objects, as we have demonstrated via examples.

6. IMPLEMENTATION ASPECTS

Although complex objects have received a lot of attention recently, not many ideas on implementation have been suggested. In this section we present some previous proposals and suggest improvements.

Clearly, one way to store complex objects is by simply storing the object hierarchy in a "flattened" way. For example, the most natural way would be to store the hierarchy representing an object in pre-order. That is, store the top-level component, then each one of its children followed by their children, etc. Although high clustering which results in fast retrieval of all the components of an object is achieved through this approach, it is very inefficient for partial retrievals and it suffers in the case where the instance of an object does not fit in one physical page. As a solution to this problem, Lorie et al. [6] suggested that the hierarchy be stored in a simple way using logical pointers to connect the various components. The reason that physical addresses are not used for pointers is because reorganization of the database would result in major reorganization of the data structures themselves. Lorie et al. suggest the Indirection Table as a solution. This table simply serves as a translation mechanism for logical pointers. Of course, the use of the indirection table has the effect of more costly retrievals since the various components of an object may be scattered to random places on the physical device. However, updates are less costly compared to the first proposal because there is no need to move data around. Another disadvantage of the approach lies in the case of sub-object retrievals. This is due to the fact that instances of a given object that fall under the same parent object are linked together through pointers, making the cost of retrieving the last record in the chain much higher than the cost of retrieving the first record.

To overcome this undesirable effect, Valduriez et al [10] suggested a different approach. Each instance of an object is assigned a unique object identifier (surrogate). All instances of an object along with their associated surrogates are stored in a relation. Surrogates are used to link the various objects with their components, in the same sense that pointers were used in the Lorie et al. proposal. However, no ordering is assumed in the way the various instances of an object are stored. To give an example, the following shows how the EMPLOYEE database of the previous section is stored using the proposal of [10]

```
EMPLOYEE(E-sur,N-sur,JOBCLASS,AGE,SALARY,D-sur)
NAME(N-sur,LAST,FIRST)
DEGREE(D-sur,TYPE,YEAR,MAJOR,S-sur)
SCHOOL(S-sur,SNAME,STATE)
```

where E-sur, N-sur, D-sur and S-sur, are used as soft pointers to EMPLOYEE, NAME, DEGREE and SCHOOL records respectively. Again, in this proposal physical independence is achieved. In addition, full retrieval of an object or partial retrieval of sub-components of an object can be done efficiently using the join operator. For example, retrieving all the degrees of the employee Susan Rogers can be performed as follows

```
{<TYPE,YEAR,MAJOR> | ∃ E-sur ∃ N-sur ∃ JOBCLASS ∃ AGE ∃ SALARY ∃ D-sur ∃ S-sur
 ( EMPLOYEE(E-sur,N-sur,JOBCLASS,AGE,SALARY,D-sur)
 & NAME(N-sur,"Rogers","Susan")
 & DEGREE(D-sur,TYPE,YEAR,MAJOR,S-sur))}
```

Notice that joins are performed on surrogates only. Since the join is a very costly operation, special support is required to accelerate its execution. In [10] the use of join indices is suggested. Join indices were originally introduced by Roussopoulos [7] and later rediscovered by Valduriez [9]. They consist of pairs of pointers to records that match on their surrogates, i.e. they are connected through the hierarchy.

The approach of [10] is very interesting because it allows direct manipulation of object sub-components. In addition, it can be easily used as an implementation of either of the proposals discussed in the previous sections (Zaniolo's proposal or the extension of database logic). Clearly, it is compatible with the relational model and can be implemented on top of any existing relational database system. One possible improvement to this scheme is the addition of a cache. Sellis in [8] discusses various caching techniques. In general the support for complex objects can range from

(1) none, in which case joins must be used to retrieve the various components, to

(2) caching surrogate pairs (join indices), in which case the surrogates provide direct access to sub-objects, to

(3) caching full object components, in which case no retrieval from the database is needed.

Clearly the cost of maintaining the above schemes increases in going from strategy (1) to (2) to (3). A compromise of the above is probably the best solution. Some objects can be stored to their whole extent, others using surrogates to identify sub-objects, etc. The specific storage requirements, and reference frequencies should be used for the most efficient implementation.

7. SUMMARY

In this paper we showed how database logic can be extended to deal with complex objects and to have deductive capabilities. A framework that ties together concepts involving deductive databases, complex objects, logic programming, and database logic was proposed. As a result, we obtained deductive heterogeneous databases, that is, systems that can be used to model inference mechanisms as well as more complicated entities such as complex objects. A heterogeneous deductive database system can be used for standard data processing applications that have a good need for representing relations, hierarchies and networks. Moreover, it can easily be used to model engineering application concepts and expert systems rules. Finally, as interesting topics for future research in the area we view the development of a formal theory for modeling complex objects as well as techniques for efficient implementation.

Acknowledgement: The authors wish to thank the National Science Foundation for patially sponsoring this research under Grants DCR-84-12662 and CDR-85-00108.

8. REFERENCES

[1] Batory, D.S. and Kim, W., Modeling Concepts for VLSI CAD Objects, ACM TODS 10 (1985).

[2] Bancillon, F. and Khoshafian, S., A Calculus for Complex Objects, Proc. of the Fifth PODS Symposium (1986).

[3] Dadam, P. at al, A DBMS Prototype to Support Extended NF^2 Relations: An Integrated View of Flat Tables and Hierarchies, Proc. of 1986 ACM SIGMOD (1986).

[4] Gallaire, H, Minker, J. and Nicolas, J.M., Logic and Databases: A Deductive Approach, Computing Surveys 16 (1984).

[5] Jacobs, B.E., Applied Database Logic Vol.I, (Prentice Hall, 1985).

[6] Lorie, R. et al., Supporting Complex Objects in a Relational System for Engineering Databases, in: Query Processing in Database Systems, W. Kim, D.S. Reiner and D.S. Batory, eds. (Springer-Verlag, 1984).

[7] Roussopoulos, N., View Indexing in Relational Databases, ACM TODS 7 (1982).

[8] Sellis, T., Efficiently Supporting Procedures in Relational Database Systems, Proc. of 1987 ACM SIGMOD (1987).

[9] Valduriez, P., Join Indices, ACM TODS 12 (1987).

[10] Valduriez, P., Khoshafian, S. and Copeland, G., Implementation Techniques for Complex Objects, Proc. of the 12th VLDB Conference (1986).

[11] Zaniolo, C., The Representation and Deductive Retrieval of Complex Objects, Proc. of the 11th VLDB Conference (1985).

FORMAL TREATMENT OF INCOMPLETE INFORMATION IN TYPE DATA BASES

Maurizio Lenzerini [1]
Dipartimento di Informatica e Sistemistica
Universitá di Roma "La Sapienza"
Via Buonarroti 12, I-00185 Roma, Italy

Abstract

The type data base is the part of a knowledge base in which all information about classes, memebership relationships between objects and classes, and interdependencies among classes, are collected. We study specific type data bases, which allow for representing different kinds of incomplete information, such as existential and disjunctive assertions. In particular, we address the problems of consistency checking and query answering, proposing efficient solutions for each of them. Our analysis is carried out in the context of the logical approach to knowledge representation, which provides a suitable formal basis for the treatment of incomplete information.

1. Introduction

The object oriented approach represents a widely diffused paradigm in various areas, such as Knowledge Representation, Data Bases and Programming Languages. The basic point of view of this approach is that modeling a real world situation is made easier if one can directly and naturally talk and reason about objects, i.e. conceptual units standing for entities in the real world.

Since entities relate with each other, a fundamental feature of an object oriented system is to provide modeling primitives for establishing various kinds of relationship among objects. One of them is classification. Classification is the modeling mechanism that allows one to establish the membership relationship between an object and the classes it belongs to. A *class* is an object that represents a set of other objects with common properties, called its instances.

Various types of relationships can in turn be established among classes. An important role is played by the so-called "interdependency" relationships (see [7]). An interdependency relationship among a collection of classes is used to assert that a certain set relation holds among the extensions of these classes. For example, disjointness is an interdependency relationship: it is used to assert that two or more classes cannot have common instances. A second example is the is-a relationship, holding when every instance of one class is also an instance of another class.

In [9] the notion of *type data base* is introduced to provide a framework for collecting all information about classes. More precisely, the type data base is considered the part of the knowledge base in which all the knowledge about the classes of interest, the membership relationships between the objects and the classes, as well as the interdependencies among classes resides. We believe that several advantages are gained by considering the type data base as an autonomous component of the knowledge base. From a theoretic point of view, it constitutes a well defined framework in which the various classification schemes that are proposed in different languages can be studied and compared. Furthermore, ad hoc techniques can be developed for dealing with specific problems such as membership and set containment inference, which are considered among the crucial aspects in the design of intelligent question-answering systems ([7], [8]).

In [6] we present a taxonomy of the fundamental interdendency relationships that can be expressed in type data bases and we study the complexity of performing various kinds of inference on such relationships. It turns out that when no limitation exists on the possible interdependencies that can be established among classes, the resulting representation schemes are so complex that even basic inferences, such as satisfiability checking, cannot be efficiently computed. On

[1] This research has been partially supported by the Italian Transportation Project of CNR. This work has been carried out while the author was visiting at University of Toronto, Department of Computer Science.

Methodologies for Intelligent Systems
Z. W. Ras and M. Zemankova, Editors

the other hand, if one accepts some limitation to the representation language, the complexity decreases and reasoning becomes feasible. Two examples of type data bases with limited expressive power are presented in [1] and [4]. The results reported in [1] demonstrates that set containment can be inferred in polynomial time in a language that includes only is-a and disjointness relationships between classes. In [4], we study the covering relationship (also called "disjunctive is-a relationship"), that is the interdependency holding when a class is a subset of the union of other classes. For example, a covering relationhip can be established between the class Student and the two classes Graduate Student and Undergraduate Student, to represent that every instance of the former is also an instance of at least one of the latter. The results reported in [4] shows that the problem of testing whether a covering relationship is implied by a set of covering relationships has a linear time solution.

In this paper we extend the above mentioned work and we investigate a class of type data bases which allow for the representation of covering relationships as well as different kinds of incomplete information, such as:

1. Existential assertions, stating that there exists an object with certain properties, without saying which is this object.

2. Disjunctive information about objects, occurring when one knows that a certain object belongs to at least one of a collection of classes. For example, a disjunctive information can represent the fact that Lily is a professor either in Computer Science or in Engineering or in both.

The main goal of our work is to develop correct and efficient methods for integrity checking, query evaluation and update management in type data bases with incomplete information. These issues are addressed in the formal framework of logic, which provides a suitable basis for a correct treatment of incomplete information in data bases (see [9]).

The paper is organized as follows. In section 2 we provide the definition of type data bases, together with other definitions that will be used in the rest of the paper. Also, we discuss the expressive power of the proposed language, pointing out its advantages and its limitations. In section 3 we present our algorithm for checking the satisfiability of a type data base with incomplete information. In section 4 such a method is applied to query evaluation. Finally, in section 5 we draw conclusions and outline future developments of our research.

In what follows, we assume the reader is familiar with the basic notions of first order logic (at the level of [2]). For the sake of brevity, only selected proofs are included in the paper. The interested reader is referred to [5] for the extended version of this paper.

2. Type Data Bases with Incomplete Information

Following the logical approach to knowledge representation, we regard a type data base as a first order theory. A theory is constituted by two components: a language and a set of sentences of such a language, called the axioms of the theory. When the language is understood, we often consider the set of axioms as the theory itself.

A type data base language is a first order language whose predicate symbols are constituted by a set of unary predicate symbols, also called types or classes, plus one distinguished binary predicate symbol: $=$. The semantics of type data base languages is based on the standard notion of interpretation in first order logic. In the intended meaning, constants represent objects and unary predicates represent classes. Also, symbol "$=$" is to be interpreted as equality.

We call *single-argument formula* any formula in prenex conjunctive normal (i.e. a formula consisting of a conjunction of clauses, a clause being a disjunction of literals) whose literals have the same argument. More precisely, a single-argument formula has one of the following forms:
1. $\forall x(\rho_1(x) \wedge \rho_2(x) \wedge \cdots \wedge \rho_n(x))$
2. $\exists x(\rho_1(x) \wedge \rho_2(x) \wedge \cdots \wedge \rho_n(x))$
3. $\rho_1(c) \wedge \rho_2(c) \wedge \cdots \wedge \rho_n(c)$
where $\rho_i(x)$ (respectively $\rho_i(c)$) denotes a clause ρ_i in which the argument of each literal is the

variable x (respectively the constant c). In this paper, whenever we talk about formulas (clauses), we refer to single-argument formulas (clauses).

The object of our investigation, namely type data bases with incomplete information, are first order theories in which several constraints are imposed on the form of the axioms. The definition of such type data bases makes use of the concepts of restricted clause and restricted formula: by restricted clause we mean a clause that contains at most one negative literal, whereas a restricted formula is a formula whose clauses are restricted.

Definition 1 *A type data base with incomplete information (ITDB) is a first order theory* $<\mathcal{L},\mathcal{A}>$*, where* $\mathcal{L}$ *is a type data base language and* $\mathcal{A}$ *is the set of axioms of the theory. In particular,* $\mathcal{A}$ *contains the unique name axioms for* $\mathcal{L}$*, the equality axioms, and a set of restricted formulas of* $\mathcal{L}$*, called the interdependency axioms of the theory.*

The axioms for equality (see, for example, [9]) are used to give the symbol "=" the intended meaning of "equal". The unique name axioms state that different constant symbols in the theory denote different objects in the real world. Finally, the interdependency axioms are used to express both general facts about the types (the interdependency relationships) and specific facts about the constants of the theory.

Restricted clauses and formulas represent the syntactic characterization of ITDB's. It is interesting, at this point, to discuss the expressive power of such theories from a semantical perspective. We shall consider in turn the different kinds of axioms that can be specified in an ITDB and provide a semantic characterization of each of them.

Let's start with the universally quantified axioms. In the general form, an axiom of this kind is constituted by the universal quantifier followed by a conjunction of clauses whose argument is the quantified variable x. For our analysis, it is sufficient to consider the case in which only one clause appears in the formula:

$$\forall x(\neg P_1(x) \vee P_2(x) \vee \cdots \vee P_n(x))$$

The above formula expresses a covering relationship between the type P_1 and the types $P_2,\ldots,P_n$: in fact, in all of its models, every instance of P_1 is also an instance of at least one of $P_2,\ldots,P_n$. From this observation, it should be easy to verify that the is-a relationship is a special case of the covering relationship, namely the one in which the involved predicates are just two.

Another special case of a universally quantified axiom occurs when no negative literal appears in the clause. In this case, the axiom represent a general indefinite assertion, which can be used to formally express that all the represented objects are contained in the union of a collection of classes. Finally, a universally quantified axiom without positive literals asserts that a certain class cannot have instances.

Let's now consider the case in which the axioms are expressed as ground formulas. Again, it suffices to consider formulas that are constituted by a single clause. The general form is:

$$\neg P_1(c) \vee P_2(c) \vee \cdots \vee P_n(c)$$

where c is a constant symbol. An axiom of this kind expresses a conditional assertion on the object represented by c. Such an assertion states that if c is an instance of P_1, then it is an instance of at least one of $P_2,\ldots,P_n$. For example, the formula:

$$\neg \text{Student(Robert)} \vee \text{MusicStudent(Robert)} \vee \text{PhilosophyStudent(Robert)}$$

can be used to represent a conditional assertion on Robert, namely that if he is a student, then he is a student in Music or in Philosophy. It is easy to see that if no positive literals appear in the clause, then the axiom expresses a negative assertion on the object c, namely that it is not an instance of a given class. On the other hand, if the clause doesn't contain the negative literal, then the axiom expresses either a positive indefinite assertion (if $n>1$), or a positive definite assertion (if $n=1$).

The last case we consider is when the axiom is expressed as an existentially quantified formula. The general form of this type of axioms is:

$$\exists x(\rho_1(x) \wedge \rho_2(x) \wedge \cdots \wedge \rho_n(x))$$

where each ρ_i is a restricted clause. These kinds of axioms can be used to specify that a collection of classes are *not* related by means of the covering relationship. For example, the formula:

$$\exists x(\mathrm{Tutor}(x) \wedge \neg \mathrm{PhdStudent}(x))$$

asserts that the class Tutor is not is-a related to the class Student, (i.e Tutor not-isa Student): in every model of the above formula there are instances of Tutor that are not instances of PhdStudent. Note that most knowledge representation languages do not provide modeling features for this type of information.

To complete our discussion on the expressiveness of ITDB's, we now mention the types of assertions that cannot be represented in these theories. There are two types of assertions that cannot be expressed in an ITDB. First, one cannot express covering relationships holding between the intersection of a collection of classes and a number of other classes. Second, indefinite negative assertions are not allowed: one cannot assert that two or more classes are mutually disjoint or that a certain object cannot simultaneously be an instance of a given collection of classes. For example, the fact that nobody is both a graduate and an undergraduate student cannot be represented in an ITDB.

The interest reader is referred to [6] for an extended discussion on the expressive power of type data bases and their complexity. Here it is worth noting that even a simple enhancement of ITDB's results in a dramatical increase of their complexity. For example, in [4] it is shown that if disjointness assertions between two classes are allowed in type data bases with incomplete information, the problem of satisfiability checking becomes NP-complete.

As we said in section 1, one of the major concerns of our work is to develop a method for checking the satisfiability of ITDB's. Recall that a theory is said to be *satisfiable* if and only if there exists an interpretation satisfying all of its axioms. Our method for checking the satisfiability of type data bases is based on the clausal form of logic. In the following, we call *Skolem ITDB* (S-ITDB) any first order theory whose predicate symbols are unary, and whose set of axioms is constituted by restricted clauses, which are either ground or universally quantified. In [5] we present a method for transforming any ITDB T into a Skolem ITDB (called the Skolemization of T, and denoted by T^{Σ}), such that T is satisfiable if and only if T^{Σ} is satisfiable. In the next section we present a method for checking the satisfiability of S-ITDB's. The above observation guarantees that such a method can be used for checking the satisfiability of any ITDB.

3. Checking for Satisfiability

The goal of this section is to present a method for checking the satisfiability of type data bases with incomplete information. The method requires an ITDB to be represented by means of a graph and is based on an algorithm that detects particular paths, called composite paths, in such a graph.

To prove the correctness of our algorithm, we first show that there is a special form of resolution, called negative unit resolution, that is sound and complete for ITDB's, and then we prove that an ITDB has a negative unit refutation (i.e. a derivation of the empty clause obtained by repeated application of negative unit resolution steps) if and only if the associated graph contains at least one composite path.

Unit resolution ([2]) is a particular form of resolution, requiring every resolution step to be applied to at least one unit clause, i.e. a clause containing only one literal. A *negative unit resolution* is a resolution step in which one of the two parent clauses contains just one negative literal.

Theorem 1 *An S-ITDB S is unsatisfiable if and only if there is a negative unit refutation of S.*

We now show how any S-ITDB S can be represented by means of a graph G^S, such that there is a negative unit refutation of S if and only if G^S contains a particular composite path.

Definition 2 *Let S be an S-ITDB. The associated graph G^S is a directed graph $<V,A>$, where:*

- *the set of nodes V is partitioned into two subsets, the P-nodes and the O-nodes. In particular, there is one P-node for each unary predicate symbol of S, and there is one O-node for each clause of S containing two or more positive literals. Moreover, the set of P-nodes include two distinguished nodes, N and Y.*
- *A is the set of arcs, labeled with the constant or variable symbols of S. For each clause $(\neg Q(w))$ in S, there is an arc $<N,Q>$ labeled with w in A. For each clause $(\neg Q(w) \vee P(w))$ in S, there is an arc $<P,Q>$ labeled with w in A. For each clause $(\neg Q(w) \vee P_1(w) \vee \cdots \vee P_n(w))$ in S, associated with the O-node M, there are arcs $<P_1,M>,\ldots,<P_n,M>,<M,Q>$, labeled with w in A. For each clause $(P_1(w) \vee \cdots \vee P_n(w))$ in S associated with the O-node M, there are arcs $<P_1,M>,\ldots,<P_n,M>,<M,Y>$, labeled with w in A. For each clause $(P(w))$ in S, there is an arc $<P,Y>$ labeled with w in A.*

In the following, any graph associated with an S-IDTB is called an S-graph. We are now in the position to define the concept of composite path in S-graphs.

Definition 3 *Let $G=<V,A>$ be an S-graph. Let θ be an element of the set of labels of G. A composite θ-path from $\{B_1,\ldots,B_n\}$ to C is an acyclic subgraph $G'=<V',A'>$ of G such that:*

- $\{B_1,\ldots,B_n,C\} \subseteq V'$
- *for each node $M \in V'$, there is a path from at least one B_i to M and a path from M to C; moreover, if M is an O-node, then all the predecessors of M in G appear also in G'*
- *every arc in A' is labeled with either x or θ.*

In the next theorem we show that there is a strong correspondence between negative unit refutations of an S-ITDB and particular composite paths in the associated graph.

Theorem 2 *Let S be an S-ITDB. Then S is unsatisfiable if and only if there is a constant symbol θ of S such that G^S contains a composite θ-path from $\{N\}$ to Y.*

```
Algorithm composite-path(G,θ,{B1,...,Bn},A)
Input S-graph G, label θ, a set of nodes {B1,...,Bn} of G, and a single node A of G
Output true, if there exists a composite θ-path from {B1,...,Bn} to A in G
        false otherwise
begin
  if n > 1
  then return(V_{i=1}^{n} composite-path(G,θ,{Bi},A))
  else if B1 is a P-node and it is marked
       then return(false)
       else begin
              mark B1
              if B1 = A
              then return(true)
              else if B1 is an O-node and some of its predecessors is not marked
                   then return(false)
                   else let S1,...,Sm be the θ-successors of B1 in G
                        in return(composite-path(G,θ,{S1,...,Sm},A))
            end
end
```

Figure 1: Algorithm *composite-path*

In figure 1 we present an algorithm that checks for the existence of a composite θ-path from nodes $\{B_1,\ldots,B_n\}$ to node A in an S-graph. Such an algorithm is the basis of our method for checking the unsatisfiability of an ITDB. Given an ITDB T, we produce the Skolemization T^{Σ}

of T, then we build the S-graph associated with T^{Σ}, and finally we check whether such a graph contains a composite c-path from {N} to Y, for some constant symbol c of T^{Σ}.

As far as efficiency issues are concerned, a precise analysis of the complexity of the proposed method is beyond the scope of this paper. However, one can notice that the above procedure is clearly polynomial in the size of the ITDB T. If n is the number of constant symbols of T, p the number of its existentially quantified axioms and m the total size of T, then one can estimate the complexity of the whole method to be $O((n+p) \cdot m)$.

4. Query Answering

In this section we apply the results presented in section 3 to the problem of query answering. In particular, we describe a function ASK that, given any ITDB T and any query expressed by means of a formula α, provides the answer to α. In order to show how such a function works, it is necessary to distinguish the case in which the query is expressed as a closed formula from the one in which it is expressed as an open formula. Suppose α is a closed formula. Then the result of applying the function ASK to T and α is:

$$\mathrm{ASK}(T, \alpha) = \begin{cases} \textit{yes} & \text{if } T \models \alpha \\ \textit{no} & \text{if } T \models \neg\alpha \\ \textit{unknown} & \text{otherwise} \end{cases}$$

In other words, the query is interpreted as a question of the type: "Assuming that all the assertions represented by T are true, is it true that α?". The answer will be *yes* if α is implied by the theory T, i.e. it is true in all the interpretations that can be attached to T. The answer will be *no* if the negation of α is implied by T, i.e. α is false in all the interpretation of T. Finally, the answer will be *unkown* if neither α nor its negation is implied by the theory, i.e. there are some interpretations of T in which α is true and others in which α is false.

On the other hand, suppose $\alpha(x)$ is an open formula. Let $\{c_1, \ldots, c_k\}$ are the constant symbols of T. The result of applying ASK to T and α is:

$$\mathrm{ASK}(T, \alpha(x)) = \{c \in \{c_1, \ldots, c_k\} \mid T \models \alpha(x/c)\}$$

where $\alpha(x/c)$ denotes the formula obtained from $\alpha(x)$ by substituting every occurrence of x with c. In this case the query is interpreted as a question of the type: "Assuming that all the assertions represented by T are true, which are the objects that satisfy condition α?". The answer will be constituted by a set of constant symbols; in particular, it will include every constant c such that the condition α, when specialized for c, is implied by the theory.

In the following, we show how the function ASK can be correctly and efficiently designed. We impose only one limitation on the form of the query α, namely it must be a single-argument formula. In other words, while the axioms of T are restricted formulas, the query α is a conjunction of single-argument clauses which may contain any number of negative literals.

We now analyze different situations that may arise, depending on the form of the query.

The first case we consider is the one in which queries are expressed as open formulas. Consider an open formula $\alpha(x)$. In order to compute the correct value of ASK(T, $\alpha(x)$), we simply consider in turn every constant symbol c of T and compute the value of ASK(T, $\alpha(x/c)$): c will be included in the answer to $\alpha(x)$ if and only if ASK(T, $\alpha(x/c)$)=*yes*. Note that $\alpha(x/c)$ is a ground formula.

Let's now analyse the case of ground queries. In particular, c onsider the problem of computing the correct value of ASK(T, $\gamma_1(c) \wedge \cdots \wedge \gamma_m(c)$). From well known results in first order logic, it follows that ASK(T, $\gamma_1(c) \wedge \cdots \wedge \gamma_m(c)$)=*yes* if and only if for each i ($1 \leq i \leq m$), ASK(T, $\gamma_i(c)$)=*yes*. Since $T \models \gamma_i(c)$ if and only if $T \bigcup \{\neg\gamma_i(c)\}$ is unsatisfiable, our problem is reduced to checking the unsatisfiability of $T_i = T \bigcup \{\neg\gamma_i(c)\}$, for each i ($1 \leq i \leq m$). Since every T_i is an ITDB, *yes*-answers to ground queries can be efficiently computed by applying the method described in section 3.

With regard to the *no*-answers, note that ASK(T, $\gamma_1(c) \wedge \cdots \wedge \gamma_m(c)$)=*no* if and only if ASK(T, $\neg\gamma_1(c) \vee \cdots \vee \neg\gamma_m(c)$)=*yes*. The query is now expressed as a formula in disjunctive normal form. Therefore, in order to reduce our problem to the case of *yes*-answer, we need to transform the formula into conjunctive normal form. Such a transformation could be costly, resulting in a substantial increase of the complexity of query answering. Notice, however, that such an increase depends only on the size of the query, and not on the size of T. Also, there are cases in which the complexity is not affected at all by the transformation. For example, this is the case when the original query is constituted by a single clause, or when every γ_i is a restricted clause. In the latter case, since $T \bigcup \{\gamma_1(c) \wedge \cdots \wedge \gamma_m(c)\}$ is an ITDB, we can simply check whether $T \bigcup \{\gamma_1(c) \wedge \cdots \wedge \gamma_m(c)\}$ is unsatisfiable: $ASK(T, \gamma_1(c) \wedge \cdots \wedge \gamma_m(c))=no$ if and only if $T \bigcup \{\gamma_1(c) \wedge \cdots \wedge \gamma_m(c)\}$ is unsatisfiable.

The case in which the queries are expressed as universally quantified formulas is analogous to the case of ground queries. It can be easily verified that $ASK(T, \forall x(\gamma_1(x) \wedge \cdots \wedge \gamma_m(x)))=yes$ if and only if for each i ($1 \leq i \leq m$), $T_i = T \bigcup \{\exists x(\neg\gamma_i(x))\}$ is unsatisfiable. Since every T_i is an ITDB, we have reduced the problem of *yes*-answers to one of checking the unsatisfiability of a number of ITDB's. Once again, we can successfully apply the method presented in section 3.

The above observation ensures us that we have an efficient method for computing several types of meaningful inferences on ITDB's. For example, testing whether the covering relationship between P_1 and $P_2 \ldots P_n$ is implied by the axioms of T, can be performed by checking whether $ASK(T, \forall x(\neg P_1(x) \vee P_2(x) \vee \cdots \vee P_n(x)))=yes$. It follows that we have an efficient method for computing all the is-a relationships that are implied by an ITDB. This, in turn, allows us to check whether two classes are equivalent, i.e. whether their extensions are the same in all the models of the knowledge base: two classes P and Q are equivalent if and only if $ASK(T, \forall x((\neg P(x) \vee Q(x)) \wedge (\neg Q \vee P(x))))=yes$. Analogously, we can test in polynomial time whether a certain class of T is invariably empty: the extension of a class P is empty in all the models of T if and only if $ASK(T, \forall x(\neg P(x))=yes$. Finally, we can check whether there exists a universal class, i.e. a class whose extension include all the objects of the type data base: a class P is a universal class if and only if $ASK(T, \forall x(P(x)))=yes$.

Turning our attention to the problem of computing the *no*-answers to universally quantified queries, note that $ASK(T, \forall x(\gamma_1(x) \wedge \cdots \wedge \gamma_m(x)))=no$ if and only if $ASK(T, \exists x(\neg\gamma_1(x) \vee \cdots \vee \neg\gamma_m(x))=yes$. The query is now in disjunctive normal form and includes an existential quantifier. It is easy to see that, in order to reduce our problem to the one of computing *yes*-answers to $\exists$-queries, we need to perform a syntactic transformation on the original $\forall$-query, which, as in the case of ground queries, can be costly.

The last case to consider is the one in which queries are expressed as existentially quantified formulas. Consider the problem of checking if $ASK(T, \exists x(\gamma_1(x) \wedge \cdots \wedge \gamma_m(x)))=yes$. The following theorem provides a method for solving such a problem.

Theorem 3 *Let T be an ITDB and let $\gamma_1, \ldots, \gamma_m$ be m clauses. Then $ASK(T, \exists x(\gamma_1(x) \wedge \cdots \wedge \gamma_m(x)))=yes$ if and only if $ASK(T^{\Sigma}, \gamma_1(x) \wedge \cdots \wedge \gamma_m(x)) \neq \emptyset$.*

The above result implies that we have an efficient method for computing other interesting inferences on the classes of the knowledge base. Two examples will motivate this observation. Suppose we want to know whether two classes have a non-empty intersection. It is easy to see that the extensions of P and Q have common elements if and only if $ASK(T, \exists x(P(x) \wedge Q(x)))=yes$. Analogously, the class P is *not* is-a related with the classes Q if and only if $ASK(T, \exists x(P(x) \wedge \neg Q(x)))=yes$.

With regard to the no-answers, note that $ASK(T, \exists x(\gamma_1(x) \wedge \cdots \wedge \gamma_m(x)))=no$ if and only if $ASK(T, \forall x(\neg\gamma_1(x) \vee \cdots \vee \neg\gamma_m(x))=yes$. Again, dealing with *no*-answers requires, in general, a syntactic transformation of the query.

5. Conclusions and Future Research

In section 4 we have shown how to use the algorithm for satisfiability checking in order to devise a sound and complete method for query answering in ITDB's. It is worth noting that the algorithm presented in section 3 can also be used for implementing a simple method for update management. Such a method fulfills what can be considered a minimal requirement, namely it ensures that the theory resulting from an update is consistent. Moreover, it allows both facts and general assertions to be inserted and deleted, coherently with the spirit of considering the type data base as a body of knowledge about a collection of objects, where assertions regarding the interdependencies among classes and those concerning the corresponding instances have the same dignity. Let's discuss the important case of insertion updates. Suppose we want to add new knowledge to an ITDB T and such a knowledge is expressed by means of a formula α. Since α can be inconsistent with T, a preliminary consistency check is needed on $T'=T \bigcup \{\alpha\}$. If T' is satisfiable, then it can be indeed considered as the result of the update; if it is unsatisfiable, then the update should be rejected. Note that such simple method allows us to construct consistent type data bases incrementally.

In the future, we aim at extending our work by eliminating some of the restrictions of ITDBs, such as the one imposing the axioms to be expressed in terms of single-argument formulas.

Also, we shall investigate the problem of integrating the presented techniques into existing data base and knowledge representation systems. Such an integration should be based on the design of a suitable module that efficiently reasons about the type data base and exchanges information with the rest of the system.

Finally, we aim at devising a more intelligent and flexible management of updates, based on a mechanism of assertion and retraction of formulas (see [3]) . For example, when a formula α is inserted into a theory T, and such a formula is inconsistent with T, one may want the system to automatically retract the minimal set S of axioms such that $(T\text{-}S) \bigcup \{\alpha\}$ is consistent. On the other hand, one may want the deletion of α from T to result in a theory that doesn't imply α; note in general this is not achieved by the syntactic elimination of α from T.

We believe that improvements of this kind are particularly appealing for type data bases, where the resulting increase of the complexity of the update algorithm could be much less severe than in the case of general first order theories.

References

[1] Atzeni P., and Parker, D.S., "Set Containment Inference", *Proc. of the International Conference on Database Theory*, Roma, Italy, 1986.

[2] Chang C.L., and Lee R.C.T., *Symbolic Logic and Mechanical Theorem Proving*, Academic Press, New York, 1973.

[3] Fagin R., Ullman J.D., and Vardi M.Y., "On the Semantics of Updates in Databases", *Proc. of the 2nd Symp. on the Principles of Database Systems*, 1983, pp. 352-365.

[4] Lenzerini M., "Covering and Disjointness Constraints in Type Networks", *Proc. of the Third IEEE International Conference on Data Engineering*, Los Angeles, California, February 1987.

[5] Lenzerini M., "Type Data Bases with Incomplete Information", Technical Report, Università di Roma "La Sapienza", Dipartimento di Informatica e Sistemistica, 1987.

[6] Lenzerini M., "Type Data Bases and Their Complexity", Technical Report, Università di Roma "La Sapienza", Dipartimento di Informatica e Sistemistica, To appear.

[7] McSkimin J.R., and Minker J., "A Predicate Calculus Based Semantic Network for Deductive Searching", in Findler N.V. (ed.), *Associative Networks: Representation and Use of Knowledge by Computers*, Academic Press, New York, 1979.

[8] Reiter R., "Deductive Question-Answering on Relational Data Bases", in Gallaire H., and Minker J. (eds.), *Logic and Databases*, Plenum Press, New York, 1978.

[9] Reiter R., "Towards a Logical Reconstruction of Relational Database Theory", in Brodie M.L, Mylopoulos J., and Schmidt J.W. (eds.), *On Conceptual Modelling*, Springer-Verlag New York Inc., 1984.

APPLYING AN EXTENDED RELATIONAL MODEL TO INDEFINITE DEDUCTIVE DATABASES

Ken-Chih Liu and Rajshekhar Sunderraman
Computer Science Department
Iowa State University
Ames, Iowa 50011

ABSTRACT

This paper presents an application of an extended relational algebra to a subclass of indefinite/non-Horn deductive databases. The semantics of the extended algebraic operators are consistent with the concept of "minimal models" of indefinite databases. Query processing involves manipulating the extended relations using the algebraic operators and answers to queries contain definite, indefinite, and "maybe" information. One of the algebraic operators, match-union, is used to combine the extended relations produced as a result of the application of recursive/non-recursive non-Horn rules.

1. INTRODUCTION

Deductive databases ([3], [4], [5]) are capable of deducing new facts from known facts and rules. Reiter ([13]) introduces two approaches to deductive databases : the model-theoretic approach, in which the database is viewed as a first-order interpretation and the proof-theoretic approach, in which the database is viewed as a first-order theory. The proof-theoretic approach is more general as any set of sentences may constitute a database. However, the only way to answer queries is to use an automated theorem prover, which can prove drastically inefficient for large databases. Although the model-theoretic approach is not general enough, the major advantage lies in the evaluation of queries with respect to the database. The algebraic approach can compute all the answers 'at once' (see [7]). The disadvantages, however, are the difficulties in expressing and manipulating disjunctive, recursive, and implicit information. In this paper, we provide a mechanism to express and manipulate some of these kinds of information in the model-theoretic approach. In [10], we introduced an extension to the relational model ([2]) for indefinite databases. Here, we apply the extended relational model to a subclass of non-Horn deductive databases (the predicate symbols in the positive literals of the clause are restricted to be the same).

Section 2 presents necessary background material on deductive databases and the extended relational model. Section 3 defines an additional algebraic operator , called the match-union operator, which is used in evaluating derived relations in indefinite deductive databases. Section 4 presents the algebraic approach to query processing in indefinite deductive databases. Recursive axioms are handled by iteration.

2. BACKGROUND INFORMATION

In this section, we present background material on deductive databases and the extended relational model for indefinite databases. For details on deductive databases, see [6]. The extended relational model for indefinite databases is defined in [10].

2.1 Deductive Databases

A deductive database is a database in which new facts may be derived from facts that were explicitly introduced. In general, a deductive database consists of a set of first-order clauses without function symbols. An *atomic formula* is of the form $P(x_1, \cdots, x_n)$, where P is a predicate symbol and the arguments to the predicate, $x_1, \cdots, x_n$, are either constant symbols or variable symbols. The general form of the clauses that can represent both facts and deduction laws is :

$$P_1, \cdots, P_k \leftarrow Q_1, \cdots, Q_l$$

where the P_is and the Q_is are atomic formulae. The P_is are called the *positive literals* and the Q_is are called the *negative literals*. An *indefinite deductive database* consists of clauses with one or more positive literals.

Methodologies for Intelligent Systems
Z. W. Ras and M. Zemankova, Editors

2.2 Extended Relational Model

The relational model is extended to include mechanisms to store and manipulate disjunctive information, also referred to as indefinite data, and information that may or may not be true. The extended relation, also referred to as an *I-table* , (I stands for Indefinite) consists of three components - definite, indefinite, and maybe. Let R be an I-table defined over the domains $D_1, \cdots ,D_n$. Then R = $< R_D ,R_I ,R_M >$ is defined as follows :

$$R_D \subseteq D_1 \times D_2 \times \cdots \times D_n ,\ R_I \subseteq 2^{D_1 \times D_2 \times \cdots \times D_n} ,\ \text{and } R_M \subseteq D_1 \times D_2 \times \cdots \times D_n .$$

The cardinality of each element of R_I is restricted to be at least 2. The elements of R_I are called *tuple sets.* R_D is the definite component, R_I is the indefinite component, and R_M is the maybe component of the I-table R. An *I-database* is a finite collection of I-tables.

Example : Consider the I-table, BG, which stores information about the bloodgroups of individuals. The table in Figure 2.1 is an instance of the I-table BG :

BG

Doug	A
Gary	B
Tom	A
Tom	O
John	A
Mary	A
Mary	B
Mike	O
James	A
James	B

Figure 2.1 An I-table - Bloodgroup

Here, the two tuples in the definite component state that the bloodgroup of Doug is A and that of Gary is B, the two tuple sets in the indefinite component state that the bloodgroup of Tom is either A or O and either the bloodgroup of John is A or the bloodgroup of Mary is A or B, and the three tuples in the maybe component state that the bloodgroup of Mike may be O, that of James may be A and that of James may be B.

Non-redundant Databases

There is no duplication of tuples or tuple sets within each component of an I-table as each of the components is defined to be a set. In order to keep "better" and "precise" information and to avoid update anomalies, duplication/redundancy of information across the three components of an I-table must be avoided. We have identified four kinds of redundancies across the components. First, a tuple present in the definite component and also in a tuple set of the indefinite component is considered redundant information. This redundancy is removed by deleting the tuple set from the indefinite component and including in the maybe component all those tuples in the tuple set except for the tuple from the definite component. Second, a tuple present in the definite component and also in the maybe component is considered redundant information. This redundancy is removed by deleting the tuple from the maybe component. Third, a tuple present in a tuple set of the indefinite component and also in the maybe component is considered redundant information. This redundancy is also removed by deleting the tuple from the maybe component. Fourth, a tuple set, u, that is a proper superset of another tuple set, v, is considered redundant. This redundancy is removed by deleting u and including in the maybe component all the tuples in u - v. We restrict all the I-tables to be non-redundant. We have defined an operator, called REDUCE, which removes the redundancy in an I-table as described above.

Extended Relational Algebra

The relational algebraic operators are extended to operate on I-tables. All these operators are defined in such a way as not to introduce redundancies. For the purposes of this paper, we describe only cartesian product, projection, and selection. Other operators are discussed in detail in [10].

Cartesian product: The cartesian product of two I-tables, R and S is denoted by T = R × S and is illustrated via an example. Consider the two I-tables in Figure 2.2. The definite component, T_D, of the cartesian product is obtained by taking the cartesian product of R_D with S_D. The indefinite component, T_I, is arrived at as follows : The two disjuncts in the single tuple set of R_I combined with the two definite tuples of S_D gives us the disjunctive formula [T(s2,p2,p1,red) and T(s2,p2,p2,blue)] or [T(s3,p3,p1,red) and T(s3,p3,p2,blue)]. Converting this formula into a conjunction of disjunctions we obtain the four tuple sets : {T(s2,p2,p1,red) , T(s3,p3,p1,red)} , {T(s2,p2,p1,red) , T(s3,p3,p2,blue)} , {T(s2,p2,p2,blue) , T(s3,p3,p1,red)} , {T(s2,p2,p2,blue) , T(s3,p3,p2,blue)}. The maybe component, T_M, is obtained by taking the cartesian product of R_D with S_M, each tuple set of R_I with S_M, R_M with S_M, R_M with S_D, and R_M with each tuple set of S_I. Using the above method we obtain the cartesian product in Figure 2.2.

R

s1	p1
s2	p2
s3	p3
s4	p4

S

p1	red
p2	blue
p3	red

T = R × S

s1	p1	p1	red
s1	p1	p2	blue
s2	p2	p1	red
s3	p3	p1	red
s2	p2	p1	red
s3	p3	p2	blue
s2	p2	p2	blue
s3	p3	p1	red
s2	p2	p2	blue
s3	p3	p2	blue
s1	p1	p3	red
s2	p2	p3	red
s3	p3	p3	red
s4	p4	p3	red
s4	p4	p1	red
s4	p4	p2	blue

Figure 2.2 : Cartesian Product

Projection: The extended projection is quite similar to the regular projection. Some tuples may migrate from the indefinite component to the definite component as a result of the projection operation. These are the tuple sets of the indefinite component all of whose tuples have the same value for the projected attributes. An example is given in Figure 2.3.

Selection: The definite and maybe tuples that satisfy the selection condition are included in the corresponding components of the extended selection. If all the tuples of a tuple set of the indefinite component satisfy the selection condition then the tuple set is included in the indefinite component of the selection. Otherwise, only those tuples in the tuple set that satisfy the selection condition are included in the maybe component of the selection. Figure 2.4 shows an example of the selection.

Remark : Since an I-database is interpreted as representing all the minimal models of the relational theory, the equality

$$\sigma_{F_1 \text{ or } F_2}(R) = \sigma_{F_1}(R) \cup \sigma_{F_2}(R)$$

does not hold any more. One has to be careful in using the extended selection operator. This observation has been made in [9].

R

s1	p1	p1	red
s1	p1	p2	red
s2	p2	p3	green
s2	p2	p3	blue
s2	p2	p3	green
s3	p3	p4	green
s3	p3	p4	red
s1	p1	p5	blue
s1	p4	p6	blue
s4	p5	p7	green
s4	p6	p8	blue
s4	p6	p9	red
s5	p5	p5	green
s1	p1	p6	red

$\Pi_{1,2}(R)$

s1	p1
s2	p2
s3	p3
s4	p5
s4	p6
s5	p5
s1	p4

Figure 2.3 : Projection

R

s1	p1
s2	p2
s3	p3
s1	p4
s4	p1
s4	p2
s5	p1
s6	p2
s7	p1
s8	p3
s9	p3
s10	p4
s11	p4
s12	p1
s13	p9
s14	p2
s15	p8

$\sigma_{(2='p1') \text{ or } (2='p2')}(R)$

s1	p1
s2	p2
s4	p1
s4	p2
s5	p1
s6	p2
s7	p1
s12	p1
s14	p2

Figure 2.4 : Selection

Semantics of I-tables and Extended Operators

An I-table can be viewed as representing the set of minimal models ([12]) of the "underlying first-order theory" ([13]) and a set of maybe tuples. Consider the I-table in Figure 2.5 (a). Tables T_1, T_2, T_3, and T_4 in Figure 2.5 (b) represent the minimal models that correspond to T and T_M in Figure 2.5 (b) is the set of maybe tuples of T.

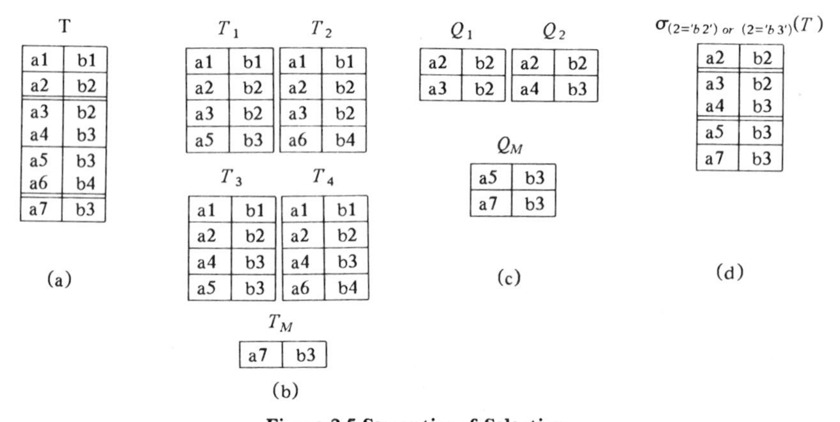

(a) T

a1	b1
a2	b2
a3	b2
a4	b3
a5	b3
a6	b4
a7	b3

(b) T_1

a1	b1
a2	b2
a3	b2
a5	b3

T_2

a1	b1
a2	b2
a3	b2
a6	b4

T_3

a1	b1
a2	b2
a4	b3
a5	b3

T_4

a1	b1
a2	b2
a4	b3
a6	b4

T_M

a7	b3

(c) Q_1

a2	b2
a3	b2

Q_2

a2	b2
a4	b3

Q_M

a5	b3
a7	b3

(d) $\sigma_{(2='b2') \text{ or } (2='b3')}(T)$

a2	b2
a3	b2
a4	b3
a5	b3
a7	b3

Figure 2.5 Semantics of Selection

The semantics of the extended algebraic operators is based on the following idea : For each operator, we consider the contribution of the operands to the minimal models. The operator is then applied to the minimal models to obtain a new set of minimal models. Finally, the result of the extended operator is obtained from this new set of minimal models. We choose the selection operator to illustrate this idea. Consider the selection $\sigma_{(2='b2') \text{ or } (2='b3')}(T)$, where T is the I-table in Figure 2.5 (a). Applying the selection to T_1, T_2, T_3, T_4, and T_M of Figure 2.5 (b) and eliminating non-minimal models, we obtain Q_1, Q_2, and Q_M of Figure 2.5 (c). Note that the tuple <a5,b3> is moved to the set of maybe tuples during the elimination of non-minimal models. Figure 2.5 (d) shows the result of the selection.

3. THE MATCH-UNION OPERATOR

In this section, we define an algebraic operator, called match-union. This operator will be used, in Section 4, to evaluate I-tables defined by a certain subclass of non-Horn rules. The motivation behind match-union is discussed now. Consider the non-Horn rule :

$$P(X_1), \cdots, P(X_k) \leftarrow Q_1, \cdots, Q_l$$

where X_i is a list of arguments (constant/variable symbols). We shall view this rule as defining the I-table, R, that corresponds to the predicate symbol P. To evaluate R, we first compute I-tables, $R_1, \cdots, R_k$, that correspond to the positive literals $P(X_1), \cdots, P(X_k)$ respectively. This is accomplished by the extended relational algebra. In order to handle the disjunction of the positive literals, the match-union operator "combines" *(unions)* tuples/tuple sets from each of the R_is based on the arguments *(patterns)* $X_1, \cdots, X_k$ to obtain R. If one tuple/tuple set from each of the I-tables $R_1, \cdots, R_k$ "match" the patterns $X_1, \cdots, X_k$, then the "union" of these tuples/tuple sets forms a tuple/tuple set of R. To formally define match-union, we need the following definition :

Definition: A *pattern*, p, is an ordered set $<t_1, \cdots, t_n>$, where each of the t_is is either a variable symbol or a constant symbol. A *ground substitution* is an assignment of constant symbols to variable symbols. Only one constant symbol is assigned to any given variable symbol. It is convenient to represent a ground substitution as a collection of independent substitution components : $\{x_1 \leftarrow c_1, \cdots, x_m \leftarrow c_m\}$. Each component, $x_i \leftarrow c_i$, of the ground substitution assigns a constant c_i to a variable x_i. A ground substitution is said to be *applicable to a pattern* p, if it has assignments for all the variable symbols of p. The *result of applying* an applicable ground substitution, σ, to a pattern, p, is a tuple denoted by pσ, which is just like p except that, all the variable symbols x_i of p are replaced by c_i, where $x_i \leftarrow c_i$ is a component of the ground substitution σ. Tuples $t_1, \cdots, t_n$ *match* patterns $p_1, \cdots, p_n$, written as $<t_1, \cdots, t_n>$ match $<p_1, \cdots, p_n>$, iff we can find a ground substitution, σ, which is applicable to all the patterns $p_1, \cdots, p_n$, such that $p_i \sigma = t_i$, $1 \leqslant i \leqslant n$.

Example: p = < John,250,x,y,10> is a pattern, where x and y are variable symbols and John, 250, and 10 are constant symbols. Let σ = {x ← Tom, y ← Red, z ← Green}. Then pσ = < John,250,Tom,Red,10>. Let t_1 = < John,25,A>, t_2 = < John,25,B>, and p_1 = < x,y,u>, p_2 = < x,y,v>. Here $<t_1,t_2>$ match $<p_1,p_2>$ because we can find a ground substitution σ = {x ← John, y ← 25, u ← A, v ← B} such that $p_1\sigma = t_1$ and $p_2\sigma = t_2$.

The match-union operator is denoted by the $\cup_p$, where p is an ordered set of patterns.

Remark : As a matter of convenience, we shall assume that the definite and the maybe components of an I-table contain singleton sets consisting of the tuples instead of the tuples themselves. This assumption is made only for defining the match-union operator.

Definition: Let $R_1, \cdots, R_n$ be n domain-compatible I-tables and let $p_1, \cdots, p_n$ be n patterns. Then, $\cup_{<p_1, \cdots, p_n>}(R_1, \cdots, R_n)$ = REDUCE(T) , where T is :

$$T_D = \{ t \mid t \in R_D^1 \text{ and } \cdots \text{ and } t \in R_D^k \}$$

$$T_I = \{ t \mid (\exists u_1) \ldots (\exists u_k)(u_1 \in R_X^1 \text{ and } \cdots u_k \in R_X^k \text{ and}$$

$$(\forall i)(1 \leqslant i \leqslant k \rightarrow (\forall t)(t \in u_i \rightarrow$$

$$(\exists t_1) \ldots (\exists t_{i-1})(\exists t_{i+1}) \ldots (\exists t_k)(t_1 \in u_1 \text{ and } \cdots \text{ and } t_{i-1} \in u_{i-1} \text{ and}$$

$$t_{i+1} \in u_{i+1} \text{ and } \cdots \text{ and } t_k \in u_k$$

$$\text{and } <t_1, \cdots, t_{i-1}, t, t_{i+1}, \cdots, t_k> \textit{matches} <p_1, \cdots, p_k>))) \text{ and } t = u_1 \cup \cdots \cup u_k)\}$$

where R_X^i is either R_D^i or R_I^i.

The definition of T_M is not presented here as it is quite cumbersome. The details are presented in [11]. In any case, T_M is not very pertinent to the discussion that follows.

Example : Figure 3.1 shows an example of the match-union operator.

R_1

Don	A
Tom	A
Gary	B
David	A
David	O
Craig	A
Craig	O
John	A
Mary	B
Liz	B

R_2

Don	A
Tom	B
David	B
Craig	A
Craig	B
John	A
John	O
Liz	A

$\cup_{<<x,u>,<x,v>>}(R_1,R_2)$

Don	A
Tom	A
Tom	B
David	A
David	B
David	O
Craig	A
Craig	B
Craig	O
John	A
John	O
Liz	A
Liz	B

Figure 3.1 Match-union

4. QUERY PROCESSING IN INDEFINITE DEDUCTIVE DATABASES

Since we are viewing an indefinite database as a collection of minimal models, the equivalence P V Q → R iff P → R & Q → R may not hold. For instance, P may be true in some minimal models and Q may be true in the rest of the minimal models, making P V Q true in the database. However, P and Q individually may not be true in the database. As a consequence, we need to generalize a clause to be of the form :

$$P_1, \cdots ,P_k \leftarrow <Q_{11}, \cdots ,Q_{1n_1}>, \cdots ,<Q_{l1}, \cdots ,Q_{ln_l}> \qquad (1)$$

where P_is and Q_{ij}s are atomic formulae (We shall omit the angular brackets in cases where there is only one atomic formula within them.). We shall refer to this form as non-Horn rules from here on (Note that this is not a clause.). The non-Horn rule is equivalent to the following logical formula :

$$P_1 \vee \cdots \vee P_k \vee \neg(Q_{11} \vee \cdots \vee Q_{1n_1}) \vee \cdots \vee \neg(Q_{l1} \vee \cdots \vee Q_{ln_l}).$$

Each $<Q_{i1}, \cdots ,Q_{in_i}>$ is termed a *conjunct*. Queries take the form :

$$Answer \leftarrow <Q_{11}, \cdots ,Q_{1n_1}>, \cdots ,<Q_{l1}, \cdots ,Q_{ln_l}>$$

where *Answer* is an atomic formula.

We shall restrict the non-Horn rules to have only one predicate symbol in all their positive literals. We shall also restrict all atomic formulae within each conjunct to involve the same predicate symbol. The non-Horn rule in (1) can be viewed as representing the following Horn rules :

$$P_i \leftarrow Q_1, \cdots ,Q_l$$

where $1 \leqslant i \leqslant k$ and $Q_j \in \{ Q_{j1}, \cdots ,Q_{jn_j} \}$, $1 \leqslant j \leqslant l$. We shall say that the non-Horn rule, (1), is *range-restricted* if every Horn rule it represents is also range-restricted. We shall restrict all non-Horn rules to be range-restricted. For the purposes of this paper, we shall also place the following restriction on the non-Horn rule, (1) : For every P_i, $1 \leqslant i \leqslant k$, the variables of P_i occur in the same "positions" on the right hand sides of all the Horn rules, with P_i on its left hand side, represented by the non-Horn rule.

In this section, we illustrate how non-Horn rules defined above can be used to generate "new" I-tables. We show the use of the match-union operator to obtain the extensions of the I-tables defined by these rules. Queries can now be answered by using the extended relational algebra ([10]), since the extensions of all the "virtual" I-tables can be computed.

4.1 Obtaining algebraic expressions from rules

Associated with each non-Horn rule of the form $P_1, \cdots, P_k \leftarrow Q_1, \cdots, Q_l$, where the Q_i are conjuncts, are k algebraic expressions, one for each of the positive literals in the rule. The algebraic expressions corresponding to the positive literals are obtained in a straightforward manner as the following example illustrates.

Example : Consider the non-Horn rule :

$$P(x,y),\ P(x,z) \leftarrow Q(x,w),\ \langle R(w,y), R(w,z)\rangle,\ S(y,z)$$

where x,y,z, and w are all variable symbols. The algebraic expression corresponding to P(x,y) is :

$$E_1 = \Pi_{1,5}(\sigma_{((2=3)\text{ and }(4=5))\ or\ ((2=3))\text{ and }(4=6))}(Q \times R \times S))$$

and the algebraic expression corresponding to P(x,z) is :

$$E_2 = \Pi_{1,6}(\sigma_{((2=3)\text{ and }(4=5))\ or\ ((2=3)\text{ and }(4=6))}(Q \times R \times S))$$

The resulting I-tables, E_1 and E_2, will be used as arguments to the match-union operator as illustrated in the next two sub-sections.

4.2 Non-Recursive Indefinite Deductive Databases

Consider a non-recursive non-Horn rule :

$$P_1(X_1), \cdots, P_k(X_k) \leftarrow Q_1, \cdots, Q_l$$

and let the predicate symbols in all the positive literals be P. Here, the X_is are lists of arguments made up of constant and variable symbols, and the Q_is are conjuncts. Then, the I-table corresponding to the predicate P is obtained as follows :

Step 1: Using the method in Section 4.1, obtain algebraic expressions for each of the positive literals in the rule.

Step 2: Compute the I-tables corresponding to each of the algebraic expressions obtained in step 1. Call the I-tables obtained $R_1, \cdots, R_k$.

Step 3: The I-table corresponding to P is

$$R = \cup_{\langle p_1, \cdots, p_k\rangle}(R_1, \cdots, R_k)$$

where p_i is obtained from X_i, $1 \leqslant i \leqslant k$.

Example: Consider the non-Horn rule :

$$\text{Dept}(x,\text{Math}),\ \text{Dept}(x,\text{CS}) \leftarrow \langle \text{Teaches}(x,231),\ \text{Teaches}(x,331)\rangle$$

which states that if x teaches the course numbered 231 or 331 then x belongs to either the Math department or the CS department. Figure 4.1 shows the extensions of the TEACHES I-table.

The algebraic expression that corresponds to the literal Dept(x,Math) is :

$$R_1 = \Pi_{1,2}(\Pi_1(\sigma_{2='231'\ or\ 2='331'}(TEACHES)) \times R_{constant\ 1})$$

where $R_{constant\ 1D} = \{\langle Math \rangle\}$, $R_{constant\ 1I} = \emptyset$, and $R_{constant\ 1M} = \emptyset$, and the algebraic expression corresponding to the literal Dept(x,CS) is :

TEACHES

John	311
Tom	231
Gary	331
David	231
Kevin	231
Craig	231
Craig	331
Joe	231

Figure 4.1 I-table TEACHES

R_1

Tom	Math
Gary	Math
Craig	Math
David	Math
Kevin	Math
Joe	Math

R_2

Tom	CS
Gary	CS
Craig	CS
David	CS
Kevin	CS
Joe	CS

Figure 4.2 I-tables R_1 and R_2

DEPT

Tom	Math
Tom	CS
Gary	Math
Gary	CS
Craig	Math
Craig	CS
David	Math
David	CS
Kevin	Math
Kevin	CS
Joe	Math
Joe	CS

Figure 4.3 I-table DEPT

$$R_2 = \Pi_{1,2}(\Pi_1(\sigma_{2='231' \text{ or } 2='331'}(TEACHES)) \times R_{constant\ 2})$$

where $R_{constant\ 2D} = \{<CS>\}$, $R_{constant\ 2I} = \emptyset$, and $R_{constant\ 2M} = \emptyset$. Evaluating these expressions we obtain the I-tables in Figure 4.2. Taking the match-union of R_1 and R_2 with respect to the patterns $<$x,Math$>$ and $<$x,CS$>$, we obtain the extension of the I-table DEPT in Figure 4.3.

4.3 Recursive Indefinite Deductive Databases

Recursion is handled by repeated application of the match-union operator and the algebraic expressions associated with a non-Horn rule until no new tuples/ tuple sets are generated. This process is guaranteed to terminate as all the databases are finite. Consider the recursive non-Horn rule :

$$P_1, \cdots, P_k \leftarrow Q_1, \cdots, Q_l$$

where the predicate symbols in all the P_is are all the same (= P) and at least one of the conjuncts on the right hand side contain atomic formulae involving the predicate symbol P. Let R be the I-table that corresponds to the predicate symbol P and Q_i be the I-table that corresponds to the predicate symbols in conjunct Q_i. R is computed as follows :

BEGIN
  i := 0
  $R^{(0)} := R_{INIT}$
  $R^* := R_{INIT}$
  REPEAT
    $R_1 := f_1(R^{(*)}, Q_1, \cdots, Q_l)$
    $R_2 := f_2(R^{(*)}, Q_1, \cdots, Q_l)$
    . . .
    . . .
    . . .
    $R_k := f_k(R^{(*)}, Q_1, \cdots, Q_l)$
    $R^{(i+1)} := \cup_{<p_1, \cdots, p_k>}(R_1, \cdots, R_k)$
    $R^* := R^* \cup R^{(i+1)}$
    i := i + 1
  UNTIL (There are no changes to r^*)
  R := R^*
END

where $f_i(R^{(i)}, Q_1, \cdots, Q_l)$ represents the algebraic expression corresponding to P_i, $1 \leqslant i \leqslant k$, R_{INIT} is the initial instance of the I-table R, and $p_1, \cdots, p_k$ are the patterns obtained from the positive literals $P_1, \cdots, P_k$. R_{INIT} may be present in the database or may be generated using another non-Horn rule, possibly non-recursive.

Example : Consider the recursive non-Horn rule :

$$BG(x,y),\ BG(x,z) \leftarrow F(x,u),\ BG(u,y),\ M(x,v),\ BG(v,z)$$

where BG(x,y) stands for 'The bloodgroup of x is y', F(x,y) stands for 'y is the father of x', and M(x,y) stands for 'y is the mother of x'. Let the database instance be as shown in Figure 4.4.

F

John	David
David	Steve
Mary	Craig
Tom	Doug

M

John	Mary
David	Pam
Mary	Liz
Tom	Lucy

$BG^{(0)}$

Steve	A
Pam	B
Craig	A
Liz	O
Doug	O
Lucy	A

Figure 4.4 A database instance

$BG^{(1)}$

David	A
David	B
Mary	A
Mary	O
Tom	A
Tom	O

$BG^{(2)}$

John	A
John	B
John	O

Figure 4.5 I-tables $BG^{(1)}$ and $BG^{(2)}$

Here, $p_1 = <x,y>$ and $p_2 = <x,z>$. The algebraic expression corresponding to the literal BG(x,y) is :

$$BG_1 = \Pi_{1,4}(\sigma_{(2=3)\text{and}(1=5)\text{and}(6=7)}(F \times BG \times M \times BG))$$

and the algebraic expression corresponding to the literal BG(x,z) is :

$$BG_2 = \pi_{1,4}(\sigma_{(2=3)\text{and}(1=5)\text{and}(6=7)}(M \times BG \times F \times BG))$$

Applying the algorithm described above, we obtain the bloodgroup I-tables $BG^{(1)}$, and $BG^{(2)}$ in Figure 4.5. $BG^{(1)}$ and $BG^{(2)}$ contain the new tuples/tuple sets generated in iteration 1 and 2 respectively. Iteration 3 does not generate any new tuples/tuple sets.

Mutually recursive rules and mutually recursive predicates for Horn rules are discussed in [1]. A similar definition can easily be made for the non-Horn rules that we are considering. To evaluate the extensions of the I-tables, we must now evaluate all the mutually recursive predicates in the REPEAT-UNTIL loop.

4.4 Queries

Consider the database in Figure 4.6.

S

s1	Jones
s3	Coady
s2	Smith
s2	Blake

SP

s1	p1
s2	p2
s3	p1
s3	p2

Figure 4.6 An I-database

ANSWER

Jones
Coady
Smith
Blake

Figure 4.7 Answer to query

and the query :

$$Answer(y) \leftarrow S(x,y),\ <SP(x,'p1'),\ SP(x,'p2')>$$

which asks for all the supplier names of suppliers who supply either part 'p1' or part 'p2'. Here, we assume that the extensions of the I-tables S and SP have already been determined, possibly by the application of one or more rules defining them. The algebraic expression corresponding to the query is :

$$Answer = \Pi_2(\sigma_{((1=3)\text{ and }(4='p1'))\ or\ ((1=3)\text{ and }(4='p2'))}(S \times SP))$$

Evaluating this expression against the database, we obtain the answer in Figure 4.7. The answer I-table is interpreted as : Jones and Coady supply either of the two parts and Smith or Blake supply either of the two parts.

5. SUMMARY AND CONCLUSION

We have used an extended relational algebra to realize the deductive component of a subclass of indefinite deductive databases. Extended algebraic operators have been defined and used to obtain the extensions of I-tables from recursive/non-recursive non-Horn rules defining them. In particular, the match-union operator is used to handle the disjunction of positive literals in the rules. The non-Horn rules are generalizations of clauses in which we allow negation of a disjunction of literals instead of just negation of literals. This was necessary because a disjunctive database consists of many minimal models and a disjunctive formula, $P \vee Q$, may be true in all the minimal models with P and Q individually being false in some minimal models. The extended relational model (algebra) as defined reduces to the regular relational model (algebra) in the absence of indefinite information.

We have not presented any significant use of the maybe component of I-tables. It was not very pertinent to the discussion presented in this paper. However, we feel that the maybe and indefinite components could play an important role in "fuzzy and uncertain" databases. By attaching a probability to the maybe tuples and tuples in the indefinite component, we can easily model "uncertain" information.

REFERENCES

[1] Bancilhon, F. and Ramakrishnan, R. An Amateur's introduction to recursive query processing strategies. Proceedings of the International Conference on Management of Data (Washington, D.C. May 28-30, 1986), ACM SIGMOD, V15 N2, June 1986, pp. 16-52.

[2] Codd, E.F. A relational model for large shared data banks, Comm. ACM, V13, N6, June 1970, pp. 377-387.

[3] Gallaire, H., and Minker, J. Logic and Data Bases. Plenum. New York. 1978.

[4] Gallaire, H., Minker, J., and Nicolas, J-M. Advances in Data Base Theory, vol. 1, Plenum. New York. 1981.

[5] Gallaire, H., Minker, J., and Nicolas, J-M. Advances in Data Base Theory, vol. 2, Plenum. New York. 1984.

[6] Gallaire, H., Minker, J., and Nicolas, J-M. Logic and databases : A deductive approach. Computing Surveys, vol. 16, No. 2, June 1984. pp. 153-185.

[7] Imielinski, T. On algebraic query processing in logical databases. In Advances in Data Base Theory, Vol. 2, H.Gallaire, J.Minker, and J-M. Nicolas Eds. Plenum press. New York and London. pp. 285-318.

[8] Ioannidis, Y.E, and Wong, E. An algebraic approach to recursive inference. Proceedings First International Conference on Expert Database systems, Charleston, South Carolina, 1986, pp. 209-223.

[9] Lipski, W. On semantic issues connected with incomplete information databases, ACM Trans. on Database Syst. V4, N3, Sept. 1979.

[10] Liu, K.C. and Sunderraman, R. An extension to the relational model for indefinite databases. Proc. of the ACM-IEEE Fall Joint Computer Conference, Dallas, Texas, Oct. 1987, (to appear).

[11] Liu, K.C. and Sunderraman, R. Applying an extended relational model to indefinite deductive databases. TR 86-18, Department of Computer Science, Iowa State University, Ames, Iowa. December 1986.

[12] Minker, J. On indefinite databases and the closed world assumption, 6th Conf. on Automated Deduction, New York, in Lecture Notes in Computer Science, N138, (Ed. D.Loveland), Springer-Verlag, 1982.

[13] Reiter, R. Towards a logical reconstruction of relational database theory. In On Conceptual Modeling, M.Brodie, J.Mylopoulos, and J.W.Schmidt, Eds. Springer-Verlag, Berlin and New York.

A Concept Version

Sung H. Myaeng[1] and Robert R. Korfhage
Interdisciplinary Department of Information Science
University of Pittsburgh

ABSTRACT

One difficult problem in information retrieval is the transformation of the user's conceptual needs into an explicit query/profile. As an attempt to tackle the problem, we propose a method of automatically constructing a structure considered as a version of term concepts embedded in a given database and investigate how it can be used to help users formulating query/profile. The use of generality/specificity relation is exploited along with other properties that can be obtained by analyzing the database. Since some expert system approaches are often criticized because of the difficulty in extending them to a large-scale database, it seems that our approach will play an important role in automating some of the processes of codifying the expert knowledge.

1. Introduction

One of the notorious problems in information retrieval (IR) systems is the difficulty in formulating a query that accurately matches the user's actual needs and contents of all and only relevant items in databases being searched. The process of transforming the user's desire or needs to an actual query usually requires the recognition of the user's anomalous state of knowledge (ASK) [1] and the efforts to express the resulting necessity in terms of his or her vocabulary. Unfortunately, in fact, terms used in an actual query are not guaranteed to cover all and only aspects of user's conceptual needs and to match those in the document databases in the retrieval system [2].

In an effort to diminish the serious effect of poor query formulation, one approach has emerged and its theoretical foundation has been established: integration of user profiles to the conventional IR systems[4]. In this approach, each individual's interests and other characteristics are maintained in a profile which allows different interpretation of a query to produce a different result and helps the initial output be tailored to the user's preference or particular needs. Furthermore, by changing the profile dynamically and automatically based on the observation of information flow between the system and the user, the system not only operates in a more intelligent and personalized manner [8] but also behaves as if implicit, long-term relevance feedbacks are incorporated. This technique of modifying the original query based on the user's relevance judgement on retrieved items has been proved to improve retrieval effectiveness[9].

While the idea of utilizing profiles seems promising, a similar problem to that in query formulation arises. When a user is allowed to explicitly manipulate his own profile at a certain point regardless of its mode, either static or dynamic, he may as well suffer from the difficulty in composing words and phrases to represent his interests among other characteristics. Even with dynamic profiles, user's creation of the initial profile seems to be a necessary component in order to avoid the possibility of misusing an unstable or incomplete profile. Given that the information obtained from the interaction between a user and a system is usually noisy and incomplete in nature, the existence of a good profiling tool seems to be as important to retrieval improvement as the integration of profiles into retrieval systems.

Thesauri have been traditionally used in information retrieval. They are some-

[1] Currently in the Department of Computer and Information Sciences at Temple University.

Methodologies for Intelligent Systems
Z. W. Ras and M. Zemankova, Editors

times accessible to the users to help selecting synonyms or used to modify queries and document representations for the purpose of improving *recall* , a term which has been used in the area of information retrieval to refer the ratio of the number of the relevant documents retrieved to the total number of relevant documents in the database. On the other hand, *precision* , which measures the ratio of the number of relevant documents retrieved to the total number of retrieved documents, is usually reduced with the use of a thesaurus although it can be increased in some situations where a term is classified into more than one groups of terms [12]. Two kinds of thesauri have been used: those constructed automatically are based on statistical similarity of terms whereas others manually constructed are semantically based, subjective, and more laborious. However they are constructed, it has been proved in experiments that the use of thesauri actually improves retrieval effectiveness [pp.11-16, 12].

With the aforementioned set of problems as a guiding motivation and the previous finding about the usefulness of thesauri as a ground, we explore in this paper an idea of automatically constructing a concept version for a given document database, which effectively goes beyond the conventional approach to the automatic construction of a thesaurus. Also proposed is a way of utilizing the term relations in the concept version as part of a profiling tool which assists users in formulating queries and profiles (thus a profiling tool). It is expected that this framework can also facilitate the development of more realistic knowledge-based information retrieval systems.

2. Construction of a Concept Version

This section presents a term organization scheme which produces a unique representation of the relations among terms in a given database. A method for assigning to the term relations values that will facilitate the utilization of the representation is also presented. The scheme effectively transforms statistical information into a meaningful structure containing hierarchical information among terms.

2.1. Overall Representation

We begin by defining the term *concept version* : it is used in this paper to refer to various meaningful terms organized in a hierarchy representing generality and specificity relations dictated from the given database. Since it is always possible for different people to organize terms in different ways using the general-specific relation interpreted by themselves, practical definitions of the two terms, generality and specificity, need to be explicated if a deterministic algorithm is to be designed for such organization purpose. Recalling that the purpose of constructing the concept version and, hence, the generality-specificity (g-s) relation between any two terms is to assist the process of user's query/profile formulation, it becomes immediately necessary to consider how typical users would interpret the g-s relation if it is available. We assume that in an actual retrieval environment, users expect that a more general term would completely or partially subsume many less general terms and retrieve more documents than any of the less general terms. Furthermore, we assume that if two terms are related in that way, users expect they are conceptually similar to some extent and therefore likely to retrieve some common documents. Motivated by the assumptions and the fact that there exists no universal g-s relation that organizes terms in the given database in a consistent manner, we now define a binary *G-S relation* that is determined by comparing two sets of documents retrieved by two terms. It should be noted that this definition is based on the existence of a target document collection.

Def. G-S relation

Two terms, t_i and t_j, are G-S related in a given database, i.e. $t_i\ R_{gs}\ t_j$, if the number of documents retrieved by t_i is greater than or equal to the number of documents retrieved by t_j, and the similarity between t_i and t_j is greater than a certain threshold. More formally

$$t\ R_{gs}\ t \text{ iff } |t_i| \geq |t_j| \text{ and } SIM(t_i, t_j) \geq \alpha$$

where |.| is the cardinality of a set of documents retrieved by a term and α is a threshold. The similarity value, $SIM(t_i, t_j)$, can be defined as follows:

$$SIM(t_i,t_j) = \frac{\sum_{k=1}^{n} t_{ik} \cdot t_{jk}}{\sum_{k=1}^{n} (t_{ik})^2 + \sum_{k=1}^{n} (t_{jk})^2 - \sum_{k=1}^{n} t_{ik} \cdot t_{jk}}$$

where n indicates the number of documents in the database and $t_{ik}(t_{jk})$ denotes the i-th (j-th) term in the k-th document [9].

Similarly, *S-G relation* can be defined as an inverse of the G-S relation. In what follows, we shall limit our discussion to the G-S relation only since the same development can be easily established for the S-G relation.

Although the G-S relation over the set of terms can be a partial ordering if we confine ourselves to the cardinality condition, the transitivity property is not guaranteed to hold with the latter condition that terms be similar in the sense as defined in the above definition. Therefore it becomes necessary to introduce another definition.

Def. Quasi-Partial Order

A relation on the set is a quasi-partial order if
i) when t_i R t_j is true, t_j R t_i is false for all i and j, $i \neq j$,
ii) t_i R t_i is false for all i, and
iii) t_i R t_j is associated with a degree in the range of (0,1) for all i and j, $i \neq j$.

While i) and ii) express anti-summetricity and irreplexivity, respectively, iii) characterizes the fuzzy nature of a relation. The G-S relation on the set of terms is a quasi-partial order provided that we have a characteristic function that determines the degree of a relation between two terms. The purpose of introducing the condition iii) will become clearer in the following subsection.

Transitivity property found in an ordinary partial order, as opposed to the quasi-partial order, seems too strong to be part of the above definition. Although the property could be observed often, we can hardly rely on this property in general since a term can have totally different meanings. For example, 'resolution' can be considered as a more specific term than 'theorem-proving' and, at the same time, as a more general term than 'pixel' in the context of computer graphics (i.e. (theorem-proving R_{gs} resolution) and (resolution R_{gs} pixel)), but it is not clear whether there is a conceptual link between 'theorem-proving' and 'pixel', let alone hierarchical information to satisfy transitivity.

In spite of the lack of definite transitivity, however, the proper containment condition in the definition of G-S relation allows the quasi-partial order to be represented by a directed acyclic graph (DAG). Since we compute the similarity value as well as the containment condition of any two meaningful terms in the database, any G-S relation that can be derived by transitivity in ordinary partial order (i.e. transitive closure) will be explicitly represented in the DAG representation in practice, eliminating the ambiguity. Focusing on a portion of the DAG as in Fig. 1, we shall use the following naming convention: A term t_i is *pivotal* with respect to another term t_j iff t_i R_{gs} t_j, while t_j is a *candidate* term with respect to t_i in the same situation. In Fig.1, for example, t_0 and t_6, but not t_3, are pivotal with respect to t_5; t_0 and t_2, but not t_1 or t_5, are candidate terms with respect to t_3.

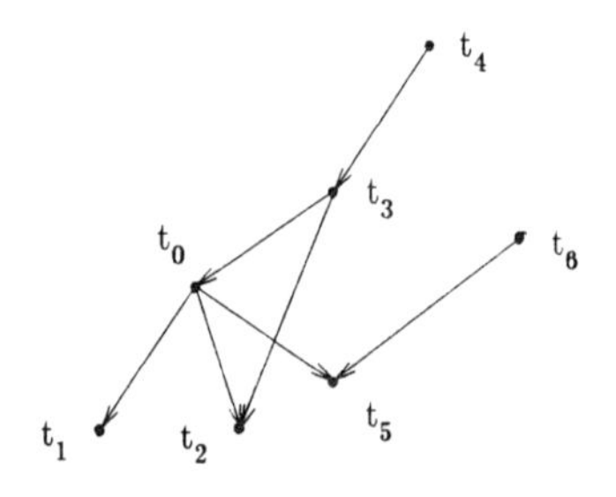

Fig. 1

2.2. Local Information

Although we have shown that the concept version can effectively be represented by a DAG, we can use some local information for immediate improvement. It is conceived that the transitive closure requirement in the DAG may reduce the potential usability of the concept version. If that restriction were not imposed, it could be possible to make use of the number of the links intervening between a pivotal term node and one of the candidate term nodes for the purpose of differentiating the degree of the specificity among all candidate terms. In the above DAG representation, however, all candidate terms are separated by one link from their pivotal term without bearing any difference in terms of the specificity. This means, for example, that given those terms as candidates for more specific terms to be used in actual retrieval session, it becomes a burden to the user to predict how each term would affect the output. To put it differently, the representation indicates neither how closely two G-S related terms are tied conceptually nor how much they differ in terms of the specificity.

At first glance, a solution to the drawback of our DAG representation of a concept version seems to lie in the use of the similarity values we compute along the process of constructing the DAG. As shown in the following, however, the use of similarity values for the purpose of enhancing the usability of the concept version constructed as such can be hardly justified. Suppose, for the sake of simplicity, that only binary values are used in similarity computation. In other words, a term is represented by a vector, where each element indicates either the corresponding document is retrieved ot not retrieved, ignoring its degree of relevancy ranking. Suppose further that we know two terms, B and C, are more specific than the term A and need to select one as an additional term in a query. Illustrated in Fig. 2 are the relationships between A and B, and A and C, respectively. Although B and C are conceptually related to A in quite different ways, it is not possible to see the actual difference between two relationships if only similarity values are available. Our knowledge regarding the difference can not be substantially improved unless we know exactly how the underlying retrieval system behaves in general, or, at least, how the similarity values are computed.

The similarity value plays an essential role in measuring symmetric closeness between two properties and therefore in classifying terms in clumps. Although many measures have been developed for different purposes [5], they all deal with symmetric characteristics of two properties and don't seem to convey much intuitive meaning when used in conjunction with the generality-specificity relation. Since our purpose is to furnish information local to a pivotal term and a set of candidate terms, as opposed to the global, structural information, the way a more general term encompasses the other one conceptually seems more appealing intuitively than the similarity value. In our framework with sets, a natural choice is the application of the set *inclusion property* which can be expressed in set notations as

$$\mathrm{INC}(A,B) = 1 - \mathrm{card}(B-A)/\mathrm{card}(B)$$

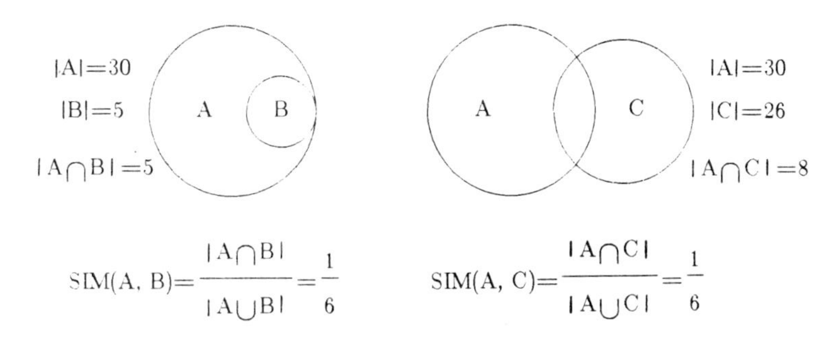

Fig. 2.

or, more practically, as

$$\mathrm{INC}(A,B) = 1 - \frac{\sum_{B_i \neq 0} |B_i - A_i|}{\sum_{j=1}^{n} |B_j|}$$

measuring an *asymmetric* characteristic of what portion of B is included in A. Here A_i and B_i (or B_j) represent weights of i-th (or j-th) document in A and B, respectively, in vector representation of terms. Our conjecture is that this value indirectly represents the likelihood of conceptual coherency of B with respect to A. In the example shown in Fig. 2, INC(A, B) = 1 and INC(A, C)= 8/26 show the adequacy of the INC value compared to the corresponding similarity values. Since the INC value in isolation doesn't carry much information about the relative size of two terms, a piece of information to supplement the INC value can be obtained by keeping track of the number of documents retrieved by each term. A graphical representation of a portion of a concept version is illustrated in Fig.3 where value on links represents the INC(pivotal term, candidate term).

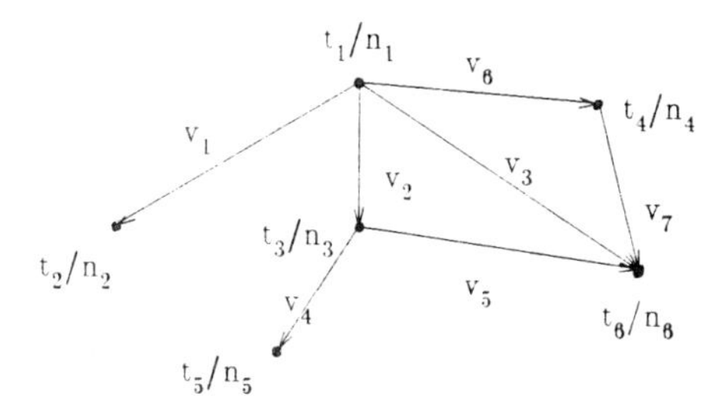

Fig. 3.

3. Application of a Concept Version

Following the trends of AI during the past decade, an expert system approach has been emerging to serve as an intelligent intermediary in the retrieval environment, sometimes simply exploiting the relevance feedback together with different search strategies [6] and other times using so-called expert knowledge for a limited domain [7,11]. Although high quality of information can be available in the approach using expert knowledge, the limitation on the domain and the size of the database seems to preclude the practical use of such systems at this point and in the foreseeable future. We expect that the approach taken here to construct a concept version can automate part of the process of codifying knowledge about the database.

It has been well known in psychology that humans' recall performance is much poorer than their recognition performance [pp 238-241,3]. This may mean that although a user may think that he knows the kinds of information desired, it should be harder to translate the conceptual information need into a verbalized query by just relying on his memory than by using a list of terms that are available in the database and possibly descriptive of rather vague information needs. Conceivably, the concept version can help increasing "user friendliness" in this sense by providing a better environment for effective query/profile formulation. We focus our attention to this aspect in this section.

Since the strength of a connection between two terms is available in our representation of a concept version, it becomes possible to make distinctions among candidate terms generated from a pivotal term which is part of a query/profile. The simplest and almost trivial case is a query -- a profile is also implied in the sequel -- with a single term. In this case, things we need to consider are those obtained by following the links from the query term in the DAG representation and the way of displaying them in a user-friendly manner, taking into account the INC value available along each link and the size on each node. It seems unreasonable to consider terms separated by more than one link since the INC value between the query term and any of those generated is zero and therefore nothing can be inferred about the conceptual coherency.

Opting for vector representation of a query, we now consider the second case where a query consists of a list of terms with no negative weights. Let T_i be a set of candidate terms that are G-S related with t_i in a query, Q, consisting of n terms, $t_1, t_2, \cdots, t_n$. Then by taking pairwise intersections of two distinct sets, T_i and T_j , and unioning the resulting sets, we have a new set called extension, E_2 , where the subscript indicates that two sets are intersected. The elements in the extension are G-S related with any two terms in the query. In similar fashion, we can take three way intersections to get E_3, and so on. After deleting common elements in E_i and E_j from E_i , where $i < j$, we obtain all candidate terms partitioned into extensions including E_1 whose elements are those pointed by a single query term only. Now we have a sequence of disjoint sets, $E_1, E_2, \cdots, E_m$, where $m \leq n$. We conjecture that the more query terms are G-S related with a candidate term, the more related the term is to the query and better qualified as a candidate term to the user. In a sense, this is to consolidate rather uncertain statistical information embedded in the concept version with additional information provided by a user's query.

Interpreting the INC value as representing the degree or probability of how much a term is conceptually close to the pivotal term, we can compute the value of *suggestive power* in such a way that it is incremented as the term is G-S related with more pivotal (query) terms. Among other possibilities, we opt for the formula used in computing the probability of two disjunctive events. Considering the INC value on each link as a default value of suggestive power with respect to the pivotal term, a new value of the suggestive power, SP'_A, of A can be computed as follows:

$$SP'_A = W_B \cdot SP_A(B) + W_C \cdot SP_A(C) - W_B \cdot SP_A(B) \cdot W_C \cdot SP_A(C) \qquad (1)$$

where $SP_A(B)$ and $SP_A(C)$ represent the suggestive power (or INC value in this particular case) of A with respect to the pivotal terms B and C, respectively, and W_B and W_C are the weights of the query terms B and C, respectively. Insofar as the computed value is order-independent and incremented systematically as more pivotal terms are involved, other formula should work as well without any substantial difference. With repeated application of this formula, the suggestive power of all elements within any E_i, $i \geq 3$, can be also newly determined.

As we conjectured earlier, we consider all terms in higher order extension are better qualified than any term in a low order extension. Considering the suggestive power associated with each term within an extension as a discriminating factor among terms, we can now place all candidate terms in a complete order in terms of the suggestive power and the qualification. In an example shown in Fig. 4, terms are ordered in this way.

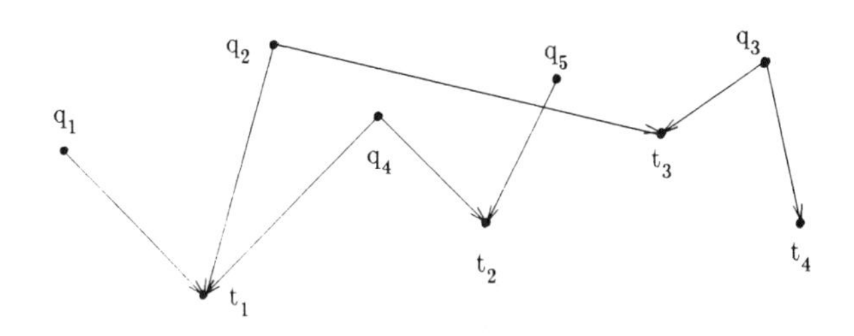

$$t_1 > t_2 > t_3 > t_4 \quad \text{if } SP_{t_2} > SP_{t_3}$$

Fig. 4.

In a more general form of a query, we allow terms to be negated. A negated weight associated with a query term usually indicates the user's desire not to retrieve documents containing the concept represented by the term, and this suggests that terms G-S related with the negated one be excluded from the positive candidates; Rather, it suggests another negative term in the query. We consider two cases: one with all negated pivotal terms and the other with the combination of plain and negated pivotal terms. In the first situation, the formula (1) used above can be applied with minor modification. Namely,

$$SP'_A = W_B \cdot SP_A(B) + W_C \cdot SP_A(C) + W_B \cdot SP_A(B) \cdot W_C \cdot SP_A(C)$$

where W_B and W_C are all negative. Since the value of the resulting suggestive power is negative, the term should be suggested as a possible supplementary term for the particular term rather than as part of the general extension.

On the other hand, the opposite signs on the weights need to be treated differently. Suppose B R_{gs} A with a negative weight and C R_{gs} A with a positive weight. Even if we assume the user expressed his intention correctly in the query, this kind of conflicting evidence toward term A can happen because of the fuzzy nature of the G-S relation, which is originated from the fact that we rely on some statistical information. Interpreting these two values as two evidences for belief and misbelief, we combine them as in [10].

$$SP'_A = W_B \cdot SP_A(B) + W_C \cdot SP_A(C).$$

As in the case dealing with all positive weights, it should be clear that the same process can be applied repeatedly to handle terms with more than one pivotal terms. Furthermore, we have been concerned only with terms more specific than a query term, but it also should be clear that the same approach can be applied to a DAG with "S-G relation" focusing on more general terms with respect a query term.

4. Discussion and Summary

We have presented the characteristics and the construction process of the concept version and its application to the development of a profiling tool. It has been shown that, since the "size" of individual terms and the generality/specificity relations among terms are contained in the concept version for a given database, a complete ordering of all the candidate terms with respect to an initial profile (query) can be available in terms of their suggestive powers to assist the user.

Traditionally computational aspects or efficiency concerns in information retrieval have been largely ignored, compared to the amount of effort devoted to the enhancement of effectiveness. Although our concern in this paper has been also focused on the representation aspect leading to the concern of effectiveness, it seems worthwhile to consider briefly about efficiency. Assuming that an inverted index has been built for the underlying retrieval system, a concept version can be constructed by reasonable amount of computation. By substituting the similarity value used to construct a DAG at the first stage by the INC value used to obtain the suggestive power on each link at later stage, the computation time is basically $O(n^2)$ with n being the number of meaningful terms in the database, and required only once in the lifetime of the database.

We have developed this framework based on a previous finding by other researchers: the use of an automatically constructed thesaurus based on similarity value only contributes to the enhancement of retrieval effectiveness. Additional information is added to the similarity-based thesaurus as an attempt to increase the quality to the point of competing with human-constructed thesaurus, yet taking advantage of objectivity. Therefore, it is conceived that this approach should perform at least as well as the similarity-based approach although experiments need to be run to determine the actual level of improvement. As future research, we need to investigate the possibility of using terms separated by more than one link in order to be less conservative in suggesting candidate terms. In the long run, we hope to be able to identify other properties that can be extracted automatically from the database and integrate them into the concept version.

REFERENCES

1. Belkin, N. J.
   Ineffable Concepts in Information Retrieval. In *Information Retrieval Experiment,* Sparck Jones (Ed), Butterworth, 1981.
2. Blair, D. C. & Maron, M. E.
   An Evaluation of Retrieval Effectiveness for a Full-Text Document Retrieval System. *CACM 28* (3), 1985, 289-299.
3. Klatzky, R. C.
   Human Memory: Structures and Processes. Freeman, 1980.
4. Korfhage, R. R.
   Query Enhancement by User Profile. In *Proc. of ACM/BCS Symposium on Research & Development in Information Retrieval,* 1984, 111-121.
5. Kuhns, J. L.
   The Continuum of Coefficients of Association. In *Statistical Association Methods for Mechanized Documentation,* Stevens, M. E. et al. (Eds), National Bureau Standards Miscellaneous Publication 269, 1965.
6. Marcus, R. S.
   An Automated Expert Assistant for Information Retrieval. In *Proc. of the ASIS Annual Meeting,* 1981, 270-273.
7. McCune, B. P. & et al.
   Rule-Based Retrieval of Information by computer. Technical report TR-1018-1. Advanced Information & Decision Systems, Mtn. View, CA. Jan., 1983.
8. Myaeng, S. H. & Korfhage, R. R.
   Towards Intelligent and Personalized Information Retrieval Systems. In *Proc. of the ACM SIGART International Symposium on Methodologies for Intelligent Systems,* 1985, 121-129.
9. Salton, G. & McGill, M. J.
   Introduction to Modern Information Retrieval. McGraw-Hill, 1983.
10. Shortliffe, E. H. & Buchanan, B. G.
    A Model of Inexact Reasoning in Medicine. *Mathematical Biosciences 23,* 1975, 351-379.
11. Shoval, P.
    Expert/Consultation System for a Retrieval Data-Base with Semantic Network of Concepts. In *Proc. of the Fourth International Conference on Information Storage and Retrieval,* 1981.
12. Sparck Jones, K.
    Automatic Keyword Classification for Information retrieval. Butterworth, London, 1971.

A First Order Calculus for Temporal Knowledge †

Mira Balaban *Neil V. Murray*

Dept. of Computer Science
State Univ. of N.Y. at Albany
Albany, NY 12222

Abstract

We describe a first order system that can represent and reason about hierarchically structured temporal knowledge. The system is a first order calculus, augmented with new interpreted symbols for dealing with time. We make extensive use of reification: the temporal context, as a whole, is an object (a term), called, a *time-structure*. We show how causal relationships, persistency as default (the frame problem), qualification problems, and contradictions, are handled in this framework. A major advantage of this formal system over more exotic ones is that well-developed proof and implementation techniques for first order logic are applicable.

1. Introduction

The notion of time is pervasive in everyday life. If AI systems are to model significant aspects of the real world, they must cope with temporal knowledge. In most proposed representations, temporal knowledge resides in separate atomic units involving single facts or events. The primitives that represent time are either intervals ([1]) or points ([18]). Non-atomic structures are developed in[14], and, less formally, in[5].

The reasoning process is the focus of most temporal AI systems. The temporal component can be implicit, e.g., in the situation calculus[8, 16], in truth maintenance systems, and in program verification systems. Time is made explicit in formal systems designed specifically for temporal reasoning. This is achieved by complicating the semantics and/or by introducing interpreted time objects. The interval calculus of[1], the modal logic of[6], the temporal logic of[18] and of[4], the logic of chronological ignorance ([22]), and the Horn-clause logic of[11] are prominent examples. Some logics are designed to capture aspects of temporal reasoning, like persistence as a default assumption ([17, 23,18]).

We describe a representation language that combines atemporal knowledge with time stamps in a hierarchical fashion. The resulting syntactic unit is called a *time structure*; it is a *term* in the calculus, and the operators are functions. Time structures can be thought of as reifications of temporal knowledge. They are similar to the notion of *chronicles* in[18], and to the notion of context in PLANNER ([9]). The inspiration for this representation language came from the structured description of music defined in[2], but its atemporal primitives can be taken from any domain.

Reasoning about time structures involves discovering what "holds" at a given time point in a given time structure. We discuss several generic reasoning processes: those that involve the operators on time structures, direct retrieval of explicit knowledge, deduction of non-explicit knowledge, and finally causal reasoning.

Capturing the context as an object in the reasoning process has several advantages: explicit contradictions can sometimes be analyzed without producing an undesired *logical* inconsistency; aspects of the frame problem are handled; switching contexts amounts to reasoning about a different time structure; some parts of the qualification problem are solved by completion of a special "HOLDS" predicate. The principal novelty of our approach is in embedding a powerful data structure for temporal knowledge within the terms of a first order logic. One of the important consequences is that implementation with logic programming

† This research was supported in part by the National Science Foundation under grant DCR-8600848.

Methodologies for Intelligent Systems
Z. W. Ras and M. Zemankova, Editors

techniques will be relatively straightforward.

2. Representation of Temporal Knowledge

We use the following notation conventions: predicates are expressed as upper case, and functions as lower case, identifiers. Variables are also lower case but are italicized; unless otherwise specified, they are assumed universally quantified. The interpreted constants introduced specifically for dealing with time appear in boldface: these are all function symbols. We use, as function symbols, &, v, $\supset$, and $\neg$; these are axiomitized to behave like functional versions of the propositional connectives $\wedge$, $\vee$, $\Rightarrow$, and $\sim$, respectively.

2.1. Time structures

We use constants or functional terms to express primitive facts, processes, or events; we refer to them formally as *primitive propositions*. For instance, we may denote by "fido_barks" the process of a dog, called fido, barking. Such a primitive proposition, by itself, has no temporal characteristics. (Not only are we ignorant of *when* fido barks, but also of *how long*. This is less obvious for 'event-like' propositions, such as "move(x, y)", where it is tempting to assume a fixed small duration relative to the time frames of other facts. In this paper, such assumptions are not made.) To express the concept of fido barking for 35 minutes, we write [fido_barks,35]. The square brackets indicate a special kind of term we call a *primitive time structure*. It expresses the notion of a primitive proposition holding or occurring for some length of time we call its *duration*. The time period starts and ends at time points zero and *duration*, respectively, with respect to the "private" time line of the primitive time structure.

The proposition of the primitive time structure can represent both static and dynamic entities. The action of blinking an eye would be represented by the constant "blink", and the fact that the color of block A is red would be represented as "color(blockA, red)". Both are assumed to have durations, though, "blink" would, probably, have a very short one. Our approach is similar to that of[24] and different from that of[1].

We require the ability to relate various events with respect to some common "time line". Suppose fido's barking occurred in the context of this somewhat richer scenario: A process called morning_routine, lasting one hour, starts at time zero, followed without delay by a brief event called owner_leaves; about one hour later fido starts barking and does so for 35 minutes. We represent this as a *composite time structure* called TS_0:

([owner_leaves,1]@1hr . ([morning_routine,1hr]@0 . ([fido_barks,35]@2hr . nil))),

which is just a list of time stamped time structures. The "@" symbol is an infix operator that acts as sugar for a special type of term called an *occurrence*. The time structure above has its own time line, taken to be a linearly ordered set like the integers or reals; the time structures that occur within it have their own time lines. But the zero point of these time lines is displaced from the zero point of the composite time structure by exactly the time stamp of their containing occurrence. So fido starts barking at time zero in the primitive time structure [fido_barks,35], but the barking starts at +2 hours in the larger time structure.

Composit time structures are lists of occurrences, that may include, themselves, time structures (a time structure is not necessarily "flat"). We use the common list notation instead of the dotted pair one. A time structure can be partially specified, as in:

([owner_leaves,1]@1hr [morning_routine,1hr]@0 [fido_barks,35]@2hr . *rest*)

where the variable *rest* stands for the unspecified part.

We write TS_{fido} ::= [fido_barks,35] to indicate that TS_{fido} may be replaced by [fido_barks, 35] wherever it appears. Let TS_{own} ::= [owner_leaves, 1] and TS_{morn} ::= [morning_routine, 1hr]. Then the time structure TS_0 can be written (TS_{morn}@0 TS_{own}@1hr TS_{fido}@2hr). (The order of the list elements is irrelevant.)

Suppose that someone in fido's neighborhood gets a headache upon being disturbed by the barking. The pain lasted 40 minutes and the neighbor called the police immediately. A possible representation is: $TS_{neighbor}$ ::= ([pain(neighbor),40]@0 [calls_police,5]@0) We may combine TS_0 with $TS_{neighbor}$ into TS_1, a day in which fido's owner leaves at 9am. Note that $TS_{neighbor}$ starts one hour later:

TS_1 ::= (TS_0@8hr $TS_{neighbor}$@10hr) = (([pain(neighbor),40]@0 [calls_police,5]@0)@10hr

([morning_routine,1hr]@0 [owner_leaves,1]@1hr [fido_barks,35]@2hr)@8hr)

2.2. Time terms

We have used terms like "1hr" to stand for a point in time at some distance from zero, where the time unit may be assumed to be one minute, and 1hr is sugar for 60. Such *time terms* may also appear as variables or functional terms. We assume that the set of time points Θ can be represented by the integers or reals. A time term is an expression denoting a member of Θ.

Among the most useful time terms are those that denote what we call ***start*** and ***clip*** times of time structures. The ***self-clip time*** of a time structure TS is written $\mathbf{clip}_{self}$ (TS); it denotes the earliest point on the time line of TS at which one of its constituent primitive propositions clips. The ***self-start time*** of TS, written $\mathbf{start}_{self}$ (TS) is similarly defined; the *duration*, written **d**(TS), is their difference. For instance, let TS be ([a,5]@-20 ([b,10]@5 [a,5]@2)@8). Then $\mathbf{clip}_{self}$ (TS) = 23 and $\mathbf{start}_{self}$ (TS) = -20; the duration is 43.

The *relative* clip and start times for a time structure TS_1 that occurs within TS_2, would be written **clip**(TS_1,TS_2) and **start**(TS_1,TS_2). As in the example above, a time structure may occur more than once in a larger time structure, and each such occurrence has a clip and start time relative to the overall structure. Therefore, **clip**(TS_1,TS_2) and **start**(TS_1,TS_2) each yield a ***list*** of time points, one for every occurrence of TS_1 in TS_2. In the previous example, **clip**([a,5],TS) = (-15 15) and **start**([a,5],TS) = (-20 10). Of course, the first argument can be composite: For example, **start**(([b,10]@5 [a,5]@2), TS) = (10). The **interval** function computes a list of pairs of time points that describe intervals during which a given time structure is "playing" within another time structure. For example, **interval**([a,5], TS) = ((-20 -15) (10 15)). The formal definition of the time functions appear in the full paper ([3]).

2.3. Term level connectives

Since our facts appear as constants or functional terms, we must provide some means of expressing logical combinations of such facts. So we write "p & q" as an infix functional term denoting the "conjunction" of p and q. We have the symbols v, $\supset$, and $\neg$ as well; they represent term level disjunction, conditional, and negation respectively. The terms formed by the term level connectives are called ***propositions***. When combined with durations they also form primitive time structures.

The inference engine for the calculus can only deal with the logic level connectives. Hence, in Section 3, we introduce certain axioms that force the term level connectives to have the intended interpretations. Our axioms do not completely characterize propositional logic, although this can be done ([20]). We are *not* quantifying over function or predicate symbols, nor are we making any use of higher order logic; although a proposition may *look* like a predicate or formula, it is merely a constant symbol or a term in our first order system.

3. Reasoning about Time Structures

We reason about knowledge with respect to its "time stamps". (This is different than [1] and[12, 13] where reasoning is done about the time objects themselves.) We try to answer questions of the form "Does p hold at a given time in a given time structure?" where x can be a proposition, or a time structure. To answer such queries we assume a predicate "HOLDS", that takes four arguments: a time-term, the query subject (a proposition or a time structure), a time-structure (the given context), and a condition, usually on the time-terms. The statement HOLDS(*t,p,ts,cond*) stands for: *p* holds at *t* in *ts*, provided that *cond* is true.

Four types of reasoning are considered: 1) Reasoning about the interpreted objects; 2) Using explicit knowledge in the time structure; 3) Using *timeless knowledge*; 4) Using causal knowledge, i.e., knowledge about the temporal impact of facts. We restrict ourselves to queries about propositions only. We assume that built-in knowledge about our syntactic sugar, about the commutativity of time structures, and about simplification of time constraints is available.

3.1. Reasoning About the Interpreted Objects

Intuitively, we want to say that a proposition p holds in a time structure ts at time point t if t falls in between corresponding start and clip times of [p,*d*], for some *d*, i.e., if $t_s \leq t < t_c$ for some $(t_s,t_c) \in$ **interval**([p,*d*] ,*ts*). For partially specified time structures, and non-explicit propositions, (Sections 3.3, 3.4), the start times and clip times cannot be computed, but still can be reasoned about.

Axiom (H1) states that for every primitive time structure $[p,d]$, the start and clip points form corresponding pairs:

$$\text{HOLDS}(t_s, \mathbf{start}([p,d]), ts, cond) \Leftrightarrow \text{HOLDS}(t_s+d, \mathbf{clip}([p,d]), ts, cond). \quad \text{(H1)}$$

(As an abbreviation, we omit the second argument of **start** and **clip** since it is present as the third argument of HOLDS.)

The start and clip points of a time structure ts_1, that **occurs** within a fully specified time-structure ts_2, satisfy HOLDS as follows:

$$\text{HOLDS}(t, \mathbf{start}(ts_1), ts_2, cond) \Leftarrow t \in \mathbf{start}(ts_1, ts_2) \quad \text{(H2)}$$

$$\text{HOLDS}(t, \mathbf{clip}(ts_1), ts_2, cond) \Leftarrow t \in \mathbf{clip}(ts_1, ts_2) \quad \text{(H3)}$$

Axiom (H4) states that a proposition holds at any time point in between corresponding start and clip points:

$$\text{HOLDS}(t, p, ts, cond \,\&\, t_s \leq t < t_s+d) \Leftarrow \text{HOLDS}(t_s, \mathbf{start}([p,d]), \text{ts}, \text{cond}) \quad \text{(H4)}$$

Using (H1) we can get an axiom similar to (H4) involving **clip**(p,d). Note that if there are no corresponding start and clip points t_s, t_c, respectively, such that $t_s < t_c$, then the proposition never holds. This axiom reflects our intuition about occurrences with zero duration.

Axiom (H5) refers to propositions that last forever.

$$\text{HOLDS}(t, p, ts, cond \,\&\, t \geq t_s) \Leftarrow \text{HOLDS}(t_s, \mathbf{start}([p,d]), ts, cond) \wedge (\forall t_c) \sim\text{HOLDS}(t_c, \mathbf{clip}([p,d]), ts, cond) \quad \text{(H5)}$$

The persistence of a death situation can be stated as

$$\text{HOLDS}(t, \mathbf{start}([\text{dead}(x),d]), ts, cond) \Rightarrow \text{HOLDS}(t', \text{dead}(x), ts, cond \,\&\, t' \geq t). \quad \text{(F1)}$$

For the term level connectives we need axioms that relate them to the logic level connectives. Recall that we use the symbols &, v, ⊃, and ¬ for the term level, and ∧, ∨, =>, and ~ for the logic level. For '&' and 'v' we assume:

$$\text{HOLDS}(t, p_1 \,\&\, p_2, ts, cond) \Leftrightarrow \text{HOLDS}(t, p_1, ts, cond) \wedge \text{HOLDS}(t, p_2, ts, cond). \quad \text{(H6)}$$

$$\text{HOLDS}(t, (p_1 \text{ v } p_2), ts, cond) \Leftrightarrow \text{HOLDS}(t, p_1, ts, cond) \vee \text{HOLDS}(t, p_2, ts, cond). \quad \text{(H7)}$$

For negation, we prefer not to propagate it to the logic level. So we have

$$\text{HOLDS}(t, \neg p, ts, cond) \Leftarrow \sim \text{HOLDS}(t, p, ts, cond). \quad \text{(H8)}$$

This decision enables us to explicitly handle term level contradictions, without having to declare logic level contradiction (see Section 3.5). The axioms for '⊃' would result from

$$\text{HOLDS}(t, p \supset q, ts, cond) \Leftrightarrow \text{HOLDS}(t, ((\neg p) \text{ v } q), ts, cond). \quad \text{(H9)}$$

3.2. Reasoning With the Explicit Knowledge

The effect of digging into the time structure is achieved by the following three axioms:

$$\text{HOLDS}(t_1, p, ([p,d]@t_2 \bullet ts), 0 \leq (t_1-t_2) \leq d). \quad \text{(H10)}$$

$$\text{HOLDS}(t_1, p, ([p,d]@t_2 \bullet ts), cond) \not\Leftarrow \text{HOLDS}(t, p, ts, cond). \quad \text{(H11)}$$

$$\text{HOLDS}(t_1, p, (ts_2@t_2 \bullet ts_1), cond) \Leftarrow \text{HOLDS}(t_1-t_2, p, ts_2, cond). \quad \text{(H12)}$$

Consider the time-structure TS_1 defined in the previous section. The query "When did the owner leave?" would be formulated as HOLDS (t, owner-leaves, TS_1, *cond*). Using rule (H12) and then (H10), *cond* is bound to $0 \leq t - 8\text{hr} - 1\text{hr} \leq 1\text{min}$ or after simplification: $9\text{hr} \leq t \leq 9.01\text{hr}$. Note that t itself is left uninstantiated. The answer is: "owner_leaves holds at any time from 9 to 9.01 a.m." (recall that our actions are not instantaneous!). If we now ask "When was the neighbor in pain?" we get the answer $0 \leq \text{t} - 10\text{hr} \leq d$ as the value of *cond*, or $10\text{hr} \leq \text{t} \leq 10\text{hr} + d$, after simplification. That is: "The neighbor was in pain at any time from 10am to 10am + d." Note that d is left unspecified. The "explicit knowledge" reasoning is no more than a retrieval procedure, and is, at worst, linear in the number of symbols in the time-structure. Our implicit-explicit distinction is related to Levesque's notion of vivid knowledge[15].

3.3. Reasoning With Timeless Knowledge

Assume that we have already established for some time structure ts_0 that

$$\text{HOLDS}\ (t_0,\ \neg\ \text{alive(FRED)},\ ts_0,\ cond_0) \qquad \text{(F3)}$$

and we now ask "When is Fred dead in ts_0?" To answer this we need the timeless information about the relationship between being not-alive and dead. If p is a term level proposition, then TRUE (p) would represent the assertion that p is timeless, i.e., always true. The following axiom expresses this understanding

$$\text{TRUE}\ (p) \Longrightarrow \text{HOLDS}\ (t,\ p,\ ts,\ cond). \qquad \text{(H14)}$$

To account for the effect of modus ponens reasoning we use axiom (H6) about term-level conjunction, and an explicit modus ponens axiom

$$\text{HOLDS}\ (t,\ p\&(p \supset q),\ ts, cond) \Longrightarrow \text{HOLDS}\ (t, q, ts, cond). \qquad \text{(H15)}$$

For the "poor Fred" example, we would have the axiom

$$\text{TRUE}\ (\ \neg\ \text{alive}(x\ ) \supset \text{dead}(x\ )\ ), \qquad \text{(F4)}$$

and from (F3), (F4), (H14), (H6), and (H15) we get HOLDS (t_0, dead(FRED), ts_0, $cond_0$). We expect that more knowledge about the term-level connectives would be needed to achieve powerful timeless reasoning.

3.4. Reasoning With Causal Knowledge

Causal relationships have been mentioned in the AI literature for over fifteen years ([1, 8, 10, 18, 24]). While general agreement on many aspects of causality is elusive, it is always related to 'flow over time' in some reference world. In our calculus, it relates occurrences along the time line of a time structure. We distinguish four parts in a causal relationship: the *precondition,* the *cause,* the *future-effect* and the *past-effect.* The precondition and the past-effect should precede, or overlap, but in no case be later than the cause; the cause should precede, or meet, but in no case overlap the future-effect. The relationship can be restricted by qualification conditions.

The precondition involves facts that must hold, for the cause to take place, provided that the qualification conditions hold. For example, the owner cannot leave the house if he is not there. The cause-future-effect relationship states that if the cause and the qualification conditions hold, then the effect should hold at some later time. For example, if a move action did take place and the table is not icy, then the moved block would be in the destination position. Note that in most systems no distinction is made between preconditions and qualification conditions. The cause-past-effect relationship refers, usually to clipping of past facts.

Causal reasoning is centered around the cause. For a cause c, a precondition p, and a qualification condition qc, the precondition-cause relationship can be expressed by PREC((c,t), $(p, f(t))$, qc) where f is a function on time terms, and $\forall\ t$, $f(t) \leq t$[1], and

$$\text{HOLDS}(t,\ c,\ ts,\ cond_1) \wedge \text{PREC}(\ (c,\ t),\ (p,\ f(t)),\ qc) \wedge \text{HOLDS}(t,\ qc,\ ts,\ cond_2)$$
$$\Longrightarrow \text{HOLDS}(f(t),\ p,\ ts,\ cond_1\&cond_2). \qquad \text{(H16)}$$

The first axiom, states that there is a precondition relation involving *c, p,* and *qc,* with the time relation given by the non-ascending function $f(t)$. For example, suppose that the action move (p_1,p_2) stands for moving the content of position p_1 to position p_2. Then an appropriate precondition axiom might be PREC((move(p_1, p_2), t), (free(p_2), t), TRUE), which means that a move cannot take place, unless the destination position is free, and there are no qualification conditions. Note that this axiom requires, by (H16), that p_2 be free along any interval of time in which move(p_1,p_2) holds. A better axiom might require it to be free only when the move clips.

[1] If the duration of the cause is known, (like in **start**($[p,d]$)), then a precondition-cause overlap means: $f(t) \leq t + d$.

For a cause c, a future-effect e, and a qualification condition qc, the cause-future-effect relationship can be expressed by CAUSE((c, t), $(e, \mathrm{f}(t))$, qc), where f is a function on time-terms, and $\forall\, t$, $\mathrm{f}(t) \geq t$, and

$$\mathrm{HOLDS}(t, c, ts, cond_1) \wedge \mathrm{CAUSE}(\ (c, t),\ (e, \mathrm{f}(t)),\ qc\ ) \wedge \mathrm{HOLDS}(t, qc, ts, cond_2)$$
$$\Rightarrow \mathrm{HOLDS}(\mathrm{f}(t), e, ts, cond_1 \,\&\, cond_2). \tag{H17}$$

For the move action, a possible axiom stating that by the time the move is completed the previous content of p_1 (i.e., a) is at p_2, provided that p_2 is not icy, would be

$$\mathrm{CAUSE}(\ (\mathbf{start}([\mathrm{move}(p_1, p_2), d]), t), (\mathrm{at}(a, p_2), t+d), \mathrm{at}(a, p_1)\ \&\ \neg\ \mathrm{icy}(p_2)\ )$$

The cause-past-effect relationship can be handled similarly to the cause-precondition relationship. The relationship would be declared by a predicate P_EFF, and an axiom schema (H18), similar to (H16). For the "move" action a possible cause-past-effect axiom is

$$\mathrm{P\_EFF}(\ (\mathbf{start}([\mathrm{move}(p_1, p_2), d_{mv}]), t\ ), (\mathbf{clip}([\mathrm{at}(a, p_1), d_{at}]), t'), \mathrm{at}(a, p_1)\ \&\ t < t' < t+d\ ).$$

As an example, Consider the following time-structure TS_{gun}, which is one possible representation for the 'loaded gun scenario' presented in[7]:

$$TS_{gun} ::= (\ [\mathrm{alive}(\mathrm{friend}),\ d_{alive}]@0,\ \ [\mathrm{loaded},\ d_{loaded}]@1,\ [\mathrm{fire\ at}(\mathrm{friend}),\ .01]@3\ )$$

The action fire_at(friend) has the following temporal impact: if the gun is loaded then friend would be dead and the gun not loaded. We assume no preconditions. The cause would be **start**(fire_at(friend)), the future-effect would be **start**(dead(friend)), and the past-effect would be **clip**(loaded). The appropriate axioms would be

$$\mathrm{CAUSE}(\ (\mathbf{start}([\mathrm{fire\_at}(\mathrm{friend}), .01]), t\ ), (\mathbf{start}(\ [\mathrm{dead}(\mathrm{friend}), d\,]),\ \ t+.01), \mathrm{loaded}\ ) \tag{F5}$$

$$\mathrm{P\_EFF}(\ (\mathbf{start}([\mathrm{fire\_at}(\mathrm{friend}), .01]), t\ ), (\mathbf{clip}([\mathrm{loaded}, d_{loaded}\,]), t\ ), \mathrm{TRUE}\ ) \tag{F6}$$

and the appropriate versions of (H17) and (H18).[(2)] The question: "When is friend not alive?" is presented by the query HOLDS($when$, $\neg$ alive(friend), TS_{gun}, $cond$). Using the axiom TRUE(dead(x) $\supset$ $\neg$ alive(x)), the axioms presented in the previous sections, and the built in arithmetical knowledge, we can prove it with the binding $\{d_{loaded} \geq 2\ \&\ when \geq 3.01 / cond\}$, which says that if the gun is loaded for at least 2 time units, friend would be not alive at any time point that is greater than or equal 3.01. (Note that the time point $when$ did not get instantiated during the proof!). The proof appears in the full paper ([3]).

3.5. Handling Term-level Contradiction

In Section 3.1 we decided not to propagate term level negation ($\neg$) within a HOLDS atom, to the logic level negation ($\sim$) (i.e., axiom (H8) was uni-directional). This decision allows us to explicitly handle potential contradictions in the term level, instead of getting a contradiction in the logic level. Consider the gun example from Section 3.4. Suppose that we want to know when friend is alive. The query would be HOLDS($when$, alive(friend), TS_{gun}, $cond$). The immediate answer, obtained, by matching (H10), as the binding for $cond$, is $0 \leq when \leq d_{alive}$. This is not very informative. A better answer can be obtained if we pose the queries for alive(friend) and $\neg$ alive(friend). Axiom (H19) turns any HOLDS query about proposition p into a pair of queries about p and $\neg$(p), and then requires that they do not hold simultaneously.

$$\mathrm{HOLDS\_NO\_CNTR}\ (t_1, p, ts, cond) \Leftarrow \tag{H19}$$

$$\mathrm{HOLDS}(t_1, p, ts, cond_1) \wedge \mathrm{HOLDS}(t_2, \neg p, ts, cond_2) \wedge \mathrm{cond} = \mathrm{resolve}(t_1, \mathrm{cond}_1, t_2, \mathrm{cond}_2)$$

where resolve is assumed to contain built-in knowledge about augmenting the constraint $cond_1$ with $cond_2$, such that t_1 and t_2 cannot overlap. For the gun example, the query HOLDS_NO_CNTR($when$, alive(friend), TS_{gun}, $cond$) yields the two HOLDS queries, which

(2) Note that if the cause would have been just fire_at(friend), and the future-effect just dead(friend), then, by (H17), we would infer that if fire_at(friend) HOLDS in between time points t_s and t_c, then dead(friend) holds in between t_s +.01 to t_c +.01, i.e., a continuous dying situation! This is not only ridiculous, but simply incorrect, since the effect of fire_at is meant to be momentary, not continuous.

are proven with the binding
$\{0 \leq when \leq d_{alive}/cond_1,\ t_2 \geq 3.01 \& d_{loaded} \geq 2/cond_2\}$, and then triggers the goal $cond$ = resolve $(when,\ 0 \leq when \leq d_{alive},\ t_2,\ t_2 \geq 3.01 \& d_{loaded} \geq 2)$. The final binding for $cond$ would be $(d_{loaded} \geq 2 \supset 0 \leq when \leq 3.01) \vee (0 \leq when \leq d_{alive})$.

4. Computing Time-Structures

Reasoning with timeless and causal knowledge gives rise to *computing time structures* that result (or are caused) by a given one. This might be interesting for the purpose of efficient reasoning (explicit knowledge), for planning, for predicting the future, for explaining the past, etc. Tentatively we want to have a rule like

$$\text{CAUSED\_TS}(ts_0,\ (\ [p\ ,d\,]@t\ \bullet\ ts_0),\ (cond\ \&\ t \leq t' \leq t+d)) \Leftarrow \text{HOLDS}(t',\ p\ ,\ ts_0,\ cond).$$

which says that if p holds in a time-structure ts_0 at time-point t' under the condition $cond$, then ts_0 causes the time-structure $([p\ ,d\,]@t\ \bullet\ ts_0)$ whenever $cond\ \& t \leq t' \leq t+d$.

For the TS_{gun} example from Section 3.4, two caused time-structures are

$TS_1 ::= (\ [\neg\text{dead(friend)},\ d_{\neg\text{dead}}]@t\ \bullet\ TS_{gun})$ with $cond = t \leq 0 \& t + d_{\neg\text{dead}} \geq d_{alive}$ and

$TS_2 ::= (\ [\text{dead(friend)},\ d_{\text{dead}}]@t\ \bullet\ TS_{gun})$ with $cond = t \geq 3.01 \& d_{loaded} \geq 2$

Let the term *ultimate-time-structure* denote a time-structure that can cause only itself. Then, if our CAUSE_TS axioms are "appropriate", the set of all ultimate-time-structures that are caused by a given time-structure represents the set of all possible futures and past explanations, or in planning terms, all possible plans. (Of course, some may be infinite.) Selecting *reasonable* ultimate-time-structures, and rejecting non-reasonable ones seems to be a common-sense issue that would evaluate the "plausibility" of the conditions of different ultimate-time-structures, based on domain knowledge.

5. Common-Sense Reasoning

The study of common-sense reasoning within the time-structures framework is still in its infancy. We have considered predicate completion for the HOLDS predicate, since all axioms presented so far are Horn in HOLDS. By Reiter's theorem[21], results obtained from the completion can also be obtained from circumscription. We indeed got the effect of "this is all" for several time-structures. Yet, the completion of HOLDS has impact on the causality axioms and on the rules about term-level connectives; in particular, the interaction with (H8) must be investigated.

The issue of distinguishing the reasonable ultimate-time-structures seems to be an issue of common-sense reasoning. We envisage that additional, domain dependent criteria, would be needed to enable "jumping to conclusions" about "preferred" ultimate-time-structures. Persistency, as a general criterion seems wrong. (If my student was working at his terminal when I left my office on Friday, and he was at the terminal when I came in on Monday, should I conclude that he spent his weekend at the terminal? Now, replace "my student was at his terminal by "my student was unemployed" and persistency does become the natural conclusion.) For the ultimate-time-structures of TS_{gun}, the condition $d_{loaded} \geq 2$ might be preferred based on some knowledge about loaded guns, and not because 'loaded' is more eager to persist than 'alive(friend)'. For the bird-animal example of [19], a criterion involving the hierarchical structure of the domain might be appropriate (like the inferential distance of[25]). The notion of chronological ignorance is a criterion that we intend to investigate. We hope that since our time-structures and conditions reside in the term level, criteria for common-sense selection of preferred ultimate-time-structures can be formulated as axioms in the logic level.

References

1. J.F. Allen, "Towards a General Theory of Action and Time," *Artificial Intelligence*, vol. 23(2), pp. 123-154, 1984.
2. M. Balaban, "The TTS Language for Music Description," submitted to *Computer Music Journal*, 1986.
3. M. Balaban and N. Murray, "Using First Order Logic to Represent and to Reason with Temporal Knowledge," *Technical Report TR87-15, Department of Computer Science,*

SUNY at Albany, Albany, NY, 1987.

4. T.L. Dean and D.V. McDermott, "Temporal Data Base Management," *Artificial Intelligence*, vol. 32(1), pp. 1-55, 1987.
5. S.E. Fahlman, *NETL: A System for Representing and Using Real-World Knowledge*, The MIT Press, Cambridge, MA, 1979.
6. J.Y. Halpern and Y. Shoham, "A propositional Modal Logic of Time Intervals," *Proc. Symp. on Logic in Computer Science, IEEE*, Boston, Ma, 1986.
7. S. Hanks and D. McDermott, "Default Reasoning, Nonmonotonic Logics, and the Frame Problem," *Proceedings, AAAI-86*, pp. 328-333, Philadelphia, PA, 1986.
8. P. Hayes, "A Logic of Actions," in *Machine Intelligence*, ed. B. Meltzer and D. Michie, vol. 6, pp. 495-520, 1971.
9. C. Hewitt, "Description and Theoretical Analysis (Using Schemata) of PLANNER: A Language for Proving Theorems and Manipulating Models in a Robot," *Report No. AI-TR-258, AI Laboratory, Massachusetts Institute of Technology*, Cambridge, MA, 1971.
10. H.A. Kautz, "The Logic of Persistence," *Proceedings AAAI-86*, pp. 401-405, Philadelphia, Pa, 1986.
11. R. Kowalski and M. Sergot, "A Logic-based Calculus of Events," *New Generation Computing*, vol. 4, pp. 67-95, 1986.
12. P. Ladkin, "Primitives and Units for Time Specification," *Proceedings AAAI-86*, pp. 354-359, Philadelphia, PA, 1986.
13. P. Ladkin, "Time Representation: A Taxonomy of Interval Relations," *Proceedings AAAI-86*, Philadelphia, PA, 1986.
14. B. Leban, D.D. McDonald, and D.R. Forster, "A Representation for Collections of Temporal Intervals," *Proceedings AAAI-86*, pp. 367-371, Philadelphia, PA, 1986.
15. H.J. Levesque, "Making Believers Out of Computers," *AI*, vol. 30(1), pp. 81-108, 1986.
16. J. McCarthy and P.J. Hayes, "Some Philosophical Problems from the Standpoint of Artificial Intelligence," in *Machine Intelligence*, ed. B. Meltzer and D. Michie, vol. 4, pp. 463-502, 1969.
17. J. McCarthy, "Applications of Circumscription to Formalizing Common-Sense Knowledge," *Artificial Intelligence*, vol. 28, pp. 89-116, 1986.
18. D. McDermott, "A Temporal Logic for Reasoning About Processes and Plans," *Cognitive Science*, vol. 6, pp. 101-155, 1982.
19. P. Morris, "Curing Anomalous Extensions," *Proceedings AAAI-87*, Seattle WA, 1987.
20. F.J. Pelletier, "Seventy-Five Problems for Testing Automatic Theorem Provers," *Journal of Automated Reasoning*, vol. 2, pp. 191-216, 1986.
21. R. Reiter, "Circumscription Implies Predicate Completion (Sometimes)," *Proceedings AAAI-82*, pp. 418-420, Pittsburgh, PA, 1982.
22. Y. Shoham, "Temporal Logics in AI: Semantical and Ontological Considerations," *Artificial Intelligence*, (to appear 1986).
23. Y. Shoham, "Chronological Ignorance, Time, Nonmonotonicity, Necessity and Causal Theories," *Proceedings AAAI-86*, pp. 389-393, Philadelphia, PA, 1986.
24. Y. Shoham, "On Domain-Independent Theories of Causation," *Experimental Draft*, 1986.
25. D.S. Touretzky, "Implicit Ordering of Defaults in Inheritance Systems," *Proceedings of AAAI-84*, pp. 322-325, Austin, TX, 1984.

KNOWLEDGE REPRESENTATION FOR PARTLY-STRUCTURED PROBLEMS

J. A. Bowen
Department of Computer Science
North Carolina State University
Box 8206
Raleigh, North Carolina 27695-8206

Abstract:
Solutions to well-structured problems are appropriately stated in block-structured procedural programming languages, while, at the other extreme, unstructured problems are appropriately addressed by flat systems of forward-chaining imperative productions. This paper presents a methodology for programming partly-structured problems which lie along the spectrum between these two extremes.

CHOICE OF PROGRAMMING PARADIGM

If a problem domain is un-structured, knowledge of it comprising a set of disjoint chunks, a production system is the most natural kind of programming language to use for solving problems in the domain; each chunk of domain knowledge is mapped onto an individual production. In contrast, whenever a problem is well-structured, it is most appropriate to use an analogously structured program in a block-structured procedural language [6].

This paper is concerned with a knowledge representation methodology for partly-structured problem domains, those which are partly well-structured and partly un-structured. For illustrative purposes, the discussion will be centered around the grocery configuration problem presented in [13].

THE GROCERY CONFIGURATION PROBLEM

Winston [13] explains the concepts underlying the R1/XCON computer configuration program [10] by making analogies with the task of configuring grocery orders. A typical performance of this latter task is shown in Figure 1.

```
INITIAL SELECTION: (one item at a time; to end type "complete")
Item please: bread.
Item please: cheese.
Item please: potato_chips.
Item please: complete.

Have added pepsi Have added butter Have added jam

FINAL SELECTION:
bag2 contains [bread, cheese, potato_chips]
bag1 contains [butter, jam, pepsi]
```

Figure 1: Configuring grocery purchases.

The user inputs his initial selection of groceries, terminating the list by typing the word *complete*. Next, the program amends this initial selection, adding any further items it believes the user has overlooked; for example, if the user has selected potato chips without selecting Pepsi, the program will add Pepsi to the selection. Then the program considers how to pack the groceries into bags, taking care to place heavy items, such as bottles of Pepsi, at the bottom of bags, where they will not crush delicate items such as packets of potato chips. Finally, the program prints out the final selection of groceries and its suggestion for how these ought to be packed, listing the top-most item in a bag first.

GRAPHICAL REPRESENTATION OF STRUCTURE

The main purpose of this paper is to present a textual approcah, which can be used in practical programming languages, for representing the structure (and lack of it) perceived in partly-structured problems. But it is also convenient to be able to represent this information in a graphical form; this can be done using a type of diagram called a *structure diagram* [3].

Consider, for example, the diagram in Figure 2 which shows the structure inherent in the grocery configuration problem. In this, as in all structure diagrams, the vertical axis represents time (with the progression being from the top of the diagram to the bottom) and the horizontal axis represents choice. Whenever there are several alternative courses of action which may be followed at a particular stage of solving a problem, these alternatives are placed side by side, orizontally, in the diagram. When execution control reaches a point where there are several alternatives, the control cycles through this set of alternative courses of action until a stage is reached where no course of action is deemed appropriate. Then, control is passed forward, that is, downward in the diagram.

Methodologies for Intelligent Systems
Z. W. Ras and M. Zemankova, Editors

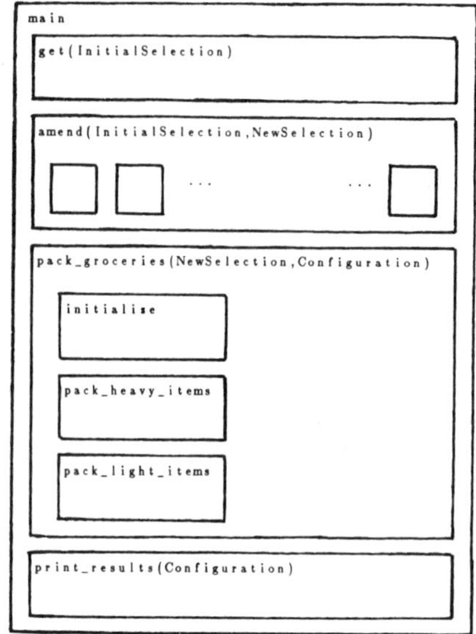

Figure 2: Structure diagram for the grocery configuration task.

Figure 2 shows that, at the topmost level, the grocery configuration task is well-structured: there are four stages: getting the initial selection; amending this selection to produce a new selection; packing the new selection of groceries into a configuration of bags; printing the final configuration.

Like other types of diagram, the amount of information shown in a structure diagram depends on the level of detail at which it is drawn. At the level of detail shown in Figure 2, the first and fourth stages of the overall task are portrayed as primitive operations, although they are, in fact, well-structured non-primitives. The second stage is shown to be ill-structured: depending on the groceries chosen for the initial selection, a wide range of different courses of action are possible. The third stage of the task is shown to be structured into three phases: initialization; packing the heavy items; packing the light items.

In this diagram, ill-structuredness was shown nested within well-structuredness. This, however, is only one of the many different relationships which may occur between well-structuredness and ill-structuredness in a partly-structured problem. Almost any relationship may occur. Ill-structuredness and well-structuredness can be inter-nested to any level. Any relationship can be shown in a structure diagram.

IMPLEMENTING PARTLY-STRUCTURED PROGRAMS

A partly-structured problem may be addressed by a set of productions. An implementation, in MUFL†, of the grocery configuration task, is given in Appendix I. However, it requires very careful reading of the program in Appendix I to determine that it does, in fact, correspond to the structure diagram shown in Figure 2. A better style is required for implementing partly-structured programs. The productions must be organized in a fashion which better reflects the inherent structure of the problem.

One approach for organizing productions was suggested by McDernott [11,12] and presented in more detail by Brownston et al [5]. In this approach, the overall task is divided into sub-tasks and working memory at various times contains flags indicating the sub-tasks of the problem that the system is "doing" at that particular time. Each production concerned with a particular task has as its first condition a test for the presence in working memory of the correct flag. Besides the productions concerned with the actual problem-solving activity, there are productions, with less specific conditions [9], for directing the flow of control between the

†MUFL (MUlti-Formalism Language) is a language which supports a range of progamming paradigms: imperative productions, declarative productions, block-structured programming, functional programming [2].

various sub-tasks, by storing and removing flags. The structure of the program can be discovered by skimming through the control-flow productions, ignoring the problem-solving productions.

The rest of this paper presents an approach, which is an elaboration of that given by McDernott, and Brownston et al., that enables the programmer to express more clearly the structure which is present in partly-structured problems. This approach is based on usage of a programming concept which bridges the gap between procedural programming and production systems.

METHODS

The *method* † [3] is a programming concept which is used to explicitly represent structure present in a partly-structured problem.

Like a procedure, a method specifies a sequence of tasks which must be executed when performing a higher level task. Also like procedures, methods may be parameterised and may be organised into hierarchies. Also like procedures, the task sequence specified by a method may contain looping and conditional constructs, and methods may be recursive. The crucial difference between a procedure and a method is that while both are used to represent structure, only a method may be used to represent structure which has underlying lack of structure.

Suppose that we have a partly-structured problem which involves two stages, *a* and *b*. Suppose that task *a* has two stages, *a1* and *a2*, and that task *b* has two stages, the first involving task *b1* and the second a repeated performance of task *a2*. Suppose that the leaf node tasks, *a1*, *a2*, and *b1*, are ill-structured. The organisation of this problem is graphically represented in Figure 3.

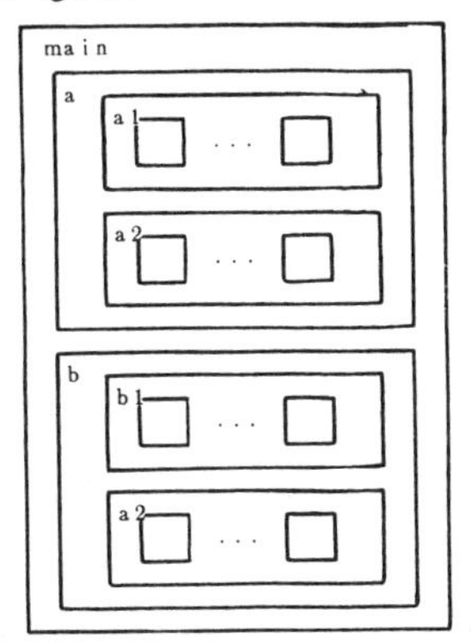

Figure 3: Structure diagram for a partly-structured problem.

The structural hierarchy present in this problem could not be implemented as a hierarchy of procedures, because the leaf node tasks, being ill-structured, must be implemented using a hierarchy of methods, as shown in Figure 4, where indentation is used to indicate nesting.

```
method(main,[a,b]).

    method(a,[a1,a2]).

        /*PRODUCTIONS for task: a1*/
        when doing(a1) and ... then ...
        when doing(a1) and ... then ...
        .
        .
        /*PRODUCTIONS for task: a2*/
        when doing(a2) and ... then ...
        when doing(a2) and ... then ...
        .
        .
    method(b,[b1,a2]).

        /*PRODUCTIONS for task: b1*/
        when doing(b1) and ... then ...
        when doing(b1) and ... then ...
        .
```

Figure 4: Method-based implementation of the partly-strucutred problem illustrated in Figure 3.

†Method is used here in a different sense to its usage in the object-oriented programming literature [1].

In this program, the first method states that the overall task invloves performing tasks *a* and *b*, while the second method states that performing task *a* involves performing tasks *a1* and *a2*. Task *a1* is implemented as a set of productions. Each such production states whenever we are *doing* task *a1* and certain other conditions are satisfied, then some sequence of actions should be performed. There is a similar set of productions for task *a2*.

The moethod for task *b* states that this task involves performing tasks *b1* and *a2*. Task *b1* is implemented as a set of productions and the earlier implementation given for task *a2* is still valid here.

This method-based program is written in MUFL. The methods are just entries in working memory and the flow of execution control which they specifiy must be imposed by a meta-level interpreter, also written in MUFL. While this interpreter and its derivation are explained in [3] someone wishing only to understand the program in Figure 4 need not refer to the interpreter.

The chief advantage of this new method-based approach is that the control structure inherent in a program is explicitly stated in the methods for the program. A separation has been achieved between the control flow information particular to solving an individual problem and the general mechanism needed to impose the required flow of control [3]. Methods can be used in other languages besides MUFL [4], such as OPS5 [7].

USING PROCEDURES, METHODS AND PRODUCTIONS TOGETHER

In a language which supports both productions and procedures, as MUFL does, the method concept can be used together with these other two formalisms, to produce a very explicit representation of the structure, and lack of it, present in a partly-structured problem. Furthermore, most of the notions used with procedures can be applied to methods. For example, parameterisation, as a way of explicitly stating the information shared between tasks, can be used not only in procedures but also in methods.

In a program which uses methods, procedures and productions to explicitly distinguish between well-structuredness and ill-structuredness, procedures are used to implement well-structuredness with no underlying lack of structure. However, well-structuredness which does have underlying lack of structure is implemented as methods. Ill-structuredness which has no underlying well-structuredness is implemented as productions with simple action parts. Ill-structuredness which does have underlying well-structuredness is implemented as productions whose action parts invoke either procedures or methods, depending on whether or not that underlying well-structuredness has further ill-structuredness underlying it at a lower level. Thus, complex interleavings of well-structuredness and ill-structuredness can be explicitly represented.

It often happens that, during the implementation of a partly-structured problem, an improved perception of the structure inherent in the problem is acquired. When the perception of a problem's structure is improved, this is reflected by a reduction in the number of productions needed: related productions coalesce. When a group of productions which implement what was previously perceived as an ill-structured task coalesce into one production, that task has become well-structured. This may have knock-on effects further up in the task hierarchy. When all the sub-tasks of a particular task which is currently implemented as a method have become well-structured, the method for that task may be replaced by a procedure. Eventually, a program which was originally composed of procedures, methods and productions may be reduced to a procedural hierarchy, if the problem has been recognised as completely well-structured.

This process may be seen at work, to a certain extent, with the grocery problem. Further consideration of the pack groceries task leads to a realization that the apparent lack of structure perceived in this task is actually incorrect. A separate production, which detects the need for a new bag and interrupts the normal packing operation, is not needed. Instead, the operation of putting an item into a bag has a bifurcated structure: a single conditional test can be used to determine the need for a new bag. This realization, leading to a new analysis of the pack groceries task, means that all un-structuredness can be removed from this task. Consequently, a procedure can be used for the task, since there is no longer any underlying lack of structure.

Consider the implementation of the grocery configuration problem which is given in Appendix II. The data structures shared between the four sub-tasks of the overall program are explicitly stated in the method for the overall program, as parameters for the tasks quoted in the method. Of the four tasks, three are now recognised to be completely well-structured. Each of these tasks is implemented as a single production which calls a procedure, or hierarchy of procedures. Only the amend selection task, still perceived as lacking in structure, has more than one production. Only the ill-structuredness present in the amend selection task prevents the replacement of the method for the overall program by a procedure. Thus, only the ill-structuredness present in the amend selection task prevents the entire program from being reduced to a procedural hierarchy.

IMPLICATIONS FOR RUN-TIME EFFICIENCY

Production system programs can be interpreted, or, for greater run-time speed, they can be compiled into run-time code where the condition parts of productions are implemented as routines that correspond to nodes in a RETE network [8].

Consider a problem which is implemented as a collection of productions, although it is inherently well-structured, and therefore amenable to implementation in a procedural style. If this production system program is compiled into a set of routines which correspond to nodes in a RETE network, the resultant code will still not execute as fast as the code that could have been generated from a procedural statement of the same problem. This is because the RETE network routines must include a large number of conditional instructions that would not be present in code generated from procedural text.

When the structure present in a partly-structured problem is explicitly stated in the program for that problem, this information can be used by a compiler to generate efficient run-time code from the program. Those parts of the program which are ill-structured, and implemented as collection of productions, can be compiled into RETE network routines, while those parts which are well-structured, and implemented as procedures or methods, can be complied into more efficient code. The code generated from a method will invoke the RETE network code generated from the productions which perform the tasks involved in the method. However, only those tasks which are implemented as two or more productions require the generation of RETE network code. RETE network code need not be generated for those tasks which involve the use of only one production; normal procedural code can be used, because these single productions essentially form bridges between methods and procedures.

CONCLUSIONS

An approach for explicitly stating all the structure perceived in a partly-structured problem has been presented. The approach, based on the use of methods, productions and procedures, can be used to develop a program from a stage where it is heavily ill-structured right through to the stage, if it is ever reached, where it is completely well-structured. At all times, the approach enables the programmer's perception of the structure inherent in a problem to be expressed in a clear way, and it enables the traditional methodology of top-down programming to be used in the step-by-step refinement of programs for partly-structured problems. The structural information so represented can be used by a compiler for generating more efficient code than would be generated in the absence of this explicit information. The approach has been presented in terms of the MUFL language. The approach should also, however, be of use in other languages, to the extent that the architecture of those languages resemble that of MUFL. For example [4], the approach can be used for programming in OPS5 [7], although certain modifications must be made, to take account of the differences between MUFL and OPS5.

REFERENCES

[1] Bobrow D g, and Stefik M, "The LOOPS Manual, A Data and Object Oriented Programming System for Interlisp", Technical Report, Xerox PARC, (1982).

[2] Bowen J A, "MUFL: A Multi-Formalism Language for Knowledge Engineering Applications", Department of Computer Science, North Carolina State University, Technical Report TR-86-16, (1986).

[3] Bowen J A , "Programming Partly Structured Problems", Department of Computer Science, North Carolina State University, Technical Report TR-86-17, (1986).

[4] Bowen J A, "Method-Based Programming in OPS5", Department of Computer Science, North Carolina State University, Technical Report TR-86-18, (1986).

[5] Brownston L, Farrell R, Kant E, and Martin N, "Programming Expert Systems of OPS5", Addison-Wesley, Reading (Mass), (1985).

[6] Davis R, and King J, An Overview of Production Systems, "Machine Intelligence", vol. 8, pp. 300-332, (1977).

[7] Forgy C L, "OPS5 User's Manual", Department of Computer Science, Carnegie-Mellon University, Technical Report CMU-CS-81-135, (1981).

[8] Forgy C L, "RETE: A fast algorithm for the many pattern/many object pattern match problem", Artificial Intelligence, vol. 19, no. 1, pp. 17-37.

[9] Jackson P, "Introduction to Expert Systems", Addison-Wesley, Wokingham (UK), (1986).

[10] McDermott J, "R1: an expert in the computer systems domain", Proceedings of the AAAI Conference, pp. 269-271, (1980).
[11] McDermott J, "Extracting Knowledge from Expert Systems", Proceedings of the Joint International Conference on Artificial Intelligence, pp. 100-107, (1983).
[12] McDermott J, "Building Expert Systems", Department of Computer Science, Carnegie-Mellon University, Draft Paper, (1983).
[13] Winston P H, "Artificial Intelligence", Addison-Wesley, Reading (Mass), (1983).

APPENDIX I

An implementation of the grocery configuration task, in which no attempt has been made to explicitly represent any of the structure which is implicit in the task.

```
/*when idle, start working, by getting the user's initial selection*/
when untrue(working)
then store working and
    output 'INITIAL SELECTION: (one item at a time; to end type "complete")'
    and newline and store selected([])
    and repeatedly do
        (output 'Item please: ' and input Item
         and provided (Item <> complete)
              do (retrieve selected(List) and make Newlist = Item plus List
                 and replace selected(List) by selected(Newlist) ) ) until (Item = complete).

/*ensure that a selection which contains bread also contains butter*/
when selected(List) and bread in List and untrue(butter in List)
then make Newlist = butter plus List and replace selected(List) by selected(Newlist).

/*ensure that a selection which contains potato chips also contains pepsi*/
when selected(List) and potato_chips in List and untrue(pepsi in List)
then make Newlist = pepsi plus List and replace selected(List) by selected(Newlist).

   /*productions concerned with other complementary items appear here*/

/*ensure that a selection which contains bread also contains jam*/
when selected(List) and bread in List and untrue(jam in List)
then make Newlist = jam plus List and replace selected(List) by selected(Newlist).

/*mark the list of selected groceries as unbagged*/
when selected(List) then replace selected(List) by unbagged(List).

/*when there are groceries to be packed, and no bag is present, fetch first bag*/
when unbagged(List) and List <> [] and untrue(bag(_,_)) then store bag(bag1,contains([])).

/*if there are any heavy items, put them into bags first*/
when unbagged(List) and Item in List and details_of(item(Item),weight(heavy))
    and bag(Bagname,contains(Contents)) and length of Contents < 3
then make Newcontents = Item plus Contents
    and replace bag(Bagname,contains(Contents)) by bag(Bagname,contains(Newcontents))
    and make Newlist = List minus Item and replace unbagged(List) by unbagged(Newlist).

/*put other items into bags*/
when unbagged(List) and Item in List
    and bag(Bagname,contains(Contents)) and length of Contents < 3
then make Newcontents = Item plus Contents
    and replace bag(Bagname,contains(Contents)) by bag(Bagname,contains(Newcontents))
    and make Newlist = List minus Item and replace unbagged(List) by unbagged(Newlist).
/*whenever there is no room in an existing bag, then start a new bag*/
when unbagged(List) and List <> []
    and untrue(bag(Bagname,contains(Contents)) and length of Contents < 3 )
    and bag(Bagname,_) and untrue(bag(Bagname2,_) and Bagname2 after Bagname)
then make Newbagname = successor of Bagname and store bag(Newbagname,contains([])).
```

```
/*when finished putting groceries into bags, commence task of printing the results*/
when unbagged([])
then remove unbagged([]) and newline
    and output 'FINAL CONFIGURATION: (top item in a bag listed first)' and newline.

/*print out the contents of a bag which have not been listed before*/
when bag(Bagname,contains(Contents))
then output Bagname & ' contains'
    and for all Item in Contents do (output ' ' & Item) and newline
    and remove bag(Bagname,contains(Contents)).

/*when finished working, then stop*/
when working then remove working and halt.
```

APPENDIX II:

This version of the grocery configuration program uses both methods and procedures.

```
/*OVERALL PROGRAM*/
method(main,[get(InitialSelection), amend_selection(InitialSelection,NewSelection),
          pack_groceries(NewSelection,Configuration), print_results(Configuration)]).

    /*GET INITIAL SELECTION*/
    when doing(get(InitialSelection)) and unbound InitialSelection
    then get(InitialSelection) and restore doing(get(InitialSelection)).

    /*AMEND SELECTION*/
    /*initially, temportarily make NewSelection = InitialSelection*/
    when doing(amend_selection(InitialSelection,NewSelection)) and unbound NewSelection
    then make NewSelection = InitialSelection
        and restore doing(amend_selection(InitialSelection,NewSelection)).

    when doing(amend_selection(InitialSelection,OldSelection))
        and bread in OldSelection and untrue(butter in OldSelection)
    then make NewSelection = butter plus OldSelection
        and change doing(amend_selection(InitialSelection,OldSelection)) to
                doing(amend_selection(InitialSelection,NewSelection)).

    when doing(amend_selection(InitialSelection,OldSelection))
        and potato_chips in OldSelection and untrue(pepsi in OldSelection)
    then make NewSelection = pepsi plus OldSelection
        and change doing(amend_selection(InitialSelection,OldSelection)) to
                doing(amend_selection(InitialSelection,NewSelection)).

   /*productions concerned with other complementary items appear here*/

    when doing(amend_selection(InitialSelection,OldSelection))
        and bread in OldSelection and untrue(jam in OldSelection)
    then make NewSelection = jam plus OldSelection
        and change doing(amend_selection(InitialSelection,OldSelection)) to
                doing(amend_selection(InitialSelection,NewSelection)).

    /*PACK GROCERIES*/
    when doing(pack_groceries(Groceries,Configuration)) and unbound Configuration
    then pack_groceries(Groceries,Configuration)
         and restore doing(pack_groceries(Groceries,Configuration)).

    /*PRINT RESULTS*/
    when doing(print_results(Configuration)) and Configuration <> []
    then print_results(Configuration).
```

```
/*PROCEDURE DEFINITIONS*/
to get(InitialSelection)
 do (output 'INITIAL SELECTION: (one item at a time; to end type "complete")'
    and newline and store selected([])
    and repeatedly do
          (output 'Item please: ' and input Item
           and provided (Item <> complete)
               do (retrieve selected(List) and make Newlist = Item plus List
                  and replace selected(List) by selected(Newlist) ) )
       until (Item = complete) and remove selected(InitialSelection)).

to pack_groceries(Groceries,Configuration)
do (pack_heavy_items(Groceries,PartialConfiguration)
   and pack_light_items(Groceries,PartialConfiguration,Configuration)).

to pack_heavy_items(Groceries,PartialConfiguration)
do (store config([]) and
   for all Item in Groceries
      do (provided details(Item,weight(heavy))
           do (retrieve config(Config) and pack(Item,Config,NewConfig)
              and change config(Config) to config(NewConfig)))
   and remove config(PartialConfiguration)).

to pack_light_items(Groceries,PartialConfiguration,Configuration)
do (store config(PartialConfiguration) and
   for all Item in Groceries
      do (retrieve config(Config) and pack(Item,Config,NewConfig)
         and change config(Config) to config(NewConfig))
and remove config(Configuration)).

to pack(Item,OldConfig,NewConfig)
do (provided (bag(BagName,contains(Contents)) in OldConfig and length of Contents < 3)
     do (make NewContents = Item plus Contents
        and make NewConfig = OldConfig minus
                         bag(BagName,contains(Contents)) plus
                         bag(BagName,contains(NewContents)))
   otherwise
     do (devise(NewName,OldConfig)
        and make NewConfig = OldConfig plus bag(NewName,contains([Item])))).

to devise(NewName,OldConfig)
do (provided (bag(Name1,_) in OldConfig and
          untrue( bag(Name2,_) in OldConfig and Name2 after Name1))
     do make NewName = successor of Name1
   otherwise do make NewName = bag1).

to print_results(Configuration)
do  (newline and output 'FINAL CONFIGURATION: (top item in a bag listed first)'
      and newline
      and for all bag(BagName,contains(Contents)) in Configuration
              do (output BagName & ' contains' and enumerate Contents)).

 to enumerate List do (for all Item in List do (display Item) and newline).

 to display Item do output ' ' & Item.
```

Frame and Inheritance Systems[1]

Minkoo Kim and Anthony S. Maida

Department of Computer Science
333 Whitmore Laboratory
Pennsylvania State University
University Park, PA 16802

Abstract

Inheritance theory is concerned with specifying the situations under which valid inferences can be computed in knowledge bases that contain exception-permitting hierarchically-organized default knowledge. Although inheritance representations are popular among AI practitioners, inheritance theory has been primarily developed for the domain of IS-A hierarchies based on Fahlman-style [4] network structures. This paper sketches a generalization of the inheritance theory of Touretzky [9] so that it can more simply be applied to a broader class of frame languages.

1. Introduction

Most AI languages based on frames and/or semantic networks include inheritance facilities of some sort (e.g., KRL [1], KL-ONE [3], NETL [4], FRL [8], KRYPTON [2], FLAVORS [10]). Some of these languages allow both exceptions to default knowledge and multiple inheritance at the same time. Although such systems seem necessary in realistic domains, formal specification of the appropriate performance characteristics of these systems has only recently begun. The complexity of exception-permitting inheritance systems stems from the fact that, in the absence of a theory of inference, the set of conclusions derivable from a realistic knowledge base is almost always ambiguous. Figure 1 illustrates this problem adapted from Touretzky [9]. This figure encodes information about a hierarchy of elephant classes. In particular: *Elephants are typically gray; Circus elephants are elephants; Royal elephants are circus elephants, but are typically not gray; Clyde is a royal elephant; Clyde is an elephant.* In Figure 1, it is unclear whether Clyde is gray. The ambiguity of the network stems from the interaction of two sources. First, we have an exception: Elephants are gray, except royal elephants. Second, we have a tangled hierarchy where Clyde is both a royal-elephant and an elephant.

One approach to this problem is to forbid the use of redundant assertions in the taxonomy and then use something called the shortest path ordering to control the inheritance process. We could apply this to Figure 1 by removing the assertion that Clyde is an elephant. With this modified network, it requires one inferential step to conclude that Clyde is not gray but three steps to conclude he is gray. By using the shortest path, we conclude that Clyde is not gray. Had we not modified the network, the path length for both conclusions would have been one, and the network would consequently have been either inconsistent or ambiguous.

---

1. This research was supported by ONR contract N00014-85-K-0521.

Methodologies for Intelligent Systems
Z. W. Ras and M. Zemankova, Editors

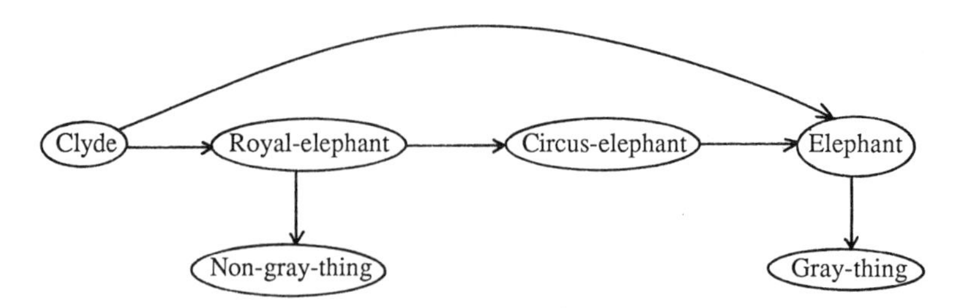

Figure 1. A portion of an ISA hierarchy.

Touretzky [9] used the inferential distance ordering as an alternative to the shortest path ordering. Touretzky's motivations for use of this measure were twofold: to maintain robust behavior in the face of redundant links; and to detect ambiguous networks. Unlike the shortest path ordering, when the network becomes redundant, conclusions derived from the inferential distance ordering remain unchanged.

The intuition underlying the inferential distance ordering is that if there is a path from "A" to "C" via "B," then "B" is between "A" and "C" and hence is closer to "A" than "C" is. This remains true even in the presence of redundant assertions.

Touretzky assumed a Fahlman-style ISA hierarchy [4] as his knowledge representation language; the inferential distance ordering was developed to apply to that kind of structure. This paper extends the inferential distance ordering to apply more general structures than ISA hierarchies. These structures will be called *inferential hierarchies*. To represent inferential hierarchies, we use a formalism based on a construct called a *knowledge packet*. We then adapt Touretzky's formalization from ISA hierarchies to the knowledge packet language so that it can be applied to a broader class of languages.

2. Generalizing Touretzky's Inheritance Theory

We propose that the inferential distance ordering can be considered for use in any domain which involves non-cyclic chains of inference. For example, consider the following set of facts.

Typically, a person who dies has a funeral.
Typically, a person who is hanged does not have a funeral.
If a person is hanged, then the person is killed.
If a person is killed, then the person dies.

These facts tend to be static and taxonomic in character. They would be stable across applications. In contrast, we will classify the fact below as *episodic* because it is likely to be true for one episode only. It is also likely to be a user assertion.

John hanged Bill.

That is, episodic infeormation is the kind of information that would change from one circumstance to another.

We will now code the taxonomic knowledge in nonmonotonic logic [7] and sketch how the inferential distance ordering can be applied to this knowledge. Later we will recode it as knowledge packets. After recoding it to knowledge packets, we will no longer use nonmonotonic logic for taxonomic knowledge.

$\forall$ (x, y) (hanged x y) ---> (killed x y)
$\forall$ (x, y) (killed x y) ---> (died y)
$\forall$ (x, y) (hanged x y) Λ M(NOT (has-a-funeral y)) ---> (NOT (has-a-funeral y))
$\forall$ (y) (died y) Λ M(has-a-funeral y) ---> (has-a-funeral y),

where M is a modal operator (c.f., [7]). Using these inferential relationships, it is possible to construct the inferential hierarchies in Figure 2. The expression (hanged x y) $\nrightarrow$ (has-a-funeral y) should be read as (hanged x y) ---> (NOT (has-a-funeral y)). The same default reasoning patterns that apply to subsumption relationships in ISA hierarchies apply also to these chains of inference. Similarly, in the previous example, using the inferential distance ordering, we can conclude "Bill does not have a funeral" rather than "Bill has a funeral."

The predicates contained in this figure are relational. Although Touretzky's scheme could apply to relational predicates, the method was cumbersome. For example, the rule $\forall$ (x, y) (hanged x y) ---> (killed x y) could not be easily represented in his scheme. At most, the rule $\forall$ (x) (hanged x John) ---> (killed x John) could be handled, since this rule can be mapped to an IS-A hierarchy where a person who hanged John is a person who killed John. Because of this, his scheme has difficulties handling relations of higher arity (c.f., [9]).

Often inference rules will have a conjunction in the antecedent as shown below.

$\forall$ (x, y) (ELEPHANT x) Λ (SNAKE y) ---> (NOT (fears x y)).

Since the expression "(ELEPHANT x)" or the expression "(SNAKE y)" each could play a role in determining the truth of the expression "(NOT (fears x y))," we will say that "(ELEPHANT x)" *constrains* "(NOT (fears x y))" and "(SNAKE y)" also *constrains* "(NOT (fears x y))."[1] We note in passing that the *constrain* relation subsumes implication. The purpose of *constrain* is to allow the inferential distance ordering to apply to cases where more than one inference chain must succeed in order to draw some conclusion. Inferential distance will be the path-length of the longest chain.

User Assertions. User assertions encode episodic knowledge that is likely to vary from domain to domain, such as illustrated in the expression below.

(hanged John Bill)

Given the data base in Figure 2, we want to conclude that Bill died but did not have a funeral. The language for user assertions is a restricted form of predicate calculus. The only connective allowed is NOT. We do not allow embedded negations. We distinguish

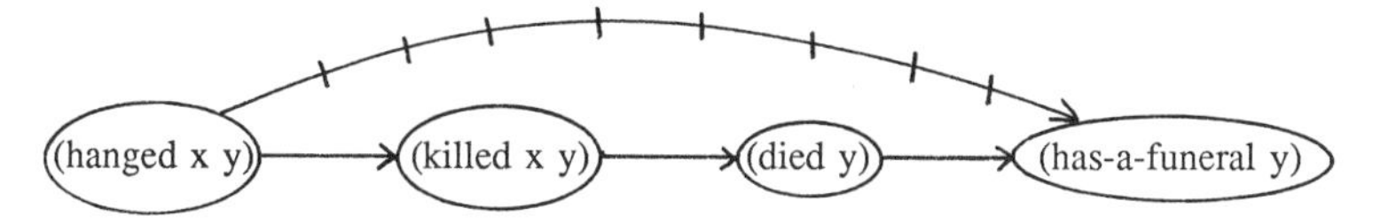

Figure 2. An inferential hierarchy.

1. In a technical report [5], we call this relation *affect*. We offer more detailed justification and discussion of this relation in the technical report.

something called *object-oriented predicates*. These are a kind of one-place predicate in which instances of the predicates are naturally viewed as objects. For instance, although both "(small John)" and "(PERSON John)" are formulas with one-place predicates, we only consider the latter formula to contain an object-oriented predicate. Object-oriented predicates are written in capitals, as well as the connective NOT. Because it is natural to express and because Touretzky used similar conventions, we allow object-oriented predicates to serve as arguments. This takes us outside of first-order logic. The first letter of a constant is capitalized. Below are possible examples of user assertions.

(ELEPHANT Clyde)
(fears Clyde SNAKE)
(SNAKE Ziggy)
(NOT (fears Clyde Ziggy))

The expression (fears Clyde SNAKE) can be translated into nonmonotonic logic [7] as:

$\forall$ (x) (SNAKE x) Λ M(fears Clyde x) --> (fears Clyde x).

To treat object-oriented predicates as arguments, we need to define the following *instantiation* process

Instantiation: Let R be a relation, C_1 and C_2 be constants, and P be an object-oriented predicate. We can substitute constants for object-oriented predicates provided that they are instances of the predicate. If we have (R C_1 P) and wish to consider substituting C_2 for P in order to get (R C_1 C_2), then we can do this if (P C_2) is true.

We call (R C_1 C_2) an *instantiation* of the formula (R C_1 P) under the set of formulas containing (P C_2). Alternatively, we say that (R C_1 C_2) is *instantiated* from (R C_1 P) by means of (P C_2).

3. Knowledge Packets

This section describes knowledge packets. Knowledge packets are used to encode taxonomic knowledge in inferential hierarchies. We use knowledge packets because they are relatively easy to formalize and have syntactic similarities to a frame language Uni-Frame [6].

We now show by example how to translate the taxonomic knowledge, which is encoded in nonmonotonic logic, into knowledge packets.

P ---> R
P ---> S
Q Λ M(P) ---> P

The above data base would be translated into two knowledge packets, one associated with the predicate of P and the other associated with the predicate of Q. The packets appear below.

[P, (R, S)]
[Q, (P)]

Below is another example encoding knowledge about elephant's attitudes toward reptiles.

[(ELEPHANT x), ((gray x))]
[(ROYAL-ELEPHANT x), ((ELEPHANT x), (NOT (gray x)))]
[(MAMMAL x), ((fears x REPTILE))]

The first two knowledge packets encode the following:

$\forall$ (x) (ELEPHANT x) Λ M(gray x) ---> (gray x)

$\forall$ (x) (ROYAL-ELEPHANT x) Λ M(ELEPHANT x) ---> (ELEPHANT x)
$\forall$ (x) (ROYAL-ELEPHANT x) Λ M(NOT (gray x)) ---> (NOT (gray x)).

The third packet contains an implicit conjunction because it encodes the formula below.

$\forall$ (x, y) (MAMMAL x) Λ (REPTILE y) Λ M(fears x y) ---> (fears x y).

This becomes important when we need to consider the *constrain* relation in formalizing the inferential distance ordering.

Elaboration. When a user assertion such as "(ELEPHANT Clyde)" is added to the knowledge base, then we can elaborate our knowledge about Clyde by invoking the packet associated with the predicate ELEPHANT. We add the expression "(gray x)" to the knowledge base with x bound to Clyde. Because of this method for deriving new facts we name the parts of a knowledge packet like the one below

$[A, (C_1, C_2, \ldots C_n)]$

as follows. A is the antecedent and "$(C_1, C_2, \ldots C_n)$" is the consequent. We call the process of elaborating our knowledge about Clyde *elaborative derivation* or *e-derivation.* A definition is given below.

> **E-derivation:** Assume a set of knowledge packets, K, containing exactly one packet associated with each predicate p. For a user assertion, $\alpha = (p\ x_1 \ldots x_n)$, if it unifies with the antecedent of the packet associated with p then the resulting substitution is applied to the consequent of the packet. From this we can get new formulas which are added to the knowledge base. These formulas are called *e-derivations* of α under K.

4. Adapting the Inferential Distance Ordering to Instantiation and E-derivation

We have modified Touretzky's formalization of the inferential distance ordering so that it applies to our knowledge packets. Recall that Touretzky's formalization has two purposes. First, given a set of default assertions, he wants to specify the set of conclusions which followed from the data base. Second, he wants to characterize the circumstances under which such a data base is either inconsistent or ambiguous.

Our formalization follows Touretzky's for the most part but we have modified his definitions and proofs to apply to the operations of *instantiation* and *e-derivation* in place of his operation *inheritable.* We also use the relation *constrain,* for which Touretzky has no analog.

First consider the sequence: $<x_1,x_2,\ldots,x_n>$, where $n \geq 1$ and each x_i is a formula which has the syntax of a user assertion. This kind of sequence will be called an *inferential sequence.* We will use the word "sequence" if it can be inferred from the context that we are talking about an inferential sequence. The inferential sequence represents the *constrain* process emerging from a user assertion on the basis of the packets in the data base. The formula x_1 is a user assertion and x_{i-1} constrains x_i for $2 \leq i \leq n$.

In the ensuring discussion, Φ will be a set of inferential sequences, and Γ will be a set of inferential sequences containing one element (e.g., $<p>$). This Γ consists entirely of user assertions. For notational convenience, p' means (NOT p), where p is a formula. Let K denote a set of knowledge packets.

Definition 1. Let Φ be a set of inferential sequences. The set of *conclusions* of Φ, written $C(\Phi)$, is the set of all formulas x_n such that an inferential sequence of the form $<x_1,\ldots,x_n>$ appears in Φ.

This set of conclusions will be used as the set of formulas implicitly believed by the inheritance system.

Definition 2. Let y be a formula. y is a *grandfather* in the set Φ to an inferential sequence $<x_1,...,x_n>$ if and only if one of the following holds.

- $y = x_i$, and $1 \leq i \leq n-2$, and $n \geq 3$.
- Φ contains a sequence $<y_1,...,y_m,x_1,...,x_i>$, such that $m \geq 1$, and y is in $\{y_1,...,y_m\}$, and $1 \leq i \leq n \geq 2$.

This definition corresponds to Touretzky's definition of *intermediary,* in that its function is to define *preclusion.* A grandfather is a formula that is an ancestor to the last element of an inferential sequence in Φ but is not a parent.

We define preclusion through which the inferential distance ordering is applied.

Definition 3. Let Φ be a set of inferential sequences. Let $<x_1,...,x_n>$ be an inferential sequence of length ≥ 2. Φ *precludes* $<x_1,...,x_n>$ if and only if there is a $\sigma = <y_1,...,y_m>$ such that the following hold.

- σ is an element of Φ.
- $m \geq 2$.
- $y_m = x_n'$.
- y_{m-1} is a grandfather in Φ to $<x_1,...,x_n>$.

To illustrate preclusion, let $\Phi = \{<A, B'> <A, C>\}$. Φ precludes $<C, B>$, since Φ contains $\sigma = <A, B'>$ and A is a grandfather in Φ to $<C, B>$. We note that preclusion has a higher priority than contradiction that is defined below.

Definition 4. Let Φ be a set of inferential sequences. Let $<x_1,...,x_n>$ be an inferential sequence of length ≥ 2. Φ *contradicts* the inferential sequence, $<x_1,x_2,...,x_n>$ if and only if there is a $\sigma = <y_1,...,y_m>$ such that the following hold.

- σ is an element of Φ.
- σ is of length ≥ 1.
- $y_m = x_n'$.
- If $m \geq 2$, then σ is not precluded by $\Phi \cup \{<x_1,...,x_n>\}$.

For example, if Φ consists of the set containing exactly <(ELEPHANT Clyde), (gray Clyde)>, then Φ would contradict the sequences <(ELEPHANT Clyde), (NOT (gray Clyde))>.

Now, we need to define a grounded expansion. This is a set of sequences that is closed under inheritance. First, we have to define when an inferential sequence is *inheritable.*

Definition 5. Let Φ be a set of inferential sequences. Let $\sigma = <x_1,...,x_n>$ be an inferential sequence of length ≥ 2. σ is *inheritable* in Φ under K if and only if Φ neither precludes nor contradicts σ and one of the following conditions holds.

- Φ contains $<x_1,...,x_{n-1}>$ such that x_n is an e-derivation of x_{n-1} under K.
- Φ contains $<x_1,...,x_{n-1}>$ and $<y_1,...,y_m>$ such that x_n is instantiated by x_{n-1} from y_m in the inferential sequence $<y_1,...,y_m>$.
- Φ contains $<x_1,...,x_{n-1},y>$ and $<y_1,...,y_m>$ such that x_n is instantiated by y_m in the inferential sequence $<y_1,...,y_m>$ from y.

Let us illustrate inheritability with an example. Assume that K consists of the knowledge packets given in Section 3. Let the user assertion, Γ, be {<(ROYAL-ELEPHANT Clyde)>, <(ELEPHANT Clyde)>}, and let $\Phi = \Gamma \cup$ {<(ROYAL-ELEPHANT Clyde), (NOT (gray Clyde))>, <(ROYAL-ELEPHANT Clyde), (ELEPHANT Clyde)>}. Then the following two sequences are inheritable in Φ under K.

<(ROYAL-ELEPHANT Clyde), (NOT (gray Clyde))>
<(ROYAL-ELEPHANT Clyde), (ELEPHANT Clyde)>

The following sequence is not.

<(ELEPHANT Clyde), (gray Clyde)>

We now move on to define a grounded expansion. The set of conclusions of a grounded expansion can be taken to be the set of facts implicitly believed by the system. If there is more than one grounded expansion, then the data base is *ambiguous*.

Definition 6. For K, Φ is closed under inheritance if and only if Φ contains every inferential sequence inheritable in Φ under K.

Let us consider the previous example. It is instructive to note that $\Phi_1 = \Gamma \cup$ {<(ROYAL-ELEPHANT Clyde), (ELEPHANT Clyde)>, <(ROYAL-ELEPHANT Clyde), (ELEPHNAT Clyde), (gray Clyde)>} is not closed under K because the sequence <(ROYAL-ELEPHANT Clyde), (NOT (gray Clyde))> is inheritable in Φ_1. Note that $\Phi_2 = \Phi_1 \cup$ {<(ROYAL-ELEPHANT Clyde), (NOT (gray Clyde))>} is closed under K.

Definition 7. Φ is an expansion of a set Γ under K if and only if Γ is a subset of Φ and for K, Φ is closed under inheritance.

Definition 8. Φ is a grounded expansion of a set Γ under K if and only if Φ is an expansion of s set Γ under K and every inferential sequence in $\Phi - \Gamma$ is inheritable in Φ under K.

In the previous example, Φ is a grounded expansion of Γ, where the set of conclusions is $C(\Phi)$ = {(ROYAL-ELEPHANT Clyde), (ELEPHANT Clyde), (NOT (gray Clyde))}. Notice that Φ_1 is not grounded because it is not closed and Φ_2 is not grounded because <(ROYAL-ELEPHANT Clyde), (ELEPHANT Clyde), (gray Clyde)> is not inheritable in Φ_2, although Φ_2 is an expansion of Γ under K. Because of this, we must conclude that Clyde is not gray.

Theorem 1. Let Φ be a grounded expansion of the set of user assertions Γ under the set of knowledge packets K. Then the conclusion set of Φ, $C(\Phi)$, is consistent if and only if the conclusion set of Γ, $C(\Gamma)$, is consistent.

Proof: The proofs of theorems and corollaries in this paper can be found in [5].

In other words, the conclusion set of a grounded expansion will be consistent if the set of user assertions is consistent.

For some set of user assertions Γ, if there is more than one grounded expansion then an ambiguity results. The following theorem and definition specify when this occurs.

Theorem 2. If the set of user assertions Γ has more than one grounded expansion under the set of knowledge packets K, for any pair of these grounded expansions, for example, Φ_1 and Φ_2, it is necessarily true that there is a formula x such that x is in $C(\Phi_1)$ (or $C(\Phi_2)$) and x' is in $C(\Phi_2)$ (or $C(\Phi_1)$).

We are going to address the circumstances under that a grounded expansion exists. Let Γ be a set of user assertions. Let K be a set of knowledge packets. We then define a knowledge base, KB, such that $KB = C(\Gamma) \cup K$. For the KB, we can consider a direct graph, CDG (Constrained Direct Graph), such that every predicate used in the KB is a vertex and every "constrain" relation between two predicates is a direct edge.

Now, we want to restrict a knowledge base such that its CDG is acyclic. An obvious reason of this restriction is ease of implementation, since it is difficult to prevent an inferential sequence to be infinite. Another reason is that it is hard to imagine a concept (predicate) can be defined in terms of itself. However, for arbitrary inference rules, a cyclic CDG can be reasonably assumed. To date, we have been unable to prove the existence of a grounded expansion in the general case. This problem remains open.

Definition 9. KB = $C(\Gamma) \cup K$ is *well-defined* if and only if Γ and K are finite, and a constrained direct graph for KB($C(\Gamma)$, K) is acyclic.

Given a knowledge base, we need to know when a grounded expansion exists and how to compute it. The following theorem and corollary give the answer.

Theorem 3. If KB = $C(\Gamma) \cup K$ is well-defined, every Γ has a grounded expansion under K.

Corollary 1. If KB = $C(\Gamma) \cup K$ is well-defined, Γ has a *constructable* grounded expansion.

5. Conclusions

Primarily, Touretzky [9] formalized the inferential distance ordering to apply to ISA hierarchies. Because of this, he could not easily apply the inferential distance ordering to a hierarchy of n-place predicates. Our initial motivation for studying Touretzky's inheritance theory was to give a formal semantics to the knowledge representation language UniFrame [6]. In this paper, we generalized Touretzky's formalism so that it can be *uniformly* applied to inferential hierarchies, including ISA hierarchies of predicates, object-oriented predicates, and relational predicates. Additionally, our scheme allows us to freely use n-place predicates.

References

1. Bobrow, Daniel G. and Winograd, Terry. An overview of KRL, a knowledge representation language. *Cognitive Science* 1(1), 1977, pp. 3-46.
2. Brachman, R. J., Gilbert, V. P. and Levesque, H. J. An essential hybrid reasoning system: knowledge and symbol level accounts of KRYPTON. *Proceedings of IJCAI-85,* 1985, Vol. 1, pp. 532-539.
3. Brachman, R. J. and Schmolze, J. G. An overview of the KL-ONE knowledge representation system. *Cognitive Science* 9(2), 1985, pp. 171-216.
4. Fahlman, Scott E. *NETL: a system for representation and using real-world knowledge.* MIT Press, Cambridge, MA, 1979.
5. Kim, Minkoo and Maida, Anthony S. Knowledge packets and inheritance systems. Technical report CS-87-17, May 1986, Department of Computer Science, Pennsylvania State University, University Park, PA 16802.
6. Maida, Anthony S. Processing entailments and accessing facts in a uniform frame system. *Proceeding of AAAI-84,* 1984, pp. 233-236.
7. McDermott, Drew and Doyle, Jon. Non-monotonic logic I. *Artificial Intelligence* 13, 1980, pp. 41-72.
8. Roberts, R. Bruce and Goldstein, Ira P. The FRL manual. AI Memo No. 409, MIT Artificial Intelligence Laboratory, Cambridge, MA, 1977.
9. Touretzky, David S. The mathematics of inheritance systems. Ph. D. Thesis, Computer Science Department, Carnegie-Mellon University, Pittsburgh, PA, 1984.
10. Weinreb, Daniel and Moon, David. *Lisp machine manual.* MIT Artificial Intelligence Laboratory, Cambridge, MA, 1981.

ON TRANSFORMATION PROPERTIES OF CONCEPTUAL STRUCTURES

ELŐD KNUTH, JÁNOS DEMETROVICS, ÁGNES HERNÁDI
Computer and Automation Institute,
Hungarian Academy of Sciences
Budapest, POB 63., H 1502 Hungary

ABSTRACT

A major practical problem of using presently available conceptual representation languages is the lack of transformability of concepts after instantiating them. This paper looks for the basic rules and conditions under which this static constraint can be resolved. Outlines of a suggested set for the most critical dynamic operations are presented.

1. INTRODUCTION

Computer aided systems presently available for conceptual representations (e.g. for database conceptual schema descriptions, see [1],[2],[3],[4],[5],[6]) rely typically on the following paradigm:

(1) First the set of abstract objects (i.e. "concepts") is formed and fixed before any instantiation can take place.

(2) Having the universe of concepts fixed, concrete objects are instantiated and maintained dynamically, however concepts themselves may not be modified any longer.

This common regime causes the following difficulty when applied in practical situations. Typically, concepts are found to be mistaken only after instantiating them, that is: we usually have a great number of various instances when recognizing that certain of our concepts were just wrong and hence need corrections. Moreover, we acquire knowledge first on concrete objects, enabling us to make abstractions over them only afterwards.

Therefore, it seems important to investigate what are the rules and conditions under which concepts can be transformed preserving integrity properties of the knowledge base. Some of them will be looked at in the sequel.

2. OPERATION CLASSES

Transformations to be performed on definitions of concepts fall into three categories:

(a) Conventional update operations like "create", "delete", "modify" etc. The problem with these operations is that they may also require transformations on instances existing already.

(b) Abstraction mechanisms like "classify", "generalize", "aggregate", etc. What is new in this case is that they are intended to be given to the users *interactively* (not restricting

Methodologies for Intelligent Systems
Z. W. Ras and M. Zemankova, Editors

them to a "design phase" only).

(c) "Conceptual transformations" which are new ones and are especially dedicated to the problem we are presently dealing with.

All the three categories have been outlined in our recent report [13]. Here we consider only the class (c) as the most important one in more depth.

3. "UNIFICATION" OF CONCEPTS

Having a set of concepts it often turns out that certain of them (treated as different ones before) are conceptually the *same* and hence they had better be modelled uniformly. For instance, we might have the pair of concepts

```
concept message;                    concept memo;
   attributes: recipient               attributes: to,
               sender,                             from,
               date,                               date,
               text;                               contents;
```

having the same meaning from conceptual point of view. As another interesting mathematical example we might mention the so called "clones" in universal algebra in comparison with "closed classes" of multiple valued logic. Both represent conceptually the same though their notations and terminologies are different.

In such cases the essential step is to find a *one-to-one mapping* between the sets of properties. Having done this, there are two possibilities from technical point of view:

i) Link concepts: by just giving the isomorphy mapping without changing the original concepts. In this case the sets of their object instances remain distinct but their union can also be retrieved.

ii) Unite concepts: under a new concept name. In this case the sets of existing instances are united. (Forming the union raises another question, namely the *identity revision* over objects themselves - not discussed here.)

4. "ABSTRACTION" OVER CONCEPTS

This operation is not the same as the widely referred "generalization" (see e.g. [1]) since the latter does not modify existing concepts.

"Abstraction", in the present sense, is the operation of extracting common properties from a set of concepts creating a new generic one. The original concepts lose the properties extracted (which will be inherited then). As a consequence the operation abstraction is always *safe*, since it does not harm object instances.

Because of the same reason as in the case of Section 3, before attempting to extract common properties we have to give the mapping between attributes to identify what are to be abstracted.

Consider e.g. the following example.

```
concept pattern matching;       concept editor;
   attributes: pattern,            attributes: input,
               text,                           commands,
               action;                         output;

               concept report generation;
                  attributes: specification,
                              input files;
```

Having these concepts, it is easy to recognize their common nature, i.e. all three are certain kinds of "information filters" (also in the sense of UNIX [11]). To make the desired transformations we first need to map attributes like these:

```
source:= text in pattern matching,
         input in editor,
         input files in report generation;

criteria:= pattern in pattern matching,
           commands in editor;
           specification in report generation;
```

Possessing these mappings we may write a command like:

```
concept filter abstraction of pattern matching,
                              editor,
                              report generation;

               attributes extracted source,
                                    criteria;

               (by mappings given)
```

Concepts participating "abstraction" may already have parent superconcepts. Thus abstraction may lead to *multiple parents* and hence concepts will then inherit properties from different parents at the same time (inheritance-network versus hierarchy).

5. "EXTENSION"

To "extend" something is meant as a "destructive" version of "abstraction" which is frequently needed in the practice. Consider the following example:

Suppose that an information systems is based on the following screen-format concepts (window types):

1) "Information section",
2) "Report specification",
3) "Report",
4) "Schema report",

all of them together with a specific set of operations associated. Now, after experimenting with the system somebody may find out that the underlying information representation scheme would permit to use a completely different interaction schema. Namely, he observes that concepts 1)-4) might all be replaced by a single one called e.g.:

5) Pattern

resulting in a much simplified model and user interface at the same time. Naturally, the condition of this conceptual transformation is the *extendibility* of the individual properties owned by concepts 1)-4) to the generic one (including their individual operations).

We do not discuss here if it can successfully be done in case of the above example. In the positive case, we can carry out the operation "abstraction" in such a way that all former concepts touched will vanish. This operation, called the "uniformization", will affect instances seriously (in contrast to pure abstraction). Their individual properties should always be extended according to the change in the definitions. We do not detail this here, though the following point suggests a direction to handle them.

6. "REQUALIFICATION" OF OBJECT

This operation changes the class an object belongs. It is reasonable to restrict such operation to changes along the qualifying super-sub concept-chain. Suppose e.g. that our knowledge base starts with the following situation:

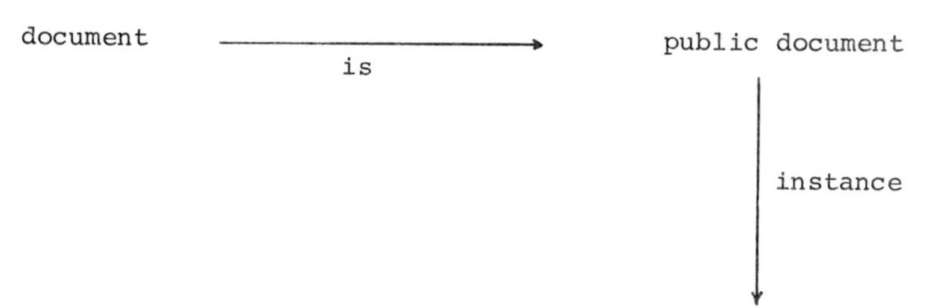

Later, we might observe that the particular document described has some generalizable properties, and it is reasonable to put them on the concepts' level like this:

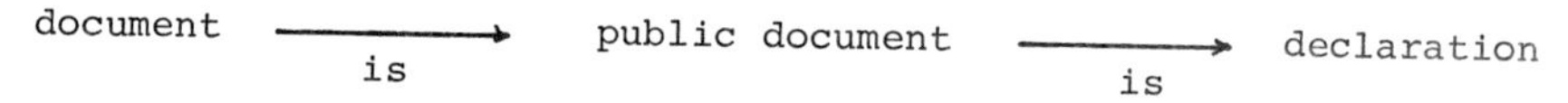

Now it is desirable to qualify the document "Declaration of Independence" as "declaration" rather than a mere public document.

In general, objects are allowed to be requalified in both directions. Requalifying in the generic direction (e.g. a "declaration" to a "public-document" above) is always safe since it does not need new information. When going, however, to the refining direction then

(a) Values for the extra attributes characteristic to the specific subconcept (i.e. those not yet possessed by the original class) should be added.

(b) Additional constraints associated to the specific subconcept should be checked.

In principle: The requalification operation should ask for the specification of all missing additional attributes. Requalification is not confirmed until they all are given and while all specific sub-constraints are not met.

7. INHERITANCE REFINEMENT

which is the operation of inserting a new concept into an existing sub-chain. Consider for example the following simple case:

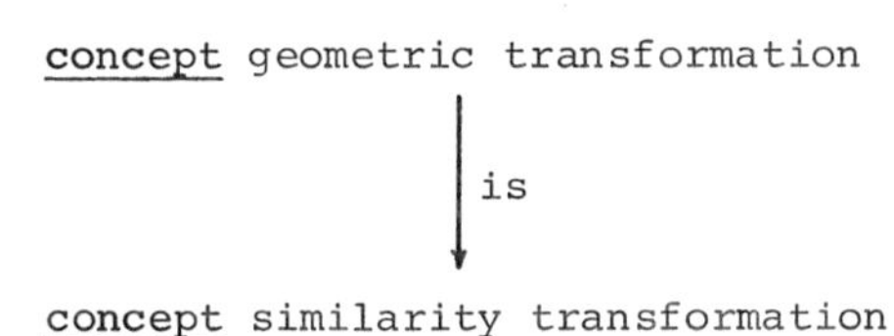

The concept of "projective transformation" (which was formulated only later during the history of mathematics), should clearly be placed between the above two:

geometric transformation
↓
projective transformation
↓
similarity transformation

A new concept created between two existing ones needs then the reallocation of their earlier attributes. By principle however, we allowe to move attributes to the generic direction only. (E.g. certain attributes of "similarity transformation" may be relocated to "projective transformation", however the concept "geometric transformation" itself can not be changed in this way.)

In general, "refinement" transforms a

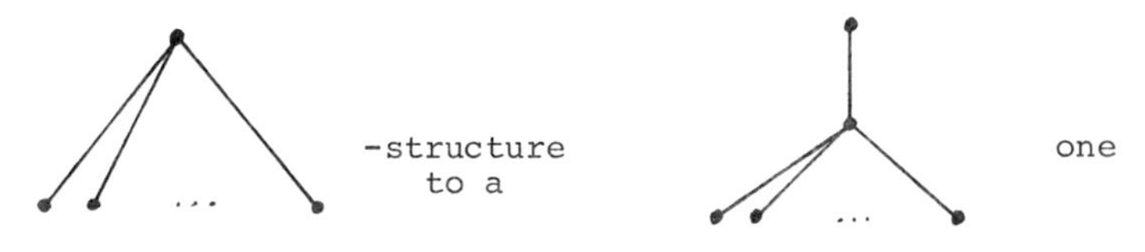

For instance, in the case of

geometric transformation

similarity transformation　　　　affin transformation

we want to get finally the configuration:

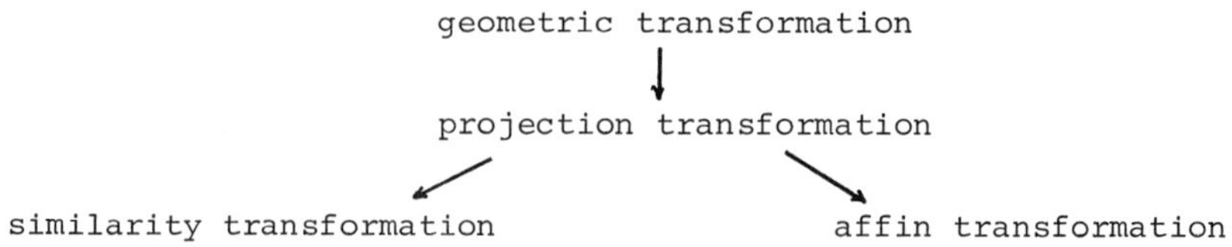

```
                    geometric transformation
                              |
                              v
                    projection transformation
                   /                         \
                  v                           v
similarity transformation              affin transformation
```

That is, "refinement" works in the same way as "abstraction" with the exception that it cannot create multiple parents (but changes existing is-a links instead). As a consequence the transformation has the same properties regarding instances as those in case of the abstraction one.

8. "CONCATENATE" CONCEPTS

is the operation of uniting two immediately subordered concepts into one single concept. Example: suppose we have

```
concept transformation;
   attributes name,
              parameters,
              domain,
              variables;

concept t-transformation is-a transformation;
   attributes timing,
              synchronization-constraints;
```

Now if we do not want to have the above distinction between the generic and specialized versions, we can request

```
concatenate (transformation, t-transformation as transformation);
```

creating a single concept with all the six *attributes* shown above.

Restriction: In principle, this operation is allowed only in the case when the generic concept has no instances at all.

9. CONCLUSION

A brief outline of a selected set of the most critical operations to transform conceptual universes has been presented. Such operations are fundamental to maintain conceptual descriptions during changes necessitated by the nature of large practical applications. At present, none of the available computer aided tools offer such transformations. A further set of operations is described in [13].

REFERENCES

1. J. Mylopoulos and H.J. Levesque, An Overview of Knowledge Representation, in: Brodie, M.L., Mylopoulos, J., Schmidt, J.W. (eds.), On Conceptual Modelling (Springer Verlag, 1984) pp. 3-18.
2. A. Albano, L. Cardielli and R. Orsini, Galileo: A Strongly-Typed Interactive Conceptual Language, ACM TODS, 10, 2, 230-260.
3. D. Teichroew, P. Macasovic, E.A.III. Hershey and Y. Yamamoto, Application of the Entity-Relationship Approach to Information Processing System Modelling. Proceedings, International Conference on Entity Relationship Approach to System Analysis and Design. Los Angeles (1979).
4. E. Knuth, F. Halász and P. Radó, SDLA, System Descriptor and Logical Analyzer, in: Olle, Sol and Veerijn-Stuart (eds.), Information Systems Design Methodologies: A Comparative Review. (North Holland, 1982) pp. 143-147.
5. D.W. Shipman, The Functional Data Model and the Data Language DAPLEX, ACM TODS, 6, 1, (1981), 140-173.
6. A. Bargida, Survey of Conceptual Modelling of Information Systems. In: On Knowledge Base Management Systems (Springer Verlag, 1986) pp. 461-470.
7. G.M.A. Verheijen and J. Van Blekkum, NIAM: An Information Analysis Method, in: Olle, Sol and Veerijn-Stuart (eds.), Information Systems Design Methodologies: A Comparative Review. (North Holland, 1982).
8. E. Knuth, L. Hannák and Á. Hernádi, A Taxonomy of Conceptual Foundations, in: Ras, Z.W., Zemankova, M. (eds.), Proceedings of the ACM SIGART International Symposium on Methodologies for Intelligent Systems, Knoxwille, Tennessee (1986), pp. 390-398.
9. O.J. Dahl, B. Myrhaug and K. Nygaard, SIMULA 67 Common Base Language, Norwegian Computer Center, Oslo (1970).
10. E. Knuth and L. Rónyai, Closed Convex Reference Schemes, in: System Description Methodologies (North Holland, 1985), pp. 435-454.
11. S.R., Bourne, The UNIX System. (Addison-Weslex, 1983).
12. J. Demetrovics, E. Knuth and P. Radó, Computer aided specification techniques (World Scientific Press, Series in Computer Science, 1, 1986).
13. E. Knuth, J. Demetrovics and Á. Hernádi, Transformation properties of conceptual structures. WP II-78/87, MTA SZTAKI, Budapest.

GENERATING QUALITATIVE REPRESENTATIONS OF CONTINUOUS PHYSICAL PROCESSES

Mieczyslaw M. Kokar
Northeastern University
360 Huntington Avenue
Boston, Massachusetts 02115
KOKAR@NORTHEASTERN.CSNET

ABSTRACT

The objective of this paper is twofold: to introduce a way of representing qualitative knowledge about continuous physical processes, and to show how such a representation could be generated automatically (to some degree) by a program. One of the representations known in the literature is called "quantity space" [5, 6]. Another approach consists of establishing a set of so called "critical points" by selecting some values of the continuous physical parameters characterizing the physical process under consideration [12, 13]. Both representations' goal is to delineate some regions of qualitatively-different behaviors of a physical system in the space of all possible behaviors. In this paper we show that these operating regions are, in most cases, delimited by some hypersurfaces in the cross-product of the continuous physical parameters - they are called here "critical hypersurfaces". The paper presents a theoretical analysis, which leads to the characterization of the class of functions describing the hypersurfaces. A general methodology for automatic generation of critical hypersurfaces is also described.

1. INTRODUCTION

Modelling of physical processes has always been an important issue in both science and engineering. Most of the scientific effort in this area was devoted to the methodology for quantitative modelling. Only recently the attention of the scientific community has been directed towards qualitative simulation. This can be attributed to the development of the AI methodology, which is mainly concerned with symbolic reasoning of which qualitative reasoning about physical processes is a part. Besides this, it is a result of some limitations of quantitative modelling. In many cases quantitative simulations are not feasible because of a very high complexity of the quantitative models. Qualitative simulation can then give some less specific results within some reasonable amount of time. Moreover, in many situations quantitative simulations are feasible, but not necessary. For instance, why should we carry out complex numeric calculations if we only want to know whether a particular physical parameter will stay within its allowable range following some changes in the controls.

Methodologies for Intelligent Systems
Z. W. Ras and M. Zemankova, Editors

2. CRITICAL POINTS

In the qualitative simulation methodology states of physical systems are characterized by some qualitative parameters which can take on a limited number of nominal values. The relationships among these parameters are described in terms of "quantity space" [5, 6]. When the relations among these parameters change, some "processes" are started or stopped. The problem is how to derive such a quantity space. Kuippers [12, 13] relates these qualitative parameters to some quantitative parameters and uses the term "critical points" to describe some specific values of physical parameters at which the physical systems change their qualitative states. In other words, critical points establish some boundaries of the regions of qualitatively-different behaviors of physical systems. For instance, the water temperatures of 0 and 100 C might constitute such boundaries for a physical system in which heat transfer is involved - below 0 C the process of "melting" takes place (assuming the transfer of heat is to the system), then the process of "water-heating" is carried out, after which the process of "boiling" is started (when the temperature gets to the point of 100 C).

3. CRITICAL HYPERSURFACES

The above example is fully justified if either the process under consideration can be characterized by only one physical parameter, or when some parameters relevant to the process remain constant (as in Figure 1). This situatuion is not a typical one. Usually processes are characterized by a number of parameters. A general situation we are dealing with can be described by a set of physical parameters, say $X_1, \ldots, X_n$. Thus the operational region of this process can be represented as a subset of the cross-product $X_1 \times \ldots \times X_n$. Delimiting some qualitatively-different subregions of this process by some critical points of the parameters X_j is equivalent to saying that these regions can be represented as rectangles for a two-dimensional space, cubes for three dimensions, and some hyper-cubes for more dimensions. This kind of situation is shown in Figure 2.

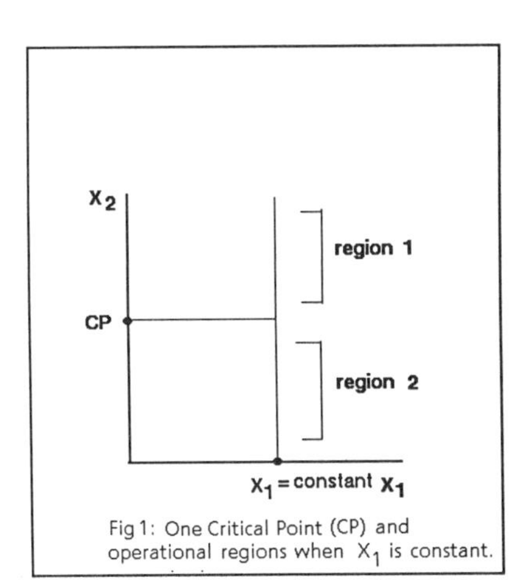

Fig 1: One Critical Point (CP) and operational regions when X_1 is constant.

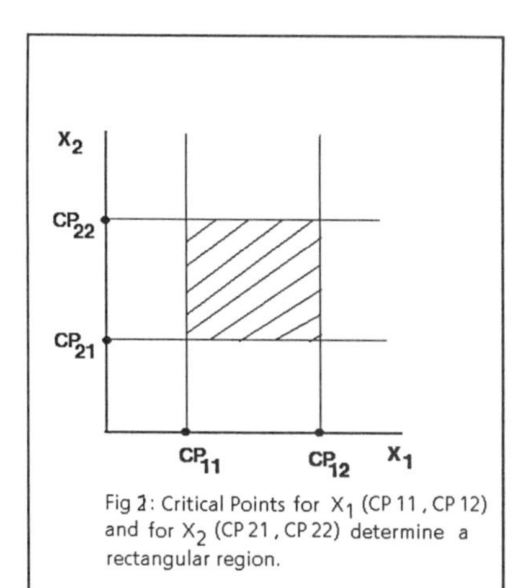

Fig 2: Critical Points for X_1 (CP 11, CP 12) and for X_2 (CP 21, CP 22) determine a rectangular region.

From the mathematical point of view it is an interesting question why should we use rectangles or cubes? A closer look at this problem from the physical point of view reveals that these regions are not really cubes. For instance, it is not possible to answer the question whether water is boiling or not when the water temperature is 98 C. To this aim one needs to know at least what is the pressure of the gas surrounding the water. This is due to the fact that the boiling temperature depends on the pressure. It is obvious that the operational regions are not delimited by some hyperplanes perpendicular to axes, they must be some more complex hypersurfaces.

The next relaxation of the form of the boundaries of operational regions in physical processes could lead to any hyperplanes in the physical process space (cf., Figure 3). Even though this assumption might look attractive from the mathematical point of view (as hyperplanes are relatively simple to handle analytically), we cannot accept it as we do not really have any relevant justification for that. Thus it is an open question what is the upper bound on the complexity of the hypersurfaces delimiting qualitatively-different regions of physical prosesses. Such a more general situation is represented in Figure 4.

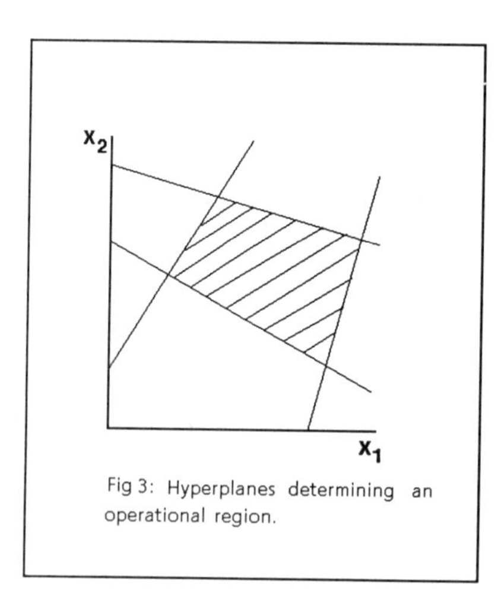

Fig 3: Hyperplanes determining an operational region.

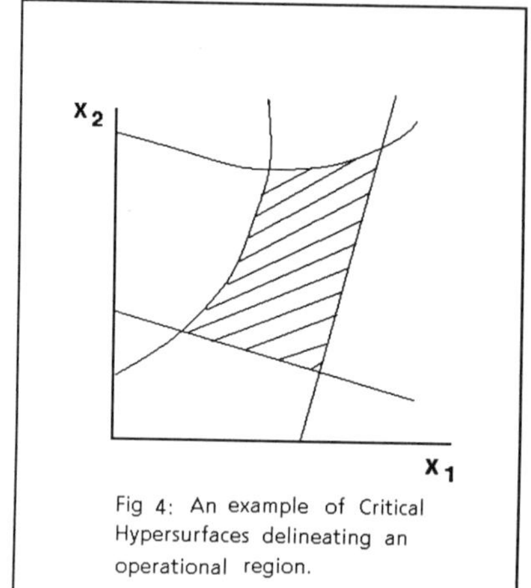

Fig 4: An example of Critical Hypersurfaces delineating an operational region.

4. THE SPACE OF HYPERSURFACES

Formally, any hypersurface in the cross-product $X_1 \times \ldots \times X_n$ can be represented as:

$$F(X_1, \ldots, X_n) = C,$$

where $X_1, \ldots, X_n$ - physical variables, F - a function, and C is a numerical constant. In this notation the above question on the complexity of hypersurfaces can be restated as what is the upper bound on the complexity of the functional formulas F, or in other words - what is the class of functions that describe hypersurfaces delimiting operational regions of physical processes?

The class of hypersurfaces can be derived from some methodological postulates related to knowledge representation for physical processes. The postulate we refer to says that functions describing physical processes must obey some syntax-semantics relations, called "dimensional invariance" [3], [18]. This postulate can be interpreted [8] as the postulate of functional substitutivity in formal logic [15]. Roughly speaking, it permits one to substitute arguments of a function by 'equal' arguments, where the equality of arguments is established by an axiom of extension (axiom of equality). In this approach two arguments are treated as equal if they represent the same physical quantity and are related by an isomorphism of the representational languages, provided these isomorphisms are identities on dimensionless numbers. Formally it is represented as:

$$F(T\ X_1,\ \ldots,\ T\ X_n) = T\ F(X_1,\ \ldots,\ X_n),$$

where T stands for a transformation of one representation language into another equivalent representation. In terms of knowledge representation theory it can be stated as "knowledge representation should be invariant under transformations of the representation language into equivalent languages", which seems to be an acceptable postulate.

Based on this postulate a theorem is proven (in the theory of dimensional analysis) that any function $F(X_1, \ldots, X_n)$, fulfilling the postulate of invariance, can be represented as:

$$f(Q_1,\ \ldots,\ Q_r),$$

where any Q_j is represented as:

$$Q_j = X_j / X_{r+1}^{aj1} \ldots X_{r+m}^{ajm}.$$

This theorem is the subject of dimensional analysis. An interested reader can find more details on this theorem, including the rules of how to calculate the exponents aj1, ..., ajm (j = 1..r), in the related literature (eg., [3], [18], [8]).

As a consequence of this theorem, any hypersurface $F(X_1, \ldots, X_n) = C$ can be represented as $f(Q_1, \ldots, Q_r) = C$. This relationship can be fulfilled if the arguments of the function f are constant: $Q_1 = C_1, \ldots, Q_r = C_r$, where $C_1, \ldots, C_r$ represent some numerical constants.

Note that in this way the problem of finding critical hypersurfaces in the cross-product $X_1 \times \ldots \times X_n$ has been decomposed into a number of simpler problems of finding r hypersurfaces $Q_j = C_j$ (j=1..r) in the cross-products $X_j \times X_{r+1} \times \ldots \times X_{r+m}$. The great advantage of this approach is that we know what are the forms of the functions describing the hypersurfaces.

At least three problems still remain open here. Firstly, we need to mention that the constanteness of the Q's is a sufficient but not necessary condition for a hypersurface. The relationship $f(Q_1, \ldots, Q_r) = C$ can also be fulfilled when the Q's are varied according to some pattern. We do not deal with this problem in this paper, it is one of the interesting topics for the further investigations. Later in this paper we show some evidence that the sufficient-condition approach is useful in practical applications.

Secondly, in order to generate a set of hypersurfaces $Q_j = C_j$ we need to be able to determine what are the values of the constants C_j. We concentrate on this topic in Section 6.

Thirdly, one more piece of information is not too easy to obtain, namely, what are the physical parameters $X_1, \ldots, X_n$ that one needs to consider. This topic is beyond the scope of this paper, some discussion of this topic is provided in [11].

5. AN EXAMPLE OF CRITICAL HYPERSURFACES

Consider the process of viscous fluid flow in a pipe [11]. It is a known fact in fluid mechanics [19, 16] that the flow can be in one of at least three different qualitative states: laminar, turbulent and transitional (unstable). In each of these states the process of fluid flow is described by qualitatively different mathematical models. Intuitively, the flow is laminar for small velocities, turbulent for large, and transitional for some intermediate velocities. Therefore, one could try to find two critical velocities (critical points), v1, and v2, delimiting the three flow regions. Unfortunately, this can work only for a very limited range of situations, namely when the pipe diameter D, fluid density ρ, and fluid viscosity η, are constant. For instance, for water in room temperature in a 1-cm-diameter pipe, turbulent flow occurs above about 0.2 m/s, while for air the critical speed is of the order of 4.0 m/s [19]. Thus the critical velocity in the latter case is twenty times higher than in the former one. This clearly shows that to reason about qualitative states of physical processes one cannot restrict the set of notions to critical points only.

In hydromechanics the transition from laminar to turbulent flow is characterized in terms of so called "Reynolds number". Reynolds number (usually described as R) is defined as a function of the above referenced parameters as:

$$R = \rho \cdot v \cdot D/\eta .$$

It is found experimentally that laminar flow occurs whenever R is less than about 2000. When R is greater than about 3000, the flow is nearly always turbulent, and in the region between 2000 and 3000 the flow is unstable, changing from one form of flow to the other (here we call it "transitional").

The relationships

$$R = \rho \cdot v \cdot D/\eta = 2000$$

and

$$R = \rho \cdot v \cdot D/\eta = 3000$$

describe hypersurfaces in the space defined by the cross-product of the continuous parameters ρ, v, D, and η.

This example shows that critical hypersurfaces, as defined in this paper, play an important role in qualitative reasoning about physical processes.

6. SEMANTICS OF CRITICAL HYPERSURFACES

In this section we concentrate on the problem of determining the values of the constants $C_1, \ldots, C_r$ in the relationships describing critical hypersurfaces. We utilize here the fact that whenever we look for critical hypersurfaces we need them for a purpose. In other words, we assume that we are interested in the behavior of a physical system which characteristic is a physical parameter Z. Assume that this parameter is dependent on the parameters $X_1, \ldots, X_n$ (as before), which formally is expressed as $Z = G(X_1, \ldots, X_n)$. In the same way as in the previous sections we can express this function using the rules of dimensional analysis:

$$Q_z = g(Q_1, \ldots, Q_r),$$

where the Q_j's are exactly the same as in the expression for f, and the additional dimensional parameter Z is transformed into

$$Q_z = Z/X_{r+1}^{a1} \ldots X_{r+m}^{am}.$$

If we know the semantics for critical points for the Z parameter, then, because Z functionally depends on the Q_j's, we can find what are the values of the Q_j's for the specific values of Z. This can be done in two different ways. If we know the form of the function g, then we can determine them by calculating the values of the Q_j's for which the value of g is equal to the specific values of Z. The other possibility is to determine these values experimentally.

The next question is then what semantics to use to determine critical points for the Z parameter. In the literature on qualitative reasoning there are known several semanics rules: sign semantics, derivatives semantics [2, 5, 6], Kuipers' QSIM semantics [12, 13], order of magnitude semantics [17].

For the example presented in the previous section none of these could be applied directly to Reynolds number (it stands here for Q_1), as neither Reynolds number, or its derivative, change their directions of growth. But flow changes from laminar to turbulent. We can utilize here the dependency of the rate of heat transfer (the Z parameter for this case) on Reynolds number. It is a known fact that the rate of heat transfer from/to the liquid in a pipe to/from the outside strongly depends on Reynolds number, it is much more intensive for $R > 3000$ than for $R < 2000$. If we take the heat exchange rate as an indicator then we can utilize, for instance, the semantics of sign of derivative, or we can apply Kuipers' semantics to the derivative of the heat transfer rate.

The interpretation of critical hypersurfaces is such that they describe boundaries between two regions of qualitatively different behaviors of a physical system. In other words, the physical system behaves similarly within the region, even though the quantitative parameters characterizing the system take on different values for different points within the region. Similar behaviors of physical systems are the subject of the similarity (or similitude) theory [1, 3]. Reynolds number referenced in the previous sections is one example of such a similarity number. It characterizes the process of flow of liquids. A set of states for which all the similarity numbers are equal is a hypersurface. The cross-product of physical parameters describing a particular process is subdivided by the relation of similarity into classes (hypersurfaces). In this paper we are concerned only with some special of the classes, the ones that we call critical hypersurfaces.

7. SUMMARY OF STEPS FOR ESTABLISHING CRITICAL HYPERSURFACES

In this section we summarize the results of the previous sections by describing several steps in which critical hypersurfaces can be established. This methodology has been described in [11].

1. Determine the characteristic parameter Z of the physical system which is to be modelled.
2. Determine what are the $X_1, \ldots, X_n$ parameters known to be relevant to this particular characteristic parameter.
3. Using methods of dimensional analysis derive a set of similarity numbers $Q_1, \ldots, Q_r, Q_z$ as functions of the physical parameters $X_1, \ldots, X_n$, and Z.
4. Using one of the available semantics (e.g., signs of derivatives) determine critical values of the characteristic parameter Z.
5. Relate the critical values of Z to the critical values of the Q's, i.e., find the critical values of the Q's for which the value of Z is equal to the critical values derived in step 4. This can be done either by analyzing the function g (if known), or by experimentation.
6. The expressions equating the monomials representing the similarity numbers with their critical values (derived in step 5) constitute descriptions of the critical hypersurfaces.

The steps 1 and 2 of this methodology are to be performed by the user. The remaining steps can be carried out automatically by a program.

8. CONCLUSIONS

This paper shows that a finite set of critical points, when understood as some special values of the continuous physical parameters, is not sufficient to determine boundaries of the regions of qualitatively-different behaviors of physical systems. We show that these regions can be delineated by some hypersurfaces in the cross-product of the parameters. We also show how such hypersurfaces can be determined semi-automatically. The procedure for establishing critical hypersurfaces utilizes the notion of critical points.

A closer analysis of the problem of determining critical hypersurfaces reveals that this task is not as easy as it may first appear. To find a set of hypersurfaces one needs some pieces of information which not always are available. One such piece is a set of all relevant continuous parameters characterizing the physical system under consideration. In many situations finding such a set is a difficult scientific task. Another problem is the form of the functional relationship characterizing the system. This is even a less trivial problem than the previous one. Automatic derivation of the complete sets of parameters and relationships among them falls into the category of automatic discovery. This is one of the research topics in machine learning. Some of the automatic discovery systems that attack these problems are BACON [14], ABACUS [4], COPER [9,10]. The progress in automatic generation of qualitative descriptions of physical systems, using the method proposed in this paper, strongly depends on the advancements in the area of automatic discovery systems.

REFERENCES

1. Birkhoff, G., (1960). *Hydrodynamics. A study in logic, fact and similitude.*, Princeton University Press, Princeton.
2. deKleer, J., Brown, S., (1982). Foundations of Envisioning, Proceedings of the National Conference on Artificial Intelligence AAAI-82, 209-212.
3. Drobot, S. (1953). On the foundations of dimensional analysis. *Studia Mathematica, 14*, 84 - 89.
4. Falkenhainer, B. & Michalski, R., S., (1986). Integrating quantitative and qualitative discovery: The ABACUS system. *Machine Learning*, 4.
5. Forbus, K., D., (1984a). Qualitative Process Theory. *Artificial Intelligence*, 24, 85-168.
6. Forbus, K., D., (1984a). Qualitative Process Theory. *Technical Report*, 789, MIT Artificial Intelligence Laboratory.
7. Forbus, K., D., (1986). Interpreting measurements of physical systems, *Proceedings of AAAI-86, Fifth National Conference on Artificial Intelligence*, Philadelphia, 113-117.
8. Kokar, M., M. (1985). *On invariance in dimensional analysis* (Technical Report MMK-2/85). Boston, MA: Northeastern University, College of Engineering.
9. Kokar, M., M., (1986a). Determining Arguments of Invariant Functional Descriptions, *Machine Learning*, 1.
10. Kokar, M., M., (1986b). Discovering functional formulas through changing representation base. *Proceedings of the Fifth National Conference on Artificial Intelligence*, Philadelphia, PA.

11. Kokar, M., M., (1987). Critical Hypersurfaces and the Quantity Space, *Proceedings of the Sixth National Conference on Artificial Intelligence*, Seattle, WA.

12. Kuipers, B., J., (1985a). Qualitative Simulation of Mechanisms. *MIT Laboratory for Computer Science, TM-274*, Cambridge, MA.

13. Kuipers, B., J., (1985b). The Limits of Qualitative Simulation, *Proceedings of the Ninth Joint Conference on Artificial Intelligence*. Los Angeles: 128-136.

14. Langley, P., (1981). Data Driven Discovery of Physical Laws, *Cognitive Science*, 5, 31-54.

15. Manna, Z., Waldinger, R., (1985). *The Logical Basis for Computer Programming, vol. 1 :Deductive Reasoning*, Addison-Wesley.

16. Monin, A., S., & Yaglom, A., M., (1973). *Statistical Fluid Mechanics: Mechanincs of Turbulence*, The MIT Press, Cambridge, MA, and London, England.

17. Raiman, O., (1986). Order of Magnitude Reasoning, *Proceedings of the National Conference on Artificial Intelligence*, Philadelphia, PA, 100-104.

18. Whitney, H., (1968), The Mathematics of Physical Quantities, part I and II, *American Mathematical Monthly*, pp. 115-138 and 227-256.

19. Young, H., D., (1964). *Fundamentals of Mechanics and Heat.*, Second Edition, McGraw-Hill Book Company.

A NEW APPROACH TO KNOWLEDGE BASE MANAGEMENT SYSTEMS

Hidefumi Kondo,* Takuo Koguchi*
*Systems Development Laboratory, Hitachi, Ltd.
1099 Ohzenji, Asao-ku, Kawasaki-shi, 215 Japan

ABSTRACT

This paper describes a knowledge base management system which has three main characteristics : ① knowledge notation by which users can store fragments of knowledge at any time without defining the data structure scheme in advance, ② a query description form in which users can query without knowing the data structure scheme of the stored knowledge, and ③ an inferential retrieval function which automatically connects related fragments of knowledge to each other.

1. INTRODUCTION

Active research has been done on the functions of knowledge base management systems [4]. However, no definite concepts about knowledge base management systems regarding functions and structure have yet been developed. A previous paper [1] reported that in the early stages of Database Management System (DBMS) development, the DBMS functions and structure were also unclear. Development of knowledge base management systems now appears to be in a similar stage.

The authors believe that knowledge base management systems have two aspects : (1) knowledge base management systems serve AI systems (expert system, etc.) by storing and retrieving objects called "knowledge" in the AI system (facts, rules, frames, etc.), in a suitable form for the AI system [2]; and (2) knowledge base management systems have a high level retrieval function and end-user interface for this purpose. Serving an AI system is similar to a Network Database supporting business on-line systems with high-speed data access (e.g. CODASYL). The high level retrieval function is similar to a Relational Database. Although the two functions have common features, the former function is generally used for AI systems, whereas the latter operates independently. This paper focuses on the high level retrieval function.

Database Management System is a typical data retrieval system. However, Database Management System deals with only fixed formatted data and queries for it must be in accordance with the scheme of the stored data. Therefore this system is suitable for routine work data processing, but not for data processing dealing with unformatted data such as fragments of knowledge. As a solution to this problem, we propose a knowledge base management system, named KBAF (Knowledge Base Administration Facility) which has three main characteristics : ① knowledge notation by which users can store fragments of knowledge at any time without defining the data structure scheme in advance, ② a query description form in which users can query without knowing the data structure scheme of the stored knowledge, and ③ an inferential retrieval function which automatically connects related fragments of knowledge to each other.

The proposed KBAF is discussed as follows : First, the general retieval model is defined (Section 2). Second, current DBMSs are studied based on the model. It is shown that DBMS is not suitable for storage/retrieval of knowledge in which data structure is unformatted (Section 3). Also, the necessary functions that the elements of the retieval model must have for storage/retrieval of knowledge are described (section 4). Third, KBAF, which has these functions, is discussed, and KBAF's knowledge representation, query notation, and retrieval mechanisms are described (Section 5).

2. THE RETRIEVAL MODEL

A retrieval system is shown in FIG. 2.1. This model has six elements: individual objects to be stored(FIG. 2.1-①), a storing function for individual objects (FIG. 2.1-②), the set of stored objects (FIG. 2.1-③), queries for the set of stored objects (FIG. 2.1-④), a function for retrieving objects from the set of stored objects in accordance with queries (FIG. 2.1-⑤), and the retrieval results of queries(FIG. 2.1-⑥). Assuming these elements to be p (object to be stored), g (storing function), M (set of stored objects), Q (contents of query), f (retrieval function), and A (retrieval results of query), the relationship between these elements can be expressed as follows :

Methodologies for Intelligent Systems
Z. W. Ras and M. Zemankova, Editors

$$M=\{m|m=g(p)\} \quad (1)$$

$$A=f(M,Q) \quad (2)$$

Equation (1) shows that the set of stored objects M is a set of individual objects p stored by the storing function g, where m represents the form of the objects when they are stored in M. Equation (2) shows that the retrieval results of query A are the consequence of the retrieval function f operating on the set of stored objects M and the contents of the query Q.

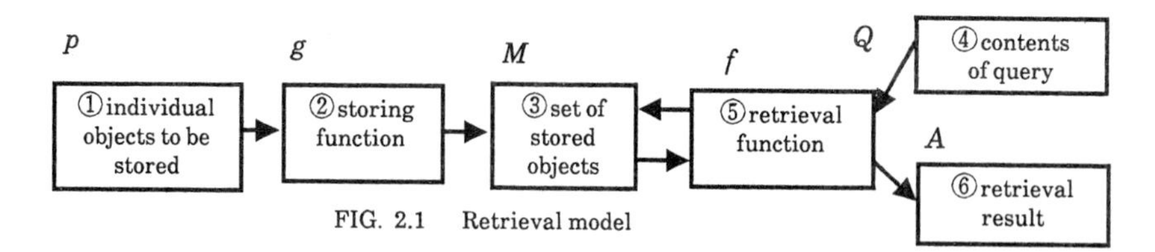

FIG. 2.1 Retrieval model

3. STUDY OF DBMS BASED ON THE RETRIEVAL MODEL

In this section the retrieval model, represented by equations(1) and (2), is applied to DBMS, and characteristics of DBMS are studied. The structure of DBMS is shown in FIG. 3.1. Each element of the retrieval model corresponds to each element of DBMS as follows:

p: individual data to be stored,
g: update program of database
(insert, delete, modify),
M: database (set of data),
Q: retrieval condition in specific query language to database,
f: retrieval program of database,
A: data retrieved by f.

This correspondence is quite favorable, as shown in FIG.3.1. Different DBMS systems are produced if different p, g, M, Q, f, and A are used.

In the following explanation a relational DBMS is used. First, the data storage function is discussed using an example in which stored data repesent company types and locations. In the case of a relational DBMS, the user enters data according to a defined table structure after creating a table of three attributes, COMPANY, TYPE, and LOCATION, as shown in FIG. 3.2. For example, consider a situation where the company name is Book Corp., its type of business is a bookstore and its stores are located in New York City and Chicago. The data will consist of two "p"s and may be entered as follows:

[Book Corp., bookstore, New York City], [Book Corp., bookstore, Chicago].

As a result, the information is stored as shown in FIG. 3.3. In the case of a relational DBMS, p is in the same form as m in equation (1). Information about companies that have ordered items and the items that they ordered is shown in FIG. 3.4. This information is stored in the same manner as in the previous example.

Next, the data retrieval function is discussed. Tables representing information on customers (FIG. 3.3) and information on their orders (FIG.3.4) are used as examples of sets of stored data. There are basic functions of DBMS which are foundations for all functions. These are retrieval of data containing the specified value, combining data which are related in the set of stored data and retrieval of combined data. The retrieval model is applied in the following manner:

M: table,
Q: the query which specifies the value used to select data and how to join data in the specific query language to the DBMS
f: the program retrieving the data which contains the specified values and is joined according to Q,
A: data retrieved by f.

For example, the query "Get name of ordered item (ORD_ITEM) and name of orderer (ORDERER) for each order of the customers (COMPANY) whose type (TYPE) is bookstore" may be expressed in the query language of the relational database as follows :

```
SELECT REC_ORD.ORD_ITEM, REC_ORD.ORDERER
FROM CUST, REC_ORD
WHERE CUST.TYPE = 'bookstore' AND CUST.COMPANY = REC_ORD.ORDERER
```

and the retrieval result is:

[library information system, Book Corp.]

As a result of this method of data storage, it is important to note the following DBMS characteristics of p, Q, and f:

p: Scheme must be defined before data are stored.

Q: Query must be in accordance with the scheme of the stored data. The relationship between data must be specified in the query. This is shown as follows :
CUST.COMPANY = REC_ORD.ORDERER

f: Data are retrieved according to search routes between the various tables specified in a query.

4. EXPECTATIONS OF KNOWLEDGE BASE MANAGEMENT SYSTEM

Knowledge can be input into the knowledge base at any time, and its data structure scheme can be unformatted. Supose that the knowledge item "There is a company called Book Corp. which is in New York City" was input at a particular time. At another time, the knowledge item "An orderer called Book Corp. ordered an item called Library information system" was input. The system should be able to store these knowledge items and then respond to a request such as "What was the ordered item that was ordered by an orderer in New York City?"

This system, which is suitable for storage and retrieval of knowledge (unformatted data), is different from DBMS as follows:

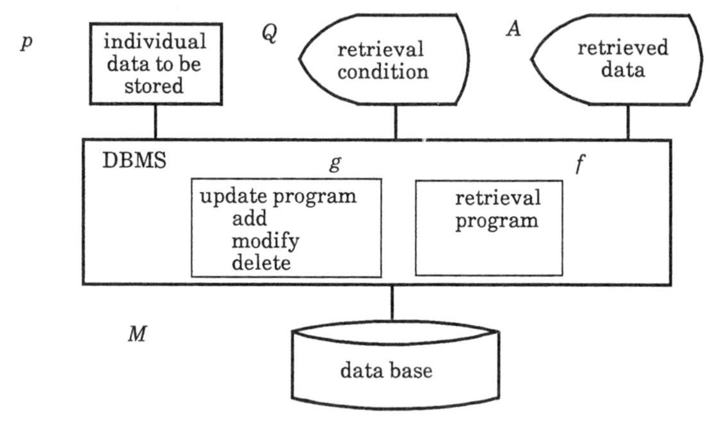

FIG. 3.1 Organization of DBMS

CUST

COMPANY	TYPE	LOCATION

FIG. 3.2 Table scheme example in DBMS

CUST

COMPANY	TYPE	LOCATION
Book Corp.	bookstore	New York City
Book Corp.	bookstore	Chicago

FIG. 3.3 Example of data input to table

REC_ORD

ORD_ITEM	ORDERER
library information system	Book Corp.
goods information system	Jones shop

FIG. 3.4 Table example

p: No fixed data structure scheme needs to be defined in advance.
Q: Users can query without knowing the schemes of the stored knowledge.
f: Users can retrieve data by automatic inference even if query representation is different from stored knowledge representation or if search routes between several individual knowledge items are not specified.

5. KNOWLEDGE BASE MANAGEMENT SYSTEM (KBAF)

5.1 Basic considerations

The knowledge base management system KBAF developed in this paper establishes p, Q, and f based on the following criteria:

p: A formal notation for representation of individual knowledge is given.
Q: A formal notation is given for query descriptions without knowing schemes of the stored knowledge.
f: KBAF must have the following five functions in order to locate destination knowledge:
- (a) understanding of different expressions of the same meaning (ex. New York City and N. Y.C.)
- (b) understanding of converseness (ex. parent and child).
- (c) understanding of the relationship between general words and specific words (ex. shop and bookstore).
- (d) understanding of incomplete query descriptions (ex. specify only last name without first name).
- (e) ability to connect related knowledge items.

A system which satisfies the criteria mentioned above is described in sections 5.2 and 5.3.

5.2 Kinds and notations of knowledge

Four kinds of knowledge are established :

- factual knowledge: individual knowledge
- rule type knowledge: knowledge for connecting related facts to each other
- dictionary type knowledge: synonyms, converseness
- generalization hierarchy type knowledge:
  words representing generalizations and specializations

Rule type, dictionary type, and generalization hierarchy types of knowledge are used to help retrieval of factual knowledge. Rule and generalization hierarchies have already been studied [5], [6] etc. Concepts from these studies are utilized in this paper.

Details of four kinds of knowledge are described in the following explanations. In the following, a{b} stands for 'a' having several 'b's.

(1) factual knowledge

A notation for individual fact is as follows (detail syntax is shown in FIG. 5.1) :

```
<fact> ::=    <item name> {<item data>} |
              <item name> {<item data>{<fact>}}
```

In this notation square brackets [], which indicate disjunctives, and braces {} and commas are terminal symbols. The following shows fact examples:

```
[K1]
Company {Book Corp.
        {Location {New York City
                  {chief{Michael Green},
                  clerk{Peter White, Tom Blue}}},
        Type{bookstore},
        Gross Sales{$1000K}}}
```

(This fact shows that Book Corp. is a company in New York City. The chief is Michael Green and the clerks are Peter White and Tom Blue. The company is a bookstore and its gross sales is $1000K.)

```
[K2]
Ordered item{Library information system{Orderer{Book Corp.}}}
```

(This fact shows that Library information system is an item that was ordered by Book Corp.)

Facts are represented in hierarchical form, as shown above. The first item name (ex. Company in [K1]) and item data (ex. Book Corp. in [K1]) are called "main item name" and "main item data". Other item names and item data are called "attribute item names" and "attribute item data". That is, main item name and main item data indicate an object described by facts, while attribute item names and attribute item data indicate an characteristics of objects.

```
<fact>    ::=      <main item name>         {   <main item data>     }  |
               <main item name>         {   <main item dataa>    {
               <characteristics description>      }}
<main item name>          ::= <word>
<main item data>      ::= <word>
<characteristics description>  ::= <item list>         |   [ <item set list> ] |
                                   <item list>     ,   [    <item set list>          ]
<item set list>         ::= {   <item list>          }  |
                            {   <item list>          },<item set list>
<item list>     ::= <item>    |    <item>,   <item list>
<item>    ::= <item name> {    <item data description>  }
<item data description>   ::= <item data list> |
                            [    <item data set list>         ]  |
                            <item data list>   ,    [    <item data set list>   ]
<item data set list>    ::=    {    <item data list>        }  |
                               {    <item data list>        },<item data set list>
<item data list>          ::= <item value> |
                                 <item value>, <item data list>
<item value> ::= <item data> |
                 <item data> {      <characteristics description>  }
<item name>       ::= <word>
<item data>  ::= <word>
```

FIG. 5.1 Syntax for facts

(2) rule type knowledge

A notation for a rule to connect related facts to each other is :

<rule> ::= <fact of (1)> :- <fact of (1)>,···

where item data may be variable.

The right side of ':-' shows how to connect related facts to each other. The left side of ':-' shows the form of knowledge which is provisionally regarded as a fact.

The following shows an example of a rule description:

[K3]

Ordered item{Y{Orderer{bookstore}} :- Company{X{Type{bookstore}}},
Ordered item{Y{Orderer{X}}}

(This rule shows that "Orderer of Ordered item Y is bookstore" is equivalent to "Type of Company X is bookstore and Orderer of Ordered item Y is X".)

(3) dictionary type knowledge

A notation for synonyms is as follows :

<synonym> ::= {<word>, <word>, ···}

The following shows an example of a synonym:

[K4]

{New York City, N.Y.C.}

A notation for converseness is as follows :

<converseness> ::= <the same form as a rule>

The following shows an example of converseness:

[K5]

person{X{child{Y}}} :- parent{X{person{Y}}}

(This example shows that "child of person X is Y" is equivalent to "parent of person Y is X".)

(4) generalization hierarchy type knowledge

A notation for a generalization hierarchy type knowledge is as follows :

<g.h.t knowledge>::={<word>{<c.c.s>{<word>{<c.c.s>{<word>{···}}}}}}

where c.c.s.: classification criteria of subordinate words.

The following is an example of generalization hierarchy type knowledge:

[K6]
{shop{ 2nd level{ bookstore{ 3rd level{ special bookstore,
general bookstore}},
drugstore,
department store}}}

5.3 INFERENTIAL RETRIEVAL OF KNOWLEDGE

5.3.1 Query description

The description syntax of queries is as follows:

<retrieval condition>::=logical expression of which the elements are <condition>s
<condition>::= <item name><comparison operator><item data>|
<item name> <comparison operator> {<condition>}
<item to be retrieved>::= <item name>{<item name>{···}}},···
<comparison operator>::= >|<|=

Content of query described by <retrieval condition> and <item to be retrieved> does not depend on the data structure scheme of the stored knowledge.

The following is an example of a query:

[Q1]
retrieval condition : Orderer = {Location= N.Y.C.}
item to be retrieved : Ordered item{Orderer}

(This query means "What is the Ordered item and who is its Orderer whose Location is N.Y.C.?")

Users may doubt if a retrieval can be carried out well when there are two facts, such as [K1] and [K2], and a synonym, such as [K4] in a query. However, it is not necessary that the user knows the data structure scheme of the stored knowledge. It is only necessary for the user to state the contents of his query using the query notation.

5.3.2 Retrieval mechanism

Basic parts of the retrieval process are shown using logic programming language [5] in FIG.5.2. This algorithm begins using getfact2(Ordered item, Y, Orderer, Location ,N.Y.C.) for the query [Q1] above. Items ⑥, ⑪, ③, ①, and ① are carried out in turn, and fact [K2] is retrieved as a result. The sequence (ⓐ~ ⓕ) in which the system searched for knowledge items in turn, is shown in FIG. 5.3. In getfact1(X, Y, Z, W) and getfact2(X, Y, Z, ZZ, W), used at the beginning of the retrieval, X and Y are item name and item data to be retrieved, and Z, ZZ, and W are two item names and item data to describe the retrieval condition. This is shown in FIG 5.2. If logical operators (AND,OR) are used in the query, the final information can be retrieved by carrying out the set operations among the fact sets that were retrieved by getfactl or getfact2. Although actual KBAF getfact functions are more complex, their algorithms are similar to the algorithm described in FIG. 5.2. Primitive predicates used in FIG. 5.2 are as follows :

(1) partfact(X, Y, Z, W)

This primitive predicate obtains the main item name, main item data, favorable attribute item name, and favorable attribute item data from the individual fact.

EX. partfact(Company, Book Corp., Location, New York City)
partfact(Company, Book Corp., chief, Michael Green)

```
①  getfact1(X,Y,Z,W)   :-  partfact(X,Y,Z,W1) ,   part_match(W,W1).
②  getfact1(X,Y,Z,W)   :-  rules(X,Y,Z,W).
③  getfact1(X,Y,Z,W)   :-  synonym(W,W1),   getfact1(X,Y,Z,W1).
④  getfact1(X,Y,Z,W)   :-  hie(W,W1), getfact1(X,Y,Z,W1).
⑤  getfact1(X,Y,Z,W)   :-  assoc1(W,W1),  getfact1(X,Y,Z,W1).
⑥  getfact2(X,Y,Z,ZZ,W)    :-  assoc2(ZZ,W,W1 ),  getfact1(X,Y,Z,W1).
⑦  syno(W,W1)     :-  W1 = W.
⑧  syno(W,W1)     :-  synonym(W,W1).
⑨  hie(W,W1) :-  syno(W,X),  hierarchy(X,Y),  syno(Y,W1).
⑩  assoc1(W,W1)  :-  getfact1(_,W1,_,W).
⑪  assoc2(ZZ,W,W1)    :-  getfact1(_,W1,ZZ,W).
```

(part-match, synonym and hierarchy are shown only for W in this Fig.)

FIG. 5.2 Retrieval process of KBAF

etc. are obtained from the fact [K1].

(2) part_match(W, W1)

This primitive predicate checks if character string W is contained in character string W1.

(3) rules(X,Y,Z,W)

This primitive predicate uses rule type knowledge. For example, this primitive utilizes the knowledge [K3] for queries like getfact1(Ordered item, Y, Orderer, bookstore).

(4) synonym(W,W1)

This primitive predicate obtains a synonym W1 of a word W.

EX.synonym(New York City, N.Y.C.) is obtained from knowledge [K4].

(5) hierarchy(W,W1)

This primitive predicate obtains a specialized word W1s of a word W.

EX.hierarchy(shop, bookstore),

hierarchy(shop,drugstore), etc. are obtained from knowledge [K6].

(6) assoc1(W, W1), assoc2(ZZ, W, W1)

Let us suppose that there are two stored facts [K1] and [K2], but there is no rule type knowledge to connect [K1] and [K2]. In this case, the following associative retrieval is carried out. If a fact contains I{w1}, but does not contain I{w} when the retrieval condition of the query contains I=w, the system thinks that a property of w is specified instead of w1. That is, the system thinks there is a fact K{w1{···L{w}}} of which the main item data is w1 and the attribute item data is w. Therefore, retrieval is carried out : first, the main item data w1 having w as an attribute item data is retrieved, next, fact having w1 as attribute item data is retrieved. Assoc1(W, W1) is used for such retrievals. Retrieval conditions such as I={ZZ=w} may be specified (ex. query [Q1]). Assoc2(ZZ, W, W1) is used in this case.

The KBAF system's organization, which includes a knowledge editor (*g*), inferential retrieval (*f*), and a knowledge base (*M*), is shown in FIG. 5.4.

6. CONCLUSION

A knowledge base management system KBAF has been developed. It has the following three characteristics: (1)Knowledge consists of four types : factual knowledge, rule type knowledge, dictionary type knowledge (synonyms, converseness), and hierarchical type knowledge (general

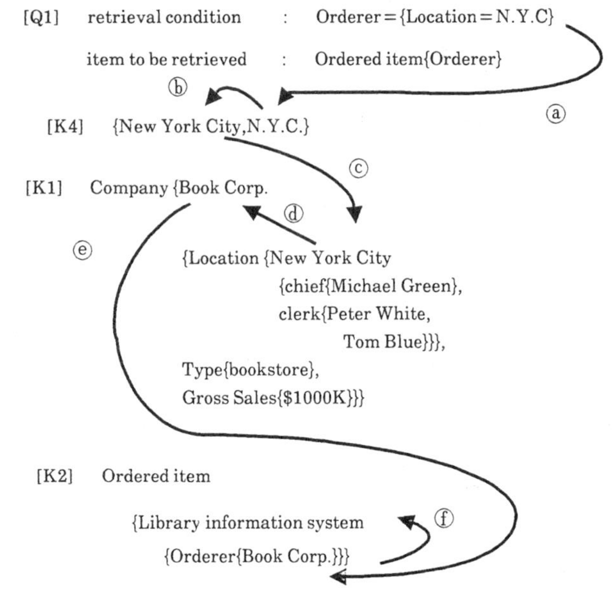

FIG . 5.3 Path of automatic knowledge search by KBAF

and specific words). (2) Retrieval conditions and items can be specified without knowing the structure of the stored knowledge. The retrieval conditions are described by logical expressions. The elements of these expressions are item names and item data. The items are described by item names. (3) The system has five important retrieval functions : synonym retrieval, generalization hierarchy retrieval (use of specialized words), retrieval using rule type knowledge (converseness retrieval is contained), associative retrieval (connection of individual facts), and partial match retrieval functions.

A first prototype implementation of KBAF was applied to storage/retrieval of the knowledge which shows titles of figures and tables in articles on computers. We are conscious, through the implementation, systems like KBAF will become convenient ones for storage/retrieval of information.

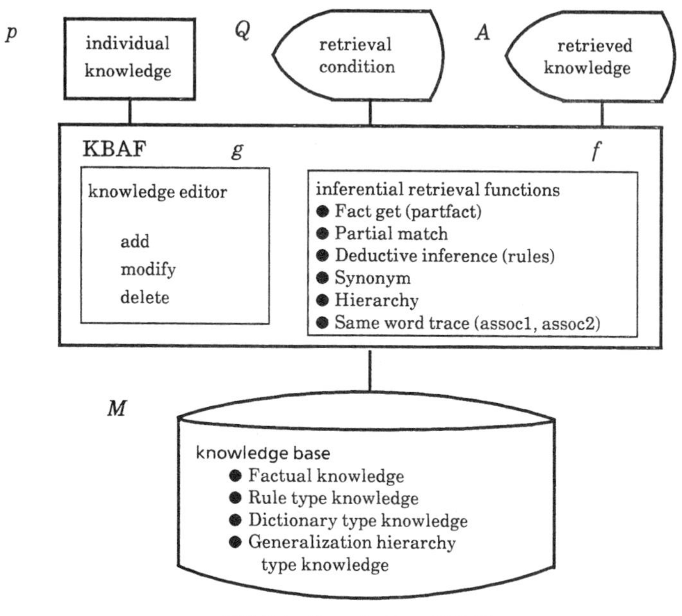

FIG. 5.4 Organization of KBAF

7. BIBLIOGRAPHY

1 L. Kerschberg : Expert Database Systems (Workshop Review), Proceedings of ACM SIGMOD Conference (1985).

2 S. Christodoulakis : Pannel : Multimedia Database Management Systems, Proceedings of ACM SIGMOD Conference (1985).

3 C. J. Date : An Introduction to Database Systems, ADDISON WESLEY Publishing Company (1981).

4 J. Mylopoulous : An Overview of Knowledge Representation, Proceedings of the workshop on Data Abstraction, Databases and Conceptual Modeling, ACM (1980).

5 W. F. Clocksin, C. S. Merish : Programming in Prolog, Springer-Verlag (1981).

6 J. M. Smith et al. : Database Abstractions : Aggregation and Generalization, ACM Transactions on Database Systems, (June 1977).

KNOWLEDGE ACQUISITION AND METAREPRESENTATION: ATTRIBUTE AUTOPOIESIS

EPHRAIM NISSAN *
*Department of Mathematics & Computer Science,
Ben Gurion University of the Negev,
P.O. Box 653, Beer-Sheva 84105, Israel

ABSTRACT

We discuss an approach to knowledge-bases where frames are conceived as nested relations, and where the structure of frames is described in a metarepresentation expressed in terms of a production system. A methodology for knowledge acquisition is described, where the metarepresentation is elicited, and focus-calibration is served by explicitly keeping a quantitative track of the plunge into knowledge-subdomains.

1. INTRODUCTION

This paper deals with a method of knowledge acquisition, that focuses on drawing a metarepresentation of a frame-base. The metarepresentation states the legal schemata of attributes in frames. It represents the organization structure of frames. Frames are conceived as being nested relations. Hierarchies (or, occasionally, networks) of attributes are developed, that express a decomposition of the knowledge of the application domain.

Moreover, our method allows to keep track, explicitly and quantitatively, of the "plunging front" of the decomposition: a structure inspired by Kiviat diagrams documents the analysis of the knowledge-domain, and its decomposition expansion, in the process of knowledge acquisition. This is important in large, multi-expert and multi-domain applications, where domain-focusing may be problematic. One should be able to avoid relying only on the individual memory of personnel, when needing access to knowledge about the evolution of the knowledge-elicitation process, and about "hot spots" focused about at given moments.

Metarepresentation of the database of the expert system is developed by individuating attributes and their relationship, in a growing hierarchy. This is useful also for the design of control, or of rules that access frames.

On the other hand, in the metarepresentation as at a given moment, the development process history does not appear through. A suitable graphic representation that we are going to expose, provides both historic documentation, and a tool for the management of knowledge acquisition while developing the current edge of the development process.

2. THE METAREPRESENTATION

The metarepresentation structure adopted is a production system, where left-hand sides are an attribute, and right-hand sides are lists of attributes that may be nested as children of the attribute in the left-hand side of the same production (see [1]).

This approach puts in evidence the potentials of development of the decomposition. The reference represented by the schema of

Methodologies for Intelligent Systems
Z. W. Ras and M. Zemankova, Editors

attributes (static metaknowledge) is a good support for the definition of dynamic aspects: constraints (e.g., productions) accessing the attributes in the frame-base, or details of the control exploiting the knowledge-base.

Elicitation translates into an autopoiesis (an organic growth) of the metarepresentation. In Negoita's terms, we

> "see a development process as an autopoietic organization which is realized as an autonomous and self-maintaining unity through a network of syntheses-producing processes such that the components, through their interaction generate recursively the same network of processes that produced them." [2] (p. 75)

On autopoiesis, see [3] and [4].

Semantically, the decomposition should account for different subdomains, and possibly for interconnections between subdomains of the application knowledge. In large projects, especially if they span on a broad range of domains, several experts may be involved, for the same domain, or for different domains. The dynamics of the knowledge-acquisition process needs an expressional support, in a syntax for allowing to describe the phases of the process effectively, and in particular, to account for "plunging" into subdomains, that is to quantify -- albeit roughly -- the depth of into which, at a given moment, specific domains have been tackled.

During the development of the preliminary metarepresentation of a frame-base, or even when knowledge is already being filled in frames, metarepresentation expansion may include various kinds of intervention in the production system expressing the attribute hierarchy:
-- new productions are introduced from scratch, or
-- existing productions in the metarepresentation are expanded with new attributes in the right-hand side (RHS), or
-- the RHS of an existing production is furtherly structured, possibly in nested sub-RHSs, or
-- new productions are introduced to replace a less sophisticated production found to be inadequate (but practically, for the sake of incrementality, you may keep the old production as well, if you have frames that were filled with the considered subframe obeying the old convention), or
-- in a given production, a left-hand side (LHS), instead of being just one attribute, is specified as a list including several attributes admitting the same RHS (legal child-set). For example, let us consider an expert system for gastronomy, where kinds of foods are organized in an inheritance network, and each kind of food owns a frame. Attributes nested under SOCIAL_INFO (where all of the social information is grouped) include OCCASIONS_RECOMMENDED_FOR, FITNESS_CONSTRAINTS, and RELIGIOUS_CONSTRAINTS. How could we organize RELIGIOUS_CONSTRAINTS? Attributes nested under it, may include an attribute, RELIGION, and also -- at the same level -- attributes where the various constraints fit: for example, ABSOLUTE_PROHIBITIONS, PERSON-IDENTITY_DEPENDENT, and TIME-DEPENDENT; the latter constraints are furtherly subdivided into calendar-dependent constraints (e.g., depending on Lent), vs. dependence from asynchronous events (as in the case of the Jewish constraint prohibiting food containing milk, if meat was eaten less than a certain number of hours before). Alternatively, you may list different religions as attributes (instead of values of RELIGION directly under the level of the attribute RELIGIOUS_CONSTRAINTS. In this case, in the metarepresentation we would have the productions (RELIGIOUS_CONSTRAINTS (MOSLEM JEWISH DRUZE HINDU)) and ((MOSLEM JEWISH ...) (ABSOLUTE_PROHIBITIONS TIME-DEPENDENT ...))

In the latter, there is a multi-attribute LHS. This means that in the frames, under any attribute indicating a particular religion, you may nest the attributes as in the RHS of the last production.

Adding attributes normally stems from the identification of new subdomains of knowledge that it is interesting to describe, with reference to the concept owning the frame. However, you may also refine the metarepresentation, adding new attributes or productions, because you seek a more sophisticated way to represent properties that are already present. For example, if, so far, you stated a certain property as applying (according to a crisp logic), now you may wish to state, e.g., numeric scores of validity of that property, or specific contexts of application. (Cf. [5].)

3. REAL CASES

In the previous section, we saw an example concerning a knowledge-base of kinds of food. The real cases from which lessons were drawn for the present discussion, are:

a) FIDEL_GASTRO, a frame-based expert adviser for gastronomy. A comparison of its architecture, with a logic-based system, "The Wine Adviser", is discussed in [6];
b) ONOMATURGE, an expert system for natural-language word-formation, that coins Hebrew neologisms, and evaluates how "good" they would seem to a conversant speaker. The control of ONOMATURGE, at present, focuses on the lexical innovation task, but the terminological frame-base is more general, and could suit also different uses of knowledge-bases in lexicography. On ONOMATURGE, see [7, 8].

The frame-base of FIDEL_GASTRO and ONOMATURGE is an essentially passive network, interpreted by task-oriented, and possibly several, programs or rulesets of control. The metarepresentation of FIDEL_GASTRO contemplates the possible use of procedural attachment ("demons" automatically triggered on retrieval), but the present control does not resort to such an option.

The demarcation between frame-base and control, makes a subdivision of task-oriented controls, manageable. The metarepresentation achieves more generality, in its content, than required by a narrowly tailored, task-specific control. This provides, e.g., FIDEL_GASTRO with the possibility of quickly-plunging implementation of one task, in a top-down functional decomposition of tasks.

The approach to frames underlying our present discussion, is the one implemented in RAFFAELLO, a knowledge-management toolbox, and is related to the nested-relation approach to databases. Both ONOMATURGE and FIDEL_GASTRO are supported by RAFFAELLO. The paper [9] illustrates the criteria underlying the salient features of the toolbox. Another paper, [10], describes didactic aspects of building expert systems with RAFFAELLO's metarepresentation. For the syntax of the CuProS metarepresentation language of RAFFAELLO, see [1]: the schema of legal frames is expressed in a production system augmented with labels. [11] discusses, in particular, the link with the nested-relation approach to databases.

4. ASPECTS OF RETRIEVAL

During the knowledge-acquisition phase, when the metarepresentation is drawn, attributes are defined, and it is only natural that ideas become concomitantly clear also about those details of control that exploit the frames.

After the metarepresentation is drawn, it may be used both as a reference by the project members, and as a guide for retrieval as performed by the frame-base management system (in particular, by RAFFAELLO).

A prototype of control is implemented, together with the first instances of frames.

Two alternative approaches to retrieval -- suiting different phases of the development of an expert system -- are reflected in the two main implemented versions of RAFFAELLO's component that manages retrieval from frames.

The general version is NAVIGATION, that is domain-independent, and retrieves from frames by consulting the metarepresentation. It is useful for rapid prototyping, while in order to optimize retrieval, in an advanced stage of the project, the other version, SIMPLE_NAVIGATION, may be cloned: an application-specific instance is easily developed.

SIMPLE_NAVIGATION is a module-base of retrieval functions, specific for certain taxonomic situations in frames, and adapted to given frame-bases. It is very easy to adapt that software, just by modifying attribute-names. Functions in SIMPLE_NAVIGATION are specialized for paths of intensive retrieval. The programmer consults the metarepresentation, while building the instance of SIMPLE_NAVIGATION: this is a shortcut with respect to the way NAVIGATION (the metarepresentation-driven version) performs retrieval. One may describe the passage from NAVIGATION to SIMPLER_NAVIGATION as manual (meta)knowledge-compilation, performed for the sake of cognitive economy: analogously, a human expert does not need to think so much to perform a task that he is accustomed to; he (or she) develops a fast procedure as a short-cut.

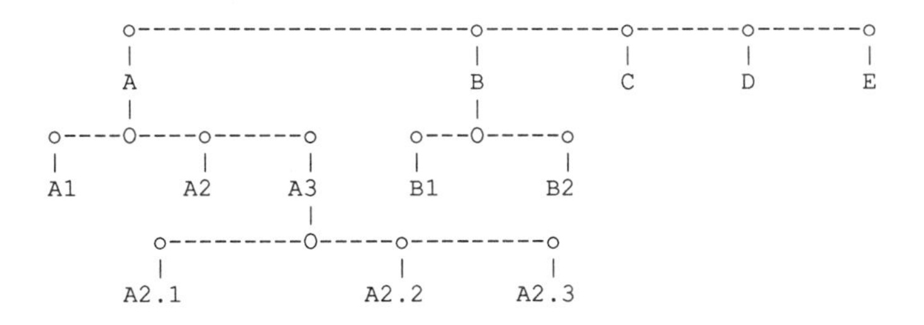

FIG. 1. A quickly plunging decomposition.

5. REPRESENTATION A' LA KIVIAT OF THE HISTORIC DIMENSION OF KNOWLEDGE ACQUISITION

Generally, the metarepresentation development is top-down. However, by analyzing particular examples, a bottom-up development may occur. Anyway, by inserting the result of "bottom-up islands" in the general schema of top-down development, the character of the latter as being a "quick-plunge" top-down decomposition will be emphasized. (See FIG. 1.)

This is not necessarily bad: an "even-descent" top-down decomposition maybe obeys the canon of classical harmony, but is not necessarily the ideal in software projects. For a similar idea in the framework of "conventional" software engineering, see, for example, [12] (p. 44).

Kiviat diagrams are resorted to, in performance evaluation and tuning of computer systems; see [13] (Sec. 3) and [14]. A Kiviat diagram is a circle with a radius plotted for each percent measure, out of a set of measures that for example include: how much time -- the CPU is active; channels are active; the CPU and channels are active; the CPU is active but no channel is active; the supervisor is executing; programs are executing; and so on.

Segments are plotted between the coordinates obtained on adjacent radiuses, and a polygon is formed; this is the way general Kiviat diagrams are generated.

In the widespread Kent version of Kiviat diagrams [15], an even number of measures appears in the circle; one half of those criteria measures good performance, while the other half includes indicators of bad performance. Radiuses corresponding to good performance, and radiuses of bad performance, alternate. The upper vertical radius is conventionally associated with a measure of good performance. A star as in FIG. 2 indicates a good performance: low values of bad measures are obtained on the "diagonals".

Kiviat diagrams are plotted, using standard alphanumeric characters, by programs included in commercial software monitors for performance evaluation, such as CUE [16].

In our new application of Kiviat diagrams, we don't adopt the Kent version. We use them to express the domain-decomposition expansion during knowledge analysis; radiuses correspond to knowledge subdomains tackled in a certain phase of metarepresentation drawing. Beside application, there is a basic difference with respect to the way Kiviat diagrams are used in the performance evaluation of computer system configurations: in the latter use, radiuses are graduated from 0% in the center, to 100% on the circumference. In knowledge acquisition, instead, we cannot assess -- a priori -- the percentage of knowledge acquisition in a (sub)domain, when we are in any given phase: in fact, we cannot reliably forecast the "size" of the decomposition as needed in future stages of the knowledge analysis process itself.

Thus, instead of plotting a circumference conceived as indicating 100%, we adopt concentrical circumferences without determining an ultimate outermost circumference. Quantification will be absolute, instead of a percentage.

Now, we have to define "sizes". Let us distinguish between:

i) the process of decomposition (attribute-autopoiesis) in the metarepresentation stating legal frame-schemata, and
ii) the process of knowledge-filling in frames.

In (i), size in our version of Kiviat diagrams may be defined as being:

#i1) the number of attributes identified in the current phase, or, at a higher level:
#i2) the number of subsectors identified so far (possibly just mentioned and tackled), and fitting in the domain represented by the radius, but not developed enough to deserve their own radius.

FIG. 3 represents a quick plunge into the subdomains 2 to 6. Adjacency of radiuses may usefully reflect semantic adjacency of subdomains.

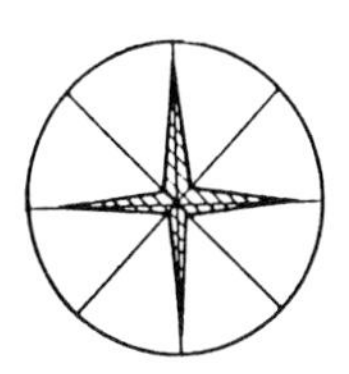

FIG. 2. A "Kent star" of good performance.

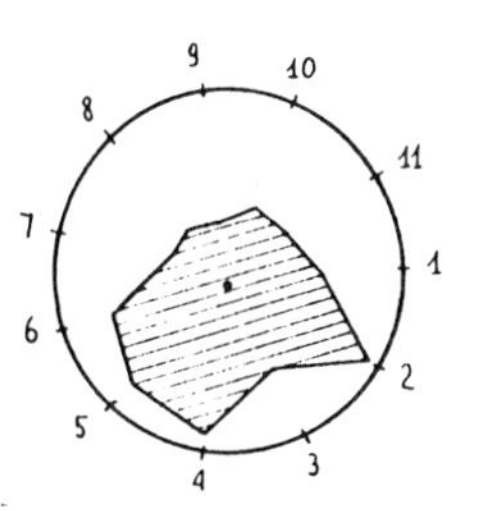

FIG. 3. A quickly plunging decomposition represented a' la Kiviat.

In case we use pseudo-Kiviat diagrams during knowledge filling (ii), then size may be defined as being:

#ii1) the number of code lines (then each radius represents a frame, or a "thematic" subframe),
or, at a higher level:
#ii2) the number of frames or of rules fitting in a certain group (represented by a radius). Cohesion into groups may stem from semantic, or even implementational considerations.

The #ii1 / #ii2 ratio is an indicator of "average" granularity of chunks of knowledge, in every knowledge-subdomain, or in every group of knowledge-representation chunks (as proper).

Granularity may be calibrated: in RAFFAELLO's frames, substructures may be repeated (instead of defining them as separate frames), thanks to the option in the syntax of the metarepresentation ([1]: the "n:" label). In [9], I discussed the benefits of calibrating granularity. A "coarse" granularity may enhance readability, because of semantic cohesion. This is the case of frames in ONOMATURGE, where there are 50-400 lines per frame, and usually 100-200 lines, with a capability of further expansion of each frame. On the other hand, a "fine" granularity may fully exploit inter-frame facilities, e.g., mechanisms that manage inheritance or propagation through message passing, in a network of active chunks of knowledge.

In ONOMATURGE, coarse granularity is natural, as frames represent lexical entries, that each may have one or several meanings ("acceptations"), with certain descriptions (e.g. of connotation) that have to be specific for the term as in a particular meaning; that is, semantic description doesn't refer only to a given meaning as abstracted from terms that may express it. Therefore, it is natural to see the description of the lexical entry in the same frame, instead of segmented in several small frames. Coarse granularity helps to bridge the gap between the needs of AI semantic representation, and the way lexicographers are accustomed to see lexical entries.
(On the knowledge-base of ONOMATURGE in the framework of the state of the art of machine dictionaries, see [8].)

The structure of particular pseudo-Kiviat diagrams, or of sets of diagrams, evolves along with the knowledge acquisition process: as the metarepresentation is expanded, or -- while filling knowledge in frames -- as new frames are added. Expanding the metarepresentation, the decomposition of knowledge subdomains brings new attributes in the production system, and also in some pseudo-Kiviat diagram. Now and then, we identify a new knowledge-subsector of further detail, or a connection with some other subdomain.

Then, a new version of some existing pseudo-Kiviat diagram, or even new pseudo-Kent diagrams, may be introduced into the set of evolving diagrams, to account for the new stage.

The autopoietic process of knowledge acquisition -- as concerning attributes (as opposed to values) -- is reflected in the metarepresentation, that at a given moment exhibits its current stage of development. A metaphor is the process of development of a natural language into its contemporary status: e.g., the modern lexicon has assimilated innovation, but the history is no longer transparent, and reconstruction provides jobs for etymologists. For project managers, instead, the project history should be at hand. We provide a documentation methodology: the process evolution is reflected in the evolving set of pseudo-Kiviat diagrams, that accounts for the history of the process: sticking, terminologically, to the analogy from linguistics, we may say that the graphic representation a' la Kiviat adds an explicit "diachronic" (i.e., historic) dimension to the written expression of the process.

In fact, the representation a' la Kiviat evolves through:

A) an increase of the number of radiuses per knowledge subdomain;
B) an increase of the number of distinct diagrams, as new diagrams are added for every detailed subdomain. There is a useful "physical" constraint on the number of radiuses in the same diagram, as to keep a good level of readability, circles should not be cluttered up with too many radiuses. Besides,
C) the development of the pseudo-Kiviat diagram set meant to describe the growth of the metarepresentation, is (roughly) followed by the development of the pseudo-Kiviat diagram set meant to historically quantify knowledge-filling in frames, whose structure has been defined in the metarepresentation.

Of course, new attributes, or even new productions, may be added to the metarepresentation at any moment, even when a frame-base already exists. Not only: you may integrate two existing frame-bases, by drawing a metarepresentation a posteriori.

6. CONCLUSIONS

As artificial intelligence is no longer confined to speculative research in the academy, and the expert systems technology has entered its industrial phase, software engineering issues are likely to become more and more important. Perhaps speaking about "knowledge engineering" is somewhat misleading, given such a context. In fact, traditionally "knowledge engineering" refers to representational issues at the object level or at the meta-level of knowledge acquisition and representation. This meaning of the compound overshadows further, emerging aspects that are also covered by "knowledge engineering". They are not put in the light they deserve: project management factors should be recognized as being a topic deserving attention on its own, in applied AI, just as software engineering gained recognition during the Seventies for non-AI software development. Therefore, people in applied AI should speak about "software engineering" as distinct from "knowledge engineering".

In this paper, I have exposed a method that integrates metarepresentation construction with an explicit, quantitative track of the diachronic dimension of the knowledge-acquisition process, in the construction of expert systems.

The process of metarepresentation growth at the attribute level ("attribute autopoiesis") is quantified and documented in an evolving set of pseudo-Kiviat diagrams. The same graphical representation is also suitable to document cu knowledge-filling in knowledge structures, and to quantify granularity organically, in order to allow a more conscious calibration of the granularity of knowledge-chunks. Domain-knowledge decomposition, and, in particular, "plunging fronts" (focuses) of knowledge analysis or filling are cast in their proper temporal dimension, quantitatively. This should help to make expert-system project management more manageable, when several experts, domains, or knowledge engineers are involved.

REFERENCES

1. E. Nissan, The Frame-Definition Language for Customizing the RAFFAELLO Structure-Editor in Host Expert Systems. In: Z. Ras and M. Zemankova, eds., Proceedings of the First International Symposium on Methodologies for Intelligent Systems (ISMIS'86), Knoxville, Tennessee (1986).
2. C.V. Negoita, Fuzzy Systems. (Abacus Press, Tunbridge Wells, Kent, U.K., 1981).
3. H.R. Maturana and F.J. Varela, Autopoiesis and Cognition: The Realization of the Living. (Kluwer Academic Publishers, Dordrecht, The Netherlands, 1980).
4. M. Zeleny, ed., Autopoiesis (North-Holland, Amsterdam, 1981).
5. E. Nissan, Exception-Admissibility and Typicalness in Proto-Representations. INFOTERM International Congress on Terminology and Knowledge Representation (Trier, FRG, 1987).
6. S. Garber, E. Nissan and A. Shur, The Wine Adviser. Technical Report, Department of Mathematics & Computer Science, Ben-Gurion University (Beer-Sheva, 1987).
7. E. Nissan, The Structure of Control in ONOMATURGE: An Expert System for Word-Formation. Computational Linguistics (accepted, pending revision).
8. E. Nissan, ONOMATURGE: An Expert System for Word-Formation and Morpho-Semantic Clarity Evaluation. INFOTERM International Congress on Terminology and Knowledge Representation (Trier, FRG, 1987).
9. E. Nissan, Development Methods and Subservient Representations With a Toolbox for Knowledge Representation: Software Engineering Aspects. Technical Report, Department of Mathematics & Computer Science, Ben-Gurion University, Beer-Sheva (1987).
10. E. Nissan, How a Metarepresentation-Driven Tool May Enhance Learning to Build Expert Systems. In: E. Bar-On and Z. Scherz, eds., Proceedings of the International Meeting on Intelligent Training (Tutoring) Systems (IMITS'86), Tel-Aviv, Israel, December 1986 (to appear).
11. E. Nissan, Nested-Relation Based Frames in RAFFAELLO. Representation & Metarepresentation Structure & Semantics for Knowledge Engineering. International Workshop on Theory and Applications of Nested Relations and Complex Objects (Darmstadt, FRG, 1987). A preliminary workshop report has been published by INRIA (Rocquencourt, France, 1987) pp. 95-99.
12. R.H. Dunn, Software Defect Removal (McGraw-Hill, 1984).
13. D. Ferrari, G. Serazzi and A. Zeigner, Le prestazioni degli elaboratori elettronici. Misura, valutazione, ottimizzazione. (Franco Angeli, Milano, Italy, 1979). English edition: Measurement and Tuning of Computer Systems. (Prentice-Hall, 1983).
14. K.W. Kolence and P.J. Kiviat, Software Unit Profiles and Kiviat Figures. ACM SIGMETRICS Performance Evaluation Review 2(3), pp. 2-12 (1973).
15. M. Morris, Kiviat Graphs: Conventions and Figures of Merit. ACM SIGMETRICS Performance Evaluation Review 3(3), pp. 2-8 (1974).
16. CUE User Guide. Version 3.5. (Boole & Babbage, Sunnyvale, CA, 1977).

TOWARDS THE DESIGN OF A KNOWLEDGE BASED SYSTEM FOR HYDROCARBON PLAY ANALYSIS

Miao-Li Pai,* Gautam Biswas,** Christopher Kendall,* and James Bezdek**
*Department of Geology, **Department of Computer Science
University of South Carolina, Columbia, SC 29208, U.S.A.

ABSTRACT

This paper describes the architecture of the knowledge-based component of the eXpert eXplorer (XX) system for hydrocarbon basin exploration. The primary purpose of this component of XX is to aid exploration geologists in defining the salient characteristics of a target hydrocarbon play, and then to retrieve data for analogous oil fields that are stored in the XX database. The knowledge base is implemented as a set of rules that models the way an experienced petroleum geologist works with incomplete and inexact information from sources such as seismic charts and well logs to identify play characteristics. A pattern clustering technique is used to find a (group of) known field(s) similar to the target play. Clustering enables the geologist to better analyze the target play and to use data from similar fields to simulate the geometry of the target facies. A sample case study illustrates the interaction between the XX system and an exploration geologist. The results of applying the pattern clustering technique are also exemplified.

1. INTRODUCTION

Oil exploration is based upon a complex mix of concepts and techniques derived from the disciplines of geology, geophysics and chemistry. Successful exploration is to a great extent based on the heuristics and experiential knowledge of exploration geologists. Advances in technology have led to the use of graphic workstations on which integrated digital mapping [1,2] and reservoir simulations [3] can be run interactively; however, many exploration tasks still require subjective interpretation. Also, the degree of confidence in an interpretation can vary greatly, depending upon the sources and quality of available information. Sophisticated techniques have been developed for direct field observations as well as indirect subsurface measurements; nonetheless, information derived from them is often evidential and not conclusive. Geologists do agree that a region must possess some basic characteristics to have oil bearing potential [4,5]. First, there must be a sedimentary basin with enough source rock to supply sufficient quantities of petroleum hydrocarbons. Permeable layers must occur in the right position to facilitate migration, and there must be suitable porous and permeable formations, such as sand, sandstone, oolitic limestone, vugular or cavernous limestone and volcanic rock to act as a reservoir. Last but not least, there must be a trap which interrupts the migration of fluids so that hydrocarbons may accumulate.

The procedure adopted by geologists for hydrocarbon exploration involves two major steps. First, data are compiled from maps, geological reports, seismic cross-sections, cores or well logs to determine the important geological characteristics of a site. In the second step, petroleum geologists compare the target area data with similar data from known fields in the same area or from other regions of the world. The idea is to apply analogical reasoning to estimate the oil bearing potential for the region under consideration.

This comparative process is based on a number of parameters and criteria. The required expertise is usually gained through years of field experience and exposure to a wide range of situations, rather than by studying textbooks and research papers in petroleum geology. Another problem with exploration is that techniques or mediums available to store data from previously explored fields are often inadequate, so previous and related studies are not readily available to other geologists. This enhances the importance of past experience to geologists. Like other complex real world processes, the data made available to or acquired by the expert is often incomplete and inconsistent, making the reasoning process even more complex.

In this paper, we concentrate on the use of a knowledge based scheme to design a guidance system for oil exploration. Our primary focus is on helping the user derive essential target play characteristics, and then using this information to compare the target play to known fields in the database and extract those that are most similar. A clustering algorithm is used to group known fields into categories, to ease their comparison with the play and to identify the common characteristics of these categories with respect to their oil bearing potential.

Section 2 of this paper describes the overall expert system architecture, the knowledge representation scheme used, and the inferencing mechanisms. Section 3 describes the similarity measures and pattern clustering techniques used. The results of applying the clustering algorithm to the database of known plays is illustrated. Section 4 contains our summary.

2. AN EXPERT SYSTEM APPROACH

The application of knowledge based system technology to real world problems is currently receiving a great deal of attention; a number of systems are being developed for geological applications. For example, PROSPECTOR [6], was designed at SRI International to aid in certain kinds of mineral exploration. Ore-deposit

Methodologies for Intelligent Systems
Z. W. Ras and M. Zemankova, Editors

models provided by various expert geologists were used for prospect evaluation, regional resource assessment, and drilling site selection. MUDMAN [7] serves as a diagnostic and treatment consultant to mud engineers, DIPMETER ADVISOR [8] interprets bore hole logs, XEOD [9] interprets environments of deposition for clastic sediments, muPETROL [10] classifies sedimentary basins, and RESOLVER [11] improves the segmentation process of seismic sections. In addition, systems are being developed for automatic seismic discrimination [12] and vibroseis field parameters determination [13]. However, a major problem with many current systems is that they are based on models with a very narrow scope, and, therefore, make improper inferences when applied to different situations. In the rest of this section, we first describe the overall structure of our system for determining hydrocarbon potential, and then develop a knowledge based approach to aid exploration geology which determines the salient characteristics of a target play.

2.1. The Overall Structure

In order to make a recommendation on the oil bearing potential of a target area, the expert geologist first collects as much information about the target area as possible, and then analyzes the geological characteristics of this area. In this decision making process, the expert invariably compares the target area to other known fields, and uses the similarities and differences in various geological characteristics to make a prediction about the target play's potential. This two step reasoning process is mirrored in the overall structure of our knowledge based system, which itself has two components (see Figure 1). The first step engages the user in a dialogue to extract salient geological characteristics of the target play; the second step uses similarity measures and pattern clustering techniques to find previously studied oil fields that are similar to the current play.

Geological characteristics for locating hydrocarbon reservoirs are based on reservoir characteristics interpreted from lithofacies studies, and trapping theories deduced from regional tectonics and local structure [14,15]. Our expert identified four major characteristics for play analysis:

1. *essential criteria,* including play location, age of the play and notes on the criteria special to the area being explored.
2. *reservoir characteristics,* which are subdivided into: general setting of the play, margin character at deposition, position of the play in the basin, sediment type, geometry of sediment, facies model -- carbonate and clastic, and post deposition structural style. Each of these in turn are expressed in terms of more specific characteristics.
3. *source characteristics, which include knowledge of* the lithologies of the source rock, such as shale, limestone, coal, and evaporite, percentage of total organic carb, and maturation level.
4. *seal characteristics, including lithologies associated with* dense limestone, shale, sabkha, shallow salina, and deep salina, as well as trap style.

Currently, the system works with 86 different characteristics, some of which are illustrated in Figure 2. There are, of course, other features which are important in this context, e.g., color of shale, clastic grain size, etc. The particular choice of these 86 features will change as our system evolves. The geological database contains a characteristics table for known plays. The rows of this table are the 86 characteristics, and each column represents a known field. Entry x_{ij}, for the ith row and j^{th} column of this table indicates that the expert's degree of confidence that the ith characteristics is present in the jth field is x_{ij}. The degree of confidence is expressed as a number in the interval [0, 1].

In addition, the system's diagnostic process must be sensitive to the information sources available to users. This raises two important issues: first, the sources of the geological information and second, the quality of the sources. The geological information for the target play may be derived from various sources, such as seismic lines, well logs, core data, well cuttings, outcrops, and previous studies that have been conducted of the target area. Each of these sources provides different kinds of information. For example, the seismic data is a good source for gross sedimentary geometry, but provides hardly any information with respect to the fauna type. On the other hand, core data reveals details of lithology and fauna, but provides very little information about the relationship of the bedding to the depositional surface. Therefore, when conducting a dialogue with the user to determine play characteristics, it is important that the system first determine information sources.

Intuitively, the more information sources available to a geologist the more characteristics should be derivable; and consequently, a more conclusive decision can be made about hydrocarbon potential. However, this may not always be true, because the quality of the source information is also very important. This becomes even more critical when different sources seem to be providing contradictory evidence. For example, when trying to determine position of the play in a basin, seismic lines that cover the entire area of interest, cross the basin margin, and allow easy identification of reflectors, provide more useful and dependable information than seismic lines that lack the above properties. Therefore, when determining sources of information available to the user, it is also important to determine the quality of these sources.

In the rest of this section, we elaborate on the expert's reasoning process on one of the major features that is used in determining the hydrocarbon potential of a field, *viz.*, the position of the play in the basin. The importance of determining the quality of the geologists' sources of information, and how it influences the system's querying process is illustrated.

2.1.1. Position of Play in Basin

Reservoir characterization is one of the essential elements for play analysis, and position of play in the basin is one way to evaluate potential reservoirs. Before the system asks any questions about characteristics that will help identify the play position in a basin, it queries the user about the sources of his information. Once specific sources are identified, the system evaluates the quality of each source by querying the user about the specific characteristics. These characteristics for seismic lines are listed below. For good quality seismic data, lines cover the area of interest and cross the basin margin; reflectors are easily identified. Reflectors are hard to identify on poor quality seismic data. If the quality of data is neither "good" nor "poor", it is considered "medium".

In order to decide the position of the play in a basin, (i.e., is it distal basin, mid basin, proximal basin, distal slope, mid slope, proximal slope, margin, proximal shelf, mid shelf or distal shelf?) our expert suggested a set of ten features which could be used to distinguish them:

1. Paleo topography, i.e., does the play lie below the break in slope, on the break in slope, or above the break in slope?
2. Bedding type, i.e., are the beds formed by a majority of chaotic, horizontal, or dipping beds? a minority of chaotic, horizontal, or dipping beds? and/or contains very little of chaotic, horizontal, or dipping beds?
3. Bedding shape, i.e., are the beds mainly parallel? are they lensed? If the beds are lensed, do they have a flat top lens shape, flat bottom lens shape, or symmetric lens shape? Are the beddings wedge shaped bedding?
4. Bedding thickness, i.e., are the beds thin bedded or thick bedded?
5. Lithology, i.e., is the lithology homogeneous or heterogeneous?
6. Vertical variation of sediment, i.e., do the sediments become coarser or finer upwards? Are they inter bedded or homogeneous?
7. Lateral variation of sediment, i.e., is the lateral variation from coarse to fine/fine to coarse, chaotic/variable, or homogeneous?
8. Fauna type, i.e., is it restricted or diverse?
9. Depth of water that fauna is associated with, is it intertidal, near shore, neritic, bathyal, or a mixture of deep and shallow water?
10. Relationship of the bedding to the depositional surface, do they curve up, truncate upward, or are they flat?

As discussed earlier, depending on the sources used to identify the required characteristics, the degrees of beliefs are assigned to user responses for each query. For instance, if "good" quality seismic cross sections are used to answer the above questions, then the responses to questions 1, 2, 3, and 10 are given a higher weight than responses to questions 8 and 9. In addition to belief values or confidence factors being attached to user responses depending on the source and quality of data, there is also inherent imprecision in the expert's judgemental rules linking characteristics to conclusions about the position of the play. The rule structure and the evidence combination scheme for making uncertain inferences is discussed in the next section.

2.2. Characteristics Analysis Phase

There are two components in our reasoning process for play analysis: the characteristics analysis phase and the play comparison phase. The goal of characteristics analysis is to extract relevant geological features of the target play by querying the user. Queries attempt to extract basic physical features of the site and other information that can be derived by studying well logs, seismic cross sections and historical information. This information is used to derive the geological characteristics discussed in Section 2.1. Expert supplied heuristics and judgmental knowledge link user supplied information to the geological characteristics. They are represented as rules in the system. It is important to note that an expert's conclusions are judgmental and have degrees of certainty associated with them. Details of the rule structure and format are presented in the next section. Often the user may not be able to supply responses to system queries. Therefore, our system is designed to reason with incomplete knowledge; an inferencing process derives that a particular characteristic exists for the target field with a confidence value between 0 and 1. Details of the reasoning scheme are presented in Section 2.2.2. The end result of this interaction with the user is to append a new numbers for the target play to the database table for known fields.

2.2.1. Knowledge Base Structure

The knowledge base is designed as a partitioned rule base, with a partition assigned to each of the major characteristics described in Section 2.1. A traditional rule format is used to link physical evidence derived from seismic cross sections, well logs, *etc.*, to desired geological characteristics. To achieve rapid prototyping, this system was implemented using EXSYS [16], an expert system building tool that is in some ways similar to EMYCIN [17]. Domain knowledge which includes facts, theories, heuristics rules and beliefs of exploration experts are encoded as rules. Examples of some rules appear below.

R51: IF the bedding types contain a majority of horizontal beds
AND the bedding shapes contain a majority of parallel beds
AND the relationship of the bedding to the depositional surface is flat
THEN the play lies on non-slope .90

R61: IF the play lies on non-slope
AND bedding thickness is thin
AND lithology is homogeneous
THEN the play lies in the basin .75,

R72: IF the play lies in the basin
AND bedding shapes contain a minor amount of symmetric lenses
THEN the play lies in the proximal basin .70
the play lies in the mid basin .20

The hierarchical structure partitions the rule into different groups; only the set of the rules relevant to current goals at a specific level are searched.

2.2.2. Inference Engine

The inference engine contains two functional components: The forward reasoning mechanism, i.e., the evidence combination mechanism, and the backward reasoning mechanism, i.e., the information derivation mechanism. The evidence combination mechanism combines the effect pieces of evidence extracted from user responses using rules in the knowledge base. The information derivation mechanism attempts to extract from the user those pieces of evidence that would lend most support to the top ranked hypothesis [18]. It does this by picking queries that are related to these evidences. In this phase, the primary characters are divided into sub-characteristics which can often be further subdivided into more specific characteristics. The expert system tries to verify the identity of the primary characteristics by using physical characteristics and indirect evidence provided by the user. However, the system queries for required information, thus guiding the interaction process. The backward reasoning mechanism is appropriate for this task.

EXSYS, like EMYCIN uses a certainty factor scheme for representing uncertainty. The certainty factor is expressed as an integer in the range 0 to 100, with 100 representing complete confidence (i.e., absolute certainty) in the conclusion, and 0 representing complete uncertainty. Adhoc functions are used for combining certainty values towards a conclusion. For example, if a rule x indicates that if a situation satisfied conditions c_{x1}, c_{x2}, ..., c_{xn}, ..., then these evidences support conclusion k with certainty factor s_x, i.e.,

Rule x
IF c_{x1}
AND c_{x2}
.
.
AND c_{xn}
.
.
THEN k (certain factor = s_x)

where s_x is a certainty factor in the range 0 - 100 supplied by the expert to indicate the strength of his belief in the conclusion.

Since the conditions c_{xn}'s are derived from user's responses to the questions asked by the system, which again could be derived from different sources, there are degrees of certainty associated with individual c_{xn}'s. Therefore, the justified certainty factor js_x for conclusion k of rule x is calculated as follows:

Let rc_{xavg} = avg(rc_{x1}, rc_{x2}, ..., rc_{xn}, ...) where rc_{xn}'s are the degree of reliabilities for conditions c_{xn}'s, respectively, and are obtained from a reliability table which was supplied by our expert geologist, using 'source and it's quality' and 'questions/features' as the keys. Then, the justified certainty factor $js_x = rc_{xavg} * s_x$.

Suppose another rule y indicates that if the situation satisfies conditions c_{y1}, c_{y2}, ..., c_{ym}, ..., then these evidences support conclusion k as well with certainty factor s_y. The system then calculates the justified certainty factor js_y, and if evidences for rule x and rule y are all known to be true, then the combined (justified) certainty factor js_{new} for conclusion k is computed by the formula:

$js_{new} = 1 - (1 - js_x) * (1 - js_y) = (js_x) + (1 - js_x) * js_y$.

Explanation facilities are also provided to explain 'why' the system needs to know the information it is requesting, and 'how' the system arrived at its final value for a specific choice. The system also provides a debugging facility that allows system designers to test the effect of changes in a user's response to the conclusions that are drawn by the system. This enables the system designer to test the importance of various pieces of evidence on the final conclusions, and in this manner debug rules. Also, it enables users of the system to check the importance of the input to the conclusion that are presented by the system.

3. THE COMPARISON PROCESS

Once the salient geological characteristics of the target play are obtained, our next goal is to compare the target play with the known fields in the database. In order to find the most similar field(s) to the target play, the system first groups all the available fields or plays (including the target play) into representative clusters. Then it examines the cluster the target play belongs to, eventually discovering a known play in the database that is most similar to the target play. It is essential for this analysis to use a similarity measure that will decide how "close" two plays are based on their overall characteristics.

3.1. Similarity Measures

The table of fields which forms the current geological database can be viewed as a pattern matrix with each field representing an individual pattern. The confidence factor assigned to each geological characteristic by the expert for known plays or derived by the Characteristic Analysis Phase (Section 2) for the target play, forms a component feature of the feature vector representing a play or field. Each play is represented as a 86-feature vector in the feature space defined in Figure 2. Note that the expert specifies that some characteristics are more important than others. To incorporate these weights into the similarity computation, a weighted measure of correlation is used, and the degree of similarity between a pair of fields is computed as follows. Let $f_i, f_j \in reals^{86}$ denote the feature vectors (86-tuples) of fields i and j, f_{ik} be the kth characteristic of field f_i, f_{jk} be the kth characteristic of field f_j, and w_k be the weighting factor for characteristic k. It is convenient to let W = diag (w_k) be the (86 x 86) diagonal matrix whose k-th element is w_k. We calculate the the weighted similarity between fields f_i, and f_j as:

$$s_W(f_i, f_j) = \frac{<f_i, f_j>_W}{//f_i//_W \; //f_j//_W} \tag{1}$$

where

$$<f_i, f_j>_W = \sum_{k=1}^{86} f_{ik} f_{jk} w_k = f_i^T W f_j$$

and

$$//f_i//_W = \sqrt{<f_i, f_i>_W} = \sqrt{\sum_{k=1}^{86} f_{ik}^2 w_k}$$

and

$$//f_j//_W = \sqrt{<f_j, f_j>_W} = \sqrt{\sum_{k=1}^{86} f_{jk}^2 w_k}$$

s_W can be interpreted as a (weighted) correlation coefficient between f_i and f_j; thus, $-1 \le s_W \le 1$. This measure plays a key role in the clustering analysis technique when we group fields into categories. Given a target play whose characteristics were derived by the expert system in Section 2, we can use this measure to compute the closest field in the database to the target play.

3.2. Pattern Clustering Method

By calculating the correlation coefficient for each pair of patterns using equation (1), a n x n symmetric matrix S = $[s_{ij}]$ is generated where n = total number of fields. Various clustering algorithms can be applied to aggregate target plays into relevant groups. In our study, we use a hierarchical single linkage clustering scheme [19,20]. The procedure is outlined below.

1. Start with n clusters, each containing a single entity and an n x n symmetric matrix of similarities S = $[s_{ij}]$ = $[\, s_W(f_i, f_j)\,]$ as in (1).
2. Search the matrix for the most similar pair of clusters. Let the value of the similarity measure between "most similar" clusters U and V be s_{UV} .

3. Merge clusters U and V. Label the newly formed cluster (UV). Update the entries in the matrix by (a) deleting the rows and columns corresponding to clusters U and V and (b) adding a row and column giving the similarities $s_{(UV)Y} = \max\{ s_{UY}, s_{VY} \}$, between clusters (UV) and the n-2 points left; $s_{UV,UV} = 1$.
4. Repeat step 2 and 3 a total of n-1 times. Record the identity of clusters that are merged and the similarity levels at which the mergers take place. The result of the aggregation can be depicted as a dendrogram, as illustrated in Figure 3.

3.3. Sample Case Study

As a case study, we collected information for 19 different fields from our geological expert. The dendrogram in Figure 3 generated by the weighted similarity measure and the single linkage clustering algorithm shows that fields #1, #2 and #3 form a cluster at similarity level of 0.99, i.e., based on overall geological characteristics, these three fields are almost identical. The three fields in question are BuHasa, Shaybah and Fateh, all of which are located in the United Arab Emirates. They are all located in basin margin, with the same general carbonate facies, a shale source and a shale seal. At the similarity level 0.72, these three fields merge into a cluster with fields #19 and #9. Field #19 is North Bridge Port of Illinois, and field #9 is a Pennsylvania Paradox Basin field formed in the four corners area of Utah, Colorado, Arizona and New Mexico. They share some characteristics: they are ramped, are located at a basin margin, and are formed of limestone sediments. However, some of the characteristics of these fields are different; i.e., the seal for the Paradox Basin field is a sabkha facies, and North Bridge Port is dense limestone, which are different from the shale of BuHasa, Shaybah and Fateh. These results are quite commensurate with expert opinion about the fields in question.

4. SUMMARY

Hydrocarbon exploration is a difficult process: geologists have to combine information from various sources of data, such as well logs, seismic cross sections and history charts. The process is further complicated by the fact that available data is often imprecise and incomplete. This paper represents the exploration geologist's reasoning approach as a two step process: first, experts try to derive salient characteristics of a target play; and then, this information is used to select analogous plays. The first step of the process is implemented as an expert system, where the system engages the user in a question-answer dialogue to extract major characteristics. The second step of this process is based on a weighted similarity measure described in Section 3.1. The knowledge based system incorporates geological experts' experiences and judgements into a rule base. A pattern clustering technique based on single link analysis was applied to a geological database of 19 known fields and depicted as a dendrogram. Results show that the clusters agree with the expert's grouping of the fields, which indicates that the weighted similarity measure and clustering algorithm produce plausible results.

5. REFERENCES

[1] Aalund, L.R., 1987, Powerful Computer Network Adds More Exploration and Production Data, Software, *Oil and Gas Journal,* January 12, pp. 33-37.

[2] Caldwell, J, H, *et al.*, 1985, ISIS: An interactive interpretation system for offshore exploration and production, *Offshore Technology Conference Paper No. 4897.*

[3] Robinson, J. E., 1982, *Computer Application in the Petroleum Industry,* Hutchinson Ross Publishing Co.

[4] Dikkers, A. J., 1985, *Geology in Petroleum Production,* Elsevier Science Publishers.

[5] Beckmann, H., 1976, *Geological Prospecting of Petroleum,* Ferdinand Enke Verlag.

[6] Duda, R., J. Gasching and P. Hart, 1979, Model Design in the PROSPECTOR Consultant System for Mineral Exploration, *Expert Systems in the Microelectronic Age,* Edinburgh Univ. Press, pp. 153-167.

[7] Kahn, G., J. McDermott, 1986, The Mud System, *IEEE EXPERT, Vol. 1, No. 1, pp. 23-32.*

[8] Smith, R. G., and J. D. Baker, 1983, The Dipmeter Advisor System: A Case Study in Commercial Expert System Development, *International Joint Conference of Artificial Intelligence,* Kerlruhse, West Germany, Vol. 1, pp. 122-129.

[9] Fang, J. H., A. W. Shultz and H. C. Chen, 1986, Expert Systems and Petroleum Exploration: An Overview, *GEOBYTE, Vol. 1, No. 5, pp. 6-11.*

[10] Miller, B. M., 1986, Building an Expert System Helps Classify Sedimentary Basins and Assess Petroleum Resources, *GEOBYTE, Vol. 1, No. 2, pp. 44-50.*

[11] Love, P. L., and M. Simaan, 1985, Segmentation of a Seismic Section Using Image Processing and Artificial Intelligence Techniques, *Pattern Recognition,* Vol. 18, No. 6, pp. 409-419.

[12] Liu, H.-H., 1985, A Rule-Based System for Automatic Seismic Discrimination, *Pattern Recognition,* Vol. 18, No. 6, pp. 459-463.

[13] Penas, C., F. Hadsell and J. Stout, 1986, An Expert System for Determining Vibroseis Field Parameters, *GEOBYTE*, Vol. 1, No. 5, pp.42-44.

[14] Wilson, J., 1982, *Carbonate Facies in Geologic History*, Spring-Verlag, New York.

[15] Miall, A. D., 1984, *Principles of Sedimentary Basin Analysis*, Springer-Verlag, New York.

[16] *EXSYS User's Manual, Version 3.1*, 1986, EXSYS Inc., New Mexico.

[17] Buchanan, B. G., E. H. Shortliffe, eds., 1984, *Rule-Based Expert Systems: The MYCIN Experiments of the Stanford HPP*, Addison-Wesley, Reading, Mass.

[18] Hayes-Roth, F., D. A. Waterman and D. B. Lenat, eds., 1983, *Building Expert Systems*, Addison-Wesley Publishing Co., Reading, Mass.

[19] Duda, R., P. Hart, 1973, *Pattern Classification and Scene Analysis*, John Wiley & Sons, New York.

[20] Johnson, R. A., D. W. Wichern, 1982, *Applied Multivariate Statistical Analysis*, Prentice-Hall.

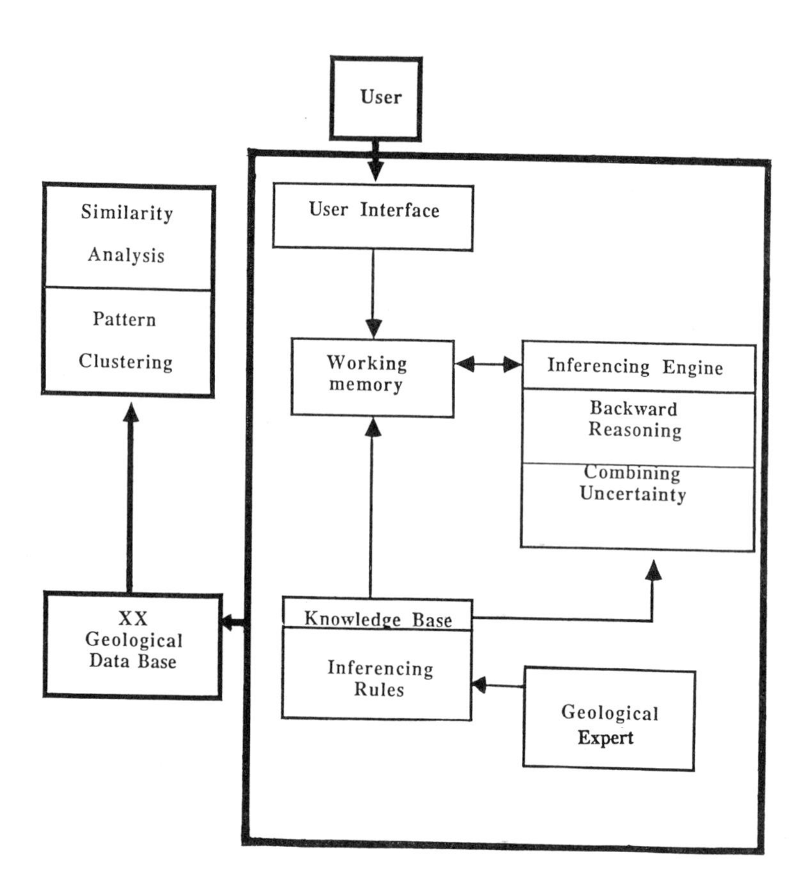

Figure 1. XX Knowledge Based System Architecture

General Setting [3%]	Basin Position	Cont Margin		
		Inner Shelf		
		Craton		
	Tectonics	Extension		
		Compression		
Margin Character at deposition [7%]	Rimmed			
	Ramped			
	Ramp to Rim			
	Block Faulted			
	Listric Growth			
	Wrench			
	Subduction			
	Overthrust			
	Salt	Turtle		
		Diapir		
Position of Play in Basin at deposition [20%]	Distal Basin			
	Mid Basin			
	Proximal Basin			
	Distal Slope			
	Mid Slope			
	Proximal Slope			
	Margin			
	Proximal Shelf			
	Mid Shelf			
	Distal Shelf			

Figure 2. Portion of Characteristics Table

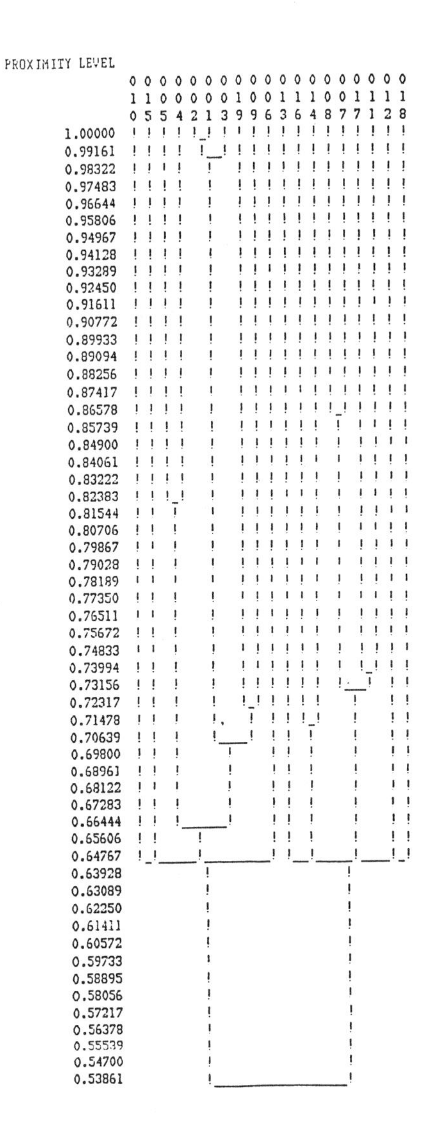

Figure 3. Dendrogram for 19 Sample Fields

ON LEARNING WITH IMPERFECT TEACHERS

ALBERTO PETTOROSSI,* ZBIGNIEW W. RAS,** MARIA ZEMANKOVA,***
*IASI-CNR, Roma, Italy; **A.I. Laboratory, UNC-Charlotte and Institute of Informatics, University of Bonn, West Germany; ***Dept. of Computer Science, University of Tennessee

ABSTRACT

The paper concerns a problem of teaching a student by several imperfect teachers. Teachers and the student are represented as knowledge base systems. By a knowledge base system we mean a structure with three main components: an information system (a data base), a knowledge base and a formal system. The knowledge base is used to store information about concepts in terms of values of attributes from the information system. The formal system (its set of axioms) provides the basis for writing procedures which generate rules of a knowledge base.

INTRODUCTION

The problem of generating rules (elements of a knowledge base) describing concepts in terms of values of attributes has been investigated by many authors. They have proposed several algorithms which minimize the number of attributes needed to describe concepts. These algorithms however do not take into consideration the relationship student-teacher. In many cases the student and a teacher may understand each other only partially. It will happen when the teacher starts to talk about concepts using either attributes or other concepts which the student does not understand. Optimization problem in this case deals with a deletion of all these attributes and concepts from the statements used by the teacher. The important step is to fix the semantics of the language used by the student and by a teacher so the meaning of the rules stored in a knowledge base is uniquely defined. The completeness theorem for the formal system (a part of a knowledge base system) proposed by us has to be proved. It is needed to avoid problems which may appear during the process of proving the correctness of algorithms developed by us. The methods of minimizing the length of terms which describe extensions of concepts have been proposed by Michalski and Larson [4], Quinlan [6], Chen and Ras [1].

BASIC DEFINITIONS

In this section we introduce the notion of an information system, an approximation space, an intension and an extension of a concept, a language which will be used by a student and by teachers, its standard interpretation and finally we introduce the notion of a knowledge base system.

By an information system we mean a sequence $S = (X, I, V, f)$, where X is a set of objects, I is a set of attributes, V is a set of values of attributes from I and f is a function and it describes an element x in terms of its attribute values. We assume that:

Methodologies for Intelligent Systems
Z. W. Ras and M. Zemankova, Editors

1) $V = \bigsqcup\{V_a : a \in I\}$ and $V_a \cap V_b = \emptyset$ for any a,b such that $a \neq b$
2) $f(x,a) \in V_a$ for each $a \in I$, $x \in X$.

To represent an information system we usually give its function f like it is done in the example below:

	Name	**Sex**	**Eyes**	**Language**	**Location**
x1	Nancy	F	Blue	German	Charlotte
x2	Robert	M	Hazel	English	Bonn
x3	Nancy	F	Blue	German	Charlotte
x4	Robert	M	Hazel	English	Charlotte

The system just described classifies objects in terms of five attributes. The objects **x1** and **x3** are not distinguishable which shows that the description of an object in the system does not have to be enough precise to specify which one we have in mind. The approximation space (defined below) introduces this idea more precisely.

Let $\sim_S$ be a relation on X defined as follows:

$$x \sim_S y \quad \text{iff} \quad f(x,a) = f(y,a) \quad \text{for any} \quad a \in I.$$

The pair $A_S = (X, \sim_S)$ is called an approximation space for S.

Let $E_S = \{[x]_S : x \in X\}$ where $y \in [x]_S$ iff $y \sim_S x$.

Elements in E_S are called elementary sets. The set $w \subseteq X$ is describable in S if w is a member of E_S or w is a union of some elements from E_S. If w is not describable in S then we can find its lower approximation in S and its upper approximation in S.

By the lower approximation of w in S we mean the set
$L(w) = \bigsqcup\{e \in E_S : e \subseteq w\}$.
By the upper approximation of w in S we mean the set
$U(w) = \bigsqcup\{e \in E_S : e \cap w \neq \emptyset\}$.
By the boundary of w in S we mean the set $B(w) = U(w) - L(w)$.

We are ready to define a formalized language L(S,C) where S = (X,I,V,f) is an information system and C is a set of concepts represented as subsets of X.

It's alphabet contains:
1) constants: $\underline{w}$ where $w \in V \cup C$ and 0, 1
2) functors: +, *, -, $\underline{L}$, $\underline{U}$, $\rightarrow$
3) predicates: =, $\leq$
4) connectives: $\vee, \wedge, \sim$
5) auxiliary symbols: (,).

The set of terms is a least set such that:
1) all constants are terms,
2) if t_1, t_2 are terms, then (t_1+t_2), (t_1*t_2), $(t_1 \rightarrow t_2)$, $-t_1$, $\underline{L}(t_1)$, $\underline{U}(t_1)$ are terms.

The set of formulas F is a least set such that:
1) if t_1, t_2 are terms, then $(t_1 = t_2)$, $(t_1 \leq t_2)$ are formulas.
2) if a, b are formulas, then $(a \vee b)$, $(a \wedge b)$, $\sim a$ are formulas.

By a standard interpretation of $L(S,C)$ we mean an interpretation M_S such that:

1) $M_S(\underline{w}) = \{x \in X : \text{if } w \in V_a \text{ then } f(x,a) = w\}$ for any $w \in V$
$M_S(\overline{w}) = w$ for any $w \in C$
$M_S(\overline{0}) = \emptyset$, $M_S(\overline{1}) = X$.

2) for any terms t_1, t_2, t:
$M_S(t_1+t_2) = M_S(t_1) \cup M_S(t_2)$
$M_S(t_1*t_2) = M_S(t_1) \cap M_S(t_2)$
$M_S(t_1 \to t_2) = M_S(-t_1) \cup M_S(t_2)$
$M_S(-t) = -(M_S(t))$
$M_S(\underline{L}(t)) = L(M_S(t))$, $M_S(\underline{U}(t)) = U(M_S(t))$

3) for any terms t_1, t_2 and any formulas a, b

$$M_S((t_1 = t_2)) = \begin{cases} T : M_S(t_1) = M_S(t_2) \\ F : \text{otherwise} \end{cases}$$

$$M_S((t_1 \leq t_2)) = \begin{cases} T : M_S(t_1) \subseteq M_S(t_2) \\ F : \text{otherwise} \end{cases}$$

$M_S((a \vee b)) = M_S(a) \vee M_S(b)$
$M_S((a \wedge b)) = M_S(a) \wedge M_S(b)$

$$M_S(\sim a) = \begin{cases} T : M_S(a) = F \\ F : \text{otherwise} \end{cases}$$

FACT 1.

The interpretation M_S is model for all statements listed below:
1) $a = \underline{L}(a)$ for any $a \in V$,
2) $\underline{L}(t) \leq t$
3) $\overline{U}(\underline{L}(t)) = \underline{L}(\underline{L}(t)) = \underline{L}(t)$
4) $\overline{L}(-t) = -\overline{U}(t)$, $\underline{U}(-t) = -\underline{L}(t)$
5) $\overline{U}(t+s) = \overline{U}(t) + \overline{U}(s)$
6) $\overline{L}(t*s) = \overline{L}(t) * \overline{L}(s)$
7) $\overline{U}(t*s) \leq \overline{U}(t) * \overline{U}(s)$
8) $\overline{L}(t) + \underline{L}(s) \leq \underline{L}(t+s)$
9) $t \to s = (-t) + s$
10) $-a = \sum\{b : b \in V_i \text{ and } a \neq b \text{ and } a \in V_i\}$ for each $a \in V$
11) axioms of Boolean algebra for terms
12) standard axioms for the predicates "$\leq$" (less than or equal) and "=" (equality) .

Assume that $(L(S,C), Ax, \{r\})$ is a formal system where Ax is a set of axioms listed in FACT 1 and r is a rule of the form below:

$$\frac{t(t_1) = t_3 \ , \ t_1 = t_2}{t(t_2) = t_3}$$

where t, t_1, t_2, t_3 are terms.

THEOREM 1. The following statements are equivalent:
1) $t_1 = t_2$ is true in all standard interpretations
2) $t_1 = t_2$ can be proved from Ax using rule r.

Let's introduce the notion of a concept more precisely.

By an extension of a concept we mean the set of all objects from X with properties that characterize the concept. Instead of saying an extension of a concept c we will just say a concept c.

By an intension of a concept we mean a set of terms describing the objects to which the concept apply. To give the intension of a concept, we have to find a set of terms describing the lower approximation of c and another set of terms describing the upper approximation of c.

Let's be more precise. By an intension of a concept c we mean a pair $(\{t_i\}_{i \in I}, \{s_i\}_{i \in J})$ such that:

$$L(c) \subseteq \bigsqcup\{ M_S(t_i): i \in I\} \subseteq c \quad \text{and} \quad L(-c) \subseteq \bigsqcup\{M_S(t_i): i \in J\} \subseteq -c$$

Let S be an information system and C be a set of concepts. By a knowledge base we mean a set K(S,C) containing the following elements:

1) sequences (c,T_c,S_c) where $c \in C$ and (T_c,S_c) is the intension of c,
2) terms $t \to c$ where $c \in C$ and t is in DNF such that: $M_S(t) \subseteq M_S(c)$,
3) terms $t \to -c$ where $c \in C$ and t is in DNF such that: $M_S(c) \subseteq M_S(-t)$.

By a knowledge base system we mean a sequence (S,(L(S,C),Ax,R), K(S,C)) where:

1) S is an information system,
2) (L(S,C),Ax,R) is a formal system,
3) K(S,C) is a knowledge base.

The knowledge base is used to store the rules representing intensions of concepts from C. The axioms Ax from the formal system are used to optimize the syntax of these rules (to minimize the number of attributes on the left hand side of the rules) and to eliminate concepts not understandable by the student.

LEARNING PROCESS

In this section we present the foundations and a sketch of a teaching protocol linking one student and two teachers. The protocol can be extended easily to several teachers. Both teachers and a student are represented as knowledge base systems. Initially the student's knowledge base is empty and the teacher's knowledge base contains only sequences (c,T_c,S_c), one sequence per each concept c in C. The knowledge base of the system "teacher" and the knowledge base of the system "student" is dynamically updated during the learning process. Rules of the form $t \to c$ and $t \to -c$ where t is a term in DNF and c is a concept are added to both systems during the process of learning the concept c.

Let's assume that a student is represented by a knowledge base system (S,(L(S,C),Ax,R),K(S,C)) where S =(X,I,V,f) and K(S,C)= Ø. The teachers (let's call them A, B) are represented by two knowledge base systems $(S_i,(L(S_i,C),Ax(i),R),K(S_i,C))$ where $S_i=(X,I_i,V_i,f_i)$, i=1,2 (respectively). We assume that $I \subseteq I_1 \cup I_2$ which means that if an attribute is known by a student then it is known by one of the teachers. However the student and the teachers may understand each other partially.

Assume that $(c,\{t1_i\}_{i \in I1},\{s1_i\}_{i \in J1})$ is a member of $K(S_1,C)$ and $(c,\{t2_i\}_{i \in I2}, \{s2_j\}_{j \in J2})$ is a member of $K(S_2,C)$. Both teachers will teach the student about the concept c.

Let's start the teaching process. It's main steps are listed below:

1) Teacher A will choose $t1_i$ and $s1_i$ from $\{t1_i\}_{i \in I1}$ and $\{s1_i\}_{i \in J1}$ respectively in order to say to the student that $t1_i \leq c$ and $s1_i \leq -c$ are true statements. However the student may not understand some attributes and some concepts used in $t1_i$ and $s1_i$.

2) Teacher A looks for DNF representation of $t1_i$ and $s1_i$. The new terms semantically equivalent to $t1_i$ and $s1_i$ have to be in a possibly optimal form. Teacher A has to minimize the number of attributes in I_1-I (the student does not understand them) and minimize the number of concepts which were not taught yet. The minimization process is based on the axiom 10 from the set Ax and on the fact that the disjunction of a concept and its negation can be replaced by the constant 1. It is also based on the fact that terms describing empty sets which are built from values of attributes can be added (using "+") to any term. The starting DNF for $t1_i$ and $s1_i$ have to be generated first (before the optimization process begins). The following three facts are used to achieve this goal.

2.1) Negation can be moved inside a term and next removed using axiom 9 from the set Ax.

2.2) Functor $\underline{L}$ can be moved inside a term. We get new $t1_{0i}$ such that $t1_{0i} \leq t1_i$ because $\underline{L}(t)+\underline{L}(s) \leq \underline{L}(t+s)$.

2.3) Functor $\underline{U}$ can be moved inside a term (if "+") or removed (if "*"). We get new $t1_{1i}$ such that $t1_{1i} \leq t1_{0i} \leq t1_i$ because $t*s \leq \underline{U}(t*s)$.

This optimization problem is NP-complete so the algorithm proposed by us is only a heuristic algorithm (it is why we say "a possibly optimal form"). We do not store the resulting "optimal" terms in the knowledge base of the teacher A because these terms are dependent on the student. If we change the student, then we need another DNF representation for $t1_i$ and $s1_i$. We do not plan to list all steps of the optimization algorithm because they are rather standard. The algorithm is based on the axioms from Ax. Let's denote the resulting terms in DNF by $t1_i^1$ and $s1_i^1$ respectively.

Teacher A sends to the teacher B the following message: $t1_i^1 \leq c$ and $s1_i^1 \leq -c$ are true statements.

3) Teacher A drops all conjuncts in $t1_i^1$ and $s1_i^1$ containing values of attributes not from I or containing concepts which were not taught yet. Let's denote the resulting terms in DNF by

t_i and s_i respectively. Teacher A sends to the student the following message: $t_i \leq c$ and $s_i \leq -c$ are true statements.

All conjuncts droped in $t1'_i$ are stored in a temporary set Y_1.
All conjuncts droped in $s1'_i$ are stored in a temporary set Z_1.

The terms $t1_i$ and $s1_i$ are removed from $T1_c$ and $S1_c$ by taking $T1_c := T1_c - \{t1_i\}$ and $S1_c := S1_c - \{s1_i\}$.

4) The student's knowledge base K(S,C) is updated by adding to it two rules: $t_i \rightarrow c$, $s_i \rightarrow -c$.

5) Teacher B drops all conjuncts in $t1'_i$ and $s1'_i$ containing values of attributes not from I_2 or containing concepts which were not taught yet. Let's denote the resulting terms in DNF by $t0_i$ and $s0_i$ respectively. Teacher B knows that the student has learned two statements: $t0_i \leq c$, $s0_i \leq -c$.

All conjuncts in $t1'_i$ built only from concepts and from values of attributes from I_2 are stored in a temporary set Y_2.

All conjuncts in $s1'_i$ built only from concepts and from values of attributes from I_2 are stored in a temporary set Z_2.

6) Teacher B will choose $t2_i$ from $\{t2_i\}_{i \in I2}$ such that $M_{S2}(t2_i) \cap M_{S2}(t0_i) \neq \emptyset$ and $s2_i$ from $\{s2_i\}_{i \in J2}$ such that $M_{S2}(s2_i) \cap M_{S2}(s0_i) \neq \emptyset$.

7) Teacher B looks for DNF representation of $t2_i$ and $s2_i$ (possibly optimal). He follows the same strategy as the teacher A does. The resulting terms are denoted by $t2'_i$ and $s2'_i$ respectively.

Teacher B sends to the teacher A the following message: $t2'_i \leq c$ and $s2'_i \leq -c$ are true statements.

Assume that t'_i (s'_i) denotes the term obtained from $t2'_i$ ($s2'_i$) by droping in $t2'_i$ ($s2'_i$) all conjuncts containing values of attributes not from I or containing concepts which were not taught yet.

Teacher B sends to the student the following message: $t'_i \leq c$ and $s'_i \leq -c$ are true statements.

All conjuncts droped in $t2'_i$ are stored in a temporary set Y_2.
All conjuncts droped in $s2'_i$ are stored in a temporary set Z_2.

Let $T2_c = \{t2_i\}_{i \in I2}$ and $S2_c = \{s2_j\}_{j \in J2}$. The terms $t2_i$ and $s2_i$ are removed from $T2_c$ and $S2_c$ by taking $T2_c := T2_c - \{t2_i\}$ and $S2_c := S2_c - \{s2_i\}$.

The student's knowledge base K(S,C) is updated by adding to it two rules: $t'_i \rightarrow c$, $s'_i \rightarrow -c$.

The steps of the learning process presented above are repeated by teachers A and B as long as the sets $T1_c$, $S1_c$, $T2_c$, $S2_c$ are not empty. If two sets representing the same teacher become empty then the teacher represented by the other sets has to continue the learning process by himself.

The last step of the process of learning the concept c is done by both teachers independently.

Teacher A takes the disjunction of all the conjuncts in Y_1 and the disjunction of all the conjuncts in Z_1. Let's denote them by y1 and z1 respectively.

Teacher A looks for possibly optimal forms for y1 and z1. During this optimization process he is trying to remove (from y1 and z1) concepts which were not taught yet and attributes which are not in I. He is following the same strategy as the one in the step 2. Let's denote the resulting terms in DNF by y1' and z1'.

Teacher A drops all conjuncts in y1' and z1' containing values of attributes not from I or containing concepts which were not taught yet. The resulting terms are denoted by y and z respectively.

Teacher A sends to the student the following message: $y \leq c$ and $z \leq -c$ are true statements.

The conjuncts in y1' containing values of attributes not from I are not understandable by the student. The part of the extension of the concept c described by these conjuncts can still be taught by the teacher A however he can teach this part only by displaying all its objects. The teacher A will apply the same strategy to the set of objects described by z1'.

The last step of the process of teaching the concept c followed by the teacher B is the same as the step just described for the teacher A.
This way the concept c is learned by the student.

The next question concerns the choice of an ordering relation for the set C. Clearly, we can not teach concepts from C in a random order. A possible strategy for ordering the concepts from C is described in [7].

CONCLUSION

This paper looks for an optimal strategy to teach one student by several imperfect teachers. The problem is NP-complete, so the strategy proposed by us is a heuristic one. The semantics M_S interprets concepts by their extensions. The formalized language is used to talk about concepts in terms of values of attributes and other concepts. The completeness theorem gives a complete set of axioms used to generate terms in DNF and next to optimize them. Let's assume that there is one teacher and several students. Clearly the teacher can not be a tutor for every student. The problem of an optimal average teaching protocol in such an environment is discussed in [2].

REFERENCES

[1] Chen, K., Ras, Z.W., "An axiomatic theory of information trees", Proceedings of CISS'85 in Baltimore, Maryland, 636-640

[2] Karpinski, M., Ras, Z.W., "An optimal average teaching protocol for a class with many students", University of Bonn
[3] Michalski, R.S., "A theory and methodology of inductive learning", Artificial Intelligence, Vol. 20, 1983, 111-160
[4] Michalski, R.S., Larson, J.B., "Selection of most representative training examples and incremental generation of VL1 hypothesis: the underlying methodology and the description of programs ESEL and AQ11", Report No. 867, Dept. of Computer Science, University of Illinois, Urbana, Illinois, 1978
[5] Pawlak, Z., "Rough sets", Internat. J. Comp. and Info. Sci., Vol. 11, 1982, 341-366
[6] Quinlan, J.R., "Learning efficient classification procedures and their application to chess end games", Chapter 15, Machine Learning: Artificial Intelligence Approach, TIOGA Publishing Comp., Palo Alto, 1983
[7] Ras, Z.W., Zemankova, M., "Rough sets based learning systems", Lecture Notes of Computer Science, Springer Verlag, No. 208, 265-275

THE INFORMATION LATTICE OF NETWORKS USED FOR KNOWLEDGE REPRESENTATION

RALPH RÖNNQUIST
Department of Computer and Information Science,
Linköping University, Linköping, Sweden

ABSTRACT

We approach the term *information content* in a graph or network on the basis of operations that intend to increase it. The amount of information contained in a network increases when arcs or nodes are explicitely added, but also when the network is contracted by means of forcing together pairs of nodes into single nodes. The network extension conforms with addition of new information, whereas the contraction conforms with an elevation of implicitly denoted information to explicit. The view is that a network's information content is the "union" of the information contained in its sub-structures.

We formalise the approach and study its effect on structuring the domain of networks. We show that the relation given through contraction and extension forms a lattice of classes of networks, where in each class the networks have the same information contents. Within each class there is a canonical element which is also the smallest network in the class; the one that cannot be contracted into a sub-structure of itself. The lattice is then a lattice on canonical elements.

INTRODUCTION

There is a rich variety of ways in which to use networks in computer science. There are flow description models, such as Information Control Nets[3], Petri Nets[7], and Augumented Transition Nets[13]. There are conceptual or semantic networks[1,12]. Networks or graphs are also used for formalising pointer structures, for instance, in the study of algorithms[6]. In the area of articficial intelligence, the term network is often understood as "semantic network"[5]. Such a network is intended to model the knowledge of an (hopefully) intelligent agent, and to be useful for the agents reasoning.

For our purpose, a network is an abstract entity which contains some amount of information; it is a "symbol" in a representation system. Comparing two networks, we are interested in which, if any, contains more information than the other. The notion of more information is then understood in terms of network operations that reflect information increase. We study two kinds of operations both of which represent information increase, namely to extend a network with new constituents (such as arcs and nodes), and to contract a network by merging pairs of nodes into single nodes. That is, we assume that a network A contains more information than a network B if A can be obtained by means of extending and/or contracting B.

Intuitively, network extension is more clearly an information increase than network contraction. At the least, to explicitely add things does not decrease the information contained. However, network contraction serves the same purpose as adding a special kind of arc to denote that two or more nodes are considered to be equivalent or same.

E.g. Consider a semantic network fragment that contains the information "John is rich". One way to represent this is to have a node denoting "John", another node denoting "rich", and an arc labelled "is" from the "John" node to the "rich" node. To add the information "Mr.Smith owns a car", represented similarily by an "owns"-arc from one node to another, has the effect of extending the network to something like figure 1 below.

Methodologies for Intelligent Systems
Z. W. Ras and M. Zemankova, Editors

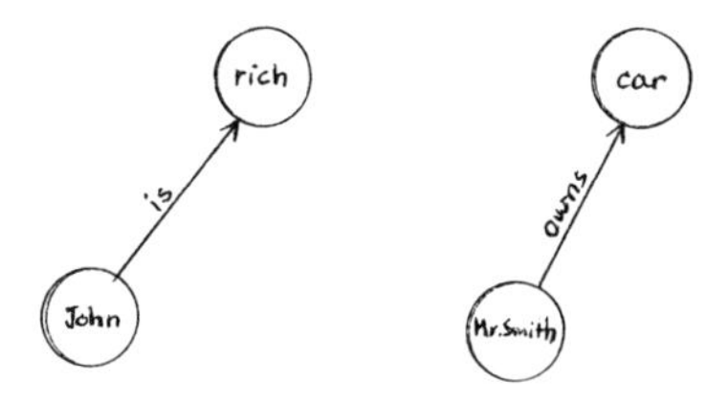

FIG. 1. John is rich and Mr.Smith owns a car

The information increase of "Mr.Smith owns a car" is thus reflected in a network extension. Now, to add the information "John is Mr.Smith", the "John" node and the "Mr.Smith" node must be equalised, which may be accomplished by a network contraction that merges these nodes into a single node. In practice, the contraction might be denoted by some equivalence constraint (as in [4]), but the system must behave as if the two nodes were actually merged.

In the present paper, we provide a collection of definitions for a formal treatment of networks. These definitions include the network extension and contraction relations, and two non-complicated algebraic operations called trivial combination and cross combination. The extension and contraction relations together defines the information increase relation. We show that this relation forms a lattice of equivalence classes, and that there is a canonical element for each class. We also show that the trivial and cross combinations accomplish the lattice *join* (least upper bound) and lattice *meet* (greatest lower bound) operations respectively.

This work is part of the study of Information Management Systems [11], and uses its definition of networks. Earlier results from the study have been reported in [9,10].

BASIC CONCEPTS

A *network* consists of *nodes*, *arcs*, and *arc labels*. It is an abstract object which may be concretely presented in a graph as follows: nodes are drawn as small circles, arcs are drawn as arrows that point from node to node, and arc labels are written in text. The figure 2 below shows a drawn network.

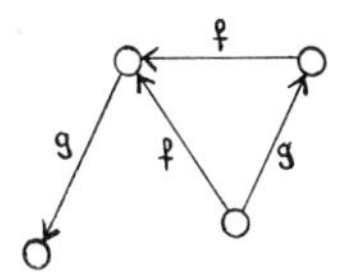

FIG. 2. A network

A *representation* of a network is a set of triples <f,m,n> of arc labels f, and node tokens m and n, which may be integers or (recursively) pairs of node tokens. The node tokens will also be referred to as node numbers. In the abstract network and in the graphical presentation the nodes are anonymous, but in the representation a unique number has been attached to each node. For instance, the network drawn in figure 2 is represented by

$$\{<f,1,2>,\ <g,1,3>,\ <f,3,2>,\ <g,2,4>\}$$

The node numbers are assigned arbitrarily to the nodes as a means of denoting them distinctly within a network. For every network, there is an equivalence class of representations, which all represent the same network, but use different node enumerations.

The set of node numbers in a representation A' is denoted N(A'), and the set of arc labels is denoted F(A').

In formulas and proofs, we use standard first order predicate logic and set theory with quantifiers and connectives defined as usual. (See, for instance, [2])

Trivial Combination

We define the *trivial combination*, A⊕B, of two networks A and B as the (unique) network represented by A'∪B', if A' and B' are representations of A and B resepectively, and the node number sets N(A') and N(B') are disjoint.

For drawn networks, the trivial combination is obtained by placing the graphs beside each other without overlay, and regarding this non-connected graph as one graph. If ⊕ is done on network representations, one of the arguments may have to be renumbered in order to guarantee that the numberings are disjoint. The node numbering in the result is therefore not uniquely determined.

We note that trivial combination is commutative and associative, i.e.

$$A \oplus B = B \oplus A \quad \text{and} \quad A \oplus (B \oplus C) = (A \oplus B) \oplus C$$

Cross Combination

We define the *cross combination*, A⊗B, of two networks A and B as the (unique) network represented by

$$\{\langle f, \langle m,r \rangle, \langle n,s \rangle \rangle \mid \langle f,m,n \rangle \in A' \wedge \langle f,r,s \rangle \in B'\}$$

if A' and B' are representations of A and B respectively.

Cross combination can be visualised in terms of a two-dimensional array whose row indices are node numbers in A', and column indices are node numbers in B'. Each entry, $\langle m,r \rangle$, denotes a (potential) node in A⊗B, and two entries are connected by an arc if and only if there are two similar arcs connecting the row indices concerned, and the column indices concerned (see figure 3).

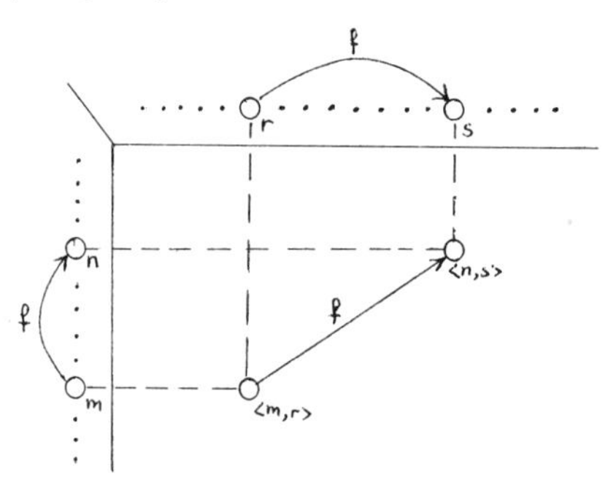

FIG. 3. Visualisation of cross combination

We note that cross combination is commutative and associative, i.e.

$$A \otimes B = B \otimes A \quad \text{and} \quad A \otimes (B \otimes C) = (A \otimes B) \otimes C$$

Extension

A network B is an *extension* of a network A, written **S**(A,B), iff for all pairs of representations, A' of A and B' of B, there is a 1-1 function **k** on node numbers such that

$$\{\langle f, \mathbf{k}(m), \mathbf{k}(n) \rangle \mid \langle f,m,n \rangle \in A' \} \subset B'.$$

We note that **S**(A,B) does not mean that A is a part of B, but rather that it is isomorphic to a part of B. Extension is therefore the same relation as sub-graph isomorphism[6]. We will also use the term *sub-structure* in reverse to extension, i.e. a network A is a sub-structure of a network B iff B is an extension to A.

The extension relation **S** is reflexive, transitive, but not symmetric. It is a partial order on networks. In particular, we note that

$$\mathbf{S}(A,B) \wedge \mathbf{S}(B,A) \rightarrow A=B.$$

Contraction

A network B is a *contraction* of a network A, written **Q**(A,B), iff for all pairs of representations, A' of A and B' of B, there is a function **k** on node numbers, such that

$$\{\langle f,\mathbf{k}(m),\mathbf{k}(n)\rangle \mid \langle f,m,n\rangle \in A'\} = B'.$$

The function **k** is called the *contraction function*, which may map two or more nodes of A into the same node in B; namely, when **k**(m)=**k**(n) for some m≠n. The contraction relation **Q** is reflexive, transitive, but not symmetric, i.e. it is a partial order on networks.

THE INFORMATION LATTICE

The information increase relation **K**(A,B) between networks A and B is now defined

$$\mathbf{K}(A,B) \equiv \exists C\colon (\mathbf{Q}(A,C) \wedge \mathbf{S}(C,B)).$$

It is easily verified that **K**(A,B) holds iff for all representations A' of A and B' of B, there is a function **k** from node numbers to node numbers, such that

$$\{\langle f,\mathbf{k}(m),\mathbf{k}(n)\rangle \mid \langle f,m,n\rangle \in A'\} \subset B'.$$

The relation **K** is reflexive, transitive, and non-symmetric, but it is not a partial order.

Proposition I: The relation **K** possesses the following properties for networks A, B, and C:

1. $\mathbf{S}(A,B) \rightarrow \mathbf{K}(A,B)$
2. $\mathbf{Q}(A,B) \rightarrow \mathbf{K}(A,B)$
3. $\mathbf{K}(A,B) \rightarrow \mathbf{K}(A\oplus C,B\oplus C)$
4. $\mathbf{K}(A,C) \wedge \mathbf{K}(B,C) \rightarrow \mathbf{K}(A\oplus B,C)$

Proof: Points 1 and 2 follows immediately from the definition of **K**, since **Q**(A,A) and **S**(A,A) are satisfied for any network A.

Point 3 is proved as follows. Let A' and B' be representations of A and B respectively, and let C' be a representation of C such that N(C') is disjoint from both N(A') and N(B'). **K**(A,B) implies that there is a function **k** from N(A') to N(B') such that

$$\{\langle f,\mathbf{k}(m),\mathbf{k}(n)\rangle \mid \langle f,m,n\rangle \in A'\} \subset B'.$$

Now, let **k**' be a function from N(A')∪N(C') to N(B')∪N(C') such that

$$\mathbf{k}'(m) = \begin{cases} \mathbf{k}(m) & \text{for } m \in N(A') \\ m & \text{for } m \in N(C') \end{cases}$$

We obtain

$$\{\langle f,\mathbf{k}'(m),\mathbf{k}'(n)\rangle \mid \langle f,m,n\rangle \in A' \cup C'\} \subset B' \cup C'$$

which implies **K**(A⊕C,B⊕C).

Point 4 is proved as follows. **K**(A,C)∧**K**(B,C) implies, by using point 3,

$$\mathbf{K}(A\oplus B,C\oplus B) \wedge \mathbf{K}(B\oplus C,C\oplus C).$$

Since C⊕B=B⊕C, and **K** is transitive, we obtain **K**(A⊕B,C⊕C). It is trivial to verify that **K**(C⊕C,C) (for any network C), and by this, we obtain **K**(A⊕B,C).

[ ]

Information Equivalence

The information increase relation **K** is not a partial order, since $\mathbf{K}(A,B) \wedge \mathbf{K}(B,A)$ does not imply $A=B$. In particular, we note that $\mathbf{K}(A,A \oplus A) \wedge \mathbf{K}(A \oplus A,A)$. That is, to put a copy of a network A beside itself is an extension and therefore an information increase which indicates that $A \oplus A$ contains more (i.e. no less) information than A. However, the network $A \oplus A$ can obviously be contracted into A, which indicates that $A \oplus A$ does not contain more information than A. We define the relation $\simeq$, for information equivalence, such that

$$A \simeq B \equiv \mathbf{K}(A,B) \wedge \mathbf{K}(B,A).$$

We also define the information equivalence class $\epsilon(A)$ for a network A as the set

$$\epsilon(A) = \{B \mid A \simeq B\}.$$

By proposition I, if a network can be contracted into a sub-structure of itself, the network and the sub-structure belong to the same equivalence class.

The Canonical Elements

Proposition II: There exists a unique element $\epsilon^*(A)$ in $\epsilon(A)$ such that $\mathbf{S}(\epsilon^*(A),B)$ for all $B \in \epsilon(A)$.

Proof: Let A and B be two networks such that $\epsilon(A) = \epsilon(B)$, and let A^* and B^* be some minimal sub-structures of A and B respectively such that $\mathbf{Q}(A,A^*)$ and $\mathbf{Q}(B,B^*)$.

Since A^* and B^* belong to $\epsilon(A)$, we have $\mathbf{K}(A^*,B^*) \wedge \mathbf{K}(B^*,A^*)$.

By the definition of **K**, there must be two networks C_1 and C_2 such that

$$\mathbf{Q}(A^*,C_1) \wedge \mathbf{S}(C_1,B^*) \wedge \mathbf{Q}(B^*,C_2) \wedge \mathbf{S}(C_2,A^*)$$

Since both **Q** and **S** imply **K**, both C_1 and C_2 belong to $\epsilon(A)$. Further, A^* is minimal in $\epsilon(A)$, which means that $\forall C \in \epsilon(A)$: $\neg \mathbf{S}(C,A^*) \vee C=A^*$. In particular, for C_2 we obtain that $C_2=A^*$.

Similarily for B^*, we obtain $C_1=B^*$, and therefore we obtain $\mathbf{Q}(A^*,B^*) \wedge \mathbf{Q}(B^*,A^*)$, which implies that $A^*=B^*$.

Thus, a network A has a unique minimal sub-structure A^* in $\epsilon(A)$ into which it can be contracted. Also, any other network B in $\epsilon(A)$ has the same unique minimal sub-structure A^* in $\epsilon(A)$ into which it can be contracted. We denote this unique minimal element by $\epsilon^*(A)$.

[ ]

The unique element $\epsilon^*(A)$ in the equivalence class $\epsilon(A)$ is called its *canonical element*. It is the smallest size network, measured in number of arcs, that contains the same amount of information as the network A.

Least Upper Bound

We define the partial order $\sqsubseteq$ on *canonical* networks A and B by $A \sqsubseteq B \equiv \mathbf{K}(A,B)$.

Proposition III: For the relation $\sqsubseteq$, $\epsilon^*(A \oplus B)$ for canonical networks A and B is the least upper bound.

Proof: From proposition I, point 4, for any three networks, A, B and C, the following is satisfied:

$$\mathbf{K}(A,C) \wedge \mathbf{K}(B,C) \rightarrow \mathbf{K}(A \oplus B,C).$$

That is, the trivial combination, $A \oplus B$, is a least upper bound for A and B. Therefore, $\epsilon^*(A \oplus B)$ is the least upper bound for A and B among canonical networks.

[ ]

Greatest Lower Bound

In this section, we show that $\epsilon^*(A \otimes B)$, is the greatest lower bound, $A \sqcap B$, for canonical networks A and B.

Proposition IV: $\mathbf{K}(A \otimes B, A)$ is satisfied for all networks A and B.

Proof: Let A and B be two networks, and let A' and B' be representations of A and B respectively. Then, the set C' defined by:

$$C' = \{<f,<m,r>,<n,s>> \mid <f,m,n> \in A' \wedge <f,r,s> \in B'\}$$

is a representation of $A \otimes B$. Now, let $\mathbf{k}$ be a function from N(C') to N(A') such that:

$$\mathbf{k}(<m,r>) = m$$

and apply this to C', to obtain the set D' defined by:

$$D' = \{<f,\mathbf{k}(<m,r>),\mathbf{k}(<n,s>)> \mid <f,m,n> \in A' \wedge <f,r,s> \in B'\} =$$

$$= \{<f,m,n> \mid <f,m,n> \in A' \wedge f \in F(B')\}$$

It is clear that $D' \subset A'$, which means that $A \otimes B$ can be contracted into a sub-structure of A, and thus $\mathbf{K}(A \otimes B, A)$.

[ ]

$\mathbf{K}(A \otimes B, B)$ follows by symmetry.

Proposition V: $A \otimes A \simeq A$

Proof: Let A be a network and let A' be a representation of A. Then, the set C' defined by

$$C' = \{<f,<m,r>,<n,s>> \mid <f,m,n> \in A' \wedge <f,r,s> \in A'\}$$

is a representation of $A \otimes A$. In particular, there is a sub-set D' of C' such that:

$$D' = \{<f,<m,m>,<n,n>> \mid <f,m,n> \in A'\}$$

which is just a renumbering of A'. That is, there is a 1-1 function $\mathbf{k}$ such that:

$$\{<f,\mathbf{k}(m),\mathbf{k}(n)> \mid <f,m,n> \in A'\} \subset C'$$

which implies that $\mathbf{K}(A, A \otimes A)$. From proposition IV, we have that $\mathbf{K}(A \otimes A, A)$, and therefore, we obtain $A \otimes A \simeq A$.

[ ]

Proposition VI: $A \otimes (B \oplus C) = (A \otimes B) \oplus (A \otimes C)$

Proof: Let A,B and C be networks, and let A',B', and C' be their respective representations, such that the node number sets are pair-wise disjoint. Then, the set D' defined by

$$D' = \{<f,<m,r>,<n,s>> \mid <f,m,n> \in A' \wedge <f,r,s> \in (B' \cup C')\}$$

is a representation of $A \otimes (B \oplus C)$. The set formation predicate is written equivalently:

$$(<f,m,n> \in A' \wedge <f,r,s> \in B') \vee (<f,m,n> \in A' \wedge <f,r,s> \in C')$$

Now, let us define the two sets:

$$D_1 = \{<f,<m,r>,<n,s>> \mid <f,m,n> \in A' \wedge <f,r,s> \in B'\}$$
$$D_2 = \{<f,<m,r>,<n,s>> \mid <f,m,n> \in A' \wedge <f,r,s> \in C'\}$$

Clearly, D_1 is a representation of $A \otimes B$, and D_2 is a representation of $A \otimes C$. Further, their node number sets are disjoint, so $D_1 \cup D_2$ is a representation of $(A \otimes B) \oplus (A \otimes C)$.

Since $D' = D_1 \cup D_2$, we obtain that any representation of $A \otimes (B \oplus C)$ is also a representation of $(A \oplus B) \otimes (A \oplus C)$.

By similar reasoning, we obtain that any representation of $(A \oplus B) \otimes (A \oplus C)$ is also a representation of $A \otimes (B \oplus C)$, and therefore it is proved that $A \otimes (B \oplus C) = (A \otimes B) \oplus (A \otimes C)$

[ ]

Proposition VII: $(A \oplus C) \otimes (B \oplus C) \simeq (A \otimes B) \oplus C$

Proof: Consider the expression $(A \oplus C) \otimes (B \oplus C)$ for any three networks A,B, and C. From proposition VI, we obtain:

$$(A \oplus C) \otimes (B \oplus C) = ((A \oplus C) \otimes B) \oplus ((A \oplus C) \otimes C) = ((A \otimes B) \oplus (C \otimes B)) \oplus ((A \otimes C) \oplus (C \otimes C)) =$$
$$= (A \otimes B) \oplus (A \otimes C) \oplus (B \otimes C) \oplus (C \otimes C)$$

Since $C \otimes C \simeq C$, we obtain

$$(A \otimes B) \oplus (A \otimes C) \oplus (B \otimes C) \oplus (C \otimes C) \simeq (A \otimes B) \oplus (A \otimes C) \oplus (B \otimes C) \oplus C$$

Further, from proposition IV, we have that $\mathbf{K}(B \otimes C, C)$, and therefore

$$(A \otimes B) \oplus (A \otimes C) \oplus (B \otimes C) \oplus C \simeq (A \otimes B) \oplus (A \otimes C) \oplus C \simeq (A \otimes B) \oplus C$$

That is, $(A \oplus C) \otimes (B \oplus C) \simeq (A \otimes B) \oplus C$.

[ ]

Proposition VIII: $\mathbf{K}(C,A) \wedge \mathbf{K}(C,B) \rightarrow \mathbf{K}(C, A \otimes B)$

Proof: From proposition VII, we have that $(A \oplus C) \otimes (B \oplus C) \simeq (A \otimes B) \oplus C$ for any three networks A, B, and C.

In particular, if C is a network such that $\mathbf{K}(C,A) \wedge \mathbf{K}(C,B)$, the left-hand side simplifies to $A \otimes B$, and we obtain $A \otimes B \simeq (A \otimes B) \oplus C$, which implies $\mathbf{K}(C, A \otimes B)$.

[ ]

Proposition IV tells us that $A \otimes B$ is below both A and B, and proposition VIII tells us that any network below both A and B is also below $A \otimes B$. Therefore, the network $A \otimes B$ is a greatest lower bound for A and B. In other words, $\epsilon^*(A \otimes B) = A \sqcap B$.

Corollary: The relation $\sqsubseteq$ forms a distributive lattice[8].

The bottom element in the lattice is the empty network. The top element is a single node, to and from which there is one arc of each arc label.

CONCLUSION

We have shown that the extension and contraction relations on networks form a lattice of equivalence classes of networks. Within each class, there is a canonical element which also is the smallest size network in the class. All elements in a class are therefore extensions to the canonical element, and they can be contracted into the canonical element.

We have also defined two operations that accomplish the lattice operations join (least upper bound) and meet (greatest lower bound). The trivial combination of two networks is the least (in information contents) larger network which contains all the information of the parts. The cross combination contains all their common information (and no more). Although trivial and cross combinations may result in non-canonical networks, their use is favoured by their computational simplicity.

A result of this work is that it enables us to deal with networks formally in a manner that resembles set theory. The intuitive notions of "union" and "intersection" of information as used in applications based on networks are given comprehensible and formal interpretations in terms of network operations. We have dealt only with a simple and particular kind of networks, consisting of anonymous nodes and labelled, directed arcs, but the basis of extension and contraction as information increase is likely to apply with similar results to any particular kind of networks.

REFERENCES

[1] Aho, Hopcroft, Ullman, *The Design and Analysis of Computer Algorithms*, Addison-Wesley Publishing Company, USA 1976.

[2] D. van Dalen, *Logic and Structure*, 2nd ed., Springer-Verlag, Germany, 1983.

[3] C. A. Ellis, *Information Control Net: A Mathematical Model of Office Information Flow*, 1979.

[4] S. E. Fahlman, *NETL: A System for Representing and Using Real-World Knowledge*, The MIT Press, Cambridge, Massachusetts, USA, 1979.

[5] N. V. Findler (ed.), *ASSOCIATIVE NETWORKS, Representation and Use of Knowledge by Computers*, Academic Press, New York, 1979.

[6] Garey, Johnson, *COMPUTERS AND INTRACTABILITY, A Guide to the Theory of NP-Completeness*, W.H. Freeman and Company, San Fransisco, USA, 1979.

[7] J. L. Peterson, *Petri Net Theory and the Modelling of Systems*, Reading, Prentice-Hall, 1981.

[8] H. Rasiowa, R. Sikorski, *The Mathematics of Metamathematics*, Polish Scientific Publishers, Warzawa, 1970.

[9] R. Rönnquist, E. Sandewall, *The Relationship between Ordered and Unordered Trees in I.M.S. Theory*, LITH-IDA-R-84-04, Linköping University, Sweden, 1984.

[10] R. Rönnquist, *Relational Algebra in I.M.S. Theory*, LITH-IDA-R-85-06, Linköping University, Sweden, 1985.

[11] E. Sandewall et al, *Theory of Information Management Systems*, Lecture Notes, Linköping University, Sweden, 1983.

[12] D. C. Tsichritzis, F. H. Lochovsky, *Data Models*, Prentice-Hall inc., New Jersey, USA, 1982.

[13] W. A. Woods, *Transition Network Grammars for Natural Language Analysis*, CACM 13:10, 1970.

KNOWLEDGE-BASED PARALLEL PROGRAMMING

PHILLIP CHEN-YU SHEU
School of Electrical Engineering
Purdue University
West Lafayette, IN 47907

ABSTRACT

In this paper we propose to use object-oriented programming for general parallel systems. To ease the task of parallel programming, we propose the framework of object-oriented knowledge bases. We consider two levels of object-oriented parallel programming at which knowledge may help. At the top level, the inheritance mechanism of object-based systems enables software reusability. Using mathematical logic as the basis of knowledge representation, we investigate the possibility of automatic object classification and procedure instantiation. At the bottom level, we consider the problem of processing structured objects parallelly subject to dynamic resource constraints.

1. INTRODUCTION

Although models object-oriented computation have been widely investigated in the field of operating systems [Lind76] [Fabr74] [Wulf75] [Wulf81] [Jone80] [Inte81] [Kahn81], programming languages [Jone76] [Lisk79] [Dod80] [Wulf76] [Gold83], and artificial intelligence [Mins75] [Bobr76] [Bobr82] [Gold80] [Hewi73] [Ther82] [FiKe85], most of the efforts have been concentrating on centralized environment.

In this paper we propose to use object-oriented programming for general parallel systems. To ease the task of parallel programming, we propose the framework of object-oriented knowledge bases. We consider two levels of object-oriented parallel programming at which knowledge may help. At the top level, the inheritance mechanism of object-based systems enables software reusability. Using mathematical logic as the basis of knowledge representation, we investigate the possibility of automatic object classification and procedure instantiation. At the bottom level, we consider the problem of processing structured objects parallelly subject to dynamic resource constraints. Special attention will also be paid to reconfigurable architectures.

2. OBJECT–ORIENTED KNOWLEDGE BASES

In general, we consider a deductive knowledge base [Gall84][Kell86](See Figure 1) to consist of a finite set of constants and a set of first order clauses without function symbols. The general form of clauses that will represent facts and deductive laws is

$$P_1 \wedge P_2 \wedge \ldots \wedge P_k \rightarrow R_1 \vee R_2 \vee \ldots \vee R_q.$$

The conjunction of the P_i's is referred to as the left-hand-side of the clause and the disjunction of the R_j's as the right-hand-side. According to the values of k and q, clauses can be classified as integrity constraint, fact, or deductive law. For all deductive laws of the form $p \leftarrow p_1 \wedge \ldots \wedge p_n$, we call *p* a *derived* predicate; Predicates other than derived predicates are called *base* predicates. Generally $q \leq 1$ in order to keep a database definite. In such databases, queries are usually represented as conjunction of predicates with uninstantiated variables. Briefly speaking, facts in deductive database are organized as relations, and a relational database can be viewed as an interpretation of a first-order language.

To incorporate the concept of object and class into a deductive knowledge base, in [Sheu86] we proposed the *framework of object_oriented knowledge base* (see Figure 1). Our first-order language consists of the following:

(1) *class(a)* is true if *a* is an object class.

(2) *instance_of(a,b)* is true if object *a* is an instance of class *b*.

This research is supported in part by the National Science Foundation under grant number CDR-85-00022.

Methodologies for Intelligent Systems
Z. W. Ras and M. Zemankova, Editors

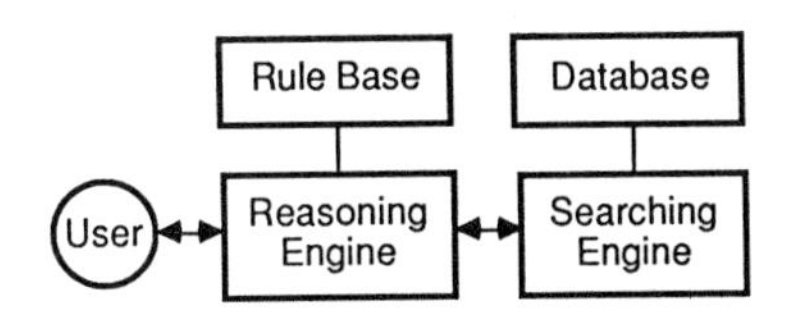

Figure 1. Knowledge Base Architecture

(3) *subclass_of(a,b)* is true if class *a* is a subclass of class *b*.

(4) *attribute(a,b)* is true if object class *a* has *b* as one of its attributes.

(5) *attribute_value(a,b,c)* is true if object *a* has *c* as the value of its attribute *b*.

(6) $c{:}a(x_1,...,x_r,y_1,...,y_p)$ is true if *a* is a method of class *c* and when *a* is executed with the input arguments $x_1,...,x_r$, the output arguments obtained are $y_1,...,y_p$. In this case, we call $c{:}a(x_1,...,x_r,y_1,...,y_p)$ a *method predicate*.

(7) $f(x_1,...,x_n)$ is true if $<x_1, ..., x_n>$ is a member of user-defined relation *f*. In this case, we call $f(x_1,...,x_n)$ a *relational predicate*.

The first order language just introduced provides us a syntax by which integrity constraints and deductive laws can be asserted. With these, the associated object base can be assured consistent and new objects can be derived from existing ones. The general form of clauses that will represent integrity constraints and deductive laws is:

$$P_1 \Lambda P_2 \Lambda ... \Lambda P_k \rightarrow R_1$$

If R_1 is a method predicate, then we call it a *derived method*; Similarly, if R_1 is a relational predicate, we call it a *derived relation*.

In general, when an object-based systems is constructed, an object-oriented knowledge base can be built accordingly. As shown above, the knowledge base is a summary of the object-based system, and the object-based system is an interpretation of the knowledge base. When new objects are added into the system or existing objects are modified, the knowledge base can be changed automatically by applying the integrity rules (due to space limitation, the details are omitted here). As will be shown later, such a knowledge base will play an important role when we program an object-based system.

3. GENERIC OBJECTS AND AUTOMATIC CLASSIFICATION

In this section we are concerned with the problem solving knowledge that is object-dependent. To this end, we shall consider the use of *generic objects* and *operation reusability*. The important idea is that if we have sufficient generic objects (and of course their related operations) defined in the knowledge base, it is very likely that a newly defined object could be an instance of a generic object. If this is true, then the operations related to the generic object can be instantiated and used as the operations for the new object.

Two possible relationships can exist between two entities A and B, where A and B can be an object or a class:

(a) object A is an instance of class B, or
(b) class A is a subclass of class B, where

case (a) holds if

(1) *instance_of(X,A)* $\rightarrow f_A(X)$

(2) $f_B(Y) \rightarrow$ *instance_of(Y,B)*, and

(3) $f_B(X)$ where *instance_of(X,A)*;

case (b) holds if

(1) *instance_of(X,A)* $\rightarrow f_A(X)$

(2) $f_B(Y) \rightarrow$ *instance_of(Y,B)*, and

(3) $f_A(X) \rightarrow f_B(X)$.

As an example, let the following integrity constraints hold:

(a) *class(flight)*

(b) *setof*($<X_1,X_2>$,*instance_of(X,flight)* Λ *attribute_value*(X,*source*,X_1) Λ *attribute_value*(X,*destination*,X_2), *f*)

(c) *instance_of(C,f)* $\wedge$ *attribute_value(C,source,C_1)* $\wedge$ *attribute_value(C,destination,C_2)* $\rightarrow$ *instance_of(C_1,city)* $\wedge$ *instance_of(C_2,city)*

(d) *instance_of(V,set)* $\wedge$ *instance_of(E,relation)* $\wedge$ *domain(E,<V,V>)* $\rightarrow$ *instance_of(<V,E>,graph)* $\wedge$ *attribute_value(<V,E>,vertex_set,V)* $\wedge$ *attribute_value(<V,E>,edge_set,E).*

By (d) we can obtain

(1) *instance_of(<city,f>,graph),* since

(2) *instance_of(city,set)* (a class is a set), and

(3) *instance_of(f,relation)* $\wedge$ *domain(f,<city,city>).*

We can define the following predicate to relate a class and its subclasses:

subclass-of(A,B) : asserts that class *A* is a subclass of class *B.*

To take care of transitive effects, we can have the following axiom:

subclass-of(A,B) $\wedge$ *subclass-of(B,C)* $\rightarrow$ *subclass-of(A,C).*

4. OPERATION REUSABILITY

As we mentioned in Section 2, one important advantage of object-based programming is that algorithms can be implemented at higher or more abstract levels of the hierarchy, and are automatically available at lower levels. There are two problems with this idea: The first problem is *user interface.* In is quite often that a user likes to define a problem for a customized object (or a set of customized objects) such that the knowledge base is able to discover an existing problem that matches the given problem. If this level of user interface is provided, a user needs not to learn all the available solutions and pick the one that is suitable for his problem. The other problem is instantiation; it happens because abstract algorithms are usually represented by abstract concepts, and different specializations may have different interpretations for these abstract concepts. For instance, associated with the abstract class *set* we can define a method *linear_search* which can be described as follows:

for each_element in the set do
  if each_element = an_element then return(each_element)
return(false)

This abstract algorithm will generate a run-time error if invoked without an overriding definition in the concrete subclass, since many of the details could not be known when the algorithm is written (e.g., the attributes of the objects that can form a set). Current implementations of object-based systems rely on users to provide the instantiation, which obviously loses the some advantages of inheritance. In the following sections, we shall discuss the possibility to automate the above processes.

4.1 Problem Instantiation

In general, a problem can be described by two parts: the *scope* of the problem (i.e., the set of objects given), and the *solution* of the problem (i.e., the solution and the constraint the solution has to obey). For a problem *p*, its scope s_p, and its solution t_p, we can define the following formulas to relate them:

(a) *scope_of(p,s_p)* $\leftarrow f_{scope(p)}(s_p)$

(b) *solution_of(p,t_p)* $\rightarrow f_{solution(p)}(s_p,t_p)$

Consequently, a problem p is an instance of another problem q if

(a) s_p is an instance of s_q

(b) t_p is an instance of t_q

(c) $f_{solution(q)}(s_p,t_p) \rightarrow f_{solution(p)}(s_p,t_p)$

For instance, if we have the following problem *shortest_path* defined for the class *graph*:

(a) $scope\_of(shortest\_path,s_p) \leftarrow graph(G,V_G,E_G) \wedge member\_of(A,V_G) \wedge member\_of(A,s_p) \wedge member\_of(B,V_G) \wedge member\_of(G,s_p) \wedge method\_of(path,graph) \wedge member\_of(path,s_p) \wedge method\_of(length,graph) \wedge member\_of(length,s_p)$

(b) $solution\_of(shortest\_path,t_p) \rightarrow \forall\ t_u\ G{:}path(t_p,A,B) \wedge G{:}length(t_p,L_p) \wedge G{:}path(t_u,A,B) \wedge G{:}length(t_u,L_u) \wedge (L_u \geq L_p)$

On the other hand, if we have the following problem defined for the class *flight*:

(a) $scope\_of(cheapest\_f\_path,s_q) \leftarrow member\_of(X,city) \wedge member\_of(X,s_q) \wedge member\_of(Y,city) \wedge member\_of(Y,s_q) \wedge member\_of(f,s_q) \wedge method\_of(f\_path,s_q) \wedge$ member_of(f_path,s_q) $\wedge\ method\_of(fare,s_q)$

(b) $solution\_of(cheapest\_f\_path,t_q) \rightarrow \forall\ t_v\ f{:}f\_path(t_q,X,Y) \wedge \wedge f{:}fare(t_q,F_q) \wedge f{:}f\_path(t_v,X,Y) \wedge f{:}fare(t_u,F_v) \wedge (F_v \geq F_q)$

Consequently, problem q is an instance of problem p if we can prove

(a) the set f is an instance of the class graph,

(b) a city is an instance of a vertex,

(c) the concept *f_path* is an instance of the concept *path*,

(d) the concept *fare* is an instance of the concept *length*,

(e) the target t_q is an instance of the target t_p,

(f) $f{:}f\_path(t_p,A,B) \wedge f{:}fare(t_p,L_p) \wedge f{:}f\_path(t_u,A,B) \wedge f{:}fare(t_u,L_u) \wedge (L_u \geq L_p) \rightarrow f{:}f\_path(t_q,X,Y) \wedge \wedge f{:}fare(t_q,F_q) \wedge f{:}f\_path(t_v,X,Y) \wedge f{:}fare(t_u,F_v) \wedge (F_v \geq F_q)$

In the above conditions, (a) and (b) have been obtained previously, (c) (d) and (e) can be obtained by following recursively the same procedure as above, and (f) is the consequence of (a)~(e).

4.2 Writing Reusable Solutions

The important criteria to write reusable procedures is to make them as general as possible, without making unnecessary assumptions. This requirement can be satisfied if we create a knowledge base parallel to the object-based system, where the knowledge base summarizes the contents of the system as we discussed in Section 3, and we

(a) allow the object-based system interacts with the knowledge base, behaving as a user, and

(b) write abstract algorithms in a way that abstract entities can be instantiated automatically.

For example, the abstract algorithm mentioned earlier can be rewritten as:

```
flag = 0;
while (member_of(X,Given_set) ∧ set(Given_set) ∧ not_nil(X)) do
      while (attribute(Given_set,Z) ∧ not_nil(Z)) do
            if      (attribute_value(Given_set,X,Z,A)      ∧      attribute_value(Given_set,
            Given_element,Z,B) ∧ (A≠B)) then (flag = 1)
      if (flag = 0) then return(X)
return(false)
```

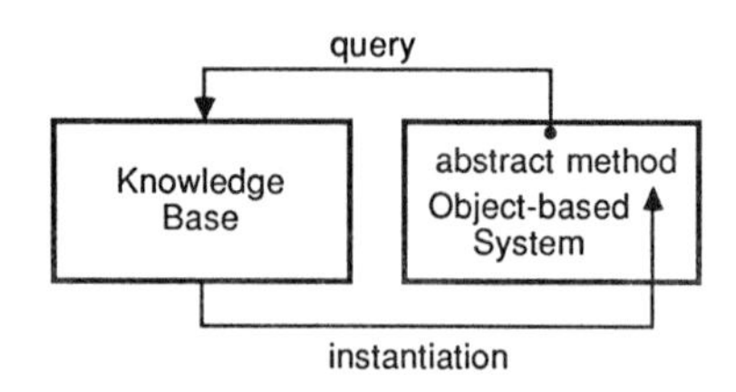

Figure 2. The Proposed Approach for Reusability

Conceptually, the above approach can be described in Figure 2. As illustrated in the above example, abstract algorithms or abstract rules in our approach are written in terms of the *structure* of an object class, and details of the structure can be instantiated at run time. Notice that this is possible since we have the existence of the knowledge base.

5. PROCESSING STRUCTURED OBJECTS PARALLELLY

An important factor to the success of our knowledge-based programming system is the availability of a rich collection of parallel algorithms; these algorithms should be stored in the knowledge base and consequently can be reused when new cases arise. In this section we are concerned with the design and representation of parallel algorithms that can process structured objects efficiently. In general, when multiple processors are available, we can decompose a large, structured object into a set of smaller objects. In order to process these sub-objects parallelly, we need to provide appropriate parallel algorithms. Although quite a few parallel algorithms have been proposed, we may need to reconsider them due to the following factors:

(a) Most of the existing parallel algorithms have assumed a shared memory model and therefore are not suitable for other models (e.g., loosely coupled MIMD models).

(b) Most of the existing parallel algorithms have assumed either unlimited amount of memory or memory capacity of one (e.g., systolic algorithms) associated with each processor. In practice we may have limited, but greater than one, memory sizes.

Obviously, in order to process large objects efficiently we need to consider the architecture on which these objects are processed. To this end our strategy is:

(a) Construct generic classes for parallel architectures; within each class *parametrization* is provided for minor variations.

(b) For each operation, we provide parallel algorithms that are most suitable for each class of architectures. The performances of these algorithms are represented as the functions of *architectural parameters* and *object parameters*.

(c) According to architectural parameters and object parameters, choose the algorithm that provides the best performance. In case the architecture is *reconfigurable*, the best algorithm and the best configuration are chosen according to exhaustive search.

A typical example to illustrate our approach is the *relation join operation* associated with the object class *relation*. Let *theta* represent any valid scalar comparison operator. The *theta-join* of relation A on attribute X with relation B on attribute Y is the set of all tuples t such that t is the concatenation of a tuple a belonging to A and a tuple b belonging to B and the predicate "$a.X$ *theta* $b.Y$" evaluates to *true*. We assume that the following information is given:

(a) The given architecture* is a processor array of size $p \times q$; each processor has memory capacity s.

(b) Each tuple in A is of length t_A (say, bytes) and each tuple in B is of length t_B.

(c) d is the largest integer by which the following relationship is satisfied:

$$s \geq dt_a + dt_B + d^2(t_A + t_B)$$

* The architecture may be static or determined ar run time if it is reconfigurable.

(d) $p = 2k$.

(e) A time unit is defined to be the time required to compare two tuples; transferring a byte from one processor to its neighbor takes α time units ($\alpha < 1$ in general).

(f) On average, $\beta n_A n_B$ tuples will be resulted from the join.

For simplicity, in the following we discuss two ways to conduct a join operation in parallel: the *systolic join algorithm* and the *parallel array join algorithm*; both of them are suitable to be implemented by a processor array.

The Systolic Join Algorithm

The above join operation can be performed easily by a systolic array [Kung80] [Kung82] [KuLe80] of size $2max(n_A,n_B) * x$, where

(a) x is arbitrary, and

(b) tuples of A enter the array from one end of the array every two time units and tuples of B enter the array from the other end of the array every time unit.

The total number of time units required to complete a join is therefore $2max(n_A,n_B)$ time units. Although this is quite desirable, in real practice it may be hard to have a systolic array of this size when n_A or n_B is very large.

Probably the only way to get around the resource shortage problem is to *segment* the relations such that concurrency can be obtained among different segment pairs. Let each relation be *k-segmented***, then the following procedure can be followed (see Figure 3a):

for $i = 1$ *to* $\lceil n_A/k \rceil$ *do*

  for $j = 1$ *to* $\lceil n_B/k \rceil$ *do*

    join the *ith* segment of A with the *jth* segment of B according to the ideal systolic algorithm.

According to the above procedure, the total time (in terms of time units) for the computation would be

$$\lceil (n_A\ n_B)/k^2 \rceil \lceil 2p \rceil = 2\lceil (n_A\ n_B)/p \rceil$$

The Parallel Array Join Algorithm

Again, the above join operation can be performed in almost one time unit if we have a processor array of size $n_A * n_B$. When $p \times q$ may be much less than $n_A \times n_B$, the following procedure can be followed (see Figure 3b):

for $i = 1$ *to* $\lceil n_A/pd \rceil$ *do*

(a) parallelly load the *((i-1)*p+1)th* thru the *(i*p)th* segments of A into row *1* thru p, respectively;

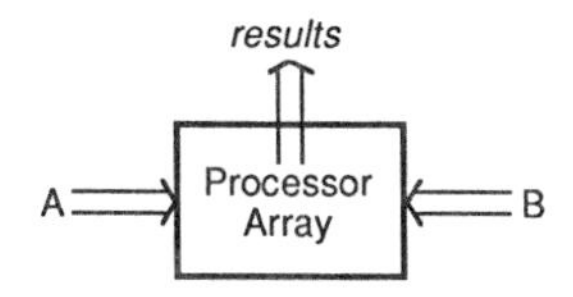

Figure 3a. The Systolic Join Architecture

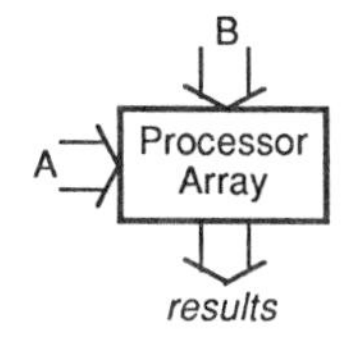

Figure 3b. The Parallel Array Join Algorithm

** I.e., each of them is partitioned into segments of size k.

(b) *for* $j = 1$ *to* $\lceil n_B/qd \rceil$ *do*

(1) parallelly load the *((j-1)*q+1)th* thru the *(j*q)th* segments of B into column *1* thru q, respectively;

(2) parallelly join the d segment pairs at all processors.

(3) transfer the resulting tuples out from the processors.

According to the above procedure, the total time (in terms of time units) for the computation would be

$$\lceil (n_A\, n_B)/pqd^2 \rceil [d^2] + \alpha[(n_A/pd)(1 + (n_B/qd))][t_A d + \beta(t_A + t_B)d^2],$$

where the first term is the time to conduct the joins and the second term is the time to load and unload the data.

Obviously, the performances of the above two algorithms depend on the parameters. Once we have different parallel algorithms designed for different architectures, the operation *join* can be written as: (assume that value of the variable *Architecture* is the architecture given when the operation is requested)

if instance_of(Architecture,processor_array) $\wedge$ *attribute_value(Architecture,number_of_rows,P)* $\wedge$ *attribute_value(Architecture,number_of_columns,Q)* $\wedge$ *attribute_value(Architecture,memory_capacity,K) then*

(perform the parallel array join algorithm) V (perform the systolic join algorithm)

if instance_of(Architecture,tree) $\wedge$ *attribute_value(Architecture,degree,P)* $\wedge$ *attribute_value(Architecture,depth,Q) then*

perform the tree algorithm;

Whenever conflicts occur, the algorithm with the best performance is chosen to be executed. Note that when an architecture can be reconfigurable to a tree or an array, both of the above two rules will be selected and conflict resolution is necessary.

6. CONCLUSION

Lets summarize the object-oriented view we have for concurrent computations:

(1) A *concurrent system* consists of a set of objects, each of them functions asynchronously.

(2) There are *virtual objects* that constitute the logical part of the system; there are *physical objects* that are the actual machines which physically carry out the computation. These physical objects constitute the *physical architecture* of the system.

(3) Operations to the objects can be customized according to the physical architecture. If the architecture is reconfigurable, the operations can be customized dynamically.

(4) It is the function of the *operating system* to decide which virtual objects should reside at each physical object. It is also the responsibility of the operating system to decide which operations should be performed at each physical object.

In this paper we have demonstrated that efficient, parallel systems can be developed with the help of knowledge engineering. In particular, we have shown that expert knowledge is useful if it is organized and abstracted well such that it can be instantiated when new cases arise. We have also shown how expert knowledge can be used to process large, structured objects parallelly and efficiently, even if even if an environment is changing dynamically. Finally, we have shown that the object computation model enables us to represent physical resources as well as logical entities in a uniform way. This capability may be very important for resource management, a critical issue which has not been discussed in this paper.

REFERENCES

[Bobr82] Bobrow, D.G., *The LOOPS Manual*, XEROX PARC, 1982.

[Dod80] *Reference Manual for the Ada Programming Language*, US Dept. of Defense, 1980.

[Fabr74] Fabry, R., "Capability-based Addressing," *CACM*,1974.

[FiKe85] Fikes, R., and Kehler, T., "The Role of Frame-based Representation in Reasoning," *CACM*, September, 1985.

[Gall84] Gallaire, H., et al., "Logic and Databases, A Deductive Approach," *ACM Computing SurveyysR, June, 1984.*

[Gold83] Goldberg, A., *Smalltalk-80: The Language and Its Implementation*, Addison Wesley, 1983.

[Hewi73] Hewitt, C., et al., "A Universal Modular Actor Mechanism for Artificial Intelligence," *Proc. IJCAI*, 1973.

[Inte81] *Intel iAPX432 General Data Processor Architecture Reference Manual*, Intel, Aloha, Oregon, 1981.

[Jack71] Jackson, M., *Principles of Program Design*, Academic Press,NY, 1971.

[John76] Johns, A., et al., "A Language Extension for Controlling Access to Shared Data," *IEEE Trans. Software Engineering*, December, 1976.

[John80] Johns, A., et al., "The Cm* Multiprocessor Project: A Research Overview," CMU-CS-80-131, CMU, July, 1980.

[Kahn81] Kahn, K.C., et al., "iMAX: A Multiprocessor OS for an Object-based Computer," *Proc. 8th Symp. on Principles of Operating Systems*, December, 1981.:36

[Kell86] Kellogg, C., "From Data Management to Knowledge Management," *Computer*, January, 1986.

[Kung80] Kung, H.T., *The Structure of Parallel Algorithms*, in *Advances in Computers*, vol. 19, 1980.

[Kung82] Kung, H.T., "Why Systolic Architectures?" *Computer*, Jan, 1982.

[KuLe80] Kung, H.T., and Leiserson, C.E., "Systolic Arrays for VLSI," in *An Introduction to VLSI Systems*, Mead and Conway Eds. Addison-Wesley, Reading, Mass., 1980.

[Lind76] Linden, T.A., "Operating System Structures to Support Security and Reliable Software," *Computing Surveys*, December, 1976.

[Lisk79] Liskov, B., et al., *CLU Reference Manual*, TR-225, CSL, MIT, 1979.

[Mins75] Minsky, M., "A Framework for Representing Knowledge," in Winston, P., (eds.) *The Phychology of Computer Vision*, McGraw-Hill, 1975.

[Parn72] Parnas, D., "On the Criteria to be Used in Decomposing Systems into Modules," *CACM*, Dec., 1972.

[Sheu86] Sheu, P. C-Y., *Query Processing in Object Bases,* Ph.D Dissertation, U.C. Berkeley, 1986.

[Wirt71] Wirth, N., "Program Development by Stepwise Refinement," *CACM*, April, 1971.

[Wulf75] Wulf, W.A., et al., "Overview ofthe HYDRA Operating System," *Proc. 5th Symp. on Operating System Principles*, November, 1975.

[Wulf76] Wulf, W.A., et al., "An Introduction to the Construction and Verification of Alphard Programs," *IEEE Trans. Software Engineering*, 1976.

[Wulf81] Wulf, W. A., HYDRA/C.mmp: An Experimental Computer System, McGraw-Hill, NY, 1981.

A Calculus for Inheritance in Monotonic Semantic Nets

Richmond H. Thomason[1], John F. Horty[2], and David S. Touretzky[3]
[1]Lingusitics Department, University of Pittsburgh, Pittsburgh, PA 15260, USA; [2]Philosophy Department, University of Maryland, College Park, MD 20742, USA; [3]Computer Science Department, Carnegie Mellon University, Pittsburgh, PA 15213, USA

1 Introduction

The research on monotonic semantic nets that we describe in this paper is part of a larger project devoted to interactions between logical theory and inheritance networks. The work shows the fruitfulness of regarding semantic nets alternatively as *models*, as *sequent calculi*, and as *interpreted languages*. In [14], we develop each of these three approaches to monotonic nets with positive and negative IS-A links, and prove them equivalent. This note summarizes our results, omitting proofs.

Though originally intended only to test our general research strategies in a simple setting, our study of monotonic inheritance turned out to be surprisingly complex. For instance, it is often assumed that monotonic inheritance networks are semantically equivalent to a fragment of classical logic, but our analysis shows that this is not so: the logic we describe, which corresponds naturally to monotonic nets, is sound and complete instead with respect to a four-valued interpretation. The sequent calculus through which this logic is presented is itself interesting as a formal system, and unusual in some respects.

As a computational application of the research, we show how it can be used in validating knowledge representation algorithms. In particular, we consider a concurrent architecture for monotonic inheritance, and prove the algorithms correct and complete with respect to our four-valued semantics.

2 Notation

Letters from the beginning of the alphabet (a, b, c) will represent *objects*, and letters from the middle of the alphabet (p, q, r) will represent *kinds* of objects. Letters from the end of the alphabet (u, v, w, x, y, z) will range over both objects and kinds.

An *assertion* will have the form $x \rightarrow y$ or $x \not\rightarrow y$, where y is a kind. If x is an object, these assertions should be interpreted as ordinary atomic statements: $a \rightarrow p$ and $b \not\rightarrow p$, for example, might represent the statements 'Jumbo is an elephant' and 'Tweety isn't an elephant'. If x is a kind, the assertions should be interpreted as necessarily true generic statements: $p \rightarrow q$ and $r \not\rightarrow q$ might represent the statements 'Elephants are mammals' and 'Birds aren't mammals'. Generic statements can be true even in the presence of exceptions: birds fly, even though penguins don't; mammals don't lay eggs, even though the platypus does. Here, however, we will limit our attention to "strict" generic statements which, if true, are true without exception, by necessity or definition.

Capital Greek letters (Γ, Δ, Π) will represent *nets*, where a net consists of a set I of individuals and a set K of kinds, together with a set of positive links and a set of negative links (both subsets

Published by Elsevier Science Publishing Co., Inc.
Methodologies for Intelligent Systems
Z. W. Ras and M. Zemankova, Editors

of $(I \times K) \cup (K \times K)$). We can identify the positive and negative links in a net with our positive and negative assertions.

3 Monotonic inheritance

The relation of *inheritance* holds between a net Γ and the individual links *supported* by Γ. Roughly, the idea is that an individual link is supported by a net Γ if it must be true whenever all the links in Γ are true, or if it is true in the situation represented by Γ. When a statement A is supported by a net Γ, we say that $\Gamma \models A$.

In order to characterize the inheritance relation, we first define the paths permitted by a monotonic net, and the statements enabled by these paths.

Definition 1 *A monotonic path is a pair of sequences* $\langle x_0, \ldots, x_n ; y_1, \ldots, y_m \rangle$, *where the first sequence* $\langle x_0, \ldots, x_n \rangle$ *is nonempty and the second sequence* $\langle y_1, \ldots, y_m \rangle$ *may be empty. A monotonic path is permitted by a net* Γ *if (1) for all* i, $0 \leq i < n$, $x_i \rightarrow x_{i+1} \in \Gamma$ *or* x_i *is a kind and* $x_i = x_{i+1}$, *(2) either* $x_n \not\rightarrow y_1 \in \Gamma$ *or* $y_1 \not\rightarrow x_n \in \Gamma$, *and (3) for all* i, $1 \leq i < m$, $y_{i+1} \rightarrow y_i \in \Gamma$ *or* y_i *is a kind and* $y_i = y_{i+1}$. *A path is positive if its second sequence is empty, and is negative otherwise. A positive path* $\langle x_0, \ldots, x_n \rangle$ *enables the positive link* $x_0 \rightarrow x_n$, *and a negative path* $\langle x_0, \ldots, x_n ; y_1, \ldots, y_m \rangle$ *enables the negative link* $x_0 \not\rightarrow y_m$.

It is then natural to define the inheritance relation itself as follows.

Definition 2 $\Gamma \models A$ *iff* Γ *permits a monotonic path that enables* A.

4 A sequent calculus

We formulate a calculus in the style of [6] for proving sequents $\Gamma \vdash A$, where Γ is a set of formulas and A a formula. Informally, this means that Γ has enough information to yield A.

Since we are considering only monotonic semantic nets, all of whose links represent statements true without exception, it might seem natural to suppose that we could embed these nets in the classical predicate calculus by translating:

$a \rightarrow p$ as pa,

$a \not\rightarrow p$ as $\neg pa$,

$p \rightarrow q$ as $\forall x[px \rightarrow qx]$, and

$p \not\rightarrow q$ as $\forall x[px \rightarrow \neg qx]$.

However, this is wrong, even in the case of monotonic inheritance. For instance, we wouldn't want to be able to prove the classically valid sequent $a \rightarrow p, a \not\rightarrow p \vdash a \rightarrow q$, since the net $\Gamma = \{a \rightarrow p, a \not\rightarrow p, a \not\rightarrow q\}$, shows us that $\{a \rightarrow p, a \not\rightarrow p\} \not\models a \rightarrow q$.

Examples such as this seem to have been generally overlooked. In fact, it seems to be a kind of "folk theorem" in artificial intelligence that the logic of semantic networks, and even frame systems, is just the classical first-order predicate calculus; often [7] is cited in support of this claim. Though it is true that some simple theories formulable in first-order logic—for instance, $\{Fa,\ \forall x[Fx \rightarrow Gx],\ \forall x[Fx \rightarrow \neg Hx]\}$—can be coded using semantic nets, it is hard to think of a natural general relation according to which the two would be equivalent. Quantifiers and classical disjunction can't be expressed easily in nets, and of course there is no straightforward way to reproduce nonmonotonic reasoning in classical first-order logic. What this example shows, though, is that even without disjunction, quantifiers, or conjunction, and even though inheritance is construed as monotonic, there is a clear sense in which logical consequence over nets diverges from the consequence relation of classical logic.

Our sequent calculus contains as its *structural rule* the schema

$$A \vdash A,$$

where A is atomic—that is, of the form $a \rightarrow p$ or $a \not\rightarrow p$. This gives us our axioms. In addition, we have *logical rules*, for introducing both $\rightarrow$ and $\not\rightarrow$, on the right and on the left of the turnstile.

$$\frac{\Gamma^a, a \rightarrow p \vdash a \rightarrow q}{\Gamma^a \vdash p \rightarrow q}\ \vdash\rightarrow$$

$$\frac{\Gamma \vdash a \rightarrow p \qquad \Delta, a \rightarrow q \vdash A}{\Gamma, \Delta, p \rightarrow q \vdash A}\ \rightarrow\vdash \qquad\qquad \frac{\Gamma \vdash a \not\rightarrow q \qquad \Delta, a \not\rightarrow p \vdash A}{\Gamma, \Delta, p \rightarrow q \vdash A}\ \rightarrow\vdash'$$

$$\frac{\Gamma^a, a \rightarrow p \vdash a \not\rightarrow q}{\Gamma^a \vdash p \not\rightarrow q}\ \vdash\not\rightarrow$$

$$\frac{\Gamma \vdash a \rightarrow p \qquad \Delta, a \not\rightarrow q \vdash A}{\Gamma, \Delta, p \not\rightarrow q \vdash A}\ \not\rightarrow\vdash \qquad\qquad \frac{\Gamma \vdash a \rightarrow q \qquad \Delta, a \not\rightarrow p \vdash A}{\Gamma, \Delta, p \not\rightarrow q \vdash A}\ \not\rightarrow\vdash'$$

In the rules $\vdash\rightarrow$ and $\vdash\not\rightarrow$, Γ^a is supposed to represent a collection of formulas not containing a. We do need both the rules $\rightarrow\ \vdash$ and $\rightarrow\ \vdash'$ to capture the meaning of $\rightarrow$ on the left of the turnstile; neither will do alone. Likewise, both $\not\rightarrow\ \vdash$ and $\not\rightarrow\ \vdash'$ are necessary.

To illustrate these rules, we provide here a sample proof, of the sequent $p \rightarrow q, q \not\rightarrow r \vdash p \not\rightarrow r$.

$$\frac{\dfrac{\dfrac{a \rightarrow p \vdash a \rightarrow p \qquad a \rightarrow q \vdash a \rightarrow q}{a \rightarrow p, p \rightarrow q \vdash a \rightarrow q}\ \rightarrow\vdash \qquad a \not\rightarrow r \vdash a \not\rightarrow r}{p \rightarrow q, q \not\rightarrow r, a \rightarrow p \vdash a \not\rightarrow r}\ \not\rightarrow\vdash}{p \rightarrow q, q \not\rightarrow r \vdash p \not\rightarrow r}\ \vdash\not\rightarrow$$

5 Soundness and completeness

Semantic nets play a dual conceptual role: we can think of them either as *models* or as *theories* (i.e., structured sets of assumptions, together with procedures for inferring conclusions from these assumptions). This may seem surprising to those who are used to the crisp division in traditional logic between semantic and proof-theoretic ideas. Semantic nets, however, belong to a different tradition, in which the distinction is less clear: in knowledge representation, it is often difficult to separate what is represented from what is doing the representing.

The analogy between nets and theories should be obvious: the links contained in a net are like hypotheses, or axioms; the links supported by a net are like the consequences derivable from a set of hypotheses; and the paths permitted by a net are like proofs. To understand their role as models, it might be helpful to place semantic nets against the background of the epistemic tradition in interpreting logics ([16], [9], [4]). This tradition is largely Bayesian, and *quantitative*: the core of the enterprise consists in interpreting formalized languages by assigning probabilities to formulas. Though, mathematically, semantic nets are very different from probability functions, they are like these functions at least in providing something that can be claimed to depict the structure of an agent's knowledge.

Thinking of nets, then, as interpretations, or models, we are able to prove the following two theorems, showing that the sequent calculus defined in Section 4 is both sound and complete with respect to the inheritance relation defined in Section 3.

Theorem 1 *If* $\Gamma \vdash A$ *is provable, then* $\Gamma \models A$.

Theorem 2 *If* $\Gamma \models A$*, then* $\Gamma \vdash A$ *is provable.*

6 A four-valued interpretation

The weak language with which we are dealing is incapable of representing many of the principles that typically distinguish classical from nonclassical logics. For example, excluded middle can't be expressed, since disjunction is not available. Still, the invalidity in nets of inferences like

$$(*) \quad a \to p, a \not\to p \vdash a \to q$$

forces a nonclassical proof-theory.

Examples such as (*) suggest, not only that we will need to look for a nonclassical interpretation of negation, but also that the models that have been developed in connection with *relevance logic* [1] should provide materials for an interpretation. Though the original motivation for relevance logic was not computational, it grew out of a belief that "fallacies of relevance" such as (*) should not be regarded as logically valid. More recently, several authors have suggested that relevance logic may have applications in computer science. Nuel Belnap has argued (in [2] and [3]) that a certain four-valued matrix, originally developed to characterize the valid inferences in a fragment of relevance logic, might be useful also as a guide for reasoning about information stored in databases. And a number of computer scientists have also explored the applications of relevance logic to problems of knowledge representation ([10], [12], [13] [11]).

We take as our truth values the four members of the set $\mathcal{T} = \{\{T\}, \{F\}, \emptyset, \{T, F\}\}$. Like Belnap, we identify values with the four information states of a database with respect to a proposition $\mathbf{p}$: (i) the state of possessing evidence for $\mathbf{p}$, and no evidence to the contrary; (ii) the state of possessing evidence against $\mathbf{p}$, and no evidence for $\mathbf{p}$; (iii) the state of possessing no evidence either for or against $\mathbf{p}$; (iv) the state of possessing evidence for $\mathbf{p}$, and evidence against p as well. These explanations should suggest why we take the power set of $\{T, F\}$ as our set of truth values: if X is one of the values from $\mathcal{T}$, '$T \in X$' means that there is evidence for any proposition bearing the truth value X, and '$F \in X$' means that there is evidence against such a proposition.

A *valuation* v on the language we have described, relative to a domain D, assigns an individual $v(a)$ in D to each individual term a of the language, and a function $v(p)$ from D to $\mathcal{T}$ to each generic term p. Where v is a valuation, v^{d}/a is the valuation like v for all terms other than a, but which assigns the value d to a. The following rules extend v to the entire language.

$v(a \to p) = [v(p)]\ (v(a))$.

$v(a \not\to p) = \mathrm{Not}(v(pa))$, where $\mathrm{Not}(\{T\}) = \{F\}$, $\mathrm{Not}(\{F\}) = \{T\}$, $\mathrm{Not}(\emptyset) = \emptyset$, and $\mathrm{Not}(\{T, F\}) = \{T, F\}$.

$v(p \to q) = \{T\}$ if for all $d \in D$, we have $T \in v^{d}/a(qa)$ if $T \in v^{d}/a(pa)$ and $F \in v^{d}/a(pa)$ if $F \in v^{d}/a(qa)$; and $v(p \to q) = \emptyset$ otherwise.

$v(p \not\to q) = \{T\}$ if for all $d \in D$, we have $F \in v^{d}/a(qa)$ if $T \in v^{d}/a(pa)$ and $F \in v^{d}/a(pa)$ if $T \in v^{d}/a(qa)$; and $v(p \not\to q) = \emptyset$ otherwise.

Given this interpretation, we define semantic implication in the usual way.

Definition 3 Γ *implies* A *if for all valuations* v, *if* $T \in v(B)$ *for all* $B \in \Gamma$, *then* $T \in v(A)$.

It can then be shown that implication in the four-valued logic characterizes the inheritance relation.

Theorem 3 $\Gamma \models A$ *iff* Γ *implies* A.

7 Parallel marker propagation algorithms

Semantic inheritance networks are attractive as formalisms for knowledge representation in part because their natural correspondence with graphs allows certain important kinds of inference to be carried out by simple graph-searching algorithms. The *graph coloring* approach to such algorithms is especially elegant. Scott Fahlman's well-known NETL [5], which introduced a novel computer architecture known as a Parallel Marker Propagation Machine (PMPM), is an AI system based on graph coloring algorithms.

A PMPM is an automaton composed of active elements that play the roles of nodes and links in a graph. Each element has a small number of internal states (maker bits, which can be on or off, representing the presence or absence of markers), and a limited ability to communicate information to the elements with which it is connected. The nodes and links in a PMPM are responsive to several marker propagation commands, each of which directs the assignment of markers to particular nodes, often by "propagating" them from one node to another through the intervening links. PMPM's are SIMD (Single Instruction stream, Multiple Data stream) machines: marker propagation commands are broadcast globally to all elements and executed in parallel by the elements to which they apply. Parallel marker propagation algorithms can be described in terms of marker propagation commands; the result of executing such an algorithm in a particular net is a *coloring*—a static assignment of colors to nodes—that can be used to convey some information about the net.

Parallel marker propagation algorithms can be presented in terms of marker propagation commands; the result of executing such an algorithm in a particular net is a *coloring*—a static assignment of colors to nodes—that can be used to convey some information about the net.

We take as our only two markers the usual truth values, T and F. Now it is standard practice (see [15]) to let the markers themselves serve as colors, so that the marker propagation commands can be seen also as propagating colors directly. In the context of our logical analysis, however, it is more natural to take as colors the four members of the matrix $\mathcal{T} = \{\{T\}, \{F\}, \emptyset, \{T, F\}\}$, from Section 6. We define the color assigned to a node by a marker propagation algorithm as the unique member of $\mathcal{T}$ containing just those markers placed by the algorithm on that node; each algorithm will then result in a total coloring of each net, with no more than one color assigned to any particular node.

The notation used here for specifying marker propagation commands is that of [15]. Commands may be either conditional or unconditional. Unconditional commands are executed by all elements regardless of their current state. The unconditional command **clear**[T], for instance, causes all elements to clear the marker bit representing T. Conditional commands are more common. The command

link-type["→"], **on-tail**[T], **off-head**[T] $\Longrightarrow$ **set-head**[T]

would be executed by any link element meeting the conditions on the left hand side of the arrow: if an element represents a link of type "→", the node at its tail bears the marker T, and the node at its head does not bear marker T, then the link will perform the action specified on the right hand side of the arrow, marking the node at its head with T. Using conditional commands, it is possible to address particular nodes by name; the node named x would be selected by placing the restriction **name**[x] on the left hand side of the conditional; only the element representing that node would then respond. This technique is used to select and mark the initial node at the beginning of a marker propagation. Looping is accomplished with a simple **loop** ... **endloop** construct, which repeats the body of the loop until no conditional command contained in the loop can be executed.

The two most common and useful parallel marker propagation algorithms for performing inferences over semantic nets are known as the upscan and downscan algorithms. (Their names, due to Fahlman, reflect the primary direction in which markers flow through the graph.) Given a net Γ and a node x, the upscan algorithm can be used to find all the statements $x \rightarrow y$ and $x \not\rightarrow y$ that are supported by Γ. It begins by assigning to x a particular marker—here we use T—and ends when: (i) the marker T has propagated to all those nodes y for which Γ supports $x \rightarrow y$, and (ii) a second marker, F, has propagated to all the nodes z for which Γ supports $x \not\rightarrow z$. (If x were the Jumbo node, for instance, an upscan of x would find all the kinds of which Jumbo is an instance, such as elephant and mammal, as well as the kinds of which Jumbo is definitely not an instance, such as bird.) We present here a version of the upscan algorithm appropriate for monotonic semantic nets. It differs from the nonmonotonic version given by Touretzky in [15], since the absence of exceptions allows contrapositive forms of reasoning, affecting the flow of markers through the network.

procedure upscan(x: **node**; T, F: **marker**) = **begin**
  clear[T,F];
  name[x] $\Longrightarrow$ **set**[T];
  loop
    link-type["→"], **on-tail**[T], **off-head**[T] $\Longrightarrow$ **set-head**[T];

```
    link-type["→"], on-head[F], off-tail[F]   ⟹  set-tail[F];
    link-type["↛"], on-tail[T], off-head[F]   ⟹  set-head[F];
    link-type["↛"], on-head[T], off-tail[F]   ⟹  set-tail[F];
  endloop
end
```

Note that a command to propagate T across a link includes the condition that T is not already on the link's head node; this makes it possible for the left hand side of the command to fail, causing the loop to terminate.

This algorithm is both correct and complete, in the following sense.

Theorem 4 *Let* $C \in \mathcal{T}$ *be the color assigned to the node* y *as the result of an upscan of the node* x *in* Γ. *Then* $\mathrm{T} \in C$ *iff* $\Gamma \models x \rightarrow y$, *and* $\mathrm{F} \in C$ *iff* $\Gamma \models x \not\rightarrow y$.

The correctness and completeness results contained in this theorem can easily be duplicated for a suitably defined downscan algorithm. (The downscan algorithm is a converse to upscan: it is used to determine all the assertions $x \rightarrow y$ and $x \not\rightarrow y$ supported by a net, given y rather than x.)

8 Conclusion

We have described in this note a number of close connections between semantic inheritance networks, on the one hand, and more traditional concepts from logic—both proof-theoretic and model-theoretic—on the other. Although these results are not logically profound, they do show, we believe, that fruitful interactions can arise between some ofthe structures that have evolved within artificial intelligence, and more traditional ideas from model theory and proof theory.

In this note we have remained within a monotonic context, and focused only on a very restricted language, but we are hopeful that this research will provide a foundation for further work. The extensions that we now envisage fall into two broad categories: developments in expressive power, and developments that provide for the ability to accommodate exceptions.

It is possible to enhance the expressive power of the language analyzed in this note while remaining entirely within a monotonic framework, by adding relational predicates, connectives, and even quantifiers. Although such networks are not realizable on a PMPM, they appear to have efficient inference algorithms on more powerful architectures, such as massively parallel message passing machines [8]; and the kind of logical analysis explored here may be useful in understanding these algorithms. The second way of extending this work is to shift to a nonmonotonic context. Here, of course, the problems are much more difficult, though some of the sequent rules presented in this report carry over unchanged to the nonmonotonic case. Still, the different approaches we have mapped out—allowing us, really, to look at the same thing from three different perspectives (semantic nets, model theory, and proof theory)—may provide new leverage for understanding the nature of nonmonotonic inheritance. The possibility of applying proof theory in this way is particularly intriguing, since it is one of the most well-developed areas of logic, and as far as we know it has never been exploited as a technique for analyzing nonmonotonic reasoning.

Acknowledgment

This material is based on work supported by the National Science Foundation under Grant No. ITS-8516313.

References

[1] A. Anderson and N. Belnap *Entailment, Vol. I.* Princeton University Press, 1975.

[2] N. Belnap. How a computer should think. In G. Ryle (ed.), *Contemporary aspects of philosophy*, Oriel Press, 1977, pp. 30–56.

[3] N. Belnap. A useful four-valued logic. In J. Dunn and G. Epstein (eds.), *Modern uses of multiple-valued logic*, D. Reidel, 1977, pp. 8–37.

[4] B. Ellis. *Rational Belief Systems.* Rowman and Littlefield, 1979.

[5] S. Fahlman. *NETL: a system for representing and using real-world knowledge.* The MIT Press, 1979.

[6] G. Gentzen. Untersuchungen über das Logische Schliessen. *Mathematische Zeitschrift.* **39**, 1934, pp. 176–210, 405–431. Translated (as Investigations into logical deduction) in M. Szabo (ed.), *The collected papers of Gerhard Gentzen*, North-Holland, 1969, pp. 68–131.

[7] P. Hayes. The logic of frames. In D. Metzing (ed.), *Frame conceptions and text understanding*, Walter de Gruyter and Co., 1979, pp. 46–61. Reprinted in R. Brachman and H. Levesque (eds.), *Readings in knowledge representation*, Morgan Kaufman, CA, 1985, pp. 287–297.

[8] D. Hillis, *The connection machine.* The MIT Press, Cambridge, 1985.

[9] H. Leblanc. Alternatives to standard first-order semantics. In D. Gabbay and F. Guenthner (eds.), *Handbook of Philosophical Logic, Vol. I,* Reidel, 1983, pp. 189–274.

[10] H. Levesque. A logic of implicit and explicit belief. *Proceedings AAAI-84*, pp. 198-202.

[11] J. Martins and S. Shapiro. Theoretical foundations for belief revision. In J. Halpern (ed.), *Reasoning about knowledge* Morgan Kaufmann Publishers, 1986, pp. 383–398.

[12] P. Patel-Schneider. A decidable first-order logic for knowledge representation. In *Proceedings IJCAI-85*, pp. 455–458.

[13] P. Patel-Schneider. A four-valued semantics for frame-based description languages. In *Proceedings AAAI-86*, pp. 344–348.

[14] R. Thomason, J. Horty, and D. Touretzky. A calculus for inheritance in monotonic semantic nets. Technical Report CMU-CS-86-138, Computer Science Department, Carnegie Mellon University (1986).

[15] D. Touretzky. *The mathematics of inheritance systems.* Morgan Kaufmann, 1986.

[16] B. Van Fraassen. Quantification as an act of mind. *Journal of Philosophical Logic*, vol. 11, 1982, pp. 343–369.

SPACE-VARYING ESTIMATION TECHNIQUE IN CONTEXTUAL CLASSIFICATION

Ming-chaun Zhang, * Kai-Bor Yu

University of North Carolina at Charlotte, Charlotte, North Carolina 28223, * Virginia Polytechnic Institute and State University, Blacksburg, Virginia 46224

Abstract:

Because of the high demand for classification efficiency and accuracy in remote sensing and machine vision, making full use of spatial information is an important problem. In this paper we develop a space-varying estimation technique for contextual classification, which can improve classification performance, as compared to noncontextual classfication and conventional contextual classification with maximum likelihood estimation for transition prbability. In addition, this technique overcomes some shortcomings in above contextual classification method, such as the assumption of homogeneity and the global operation produces unsatisfactory results, when the image contains discontinuities (ie. edges and boundaries of regions). Finally, simulated and real experimametal result for space-variying estimation techniqure are shown that space-varying estimation methold can improve classification performance, as compared to maximum likelihood estimation methold.

(1) Introduction :

Making full use of spatial information is an important problem in computer vision and pattern recognition. In recent years, the effort to incorporate spatial information into the classification has become increasingly prevalent, and progress has been made. The use of context in pattern classification has been described by many papers [1 - 6]. Spatial information used for improving classification results are usually from two main sources of context: 1) spatial pixel category depedences and 2) two-dimensional correlation between pixels.

In [1] and [2], we proposed two context classification schemes. The dynamic programming approach [1] is based on a recursive procedure for optimal estimation of the state of a two-dimensional discrete Markov Random Field. How to estimate the transition probabilities $P(C_{ij} \mid C_{ij+1} , C_{i+1j})$ efficiently and accurately is an important aspect in utilizing the technique. In the stochastic relaxation scheme [2], the decision making minimizes the potential function. Here, also estimating the transition probabilities $P(C_{ij} \mid C_{ij-1})$ and $P(C_{ij} \mid C_{i-1j})$ is an important aspect in utilizing the technique.

Conventional maximum likelihood estimation of transition probabilities was employed in [1] and [2]. In sections 3, with theoritial analysis and simulated experiments we show that the technique produce unsatifactry results when the image contains discontimutes such as edges, and boundaries of region. In order to solve this probelm, a space-varying estimation method for transition probability is proposed in section 4. The key idea of the technique is that we use local statistic (ie. space-varying estimation) instead of global statistic (ie. maximum likelihood estimation).

In view of the sampling theory, to obtain a smaller confidence interval of

Methodologies for Intelligent Systems
Z. W. Ras and M. Zemankova, Editors

transition probability estimation at a high confidence level, more observations are necessary. However, for a typical image, the local statistics of the image are position dependent. A large sample size will affect the accuracy of estimation of these local statistics. A technique for determined a projected sample size required for a desired estimation accuaracy proposed by Young(1977) is employed in our procedure. It will guqranted to offer the best compromise between increasing the number of observation and maintaing the homogaety and to satisfy given accuracy. Finally, simulated and real experimental results for space varying estimation technique are shown in section 4. It indicates that space-varying estimation methold can improve classification performance, as compared to maximum likelihood estimation methold.

(2) Contextual classification technique :

From the Bayesian Model, the context classification problem can be stated as follows: to assign labels C to the pixels in the neighborhood of pixel (i,j) which minimizes the expected loss

$$\sum_{C^*} \text{Los}(C, C^*) P(C^* \mid D_{ij}, Q) \tag{2.1}$$

where $P(C^* \mid D_{ij}, Q)$ is the probability that true labeling of the pixels is C^* given i) the measurements D_{ij} of the pixels in the neighborhood of pixel (i,j) ii) the prior information Q we have about pixel dependencies. And where $\text{Los}(C,C^*)$ is the loss incurred for the assignment of interpretation C to the pixels in the neighborhood of pixel (i,j), when the true interpretation is C^*.

With the loss function defined by following equation :

$$\text{Los}(C, C^*) = \begin{cases} 0 & \text{where } C=C^* \\ 1 & \text{otherwise} \end{cases}$$

[2] derived that the best decision procedure is to choose interpretation C which satisfies the maximality condition

$$\prod_{(l,k) \in N_{ij}} P(d_{lk} \mid C_{lk}) P(C) \geqslant \prod_{(l,k) \in N_{ij}} P(d_{lk} \mid Z_{lk}) P(Z) \quad \text{for all } Z \in \Omega$$

The choice of C satisfying this maximality condition cannot be independently done pixel by pixel.

From the Markov-Gibbs model assumption, we have

$$P(D_{ij}, C) = \frac{1}{Z} e^{-\frac{U(D_{ij},C)}{KT}} \tag{2.2}$$

where $U(D_{ij},C)$ is an energy function associated with distribution $P(D_{ij}, C)$.

[2] finally derived that the assigned category is determined by minimizing

$$U(D_{ij}, C) = \sum_{(l,k)} \log P(d_{lk} \mid C_c) + U(C)$$

$$\text{where} \quad U(C) = \sum_{(l,k)} \log P(d_{lk} \mid C_c) + \sum_{(l,k) \in N_{(ij)}} \log P(C_{lk})$$

$$+ 2 * \sum_{(l,k) \in N_{(ij)}} \log P(C_{lk} \mid C_{l+1k})$$

$$+ 2 * \sum_{(l,k) \in N_{(ij)}} \log P(C_{lk} \mid C_{lk+1}) \tag{2.3}$$

Because of the existence of many local extrema, the computation cost of maximizing the posterior probability for Bayes classification is usually computationally high. The identification of even a near-optimal solution is surprisingly difficult for such a relatively complex function. Stochastic relaxation procedure overcomes the computational difficulty remarkably well.

The method used in this context classification is essentially a variant of a Monte Carlo procedure, in which maximizing the posterior probability (MAP) is based on stochastic relaxation, an annealing optimization method. The procedure can be briefly described as follows. For each state D_{ij} of a model D, a random perturbation is made. The change in energy, ΔU is computed. If $\Delta U \leqslant 0$, the perturbation is accepted, that is the new pattern configuration, which corresponds to the new "energy", $U' = U_0 + \Delta U$, replaces the original one. If ΔU is positive then the perturbation is accepted with probability

$$P(\Delta U) = e^{\frac{-\Delta U}{T}} \tag{2.4}$$

This conditional acceptance is easily implemented by choosing a random number R uniformly distributed between 0 and 1. If $R <= P(\Delta U)$ then the perturbation is accepted; otherwise the existing model is retained. Random perturbation according to these rules eventually causes the system to reach equilibrium, or the configuration θ corresponding to maximum probability. The technique used here slowly lowers the temperature T during execution of the iterative procedure. If the system is cooled sufficiently slowly and equilibrium conditions are maintained, the model converges to a state with minimum energy or maximum a posterior probability.

In summary, the stochastic relaxation context classification procedure can be implemented as follows: (i) Evaluate training statistics. This includes the mean vector and covariance required for the Gaussian class conditional distribution. (ii) Preclassify the image using a pixel independent or context free Bayes classification technique. (iii) Evaluate the transition probabilities: $P(C_{ij} \mid C_{i,j+1})$ and $P(C_{ij} \mid C_{i+1,j})$ from the preclassification results. (iv) Using equations (2.2-2.4) implements the stochastic relaxation and annealing optimization procedure.

(3) Maximum likelihood estimator for transition probability :

In [1] and [2] we employed a conventional maximum likelihood estimator for transition probability, denoted as $\hat{P}_{kl} = \frac{m_{kl}}{m_k}$.

Most of digital image processing and contextual pattern classification algorithms are designed with the assumption that image processing is based on stationary spatial statistics. In view of the great variety of real world scenes, the stationary and homogeneous assumptions are not supposed to be exactly true. Thus, there is no guarantee that the estimation of statistical parameters is still satisfactory and reliable for the implementation of the algorithms. However, we still hope that the minor error in the mathematical model should cause only a small error in the final conclusions. Unfortunately, this does not always hold.

The maximum likelihood estimation technique we used here is basically a global operation, and the result is a global statistic parameter (ie., an average of transition count value through the entire image). When the image contains discontinuities such as edges and boundaries of regions, the assumption of homogeneity and the global operation produce unsatisfactory results.

To show an extreme example in our application problem, a three class pseudo-vandom Markov image is used as test image (figure 1). The left half part of the simulated image has high transition probability from class k to class l; and low transition probability from class k to class l, (k,l = 1,2,3 and k ≠ l), but the right half part has a reverse situation.

$$P_{lf} = \begin{bmatrix} 0.8 & 0.1 & 0.1 \\ 0.1 & 0.8 & 0.1 \\ 0.1 & 0.1 & 0.8 \end{bmatrix} \qquad P_{rt} = \begin{bmatrix} 0.25 & 0.375 & 0.375 \\ 0.375 & 0.25 & 0.375 \\ 0.375 & 0.375 & 0.25 \end{bmatrix}$$

The maximum likelihood estimation result is given by

$$P_{kl} = \begin{matrix} 0.525 & 0.238 & 0.238 \\ 0.238 & 0.525 & 0.238 \\ 0.238 & 0.238 & 0.525 \end{matrix}$$

Figure 2 shows the estimation curves of transition probability vs x-coordinate of the test image. From it, we can see that the maximum likelihood estimator introduces a large error into the estimation of transition probability matrix.

(3) Space-varying Estimation Method for Transition Probability:

Various researchers proposed estimation of local statistics for digital processing of nonstationary images. Some researchers [N.E. Nahi and Habibi 8] considered partitioning the image into homogeneous regions. Another [S.A. Saralar and R.J. Defigweeidi 9] use a continuously adaptive technique where the parameters are, during a scan, are updated based upon a local window. Wallis [10] and Lee [11] use local statistics for noise filtering.

In order to solve the local statistics estimation problem, we introduce a "robust" estimation method called a space-varying estimation technique, which should have an optimal or nearly optimal efficiency for the assumed model. It should be robust in the sense that smaller deviation from the model assumptions should impair the performance only slightly, and somewhat larger deviations from the model should not cause a catastrophe.

Let $p_{kl}(i,j)$ be transition probability from class k to class l at pixel (i,j). The proposed space-varying estimation method can be described in a general manner by an expression of the following form.

$$p_{kl}(i,j) = \frac{\sum_{(u,v)\epsilon N} W(i,j,u,v)d_{kl}(u,v)}{\sum_{(u,v)\epsilon N} W(i,j,u,v)d_k(u,v)} \tag{3.1}$$

where N is the window from which the sample data are taken, and pixel (i,j) is a central point in the block, pixel (u,v) is a sampling point within the block window N, and $d_{kl}(u,v)$ called unit transition from class k to class l is a function of transition count. It has

$$d_{kl}(u,v) = \begin{cases} 1 & \text{if there is a state change from class k to class l at pixle (u,v)} \\ 0 & \text{otherwise} \end{cases}$$

$d_k(u,v)$ is an unit transition from class k. It has

$$d_k(u,v) = \begin{cases} 1 & \text{if there is a state change from class k to class l at pixle (u,v)} \\ 0 & \text{otherwise} \end{cases}$$

W(i,j,u,v) is a weighting function that quantifies the importance of pixel (u,v) with respect to the central pixel (i,j).

When W(i,j,u,v) = constant then P_{kl} is position invariant, which is the common maximum likelihood estimation. When the weighting function has the form W(x-u,y-v), it becomes the increasingly popular M-estimators, which can be written as

$$p_{kl}(i,j) = \frac{\sum_{(u,v)\in N} W(x-u,y-v)d_{kl}(u,v)}{\sum_{(u,v)\in N} W(x-u,y-v)d_i(u,v)} \tag{3.2}$$

where W(.) is usually a positive symmetric decreasing function. The M-estimators have good asymptotic properties and are robust with respect to a variety of distribution function.

The estimation procedure proposed here is one that fits into the general description of equation 4.1, but which has the feature that its computation is very simple, not requiring the solution of nonlinear equations. It is of the form

$$p_{kl}(i,j) = \frac{\sum_{(u,v)\in N} W(u,v)d_{kl}(u,v)}{\sum_{(u,v)\in N} W(u,v)d_k(u,v)} \tag{3.3}$$

where W(u,v) is a positive function, whose value is decreased by increasing the distance between pixel (u,v) and central pixel (i,j). For simplicity, we assume W(u,v) = 1/D(u,v) , where D(u,v) is the distance between pixel (u,v) and central pixel (i,j).

For the space-varying estimation technique an important problem is choosing a suitable block window size. In view of the sampling theory, to obtain a smaller confidence interval at a high confidence level, more observations are necessary. However, for a typical image, the local statistics of the image are position dependent. A large sample size will affect the accuracy of estimation of these local statistics. A compromise between increasing the number of observations and maintaining the homogeneity is desired.

In order to solve this problem we use the "projected sample determination technique" proposed by Young (1977) to create a nearly minimum size of estimation window, in which the space-varying estimation is guaranteed to satisfy a given accuracy. The technique for determining a projected sample size first required estimation of confidence intervals of transition probabilities. The major steps and final results for the confidence interval estimation and projected sample size determination see [15].

(4) Experiments results for space-varying estimation technique:

To understand the performance of the space-varying estimation tecunique, we examine its behavior on simulated data sets and on real remote sensing images. As mentioned in section 2, for some extreme cases such as the simulated image in Figure 1, a large estimation error is introduced when using the common maximum likelihood estimator.

But the space-varying estimation technique can achieve better classification results. In order to show the performance of the "space-varying" estimation, a simulated image of size 50 X 50 pixels is used as first test image. It consists of two equal size pseudo-random Markov images. (Figure 1)

The left part of image has transition probability matrix p_l and the right part of image p_r are as follows

$$P_l = \begin{bmatrix} 0.8 & 0.1 & 0.1 \\ 0.1 & 0.8 & 0.1 \\ 0.1 & 0.1 & 0.8 \end{bmatrix} \qquad P_r = \begin{bmatrix} 0.25 & 0.375 & 0.375 \\ 0.375 & 0.25 & 0.375 \\ 0.375 & 0.375 & 0.250 \end{bmatrix}$$

The maximum likelihood estimation result is given by:

$$P_{ij} = \begin{bmatrix} 0.525 & 0.238 & 0.238 \\ 0.238 & 0.525 & 0.238 \\ 0.238 & 0.238 & 0.525 \end{bmatrix}$$

The "space-varying" estimations for each pixel are calculated from the equation (3.3), and the numerical results are shown in the figure 2

From the figure, it is observed that the estimation accuracy using the robust technique is much better than maximum-likelihood estimation for mo... pixels, except for those pixels near the boundary.

Then we apply the stochastic relaxation contextual classification method to the test image using transition probability from both the common maximum likelihood estimator and the "space-varying" estimator. Tables 1 shows the contingency tables for classification results of the pixel independent Bayes' context free classification, and the stochastic relaxation contextual classification methods using the maximum likelihood transition probability estimation and the "space-varying" estimation, respectively. They indicated that the contextual classifier based on the maximum likelihood estimation gained a 1.0 % increase in overall classification accuracy over the pixel independent Bayes' classifier, and that the "space-varying" contextual classification gained a 2.3% increase over the pixel independent Bayes' classification. Obviously, the accuracy improvement of a "space-varying" estimation technique is significant.

In order to examine the behavior of the technique, we use the Landsat MSS data, which was a subset of the 13 April 1976 MSS scene of Roanoke, VA., and has been used in [1] and [2]. From the previous section we konw that the local statistics of the image (eg. transition probability matrix) are position depedent. A large sample size will affect the accuracy of estimation of these local statistics. But to obtain a smaller confidence interval at a high confidence level, more observations are neccessary. In order to find a possible minimum sample size under a given confidence interval at the given confidence level, we use Young's technique to determine the projected sample's size. Then the minimum size of block window in which the number of pixel is equal to the projected number of observations is created for the space-varying estimation technique. For this test image, a window size of 11 x 11 is satisfied to the confidence interval (-0.1, +0.1) at the given confidence level of 0.05. The experimental results, shown in table 2, indicate that the space-varying estimation technique can improve the classification accuracy, especially for discontinuous images. (see Figure 3)

The second real test image is a subset of MSS image for Clarke Oregon. The overall classification accuracies of pixel independent classifier and stochastic relaxation context classifiers using the maximum likelihood transition probability estimation and "space-varying estimation" are shown in table 4. Examining the results in table 4, it can again be seen that the context classification using "space-varying" estimation is superior to the maximum - likelihood estimation. (See Figure 4)

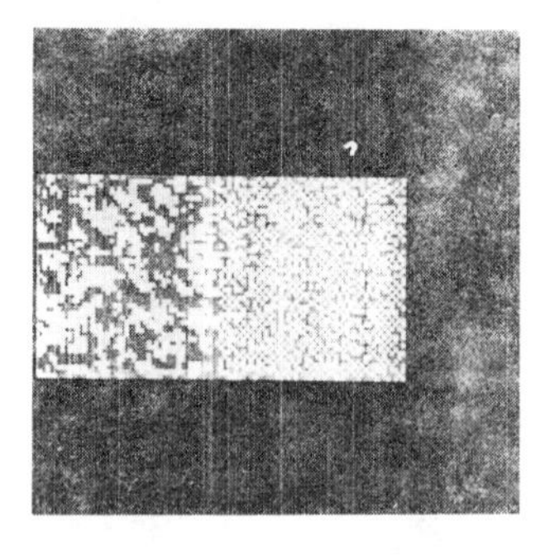

Fig. 1

Simulated experience of transition. Probability estimation using robust estimation technique. This image has two parts in which there are two extreme different transition probability matricies

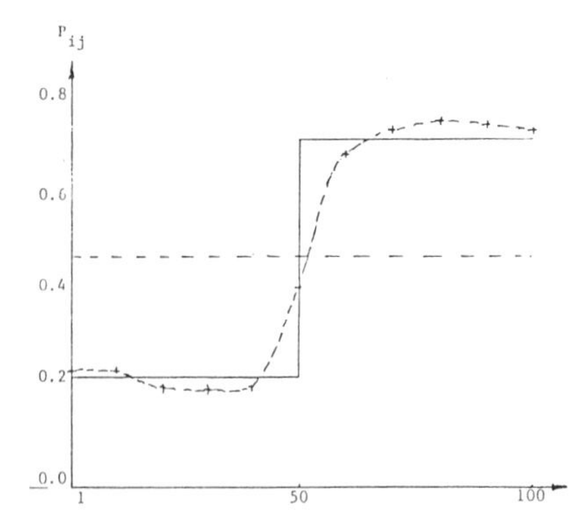

Figure 2 Estimation curves of transition probability vs x-coordinate of the test image. curve 1 - true of Pij curve 2 - maximum likelihood estimation curve 3 - space varying estimation

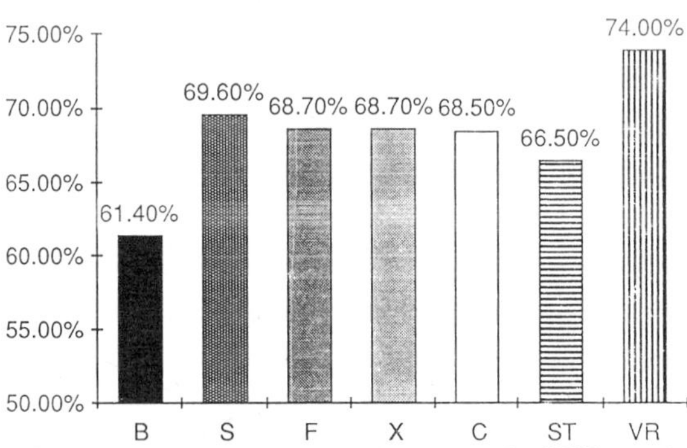

Figure 3 Comparison of overall classification accuracies of MSS scene of Roanoke, VA., using different classifiers. B : pixel indepedent Bayes classifies; S: two pass forward-backward look-ahead; F : four pass; X : one step context look-ahead; C : no context look-ahead; ST : stochastic relaxation. VR : contextual stochastic relaxation classification using space-varying estimation technique.

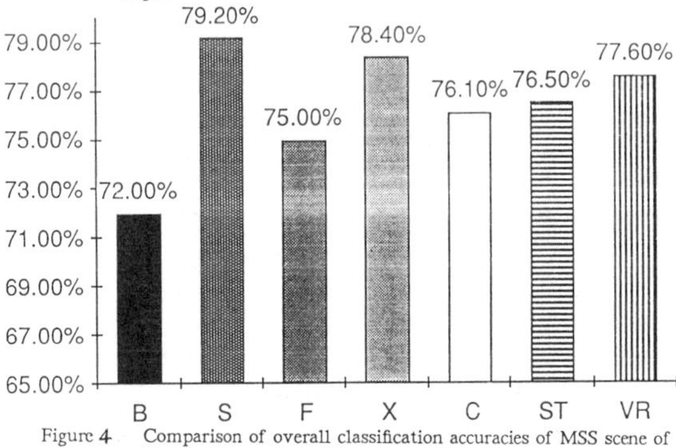

Figure 4 Comparison of overall classification accuracies of MSS scene of Clarke, OR., using different classifiers. B : pixel indepedent Bayes classifies; S: two pass forward-backward look-ahead; F : four pass; X : one step context look-ahead; C : no context look-ahead; ST : stochastic relaxation. VR : contextual stochastic relaxation classification using space-varying estimation techniq.

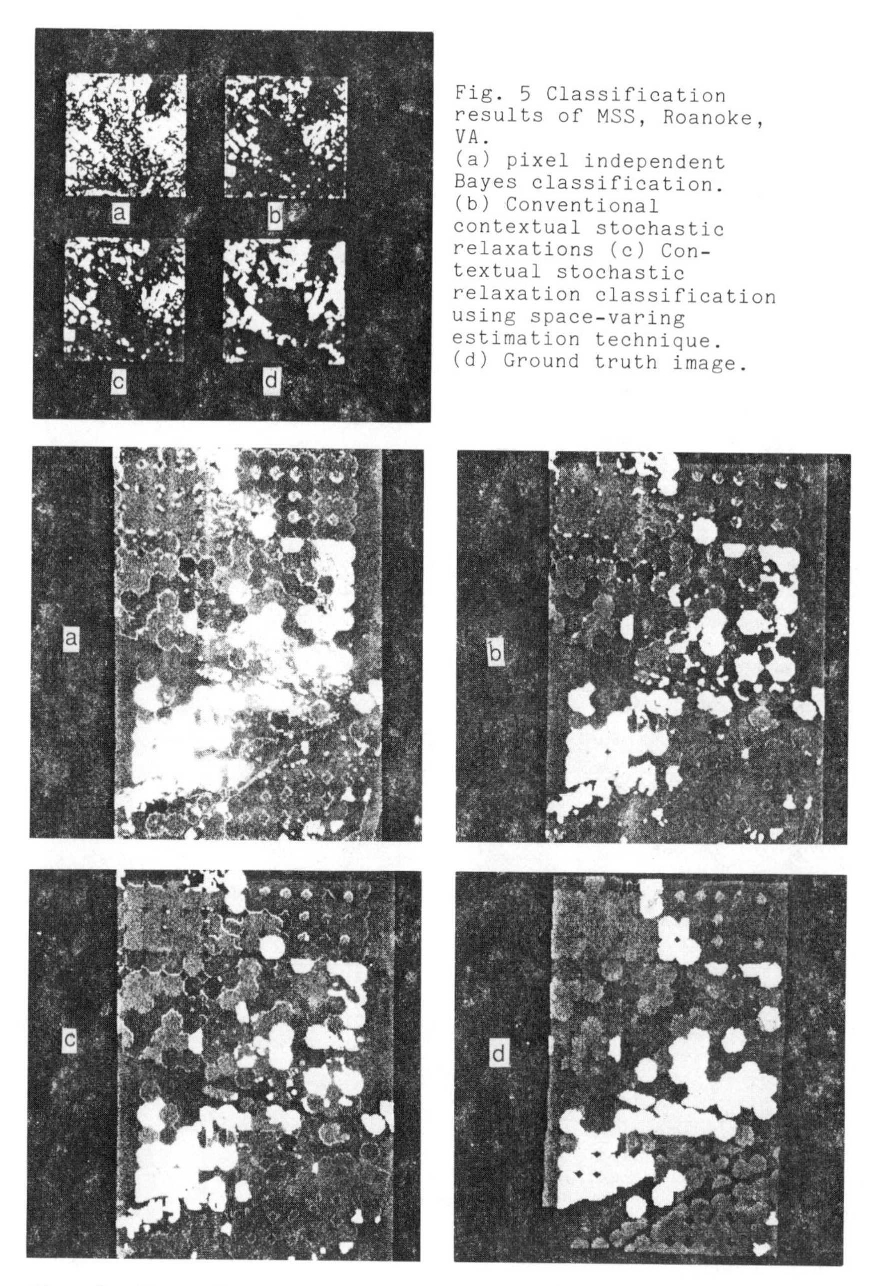

Fig. 5 Classification results of MSS, Roanoke, VA.
(a) pixel independent Bayes classification.
(b) Conventional contextual stochastic relaxations (c) Contextual stochastic relaxation classification using space-varing estimation technique.
(d) Ground truth image.

Fig. 6. Classification results of MSS, Clarke, Oregon
(a) pixel independent Bayes classification. (b) Conventional contextual stochastic relaxations. (c) Contextual stochastic relaxation classification using space-varing estimation technique. (d) Ground truth image.

(C) Context classification result using space-varying transition probability estimation technique.

CLASS	URB	AGR	RNG	FST	TOTAL	ACC(%)*
URB	533	99	0	4	636	83.3%
AGR	122	168	0	13	304	55.0%
RNG	0	0	0	0	0	-
FST	18	1	0	39	61	67.0%
TOTAL	737	170	0	53	1000	74.0%

Table 3 Contingency tables for classification results of MSS scene of Clark, OR.

COL = ASSIGNED CAT ROW = TRUE CAT

(A) Pixel independet Bayes' classification result:

CLASS	WHT	ALF	POT	CRN	PAS	RNG	TOTL	ACC(%)
WHT	1560	31	110	8	10	132	1851	84.3%
ALF	44	295	241	25	167	125	897	32.3%
POT	88	46	1219	25	45	138	1561	78.1%
CRN	4	8	5	351	3	22	393	89.3%
PAS	0	0	2	0	15	1	18	83.3%
RNG	15	14	13	27	12	99	180	55.0%
TOTL	1711	394	1590	436	252	517	4900	72.2%

(B) Context classification result by stochastic relaxation using maximum likelihood estimation technique:

CLASS	WHT	ALF	POT	CRN	PAS	RNG	TOTL	ACC(%)
WHT	1643	9	112	5	2	80	1851	88.7%
ALF	46	299	296	21	116	119	897	33.3%
POT	72	22	1361	21	24	61	1561	87.1%
CRN	7	8	6	351	2	19	393	89.3%
PAS	0	0	3	0	14	1	18	77.7%
RNG	26	6	42	21	7	78	180	43.3%
TOTL	1794	344	1820	419	165	358	4900	76.4%

(C) Context classification result by stochastic relaxation using space-varying transition probability estimation technique:

CLASS	WHT	ALF	POT	CRN	PAS	RNG	TOTL	ACC(%)
WHT	1845	1	2	0	0	3	1851	99.6%
ALF	251	584	11	8	0	43	897	65.1%
POT	507	13	1015	9	0	17	1561	65.1%
CRN	64	14	5	288	0	22	393	73.3%
PAS	0	0	0	0	18	0	18	100.%
RNG	105	14	2	4	0	55	180	58.3%
TOTL	2772	626	1035	309	18	140	4900	77.6%

* Classification accuracy.

** Overall classification accuracy : ratio of the number correctly classified pixels to the number of total classified pixels.

WHT – Wheat
ALF – Alfalfa
POT – Potatoes
CRN – Corn
RNS – Beans
APL – Apples
PAS – Pasture (irrigated)
RNG – Rangeland

Table 1 Contingency tables for classification results of simulated test image of Figure 6.2

COL = assigned categories   ROW = true categories

(A) Bayes classification result

CLASS	1	2	3	TOTAL	#ERR	ACC(%)*
1	998	45	45	1088	90	91.73%
2	27	653	55	735	82	88.85%
3	27	2	648	677	29	95.4%
TOTAL	1052	700	748	2500	201	91.96%

(B) Context classification result using maximum likelihood estimation technique

CLASS	URB	AGR	RNG	FST	TOTAL	ACC(%)*
URB	454	173	0	8	635	71.0%
AGR	94	200	0	9	303	66.0%
RNG	0	0	0	0	0	-
FST	26	15	0	19	60	32.0%
TOTAL	574	388	0	36	998	67.5%

(C) Context classification result using space-varying transition probability estimation technique.

CLASS	1	2	3	TOTAL	#ERR	ACC(%)*
1	1053	26	9	1088	35	96.8%
2	36	687	12	735	48	93.5%
3	41	19	617	677	60	91.4
TOTAL	1130	732	638	2500	143	94.3%

Table 2 Contingency tables for classification results of 13 April 1976 MSS scene of Roanoke, VA. Scale factor of the number of pixels 10 ** 1

COL = assigned categories   ROW = true categories

(A) Bayes classification result

CLASS	URB	AGR	RNG	FST	TOTAL	ACC(%)*
URB	398	210	0	635	635	63.0%
AGR	86	181	0	36	303	60.0%
RNG	0	0	0	0	0	-
FST	20	7	0	34	61	56.0%
TOTAL	504	398	0	97	999	61.4%

(B) Context classification result using maximum likelihood estimation technique

CLASS	1	2	3	TOTAL	#ERR	ACC(%)*
1	1046	16	26	1088	42	96.1%
2	47	647	41	735	88	88.1%
3	40	4	633	677	44	93.5%
TOTAL	1133	667	700	2500	174	93.0%

Reference

[1] Haralick, R. M. , M. C. Zhang and J. B. Campbell, 1984. "Multispectral Image Context Classification Using the Markov Random Field". PECORA, Proceedings, 1984, Oct..

[2] Zhang, M. C. , R. M. Haralick and J. B. Campbell, 1985. "Context Classification by Stochastic Relaxation". IEEE Computer Society Workshop on Computer Architecture for Pattern Analysis and Image Database Management. Nov. 18-20, 1985.

[3] Yu T. S. and K. S. Fu, 1983. "Recursive Contextual Classification Using a Spatial Stochastic Model Pattern Recognition". Vol., 16, No. 1, pp 89-106.

[4] Swain P. H. , S. B. Vardeman and J. C. Tiltor, 1981. " Contextual Classification of Multispectral Image Data". Pattern Recognition Vol, 13. No., 6, pp 428-441.

[5] Swain P. H. , H. J. Siegel and B. W. Smith, 1979. " A Method for Classifying Multispectral Remote Sensing Data Using Context". 1979, Machine Processing of Remote Sensed Data Symposium, pp 343-353.

[6] Gurney, C. M. , and Townshend, 1983. "The Use of Contextual Information in the Classification of Remote Sensing Data". Photogrammetric Engineering and Remote Sensing, Vol, 49, No. 1, Jan., 1983.

[7] Haralick, R. M. , 1983. "Decision Making in Context". IEEE, Trans. on Pattern Analysis and Machine Intelligence, Vol, PAMI-5, No. 4, July.

[8] Nahi, N. E. and A. Habihi, 1975. "Decision-Directed Recursive Image Enhancement". IEEE Trans. Circuits Syst. Vol, CAS-22 pp. 286-293, Mar. 1975.

[9] Saralar, S. A. and R. J. DeFiguereido, 1981. "Adaptive Image Restoration by a Modified Kalman Filtering Approach". IEEE, Acoust., Speech, Signal Processing, Vol. Ass p-29, pp. 1033-1042, Oct. 1981

[10] Wallis R. , 1976. "An Approach to Space-Variant Restoration and Enhancement of Images". in Proc. Symp. Currenr Math. Prob image Sci. Naval Postgraduate School, Monteriy, CA. Nov. 1976.

[11] Lee, J. S. , 1980. "Digital Image Enhacement and Noise Filtering by Use Local Statistic". IEEE Trans. Pattern Anal. Math. Intell, Vol, PAMI-2, Mar., 1980.

[12] Young R. E. , 1977. "Transition Probability Estimation for Discrete State Markov Chains". Thesis, Purdue University, 1977.

[14] Sminov, N. V. , O. V. Sarmanov, and V. K. Zahrov, 1966. "A Local Limit Theorem for Transition Numbers in a Markov Chain, and its Applications". Soviet Math., Doklady, Vol. 7 (Mar.-Apr. 1966) No. 3.

[15] Zhang, M. C. , 1986. " Advanced Spatial Information Processes - Modeling and Application ". Thesis, Viginia Tech, 1986.

LEARNING IN THE LIMIT IN A GROWING LANGUAGE

RANAN B. BANERJI,
Department of Math and CSC, Saint Joseph's University, Philadelphia, Pa
19131 (rbanerji@sju.edu)

ABSTRACT

This paper describes the design of an algorithm which learns a class of theories in the limit in a sublanguage of a first order language. The introduction describes the background of the work and establishes the need. The next section gives a summary of the technical concepts involved. Subsequent sections introduce the sublanguage and the learning algorithm. The conditions for the convergence of the algorithm are then established and the average complexity discussed.

INTRODUCTION AND BACKGROUND

In this paper the work "learning" will be used in the sense of "developing class descriptions from examples of the members of the class". The work described here is a continuation of a series of efforts [1,2,3,4] to simulate the kind of learning process where the efficiency of the learned description increases with increase in knowledge. The major ingredient of such a process is its ability to use the name of one class in the description of another. Such a process is often called "Multilevel Learning". In the past it has also been called, "learning in a growing language", since the wherewithal for the description grows from the initial features of the language to include the names of previously learned concepts as well as names of internally generated concepts used as additional features. The learning algorithm described here does not use any previous knowledge of the language used. Instead it learns the language as it learns the descriptions.

Around 1964, Pennypacker [1] attempted to use this idea with descriptions written in propositional calculus. This work was described by the present author [2,5] who also pointed out that (1) the Pennypacker techniques could compress disjunctive descriptions by using the name of one disjunctively described class in another, (2) to take full advantage of the idea one would have to include in the language the descriptions of relations as well as those of classes and (3) the descriptions of relations could be learned using the same technique as is used in learning the descriptions of classes.

Various later authors [10,11,12] incorporated binary predicates among the features describing examples. However, efforts were not made to learn disjunctive descriptions, nor were any efforts made at that time to have the learning algorithms learn descriptions of relations (i.e. to learn binary or higher order predicates). These were taken up by Cohen [2] and extended by Sammut [3]. These essentially collaborative pieces of work were joined independently by various workers about this time - developing learning algorithms for various purposes [6,7].

At about this time Shapiro [8] extended the concept of "Learning in the Limit" (developed by Gold [9] as a model for learning languages) to the learning of theories from facts in first order logic. Since the descrip-

Methodologies for Intelligent Systems
Z. W. Ras and M. Zemankova, Editors

tions of classes can be looked up as sets of Horn Clauses, his general technique was applicable to the learning of the descriptions of classes and relations. Also the technique did not need that the examples be presented to the learning mechanism by a helpful teacher, as was assumed by some of the authors mentioned here.

The present work describes our attempt to use Shapiro's techniques to learning descriptions of classes and relations using a more general language than used in Shapiro's experiments. The language chosen by us seem much more suitable to the purpose of concept learning. Certain improvements to the technique have been made for pruning the search for descriptions in the chosen language. Also, unlike Shapiro's work, it has not been assumed that the language is available to the learning algorithm: the algorithm learns the language as it learns the descriptions. Apart from this, the work follows Shapiro's guidelines quite faithfully.

In what follows we shall present the essential points of Shapiro's approach and then proceed to describe the specifics of our algorithm.

Conditions for Learning in the Limit

The essential points of Shapiro's approach were as follows:

(1) There exists a first order language (with a fixed number of predicate and function symbols). A sublanguage L_h of this language is adequate for expressing the axioms of some model of the language. There is a sub-language L_o of L_h whose sentences can be used to express results of observations on the model. For the learning algorithm to function correctly, L_h and L_o are supposed to form an admissible pair in that if a false sentence occurs in the theory then there will be a sentence in L_o false in the model, that will be deducible from the theory. (See Shapiro for examples of admissible and inadmissible pairs of languages).

(2) A sequence of facts are presented by the environment to the learning algorithm. A fact consists of a sentence in L_h, with a mark to indicate whether the sentence is true or false in the model. In the languages of interest, L_o is infinite albeit denumerable; it is required that the method of presentation be such that every sentence in L_o appears at some point in the (denumerable) sequence. At some points the learning algorithm presents sentences to the environment (i.e. performs an experiment) and asks the environment to mark it true or false. From time to time the learning algorithm outputs a finite set of axioms for a theory for the model. The algorithm is said to learn the model in the limit if at some finite time the learning algorithm produces a correct set of axioms for the model and does not output any new set of axioms afterwards.

Shapiro has indicated the outline of a learning algorithm which both he and the present author has followed for the specific languages used. To prove the convergence of the algorithm, a few requirements had to be met by the theory to be learned, in addition to its expressibility in L_h.

(3) A computable function h exists such that given any true sentence s, its proof would not need more than h(s) steps. That is, given a false sentence it was decidable in finite time that it was unprovable.

Because of certain differences between the L_o used by Shapiro and the ones used in the present work, another condition was needed.

(4) Given the resolution proof of any sentence in L_o, one could construct a proof of it where at each step of the proof one of the resolvents belong

to L_o. Shapiro's algorithm used the resulting proof tree to isolate erroneous axioms in the theory which proved false sentences to be true. The process asked questions of the environment about the truth of one of the resolvents - hence it had to be in L_o.

On the basis of these and a few other conditions (some of which have been violated in the present work) Shapiro proved that the algorithm learns in the limit. The language and models used in the present work allow one to assume admissibility. It has been proved in this work that in any theory using the languages here, condition (3) above is also met. Condition (4), which was trivially met in the languages used by Shapiro, is somewhat difficult in the present case and its validity had to be proved separately. The violation of some of the other Shapiro conditions also made it necessary to prove separately that the learning algorithm converges.

The next section describes and motivates the language used in the present work.

The Class of Languages

In the first order languages used here for forming descriptions, there are variables, constants and unary function symbols. No binary or higher arity function symbols are used. The work is motivated by the underlying belief that objects are manifested by the results of measurements made on them. Measurements are functions with objects as inputs. Measurements made on different parts of an object are in fact the composition of two measurements - one which isolates a part and one that makes the measurement on the part. Thus instead of saying that the object x is related by "has-as-left-part" to a different object which is related in turn by relation "has-color" to RED, in this language one would say that the object x satisfies the statement color-of(left-part-of(x))=red. More precisely stated, an _atomic sentence_ or _atom_ consists of a term followed by an equals sign followed by a constant. A _term_ is either a variable or a function symbol followed by a term enclosed in parentheses. A _predicate_ is either an atom or consists of a predicate letter of arity n, followed by n terms separated by commas. Such a predicate is called a _defined predicate_. If all the terms occurring in a defined predicate are variables, then the predicate is called a _leftside_. A _sentence_ consists of a Horn clause, whose head is a leftside and whose body contains predicates.

For the purposes of this work, some of the predicate letters are considered to be in a special class: these are called _concept letters_. A leftside formed with a concept letter is called a _definiend_.

Predicates formed by concept letters are the ones which name concepts to be learned. Predicate letters other than concept letters can be generated internally by the learning algorithm to simplify complex descriptions which can not be simplified by the use of concept letters. These are what people often call "features" in pattern recognition parlance. The processes of "feature extraction" and compression will be described in the section on algorithms.

Sentences as described above form the hypothesis language L_h. The observation language L_o consists of _ground sentences_, i.e., those whose head is a definiend and whose body consists entirely of atoms.

A _theory_ will be defined to be a set of sentences and the definition of proofs and the definition of a theory implying a sentence is standard.

Of course, because of the very restricted nature of sentences in this language, proof procedures are much simpler than in the case of general logics. Moreover, the learning algorithm can be proven to learn only such models whose theories obey certain restrictions inside L_h. These restrictions will be discussed when convergence is discussed.

Instead of defining the model of a theory by an abstract mathematical structure, we shall define the word syntactically. Given a theory, a ground sentence P:-B will be called minimal in the theory if it is implied by the theory and no ground sentence P:-A, with A a subset of B, is implied by the theory.

It may be worthwhile at this point to give some examples of the syntactic objects discussed above.

Let us think of binary numbers as lists of binary digits. These lists will have two functions defined on them. The function "end" will isolate the least significant digit and "rest" will be the rest of the list, which is either another list or the constant "none". For exemplifying various processes, let us consider the following theory, where the predicate "num" stands for a binary numeral. In this theory, num is the only concept letter. d1 and d2 are internally generated for compressing theories by feature extraction.

```
num(x):-d1(end(x),d2(rest(x);.....(1)
d1(x):-x=0;.......................(2)
d1(x):-x=1;.......................(3)
d2(x):-x=none;....................(4)
d2(x):-num(x);....................(5)
```

For the purposes of clarifying terms, notice that the head of (1) above is the only leftside that is a definiend. Atoms occur in the body of (2),(3), and (4). The bodies of (1) and (5) consist only of defined predicates - although in general a body can contain both atoms and defined predicates. In this theory the terms that occur do not have deep nestings. But they do occur in ground sentences implied by the theory, e.g., in

```
num(x):-end(x)=0,end(rest(x))=1,end(rest(rest(x)))=1(rest(rest
        (rest(x)))=none, font(x)=bold,color(end(x))=red;
```

The above ground sentence is not minimal in the theory. The following one, whose body is a subset of the above, is.

```
num(x):-end(x)=0,end(rest(x))=1,end(rest(rest(x)))=1,rest(rest
        (rest(x)))=none;
```

Some other members of the model of the theory are:

```
num(x):-end(x)=1,rest(x)=none;
num(x):-end(x)=1,end(rest(x))=0;rest(rest(x))=none;
```

and infinitely many more. The theory has an infinite model because of the recursions involved.

Before going on to describe the learning algorithm, we proceed to show informally that given a ground sentence one can predict how long a proof of it from a theory is going to be, as required by Shapiro's requirement discussed above. Formal proof of this and other claims will be published elsewhere [13].

Recall that all the sentences in the theory are Horn clauses in which only variables occur in the head, which is always a defined predicate. As we shall indicate later, in all theories learned by the algorithm all variables that occur in the body of a clause also occur in the head. Also, in all resolutions, the positive literal resolved, being a definiend, has its variables replaced by terms, and so no unification decreases the nesting of any term. Moreover, no resolution can decrease the number of literals in the body. Given a ground sentence to prove, one thus knows that if a clause is generated by the proof process which has either more literals or terms of greater degree of nesting than the body of the clause to be proved, then that clause can not be used to prove the given ground sentence. The number of possible clauses with limited size of the body and limited nestings of the terms being finite, all proofs of length greater than a fixed computable length will involve clauses with greater size than the ones to be proved, and either a proof will be found within this size and nesting or will not be found at all.

We also have to show that if a ground sentence can be proved from the theory, then it can be proved in such a way that at every step of the proof, one of the resolvents is a ground sentence. This is proved exhibiting an algorithm which, given any proof, can convert it into a proof of the desired form. The major point to the algorithm is as follows: Let us assume that at some step of the proof, one resolves the clauses A:-B and C:-D where a substitution instance of C occurs in B, yielding the resolvent A:-E. Let a certain defined predicate X occur in D and hence some substitution instance of it would occur in E. Let all steps of the proof after this one be such that at least one of the resolvents is a ground sentence. Since the last step of the proof is a ground sentence, X must be the substitution instance of the head of some ground sentence which is used as a resolvent. The algorithm modifies the proof by resolving this ground sentence with C:-D first, removing X from E. The process is repeated as often as necessary to get rid of defined predicates yielding a proof with the desired property.

This algorithm yields proofs in the form required by Shapiro to initiate a process called "contradiction back-trace" for what is known as "credit assignment" in the field, i.e. to find out which sentences in a theory lead to proofs of false sentences. If a fact defines a certain ground sentence to be false and a proof for it exists from a theory, then the axiom to blame is found as follows. At each step of the proof the algorithm asks of the environment whether the ground resolvent is true (the sentence being in L_o, it is legal to ask the question). If it is false, one of the axioms used in its proof must be false. Else the axioms involved in the proof of the other, non-ground resolvent must be false. The algorithm asks the same question at the different steps of the "guilty" tree till it isolates the false axiom.

The learning algorithm described in the next section will use this algorithm as well as the check on provability described above.

The Algorithm and its Convergence

As has been mentioned before, the algorithm described here does not use any previous knowledge about the language used. Instead it learns the language from the facts presented to it to the extent it sees the need for the learning, avoiding to the extent feasible having to learn about terms unnecessary to developing the theory. Thus at any point in its operation, the learning program's knowledge has two components: the knowledge of the language and the theory developed so far. The structure of the theory has been discussed already. The knowledge of the language associates with each concept letter a set of atoms which occur in some positive examples of the concept (i.e., facts with the concept at the head and marked true).

There are several major procedures used by the learning algorithm. the first one is:

(1) ADD: This procedure is invoked when the program encounters a positive example of a concept which is not implied by the current theory. It adds to the language by associating with the predicate at the head of the fact all the atoms in the body of the fact (unless the atom was already there). At the first occurrence of a positive example of the concept the concept is associated with all the atoms in the body of the example.

ADD also modifies the theory. At the first occurrence of a positive example of the concept, the theory is augmented by P:-, where P is the definiend corresponding to the concept. The body of the sentence is empty, indicating that "everything is a P." Else it augments the theory by adding the Sentences P:-A, where A is one of the atoms just added to the language. There is one such sentence added for each new atom.

(The reader will note that the theory learned by the algorithm has a lot of disjunctions. But the disjuncts are not the positive examples themselves, as in rote learning. Rather the disjuncts are alternative generalizations of the examples.)

The next major procedure is

(2) SHRINK: This one is invoked when it is found that the theory implies a ground sentence which has been marked false. First the algorithm locates the (or one of the) sentences at fault in the theory (asking questions of the environment as described in the previous section). As the algorithm below shows, the culprit sentence is removed from the theory if its body contains any defined predicate (since it was a generalization (vide ultra) of sentences already in the theory and has been found to be untrue). If the culprit is a ground sentence, then SHRINK adds to (i.e., forms the conjunction with) the body one of the atoms in the language associated with the predicates at its head. In doing so care is taken that the resulting sentence is not implied by any other sentence of the theory.

It can be shown that if the model is consistent (i.e. if no false ground sentence has a body which contains the body of a true ground sentence with the same head), then the process of shrink excludes at least one false ground sentence without excluding any known true ground sentence whose body is contained in the language associated with its head. If SHRINK excludes a true ground sentence than ADD enhances the language by the new atoms in the ground sentence so as to include this sentence. Any false sentence implied by these are then removed by SHRINK. Given any finite model, an alternation of SHRINK and ADD can thus produce a theory consistent with it.

However, the resulting theory can be unnecessarily complex. Moreover, since these processes only learn theories with ground sentences, no infinite model can be explained with such theories. this drawback can be rectified with the following procedure.

(3) GENERALIZE: This process is invoked only after the two previous processes working in two cooperating loops have resulted in a theory with ground sentences explaining all the known facts. GENERALIZE brought into action if the previous loops have added to or shrunk the ground part of the theory in their current invocation. At this point, the algorithm looks for

all pairs of sentences in the theory in which the body of the first contains an instance of the body of the second. In this case, the involved part of the body of the first is replaced by the substitution instance of the head of the second. We shall illustrate the process in the next section.

One other process is invoked for compression of the sentences of the theory. It is called DREAM and is merely a generalization of an application of the distributive law of Boolean logic and can probably best be explained by examples. DREAM is responsible for introducing the internally generated feature names.

A skeleton of the algorithm follows.

```
Begin
  F+:=ϕ;F =ϕ;L:=ϕ;T:=ϕ;
  Do forever
    begin
      read a fact <M,v> and place M in Fv;
      FLAG:-false;
      while there is a MεF+ not implied by T or
            there is a MεF_ implied by T do
        begin
          while there is an MεF_ implied by T do
            begin
              locate Q:-BεT responsible for error;
              if B contains a defined predicate
                then T = T -{Q:=B}
                else begin T:=SHRINK (T,L,Q:-B); flag:=true end
            end
          if there is P:-AεF+ not implied by T
            then (T,L):=ADD(T,L,P:-A)
        end;
      if FLAG then for every pair of sentences in T allowing
        GENERALIZE, apply it, provided no MεF_ is implied by
        the sentence added;
      apply DREAM to all applicable cases
    end
  end
end.
```

As was indicated during the discussion of Shapiro's algorithm, the main loop works infinitely, verifying the current theory continuously, changing it only when facts demand it. The point to be made here is that the algorithm is such that as long as a theory exists in the language, it can be found in a finite period of time and no modification is needed after that.

The main loop of the algorithm consists of two other loops, the first working with ADD and SHRINK and the other working with GENERALIZE and DREAM. It has already been indicated that the first loop always terminates with a ground theory for the finite set of facts currently available in F_+ and F_-. The second loop only introduces those generalizations that do not imply any known false facts - it does not remove any true known facts. It is possible that the generalizations introduced will explain true facts as well as false facts as the outer loop continues. It can, however, be shown that in the kind of infinite models that theories of this class of languages can express, sentences are bound to occur which lead to generalizations which explain only the true facts, provided that if any sentence of the theory contains two defined predicates in its body, the two predicates model disjoint sets of ground sentences. Thus the algorithm does learn theories of infinite models in the limit in this restricted class of theories. Finite models, of course, are learned as soon as all the minimal true sentences are constructed by ADD and SHRINK.

Some Examples and Discussion of Efficiency

In this section we propose to illustrate how the learning algorithm would construct a theory like the one exemplified by equations (1)-(5) in section 2 and to discuss our present understanding of the efficience of the algorithm. Unfortunately, a complete run-down of an example would be prohibitively long. We shall, therefore, describe some specific steps in its action to illustrate the operation of the procedures discussed in the previous section. Also, to simplify the presentation a "compassionate" environment will present well-chosen facts in a convenient sequence.

Let the initial fact be

num(x):-end(x)=0,rest(x)=empty.

Then L contains the order pair

<num, {end(x)=0,rest(x)=empty}>

and the theory contains the lone sentence

num(x):-.

This is done by ADD. The next example could be marked false, with num(x) at the head and some nonsense as the body. SHRINK would then change the theory to the following set of sentences:

{num(x):-end(x)=0;num(x):-rest(x)=empty}

One could then have a false fact with num(x) at the head and the body containing end(x)=0 and some nonsense. This would remove end(x):=0 from the theory but would not replace it by its conjunction with rest(x)=empty since that conjunction would be implied by the other sentence in the theory. However, if this false fact was followed by another containing rest(x)=empty and some nonsense, then we would have the theory

{num(x):=end(x)=0,rest(x)=empty}.

A similar exercise starting with num(x):-end(x)=1,rest(x)=empty (invoking ADD once more, followed by more calls to SHRINK) would add the sentence

{num(x):-end(x)=1,rest(x)=empty}

to the theory. At this point DREAM would convert the theory to:

{num(x):-dl(end(x)),rest(x)=empty;dl(x):-x=0,dl(x):-x=1}

by taking end(x)=1 and end(x)=0 in the two previous sentences and "factoring them out" into two new sentences, after replacing "end(x)" by "x".

By the time the sentence

num(x):-dl(end(x)),dl(end(rest(x))),rest(rest(x))=empty

has been added to the theory, GENERALIZE would unify the last two conjuncts in the body with the body of the first sentence in the theory above to yield

num(x):-dl(end(x)),num(rest(x))

We shall leave the rest of the construction, with one more call to DREAM, to the imagination of the reader. At the present, no exact calculations have been made of the efficiency of the algorithm. Actually, there are two distinct phenomena that affect its time efficiency. On the one hand, there is the limit to the number of times the three successive inner loops to the program would be entered to make the theory compatible with the currently available examples. Calculation of the average efficiency would be difficult and perhaps even meaningless in the absence of a believable statistical property of the source of the examples. One is thus forced to look at the worst case complexity, at least as far as the inner loops are concerned. At a first glance, our conjecture is that the time complexity would be exponential in the number of atoms that appear in the language conjecture L. So the overall efficiency of the program really depends on whether it can develop the theory as soon as it has gathered the minimal number of atoms the theory needs.

The answer to this latter question depends very heavily on the second aspect of the efficiency, to wit, how many times the main loop will have to be entered before the correct theory can be discovered by the algorithm. Unfortunately, the answer to the question is entirely dependent on the property of the input sequence. It is our conjecture looking at some example theories that one can surmise for each theory a minimal set of examples which suffices to make the algorithm discover the theory. A "compassionate teacher", of course, could show these in a correct sequence resulting in a fast convergence. But the real question is what happens when the teacher is NOT compassionate (we are entirely neglecting "noise", i.e. the effect of a dishonest teacher!). Here one can only make a probabilistic estimate of how late it will before the crucial examples are presented to the algorithm.

Presently an experiment is being carried out on this matter using a Markov model as source of examples. It is intended that this model will also be used in the theoretical estimation of the average efficiency of the overall algorithm.

Acknowledgements

The work described in this paper was supported by the National Science Foundation under grant DCR-8504223 to the Saint Joseph's University. The preparation of the manuscript was supported by the Saint Joseph's University as a part of the contribution to research in Machine Learning undertaken in cooperation with the Benjamin Franklin Partnership with the Commonwealth of Pennsylvania and with Expert Systems International, Inc.

Reference

1. Pennypacker, J., An Elementary Information Processing Program for Object Recognition, Report no. SRC 30-1-63, Case Institute of Technology, Cleveland, OH (1963).
2. Banerji, R.B., Theory of Problem Solving: An Approach to Artificial Intelligence, American Elsevir, NY (1969).
3. Cohen, R., Confucius: A Structural Pattern Recognition and Learning System, Proceedings of the International Conference on Cybernetics and Society, p. 1443, (Kyoto, 1978).
4. Sammut, C., Learning Concepts by Performing Experiments, Ph.D. Dissertation, University of New South Wales, Kingston (1981).
5. Banerji, R.B., The Logic of Learning: A Basis for Pattern Recognition and for Improvement of Performance, Advances in Computers, 24, 178 (1985), Academic Press, NY
6. Carbonell, J., Michalski, R., and Mitchell, T. (Eds.), Machine Learning, Tioga Press, Palo Alto (1983).
7. Carbonell, J., Michalski, R., and Mitchell, T. (Eds.), Machine Learning II, William Kaufman, CA (1985).
8. Shapiro, E., Induction Inference of Theories from Facts, Technical Report No. 193, Computer Science Department, Yale University, New Haven, CN (1981).
9. Gold, E.M., Language Identification in the Limit, Information and

Control, 10, 447 (1965).
10. Winston, P., Learning Structural Descriptions from Examples, Report No. AI-TR-231, Artifical Intelligence Lab., Massachussetts Institute of Technology, Cambridge, MA (1970).
11. Hayes-Roth, R., Collected Papers on the Learning and Recognition of Structured Patterns, Department of Computer Science, Carnegie-Mellon University, Pittsburgh, Pa (1975).
12. Vere, S., Induction of Concepts in the Predicate Calculus, Department of Information Engineering, University of Illinois at Chicago Circle (1975).
13. Banerji, R.B., An Algorithm for Learning Theories in a Growing Language, Report from the Laboratory for Research in Computer Learning, Saint Joseph's University, Philadelphia, Pa (1987).

INTEGRATING EBL AND SBL APPROACHES TO KNOWLEDGE BASE REFINEMENT

F.Bergadano, A.Giordana and L.Saitta

Dipartimento di Informatica, Universita' di Torino, C.so Svizzera 185 10149 - Torino, Italy Tel. 39-11-755677

ABSTRACT

In this paper we present a methodology for knowledge base refinement in noisy environments. The knowledge is represented in two separate bodies: a knowledge base (KB) describing the typical cues found in the phenomenon and a deformation theory giving the possible modifications of the objects to be considered. An algorithm for Explanation Based Learning (EBL) in incomplete theories is used for refining the knowledge base KB, by using the deformation theory in order to find the explanations. On the contrary, Similarity Based Learning (SBL) is advocated for refining and improving the degradation theory itself. The resulting procedure is able to integrate the two approaches and allows the system to achieve better and better performances incrementally.

1. INTRODUCTION

The relevant time cost for building a high performance expert system is not only spent in acquiring the initial knowledge base but is also spent in a refining phase, lasting until satisfactory performances are obtained. In fact, it is often quite easy to define an initial kernel of knowledge capturing the most relevant phenomena of the domain, whereas it may become tedious and difficult to add new rules for taking into account borderline and exceptional phenomena and for optimizing the knowledge base efficiency.

In several domains automated learning is the only reasonable approach for dealing with the above mentioned problem. The literature offers today examples of applications of learning techniques to the knowledge base refinement problem [1-5], and to the compilation of shallow knowledge starting from deep models [6-7]. A fundamental technique used in solving this task is Explanation Based Learning (EBL), described, for example, by Mitchell, Keller and Kedar-Cabelli [8] and by DeJong and Mooney [9].

This paper addresses the problem of refining a knowledge base containing rules for classifying an instance of a concept starting from its symbolic description. This is a crucial problem in important tasks such as scene analysis, pattern interpretation and medical diagnosis.

The setting of the problem can be described as follows: let us consider a set of concepts and let us assume to have a knowledge base of decision rules, given by a teacher or automatically acquired, allowing a subset of all the possible instances of the concepts to be correctly classified. The basic assumption is that this knowledge base should capture the most relevant and reliable aspects of the concepts and, therefore, the instances classified by it can be considered as "typical", for instance, in the sense defined by Zadeh [10].

The rules contained in the knowledge base give an initial, prototypical definition of the concepts. However, in real domains, many instances of the concepts will not exactly correspond to the typical ones, because of noise and of intrinsic concept variability, and then they will fail to be recognized.

On the other hand, deviations from standard instances cannot usually be totally unpredictable and a domain knowledge is often available, on the basis of which at least some broad classes of deformations, possibly occurring in the instances, can be expected. These predictions, collected as a set of transformation rules, will constitute a **'deformation theory'**. Usually this theory can only be very general, based on the a-priori knowledge of the concepts and of the domain. The precise conditions under which a given deformation rule can be applied are unknown, and the assumption of having a perfect theory as in [8] is not realistic.

Given this scenario, a large room for classification improvements through learning is left. In particular, a sequence of non typical examples can be presented to the knowledge base together with their correct classification. By applying the deformation theory, an explanation of why a given example was misclassified can be built up and the knowledge base can be updated accordingly, by remembering what particular deformations actually occurred. On the other hand, the deformation theory itself can be modified and made more specific, by analyzing the particular context in which the deformation rules have been used in the given examples.

Hence we developed an integrated EBL and SBL method, which, as mentioned before, allows both the knowledge base to be refined and made more robust, and the deformation theory to be improved and made more specific. In this way it is possible to obtain a self-adaptive system which starts working on simple tasks of a given domain and becomes capable to deal with more and more complex tasks of the same domain.

Finally, the necessity to cope with imperfect theories led to the introduction of statistical techniques to be coupled with the logical reasoning performed in the explanation process.

Methodologies for Intelligent Systems
Z. W. Ras and M. Zemankova, Editors

2. KNOWLEDGE REPRESENTATION: CLASSIFICATION RULES AND DEFORMATION THEORY

The concept instances to be classified are described as a collection of elementary objects (which are called *primitive*), each one characterized by a vector of linguistic or numeric attributes. This type of representation is quite usual in the domains of pattern recognition and scene analysis and has already been used by the authors in other papers on related subjects [11,12].

Let $H^{(0)} = \{h_i | 1 \leq i \leq M\}$ be the set of the considered concepts. The knowledge base, used to recognize their instances, consists of a set of **classification rules**, expressed in the form

$$\phi(x_1, \ldots, x_n) \xrightarrow{w} H \tag{1}$$

where H is a subset of concepts belonging to $H^{(0)}$ and $\phi(x_1, \ldots, x_n)$ is a formula of a first order logic based language L. If the formula ϕ holds in a given pattern f, then, according to rule (1), f is an instance of one of the concepts belonging to H. The weight w [11] is a measure of the reliability of the rule, estimating the probability that f is an instance of H, given that the precondition ϕ holds. The use of weak implication allows the knowledge base to neutralize the effect of incorrect rules which can be added during the learning process. This point will be clarified in Section 5.

For the sake of exemplification, let us consider the set of concepts $H^{(0)}$ = {car, truck, train} in a block's world like problem (see Fig. 1). Further, let's assume a knowledge base of classification rules such as (1), is given:

$$rectangle(x) \wedge small(x) \wedge \neg square(x) \longrightarrow \{\text{car, train}\} \tag{2}$$

$$rectangle(x) \wedge big(x) \wedge \neg square(x) \longrightarrow \{\text{train, truck}\} \tag{3}$$

$$rectangle(x) \wedge triangle(y) \wedge above(y,x) \longrightarrow \{\text{car}\} \tag{4}$$

$$square(x) \wedge (big(x) \vee (square(y) \wedge inside(y,x))) \longrightarrow \{\text{car, truck}\} \tag{5}$$

$$square(x) \wedge rectangle(y) \wedge right\_of(y,x) \longrightarrow \{\text{car}\} \tag{6}$$

The instances of Fig. 1 are "typical" in the sense that they are consistent with each one of the rules (2)-(6), i.e. they satisfy a rule antecedent $\phi(x_1, \cdots, x_n)$ if and only if they are instances of a concept belonging

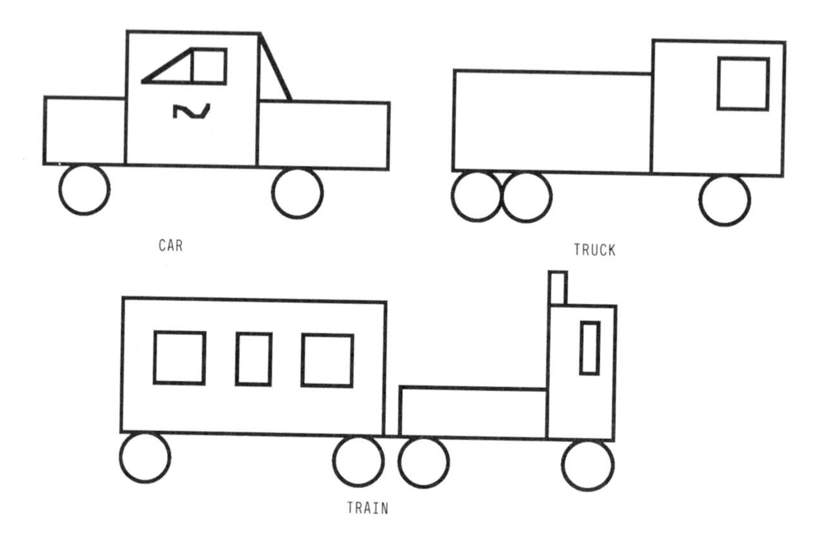

Fig. 1 - Typical instances of the concepts $H^{(0)}$ = {car, truck, train}

to the rule consequent H. Rules (2)-(6) could be seen as given by an expert or automatically learned from a set of examples of the concepts in $H^{(0)}$ = {car,truck,train}.

The semantics of the language L is defined starting from a set of functions associated to the basic predicates. In particular, for every predicate $P(x_1, \ldots, x_k) \in L$ we associate a function $f_P(\mathbf{A}(x_1),\ldots,\mathbf{A}(x_k))$, evaluating the truth value $\mu(P(x_1, \ldots, x_k))$. The value f_p is computed on the basis of the attribute values of the objects in the symbolic description of the instances. If we choose a continuous valued logic, then $\mu: L \longrightarrow [0,1]$, whereas, for a binary logic $\mu: L \longrightarrow \{0,1\}$. A continuous valued logic has actually been used in [12,13], where a technique for combining evidences and weights has been supplied. Nevertheless the algorithms proposed in this paper do not depend on the particular semantics of the language L and then the binary case will be considered for the sake of simplicity. For example, consider the predicate "big" used in some of the rules (2)-(6), and suppose that the instances of Fig. 1 are represented in a symbolic description giving the shape, area and coordinates of every object (i.e. geometric figure) composing the pattern. Then, in the case of binary logic, the function f_{big} could be defined as:

$$f_{big}(<shape_x, area_x, coordinates_x>) = \begin{cases} 0 & \text{if } area_x < 10 \\ 1 & \text{if } area_x \geq 10 \end{cases}$$

It should be noted that, by using rules of the form (1), the following implication holds:

$$\frac{\phi_1 \xrightarrow{w_1} H_1,\ \phi_2 \xrightarrow{w_2} H_2}{\phi_1 \wedge \phi_2 \xrightarrow{w} H_1 \cap H_2} \tag{7}$$

In (7) the range of values assumed by the weight w depends on w_1 and w_2. Implication (7) states that a narrower (more precise) classification may be obtained, for a given pattern, starting from broader ones. In the following we will assume that, for typical patterns, an unambiguous, correct classification may be reached using implication (7), possibly more than once.

The second important knowledge source of the system is the **deformation theory;** it is not directly related to the classification process, and describes how an instance can be modified because of noise, errors or differences which can occur among instances of the same class. This kind of knowledge is represented as a set of deformation rules of the type:

$$G: \quad \psi(x_1, \ldots, x_m) \Longrightarrow z_1 = g_1(y_1,\ldots,y_k)\ ;\ \cdots\ ;\ z_r = g_r(y_1, \cdots, y_k) \tag{8}$$

being g_i operators describing elementary transformations among objects, such as composition, decomposition, substitution and so on; $\psi(x_1, \ldots, x_m)$ is a formula of L describing a precondition which must hold in the concept instance in order to apply the transformation. The transformation consists in substituting the set of objects $\{y_1, \cdots, y_k\}$ in the pattern with the set of objects $\{z_1, \cdots, z_r\}$.

In the context of the example of Fig. 1, two deformation rules could be

$$G1: \quad trapezoid(x) \Longrightarrow z_1 = edge(x),\ z_2 = body(x) \tag{9}$$

$$G2: \quad trapezoid(x) \Longrightarrow z_1 = make\_straight(x) \tag{10}$$

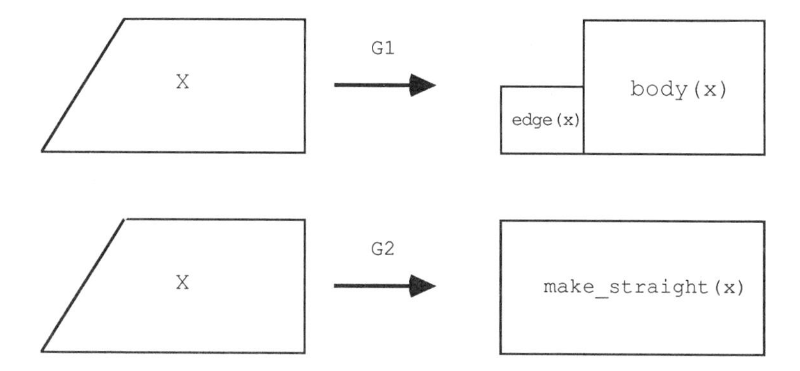

Fig. 2 - graphical description of deformation rules (9) and (10)

where *make_straight*, *edge* and *body* are functions which perform, in the symbolic description, the transformations described in Fig. 2.

3. EXPLANATION BASED LEARNING

During the normal operation of the system, the knowledge base (KB) of production rules is used to classify new instances of the concepts. Though, when an instance f of a concept h has not been correctly classified, or has not been sufficiently disambiguated (i.e h is still confused in a set of classes H), an explanation based learning phase is activated. This process takes place in two steps: explanation and extraction of new knowledge. The explanation step is aimed at showing why the instance f could not be classified and how it can be transformed in order to solve the problem. First of all, three sets of rules in *KB* can be distinguished, after they have been applied to f:

- A set $R_T = \{ \phi_i \xrightarrow{w} H_i |\ h \in H_i \ and \ \mu(\phi_i) = 1\}$. The rules in R_T are those which correctly succeeded in classifying f as an instance of a class in H_i.
- A set $R_F = \{ \phi_j \xrightarrow{w} H_j |\ h \in H_j \ and \ \mu(\phi_j) = 0\}$. The rules in R_F failed in classifying f, but they should have succeeded.
- A set $R_E = \{\phi_k \xrightarrow{w} H_k |\ h \notin H_k \ and \ \mu(\phi_k) = 1\}$. The rules in R_E incorrectly classified f and should not have succeeded.

The goal of this step is to find one or more deformation rules that, when applied to the objects of the concept instance, transform it into a new one such that:

(a) All the rules in R_T are still verified.
(b) As many rules in R_F as possible become verified.
(c) Hopefully all the rules in R_E fail. This condition will be considered as a secondary goal, not mandatory, because contradiction is accepted, owing to the use of weak implication.

The algorithm to perform this task is organized as a state space search where:

- The states are pattern descriptions.
- The operators are the deformation rules available to the system.
- the initial state is the initial description of the instance f, which was not classified correctly.
- "Goal" states must satisfy the conditions (a),(b),(c) given above.

If we consider the example of classification rules (2)-(6) and deformation rules (9) and (10), we would get a search tree such as the one given in Fig. 3. Suppose we want to classify the instance of "car" given in the root n_0 of the tree. None of the preconditions of rules (2)-(6) is verified by this pattern (since there are no rectangles and no squares), thus R_T and R_E are empty and this instance cannot be classified. On the contrary, rules (2),(4),(5),(6) should be verified because "car" is included in their right hand side, and thus they belong to R_F. These contents of R_T, R_E and R_F are written near the root node of the tree in Fig. 3.

The first step in the explanation based learning process will consist in the expansion of this search tree, where the operators, in our example, are the operators (9) and (10). For instance, by applying transformation rule G1 to $n0$ (where x has been bound to b) we will generate the pattern in node $n4$, since the trapezoid b has been split in edge(b)=c and body(b)=d. Classification rules (2) and (5) can now be correctly verified by binding x to c and d, respectively. The other rules remain in R_F. Similar considerations can be made for the other nodes. The contents of R_T, R_E and R_F are given, for each node, in Fig. 3. Node $n6$ can be considered as a goal node since all the rules whose consequent contains "car" are verified, and no other is.

In general, the search is supposed to be guided by heuristics such as "better nodes have more rules in R_T", "better nodes have no rules in R_E", "prefer simpler transformations" and so on.

The output of this step, if successful, will be one or more sequences of operators which transform the original pattern into a goal node. In our example, a solution could be t=<G1(a),G2(b)>.

From a transformation t, which explains a particular misclassification (or insufficient classification), two types of knowledge can be extracted: a set of new rules $\{\psi'_i \xrightarrow{w} H'_i \mid h \in H'_i\}$ which can correctly classify the original instance, and more specific deformation rules which can be more efficiently and reliably used in searching for an explanation in further instances affected by the same type of deformation. The refinement of the deformation theory will be the topic of the next section; here we will discuss the extraction of the first type of knowledge.

Given an instantiated deformation rule:

$$g_1(a): \quad \psi(a) \longrightarrow z=f(a) \tag{11}$$

belonging to solution of step 1, and a classification rule

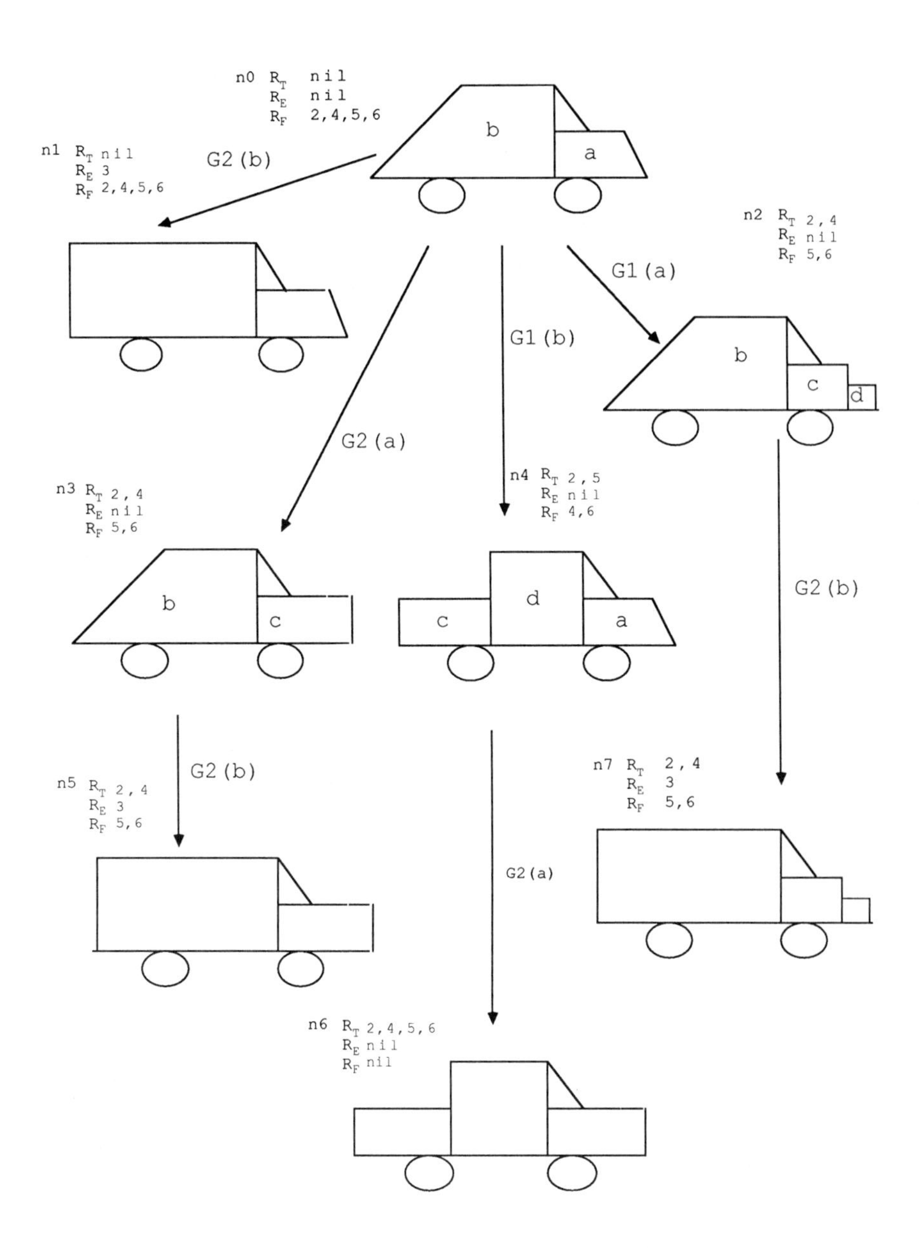

Fig. 3. Search tree for rules (2)-(6), deformations (9)-(10), and instance of car given in the root.

$$\phi(y) \longrightarrow H \tag{12}$$

belonging to R_F in the initial pattern, but belonging to R_T in the goal node, due to the application of (11), a new classification rule can be learned:

$$\phi(f(a)) \wedge \psi(a) \longrightarrow H \tag{13}$$

If, in (11), the object "a" was generated by other transformations in the solution sequence, then these transformations should also be included in (13). Rules (11)-(13) can be easily generalized to the case of more than one variable. As an example, consider again Fig. 3. Given classification rule (2) and the instantiated deformation rule G1(b), the following rule can be learned:

$$trapezoid(x) \wedge rectangle(edge(x)) \wedge small(edge(x)) \wedge \neg square(edge(x)) \longrightarrow \{car,\ train\} \tag{14}$$

Given rule (4) and deformation G2(a), the following can be learned:

$$trapezoid(x) \wedge rectangle(make\_straight(x)) \wedge triangle(y) \wedge above(y,make\_straight(x)) \longrightarrow \{car\} \tag{15}$$

One more thing should be mentioned: suppose that the following two rules

$$\phi_1(y) \longrightarrow H_1 \tag{16}$$

$$\phi_2(y) \longrightarrow H_2 \tag{17}$$

belong to R_F in the initial pattern, and are verified in the goal node because of the application of the same deformation rule (11). Then the rule to be learned must contain the fact that the transformation is the same:

$$\psi(a) \wedge \phi_1(f(a)) \wedge \phi_2(f(a)) \longrightarrow H_1 \cap H_2 \tag{18}$$

As an example, consider rules (2) and (5) and transformation G1(b), then the following rule can be learned:

$$\begin{aligned} &trapezoid(x) \wedge square(body(x)) \wedge big(body(x)) \wedge \\ &rectangle(edge(x)) \wedge small(edge(x)) \wedge \neg square(edge(x)) \longrightarrow \{car\} \end{aligned} \tag{19}$$

Some of the rules (14),(15) and (19) can be added to the knowledge base KB of classification rules, and will be able to classify modified car patterns similar to the one given in the root node of Fig. 3.

Some comparisons must be made between the classic EBL method [8] and the one given here, since there are some substantial differences. The EBL described by Mitchell, Keller and Kedar-Cabelli is based on a monotonic deduction process and the theory is assumed to be perfect; then every explanation found is good by definition and then all the alternative explanations are considered equivalent from the point of view of the reliability. This is not the case here; the explanation process is potentially non-monotonic, since the deformation rules change the pattern and may invalidate the conditions used in different explanations. This process cannot be a simple deduction, and is considered as a problem solving activity, where these kinds of constraints are taken into account. For this reason, the degradation theory is kept separate from the knowledge base KB.

On the other hand, the theory is imperfect, and many explanations can be found for the same pattern. Some of them might be wrong in the sense that the same explanation might lead to an erroneous classification for a different instance. This happens because the preconditions of the degradation rules are not sufficiently precise and then the rules might be used improperly. In the following we will consider as "good" the explanations which obtain a significant statistical confirmation in other examples. "Good" degradation rules will be the ones which generate "good" explanations. In the next section we suggest a method for improving the degradation theory in this sense.

4. DEFORMATION THEORY REFINEMENT

The refinement of the deformation rules is a crucial point for increasing the performances of the explanation based learning process. In fact, a good deformation theory should allow good explanations to be found quickly and reliably. For this reason, the deformations rules should be powerful and well directed by strong preconditions stating when and how they can be applied.

EBL essentially deduces from the theory what is already known and transforms it into a form which is more explicit and usable. Therefore, EBL alone cannot be used to improve the theory itself. Nevertheless, EBL generates examples ("good" and "wrong") of theory applications over the instances. Such examples could be used by an SBL algorithm to induce a stronger theory. Here we try to formalize this problem in terms of learning from examples and counterexamples.

Let t be a deformation; we want to learn a precondition ψ such that when ψ is verified, then t is applicable. The pattern descriptions where t has been applied during the EBL process are examples of t and all the others are counterexamples.

Nevertheless, the problem is not so simple and must be specified more precisely. Since, in this framework, the concepts to be learned by the SBL algorithm are the transformations applicable to the patterns, a first point involves the selection of the transformations which are really representative. A generic deformation $t=<G_1, \cdots, G_n>$, found in the explanation process, could be very complex, due to the random occurrence of several independent and simpler deformations. If every generic deformation t had to be considered, then the number of concepts to be learned would be too high. A reasonable choice is to consider as concepts only the groups of elementary deformations $T_i=<G_1, \cdots, G_n>$ which have a significant statistical occurrence, either alone or inside some more complex transformation.

A second point involves the selection of the examples and of the counterexamples of a given transformation T_i. Obviously, the patterns where T_i has been applied successfully are examples of T_i, but there exist also many cases where T_i has not been applied because of the limited search effort in the explanation process, but would have given good results. On the other hand, all the cases where T_i led to wrong or incomplete explanations are counterexamples of T_i. Such a set of examples and counterexamples would be of unmanageable size and has to be restricted. In our choice, the examples are the patterns where T_i has been actually applied and the counterexamples are the other patterns, where explanations not involving T_i have been chosen. This strategy relies on the assumption that good explanations must be repetitive and have a statistically significant occurrence. Therefore, if a transformation T_1 is used more frequently (in similar cases) than another transformation T_2, then T_1 is considered to be better than T_2.

The last point involves the choice of the induction algorithm. This task is characterized by the following requirements:

a) The concepts are not mutually exclusive, i.e. there are examples of more than one deformation at the same time.

b) It is essential that the precondition ψ_i of T_i is selected by taking into account the statistical relevance of the set of examples covered by ψ_i.

c) It is necessary to accept that, in the general case, the concept discrimination rules ψ_i be approximate, i.e. cover also a fraction of the counterexamples. This is due to the statistical nature of the problem.

This is a precise multi-concept induction problem, and any appropriate algorithm could be used. We propose the algorithm adopted by the BIMBO system (described in [11]), which has been especially designed fo concept acquisition in applications strictly related to the one described here.

5. LONG TERM KNOWLEDGE REFINEMENT PROCESS

In the previous sections we have shown how Explanation Based Learning and Similarity Based Learning can cooperate to refine both a knowledge base KB and a deformation theory at the same time. Here we will present some considerations on the long term behavior of a knowledge base maintained using the described techniques, and, in particular, we will analyze how weak implication helps in attributing relevance to the most reliable rules and to neutralize the others.

Let the initial knowledge base KB be given by a human expert, or acquired in some other way, and let a deformation theory be available to formalize the most elementary deformations of the pattern. Then the experimentation begins on a task of the domain and a set of samples is proposed for classification. If the response of the knowledge base is successful, then only the weights of the rules which have been activated is updated according to the statistical contribute of the new examples; otherwise, the following steps are performed:

a) The weights of the rules in the set R_T and of the set R_E are updated (the first ones are raised and the second ones are lowered).

b) An explanation is searched as sketched in Section 3. It may happen that no explanation can be found because the theory in not sufficiently developed and/or the search space is too large.

c) In the case that the explanation t is found, new rules to update KB are generated and the concept instance is recorded as an example of the deformations in t.

When a set of explanations which is large enough has been recorded, a step of theory refinement is made and new, more specific deformation rules can be added to the deformation theory. The rules which are more specific and which occur more frequently will receive a higher score, in order to privilege their use in the first phase of the explanation process (see Section 3). Then a new phase of experimentation, using the refined theory for obtaining new explanations, follows. Note that the new theory has now more chances of generating an explanation for some of the cases previously unsolved. Moreover, the rules which are not robust, added to KB owing to weak explanations, will gradually receive lower weights, whereas, on the other hand, the system will be forced to generate alternative rules for resolving the cases which were not previously classified.

6. CONCLUSIONS

A method has been described for refining a knowledge base of rules which perform the classification of concept instances, using a theory which describes the elementary deformations that can be found in a concept example with respect to what has been called its "typicality". The novelty of the method consists in the integrated use of explanation based and similarity based learning techniques which allow the refinement both of the knowledge base and of the deformation theory.

This method has been developed thinking to applications in the domain of pattern recognition and of scene analysis and is being integrated into the complex system BIMBO [11] especially designed for for this kind of domains.

The explanation based technique described in Section 3 has been already experimented into a system for pattern classification presented in [12,13], where the results obtained for speech patterns are also presented. The deformation theory refinement, based on the use of the BIMBO system, has been already applied to a complex task of speech recognition in which rules describing how the word utterance can be deformed with respect to the standard one, have been automatically learned.

REFERENCES

[1] - R.Davis: "Interactive Transfer of Expertise, Acquisition of New Inference Rules" Artificial Intelligence 12, 121-157, 1979.

[2] - A. Ginsberg, S. Weiss, P. Politakis: "SEEK2: A Generalized Approach to Automatic Knowledge Base Refinement", *Proc. IJCAI*, 367-374, 1985.

[3] - J.C. Schlimmer and R.H. Granger, Jr. :"Incremental Learning from Noisy Data", *Machine learning*, 1, 317-354, 1986.

[4] - R.Rada:"Gradualness Facilitates Knowledge Refinement", IEEE Trans. Pattern Analysis and Machine Intelligence, *PAMI-7*, 523-530 (1985).

[5] - R.G.Smith, H.A. Winston, T.M. Mitchell, B.G. Buchanan: "Representation and Use of Explicit Justifications for Knowledge Base Refinement", *Proc. IJCAI*, 673-680, 1985.

[6] - J.E. Laird, P.S. Rosenbloom and A. Newell: "Chunking in Soar: the Anatomy of a General Learning Mechanism", *Machine learning*, 1, 11-46, (1986).

[7] - W. Van de Velde: "Learning Heuristics in Second Generation Expert Systems", *Proc. 6th. Int. Workshop on Expert Systems & their Applications*, Avignon (France) 1986.

[8] - T.M.Mitchell, R.M.Keller, S.J.Kedar-Cabelli: "Explanation Based Generalization: a Unifying View", *Machine learning, 1*, 47-80 (1986).

[9] - G. DeJong and R. Mooney: "Explanation-Based Learning: An Alternative View", *Machine learning*, 1, 145-176, (1986).

[10] - L.A. Zadeh: "The Concept of a Generalized Assignment Statement and its Application to Common Sense Reasoning", invited lecture of the *Int. Symposium on Methodologies for Intelligent Systems*, (Knowville - USA 1986).

[11] - F. Bergadano, A. Giordana, L. Saitta: "Approximate Reasoning in Knowledge Acquisition", in 'Fuzzy Logic in Knowledge Engineering' C. Negoita, H. Prade (Eds.), Verlag TUV Rheinland (Koln, Germany, 1986), pp. 127-148.

[12] - F.Bergadano, A.Giordana: "A Framework for Knowledge Representation and Use in Pattern Recognition", Proc. Int. Symposium on Methodologies for Intelligent Systems, 423-431 (Knoxville USA 1986).

[13] - F. Bergadano, A. Giordana: "Evidential Reasoning in Hierarchical Rule Networks", invited for the second IFSA congress, Tokyo 1987.

A LEARNING ALGORITHM FOR A CLASS OF CONTEXT-FREE LANGUAGES (EXTENDED ABSTRACT)

PIOTR BERMAN[1] , ROBERT ROOS[2]

Computer Science Department
The Pennsylvania State University
University Park, PA 16802

ABSTRACT

We demonstrate that the class of languages accepted by deterministic one-counter automata, or DOCAs (a natural subset of the context-free languages), is learnable in polynomial time. Our learning protocol is based upon Angluin's concept of a "minimally adequate teacher" who can answer membership queries about a concept and provide counterexamples to incorrect hypothesized concepts. We also demonstrate that the problem of testing DOCAs for equivalence may be solved in polynomial time, answering a question posed by Valiant and Paterson.

1. INTRODUCTION.

Until recently, studies in concept learning (see, e.g., [9]) have devoted little attention to examining the computational complexity of learning. In [14] Valiant proposes a methodology for developing a rigorous *learnability theory*, the goal of which is to identify those concepts that may be feasibly learned under plausible learning protocols. In his model, the student observes positive and negative instances of an investigated concept. The concepts in [14] are assumed to be described by boolean formulas from various restricted classes. If the student can, with high probability, find a formula that closely matches the target formula we say the class of formulas is *learnable*. A class of formulas is *feasibly learnable* if the student succeeds within time polynomial in the formula size.

Angluin [1] considers protocols consisting of a dialogue between a student and a "minimally adequate teacher" who wishes to teach a concept C to the student. The student may ask two kinds of questions of the teacher. *Membership queries* have the form, "Is c an example of concept C?" Here, the teacher behaves like a "black box" for the concept and merely replies yes or no. *Equivalence queries* look like, "Is concept D equivalent to C?" The teacher responds "Yes" or provides a counterexample, i.e., an example belonging to one but not both concepts. The student is required to learn the concept exactly. Performance in this model is gauged by the worst case time required by the student to learn the concept as a function of the concept description size and the size of the largest counterexample provided by the teacher. The concept is feasibly learnable if the time is a polynomial in these parameters.

Angluin's protocol allows us to study feasible learnability in the following setting: the student is a scientist, Nature is the teacher. The scientist observes Nature (looking for counterexamples/examples) and performs experiments (corresponding to membership

[1]Research supported by National Science Foundation grant DCR-8407256.

[2]Research supported by Office of Naval Research grant N00014-80-C-0517.

Methodologies for Intelligent Systems
Z. W. Ras and M. Zemankova, Editors

queries). The scientist must form a theory consistent with all observed and experimental data. This task is feasible if there is a polynomial bound (in terms of the minimal size for the description of the desired theory and the description of observed facts) for (a) the time needed to form a theory consistent with all that is known so far, and (b) the number of times the scientist may be forced to change the theory upon observing a counterexample.

Angluin studies the learnability of classes of formal languages, and proves that the class of regular languages (those accepted by deterministic finite state automata) can be feasibly learned. Using her protocol, we extend this result to languages accepted by deterministic one-counter automata, or DOCAs. We also solve an open problem posed by Valiant and Paterson [16] and partially answered by Tomita and Goto [13] on the difficulty of deciding equivalence of DOCAs. machines.

References [3], [7], [8], [10], [11], and [15] expand Valiant's results to other classes of boolean formulas ([3] considers also the effects of errors in the examples), while in [4] the focus is on geometric concepts. In [2] Angluin discusses the influence of learning protocols on feasible learnability. E.g., *disjointness queries* were used in the construction of an automatic Prolog program debugger [12]. In a way, this debugger 'learns' the correct program by querying the programmer.

2. DEFINITIONS AND NOTATION.

Let $\mathbf{Z}$ stand for the set of integers, $\mathbf{N}$ stand for the set of non-negative integers. The notation $poly(n)$ will stand for some unspecified polynomial in n. If Σ is an alphabet, Σ^* and Σ^+ stand for all words over Σ and all nonempty words over Σ, respectively. If w is a word, $|w|$ is the length of w. The empty word is denoted by λ. Finally, if L_1 and L_2 are subsets of Σ^*, we denote their symmetric difference by $L_1 \oplus L_2$.

A *deterministic finite automaton* (DFA) is a 5-tuple $<\Sigma, Q, q_0, F, \delta>$, where Σ is the *alphabet*, Q is a finite set of *states*, q_0 is the *initial state*, $F \subseteq Q$ is the set of *final states*, and $\delta: Q \times \Sigma \to Q$ is the *transition function*. A *general automaton* is similarly defined, except that Q can be infinite. These automata are *acceptors* of languages (see [6]).

We will use Angluin's procedure for learning DFAs as a subroutine in our algorithm for learning DOCAs. Our approach will be to define a type of machine called a "linear pattern automaton" (LPA), show that it is equivalent to a DOCA, and then demonstrate an algorithm to produce an LPA of size $poly(n)$ which is equivalent to the LPA of size n known to the teacher. (We have no feasible procedure to obtain a "unique minimal" DOCA or LPA, so we are content to learn an LPA of size poly(n).) We now formally define these machines.

A *deterministic one-counter automaton* (DOCA) M is a 5-tuple $<\Sigma, Q, q_0, F, \delta>$, where Σ is a finite alphabet, Q is a finite set of states, q_0 is the initial state, $F \subseteq Q$ is the set of final states, and $\delta: Q \times \Sigma \times \{0,1\} \to Q \times (\mathbf{Z} \cup \{clear\})$ is the transition function.

A *configuration* of M is a pair (q, i) from $Q \times \mathbf{N}$. Initially, the DOCA is in configuration $(q_0, 0)$. Transition $\delta(p, a, j) = (q, d)$ means "If the current configuration is (p, i), the current input is a, and $sign(i) = j$, go to configuration $(q, i+d)$, or to $(q, 0)$ if $d = clear$." If adding d to the counter causes it to become negative, the DOCA fails and rejects the input. The DOCA accepts the input if it ends in a state from the set F. The *size* of a DOCA is defined to be $|Q| + \sum_{i=1}^{k} |d_i|$, where $d_1, d_2, \cdots, d_k$ are all of the increment values appearing in the definition of δ.

We identify a DOCA with a general automaton, the states of which are DOCA configurations. The infinite graph corresponding to this automaton will have a repeating structure, since configurations which differ only in their (non-zero) counter values will be "locally indistinguishable."

A *partial finite automaton over alphabet* Σ is a triple $<Q, F, \delta>$, where Q is the set of states, $F \subseteq Q$ contains the final states, and δ is a partial function from $Q \times \Sigma$ to Q.

A *linear pattern automaton* (LPA) M is a 5-tuple $<\Sigma, C, q_0, \mathbf{P}, \mathbf{E}>$, where Σ is the alphabet, C (the *core*) is a partial finite automaton $<Q_0, F_0, \delta_0>$ over Σ, and q_0 is an element of Q_0. $\mathbf{P}$ is a finite set $\{P_1, P_2, \cdots, P_k\}$ of *patterns*, where each P_i is a partial finite automaton $<Q_i, F_i, \delta_i>$ over Σ. We require that $Q_i \cap Q_j = \emptyset$, $0 \leq i \neq j \leq k$. Finally, if we define $Q_i' = Q_i \cup Q_0$, $\mathbf{E}$ is a finite subset of $\bigcup_{i=0}^{k} Q_i' \times Q_i' \times \mathbf{N}$. We call $\mathbf{E}$ the set of *state identifications* of M.

An LPA $M = <\Sigma, C, q_0, \mathbf{P}, \mathbf{E}>$ defines a general automaton $<\Sigma, \mathbf{Q}, \mathbf{q}_0, \mathbf{F}, \Delta>$ as follows. Let $Q = \bigcup_{i=0}^{k} Q_i$. The set of states, $\mathbf{Q}$, forms a partition of $Q \times \mathbf{N}$. Let $[p, i]$ denote the element of the partition containing (p, i). Then $\mathbf{Q}$ is the finest partition of $Q \times \mathbf{N}$ satisfying:

(i) if $p \in Q_0$, then $[p, i] = [p, j]$ for all i, j;
(ii) if $(p, q, a) \in \mathbf{E}$, $p \notin Q_0$, then $[p, i] = [q, i+a]$ for all i.
(iii) if $(p, q, a) \in \mathbf{E}$, $p \in Q_0$, then $[p, 0] = [q, a]$.

The initial state, $\mathbf{q}_0$, of the general automaton is $[q_0, 0]$. (Bold-faced lower case letters represent states in the general automaton.) We define the transition function Δ as follows: If there exists $(q, 0) \in \mathbf{q}$ such that $\delta_0(q, a)$ is defined, $\Delta(\mathbf{q}, a) = \{[\delta_0(q, a), 0]: (q, 0) \in \mathbf{q}\}$; otherwise, $\Delta(\mathbf{q}, a) = \{[\delta_i(q, a), j]: (q, j) \in \mathbf{q}\}$. This separation into two cases assures that the core takes precedence in defining the transition (i.e., the equivalent DOCA knows when its counter is zero). If this does not define $\Delta(\mathbf{q}, a)$, we assume that $\Delta(\mathbf{q}, a)$ consists of some non-accepting "dead state." The final states, $\mathbf{F}$, are those $\mathbf{p}$ such that for some $(p, i) \in \mathbf{p}$, there exists $j \leq k$ with $p \in F_j$. If, for every $\mathbf{p} \in \mathbf{Q}$ and for every $a \in \Sigma$, $\Delta(\mathbf{p}, a)$ is a singleton, we say that M is a *deterministic* LPA.

Think of a pattern as a kind of "tile" which is placed over a set of configurations of a DOCA. Tiles corresponding to different patterns may overlap at one or more configurations. The copy numbers of these two types of tiles needn't be the same, so it is not obvious what counter value to assign to states in the overlap. Working only with patterns allows us to separate these overlaps and choose a consistent counter action.

Define the *size* of an LPA to be $|Q| + \sum_{(p,q,a) \in \mathbf{E}} a$. For some indexing of the pattern and core states define two functions on the states $\mathbf{Q}$:

$st(\mathbf{q}) = p$, where p is the element of lowest index such that $\mathbf{q} = [p, i]$ for some i;
$ht(\mathbf{q}) = \min\{i: \mathbf{q} = [st(\mathbf{q}), i]$.

If $\mathbf{p}$ is a state of the LPA, c is an integer, and $w \in \Sigma^*$, define the following:

$\mathbf{p} + c$ is the state satisfying $st(\mathbf{p}+c) = st(\mathbf{p})$ and $ht(\mathbf{p}+c) = ht(\mathbf{p}) + c$;

$mode(\mathbf{p}, w) = 1$ if $\Delta(\mathbf{p}, w) \in \mathbf{F}$, 0 otherwise; $mode(\mathbf{p}) = mode(\mathbf{p}, \lambda)$;

the *computation of* $\Delta(\mathbf{p}, a_1 \cdots a_r)$ is the sequence $\mathbf{p}^0 = \mathbf{p}, \mathbf{p}^1, ..., \mathbf{p}^r$ such that $\mathbf{p}^i = \Delta(\mathbf{p}, a_1 \cdots a_i)$. A computation is *positive* if $ht(\mathbf{p}^i) > 0$ for $i < r$.

Finally, if $\mathbf{p}$ is a state and p is either a pattern state or a core state, we say that $\mathbf{p}$ is:

a *p-state* if $(p, i) \in \mathbf{p}$ for some i;
a *positive state* if $ht(\mathbf{p}) > 0$, a *0-state* otherwise.

3. STATE EQUIVALENCE IN LPAS.

In order for our learning algorithm to work, we need a feasible way to determine equivalence of states and their height. We recall a method for minimizing DFAs (see [6], p. 74): begin by partitioning the states into two sets according to mode. At any stage of the minimization, if $a \in \Sigma$ is an input symbol and Π is the current partition, refine Π to get Π' using the rule, "p is equivalent to q (with respect to Π') if and only if $\delta(p, a)$ is equivalent to $\delta(q, a)$ (with respect to Π)." The process induces a set of "witness strings" to the nonequivalence of pairs of classes.

We will apply an infinite version of this algorithm to LPAs. At stage 0 we begin with a partition Π_0 of states of the LPA into two sets according to mode, and a witness set $W_0 = \{\lambda\}$. At stage i we form a suffix-closed set of strings W_i, properly containing W_{i-1}, and a partition Π_i, a proper refinement of Π_{i-1}, such that $\mathbf{p}$ and $\mathbf{q}$ belong to different sets in Π_i if and only if, for some witness $w \in W_i$, $mode(\mathbf{p}, w) \neq mode(\mathbf{q}, w)$. In this case we say that w *separates* $\mathbf{p}$ *from* $\mathbf{q}$. A string $w \in W_i$ is labelled *useful* if and only if, for some $a \in \Sigma$, aw induces a further splitting (and hence is a candidate for membership in W_{i+1}). Associated with every pattern state will be a set (initially empty) of strings called *loops*.

We distinguish between *ordinary* stages and *extrapolation* stages. Perform an extrapolation stage whenever an *extrapolation condition* is satisfied. Otherwise, if a useful witness exists, perform an ordinary stage.

EXTRAPOLATION CONDITION. It is possible to perform an extrapolation stage if, at the end of stage i, there is a useful witness $w \in W_i$ such that

(i) for some states $\mathbf{p}_1$ and $\mathbf{p}_2$, w separates $\mathbf{p}_1$ from $\mathbf{p}_2$;

(ii) w can be written in the form $\beta\gamma$ where, for every $k > 0$, $\beta^k\gamma$ also causes a splitting to occur. (The string β is called a *descending loop* because it must be the case that, for some state $\mathbf{p}$, $\Delta(\mathbf{p}, \beta) = \mathbf{p} - l$ and is a positive computation. Call l the *drop* of the loop β.)

The extrapolation condition is actually a bit more technical.

ORDINARY STAGE. Form W_i (where i is the stage number) by extending a shortest useful witness in W_{i-1} by a one-letter prefix to obtain a refinement of Π_{i-1}.

EXTRAPOLATION STAGE. Let $w = \beta\gamma$ be the witness satisfying the extrapolation condition, where β is the loop. Suppose its drop is l. The new witness set W_i is formed by adding infinitely many strings of the form $\alpha\beta^m\gamma$. This is a reflection of the fact that, since the computation along β is positive and descending for some state $\mathbf{p}$, we have $\Delta(\mathbf{p} + ml, \beta^m) = \mathbf{p}$ for all $m \geq 0$. If $\Delta(\mathbf{q}, \alpha) = \mathbf{p}$ for some state $\mathbf{q}$, where the computation is positive, then it is also true that $\Delta(\mathbf{q} + ml, \alpha\beta^m) = \mathbf{p}$ for all $m \geq 0$. Thus, one may separate $\mathbf{q}$ from $\mathbf{q} + l$, $\mathbf{q} + l$ from $\mathbf{q} + 2l$, and so on. The witness strings $\alpha\beta^m\gamma$ may induce separations of other state pairs in the LPA as well. We extend a witness only if at least one of the separating computations induced by it is positive over α.

Extrapolation allows us to assign "linguistic heights" (defined in section 4) to an infinite set of states. We will see later that strings α, β, γ, having polynomially bounded lengths, can be found algorithmically during learning.

Lemma 1. An extrapolation stage adds strings of the form $\alpha\beta^m\gamma$ where $|\alpha|$ is bounded by a polynomial in n. At the conclusion of an extrapolation stage, there are only polynomially many useful witnesses in W_i.

Proof: To appear in the final paper. □

At the conclusion of the extrapolation stage we can use the elements of *loops*$(st(\mathbf{p}))$ to further refine the partition—details are left to the full paper. Once this has been done, β is added to *loops*$(st(\mathbf{p}))$.

Lemma 2. At most a polynomial number of ordinary stages and a polynomial number of extrapolation stages are required in order to fully differentiate the equivalence classes of an LPA of size n.

Proof: To appear in the final paper. The proof uses the more technical definition of extrapolation. □

These lemmas are sufficient to enable us to prove the main theorem of this section.

Theorem 3. If M is an LPA of size n and $\mathbf{p}$ and $\mathbf{q}$ are nonequivalent states of M, there is a witness to their nonequivalence of the form $w = \alpha\beta^h\gamma$, where $|\alpha|$, $|\beta|$, and $|\gamma|$ are all $poly(n)$ and $h \leq min(ht(\mathbf{p}), ht(\mathbf{q}))$. □

Corollary 4. ("Polynomial sized counterexamples") If M_1 and M_2 are nonequivalent LPAs of sizes $\leq n$, accepting languages L_1 and L_2 respectively, then there is an element in $L_1 \oplus L_2$ of length $poly(n)$.

Proof: By theorem 3, the initial states, considered as states in an LPA formed by taking the union of M_1 and M_2, are equivalent or have a $poly(n)$-length witness. □

4. LPAS AND DOCAS.

We say an LPA is *normalized* if, whenever $[q, i] \neq [q, j]$, states $[q, i]$ and $[q, j]$ are nonequivalent. (In other words, the counter is always used with a reason.) Our learning algorithm always constructs a normalized LPA. We now show the equivalence of DOCAs, LPAs, and normalized LPAs. Note that we can define 0-configurations, positive configurations, and positive computations of DOCAs in a manner completely analogous to the definition for LPAs.

Theorem 5. Let M_1 be a size n DOCA. Then there is a normalized LPA M_2 of size $poly(n)$ which accepts the same language. Conversely, if M_1 is an LPA of size n, there is a $poly(n)$-size DOCA M_2 which accepts the same language.

Proof: (Sketch) If M_1 is a DOCA, we find configurations (q, i) and $(q, i+k)$, $k > 0$, with no 0-configurations (i.e., configurations with counter value of zero) along the path from (q, i) to $(q, i+k)$. By iterating this path we can visit $(q, i + lk)$ for $l = 0, ..., 2n$. From each such configuration we perform a breadth-first search. These searches, performed synchronously in parallel, will collide with one another or with 0-configurations, defining a pattern and a set of state identifications. Remaining patterns are detected similarly, and whatever is left defines the core. Some additional work is required to normalize.

Given an LPA M_1, we define a DOCA so that states correspond to equivalence classes of the pattern and core states of the LPA, using the equivalence relation on these states induced by "both p and q appear in some identification triple." DOCA transitions are defined using the LPA transition functions δ_i. The size of the counter change is determined by the state identification triples. Discrepancies in consistent state-naming can be handled with a little extra work. □

From now on, LPA will always mean deterministic normalized LPA. Now we can say something about equivalence testing of DOCAs, answering a question in [16].

Theorem 6. There is an algorithm running in time $poly(n)$ that can determine whether M_1 is equivalent to M_2 for any DOCAs M_1 and M_2 of size n or less.

Proof: (Sketch) Convert the DOCAs to DFAs by adding states to reject inputs exceeding a certain polynomial length. Now test these DFAs for equivalence. □

The following definitions and theorems provide us with useful tools for learning the LPA represented by some black box. Note that we need *normalized* LPAs for the theorems to hold.

Let M be a size n LPA, let p be a pattern state of M. An $\alpha\beta\gamma$*-set* B *for* p is a set of triples $<\alpha, \beta, \gamma>$ of strings, $|B| \leq n$, satisfying:

(i) $|\alpha\beta| \leq n$, $|\gamma| \leq poly(n)$ for all $<\alpha, \beta, \gamma> \in B$;

(ii) There exist constants k, l with $|k|, l \leq n$ such that if $ht(\mathbf{p}) > n$ and $\mathbf{p}$ is a p-state , then for some $<\alpha, \beta, \gamma> \in B$, $mode(\mathbf{p}, \alpha\beta^m\gamma) \neq mode(\mathbf{p}, \alpha\beta^i\gamma)$ for all $i < m$, where $m = \lfloor (ht(\mathbf{p})+k)/l \rfloor$.

A triple $<\alpha, \beta, \gamma>$ defines a *linguistic height* for states containing a given pattern state by means of a 'test set' $\{\alpha\gamma, \alpha\beta\gamma, \alpha\beta^2\gamma, \cdots\}$. The size of this set is related to the true height by a linear function with coefficients bounded by n.

Theorem 7. Let M be an LPA. Every pattern state p of M has an $\alpha\beta\gamma$-set.

Proof: This follows directly from the arguments of the proof of theorem 3. □

Let M be an LPA of size n, $\mathbf{q}$ a state of M, and let α, β, γ be strings. Define $m(\mathbf{q}, \alpha, \beta, \gamma)$, the *height of* $\mathbf{q}$ *with respect to* α, β, γ, to be

$$m(\mathbf{q}, \alpha, \beta, \gamma) = \min \{k: mode(\mathbf{q}, \alpha\gamma) \neq mode(\mathbf{q}, \alpha\beta^k\gamma))\}.$$

When the strings α, β, γ are understood from the context, we write simply $m(\mathbf{q})$.

Theorem 8. Let M be an LPA of size n. Fix α, β, γ satisfying $|\alpha\beta| \leq n$ and $|\beta_3| \leq poly(n)$. For pattern state q, define $S(q) = \{\mathbf{q}: st(\mathbf{q}) = q$ and $n^3 < m(\mathbf{q}) < \infty\}$. Then there exist integers j, k, l with $k \leq n$ and $|j|, l \leq n^2$, such that, for any $\mathbf{q} \in S(q)$,

$$0 \leq m(\mathbf{q}) - k \lfloor (ht(\mathbf{q})+j)/l \rfloor \leq n.$$

Proof: (Sketch) Any computation $\Delta(\mathbf{q}, \alpha\beta^i\gamma)$ will be positive and cyclic over β^i if $\mathbf{q}$ is sufficiently high. It is not too difficult to show that the condition $m(\mathbf{q}) < \infty$ implies that the computation is descending on β^i. From this point on, the argument is similar to that in the previous theorem. □

5. THE LEARNING ALGORITHM.

Using Angluin's algorithm, construct a DFA of $poly(n)$ states. Note that the machines passed to the teacher for equivalence testing in this preliminary phase will be DFAs, which are trivial examples of LPAs. Once the DFA is large enough, perform a triply-nested series of breadth-first searches through the automaton, beginning at the initial state. (This is actually a search for strings used in the extrapolation stage of equivalence testing.) These BFSs will use membership queries to the teacher to fill in missing transitions, i.e., transitions whose correctness has not been attested to by earlier queries.

Let us call two states $\mathbf{p}$ and $\mathbf{q}$ *conformable* if it is possible to define a pattern and a set of state identifications such that these definitions are consistent with the current LPA, and such that $st(\mathbf{p}) = st(\mathbf{q})$. The outer BFS selects a candidate for a copy of a pattern state, call it $\mathbf{q}_1$. This BFS will terminate when all but $poly(n)$ states have been covered by patterns. (These uncovered states will form the core of the new LPA.) From this candidate, perform another BFS, the purpose of which is to locate a state $\mathbf{q}_2$ which is conformable with $\mathbf{q}_1$. This BFS will terminate when we either detect a pattern or exceed some polynomial distance from $\mathbf{q}_1$. If w is the string of input symbols used to reach $\mathbf{q}_2$ from $\mathbf{q}_1$, determine states $\mathbf{q}_3, \cdots, \mathbf{q}_n$ by iterating w. If $\mathbf{q}_1$ and $\mathbf{q}_2$ are indeed conformable, this implies the conformability of the rest of these states.

From all $\mathbf{q}_i$s perform, in parallel, breadth-first searches. If the $\mathbf{q}_i$s are conformable then at identical stages of each BFS we should collide with other BFSs at identical states (exceptions can occur for values of i near 1 and near n). There are other consistency checks that must be performed—for example, states at identical stages in the BFSs should have the same mode. The full paper addresses these consistency issues in more detail. We know that we have detected a pattern if some consecutive subsequence $\mathbf{q}_i, \mathbf{q}_{i+1}, \ldots, \mathbf{q}_{i+s}$ of the $\mathbf{q}$s corresponds to a set of isomorphic partial FAs, if all of these FAs were produced by BFSs which terminated through collisions with BFSs running in parallel with them, and if no inconsistencies were found. The transitions from $\mathbf{q}_1, \cdots, \mathbf{q}_{i-1}$ which don't fit the pattern determine pattern-to-core state identifications. Later stages of the outer BFS identify core-to-pattern state identifications. Overlaps in the parallel BFSs determine pattern-to-pattern state identifications.

During the inner breadth-first searches, we explicitly construct $\alpha\beta\gamma$-systems in a way similar to that used in our proof of theorems 7 and 8. Such systems are useful in checking some of the consistency conditions in the innermost breadth-first searches.

In summary, the ideas behind the algorithm are simple. There are three nested levels of breadth-first search that seek to do the following:

Outer BFS: find candidates $\mathbf{q}_1$ for "roots" of patterns.
Middle BFS: given candidate $\mathbf{q}_1$, find candidates for conformable $\mathbf{q}_2$s.
Inner BFSs: find candidates for patterns and check them for consistency.

All of the work can be done in polynomial time.

6. CONCLUSIONS AND OPEN PROBLEMS.

We described an algorithm for learning DOCA languages that runs in time polynomial in the size of the LPA and the length of the longest counterexample. The polynomial is of very high degree. However, we feel we can reduce this to obtain a "practical" running time.

Another definition of LPAs would permit copies of different patterns to overlap. This would require a modification of the notion of "state identifications" to permit things of the form $(p, q, a, b) \in Q \times Q \times \mathbf{N} \times \mathbf{N}$. States in the automaton would be determined by the smallest partition in which $(p, q, a, b) \in \mathbf{E}$ would imply $[p, i]=[q, ai+b]$. This gives rise to a type of machine more powerful than a DOCA (for example, one which can recognize the language $\{a^i b^{\lceil \log i \rceil}\}$). It seems that our methods should be able to produce a learning algorithm for this more general type of machine.

REFERENCES

[1] Angluin, D. Learning regular sets from queries and counter-examples. Yale University Department of Computer Science report YALEU/DCS/TR-464 (March 1986).

[2] Angluin, D. Types of queries for concept learning. Yale University Department of Computer Science report YALEU/DCS/TR-479 (June 1986).

[3] Angluin, D., and P. D. Laird. Identifying k-CNF formulas from noisy examples. Yale University Department of Computer Science report YALEU/DCS/TR-478 (June 1986).

[4] Blumer, A., A. Ehrenfeucht, D. Haussler and M. Warmuth. Classifying learnable geometric concepts with the Vapnik-Chervonenkis dimension. University of California at Santa Cruz Computer Research Laboratory report UCSC CRL-86-5 (March 1986). Also in *Proceedings of 18th Annual Symposium on Theory of Computing* (1986), 273-282.

[5] Harrison, M. A. *Introduction to Formal Language Theory* (Addison-Wesley, 1978), 312.

[6] Hopcroft, J., and J. Ullman. *Introduction to Automata Theory, Languages, and Computation* (Addison-Wesley, 1979).

[7] Kearns, M., M. Li, L. Pitt, and L. G. Valiant. Recent results on boolean concept learning. Workshop on Machine Learning, Irvine (June 1987).

[8] Kearns, M., M. Li, L. Pitt, and L. G. Valiant. On the learnability of boolean formulae. *Proceedings of 19th Annual Symposium on Theory of Computing* (1987), 285-295.

[9] Michalski, R., J. Carbonell, and T. Mitchell. *Machine Learning* (Tioga, 1983).

[10] Natarajan, B. K. On learning boolean functions. *Proceedings of 19th Annual Symposium on Theory of Computing* (1987), 296-304.

[11] Pitt, L., and L. G. Valiant. Computational limitations on learning from examples. Harvard University Aiken Computation Laboratory report TR-05-86 (July 1986).

[12] Shapiro, E. *Algorithmic Program Debugging*. Ph. D. thesis, Yale University Computer Science Dept., 1982. (MIT Press, 1983.)

[13] Tomita, E., and M. Goto. A polynomial time algorithm for deciding the equivalence problem for deterministic one counter automata. University of Electro-Communications technical report (1982). (In Japanese)

[14] Valiant, L. G. A theory of the learnable. *Communications of the ACM* 27 (1984), 1134-1142 .

[15] Valiant, L. G. Learning disjunctions of conjunctions. *Proceedings of 9th IJCAI* (1985), 560-566.

[16] Valiant, L. G., and M. Paterson. Deterministic one-counter automata. *Journal of Computer and System Sciences* 10 (1975), 340-350.

Learning from Examples based on Rough Multisets

Jerzy W. Grzymala-Busse
Department of Computer Science
University of Kansas
Lawrence, KS 66045

Abstract.

A new concept of rough multisets is introduced. This concept generalizes the ordinary rough set, introduced by Z. Pawlak in 1981. It is shown that this new tool enables one to simplify the information system used until now. The new system, called an information multisystem, is obtained from the old one by eliminating the category of objects. It is also shown that due to rough multisets, in spite of the fact that we start from a simpler system (in which examples are stored), we end up with the same rules as if we were using an ordinary information system. Uncertainty is represented by inconsistent actions of experts. Thus two sets of rules are produced: certain and possible.

1. Introduction

The problem of knowledge acquisition under uncertainty is extremely popular nowadays and a number of different approaches are being used [7].

This paper represents the rough-set approach to learning from examples. Each example represents an expert's actions taken on the basis of some conditions. Examples may contradict each other, i.e. for different examples actions may differ in spite of the fact that corresponding conditions are equal. Such inconsistencies are taken into account in the production of rules.

We will use rough set theory to manage uncertainty. The concept of a rough set was introduced by Z. Pawlak in 1981 [11]. The bibliography of papers and reports on rough set theory and its applications exceeds one hundred items. There are successful implementations of systems in industry and medicine (see e.g. [1, 3, 9]) built applying rough set theory.

It was shown that rough sets and fuzzy sets are independent [2, 14] and offer alternative solutions. Similarly, the probabilistic approach to uncertainty (see e.g. [15]) was compared with the rough-set approach in [19]. Rough set theory is somewhat similar to Dempster-Shafer theory [16], as it was pointed out in [5, 18].

In the presented paper rough sets are generalized, resulting in a new concept - rough multisets. The new concept is defined by means of multiset theory. There is a number of reasons for that new concept. In general, lower or upper approximations of a classification, determined by means of ordinary rough theory, are not sets but multisets. The new concept makes it possible to produce the same rules from a simpler system used to store data. So far, the information system, consisting of objects, attributes, values, and a description function was used. It was not an ordinary database since it contained duplicate rows. The concept of a rough multiset makes it possible to work with a system, called here an information multisystem, in which objects are eliminated, and the resulting system stores n-tuples of values of attributes. It resembles a relational database. The difference is that duplicates among n-tuples are permitted, thus the basic structure is not a relation but a multirelation, which is a multiset. The information multisystem is simpler than an information system, yet by using rough multisets we may produce identical rules as for ordinary information systems and ordinary rough sets. Finally, for the same problem, in general, a rough multiset has a smaller cardinality than a rough set.

2. Rough Sets

The concept of rough set was introduced in [11], and later on further developed in more than a hundred papers and reports, see e.g. [2, 12-14].

Methodologies for Intelligent Systems
Z. W. Ras and M. Zemankova, Editors

Let U be a nonempty set, called the *universe*, and let R be an equivalence relation on U, called an *indiscernibility relation* . An ordered pair $A = (U, R)$ is called an *approximation space*. For an element x of U, the equivalence class of R containing x will be denoted by $[x]_R$. Equivalence classes of R are called *elementary sets in A*. We assume that the empty set is also elementary. Any finite union of elementary sets in A is called a *definable set in A*.

Let X be a subset of U. We wish to define X in terms of definable sets in A. Thus, we need two more concepts. A *lower approximation of X in A*, denoted by $\underline{R}X$, is the set

$$\{x \in U \mid [x]_R \subseteq X\}.$$

An *upper approximation of X in A*, denoted by $\overline{R}X$, is the set

$$\{x \in U \mid [x]_R \cap X \neq \emptyset\}.$$

The lower approximation of X in A is the greatest definable set in A, contained in X. The upper approximation of X in A is the least definable set in A containing X.

Concepts of lower and upper approximations of X in A correspond to inner and outer reductions from Dempster-Shafer theory (p. 117 of [16]).

Let X and Y be subsets of U. Lower and upper approximations of X and Y in A have the following properties

$$\underline{R}X \subseteq X \subseteq \overline{R}X,$$

$$\underline{R}U = U = \overline{R}U,$$

$$\underline{R}\emptyset = \emptyset = \overline{R}\emptyset,$$

$$\underline{R}(X \cup Y) \supseteq \underline{R}X \cup \underline{R}Y,$$

$$\overline{R}(X \cup Y) = \overline{R}X \cup \overline{R}Y,$$

$$\underline{R}(X \cap Y) = \underline{R}X \cap \underline{R}Y,$$

$$\overline{R}(X \cap Y) \subseteq \overline{R}X \cap \overline{R}Y,$$

$$\underline{R}(X - Y) \subseteq \underline{R}X - \underline{R}Y,$$

$$\overline{R}(X - Y) \supseteq \overline{R}X - \overline{R}Y,$$

$$\underline{R}(-X) = -\overline{R}X,$$

$$R(-X) = -\underline{R}X,$$

$$\underline{R}X \cup \overline{R}(-X) = X,$$

$$\underline{R}(\underline{R}X) = \overline{R}(\underline{R}X) = \underline{R}X,$$

$$\overline{R}(\overline{R}X) = \underline{R}(\overline{R}X) = \overline{R}X,$$

where $-X$ denotes the complement U-X of X.

A *rough set in A* (or *rough set*, if A is known) is the family of all subsets of U having the same lower and upper approximations in A.

3. Multisets

The name 'multiset' has been suggested by N.G. deBruijn [6] for a collection of elements, in which *multiple* occurrences of elements are permitted. It is convenient to use the same notation as for ordinary sets, thus {a, a, b, c, c, c} (or {2·a, b, 3·c}) denotes a multiset X with elements a, b, and c occurring in X twice, once, and three times, respectively. In the sequel, some definitions are cited from [4] and [6]. The *empty multiset* $\emptyset$ is the same as the empty set. The fact that an element x occurs at least once in X will be denoted by $x \in X$. The *cardinality of multiset X* is the total number of occurrences of elements of X. A multiset X is a *sub-multiset of a multiset Y* (denoted $X \subseteq Y$) iff each element of X is also an element of Y at least as many times. Two multisets X and Y are *equal* iff $X \subseteq Y$ and $Y \subseteq X$.

Let X and Y be multisets. The *union of X and Y* (denoted $X \cup Y$) is a multiset of all elements which are members of X or Y, and the number of occurrences of each element x in $X \cup Y$ is the maximum of the two numbers: the number of occurrences of x in X and the number of occurrences of x in Y. Similarly, the *intersection of X and Y* (denoted $X \cap Y$) is a multiset of all elements which are members of X and Y, while the number of occurrences of each element x in $X \cap Y$ is the minimum of the two numbers: the number of occurrences of x in X and the number of occurrences of x in Y. The *difference of X and Y* (denoted $X - Y$) is a multiset of all elements x of X for which the difference between the number of occurrences of x in X and the number of occurrences of x in Y is a positive number, if that difference is positive then it serves also as a number of occurrences of x in $X - Y$. The *sum of X and Y* (denoted $X + Y$) is a multiset of all elements which are members of X or Y, where the number of occurrences of each element x in $X+Y$ is the sum of the number of occurrences of x in X and the number of occurrences of x in Y.

A *multipartition* $\mathcal{X}$ *on a multiset* X is a multiset $\{X_1, X_2,..., X_n\}$ of multisets $X_1, X_2, ..., X_n$ (some of $X_1, X_2, ..., X_n$ may be mutually equal), such that

$$\sum_{i=1}^{n} X_i = X .$$

If X is an ordinary set then $\mathcal{X}$ is an ordinary partition.

Let $A_1, A_2,..., A_n$ be ordinary sets, where $n \in \{1, 2,... \}$. A multiset with elements from $A_1 \times A_2 \times \cdots \times A_n$ will be called a *multirelation* on $A_1 \times A_2 \times \cdots \times A_n$.

Note that multisets provide great convenience as a tool, as it may be recognized from [6] (see also [4]).

4. Rough Multisets

For the rest of the paper we will use the following notation. Let M be a multiset. Let a be an element of M whose number of occurrences in M is n. The sub-multiset $\{n \cdot a\}$ will be denoted by $[a]_M$ .Thus M may be represented as union all $[a]_M$'s, where $a \in M$. A multiset $[a]_M$ is called an *elementary multiset in* M. We also assume that the empty multiset is elementary. A finite union of elementary multisets is called a *definable multiset in M*.

Let X be a sub-multiset of M. A *lower approximation of X in M* (denoted $\underline{X}$) is the multiset

$$\{x \in M \mid [x]_M \subseteq X\} = \bigcup_{[x]_M \subseteq X} [x]_M .$$

An *upper approximation of X in M* (denoted $\overline{X}$) is the multiset

$$\{x \in M \mid [x]_M \cap X \neq \emptyset\} = \bigcup_{[x]_M \cap X \neq \emptyset} [x]_M .$$

A *rough multiset in M* is the family of all sub-multisets of M having the same lower and upper approximations in M. The name 'rough multiset' is used here to keep the name brief and to distinguish it from ordinary rough sets. However, a rough multiset is an ordinary set, whose elements are multisets.

Let X and Y be sub-multisets of M. Every property of lower and upper approximations of sets in A from the preceding section may be translated into multisets, e.g.

$$\underline{X} \subseteq X \subseteq \overline{X},$$

$$\underline{M} = M = \overline{M},$$

etc. The additional properties are

$$\underline{X + Y} \supseteq \underline{X} + \underline{Y}$$

and

$$\overline{X + Y} \subseteq \overline{X} + \overline{Y}.$$

5. Information Systems

We will quote the definition of an information system from [10] (see also [5, 8, 13]). The information system is also known as a data matrix [17] and is similar to a database. The difference between a database and an information system is that the entities of the information system do not need to be distinguished by attributes. The information system contains training instances (examples), from which rules are produced. Thus, attributes are divided into two categories: conditions and decisions. Entities (called objects) are described by values of conditions while classifications of experts are described by values of decisions.

Therefore, an *information system* S is a quadruple (U, Q, V, ρ), where

U is a nonempty finite set, and its elements are called *objects of* S,

$Q = C \cup D$ is a set of *attributes*, where C is a nonempty finite set; its elements are called *conditions of* S and D is also a nonempty set; its elements are called *decisions of* S, $D \cap C = \emptyset$,

$V = \bigcup_{q \in Q} V_q$ is a nonempty finite set, and its elements are called *values of attributes*, where V_q is the set of values of attribute q, called the *domain of* q, and

ρ is a function of $U \times Q$ onto V, called a *description function of* S, such that $\rho(x,q) \in V_q$ for all $x \in U$ and $q \in Q$.

Let P be a nonempty subset of Q, and let x, y be members of U. Objects x and y are *indiscernible by P in S*, denoted by $x \underset{P}{\sim} y$, iff for each q in P, $\rho(x, q) = \rho(y, q)$. Obviously, $\underset{P}{\sim}$ is an equivalence relation on U. Thus P defines a partition on U; such a partition is a set of all equivalence classes of $\underset{P}{\sim}$. This partition is called a *classification of U generated by P in S*.

For a nonempty subset P of Q, an ordered pair $(U, \underset{P}{\sim})$ is an approximation space A. For the sake of convenience, for any $X \subseteq U$, the lower approximation of X in A and the upper approximation of X in A will be called *P-lower approximation of X in S* and *P-upper approximation of X in S*, and will be denoted by $\underline{P}X$ and $\overline{P}X$, respectively. A definable set X in A will be also called *P-definable in S*. Thus, X is P-definable in S iff $\underline{P}X = \overline{P}X$.

Example. An information system is given by table 1.

Table 1

	Q			
	C		D	
	a	b	c	d
x_0	0	2	4	7
x_1	0	3	4	7
x_2	1	2	5	7
x_3	0	2	4	7
x_4	0	2	4	7
x_5	0	3	4	6
x_6	1	2	5	7
x_7	0	2	4	6
x_8	1	2	5	6
x_9	1	3	5	6

Table 2

Q			
C		D	
a	b	c	d
0	2	4	7
0	3	4	7
1	2	5	7
0	2	4	7
0	2	4	7
0	3	4	6
1	2	5	7
0	2	4	6
1	2	5	6
1	3	5	6

A classification of U generated by C is

$$\{\{x_0, x_3, x_4, x_7\}, \{x_1, x_5\}, \{x_2, x_6, x_8\}, \{x_9\}\}.$$

Let $X = \{x_8, x_9\}$. The set X is characterized as the set of all elements of U for which $c = 5$ and $d = 6$. Then

$$\underline{C}X = \{x_9\}$$

and

$$\bar{C}X = \{x_2, x_6, x_8, x_9\}.$$

The set X implies the following rough set

$$\{\{x_2, x_9\}, \{x_6, x_9\}, \{x_8, x_9\}, \{x_2, x_6, x_9\}, \{x_2, x_8, x_9\}, \{x_6, x_8, x_9\}\}.$$

For any member of the above rough set, the lower approximation is $\{x_9\}$ and the upper approximation is $\{x_2, x_6, x_8, x_9\}$.

Let P be a nonempty subset of Q and let $\mathcal{X} = \{X_1, X_2, ..., X_n\}$ be a partition on U. Such $\mathcal{X}$ is called a classification of U for a system $S = (U, Q, V, \rho)$. *P-lower* and *P-upper approximations of $\mathcal{X}$ in S* (denoted $\underline{P}\mathcal{X}$ and $\bar{P}\mathcal{X}$, respectively) are the following sets

$$\underline{P}\mathcal{X} = \{\underline{P}X_1, \underline{P}X_2, ..., \underline{P}X_n\}$$

and

$$\bar{P}\mathcal{X} = \{\bar{P}X_1, \bar{P}X_2, ..., \bar{P}X_n\}.$$

Example (cont'd). A classification $\mathcal{X}$ of U generated by D in S is equal to

$$\{\{x_0, x_1, x_3, x_4\}, \{x_2, x_6\}, \{x_5, x_7\}, \{x_8, x_9\}\}.$$

Moreover,

$$\underline{C}\{x_0, x_1, x_3, x_4\} = \emptyset, \qquad \bar{C}\{x_0, x_1, x_3, x_4\} = \{x_0, x_1, x_3, x_4, x_5, x_7\},$$
$$\underline{C}\{x_2, x_6\} = \emptyset, \qquad \bar{C}\{x_2, x_6\} = \{x_2, x_6, x_8\},$$
$$\underline{C}\{x_5, x_7\} = \emptyset, \qquad \bar{C}\{x_5, x_7\} = \{x_0, x_1, x_3, x_4, x_5, x_7\},$$
$$\underline{C}\{x_8, x_9\} = \{x_9\}, \qquad \bar{C}\{x_8, x_9\} = \{x_2, x_6, x_8, x_9\}.$$

Thus

$$\underline{C}\mathcal{X} = \{\emptyset, \{x_9\}\},$$

and

$$\bar{C}\mathcal{X} = \{\{x_0, x_1, x_3, x_4, x_5, x_7\}, \{x_2, x_6, x_8\}, \{x_2, x_6, x_8, x_9\}\}.$$

Let us make some observations. First, $\underline{C}\mathcal{X}$ has two elements, while $\mathcal{X}$ has four, since $\emptyset$ is the lower approximation of three different elements of $\mathcal{X}$. Similarly, $\bar{C}\mathcal{X}$ has only three elements, since upper approximations of two different elements of $\mathcal{X}$ are identical. It is clear that $\underline{C}\mathcal{X}$ and $\bar{C}\mathcal{X}$ presented as multisets, with duplicate elements, will describe the situation more accurately.

6. Information Multisystems

The new concept of an information multisystem will be introduced here as the simplification of the above concept of an ordinary information system. The main difference is in omitting objects. The only reason why objects were necessary for ordinary information systems was naming rows of the table of the information system to make a distinction between two otherwise identical rows (i.e. rows with identical values for each attribute). The information about objects is not included into the set of resulting rules, anyway. Our basic tool is a multiset, therefore we do not have to distinguish between two identical rows.

Thus an *information multisystem* (or briefly *multisystem*) S is a triple $(Q, V, \boldsymbol{Q})$, where Q and V are defined as for an ordinary information system, and $\boldsymbol{Q}$ is a multirelation on $\times_{q \in Q} V_q$, called an *information multirelation of S*.

In many applications we are interested in some selected domains only, i.e. in some *projection* of $\boldsymbol{Q}$. Thus, if P is a subset of Q, we define a *projection of $\boldsymbol{Q}$ onto P* as the multirelation $\boldsymbol{P}$, obtained by deleting the columns corresponding to attributes in $Q - P$. Note that duplicate tuples in $\boldsymbol{P}$ are not removed. Therefore $|\boldsymbol{Q}| = |\boldsymbol{P}|$.

An information multisystem is a generalization of the concept of a relational database. The difference is that in an ordinary relational database the basis is a n-ary relation, while an information multisystem is based on a n-ary multirelation, where n is equal to the cardinality $|Q|$ of the set Q. In other words, an information multisystem permits duplication of n-tuples.

For each ordinary information system there exists unique information multisystem which is based on omitting objects.

Thus, for an information system from table 1 there corresponds the information multisystem presented in table 2.

Example (cont'd). The multirelation $\boldsymbol{C}$ is

$$\{4\cdot(0, 2), 2\cdot(0, 3), 3\cdot(1, 2), (1, 3)\}.$$

Let X be the following sub-multiset of $\boldsymbol{C}$

$$\{(1, 2), (1, 3)\}.$$

Note that we may characterize X as the multiset of all elements from $\boldsymbol{C}$ for which $c = 5$ and $d = 6$. Then

$$\underline{C}X = \{(1, 3)\},$$

and

$$\overline{C}X = \{3\cdot(1, 2), (1, 3)\}.$$

The set X implies the following rough multiset

$$\{\{(1, 2), (1, 3)\}, \{2\cdot(1, 2), (1, 3)\}\}.$$

The above rough multiset is much simpler than the ordinary rough set (consisting of 6 elements), describing corresponding information system from the first part of the example.

7. Classifications

In ordinary information systems, classifications are partitions on the set of all objects. Our basic model is an information multisystem, hence classifications are multipartitions.

Let $S = (Q, V, \boldsymbol{Q})$ be an information multisystem. Let A, B be subsets of Q. Let $\boldsymbol{A}$ be a multirelation, i.e. a projection of $\boldsymbol{Q}$ onto A, and let $|A| = i$ and $|B| = j$. The subset B of Q generates a multipartition B_A on $\boldsymbol{A}$ defined as follows: each two i-tuples determined by A are in the same multiset $X \in B_A$ iff their associated j-tuples, determined by B, are equal.

Example (cont'd). For an information multisystem from table 2 and for multirelation $\boldsymbol{C}$, multipartition D_C on $\boldsymbol{C}$ is given below

$$D_C = \{\{(0, 2), (0, 3)\}, \{3\cdot(0, 2), (0, 3)\}, \{(1, 2), (1, 3)\}, \{2\cdot(1, 2)\}\}.$$

E.g., $\{(0, 2), (0, 3)\} \in D_C$ since for (0, 2), (0, 3), their associated pairs (4, 6), (4, 6), respectively, determined by D, are equal. Furthermore, $\{3\cdot(0, 2), (0, 3)\} \in D_C$ since all members of it are associated with the same pair (4, 7), determined by D.

Similarly,

$$\boldsymbol{D} = \{\{2\cdot(4, 6)\}, \{4\cdot(4, 7)\}, \{2\cdot(5, 6)\}, \{2\cdot(5, 7)\}\},$$

$$C_D = \{\{(4, 6), 3\cdot(4, 7)\}, \{(4, 6), (4, 7)\}, \{(5, 6), 2\cdot(5, 7)\}, \{(5, 6)\}\}.$$

Let P be a subset of Q and let X be a sub-multiset of $\boldsymbol{P}$. A *P-lower approximation of X in S* (denoted $\underline{P}X$) is the lower approximation $\underline{X}$ of X in $\boldsymbol{P}$. A *P-upper approximation of X in S* (denoted $\overline{P}X$) is the upper approximation $\overline{X}$ of X in $\boldsymbol{P}$. For an information multisystem S, a definable multiset X in $\boldsymbol{P}$ will be called P-definable in S. Thus, X is *P-definable* iff $\underline{P}X = \overline{P}X$.

Note that in the case of rough multisets and information multisystems we do not need to introduce explicitly the concept analogous to that of indiscernibility relation for ordinary information systems in order to define P-lower and P-upper approximations.

Let $X = \{X_1, X_2, ..., X_n\}$ be a multipartition on $\boldsymbol{Q}$. We will call X a *classification of* $\boldsymbol{Q}$ *in S*. *P-lower* and *P-upper approximations of X in S* (denoted $\underline{P}X$ and $\overline{P}X$, respectively) are the following multisets

$$\underline{P}X = \{\underline{P}X_1, \underline{P}X_2, \ldots, \underline{P}X_n\}$$

and

$$\overline{P}X = \{\overline{P}X_1, \overline{P}X_2, \ldots, \overline{P}X_n\}.$$

Note that both $\underline{P}X$ and $\overline{P}X$ may consist of multiple occurrences (see example below). However, the only member of $\underline{P}X$ which may occur more than once is the empty set.

Example (cont'd). Below are the approximations of some multipartitions for an information multisystem from table 2.

$$\underline{C}D_C = \{\emptyset, \emptyset, \{(1, 3)\}, \emptyset\},$$

$$\overline{C}D_C = \{2 \cdot \{4 \cdot (0, 2), 2 \cdot (0, 3)\}, \{3 \cdot (1, 2), (1, 3)\}, \{3 \cdot (1, 2)\}\},$$

$$\underline{C}\{c\}_C = \{\{4 \cdot (0, 2), 2 \cdot (0, 3)\}, \{3 \cdot (1, 2), (1, 3)\}\} = \overline{C}\{c\}_C,$$

$$\underline{C}\{d\}_C = \{\{(1, 3)\}, \emptyset\},$$

$$\overline{C}\{d\}_C = \{\{4 \cdot (0, 2), 2 \cdot (0, 3), 3 \cdot (1, 2), (1, 3)\}, \{4 \cdot (0, 2), 2 \cdot (0, 3), 3 \cdot (1, 2)\}\},$$

$$\underline{D}C_D = \{\emptyset, \emptyset, \{2 \cdot (5, 7)\}, \emptyset\},$$

$$\overline{D}C_D = \{2 \cdot \{2 \cdot (4, 6), 4 \cdot (4, 7)\}, \{2 \cdot (5, 6), 2 \cdot (5, 7)\}, \{2 \cdot (5, 6)\}\}.$$

As follows from the above example, both $\overline{C}D_C$ and $\overline{D}C_D$ contain the same multiset twice ($\overline{C}D_C$ contains the multiset $\{4 \cdot (0, 2), 2 \cdot (0, 3)\}$ twice while $\overline{D}C_D$ contains the multiset $\{2 \cdot (4, 6), 4 \cdot (4, 7)\}$ twice). This is true in general, i.e. *for any $A, B \subseteq Q$, $\overline{A}B_A$ contains a multiset more than once iff $\overline{B}A_B$ contains a multiset more than once.*

8. Certain and Possible Rules.

Actions of experts may be represented by rules. Such a rule is a conditional statement that specifies an action under conditions. Rules are built from constants 0 and 1, atomic expressions of the form $(a{:=}v)$, where a is an attribute and v is an attribute value, and symbols $\neg$, $\vee$, $\&$, $\Rightarrow$, and $\Leftrightarrow$ (negation, disjunction, conjunction, implication, and equivalence, respectively). 0 means the empty set, 1 means the universe, an atomic expression $(a{:=}v)$ means the set of all elements of the universe with the value of attribute a equal to v. The universe in the case of an ordinary information system is U, in the case of an information multisystem is the projection of $\boldsymbol{Q}$ onto C. In both cases we may produce the same set of rules, although the basis is different. The first case was presented in a number of papers, e.g. [5, 9, 19]. Here we will present the second case.

The only multisets which may be described by rules, using the set C of conditions, are C-definable. If a multiset X is not C-definable we can not represent it by a single set of rules, but we may represent sets $\underline{C}X$ and $\overline{C}X$ by the rules. If either $\underline{C}X$ or $\overline{C}X$ is the empty set, then the corresponding rule has an antecedent equal to 0. If it is the universe, then the corresponding rule has an antecedent equal to 1. A rule derived from $\underline{C}X$ is certain, a rule derived from $\overline{C}X$ is possible.

Example (cont'd). In the example we disregard rules with antecedents equal to 0 or 1. The certain rules for members of the decision set D may be derived from $\underline{C}\{c\}_C$ and $\underline{C}\{d\}_C$.

For $\underline{C}\{c\}_C$, the multiset $\{4 \cdot (0, 2), 2 \cdot (0, 3)\}$ is associated with the value 4 for c, and the multiset $\{3 \cdot (1, 2), (1, 3)\}$ with value 5 for c, hence the certain rules are

$$(a{:=}0) \& (b{:=}2) \vee (a{:=}0) \& (b{:=}3) \Rightarrow (c{:=}4)$$

and

$$(a{:=}1) \& (b{:=}2) \vee (a{:=}1) \& (b{:=}3) \Rightarrow (c{:=}5),$$

or in the simplified form

$$(a{:=}0) \Rightarrow (c{:=}4)$$

and

$$(a{:=}1) \Rightarrow (c{:=}5).$$

The only nonempty multiset in $\underline{C}\{d\}_C$ is $\{(1, 3)\}$, associated with value 6 for d, so that

$$(a{:=}1)\&(b{:=}3) \Rightarrow (d{:=}6)$$

is the only certain rule. The only possible rule (different from certain rules and with antecedent different from 1) may be derived from $\overline{C}\{d\}_C$, and it is

$$\neg((a{:=}1)\&(b{:=}3)) \Rightarrow (d{:=}7).$$

9. Conclusions

The concept introduced here, of the rough multiset, generalizes the concept of an ordinary rough set. Although some definitions may look more complex at the first glance, all necessary computations needed to produce approximations first and rules later on are of the same complexity. The main advantage is that the category of objects, a necessity in ordinary information systems, is eliminated from the definition of an information multisystem. The resulting system resembles a relational database. Moreover, the rough multiset itself, in general, is of smaller cardinality than a corresponding ordinary rough set.

References

1. T. Arciszewski, W. Ziarko. Adaptive expert system for preliminary engineering design. *Proc. 6th Internat. Workshop on Expert Systems and Their applications, April 28-30, 1986, Avignon, France,* Vol. 1, 696-712.
2. D. Dubois, H. Prade. Twofold fuzzy sets and rough sets. *Fuzzy Sets and Systems* 17 (1985).
3. J. Fibak, K. Slowinski, R. Slowinski. The application of rough set theory to the verification of indications for treatment of duodenal ulcer by HSV. *Proc. 6th Internat. Workshop on Expert Systems and Their Applications, April 28-30, 1986, Avignon, France,* Vol. 1, 587-599.
4. J.A. Goguen, Jr. Concept representation in natural and artificial languages: axioms, extensions and applications to fuzzy sets. In *Fuzzy Reasoning and its Applications, (E.H. Mamdani and B.R. Gaines, eds.)* , Academic Press, 1981, 67-115.
5. J.W. Grzymala-Busse. Rough-set and Dempster-Shafer approaches to knowledge acquisition under uncertainty - a comparison. *To appear.*
6. D.E. Knuth. *The Art of Computer Programming, vol. II, Seminumerical Algorithms,* Addison-Wesley, 1981, *vol. III, Sorting and Searching,* Addison-Wesley, 1973.
7. A. Mamdani, J. Efstathiou, D. Pang. Inference under uncertainty. *Expert Systems 85. Proc. 5th Tech. Conf. British Computer Soc., Specialist Group on Expert Systems, Dec. 17-19, 1985,* 181-194.
8. W. Marek, Z. Pawlak. Information storage and retrieval systems: mathematical foundations. *Theoretical Computer Science* 1 (1976), 331-354.
9. A. Mrozek. Information systems and control algorithms. *Bull. Polish Acad. Sci., Tech. Sci.* 33 (1985), 195-204.
10. Z. Pawlak. Mathematical foundations of information retrieval. *Institute Comp. Sci. Polish. Acad. Sci. Rep.* #101 (1973).
11. Z. Pawlak. Rough sets. Basic notions. *Institute Comp. Sci. Polish. Acad. Sci. Rep.* #431 (1981).
12. Z. Pawlak. Rough sets. *Internat. J. Computer Information Sci.* 11 (1982), 341-356.
13. Z. Pawlak. Rough classification. *Internat. J. Man-Machine Studies* 20 (1984), 469-483.
14. Z. Pawlak. Rough sets and fuzzy sets. *Fuzzy Sets and Systems* 17 (1985), 99-102.
15. J.R. Quinlan. INFERNO: A cautious approach to uncertain inference. *Computer Journal* 26 (1983), 255-269.
16. G. Shafer. *Mathematical Theory of Evidence,* Princeton University Press, 1976.
17. H. Spaeth. *Cluster Analysis Algorithms for Data Reduction and Classification of Objects,* Ellis Horwood Ltd., 1980.
18. S. Wierzchon. Decision making with upper and lower probabilities. *Institute Comp. Sci. Polish Acad. Sci. Rep.* #550, 1984.
19. S.K.M. Wong, W. Ziarko, R. Li Ye. Comparison of rough-set and statistical methods in inductive learning. *Internat. J. Man-Machine Studies* 24 (1986), 53-72.

RULE-DISCOVERY FROM EXAMPLES USING A COMBINATION OF SYNTACTIC AND SEMANTIC INFORMATION

Sukhamay Kundu, Computer Science Department, Louisiana State University, Baton Rouge, LA 70803, USA

ABSTRACT.

Given a set of initial-final state pairs (S_{i_1}, S_{i_2}), $1 \leq i \leq n$, a fundamental problem in machine learning is to find a transformation rule or query Q, if any, which transforms each initial state S_{i_1} to the corresponding final state S_{i_2}. We study this problem where a state is characterized by a syntactic component and a semantic component. A query Q may refer to both the syntactic and the semantic properties. We develop a systematic method for the discovery of Q in the context where each S_{i_j} is a two dimensional scene with spatial relationships among its objects. The combination of the syntactic and the semantic characteristics allow us to solve a larger class of problems than is possible using either of the two separately. It also tends to make the solution query Q simpler.

1. INTRODUCTION.

We consider here the problem of rule-discovery by analysis of example situations. Each example situation is an input-output pair, where the output is obtained by the application of an unknown transformation Q to the input. The transformation Q is variously called a *rule* or a *query*. For two dimensional scenes, which is used for illustration in this paper, Q is viewed as a transformation. For the database environments, the input is a database state, Q a database query, and the output is the result of the query, which may be a new database state or simply an output relation. In the physical world, Q may be viewed as a natural law which describes the changes to an input state due to a physical or chemical process. In each of these cases, the basic problem is to discover Q by studying a set of input-output pairs. The discovery of Q may be thought of as a case of learning from examples. This type of rule-learning differs from those considered in [7, 8], where the goal is find a logical expression that discriminates (gives yes/no values) a set of 'positive' instances from a set of 'negative' instance. The underlying principles in 'concept learning' in [12] from 'positive' examples and 'near misses' is not fundamentally very different from the discriminator finding problem. (In [12], the learned concept is represented as a semantic net rather than as a logical expression as in [7, 8].) Another form of learning, namely, that of finding a better evaluation function in game playing or refining of an heuristic function in a search [10, 11] is comparatively a simpler type of learning than [7, 8] or that of ours because of the structural simplicity of what is to be learned. The most complex form of learning that has been considered in the literature is the learning of automated programming from examples [1, 2, 4, 5]. Our rule-discovery problem can be thought of as a simple case of automated programming, the main difference being in the nature of input/output description language, i.e., in the nature of 'programs' to be learned. The rule learning considered in [6] consists of deriving equations from dimensional (mass, distance, time) considerations of the physical quantities. This is a very simple form of rule discovery compared to what we consider here.

2. THE BASIC CONCEPT OF A SCENE AND A QUERY.

2.1. The Syntactic Component of a Scene.

We assume that there is a set of objects B = $\{b_1, b_2, ...\}$ and a set of relationship types R = $\{r_1, r_2, ...\}$, where each r_j is a *binary* relation on B. A scene S consists of a *finite* subset of the objects B and a *finite* set of relationship instances of the various types r_j among those objects. The relationship instances in a scene comprise its *syntactic* structure. For the purpose of illustrations in this paper, we use the objects {dot, circle, triangle, square}, and the spatial relationships R = {L = left, I = inside}. We write L(x, y) for "x left of y" and I(x, y) for "x inside y". A scene S can be represented by an *ordered* tree T(S) as shown in Fig. 1, where the terminal nodes are the scene objects; each object is shown here as a labeled circle. The intermediate nodes in T(S) are labeled L or I and have two or more children each. A node with the label L is called an *L-node*, and a node with the label I is called an *I-node*. Each child of an L-node can be either a terminal node or an I-node. For an I-node, the first child can be a terminal node or an L-node, and the other children are terminal nodes. Given a subset S′ of the objects in S, we identify S′ with the *subscene* of S on S′. The tree representation of the subscene

Methodologies for Intelligent Systems
Z. W. Ras and M. Zemankova, Editors

on S′ is obtained by basically deleting the terminal nodes in T(S) which are not in S′ (followed by some additional simplifications of the resulting tree to bring it to the proper form). For any two objects x and y in a scene S, exactly one of L(x, y) and I(x, y) is true, and this is defined by the tree T(S) in a straight forward manner. (It may be noted that the relationships L and I are of fundamentally different nature in that there are more inference rules for determining the L-relationship than those for determining the I-relationships.)

2.2. The Semantic Component of a Scene.

It is desirable that the semantic component of a scene S be at least partially independent of its syntactic component. In this paper, we use a linear ordering: $b_i < b_j$ of the objects in B as a simple model of such a semantic property. Thus we talk of the smallest object, the largest object, etc. in a scene independently of the syntactic structure of the scene. For the objects {dot, circle, triangle, square}, we assume that dot < circle < triangle < square.

2.3. The Structure of a Query.

A rule or a query Q is a *mapping* which transforms a scene S_1 to a scene S_2 = Q(S_1), or equivalently, transforms the tree T(S_1) of S_1 to the tree T(S_2) of S_2. A transformation may consists of addition, deletion, or replacement of one or more nodes (subtrees) to T(S_1). A general transformation can be thought of as a series of elementary transformations, each of which adds, deletes, or replaces exactly one node to the tree. The complexity of determining a general query comes from the fact that the same final effect can be obtained by using a different set of elementary transformations and applying them perhaps in a different order. We illustrate the various issues associated with the rule-discovery problem and our solution technique by considering the elementary queries of the form Q = del(x), meaning "delete the object x". The main problem now is finding a specification (= a formula or a program) for the object x. An object x can be specified, for example,

(1) simply by naming it explicitly, x = b_j, or

(2) in terms of the syntactic and semantic properties of x in relation to the other objects in the scene; e.g., x = the leftmost object in S. The relationships used in defining x may themselves be obtained via other objects and the relationships involving those objects; for example, "if r = I is the most frequently occurring relationship involving y = the smallest object, then x = the largest object inside y, else ...."

A specification of type (2) is more general than one of type (1), and is applicable to more scenes .† Given a set of scene pairs $P_i = (S_{i_1}, S_{i_2} = S_{i_1} - b_i)$, $1 \le i \le n$, a more general specification is more likely to succeed in identifying b_i in S_{i_1}. We use the terms "query" and "specification" interchangeably.

We now formally define the specification language. We assume that there is a finite set of elementary or *primitive* functions $\{f_1, f_2, ..., f_k\}$.§ Next, we assume that there is one or more rules for combining the primitive functions f_j to generate more complex specifications. We use the ordinary *function composition* rule and the *set operations* (union and intersection) to combine the primitive functions f_j. This defines the search space of all possible specifications for an object x and also a structure of the search space. It is unlikely that without some structure on the search space one could provide a systematic method for searching through that space for the desired query.

2.4. Primitive Functions.

For the sake of definiteness, we use the following primitive functions in the remainder of the paper. Within each group, there are some functions which are classified as *syntactic* because the results of applying these functions depend on the syntactic structure of the scene, and the remaining functions are classified as *semantic*. (One could add to this list many other functions such as "the insidemost object in S", etc.)

---

† If Q = del(b_j) and b_j is not an object in S, then one could define Q(S) = S.

§ A constant function such as $f_1(S) = b_j$ is equivalent to naming the specific object b_j. The functions f_j may, in general, be partial functions in the sense that they need not be applicable to every scene. For example, the function rep(x, y), meaning "replace x by y", requires that x ∈ S in order for it to be applicable. For the function add(x, p), meaning "add x at position p in the tree of the scene", there must be certain primitive functions to specify the position p.

1. The argument S in the following functions is typically the initial scene or a subscene of it.

   a) $f_1(S)$ - the leftmost object in S.
   b) $f_2(S)$ - the rightmost object in S.
   c) $f_3(S)$ - the smallest object in S in the order "<".
   d) $f_4(S)$ - the largest object in S in the order "<".
   e) $f_5(S)$ - a specific named object b_j in S.

2. The following functions take two arguments each: the first argument is an object x and the second argument is a scene S. The result of the operation is a subscene of S. We may also allow forming union and intersection of these subscenes to form new subscenes.

   a) $g_1(x, S)$ - the objects to the left of x in S.
   b) $g_2(x, S)$ - the objects to the right of x in S.
   c) $g_3(x, S)$ - the objects inside x in S.
   d) $g_4(x, S)$ - the objects smaller than x in S.
   e) $g_5(x, S)$ - the objects larger than x in S.

We shall limit the use of $f_5(S)$ where $b_j \in S$. For a scene which contains duplicate occurrences of an object, the functions f_3, f_4, and f_5 may become undefined. Similarly, in applying a g-function $g_j(x, S)$, the particular copy of a multiply-occurring object x must be uniquely identified (say, by using the syntactic functions). The following examples show how one can combine the above f- and g-functions to create more complicated specifications.

$$\text{Second-leftmost}(S) = f_1(g_2(f_1(S), S)), \qquad \text{Second-smallest}(S) = f_3(g_5(f_3(S), S)).$$

The notion of "leftmost" in the above example needs a little explanation. If there are no occurrence of the inside-relationship in S, then the leftmost object in S is simply the leftmost terminal node in T(S). However, in presence of a relationship $I(b_i, b_j)$, we take the view that parts of the object b_j extends to the left of b_i and so b_i is considered "less" to the left than is b_j, and hence b_i may be ignored in determining the leftmost object. Similarly, b_i may be ignored in determining the rightmost object. In Fig. 1(ii), b is the leftmost object and g is the rightmost object. If we delete the objects {a, b, c}, then g becomes both the leftmost and the rightmost object. The applications of $g_j(x, S)$ with $x \in S$ is of particular interest in this paper and are considered in more detail in the next section.

2.5. The Query Tree.

A tree whose root node is a scene S and whose edges along each path from the root are labeled alternately by an f-function and a g-function is called the *query-tree* $\Omega(S)$ for S. If the edge (x, y) is labeled f_j, then $y = f_j(x)$ is called an *object-node*; if the edge (x, y) is labeled g_j, then $y = g_j(x, z)$, where z is the parent node of x, is called a *scene-node*. Since we do not allow an object-node to have a descendent object-node with the same object, it follows that the tree $\Omega(S)$ is finite. Each object-node (more precisely, the path from the root node to the object-node) represents a query. A query Q which involves an application of a g-function $g_j(x, S)$, where $x \notin S$, is called a *non-linear* query; otherwise Q is called *linear*. A query Q is called *superlinear* if for every application of a g-function $g_j(x, z)$ in Q, we have $x = f_i(z)$. Thus $\Omega(S)$ consists precisely of all superlinear queries on S. The path in $\Omega(S)$ to an object-node is called a *specification* of the object at that node. The terms "path" and "specification" are used synonymously. It is not difficult to show that for any object $b \in S$ there is a superlinear query Q for b which involves only the functions $\{f_1, g_2, g_3\}$; Q is called a *syntactic* query for b. The particular form of Q for a given syntactic position (such as the rightmost object) in T(S) depends, however, on T(S). Thus the functions $\{f_1, g_2, g_3\}$ are not sufficient to determine a common query unless the trees $T(S_{i_1})$ themselves are syntactically identical (i.e., they differ only in the labels of the terminal nodes) and the objects $b_i \in S_{i_1}$, where $S_{i_2} = S_{i_1} - b_i$, are in the same syntactic position in each $T(S_{i_1})$. Thus we cannot eliminate the other f- and g-functions (such as f_2, g_1, etc.) from the consideration without sacrificing our ability to discover a common Q for certain sets of scene pairs. In general, having more primitive functions means that more alternative specifications can be obtained for an object in a scene and therefore there is more chance of finding a common specification for a class of scenes. Fig. 2 shows two scene pairs for which $Q = \text{del}(f_3(S))$ is the common rule, but there is no common syntactic specification of the respective objects in those two scenes.

Fig. 3 shows a scene S and a subtree of $\Omega(S)$ containing a query formed out of $\{f_1, g_2, g_3\}$ for each of its objects. In general, there may be more than one ways of specifying a node in T(S) using the functions f_1, g_2, and g_3. For example, two distinct specifications of the object circle in the scene in Fig. 3 are $f_1(g_2(\bullet, S))$ and $f_1(g_2(\Delta, S)$, of which the first one is not a superlinear query. For any scene S using the relationships L and I, there is basically a unique minimal (with minimum number of function applications) specification using $\{f_1, g_2, g_3\}$ for each of its objects. An alternative superlinear specification for the object dot in Fig. 3 is $f_2(g_3(f_1(S),$

S)). We may regard the syntactic specifications in terms of $\{f_1, g_2, g_3\}$ as a specifications *from the left*. The primitive functions $\{f_2, g_1, g_3\}$ also suffice to form a syntactic specification of each object in a scene S; such a specification may be called the specification *from the right*. There can be many alternative *mixed* syntactic specifications if we allow the use of all five primitives $\{f_1, f_2, g_1, g_2, g_3\}$.

3. RULE DISCOVERY.

In the remainder of this paper, we consider only the superlinear queries. Our general approach to the rule-discovery will be the following. Let $P_i = (S_{i_1}, S_{i_2})$ be a given scene-pair. We first identify the object b_i such that $S_{i_2} = S_{i_1} - b_i$. This is easily done by comparing the objects in S_{i_1} and S_{i_2}, if there are no duplicate objects; otherwise, one must consider the trees T(S_{i_1}) and T(S_{i_2}) in order to determine which copy of the object is deleted. (In some cases, it may not be possible to definitely say which copy has been deleted from S_{i_1}; for example, if S_{i_1} consists two dots inside a triangle, the result of deleting the left dot is no different from that of deleting the right dot.) Next, generate all specifications q_{ij} of b_i in S_{i_1}. If S_{i_1} contains multiple copies of b_i, then one needs to generate the specifications Q_i for each copy of the object b_i in S_{i_1} whose deltion gives S_{i_2}, and the union of these specifications is the final $Q_i = \{q_{i_0} = b_i, q_{i_1}, q_{i_2}, ...\}$. The process is repeated for each of the scenes pairs P_i, $1 \le i \le n$. Finally, we identify a common specification Q $= q_{1i_1} = q_{2i_2} = ... = q_{ni_n}$, say, among the sets Q_i.

A simple definition of the complexity of a query is the number of function symbols in it, i.e., the length of the associated path in Ω(S). More generally, one could assign a non-negative weight $w_i \ge 0$ to each of the primitive functions and take the sum of the weights of the edges (functions) in a specification path to be the weight of the query. The least complex query is the query of least weight. The minimum weight common query Q can be obtained by a breadth-first search of the trees $\Omega(S_{i_1})$. Let Ω_b(S) be the subtree of Ω(S) obtained by deleting all scene-nodes, including their descendents, which do not contain the object b (or the particular copy of b which is deleted from S, in presence of multiple copies of b in the scene); an object node which equals b is, by definition, a terminal node in Ω_b(S). In order to obtain a common query, the search can be limited to the subtrees $\Omega_{b_i}(S_{i_1})$ $\subseteq \Omega(S_{i_1})$, $1 \le i \le n$; we may also assume that f_5 is applied only to the original scene at the root node. We identify the subtrees $\Omega_{b_i}(S_{i_1})$ with the query sets Q_i.

3.1. An Extended Example.

Fig. 4(i) shows two scenes S_{11} and S_{21}. Let $S_{12} = S_{11} - b_1$, where b_1 = dot, and $S_{22} = S_{21} - b_2$, where b_2 = circle. A common specification for b_1 in S_{11} and b_2 in S_{21} is

$Q = f_1(g_4(f_1(S), S))$ = The leftmost object among those which are smaller than the leftmost object. (This is not the same as the second leftmost object!)

We describe the processing of the query trees $Q_1 = \Omega_{dot}(S_{11})$ and $Q_2 = \Omega_{circle}(S_{21})$ leading to the discovery of Q. In particular, we show that the *parallel* and *increamental* development of Q_1 and Q_2 can greatly reduce the required computation by pruning parts of these trees which do not contain a desired solution Q. Basically, these trees are developed level by level, eliminating a subpath whenever possible so that extensions of those subpaths are not formed. A subpath is eliminated when it belongs to one query tree Q_j but does not belong to the other. (Although the search process shown here proceeds in a breadth-first manner, one could alternatively use a depth-first search or a combination of the two, particularly, if we were interested in just a common query. The breadth-first search gives the 'simplest' query. For simplicity, we do not consider the union and intersection operations on subscenes in this example.) Fig 4(ii) shows the first two levels of the tree Q_1 and a part of the third level used in computing the common query Q. Consider the first level from the root. The application of f_5 at the root with the named object b_1 = dot is indicated by the label f_{dot}. The nodes $f_3(S_{11}) = f_5(S_{11}) = b_1$ are terminal nodes, and are indicated by an underscore. Fig. 4(iii) shows only that part of Q_2 which can potentially lead to a common query Q. Since $f_3(S_{11})$ is a terminal node in Q_1 and $f_3(S_{21})$ is not a terminal node in Q_2 (by definition), they are deleted from the respective query trees. The deletion is indicated by the mark "X" below the node. Similarly, the nodes $f_{dot}(S_{11})$ in Q_1 and $f_{circle}(S_{21})$ in Q_2 are deleted. This completes the processing of the first level in Q_1 and Q_2.

At the level two, there are only two edges leading from $f_1(S_{11}) = \Delta$ in Fig. 4(ii), which are labeled g_3 and g_4; all other g-functions at $f_1(S_{11})$ result in subscenes not containing b_1 and hence they are not in Q_1. In Q_2, we consider only the applications of g_3 and g_4 at $f_1(S_{21})$. Among them, only g_4 leads to a subscene containing

b_2 and thus the path f_1-g_3 is eliminated in Q_1. Similarly, the paths f_2-g_4 and f_4-g_1 are also eliminated from Q_1. The end points of each these paths are marked by "X". This completes the processing of level two nodes in Q_1 and Q_2. Next we proceed to the level three. (Note that at any node we could develop either of Q_1 and Q_2 first, and then use the other query tree to perform the pruning.) The extensions f_1 and f_3 of f_1-g_4 in Q_1 lead to terminal nodes. Among the corresponding extensions in Q_2, only f_1 leads to a terminal node. Thus f_3 at f_1-g_4 is eliminated from both Q_1 and Q_2; similarly, f_4 at f_1-g_4 is also eliminated from Q_1 and Q_2. The common path f_1-g_4-f_1 gives the query Q given above.

If we continue the analysis, the next common path found is f_2-g_1-f_3. This gives the common query for b_1 = dot in S_{11} and b_2 = circle in S_{21} as $Q' = f_3(g_1(f_2(S), S))$ = the smallest object which is to the left of the rightmost object. (There are many other common queries.) If we chose b_2 = square in Fig. 4 instead of b_2 = circle, then it is easy to see that there is no common specification for b_1 = dot in S_{11} and b_2 = square in S_{21} using the f_j's and g_j's given here, and the search method terminates unsuccessfully. A common query can, however, be found if we use a different set of primitive functions. (We leave it to the reader to find such a set of primitives.) This example illustrates the point that the specification of the primitive queries f_j and g_j's is an important step in posing the discovery problem of Q.

When there are n ≥ 3 scene pairs (S_{i_1}, $S_{i_2} = S_{i_1} - b_i$), we can repeat the pruning process at each level by pairwise comparison of all partially developed query trees Q_i and Q_j, $1 \le i < j \le n$. A complete algorithm based on this approach for finding a common query is given in [13]. One may alternatively proceed by first finding a query in Q_1, and then verifying if it also belongs to the other Q_i, i > 1; if a failure occurs, then go back and generate another query in Q_1, and so on.

3.2. Developing the Syntactic Part of Query Q First.

One of the attractiveness of the syntactic specification of an object is that they are relatively easy to compute since it does not need the construction of intermediate subscenes. If the root of T(S) is an L-node, the syntactic specification for all nodes in the subtree at the kth leftmost child of the root, k ≥ 1, begins with the path "f_1-g_2-f_1-g_2- ...-g_2-f_1" where the group "g_2-f_1" is repeated (k-1) times. Similarly, for the pair $\{f_2, g_1\}$, giving syntactic specifications from the right. Similar expressions also exist if the root is an I-node. One useful heuristics for searching a common query of the objects b_i in S_{i_1} is to first determine the maximum value of k ≥ 0 such that for each i the ancestor a_i of b_i at level k in $T(S_{i_1})$ has the same syntactic position (either from left or from right). If S'_{i_1} is the subscene of S_{i_1} corresponding to the subtree at a_i, then next determine a common g-function which creates a subscenes S''_{i_1} of S'_{i_1} containing b_i, for each i. Now repeat the process with the subscenes S''_{i_1} and $b_i \in S''_{i_1}$. This method may not, however, always succeed in finding a common query, even if one exists. In other words, one may not always be able to give a preference to determining as much syntactic specification as possible before using semantic part of the specification.

3.3. Multiple Object Deletion

A natural generalization of the query del(x) is where x is replaced by a set of objects b = $\{x_1, x_2, ..., x_k\}$. There are two distinct view points for such a query.

(1) del($\{x_1, x_2, ..., x_k\}$) = k successive instances of single object deletions. This requires that the specification of x_j be given in terms of the subscene S - $\{x_1, x_2, ..., x_{j-1}\}$ obtained by the deletion of the first (j-1) objects. The main difficulty with this view is that the specification of x_j is dependent on the order in which the objects are deleted, giving a very large number of specifications of the full query Q. If there are N specifications of an object in S (and its subscenes) on the average, then the total number of specifications of Q is (k!).N^k.

(2) del($\{x_1, x_2, ..., x_k\}$) = simultaneous deletion of all k objects. This requires that each x_j be specified in terms of the original scene S. The possible alternative specifications of Q is now only N^k.

The two views are, however, not too different in terms of the amount of computation they require. In view (2), one must still find a separate ordering of the objects for each S_{i_1} so that for the objects in each particular position in those orderings, a common specification for those objects in the respective S_{i_1}, $1 \le i \le n$, exists.

It is clear that the use of union and intersection of subscenes can lead to shorter queries for multiple object deletion. However, finding a query with the set operations may not be easier. This is because the set $\{x_1, x_2, ...,$

$x_k\}$ may be expressed in many alternative ways as a union, making the search space much larger. One advantage of using the set operations is, however, that it allows us to delete different number of objects from each scene. If we do not insist on a query which has the minimum number of set operations, then finding a query using set union is actually as simple as the case of a single object deletion. We modify the definition of $\Omega_b(S)$ for a set of objects b (which may be empty) by allowing any object-node or a scene-node to be a terminal node provided the objects at that node is a subset of b. We form all common paths in the query-trees Q_i until sufficiently many paths have been found such that the union of the terminal nodes of those path in each Q_i equals the corresponding b_i. If no such collection of paths are found, then there is no common query for $b_i \subseteq S_{i_1}$. For b_1 = {dot, square} $\subseteq S_{11}$ and b_2 = {square} $\subseteq S_{21}$ in Fig. 4, a common query is $Q = g_3(f_1(S), S) \cup f_4(S)$.

4. CONCLUSION

We have given here an effective technique for discovering an unknown transformation (rule or query) Q from a given set of instances $(S_{i_1}, S_{i_2} = Q(S_{i_1}))$, $1 \leq i \leq n$, of that transformation, when the search space for Q is defined in terms of a set of primitive transformations and a set of composition rules for forming more complex transformations by combining two or more primitive transformations. The two main parts in a general discovery-problem are: (1) modeling of the search space of Q, and (2) defining a search algorithm. The problem of finding an appropriate model of a search space at present remains primarily a human intelligence activity, and is not addressed here. The success of the search process, on the other hand, depends heavily on the model of the search space. Our primary contribution in this paper has been the development of a specific search space structure and show that such a search space can be effectively searched to discover the desired query Q. The notion of a superlinear query is introduced here to make the search process for such a query particularly simple.

5. REFERENCES

1. Bauer, M. A., Programming by examples, Artificial Intelligence, *12*(1979), pp. 1-21.
2. Barstow, D. R., An experiment in knowledge-based automatic programming, Artificial Intelligence, *12*(1979), pp. 73-119.
3. Evans, T. G., A heuristic program to solve geometric analogy problems, in "Semantic Information Processing", ed. by M. Minsky, MIT Press, Cambridge, MA, 1968.
4. Green, C., Shaw, D., and Swartout, W., Inferring LISP programs from examples, Fourth International Joint Conference on Artificial Intelligence IJCAI '74, Tbilisi, USSR (1974).
5. Kant, E., On the efficient synthesis of efficient programs, Artificial Intelligence, *20*(1983), pp. 253-305.
6. Kokar, M. W., Discovering functional formulas through changing representation base, Proceedings of the 5th National Conf. on Artificial Intelligence, AAAI-86, Philadelphia, 1986, pp. 455-459.
7. Michalski, R. S., A theory and methodology of inductive learning, Artificial Intelligence, *20*(1983), pp. 111-161.
8. Michalski, R. S. and Chilausky, R. L., Learning by being told and learning from examples: an experimental comparison of the two methods in the context of developing an expert system for Soybean disease diagnosis, International J. of Policy Analysis and Information Systems, *4*(1980).
9. Michalski, R. S., Carbonell, J. G., and Mitchell, T. M. (eds.), Machine learning - an artificial intelligence approach, Tioga Publ. Co., Palo Alto, CA, 1983.
10. Rendall, L., A new basis for state-space learning systems and a successful implementation, Artificial Intelligence, *20*(1983), pp. 369-392.
11. Samuel, A. L., Some studies in machine learning using the game of checkers, in Computers and Thought (Feigenbaum and Feldman, eds.), 1963.
12. Winston, P. H., Artificial Intelligence (2nd edition), Addison-Welsey Publ. Co., Reading, MA, 1984.
13. Kundu, S., Rule-discovery from examples using a combination of syntactic and semantic information, Tech. Rept. 87-001, Lousiana State University.

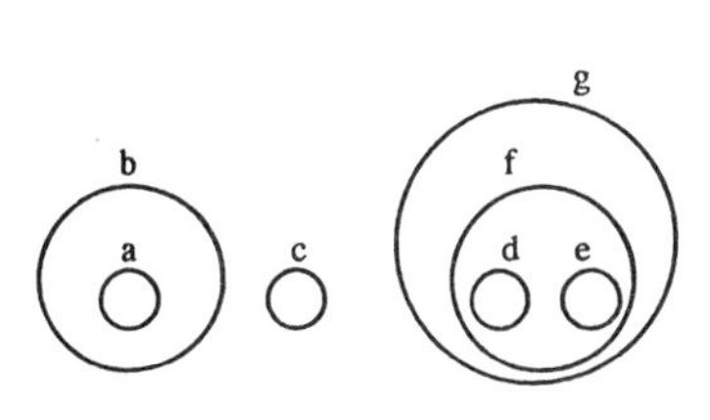

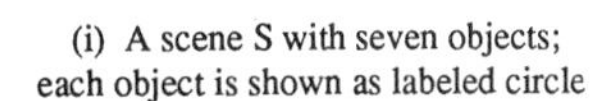
(i) A scene S with seven objects; each object is shown as labeled circle

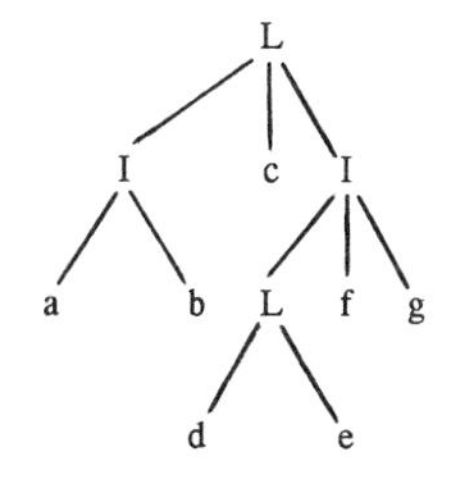

(ii) The tree representation T(S) of the scene in (i).

Figure 1. A scene and its tree representation.

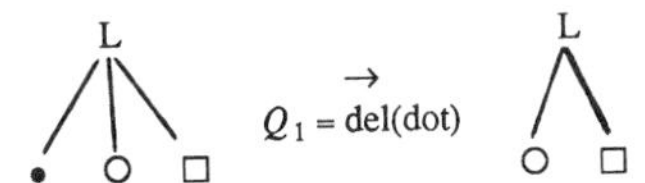

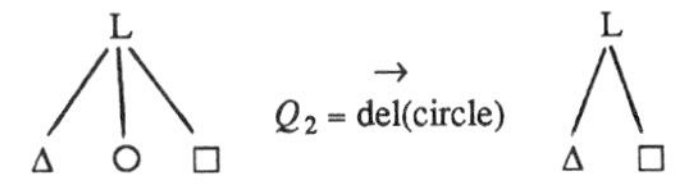

Figure 2. A common query for the two scene-pairs is Q = del(f_3(S)). However, there is no common syntactic specification for the object "dot" in S_{11} and the object "circle" in S_{21}.

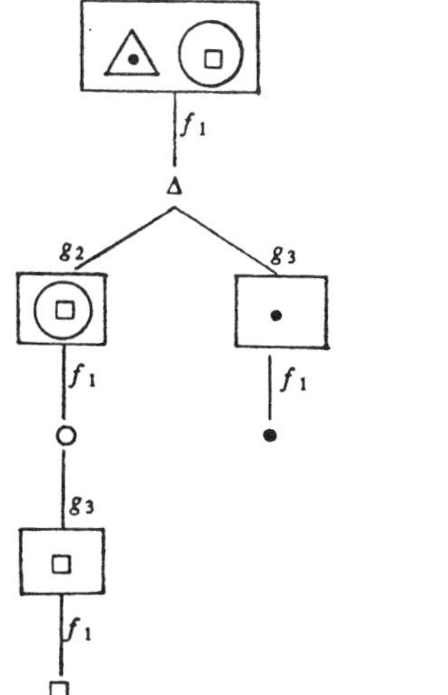

Δ $= f_1(S)$
• $= f_1(g_3(\Delta, S)) = f_1(g_3(f_1(S), S))$
○ $= f_1(g_2(\Delta, S)) = f_1(g_2(f_1(S), S))$
□ $= f_1(g_3(f_1(g_2(\Delta, S)), g_2(\Delta, S)))$
$= f_1(g_3(f_1(g_2(f_1(S), S)), g_2(f_1(S), S)))$

Figure 3. Part of the tree Ω(S), where S is the scene at the root of the tree, and the corresponding syntactic specifications for the four objects in S in terms of $\{f_1, g_2, g_3\}$.

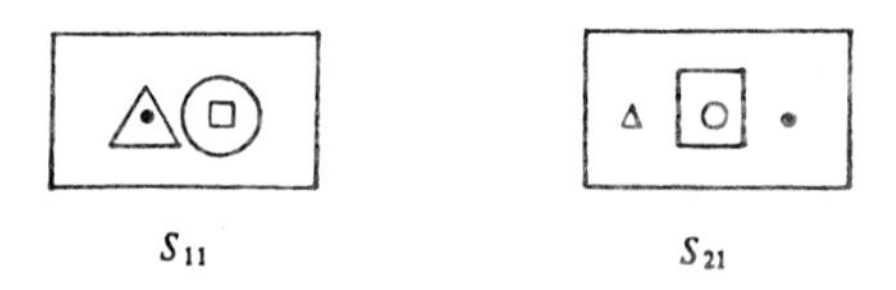

(i) Two scenes S_{11} and S_{21}.

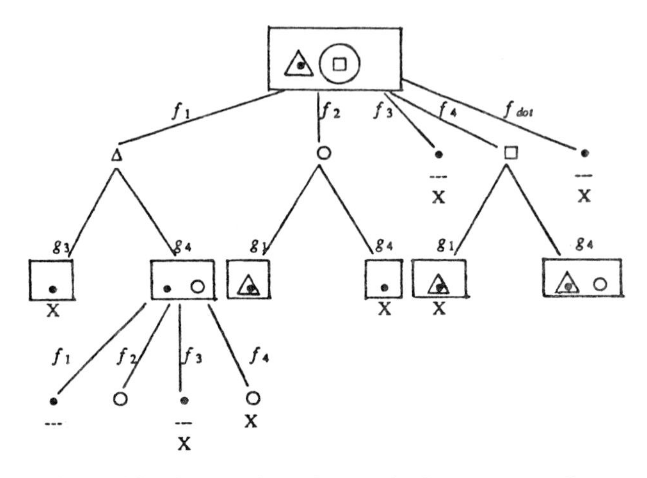

(ii) Part of $\Omega_{dot}(S_{11})$ which is used in computing the common query Q.

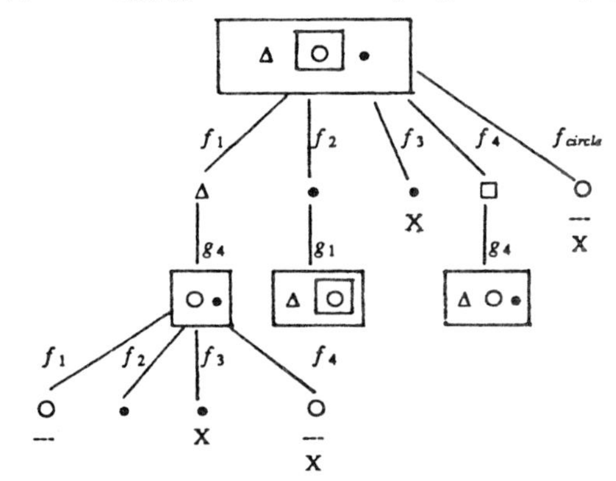

(iii) Part of $\Omega_{circle}(S_{21})$ which is used in computing the common query Q.

Figure 4. Computation of a common query using parallel development of the query trees with the early elimination of paths which do not lead to successful solutions.

CLASSICAL CONDITIONING AS AN EXAMPLE OF NATURAL MODELS USEFUL IN MACHINE LEARNING

WILLIAM W. MCMILLAN
Department of Computer Science
Eastern Michigan University
Ypsilanti, MI 48197

ABSTRACT

Artificial intelligence might make more progress toward its practical goals if models of learning from the natural sciences are considered as the basis for machine learning procedures. Potentially fertile sources of ideas are the fields of classical and operant conditioning. An adaptive operating system command monitor based on classical conditioning is described as an illustration. Other possible applications of classical conditioning are suggested, as well as the value of exploring issues in operant conditioning.

INTRODUCTION

Deken [2] posited that artificial intelligence (AI) needs more techniques that are derived from the study of natural systems if it is to make significant progress toward robust, adaptive software. The goal of AI is to model the behavior of biological intelligent systems at some level of correspondence. Engineering-oriented work focuses on correspondence in capability or gross performance, with little concern for correspondence in underlying processes. Work oriented toward natural science is concerned more with modelling underlying mechanisms, sometimes sacrificing immediate payoff in gross performance. Deken's point is that we might make more long-term progress toward the engineering goal if we pay more attention to psychological and physiological goals.

Machine learning is one sub-field of AI in which natural models may lead to advances. The machine learning literature distinguishes between many kinds of learning, including rote learning, parameter learning, concept learning, analogy learning, discovery learning, and so on. But only a few researchers have attempted to model natural learning directly, with the goal of creating practical tools. Laird, Rosenbloom, and Newell [8,10] have achieved automated learning in domains such as motor performance and expert systems using a process observed in human learning: subgoal chunking. In a similar vein, Anderson [1] employed psychologically-based techniques to implement knowledge "compilation." Holland [6,7] borrowed ideas from genetics to create relatively robust learning procedures. A cognitive model of memory organization is the basis of research by Schank [11] and his students in learning from natural language. Research by connectionists (e.g., Fahlman and Hinton [3]) is related to models of neural nets. Psychological theory about how an organism samples stimuli in its environment inspired a program that can learn many simultaneous concepts in the presence of extraneous and noisy stimuli (Ferguson and McMillan [4]).

If it may be profitable to employ natural models, some more attention to the kinds of learning distinguished by those who study natural learning is in order. The simplest form of learning studied by psychologists is habituation, the gradual attentuation of a response with repeated presentations of the stimulus that elicits the response. Somewhat more

Methodologies for Intelligent Systems
Z. W. Ras and M. Zemankova, Editors

complex is classical conditioning, which brings a reflex under the control of a stimulus previously unassociated with the reflex. Classical conditioning is the basis of the implementation reported in this paper, and is described in more detail below. Operant conditioning is learning based on reinforcement; an organism operates on the environment and the consequences of its operations shape its behavior. The issues that arise in operant conditioning include the manner in which reinforcement schedules affect patterns of behavior, how an organism learns chains of behaviors, and so on. In more cognitive studies of learning, the taxonomy is more similar to that discussed in AI, e.g. concept and analogy learning. Summaries of psychological studies of learning have been provided by Hilgard and Bower [5], Mackintosh [9], and others.

In the belief that a good test of a more natural approach to learning is to explore relatively simple mechanisms, this paper focuses on classical conditioning. Below is a description of classical conditioning, followed by a report of a simple, useful implementation, and a discussion of other possible applications in machine learning.

CLASSICAL CONDITIONING

A reflex is an innate association between a stimulus and a response, such as between an air-puff directed at the eye and an eye-blink. The stimulus is called an uncontioned stimulus (UCS) and the response is called an unconditioned response (UCR). Classical conditioning is a procedure by which a UCR comes under the control of a stimulus that did not originally control it. For example, a tone might be paired on many occasions with an air-puff, leading to the elicitation of an eye-blink to the tone alone. The new controlling stimulus is called a conditioned stimulus (CS) and the response to it is called a conditioned response (CR). (The CR is usually somewhat different in strength or nature from the UCR.) Reflexes are associations that have so much adaptive value that they have been incorporated into the genetics of an animal. Classical conditioning allows the animal to "anticipate" a stimulus that demands a response.

Despite its apparent logical simplicity, the intricacies of classical conditioning have occupied the professional lives of many hundreds of experimental psychologists. Some questions that have been addressed: What is the optimal delay between presentations of the UCS and the CS? How long does it take for an animal to "forget" the CS-CR association? After forgetting, why does the CS-CR association spontaneously reappear in a later experimental session? Are some CSs more easily associated than others with a UCR? To what extent does conditioning generalize to stimuli somewhat different from the CS? What is the nature of second order conditioning, in which a secondary CS comes to elicit a CR, solely on the basis of pairings with a primary CS? The list could be extended to outlast the most patient reader.

Of course, the fact that psychologists find classical conditioning interesting is not in itself a justification for its use in machine learning. It is undeniable, though, that nature has provided a complex mechanism to support a relatively simple capability, and that this capability must have adaptive value in dealing with natural environments. AI must become more successful in creating tools that work outside of contrived environments. Perhaps classical conditioning should be in the toolbox.

AN IMPLEMENTATION

To demonstrate the potential value of classical conditioning in a practical application, a learning module for a hypothetical operating system command monitor was written. The program is called Pavlov-OS.

The first question in applying classical conditioning in machine learning is, What is a reflex? Reflexes in the present domain are 1) the invocation of the appropriate system program when a command is received, e.g., the print spooling program when a PRINT command is entered by the user, and 2) the retrieval of a file when its name is used as a command parameter. The conditioning implemented allows the monitor to anticipate the user's next command on the basis of past command sequences, and to anticipate parameters that are likely to be used with a command. For example, a user might often give the LINK command after giving the COMPILE command. Another user might be more likely to give the EDIT command after the COMPILE command. Some commands might often be given with the same parameter during a session.

For conditioning that leads to command predictions, the UCS is the current command, the UCR is the appropriate operating system action, the CS is the previous command, and the CR is the operating system action called for by the anticipated command. Since it would be rash to simply execute the action associated with the anticipated command, Pavlov-OS displays a menu of the anticipated commands, so that the user can quickly select the next command if the program has guessed accurately. For predicting command parameters, the UCR is finding the appropriate file, the CS is the current command, and the CR is using the anticipated file. As with commands, a menu of anticipated parameters is presented. In a monitor that has dozens of commands, especially if a mouse is available to select a menu option, this adaptive interface could speed up a user's work significantly.

Acquisition curves for classical conditioning can vary a great deal, depending on the animal being conditioned, the reflex involved, and other factors. A typical conditioning function approximates the cumulative normal distribution, so that function was employed here. Positive conditioning values can range from 0.0 to 1.0. The mean of the normal distribution employed was 5 trials, with a standard deviation of 2.5. (A trial is the entering of a single command.) This means that nearly maximal conditioning is achieved after 10 trials (if there are no inhibitory trials, which are discussed below).

An important issue is whether inhibitory conditioning is employed. That is, when stimulus i is NOT followed by stimulus j, does the system take note and learn that behaviors associated with stimulus j are unlikely to be required when stimulus i is encountered? There is strong evidence that inhibitory conditioning occurs in animals, so it is employed in Pavlov-OS. Inhibitory conditioning values are acquired similarly to positive conditioning values. The acquisition function is the negative of the cumulative normal distribution, but with a mean of 7 and standard deviation of 3.5. This means that inhibitory conditioning occurs more slowly than positive conditioning. Inhibitory values range from -1.0 to 0.0.

Command conditioning is encoded in a two-dimensional matrix where each dimension is indexed by monitor commands. Cell (i,j) indicates the expectation that command j will follow command i. Three values are stored in each cell: 1) a conditioning value, ranging from -1.0 to 1.0, which is the sum of positive and inhibitory conditioning from previous trials, 2) the number of times j has followed i, and 3) the number of times j has not followed i. The latter two values are required to determine the correct increment in positive or inhibitory conditioning on each trial.

For parameter conditioning, each command is associated with a list of parameters that have been used with that command in the past. The same variables are stored for each command-parameter pair as for each command-command pair. The count of the number of times a parameter p has NOT followed a command i commences after p has been used with i on one occasion.

On each trial, Pavlov-OS reads a command, guesses the first parameter for the command, reads parameters, and then guesses the next command. To form a list of anticipated parameters for a particular command, the program searches the list of parameters that have been used with that command in the past, and adds to the list all that have conditioning values above a threshold value. To form a list of anticipated commands given the current command i, the program finds all commands j for which the conditioning value i,j is greater than a threshold. (Reasonable thresholds seem to be approximately 0.5 to 0.7.) Conditioning values are updated for 1) the current command i as a predictor of the current parameter p, and 2) for the previous command k as a predictor of the current command i. Updating involves making positive increments in the (i,p) and (k,i) conditioning values, and negative increments for all command-parameter pairs (i,g), g <> p, and all command-command pairs (h,i), h <> k.

In its present version, Pavlov-OS only looks at the current and previous trial when it increments conditioning values. An extension would save several previous trials and use them all for conditioning, suitably attentuated for age. Presently, the system appears to anticipate parameters and commands appropriately and conservatively, although extensive tests with actual users have not been carried out. Only empirical studies can determine optimal values for the parameters of conditioning, such as the mean values for the normal distributions. Another possible extension is to implement generalization. For example, given a measure of similarity between commands, the program could include in the menu commands that are related to the anticipated command if the conditioning to the anticipated command is sufficiently strong.

It might be argued that this system could be implemented without consideration of natural classical conditioning, e.g., by a Bayesian inference system. Other techniques may indeed be helpful, but if one implements a system in which there are associations that correspond to reflexes and learning is in the form of associations between stimuli, then one *is* implementing classical conditioning. Doing so without knowledge of classical conditioning in natural systems may simply deprive the implementer of some valuable ideas.

OTHER APPLICATIONS

The command monitor application described above is intended to be illustrative, but it may not be extremely compelling because it is relatively simple. It is easy, though, to imagine more significant applications. Consider an automated communication system used by a handicapped person. If such a system could anticipate commands or messages and present a menu that is likely to include the user's next command, it would greatly reduce the information that the user would have to supply. When the cost of providing information is high, as it is for a user with motor deficits, the value of accurate predictions that reduce information requirements is also high.

Another possible application is in a real-time monitoring system, as in a factory. A reflex might be calling an emergency crew when certain conditions, such as temperature, become critical. Classical conditioning could allow such a system to anticipate the emergency and alert relevant personnel early.

To return to the realm of operating systems, a classical conditioning system could allow a supervisory program to anticipate situations in which it must redistribute computational loads or storage. For example, when conditions related to high load are observed, the operating system might change its cache replacement algorithm to avoid predicted unpleasantness. With experience, the system could be expected to learn about relationships between conditions about which its human supervisors are unaware.

Classical conditioning cannot satisfy the requirements of all machine learning endeavors, of course. The point is that, in a system that employs more than one technique to deal with its problems, classical conditioning might have an appropriate place.

DISCUSSION

For nearly one hundred years, physiologists and psychologists have pursued a science of learning. Most of the resulting empirical facts and theories have been ignored by the AI community. This is probably because AI has looked most often to cognitive psychology for its understanding of natural systems, and cognitive psychologists have worked mightily over the last 20 years or so to divorce themselves from the constraints of behaviorism. The benefits are undeniable: psychology was freed to consider problems that behaviorist vocabulary and methodology had all but banned, such as complex problem solving and memory. Now that AI needs a fresh infusion of ideas about natural systems, though, it might be a good idea to dust off our books by Pavlov, Hull, and Skinner.

This paper has considered classical conditioning because it provides a relatively simple illustration of the use of natural models. A more complex area, and one that might provide ideas more directly relevant to complex applications in AI, is operant conditioning. An example of an operant conditioning issue that might interest AI researchers is the manner in which animals make choices. A major question, in AI parlance, is whether animals working for reinforcement use hill-climbing or some technique that allows more global optimization.

The AI researcher who begins to explore natural learning models this year cannot expect to have a master-level chess program next year. Immediate gains in gross performance would be traded for a better understanding of fundamental processes in intelligence, which in the long run will be necessary to fulfill the promise of AI.

REFERENCES

1. J. R. Anderson in: Machine Learning: An Artificial Intelligence Approach, Vol. 2, R. S. Michalski, J. G. Carbonell, and T. M. Mitchell, eds. (Morgan Kaufman, Los Altos, CA 1986) pp. 289-310.
2. J. Deken, presented at the ACM SIGART International Symposium on Methodologies for Intelligent Systems, Knoxville, TN, 1986.
3. S. E. Fahlman and G. E. Hinton, Computer 20, 100-109 (1987).
4. R. C. Ferguson and W. W. McMillan, presented at the 13th Annual ACM Computer Science Conference, New Orleans, LA, 1985.
5. E. R. Hilgard and G. H. Bower, Theories of Learning, 4th Ed. (Prentice-Hall, Englewood Cliffs, NJ 1975).
6. J. H. Holland, Adaptation in Natural and Artificial Systems (University of Michigan Press, Ann Arbor 1975).

7. J. H. Holland in: Machine Learning: An Artificial Intelligence Approach, Vol. 2, R. S. Michalski, J. G. Carbonell, and T. M. Mitchell, eds. (Morgan Kaufman, Los Altos, CA 1986) pp. 593-623.
8. J. E. Laird, A. Newell, and P. S. Rosenbloom, Technical Report 2 (Cognitive Science and Machine Intelligence Laboratory, University of Michigan, Ann Arbor 1987). (To appear in Artificial Intelligence.)
9. N. J. Mackintosh, The Psychology of Animal Learning (Academic Press, London 1974).
10. P. S. Rosenbloom and A. Newell in: Machine Learning: An Artificial Intelligence Approach, Vol. 2, R. S. Michalski, J. G. Carbonell, and T. M. Mitchell, eds. (Morgan Kaufman, Los Altos, CA 1986) pp. 247-288.
11. R. C. Schank, Dynamic Memory: A Theory of Reminding and Learning in Computers and People (Cambridge University Press, Cambridge 1982).

Relating Boltzmann Machines to Conventional Models of Computation

Ian Parberry

Georg Schnitger†

Department of Computer Science,
333 Whitmore Laboratory,
The Pennsylvania State University,
University Park, Pa. 16802.

ABSTRACT

We show that Boltzmann machines are equivalent in computing power to combinational circuits built from gates which compute Boolean threshold functions and their negations. In particular, the connection graph of a Boltzmann machine can be made acyclic, randomness can be removed, and edge-weights can be made equal to unity. The running-time is increased by only a constant multiple, and the number of processors by a polynomial.

1. Introduction.

Connectionist models of the brain have recently regained popularity amongst researchers in Artificial Intelligence. The connectionist model is a parallel system which has a large number of simple processing elements. Computation is performed by increasing or decreasing the strength of communications between physically connected processors. One such model is the *Boltzmann machine* [1, 5, 6], a directed graph in which vertices represent processors, and edges represent (directed) links between processors. Each vertex is labelled with a *threshold value,* and each edge with a *weight,* both of which are integers. Each processor can be in one of two states, which we will call *active* and *inactive*. The computation occurs synchronously as follows. At time t, a processor computes the sum of the weights of the edges connecting it to its active neighbours. That processor is active at time t+1 with probability depending on the difference between that sum and its threshold (with probability tending to zero below the threshold, exactly one-half at the threshold, and tending to one above it). At the start of the computation a distinguished set of input vertices is held in either the active or inactive state, to represent the input in binary. The output is similarly encoded in the states of a distinguished set of output vertices on completion of the computation. The computation is completed when the energy of the system is at a local minimum.

One of the interesting open problems in Artificial Intelligence is the development of a low-level model of cortical activity. The Boltzmann machine is one of the many such models proposed in the literature. Much research is currently aimed at determining whether these low-level models can emulate high-level cortical functions, such as learning. We believe that it is important to investigate the computational power of these models. An outer limit on what can be computed is a conservative outer limit on what can be learned. Special-purpose computational algorithms may be used to derive efficient learning algorithms in specific domains.

† Research supported by NSF grant DCR-84-07256.

Methodologies for Intelligent Systems
Z. W. Ras and M. Zemankova, Editors

We will measure the resources of *running-time* and *hardware* as functions of the size of the problem which the machines are to solve. We will show that the connection graph can be made acyclic, the machine can be made deterministic (that is, all random behaviour can be removed), and all edge-weights can be made equal to unity. That is, we show that a Boltzmann machine can be reduced to a *combinational circuit*. The resulting machine will have its running-time increased by a constant multiple, and its hardware requirement increased by a polynomial.

The main body of this paper is broken up into six major sections. In the first section we give a more formal definition of our Boltzmann machine model. In the second section we note that cycles can be removed from the connection graph of the machine. The third section shows how probabilism can be removed from the processors, and replaced by probabilistic inputs. The fourth section shows how probabilism can be removed entirely using a standard sampling technique. The fifth section removes edge-weights and compares the computing power of the resulting Boltzmann machines to standard complexity classes from the literature. The sixth and final section considers some generalizations of our simplified Boltzmann machine model.

2. The Boltzmann Machine.

We wish to study the computing power of resource-bounded Boltzmann machines. The two resources of interest are time and hardware. It is customary in complexity theory to measure resources as a function of input size. We will therefore make minor modifications to the standard definition of Boltzmann machines to make such a measurement possible. We will consider a Boltzmann machine to be an infinite family $B = \langle B_1, B_2, \ldots \rangle$ of finite machines, one for each input size. This is customary when modelling a machine which is finite, yet is large enough for all reasonable requirements. Each finite machine B_n consists of:

(i) A directed graph $G_n = (V_n, E_n)$. The vertices in V_n are termed *processors*.

(ii) A distinguished set of *input processors*, $I_n \subseteq V_n$.

(iii) A distinguished set of *output processors*, $O_n \subseteq V_n$.

(iv) A distinguished set of *initially-active processors*, $A_n \subseteq V_n$, $A_n \cap I_n = \{\}$.

(v) A threshold assignment, $h_n : V_n \rightarrow \mathbf{Z}$, which assigns a *threshold* to every processor.

(vi) A weight assignment, $w_n : E_n \rightarrow \mathbf{Z}$, which assigns a *weight* to every edge. We adopt the useful convention that if $(u,v) \notin E_n$ then $w_n(u,v)$ is defined to be zero. Note that we require that edge-weights remain constant, that is, they do not vary with time. The modification of weights during the computation is crucial to the learning algorithms of [1, 5, 6]; however, each computation consists of a series of sub-computations with fixed weights. We will further discuss weight modification schemes in Section 6.

We will depict each finite Boltzmann machine (for a fixed number of inputs) using circles for vertices, and lines connecting them for edges. Arrows will indicate the direction of communication along these edges. Threshold values will be placed inside the appropriate vertices, and weights alongside the appropriate edges. Each vertex will be named using numbers and letters if necessary, the name appearing next to the relevant vertex. Figure 2.1 shows a simple three-processor machine.

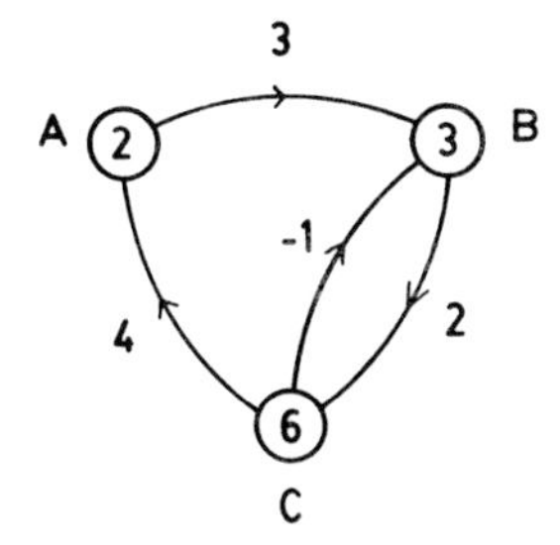

Figure 2.1 A Boltzmann machine with 3 processors, labelled "A", "B" and "C". $I_n = \{A\}$, $O_n = \{B\}$ and $A_n = \{\}$.

A *computation* of B on an input x consisting of n bits (we write $x \in \{0,1\}^n$) is defined as follows. At time $t = 0$ the input processors of B_n are placed into states which encode x. That is, the processors in I_n are numbered consecutively, and the ith such processor is held in the active state if the ith bit of x is one. The processors of A_n are also held in the active state. All other processors are held in the inactive state. Define the *output* of processor v at time t, written U(v,t), to be 1 if v is active at time t and 0 if it is inactive. Define the *input* to processor v at time $t > 0$, written $W_n(v,t)$, to be the sum of the weights of edges connecting it to processors which were active in the previous step, that is:

$$W_n(v,t) = \sum_{u \in V_n} w_n(u,v)U(u,t-1)$$

We wish v to be active at time t with probability $p(W_n(v,t)-h_n(v))$ where:

$$p(\Delta) = \frac{1}{1+e^{-\Delta/\tau}}$$

and τ is a parameter that acts like "temperature" [1, 5, 6]. We insist that at any time during the computation, τ is the same for all processors. We also insist that while τ may vary with time (for example, when performing simulated annealing [7]), it must depend on the input size, not on the particular input being processed (the standard term *oblivious* is used to describe any parameter which is the same for all inputs of any fixed size, but may vary with size). Note that $p = 0.5$ when $W_n(v,t) = h_n(v)$, $p \to 1$ as $W_n(v,t) \to \infty$ and $p \to 0$ as $W_n(v,t) \to -\infty$. We are considering *synchronous* computation, in which all processors change state simultaneously.

Let us assume that there is some pre-defined termination convention. That is, for each n there is some finite time T(n) at which the computation is deemed to be over. The output of B is encoded in the states of the output processors (analogously to the way that the input was encoded in the states of the input processors) at this time. The *running-time* of B is is then said to be T(n). Note that the exact details of the termination condition are not crucial to this definition. T(n) can be taken to be the worst-case running-time over all inputs of size n provided there is some method of maintaining the output for up to T(n) steps, should the computation terminate at some earlier point for any particular input. This can be achieved with careful design and self-loops. B is said to have *size* (at most) Z(n) if for all $n \geq 1$, $|E_n| \leq Z(n)$. We will use size as a measure of hardware requirements. We assume that $|E_n| \geq |V_n|$, which is the case for all but degenerate machines, so that the number of edges is a reasonable measure of size to within a polynomial. We also assume that the absolute values of the edge weights (and therefore the thresholds) are bounded above by $Z(n)$. This ensures that $Z(n)$ is, to within a polynomial, a good measure of the number of bits required to describe B_n. This is a reasonable assumption because there is evidence [5] that the performance of learning algorithms is enhanced when the weights are kept small.

Suppose we restrict our Boltzmann machines to a single output, that is $|O_n| = 1$ for all n. If $x \in \{0,1\}^n$, we say that B *accepts* x if the computation of B_n on input x terminates with the output of the output processor equal to 1, and *rejects* x otherwise. A *language* L is a set of strings of zeros and ones (we write $L \subseteq \{0,1\}^*$). We say that B *recognizes* a language $L \subseteq \{0,1\}^*$ if it can determine whether or not an input x belongs to L with probability of error bounded away from 0.5. That is, it recognizes L iff there is a real number $\epsilon > 0$ such that:

(i) for all $x \in L$, the probability that B accepts x is $\geq 0.5+\epsilon$.

(ii) for all $x \notin L$, the probability that B rejects x is $\geq 0.5+\epsilon$.

This is often called *two-sided bounded-error probabilism* and has a well-studied analogue for sequential computation.

Note that our results hold equally well for Boltzmann machines which compute functions. Let $f:\{0,1\}^n \rightarrow \{0,1\}^m$. A Boltzmann machine is said to *compute* f if for all inputs x and for all i, the machine terminates with the ith bit of its output equal to the ith bit of f(x) with probability $0.5+\epsilon$. Given a machine with m outputs, we can make m copies of it and take one bit of output from each. Each independent copy can then be treated as a language recognizer. The new composite machine has time identical to the original, and size larger by at most a square factor.

3. Removal of Cycles.

The Boltzmann machine may have cycles (i.e. feedback loops) in its connection graph. We can use a standard technique from Savage [12], Goldschlager and Parberry [4] and Parberry and Schnitger [8, 10] to remove these cycles. For each machine with cycles we can produce a new machine without cycles which has the same input-output behaviour (in particular, which recognizes the same language) with a polynomial increase in size and no increase in time. Consider a Boltzmann machine B, possibly with cycles, of size $Z(n)$ and running-time $T(n)$. The acyclic machine $\hat{B}$ consists of $T(n)+1$ "snapshots" of B, one at each point in time. As a consequence, $\hat{B}$ will have size $O(T(n)Z(n))$ and run in time $T(n)$. For more details see Parberry and Schnitger [9]. If we restrict $T(n)$ to be at most a polynomial in $Z(n)$ then the increase in size is at most a polynomial. This is a reasonable restriction if we are interested primarily in machines with running-time very much smaller than size, in particular, if we are using the Boltzmann machine as a low-level model of the brain. (The human brain appears to have around 10^{10} neurons, with a firing time of around one millisecond. Many discrete computations appear to take place within seconds or minutes, that is, if the firing time of a neuron is taken to be the time unit, in around 10^5 steps.)

4. Deferral of Probabilism to the Inputs.

A slightly simpler model of the Boltzmann machine has deterministic processors, of two different types. An *upper-threshold* processor, v, is active at time t iff $W_n(v,t) \geq h_n(v)$. A *lower-threshold* processor, v, is active at time t iff $W_n(v,t) \leq h_n(v)$. We will depict each deterministic processor as a circle with a symbol " $\leq$ " for a lower-threshold and " $\geq$ " for an upper-threshold processor, followed by the threshold value. It is easy to produce processors which compute the Boolean AND and Boolean OR of the states of a set of processors. An AND processor is an upper-threshold processor with threshold k, with edges of weight 1 connecting it to k other processors. We depict an "AND" processor as a circle containing the symbol " $\wedge$ ". An OR processor is an upper-threshold processor with threshold 1, with edges of weight 1 connecting it to k other processors. We depict an "OR" processor as a circle containing the symbol " $\vee$ ".

We also augment the model with a set of *random inputs,* $R_n \subseteq V_n$, $R_n \cap I_n = \{\}$, $R_n \cap A_n = \{\}$, each of which is independently assigned a state from the appropriate probability distribution at the start of each computation. We will depict a random input using a circle containing the word "random" and the probability that it is active. This probability must be a constant.

It is possible to replace each processor of the Boltzmann machine with a small number of processors and random inputs. A processor with threshold-value k, and s inputs with weights $w_1,...,w_s$ can be replaced by the circuit in Figure 4.2. The circuit makes use of an *equality processor.* An equality processor v is active at time t iff $W_n(v,t) = h_n(v)$. An equality processor can be constructed from an upper-threshold, a lower-threshold and an AND processor as in Figure 4.1. Then a probabilistic processor with threshold value k and s inputs in a Boltzmann machine with size Z(n) is replaced by $2Z(n)^2+1$ random inputs, equality processors and AND processors, and a single OR processor. The key is to provide a

Figure 4.1 An equality processor and its implementation.

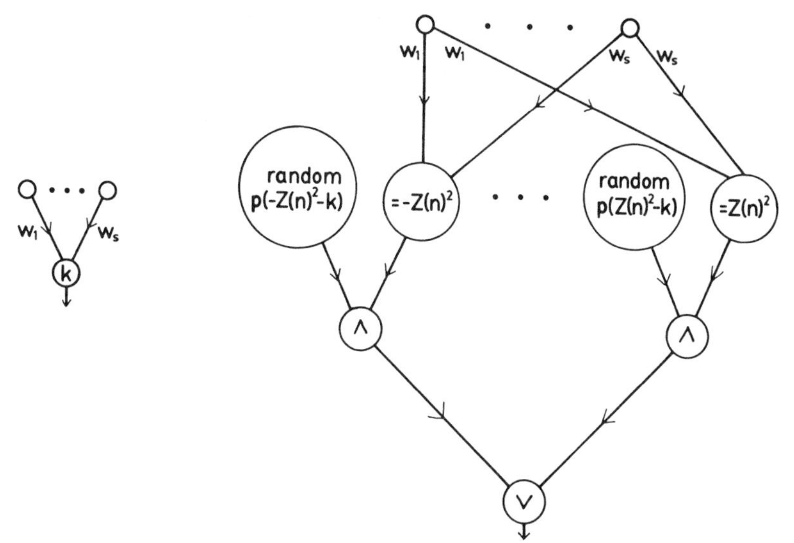

Figure 4.2 A probabilistic Boltzmann processor and its implementation.

random input for each possible probability. The probability depends on the threshold value, k, which is fixed, and the sum of the weights of edges connecting the processor to active neighbours, which, since s is bounded above by Z(n) and each weight is bounded above in absolute value by Z(n), is bounded above in absolute value by $Z(n)^2$. The random input which is active with the correct probability value is "selected out" by the rest of the circuit.

Thus every Boltzmann machine can be simulated by one with deterministic processors and a small number of random inputs, with at most a polynomial increase in size and a constant-multiple increase in running time.

5. Complete Removal of Probabilism.

Given a Boltzmann machine B with random inputs, as described in the previous Section, we show how to produce a new machine $\hat{B}$ which is deterministic and recognizes the same language as B, with only polynomially more processors and time differing by at most a constant multiple. Suppose $B = \langle B_1, B_2, \ldots \rangle$ recognizes L with error probability $0.5-\epsilon$, where $\epsilon > 0$ is a real number. We will construct a completely deterministic machine which recognizes L (with no error). If B_n is a finite Boltzmann machine with n inputs, and r is a fixed string of zeros and ones of the appropriate size, let $B_n(r)$ be the machine obtained by fixing the random-inputs according to r. That is, if the ith bit of r is 1, then the ith random input is placed in A_n. Suppose we pick cn such strings at random, where $c > (1-2\epsilon)(\log_e 2)/\epsilon^2$, choosing each random input independently from the appropriate distribution. We claim that there is a choice of such an $r_1, \ldots, r_{cn}$ such that the deterministic machine $\hat{B}_n$ depicted in Figure 5.1 recognizes the same language as B_n with no error. $\hat{B}_n$ consists of a copy of each of $B_n(r_1), \ldots, B_n(r_{cn})$. Each of those sub-circuits is a sample of the random circuit B_n. $\hat{B}_n$ decides which output to produce by taking a majority decision of the outputs of those samples (we assume that c is even).

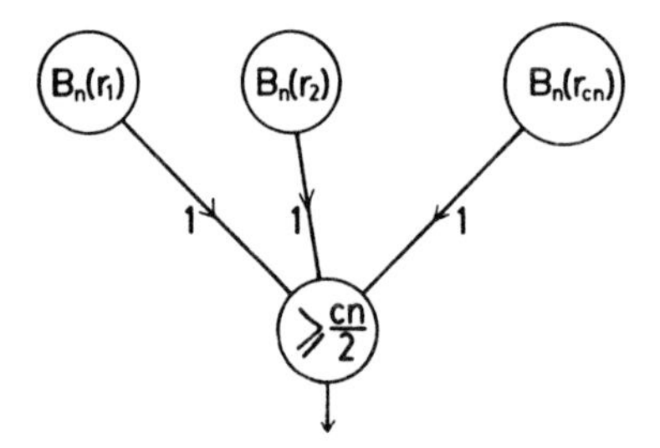

Figure 5.1 A deterministic machine $\hat{B}_n$ constructed from cn copies of B_n.

Let x be an input of size n. Let

$$\text{Failures}(x) = \{(r_1, \ldots, r_{cn}) \mid \hat{B}_n \text{ gives the wrong output}\}$$

We claim that if the sequence $r_1, \ldots, r_{cn}$ is picked at random, then the probability that it is in Failures(x) is $< 2^{-n}$. The proof requires a well-known result from probability theory, which we will adopt from [2, 13]. Suppose we perform N independent Bernoulli trials each with probability p. Let B(k,N,p) be the probability that at least k of the trials succeed. Then:

Proposition. If $k = Np(1+\beta)$ for some $0 \leq \beta \leq 1$ then $B(k,N,p) \leq e^{-0.5\beta^2 Np}$.

If we pick any r at random, the probability that it fails is $\leq 0.5-\epsilon$. If we perform cn independent Bernoulli trials to pick $r_1,...,r_{cn}$, where $c > (1-2\epsilon)(\log_e 2)/\epsilon^2$, and take $N = cn$, $p = 0.5-\epsilon$, $\beta = 2\epsilon/(1\text{-}2\text{epsilon})$, $k = cn/2$, then by the proposition, the probability that there are at least cn/2 failures out of cn trials is:

$$B(cn/2,cn,0.5-\epsilon) \leq e^{-0.5cn(0.5-\epsilon)} < 2^{-n}.$$

Therefore if we pick $r_1,...,r_{cn}$ at random, the probability that it is in $\bigcup_x \text{Failures}(x)$ is less than one (since there are only 2^n possible strings x of length n). Therefore there must be at least one choice of cn strings $r_1,...,r_{cn}$ that make $\hat{B}_n$ work correctly for all inputs of size n. Therefore $\hat{B}$ recognizes the same language as B.

6. Boltzmann Machines and Threshold Circuits.

To complete our result, it is sufficient to observe that all edge-weights can be made equal to one [8, 10]. Thus Boltzmann machines are, under the assumptions listed in the Introduction, equivalent to unbounded fan-in circuits built from gates which compute Boolean threshold functions. These so-called unbounded fan-in threshold circuits are a sub-model of the Boltzmann machine which has been greatly studied in the recent literature (see, for example, [3, 8, 10, 11]).

It is perhaps surprising that so many of the key features of the Boltzmann machine (such as probabilism and the ability to do simulated annealing) are unimportant. However, having shown that Boltzmann machines are weaker than they appear, it must be noted that even threshold circuits of polynomial size and constant depth are extremely powerful. For example, they can multiply two integers [3], approximate convergent rational power series, perform integer and polynomial division, fast Fourier transform, polynomial interpolation, Chinese remaindering, compute elementary symmetric functions, and banded and triangular Toeplitz matrix inverses [11]. Thus Boltzmann machines are more powerful than the classical sequential or parallel models of computation.

7. Weight-Modification and Asynchrony.

We have assumed that the edge-weights remain constant throughout the computation. However, one of the key features of the Boltzmann machine is its ability to learn by modifying its edge-weights. If the weight of an edge at a particular point in time can be computed by a polynomial size, constant depth threshold circuit from the states of the processors in previous steps, then an edge of variable weight can be simulated by providing an edge of each possible weight, and "selecting out" the appropriate edge using a small circuit of AND and OR gates. The size of the new circuit will increase by a polynomial, and the running time by a constant multiple.

We have also assumed that the model is synchronous, that is, the processors are synchronized. Our results work equally well for a Boltzmann machine in which each processors makes a decision on whether to fire based upon any function which is computable from the states of its neighbours in constant time by a constant-depth, polynomial-size threshold circuit, even when that decision is made probabilistically. As before, the number of processors will increase by a polynomial, and the running time by a constant multiple.

References

1. D. H. Ackley, G. E. Hinton, and T. J. Sejnowski, "A learning algorithm for Boltzmann machines," *Cognitive Science*, vol. 9, pp. 147-169, 1985.

2. D. Angluin and L. Valiant, "Fast probabilistic algorithms for Hamiltonian circuits and matchings," *Proc. 9th Ann. ACM Symp. on Theory of Computing*, 1977.
3. A. K. Chandra, L. J. Stockmeyer, and U. Vishkin, "Constant depth reducibility," *SIAM J. Comp.*, vol. 13, no. 2, pp. 423-422, May 1984.
4. L. M. Goldschlager and I. Parberry, "On the construction of parallel computers from various bases of Boolean functions," *Theor. Comput. Sci.*, vol. 43, no. 1, pp. 43-48, May 1986.
5. G. E. Hinton and T. J. Sejnowski, "Learning and relearning in Boltzmann machines," in *Parallel Distributed Processing: Explorations in the Microstructure of Cognition*, vol. 1, pp. 282-317, MIT Press, 1986.
6. G. E. Hinton, T. J. Sejnowski, and D. H. Ackley, "Boltzmann machines: Constraint satisfaction networks that learn," Technical Report CMU-CS-84-119, Dept. of Computer Science, Carnegie-Mellon Univ., May 1984.
7. S. Kirkpatrick, C. D. Gelatt, Jr., and M. P. Vecchi, "Optimization by simulated annealing," *Science*, vol. 220, pp. 671-680, 1983.
8. I. Parberry and G. Schnitger, "Parallel computation with threshold functions (Preliminary Version)," in *Proc. Structure in Complexity Theory Conference*, Springer-Verlag Lecture Notes in Computer Science, vol. 223, pp. 272-290, Berkeley, California, June 1986.
9. I. Parberry and G. Schnitger, "Relating Boltzmann machines to conventional models of computation," Technical Report CS-87-07, Dept. of Computer Science, Penn. State Univ., Mar. 1987.
10. I. Parberry and G. Schnitger, "Parallel computation with threshold functions," *J. Computer and System Sciences*, To Appear.
11. J. Reif, "On threshold circuits and polynomial computation," *Proc. 2nd Structure in Complexity Theory Conference*, Ithaca, NY, June 1987.
12. J. E. Savage, "Computational work and time on finite machines," *J. ACM*, vol. 19, no. 4, pp. 660-674, 1972.
13. L. G. Valiant and G. J. Brebner, "A scheme for fast parallel communication," *SIAM J. Comp.*, vol. 11, no. 2, pp. 350-361, 1982.

LEARNING CONCEPTS IN ROUGH ENVIRONMENT, AN OPTIMIZATION PROCEDURE

ZBIGNIEW W. RAS,* CEZARY JANIKOW **
*UNC-Charlotte, A.I. Lab. and Univ. of Bonn, Institute of Informatics, West Germany; **UNC-Chapel Hill and UNC-Charlotte, Dept. of Computer Science

ABSTRACT

We have two knowledge base systems. One represents a student and the other represents a teacher. Student's knowledge is initially limited to the descriptions of objects from some set X in terms of values of attributes from I. The teacher's knowledge about objects from X is minimum as good as student's knowledge but in general we assume that the teacher knows more about objects from X than the student does. The teacher knows concepts (their extensions) from C and the student does not. The paper presents the foundations of a teaching protocol to be followed by the teacher to teach the student all concepts from C.

INTRODUCTION

The paper concerns learning intensions and extensions of concepts. By the extension of a concept we mean a set of objects with properties that characterize the concept. By an intension of a concept we mean a set of properties characterizing the objects to which the concept apply. The student knows descriptions of objects from X in terms of attributes from I1. The teacher knows descriptions of objects from X in terms of attributes from I2. We assume that I1 $\subseteq$ I2. Additionaly the teacher knows the extension and an intension of any concept c (he can use attributes from I2 and concepts different from c to describe c) from a set C. To teach the extension of a concept c from C he has to teach first its intension (the corresponding part of the extension of c can be generated by the system "student"). The remaining part of the extension of a concept c can be taught by displaying to the student all its objects.

1. BASIC DEFINITIONS

In this section we introduce the notion of a knowledge base system. By a knowledge base system we mean an information system ([5,7]) extended by adding to it a set of rules. Rules are used to represent approximations of concepts in terms of values of attributes and other concepts. The set of rules representing the student's knowledge about concepts is initially empty. Rules used in this paper are generalizations of rules used by Michalski in his **AQ11** system ([4]) and by Quinlan in his **ID3** system ([6]).

By an information system ([5]) we mean a sequence S=(X,I,V,f), where X is a set of objects, I is a set of

Methodologies for Intelligent Systems
Z. W. Ras and M. Zemankova, Editors

attributes, V is a set of values of attributes from I and f is a function from $X^{x}I$ into V. The function f is called an information function and it describes an element x in terms of values of attributes from I. We assume that:

$f(x,a) \in V_a$ for each $x \in X$

$V = \bigcup\{V_a : a \in I\}$ and $V_a \cap V_b \neq \emptyset$ for any a,b where $a \neq b$.

Assume for example that S = (X,I,V,f) is represented by a table below:

	NAME	SEX	EYES	LANGUAGE	LOCATION
x1	Nancy	F	blue	German	Chicago
x2	Robert	M	hazel	English	Charlotte
x3	Nancy	F	blue	German	Chicago
x4	Robert	M	hazel	English	Charlotte
x5	Ingmar	M	hazel	German	Chicago
x6	Nancy	F	blue	German	Chicago
x7	Nancy	F	blue	German	Bonn

Assume that {x2, x4, x6} is a set of persons in the system above who are lawyers. Can we describe this set precisely in terms of values of attributes from I?

The answer is negative because the object x6 has the same description as the object x3 and only one of them is a member of the set "lawyers". However the set "lawyers" can be described by giving its lower bound and its upper bound in terms of the approximation space for S. Let's start with the definition of an approximation space for S and show how to approximate concepts.

Assume that $c \subseteq X$ is a set representing some concept (its extension) and $\sim$ is an equivalence relation on X defined below:

$$x \sim y \quad \text{iff} \quad (\forall a \in I)[\ f(x,a) = f(y,a)].$$

The pair $(X, \sim)$ is called an approximation space for S. The set of equivalence classes (elementary sets) of the relation "$\sim$" is denoted by E_S. A concept can be described precisely in terms of attributes from I if it is a union of some elements from E_S. In the opposite case we can give only its rough description.

By the lower approximation of a concept c in S we mean the set $L(c) = \bigcup\{e \in E_S : e \subseteq c\}$.

By the upper approximation of a concept c in S we mean the set $U(c) = \bigcup\{e \in E_S : e \cap c \neq \emptyset\}$.

By the boundary of a concept c in S we mean the set

$$B(c) = U(c) - L(c).$$

In our example L("lawyers")= {x2, x4} and U("lawyers")= {x1, x2, x3, x4, x6}.

It is easy to observe that:

if we add new attributes (independent from I) to the system S then usually concepts can be described more precisely (the approximation space has smaller elementary sets).

Let's introduce the notion of a concept more precisely.

By an extension of a concept we mean the set of objects from X with properties that characterize the concept. Instead of saying an extension of a concept c we will just say a concept c.

By an intension of a concept we mean a set of terms describing the objects to which the concept apply. So, the intension of a concept is introduced rather roughly. To give the intension of a concept c we will have to find a term describing the lower approximation of c in S and another term describing the upper approximation of c in S.

We assume that a teacher knows all concepts (their extensions) from the set C and his knowledge about the intension of any concept c from C is represented as a pair of terms (t_1,t_2) where t_1 is a description of L(c) and t_2 is a description of -U(c). The rule corresponding to a concept c (in the knowledge base system "teacher") has a form (c,t_1,t_2). So, the teacher can describe concepts only with some roughness. The optimal representation for terms t_1 and t_2 is the disjunctive normal form. This way, because of the table representation of an information system, we can go easily from intensions to extensions of concepts. The strategies for generating (learning) intensions of concepts from their extensions were proposed by Michalski [4], Quinlan [6] and others. The boundary B(c) of a concept c can be taught by displaying all objects from B(c) with a message saying which objects belong to the concept c and which do not. We assume that the terms t_1 , t_2 in a rule (c,t_1,t_2) do not have to be in DNF. The main goal in this paper is to show how to transfer terms (of the language used by the system "teacher") to the disjunctive normal form and how to use them to construct rules for the system "student".

2. LANGUAGE USED BY SYSTEMS "STUDENT" AND "TEACHER"

The language used by a teacher and its standard interpretation will be defined in this section. The student (at the end of the teaching process) will use the same language as the teacher does but he can interpret terms (rules) differently than the teacher. Initially the teacher will use statements built only from values of attributes in I. With each concept c learned by the student, the language used by the "teacher" will be extended by adding c to the set of its constants. We will give a complete and sound set of axioms for the semantics introduced in this section. These axioms will be used to construct the rules in the system "student".

Let's assume that S=(X,I,V,f) is an information system which represents a student and C is a set of concepts. The language L(S,C) is defined below.

Its alphabet contains:
1) constants: $\underline{w}$ where $w \in V \cup C$ and 0, 1
2) functors: +, *, - , -->, $\underline{L}$, $\underline{U}$

3) predicates: =, $\leq$
4) connectives: $\vee$, $\wedge$, $\sim$
5) auxiliary symbols: (,).

The set of terms T is a least set such that:
1) all constants are terms
2) if t_1, t_2 are terms, then (t_1+t_2), (t_1*t_2), $(t_1\text{-->}t_2)$, $-t_1$, $\underline{L}(t_1)$, $\underline{U}(t_1)$ are terms.

The set of formulas F is a least set such that:
1) if t_1, t_2 are terms then $(t_1 = t_2)$, $(t_1 \leq t_2)$ are formulas
2) if **a**, **b** are formulas then $(\mathbf{a} \vee \mathbf{b})$, $(\mathbf{a} \wedge \mathbf{b})$, $\sim \mathbf{a}$ are formulas.

The language L(S,C) is used by the teacher only if C is a set of concepts already taught by him. So, L(S,C) can be seen as a growing language. If c is a new concept learned by a student, then L(S,C) is extended by adding c to the set C.

By a standard interpretation of L(S,C) we mean an interpretation M_S such that:

1) $M_S(\underline{w}) = \{ x \in X:$ if $w \in V_a$ then $f(x,a) = w\}$ for any $w \in V$
$M_S(\overline{w}) = w$ for any $w \in C$
$M_S(\overline{0}) = \emptyset$, $M_S(1) = X$

2) for any terms t_1, t_2, t
$M_S(t_1+t_2) = M_S(t_1) \cup M_S(t_2)$
$M_S(t_1*t_2) = M_S(t_1) \cap M_S(t_2)$
$M_S(t_1\text{-->}t_2) = M_S(-t_1) \cup M_S(t_2)$
$M_S(-t) = -M_S(t)$
$M_S(\underline{L}(t)) = L(M_S(t))$, $M_S(\underline{U}(t)) = U(M_S(t))$

3) for any terms t_1, t_2 and any formulas **a**, **b**

$$M_S((t_1 = t_2)) = \begin{cases} T: & M_S(t_1) = M_S(t_2) \\ F: & \text{otherwise} \end{cases}$$

$$M_S((t_1 \leq t_2)) = \begin{cases} T: & M_S(t_1) = M_S(t_2) \\ F: & \text{otherwise} \end{cases}$$

$$M_S((\mathbf{a} \vee \mathbf{b})) = M_S(\mathbf{a}) \vee M_S(\mathbf{b})$$
$$M_S((\mathbf{a} \wedge \mathbf{b})) = M_S(\mathbf{a}) \wedge M_S(\mathbf{b})$$

$$M_S(\sim \mathbf{a}) = \begin{cases} T: & M_S(\mathbf{a}) = F \\ F: & \text{otherwise} \end{cases}$$

Let's make some comments about the language L(S,C) and the semantics M_S introduced above. L(S,C) will be used by the teacher to teach a concept c only if c is not in C and all the concepts from C are already taught. L(S,C) does not have to be enough powerful to describe precisely the extension of c. This way the concept c will be learned only rougly (the intension of c expressed in terms of the language L(S,C) will describe the lower bound and the upper bound of c). The equivalence classes of the approximation space corresponding to L(S,C) are geting smaller with each new concept learned by the student (we assume that the student can learn extensions precisely).

The term $t_1 \dashrightarrow t_2$ where $M_S(t_1) \subseteq M_S(t_2)$ is called a generalization rule.

The term $t_1 \dashrightarrow t_2$ where $M_S(t_2) \subseteq M_S(t_1)$ is called a specification rule.

Fact 1. The interpretation M_S is a model for all statements listed below:

1) $a = \underline{L}(a)$ for any $a \in V$
2) $\underline{L}(t) \leq t$
3) $\overline{U}(\underline{L}(t)) = \underline{L}(\underline{L}(t)) = \underline{L}(t)$
4) $\underline{L}(-t) = -\overline{U}(t)$, $\overline{U}(-t) = -\underline{L}(t)$
5) $\overline{U}(t+s) = \overline{U}(t) + \overline{U}(s)$
6) $\underline{L}(t*s) = \underline{L}(t) * \underline{L}(s)$
7) $\overline{U}(t*s) \leq \overline{U}(t) * \overline{U}(s)$
8) $\underline{L}(t) + \underline{L}(s) \leq \underline{L}(t+s)$
9) $t \dashrightarrow s = (-t) + s$
10) $-a = \sum\{b : b \in V_i \text{ and } a \neq b \text{ and } a \in V_i\}$ for each $a \in V$
11) axioms of Boolean algebra for terms
12) standard axioms for predicates "=" and "$\leq$".

Assume now that (L(S,C),Ax,R) is a formal system where Ax is a set of axioms listed in FACT 1 and R is one-element set of rules. The rule r from R has the following form:

$$\frac{t(t_1) = t_3 \ , \ t_1 = t_2}{t(t_2) = t_3}$$

where t, t_1, t_2, t_3 are terms.

Theorem 1. The following statements are equivalent:
1) $t_1 = t_2$ is true in all standard interpretations
2) $t_1 = t_2$ can be proved from Ax using rule r.

Let's make some additional comments. The teacher will use terms from L(S,C) to describe an intension of a concept c. Let's assume that the final result of teaching a concept c is described by a sequence (c, t_1, t_2) where $t_1 \leq c$ and $c \leq -t_2$ are true in all standard interpretations. Terms t_1, t_2 do not have to be in DNF. However, we can construct new terms t_1', t_2' (where $t_1' \leq t_1$, $t_2' \leq t_2$ are true in all standard interpretations) in DNF by:

1) Moving negation inside terms t_1, t_2
2) Removing negation by applying axiom 10
3) Moving functors $\underline{L}$ and $\overline{U}$ inside both terms by applying axioms 2-9.

The result of the above steps is stored as a sequence (c, t_1', t_2').

3. LEARNING CONCEPTS BY THE SYSTEM "STUDENT"

The foundations of a teaching protocol will be discussed in this section. The student is represented as an information system S with the set of rules which is initially empty.

Let's assume that S=(X,I,V,f) is an information system representing a student who needs to learn concepts from some set C. He will learn them one by one with teacher's help.

Initially, we assume that the order in which these concepts are taught is arbitrary. Let $c_1, c_2, \ldots, c_n$ is a list of concepts to be taught. The set of rules R representing the student's knowledge about concepts is initially empty.

The result of learning the concept c_1 is described by the rule (c_1,t_1,s_1), where t_1, s_1 are terms in $L(S,\emptyset)$ describing $L(c_1)$, $-U(c_1)$ respectively.

The result of learning the concept c_2 is described by the rule (c_2,t_2,s_2), where t_2, s_2 are terms in $L(S,\{c_1\})$ such that $t_2 \leq c_2$, $c_2 \leq -s_2$ are true in all standard interpretations. For the simplicity reason we will say from now $t_1 \leq t_2$ instead of saying $t_1 \leq t_2$ is true in all standard interpretations.

Assume that after n-1 steps $R=\{(c_i,t_i,s_i): i \leq n-1\}$ and c_n is the next concept to be learned. The teacher can teach either its extension or its intension. To teach the extension of a concept he has to provide examples of objects representing the concept. Assume that the teacher will teach an intension of a concept. In this case he has to provide two terms t_n, s_n from $L(S,\{c_i\}_{i<n-1})$ such that $t_n \leq c_n \leq -s_n$. Terms t_n, s_n are transformed to t_n', s_n' both in DNF. This transformation is done by moving first the negation inside terms, removing the negation and finally moving functors $\underline{L}$ and U inside resulting terms. We will get $t_n' \leq t_n \leq c_n \leq -s_n \leq -s_n'$.
Conjuncts in t_n' and s_n' have the form $r_1 * r_2 * \ldots * r_m$ where $r_i=\underline{w}$ or $r_i = \underline{L}(\underline{w})$ or $r_i = \underline{U}(\underline{w})$. We are assuming here that w is either a member of V C or the negation of a concept (if we know a concept, then we know its negation).

Let's denote by t_{n2}, s_{n2} terms obtained from t_n', s_n' (respectively) by replacing $\underline{L}(\underline{c}_i)$ by t_i and $\underline{U}(\underline{c}_i)$ by $\underline{c}_i$.

Let's denote by t_{n3}, s_{n3} terms obtained from t_n', s_n' (respectively) by replacing $\underline{L}(\underline{c}_i)$ by $\underline{c}_i$ and $\underline{U}(\underline{c}_i)$ by $-s_i$.

The result of learning the rule (c_i, t_i, s_i) is described in four statements below:

1) Objects described by t_{n2} are in the extension of c_n,

2) Objects described by s_{n2} are not in the extension of c_n,

3) It is quite probable that the objects described by t_{n3} and neither described by t_{n2} nor s_{n3} are in the extension of c_n,

4) It is quite probable that the objects described by s_{n3} and neither described by s_{n2} nor t_{n3} are not in the extension of c_n.

It is the time to propose some strategy to order the concepts from C before the teacher starts to teach them. Let's assume that the set of concepts C is ordered by the relation $\leq$ defined below:

$c_1 \leq c_2$ iff the extension of c_1 is a subset of the extension of c_2.

Now, we will list the main steps of the algorithm which orders the concepts during the teaching process.

1) Teach the concepts which are members of the greatest antichain in $(C,\leq)$. Exit if C is empty.

2) Remove from C all the concepts you taught and denote the resulting set again by C

3) Go back to 1).

REFERENCES

[1] Banerji, R.B., "Learning in the limit in a growing language", Saint Joseph's University, 1987

[2] Michalski, R., "A Theory and Methodology of Inductive Learning", Artificial Intelligence, Vol. 20, 1983, 111-160

[3] Michalski, R., Chilausky, R., "Learning by being told and learning from examples", Internat. J. Policy Anal. Inform. Systems, Vol. 4, No. 2, 1980, 125-160

[4] Michalski, R.S., Larson, J.B., " Selection of most representative training examples and incremental generation of VL1 hypothesis: the underlying methodology and the description of programs ESEL and AQ11", Report No. 867, Dept. of Computer Science, University of Illinois, Urbana, Illinois, 1978

[5] Pawlak, Z., "Rough Sets", Internat. J. Comp. and Info. Sci., Vol. 11, 1982, 341-366

[6] Quinlan, J.R., "Learning efficient classification procedures and their application to chess end games", Chapter 15, Machine Learning: Artificial Intelligence Approach, TIOGA Publishing Comp., Palo Alto, R.S. Michalski, J. Carbonell, T. Mitchell (Editors), 1983

[7] Ras, Z.W., Zemankova, M.,"Rough sets based learning systems", Lecture Notes of Computer Science, Springer Verlag, No. 208, 265-275

COGNITIVE SIMULATION FOR INTELLIGENT DECISION SUPPORT: SCENARIO-LEARNING FROM EPISODES AND EXPECTATION-DRIVEN PREDICTION

Tetsuo SAWARAGI* and Sosuke IWAI*

* Dept. of Precision Mechanics, Faculty of Eng.
Kyoto University, Kyoto 606, JAPAN

ABSTRACT

Human experts are characterized by their abilities to adaptively construct an internalized world model from their experiences as well as to make a model-driven prediction even for a newly-encountering situation. What is required of a knowledge-based decision support system for ill-structured and open world problems is an installation of these abilities. In this paper, a methodology for learning models as expected scenarios from episodes is presented. Then, to measure fitness of a world reality to the model, an idea of prototypicality is introduced, and experts' expectation-driven cognitive process is formulated.

INTRODUCTION

Human experts interpret new cases in terms of something with which they are already familiar, but when knowing some information does not fit to the available pre-existing pattern, they try to adapt past experiences to newly encountering situation that are similar but not identical to the old. This process is a learning capability, whose task is to compare a whole range of similar experiences and derive somehow the "essence" of these experiences. The combined "essence" of past experiences will ultimately amount to an internalized model of the real world in their own views and to governing principles or laws. People behave rationally with respect to this model, and such behavior may not be even approximately optimal with respect to the real world, but at least satisfactory to them.

As for a general architecture of DSS (Decision Support System), a knowledge-based approach has been proposed (Sawaragi et al, 1986a,1986b), where the predecision stages were supported, that is, helping the user identify and explicate the problem he was facing, through an interactive conversation with an enormous amount of domain-specific knowledge. This knowledge base was a collection of relevant historical cases or episodes consisting of a large variety of causally interrelated events and are originally documented statements.

To provide a model-learning capability with the knowledge base, we introduce an idea of *scripts*. A script is a kind of psychological schemata in a form of a consistent, coherent pattern as a series of events linked together in a narrative form. The system can adaptively organize scripts based on the familiar episodes that are relevant to the input information from the user and stored in the knowledge base. Then, prediction of high-consequence events as well as interpretation of prior episodes are performed based on the constructed script. For this purpose, we first develop a methodology for aggregating a detailed causal network into a more essential sequence of larger conceptual units of social events. Next, we suggest an algorithm for organizing a script as a sequence of generalized events from

Methodologies for Intelligent Systems
Z. W. Ras and M. Zemankova, Editors

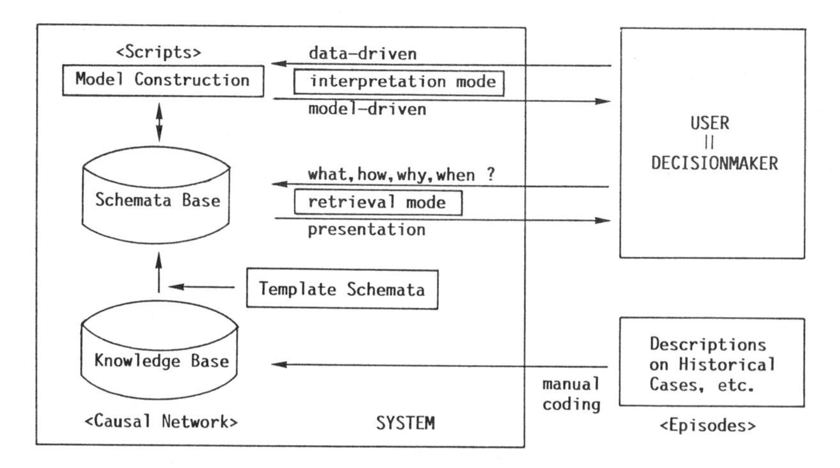

Fig.1 An overview of the system

these extracted sequences. Finally, a methodology for model-driven prediction is suggested based on the organized scripts using an idea of prototype theory from the psychological domain. Fig.1 shows an overview of the system.

AGGREGATION OF DOCUMENTED EPISODES INTO A SEQUENCE OF EVENTS

In previous papers, we have developed an method for encoding documentary data, that is, causal assertions stated by experts, of some episodic cases into causally-chained networks (Sawaragi et al., 1986a, 1986b). Three kinds of nodes (P:*Perception*, D:*Decision*, V: *Value-Belief* Nodes) as well as four kinds of links (C:*Cause*, T:*Terminate*, +S and -S:*Positive and Negative Sentiment* Links) were introduced. Based on these classifications of nodes and links, a number of descriptor units for human social behavior, called *primitive events*, are defined, and a more complex patternized social event including actors' purposes and intentions is defined as an ordered set of primitive events, called *complex events*. Fig.2(a) illustrates a causal network encoded from the documented description on "Japan-US Trade Friction Problem" with regards to three actors, "Japan Steel Industries (JSI)," "US Steel Co. (USS)," and "Steel Chocus(SC)(A league of congressmen)":

"JSI's inroads into US steel market (P11->V11) increased the steel exports of Japan to US (P11->P13), which did harm against USS (P13->V12). Then, USS petitioned to SC and SC supported USS's request of raising steel imports prices (P13->D11->D12->P14->V15), which was welcome by USS (P14->V14) and forced a significant burden on JSI (P14->V13). In reply to this, SC decided to set the Trigger Prices, which obliged JSI to abide by that and had to perform the voluntary restriction of steel exports against its will (P14->D13->P15->D14 ->P16->V17)."

For the primitive and complex events, the system stores their general specification forms as *template schemata*. Each template schema has a corresponding set of attributes of events as slots, and the variables that are to be filled with some specific values. For instance, as shown in Fig.3(a), the slot-value pairs such as event-type, actors, and contents are

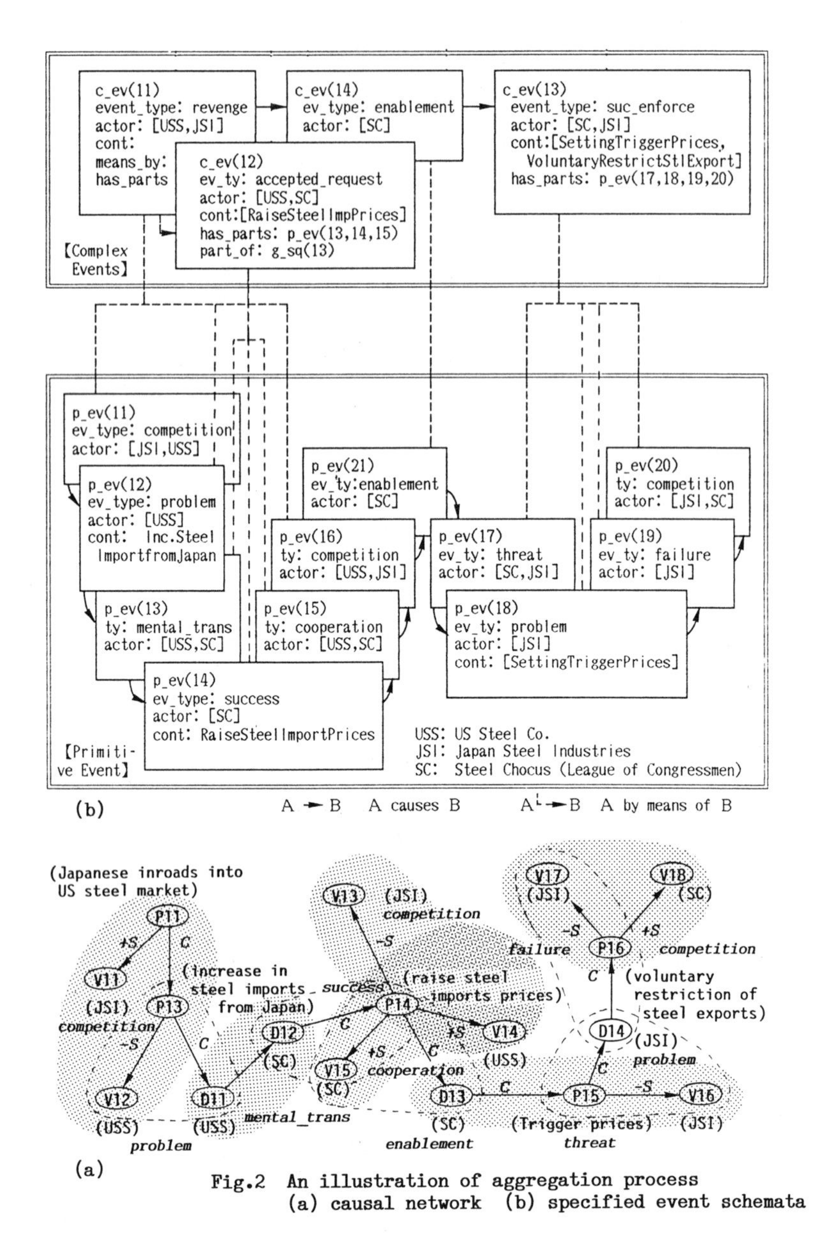

Fig.2 An illustration of aggregation process (a) causal network (b) specified event schemata

prepared, where the numbers of actors or contents are determined according to event-types. The same entities in the template schemata bind the corresponding variables to the identical values, and this is made clearer in Fig.3(b) that illustrates a template schema of a complex event "revenge" in semantic networks. As this figure shows, the template schema has an ordered set of primitive events as its parts through a *has-parts* link. Each primitive event is to be specified from the causal network according to its

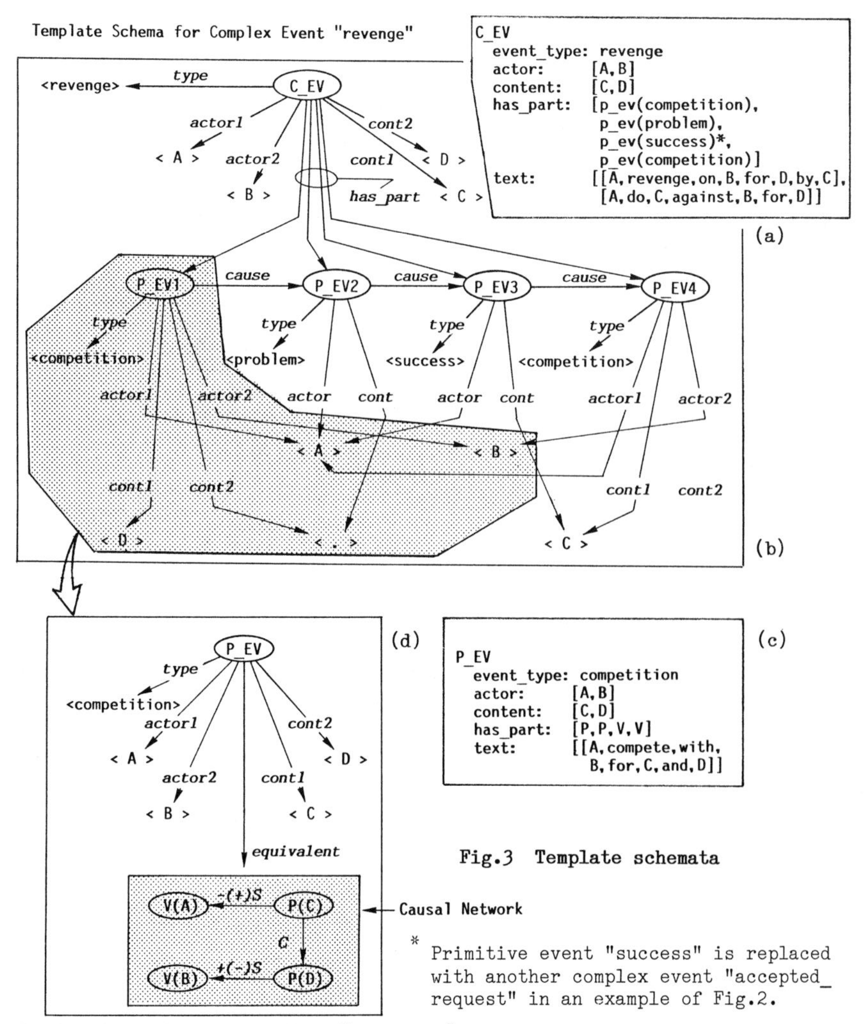

Fig.3 Template schemata

* Primitive event "success" is replaced with another complex event "accepted_request" in an example of Fig.2.

Template Schema for Primitive Event "competition"

template schema as illustrated in Fig.3(c) and (d) for a primitive event "competition". The slot of text defines in list form the natural language expressions that can be used to represent the conceptual meaning of the event in retrieving the specified event schemata.

For a focused sub-region of the knowledge base, the system instantiates the corresponding template schemata and transforms the network into a series of event schemata with a finite set of event features. For instance, for the network of Fig.2(a), the template schemata for three complex events, "revenge", "accepted_request" and "successful_enforcement", as well as ones for their component primitive events, are instantiated. As a result, the system generates event sequences at two different abstraction levels as shown in Fig.2(b), which are to be stored in a schemata base.

ADAPTIVE SCRIPT FORMATION FROM EPISODES

Since the transformed event schemata represent conjunctions of relational statements in the form of [Slot = Value], now it is possible to compare a whole range of similar episodes.

From the collections of event schemata composing different episodes, such general descriptions called *generalized event schemata (GES)* can be generated that implies some of event schemata as its instances. We refer to those event schemata implied by GES as *instance event schemata (IES)* here after. The generalization proceeds according to the *climbing generalization tree rule* as shown in Fig.4, where CTX stands for some arbitrary set of relational statements that are commonly shared by a pair of IES, and s represents the lowest parent node whose descendents include node a and b in the a-kind-of hierarchy of values for slot L. By repetitive application of this rule under a constraint for avoiding over-generalization to all the IES as well as to the generated GES, the GES at different levels of generalization are formed, which produces a hierarchical tree structure for event concepts where the upper nodes represent such GES whose component slots have the more general values and implies the more IES.

When some newly observed event is given, the consequent expected scenarios following this event can be generated by successive applications of the above mentioned generalization process. These are predictable coherent sequences of generalized events, and we call them *scripts* (Schank and Abelson 1977, Abelson 1981).

Suppose that for a provided e_t that represents some situation, episodes in Fig.5(a) are retrieved, all of which are preceded by the events similar to e_t. As shown above, GES $E_k^{(1)}$ (k=1,..,n) are generated from stored IES $e_{1,1}$-$e_{10,1}$ as well as from e_t at various generalization levels. At first, for a set of IES covered by $E_1^{(1)}$, that is, for IES $e_{1,1}$-$e_{3,1}$, another set of IES, $\varepsilon_1^{(1)}$= [$e_{1,2}$ - $e_{6,2}$], is determined whose elements are those directly caused by one of the IES of $E_1^{(1)}$ in the collection of episodes. Then, to this set $\varepsilon_1^{(1)}$ the generalization process is applied. If such GES $E_1^{(2)}$ is generated that can cover almost all the IES of $\varepsilon_1^{(1)}$ as illustrated in Fig.5(a), an event class described by GES $E_1^{(2)}$ can be regarded as representative, i.e., uniquely predictable. Otherwise, the script preceded by $E_1^{(1)}$ terminates, and another upper GES $E_k^{(1)}$ (k=2,3,..) is tried whether any script can be formed preceded by it at this k-th level.

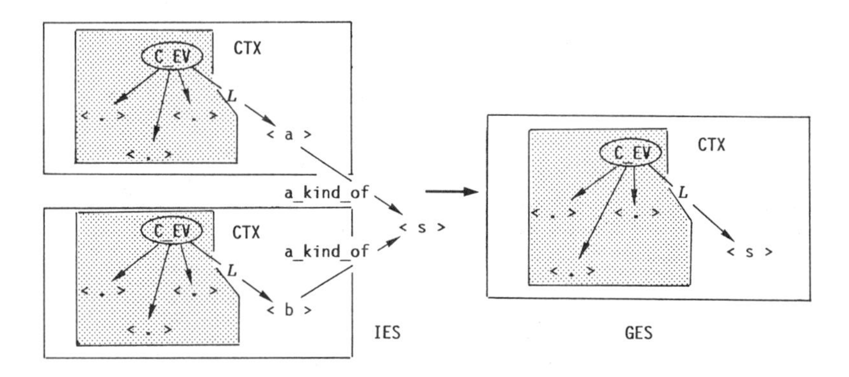

Fig.4 Climbing generalization tree rule

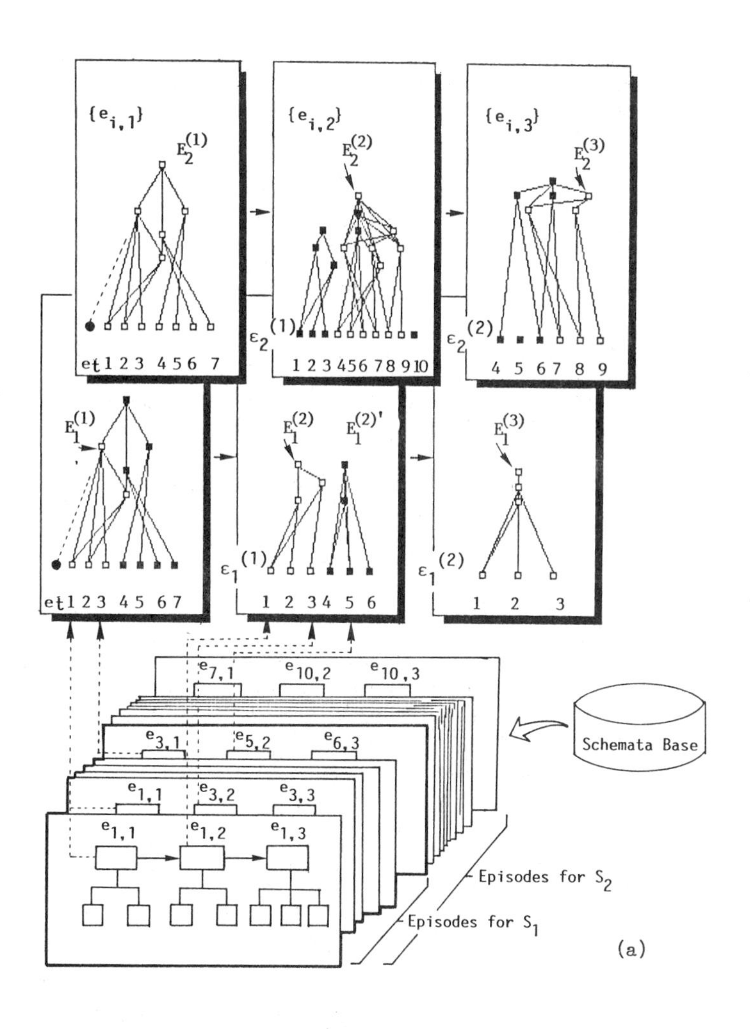

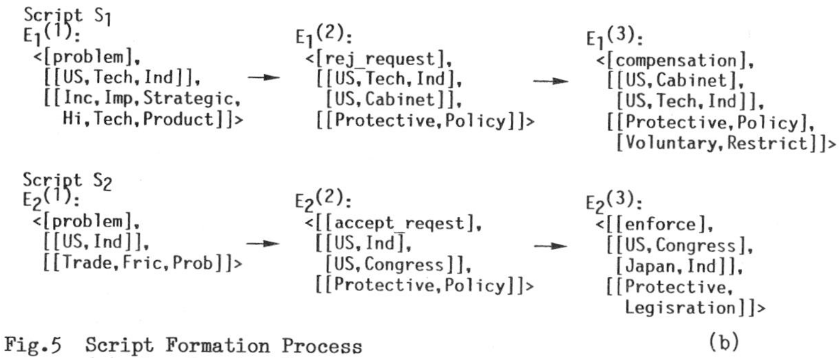

Fig.5 Script Formation Process
(a) Step-by-step Generalization of event schemata
(b) Illustrations of generated scripts

In this way, at each level of GES formed above e_t, the scripts S_k, are organized in parallel. That is, if we adopt the lower $E_k^{(1)}$, a script from the narrower viewpoint is generated based on the fewer episodes, while a global script is formed from a lot of episodes when we adopt an upper $E_j^{(1)}$ ($j > k$). Fig.5(b) illustrates the generated scripts on the basis of episodes concerning with "Japan-US trade friction problem," with a triggering event e_t represented as:

<[event-type=problem],[actor=UCW],
[content=[Increase,in,Imports,of,Electric,Devices,from,Japan]]>.

Note that even though $E_1^{(1)}$ is a subset of $E_1^{(2)}$, the sets of episodes based on which scripts are formed would not necessarily maintain the set-inclusion relationship. Therefore, the scripts following them might differ from each other; for instance in the above example, a "liberalistic" script S_1 and a "protective" one S_2 are generated.

QUANTIFICATION OF MODEL-DRIVEN INTERPRETATION BASED ON PROTOTYPE THEORY

The generated scripts are models that represent expected scenarios when e_t happens. Each model maps input information, i.e., either any stored prior episode or hypothetical one that are not found in the schemata base, onto its corresponding interpretation, so the most promising is a system in which scores are computed according to "fit" of the input information to the models. We assume that some kind of "tuning function" is constructed for each script according to episodes based on which the script is generated. The tuning function for a glovally-viewed script is broad, while the one for a narrowly-viewed script is more finely tuned relative to the former as shown in Fig.6. For instance, while a hypothetical episode H_1 activate the global script less strongly than another episode H_2, the former will activate the specific script more strongly than a global one will.

In order to calculate such activation scores, we introduce an idea of *prototypicality* (Rosch & Lloyd, 1977). Being provided with the individual instances as stimuli, we form a *prototype* as a redundancy structure of the category, and our psychological category are considered to be formed around this prototype. Members of a category come to be viewed as prototypical of the category in proportion to an extent to which they bear a resemblance to this prototype.

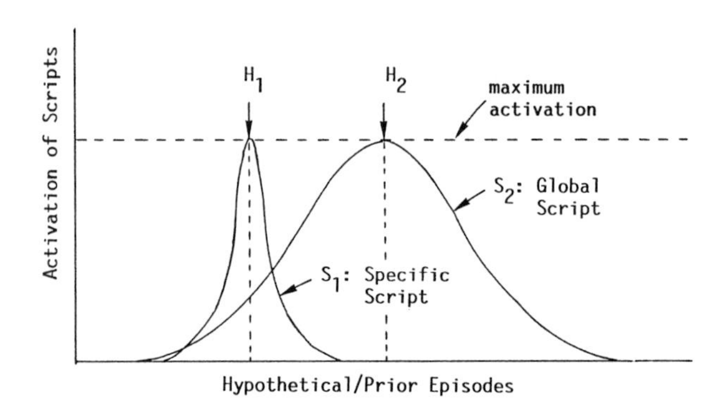

Fig.6 Tuning functions formed by activation of scripts

Based on these ideas, we calculate a degree of prototypicality of IES e_i under GES E_j as follows: for a member IES, e_i, we define a set of relational statements as $RS(e_i)$, which includes not only those composing IES but also ones concerning with their upper values through the a-kind-of relations. Then, comparing the $RS(e_i)$ for all members of E_j, we can make such a set of common relational statements $CRS(E_j)$ each of which is commonly shared by no less than half of the members, and we define this set as prototype of E_j. $prot(e_i|E_j)$ can be defined as a degree of semantic similarity of e_i to the prototype according to the following:

$$prot(e_i|E_j) = \frac{(CRS(E_j) \cap RS(e_i))^{\#}}{(CRS(E_j) \cup RS(e_i))^{\#}} \qquad (0 \leq prot(e_i|E_j) \leq 1.0), \quad (1)$$

where $\cap$ and $\cup$ denote an intersection and an union in a set-theoretical sense, respectively, and the superscript # means a number of elements of the set. The fitness of a hypothetical episode $H{:}e_t, e_{p1}, \ldots, e_{pk}$, to script S_i: E_1, $E_2, \ldots$ can be calculated using $prot(e_i|E_j)$ according to the following:

$$prot(H|S_i) = prot(e_t, e_{p1}, \ldots, e_{pk}|S_i)$$
$$= \frac{1}{k+1}\left[\sum_{i=1}^{k} \{\max_j prot(e_{pi}|E_j)\} + prot(e_t|E_1)\right]. \qquad (2)$$

The most plausible interpretation of H is the one that has the maximum fitness with H.

CONCLUSIONS

An ill-structured problem is defined as one putting demands on knowledge as prior experiences, and what is considered as evidence of some judgment's truth or plausibility is the empirical knowledge itself rather than any deductive inferences in an analytical way. Moreover, the boundary of required knowledge is not definite, so the system should be designed to deal with "open" world. Our suggested methodology to adaptively construct models based on familiar episodes and to quantify the model-driven interpretation using prototype theory will contribute much to realizing an intellectual decision support for such ill-structured, open world problems.

References

Abelson, R.P.,"Psychological Status of the Script Concept," Amer. Psychologist, 36, 715-729, 1981.

Rosch, E. and B.B. Lloyd, "Cognition and Categorization," Lawrence Erlbaum Assoc., Hillsdale, N.J., 1978.

Sawaragi, T., S. Iwai, and O. Katai, "An Integration of Qualitative Causal Knowledge for User-Oriented Decision Support," Control-Theory and Advanced Technology, 2, 451-482, 1986a.

Sawaragi, T., S. Iwai, and O. Katai, "Human-Friendly Interface System for Decision Support Based on Self-Organized Multi-Layered Knowledge Structure," Preprints of 7th International Conference on Multiple Criteria Decision Making, Kyoto, 1986b, 674-683.

Schank, R.C. and Abelson, R.P., "Scripts, Plans, Goals, and Understanding," Hillsdale, N.J., Lawrence Erlbaum Associates, 1977.

An Inductive Learning System – ILS

J.H. Wong and S.K.M. Wong

Department of Computer Science
University of Regina
Regina, Saskatchewan
Canada. S4S 0A2

Abstract : *An inductive learning system (ILS) is proposed. The ILS system is designed based on the concepts of Core and Reduct to ensure that the generated decision rules contain no superfluous attributes. An efficient and effective method of selecting attributes is suggested for generating decision rules. This new approach is compared with the learning systems ID3 and AQ11. ILS has been implemented and applied to the diagnosis of soybean bean diseases based on the samples given by experts in plant pathology.*

1. Introduction

The main objective of inductive learning system is to infer decision rules from a set of sample decisions provided by an expert. There have been many methods suggested [1, 2, 3, 4] for the design rule-guided expert systems by inductive inference. Based on the theory of information, Quinlan [3] proposed a method (ID3) to construct a decision tree. ID3 starts with selecting an attribute and partitions the samples into disjoint subsets characterized by the values of the attribute. The same procedure is applied recursively until all objects in the samples are classified correctly. Obviously, this method depends very much on how well the attribute is selected in the construction of the decision tree. It is important to note that such a tree may contain superfluous attributes. In order words, the decision rules obtained in this way are not necessarily generalized. An alternative attribute selection criterion can be formulated based on the theory of *Rough Set* [5, 6]. It has been shown in [4, 7] that this criterion is, in fact, a special case of the statistical approach in ID3. Another inductive method (AQ11) to construct decision rules was proposed by Michalski [2]. Given a set of events representing a *concept*, the main task in AQ11 is to build a *star* for an event belonging to this concept against the negative event set. It can be seen that when there are many events belonging to the concept, the computational complexity can easily become intractable. To make it practical, AQ11 has a parameter called *maxstar* which controls the maximum possible number of generated complexes at each set-theoretic multiplication.

In this paper, we suggest an inductive learning algorithm (ILS) [8]. Any superfluous attributes are automatically eliminated. The attribute selection criterion in ILS is based on the minimization of error rate (Bayes decision procedure). We also present a detailed comparison of our method with ID3 and AQ11. We conclude by commenting on the advantages and disadvantages of the various inductive learning systems.

2. Basic Concepts and Knowledge Representation

In many problems of artificial intelligence such as machine learning and expert system, the knowledge about a given set of objects is expressed by some features (attributes) and their descriptions (attribute values). Such a knowledge representation system S can be formally defined as follows :

$S = < U, C, d, V, f >$, where U is a finite set of objects ,

$T = C \cup d$ is a set of attributes of which C and d are referred to as student (condition) and expert (decision) attributes, respectively ,

$V = \bigcup_{x \in T} V_x$ is a set of attribute values (where V_x is the domain of attribute $x \in T$) , and

$f : U \times T \rightarrow V$ is an information function such that $f(e,x) \in V_x$, for each $e \in U$ and $x \in T$ (i.e. f assigns a set of attribute values to each object in U) .

Methodologies for Intelligent Systems
Z. W. Ras and M. Zemankova, Editors

Example 2-1 : A knowledge representation system S can be represented in a tabular form.

U	x_1	x_2	x_3	x_4	d	U	x_1	x_2	x_3	x_4	d
e_1	0	3	3	0	+	e_{17}	0	0	1	0	–
e_2	0	3	2	1	+	e_{18}	1	2	1	2	–
e_3	1	2	3	0	+	e_{19}	0	2	0	1	–
e_4	1	3	3	1	+	e_{20}	1	1	1	1	–
e_5	0	2	3	1	+	e_{21}	3	3	3	2	–
e_6	1	3	2	1	+	e_{22}	2	3	3	2	–
e_7	1	2	2	0	+	e_{23}	2	3	3	0	–
e_8	1	2	3	1	+	e_{24}	3	3	2	3	–
e_9	3	0	0	3	+	e_{25}	3	0	3	0	–
e_{10}	2	1	0	3	+	e_{26}	2	1	3	1	–
e_{11}	2	0	1	2	+	e_{27}	0	3	1	3	–
e_{12}	3	1	1	2	+	e_{28}	0	2	0	3	–
e_{13}	2	1	1	2	+	e_{29}	3	3	3	0	–
e_{14}	3	1	0	4	+	e_{30}	2	0	3	2	–
e_{15}	2	0	0	2	+	e_{31}	0	1	1	1	–
e_{16}	3	0	1	2	+	e_{32}	1	1	0	1	–

Table 2-1 A knowledge representation system S.

2.1 Equivalence Relations

For any subset of condition attributes $B = x_1x_2...x_m \subseteq C$ in a knowledge representation system $S = <U, C, d, V, f>$, an equivalence relation $\theta(B)$ on U can be defined as follows :

$(e_1,e_2) \in \theta(B)$ *iff* $f(e_1,x_j) = f(e_2,x_j)$ for every attribute $x_j \in B$.

In particular when $B = C$, $\theta(C)$ is known as the *atomic* partition. Each equivalence class Y_i of $\theta(B)$ has a unique description $Des(Y_i)$ defined by a Boolean conjunctive expression in terms of the values of the attributes in B as follows :

$Des(Y_i) = f(e,x_1) \wedge f(e,x_2) \wedge ... \wedge f(e,x_n)$, where e is a typical element that belongs to Y_i.

In this paper, we consider only those equivalence relations whose individual equivalence classes can be described by conjunctive Boolean expressions of the attribute values.

2.2 Decision Rules

Given a knowledge representation system $S = <U, C, d, V, f>$, let $\theta(d) = \{E_1, E_2,...., E_n\}$ denote the partition (equivalence relation) on U induced by the expert attribute d and let $V_d = \{a_1, a_2,...., a_n\}$ be the domain of d. Each E_i represents an expert concept a_i (i.e. $Des(E_i) = a_i$).

Given a partition $\bar{B} = \{Y_1, Y_2,...., Y_m\}$, the set of decision rules for each expert concept a_i can be expressed in terms of the descriptions of the equivalence classes of $\bar{B}$ as follows :

$\{r_{ij}\} = \{Des(Y_i) \rightarrow a_j \mid 0 < P(E_j \mid Y_i) \leq 1\}$, where $P(E_j \mid Y_i) = P(E_j \cap Y_i) / P(Y_i)$ is the conditional probability.

A decision rule r_{ij} is said to be deterministic if and only if $P(E_j \mid Y_i) = 1$, namely, $r_{ij} : Des(Y_i) \rightarrow a_j$. That is, if $Des(Y_i)$ uniquely implies a_j, then rule r_{ij} is deterministic; otherwise r_{ij} is non-deterministic.

2.3 The Concepts of Core and Reduct

The information in a knowledge representation system $S = <U, C, d, V, f>$ is described by means of attributes and attribute values. A question is whether all available attributes are necessary to describe a subset of objects representing an expert concept. In order to facilitate the discussion of superfluous attributes [9], the concepts of Core and Reduct [8] are introduced below.

If the knowledge representation system S contains no identical rows, the atomic partition $\theta(C)$ is an identity relation. In this case, the set of equivalence relations, $L = \{ \theta(B) \mid B \subseteq 2^C \}$, forms a partition lattice based on the partial ordering $\leq$ defined as follows: for any $\theta, \theta' \in L$,

$\theta \leq \theta'$ *iff* $(e_i,e_j) \in \theta$ implies that $(e_i,e_j) \in \theta'$.

Note that a knowledge representation system is deterministic if $\theta(C) \leq \theta(d)$.

Definition 2.3–1 : Suppose $\theta(B) \leq \theta(d)$ holds for a subset of attributes $B \subseteq C$ in a knowledge representation system $S = \langle U, C, d, V, f \rangle$. An attribute x is superfluous in B with respect to d if $\theta(B - \{x\}) \leq \theta(d)$; otherwise x is non-superfluous in B with respect to d if $\theta(B - \{x\}) \nleq \theta(d)$.

Definition 2.3–2 : Let R be a subset of attributes of C in S . R is a Reduct with respect to d if $\theta(R) \leq \theta(d)$ and there exists no superfluous attribute in R.

Lemma 2.3–1 : An attribute x is non-superfluous in C with respect to d *iff* no Reduct exists in $(C - \{x\})$.

($\Rightarrow$) Since $x \in C$ is non-superfluous, by definition 2.3-1, $\theta(C - \{x\}) \nleq \theta(d)$. Suppose there exists a Reduct $R \subseteq (C - \{x\})$, this implies $\theta(C - \{x\}) \leq \theta(R)$ and $\theta(R) \leq \theta(d)$. Since $\leq$ is transitive, $\theta(C - \{x\}) \leq \theta(d)$. This is in contradiction with the assumption.

($\Leftarrow$) Since no Reduct exists in $(C - \{x\})$, this implies $\theta(C - \{x\}) \nleq \theta(d)$. Suppose $x \in C$ is superfluous, by definition 2.3-1, $\theta(C - \{x\}) \leq \theta(d)$. This is in contradiction with the assumption.

Lemma 2.3–2 : An attribute x is superfluous in C with respect to d *iff* there exists at least one Reduct which does not contain the attribute x.

($\Rightarrow$) Given $x \in C$ is superfluous with respect to d. Suppose x does not exist outside any Reduct. This means that x exists in $\bigcap_{i=1}^{n} R_i$, the intersection of all Reducts. Obviously, if this attribute x is removed from C, then no Reduct exists in $(C - \{x\})$. Therefore, by Lemma 2.3-1, x is non-superfluous and this is a contradiction.

($\Leftarrow$) Suppose $x \in C$ exists outside a Reduct R, then, $R \subseteq (C - \{x\})$. It immediately follows that $\theta(C - \{x\}) \leq \theta(R) \leq \theta(d)$. By definition 2.3-1, x is superfluous with respect to d.

Definition 2.3-3 : The Core is a set union of all non-superfluous attributes in C with respect to d in a knowledge representation system S.

Theorem 2.3-1 : Let $\{R_i \mid i = 1, 2, \ldots, n\}$ be the set of all Reducts. Then $\bigcap_{i=1}^{n} R_i = \text{Core}$.

($\Rightarrow$) Let $x \in \bigcap_{i=1}^{n} R_i$, which means that x exists in all the Reducts. Suppose $x \notin$ Core. That is, x is superfluous. By Lemma 2.3-2, x exists outside at least one Reduct. This is a contradiction. Hence, x also exists in the Core.

($\Leftarrow$) Let $x \in$ Core. By definition 2.3-3, x is non-superfluous. Suppose $x \notin \bigcap_{i=1}^{n} R_i$. This implies that x exists outside at least one reduct. By Lemma 2.3-2, x is superfluous and this is a contradiction.

The Core can be easily determined by finding all non-superfluous attributes in C. In a deterministic knowledge representation system S, there may exist more than one Reduct in C with respect to d. If the Core is not empty, it may be used as the starting point to find a Reduct. It should, perhaps, be emphasized here that there are many ways to obtain a Reduct. In Section 5, a method for finding a desirable Reduct is proposed.

3. The ID3 System

In ID3 the decision rules are expressed in the form of a decision tree. Each node represents an attribute. The edges out of a node are labeled with the possible values of the attribute or conditions. Each leaf node consisting a set of objects is labeled by an expert class. Any given object is characterized by a unique path or decision rule from the root of the tree to the leaf. The class label at the leaf node indicates the expert class assigned to the object. The construction of a decision tree for a given set of objects belonging to different expert classes is achieved by associating the set of objects with a root and then recursively sprouting nodes in an attempt to split the objects into consistently defined classes. The salient feature of this method lies in selecting a proper subset of relevant attributes to construct a decision tree based on the *entropy* function [10].

Example 3–1 : To illustrate the method of ID3, consider the knowledge representation system of Table 2-1. The probability of occurrence of objects in class "+" is $p^+ = 16/32$ and in class "–" is $p^- = 16/32$. The entropy H for the set of probabilities $\{p^+, p^-\}$ is given by

$$H_{\varnothing} = -(p^+ \log p^+ + p^- \log p^-)$$
$$= -(16/32 (\log_{10} 16/32) + 16/32 (\log_{10} 16/32)) = 0.3010.$$

$H_{\varnothing}$ is called the *initial entropy* because it measures the information uncertainty of the system in its initial state. If we select attribute x_1 to partition the system, the resulting expected entropy H_{x_1} is given by

$$H_{x_1} = 8/32[-3/8(\log_{10} 3/8) - 5/8(\log_{10} 5/8)] + 8/32[-5/8(\log_{10} 5/8) - 3/8(\log_{10} 3/8)]$$
$$+ 8/32[-4/8(\log_{10} 4/8) - 4/8(\log_{10} 4/8)] + 8/32[-4/8(\log_{10} 4/8) - 4/8(\log_{10} 4/8)]$$
$$= 0.2942.$$

The partition of the set of objects based on the values of the attribute x_1 thus reduces the information uncertainty by

$$\beta_{x_1} = H_{\varnothing} - H_{x_1} = 0.3010 - 0.2942 = 0.0068.$$

Similarly, the reduction of information uncertainty for each of the remaining attributes are computed and summarized below :

$$\beta_{x_2} = 0.0046 , \beta_{x_3} = 0.0111 , \beta_{x_4} = 0.0125.$$

Note that the reduction of information uncertainty is maximum for attribute x_4. Hence, x_4 is chosen to be the root of the tree. The above procedure can be repeatedly applied to obtain the entire decision tree which leads to the following decision rules :

$(x_4 = 4) \rightarrow (\{e_{14}\} = +)$, $(x_4 = 3) \wedge (x_2 = 1) \rightarrow (\{e_{10}\} = +)$,
$(x_4 = 0) \wedge (X_2 = 2) \rightarrow (\{e_3,e_7\} = +)$, $(x_4 = 1) \wedge (x_2 = 2) \wedge (x_3 = 3) \rightarrow (\{e_5,e_8\} = +)$,
$(x_4 = 1) \wedge (x_2 = 3) \rightarrow (\{e_2,e_4,e_6\} = +)$, $(x_4 = 2) \wedge (x_2 = 0) \wedge (x_3 = 0) \rightarrow (\{e_{15}\} = +)$,
$(x_4 = 2) \wedge (x_2 = 1) \rightarrow (\{e_{12},e_{13}\} = +)$, $(x_4 = 2) \wedge (x_2 = 0)(x_3 = 1) \rightarrow (\{e_{11},e_{16}\} = +)$,
$(x_4 = 3) \wedge (x_2 = 0) \rightarrow (\{e_9\} = +)$, $(x_4 = 0) \wedge (x_2 = 3) \wedge (x_3 = 3) \wedge (x_1 = 0) \rightarrow (\{e_1\} = +)$,
$(x_4 = 0) \wedge (x_2 = 0) \rightarrow (\{e_{17},e_{25}\} = -)$, $(x_4 = 3) \wedge (x_2 = 3) \wedge (x_3 = 3) \rightarrow (\{e_{24},e_{27}\} = -)$,
$(x_4 = 1) \wedge (x_2 = 1) \rightarrow (\{e_{20},e_{26},e_{31}, e_{32}\} = -)$, $(x_4 = 1) \wedge (x_2 = 2) \wedge (x_3 = 0) \rightarrow (\{e_{19}\} = -)$,
$(x_4 = 2) \wedge (x_2 = 2) \rightarrow (\{e_{18}\} = -)$, $(x_4 = 2) \wedge (x_2 = 0) \wedge (x_3 = 3) \rightarrow (\{e_{30}\} = -)$,
$(x_4 = 2) \wedge (x_2 = 3) \rightarrow (\{e_{21},e_{22}\} = -)$, $(x_4 = 0) \wedge (x_2 = 3) \wedge (x_3 = 3) \wedge (x_1 = 2) \rightarrow (\{e_{23}\} = -)$,
$(x_4 = 3) \wedge (x_2 = 2) \rightarrow (\{e_{28}\} = -)$, $(x_4 = 0) \wedge (x_2 = 3) \wedge (x_3 = 3) \wedge (x_1 = 3) \rightarrow (\{e_{29}\} = -)$.

It should be noted that *all* attributes x_1, x_2, x_3, and x_4 are involved in the above decision rules.

4. The AQ11 System

The AQ11 learning system proposed by Michalski generates decision rules from a set of training samples. The decision rules are expressed in terms of the variable-value logic calculus consisting of *selectors* and *complexes* [11]. The basic building block of the AQ11 learning system is the covering algorithm A^q [2] which generates a *cover* $C(E_1 \mid E_2)$ of one event set E_1 against another event set E_2. Such a cover can be interpreted as a set of complexes which is satisfied by every event in E_1 and not satisfied by any event in E_2.

A more detailed description of AQ11 can be found in [2, 11, 12]. It can be seen that when there are many events, the computational complexity will eventually explode. To make it practical, AQ11 has a parameter called *maxstar* which controls the maximum possible number of generated complexes. To illustrate the concept of a cover, Michalski also introduced the generalized logical diagram (GLD) [11] which serves as a visual aid to interpret what a cover is. The event (vector) space $U(h_1, h_2,...., h_n)$ defined by the attribute set $\{x_1, x_2,...., x_n\}$, where $h_i = \{0, 1,...., h_i-1\}$ is the domain of attribute x_i, can be represented by an n-dimensional grid spanned from the $h_1, h_2,...., h_n$ points on axes $x_1, x_2,...., x_n$, respectively. Each event vector $e_j = (v_1, v_2,...., v_n)$, $v_j \in h_i$, is then mapped onto the corresponding grid of the GLD. Michalski applied the ideas of star and cover to the design of AQ11 system.

In should be emphasized that the procedure to generate a cover is computationally a very complex problem. If the event space is small enough (say, $n \leq 8$ and every $h_i \leq 4$), then a star can be determined graphically from the GLD by visual inspection.

Example 4-1 : The event space U(4,4,4,5) is defined by the attributes $x_1 = \{0,1,2,3\}$, $x_2 = \{0,1,2,3\}$, $x_3 = \{0,1,2,3\}$, and $x_4 = \{0,1,2,3,4\}$. $E_1 = \{ e_1, e_2,..., e_{16} \}$ and $E_2 = \{ e_{17}, e_{18},..., e_{32} \}$ represent expert concepts "+" and "–", respectively. The cover for the knowledge representation system given by Table 2-1 can be constructed visually by using the GLD as shown in Figure 4-1.

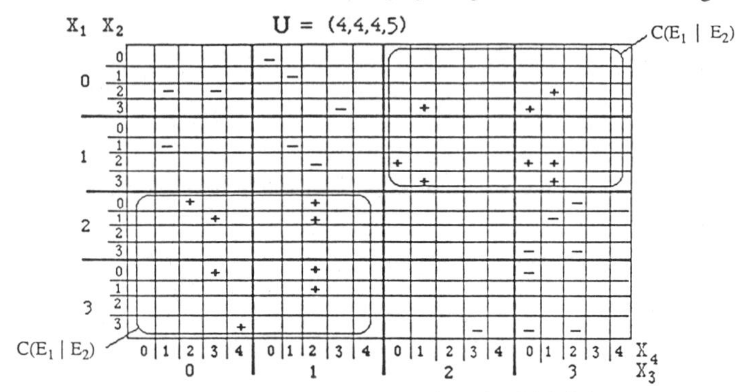

Figure 4-1 The Cover $C(E_1 \mid E_2)$ for Table 2-1.

The decision rules derived from the cover $C(E_1 \mid E_2)$ are:

$(x_1 = 0) \wedge (x_3 = 2) \rightarrow (\{e_2\} = +)$, $(x_1 = 2) \wedge (x_3 = 0) \rightarrow (\{e_{10},e_{15}\} = +)$,

$(x_1 = 0) \wedge (x_3 = 3) \rightarrow (\{e_1,e_5\} = +)$, $(x_1 = 2) \wedge (x_3 = 1) \rightarrow (\{e_{11},e_{13}\} = +)$,

$(x_1 = 1) \wedge (x_3 = 2) \rightarrow (\{e_6,e_7\} = +)$, $(x_1 = 3) \wedge (x_3 = 0) \rightarrow (\{e_9,e_{14}\} = +)$,

$(x_1 = 1) \wedge (x_3 = 3) \rightarrow (\{e_3,e_4,e_8\} = +)$, $(x_1 = 3) \wedge (x_3 = 1) \rightarrow (\{e_{12},e_{16}\} = +)$.

The same procedure can be applied to find the cover $C(E_2 \mid E_1)$ which leads to the following decision rules:

$(x_1 = 0) \wedge (x_3 = 0) \rightarrow (\{e_{19},e_{28}\} = -)$,

$(x_1 = 0) \wedge (x_3 = 1) \rightarrow (\{e_{17},e_{27},e_{31}\} = -)$, $(x_1 = 2) \wedge (x_3 = 3) \rightarrow (\{e_{22},e_{23},e_{26},e_{30} \} = -)$,

$(x_1 = 1) \wedge (x_3 = 0) \rightarrow (\{e_{32}\} = -)$, $(x_1 = 3) \wedge (x_3 = 2) \rightarrow (\{e_{24}\} = -)$,

$(x_1 = 1) \wedge (x_3 = 1) \rightarrow (\{e_{18},e_{20}\} = -)$, $(x_1 = 3) \wedge (x_3 = 3) \rightarrow (\{e_{21},e_{25},e_{29} \} = -)$.

Unlike the decision rules generated by ID3 (see Example 3-1), there are only two attributes x_1 and x_3 involved in this example. The decision rules obtained from AQ11 are more compact but at a higher cost of computationally complexity.

5. The Inductive Learning System – ILS

Based on the notions of Core, Reduct introduced in section 2.3, and Bayes decision procedure [13], an inductive learning algorithm ILS [8] is proposed. In order to facilitate the construction of a Reduct, the Core is first computed. There are many possible ways to find a Reduct. Here, we adopted the Bayes decision procedure as a plausible attribute selection criterion for obtaining a Reduct which is then used to build the decision tree.

5.1 Bayes Decision Procedure

Let the equivalence classes of the partition $\theta(d) = \{E_1, E_2,...., E_m\}$ on U represent m expert concepts in a knowledge representation system S = <U, C, d, V, f>. Let $P(E_i)$ be the *a priori probabilities* of the expert concepts E_i, i = 1, 2,...., m. If these $P(E_i)$ are the only available information, it seems reasonable to make the following decision, decide E_i if $P(E_i) > P(E_j)$; otherwise decide E_j . However, it seldom happens that, one is asked to make decisions with so little information.

Let $G = \{Z_1, Z_2,...., Z_n\}$ denote a partition on U. Let $\{\bar{a}_1, \bar{a}_2,...., \bar{a}_m\}$ be the set of all possible actions. In classification problems, action $\bar{a}_i$ may be interpreted as the decision that the expert class is E_i. That is, if action $\bar{a}_i$ is taken and the expert class is E_j , then the decision is correct if i = j, and in error if $i \neq j$. Let $\sigma(\bar{a}_i \mid E_j)$ denote a loss function for taking action $\bar{a}_i$ when the expert class is E_j. It is convenient to define a zero-one loss function as follows :

$$\sigma(\bar{a}_i \mid E_j) = \begin{cases} 0 & \text{if } i = j \\ 1 & \text{if } i \neq j. \end{cases} \quad (i , j = 1, 2,...., m) \tag{5.1-1}$$

That is, the above loss function assigns no loss to a correct decision, and assigns a unit loss to any error. All errors are regarded to be equally costly.

If the a posteriori probabilities $P(E_j \mid Z_k)$ are known, the expected loss associated with decision $\bar{a}_i$ is given by

$$\Gamma(\bar{a}_i \mid Z_k) = \sum_{j=1}^{m} \sigma(\bar{a}_i \mid E_j)P(E_j \mid Z_k), \tag{5.1-2}$$

which is commonly known as the conditional risk. If errors are to be reduced, it is natural to seek decision rules that minimize the average probability of error. Now, if the zero-one loss function is assumed, then for each Z_k the expected loss associated with making decision $\bar{a}_i$ can be written as

$$\Gamma(\bar{a}_i \mid Z_k) = \sum_{j=1}^{m} \sigma(\bar{a}_i \mid E_j)P(E_j \mid Z_k) = \sum_{j \neq i} P(E_j \mid Z_k) = 1 - P(E_i \mid Z_k), \tag{5.1-3}$$

where $P(E_i \mid Z_k)$ is the conditional probability that decision $\bar{a}_i$ is correct. The Bayes decision procedure to minimize the overall risk calls for selecting the decision that minimizes the conditional risk. Thus, one should select the decision $\bar{a}_i$ that maximizes the a posteriori probability $P(E_i \mid Z_k)$ in equation 5.1-3. In other words, for minimum-overall-risk one may choose for each Z_k the following decision procedure:

$$\text{Decide } E_i \text{ if } P(E_i \mid Z_k) > P(E_j \mid Z_k) \text{ for all } i \neq j. \tag{5.1-4}$$

Let $\bar{a}(k)$ denote the optimal decision for Z_k. It can be easily verified that the overall risk, ψ_G, as a result of the partition $G = \{Z_1, Z_2,...., Z_n\}$,

$$\psi_G = \sum_{k=1}^{n} \Gamma(\bar{a}(k) \mid Z_k)P(Z_k), \tag{5.1-5}$$

is indeed minimum.

5.2 Attribute Selection Criterion based on Bayes Decision Procedure

In contrast to ID3, one can use the Bayes decision procedure to construct a decision tree. For any condition attribute $x_i \in C$, let ψ_{x_i} denote the minimum-overall-risk as a result of the partition induced by x_i . The attribute x_k with the smallest minimum-overall-risk ψ_{x_k} in the set $\{\psi_{x_i} \mid i = 1, 2, ..., n\}$ is chosen to be the root of the tree. Similarly, any sub-node of the tree containing objects of mixed expert classes can be further subdivided by selecting the attribute corresponding to the smallest value in $\{\psi_{x_i}\}$ excluding those attributes which are not the parents of this sub-node.

However, the resulting decision tree obtained in this way (or from ID3) may contain superfluous attributes. Recall that a Reduct in a knowledge representation system can be easily determined by successively eliminating the superfluous attributes outside the Core in an arbitrary order. Since there may exist many Reducts, the problem is how to choose an appropriate Reduct to build a decision tree. We suggest here to use the Bayes decision procedure for eliminating superfluous attributes. Based on our experimental results, the Reduct obtained by the proposed method is a reasonable one.

A Reduct can be constructed by first eliminating the superfluous attribute $x_j \in (C - \text{Core})$ with the largest minimum-overall-risk ψ_{x_j}. This procedure can be successively applied until all superfluous attributes outside the Core are eliminated. The desired Reduct consists of the remaining attributes which are then used to construct the decision tree. The attribute in the Reduct, which has the smallest minimum-overall-risk, is chosen as the root in deriving the decision tree. This procedure is applied recursively to the individual sub-node of the tree, which consists of more than one class of objects.

5.3 The ILS Algorithm

The major steps of the ILS algorithm are outlined below :

INPUT – A knowledge representation system $S = \langle U, C, d, V, f \rangle$.

PROCEDURE –

Step 1 : Find the Core of S (see Example 5.3-1).

Step 2 : If Core $\neq \varnothing$ and $\theta(\text{Core}) \leq \theta(d)$, then the Core is the only Reduct; else find a Reduct (see Example 5.3-2).

Step 3 : Use the Reduct obtained from Step 2 to construct a decision tree (see Example 5.3-2).

OUTPUT – Generalized decision rules for S.

Example 5.3-1 : Consider the knowledge representation system of Table 2-1. Note that there are two expert classes $Des(E_1)$ = "+" and $Des(E_2)$ = "–" in $\theta(d)$. According to the Bayes decision procedure, the minimum-overall-risk for each attribute of C is computed and listed as follows :

$$\psi_{x_1} = p(x_1{=}0)[\ \min(p(+\mid x_1{=}0),\ p(-\mid x_1{=}0)\ ] + p(x_1{=}1)[\ \min(p(+\mid x_1{=}1),\ p(-\mid x_1{=}1)\ ]$$
$$+\ p(x_1{=}2)[\ \min(p(+\mid x_1{=}2),\ p(-\mid x_1{=}2)\ ] + p(x_1{=}3)[\ \min(p(+\mid x_1{=}3),\ p(-\mid x_1{=}3)\ ]$$
$$= (8/32)(3/8) + (8/32)(3/8) + (8/32)(4/8) + (8/32)(4/8) = 14/32\ .$$

Similarly,

$$\psi_{x_2} = (7/32)(3/7) + (8/32)(4/8) + (7/32)(3/7) + (10/32)(4/10) = 14/32\ ,$$
$$\psi_{x_3} = (7/32)(3/7) + (9/32)(4/9) + (4/32)(1/4) + (12/32)(5/12) = 13/32\ ,$$
$$\psi_{x_4} = (7/32)(3/7) + (10/32)(5/10) + (9/32)(4/9) + (5/32)(2/5) + (1/32)(0) = 14/32\ .$$

It can be easily verified that $\theta(x_1x_2x_3x_4) \leq \theta(d)$ holds. This means that the given knowledge representation system S is deterministic. In order to find the Core in $C = \{x_1,x_2,x_3,x_4\}$ with respect to d, the set of superfluous attributes in C is first determined. It is found that $\theta(x_2x_3x_4) \not\leq \theta(d)$, $\theta(x_1x_3x_4) \leq \theta(d)$, $\theta(x_1x_2x_4) \not\leq \theta(d)$, and $\theta(x_1x_2x_3) \leq \theta(d)$. This implies that x_2 and x_4 are superfluous in C with respect to d. Therefore, the Core is equal to x_1x_3. In fact, $\theta(x_1x_3) \leq \theta(d)$ and, therefore, x_1x_3 is the only Reduct. The decision rules corresponding to the Reduct x_1x_3 are identical to those obtained from AQ11 (see Example 4-1). This example clearly illustrates that the ILS provides a more efficient method to infer decision rules for a given knowledge representation system.

In general, the Core may not necessarily be the Reduct. In this case, the Reduct can be computed as shown by the following example.

Example 5.3-2 : Consider the following knowledge representation system Table 5.3-1 :

U	x_1	x_2	x_3	x_4	d
e_1	0	0	1	0	+
e_2	1	0	0	0	+
e_3	0	1	1	1	+
e_4	1	1	0	1	−
e_5	1	1	1	1	−
e_6	1	1	1	0	−

Table 5.3-1 An example of a knowledge representation system S.

From the above table, we obtain

$$\theta(x_2x_3x_4) \not\leq \theta(d)\ ,\ \theta(x_1x_3x_4) \leq \theta(d)\ ,\ \theta(x_1x_2x_4) \leq \theta(d)\ ,\ \theta(x_1x_2x_3) \leq \theta(d)\ .$$

This implies that x_2, x_3, and x_4 are superfluous attributes in C with respect to the expert attribute d. Therefore, the Core is x_1. Since $\theta(x_1) \not\leq \theta(d)$, there exist at least two or more Reducts. The minimum-overall-risks for the individual attributes are :

$$\psi_{x_1} = (0)(2/6) + (1/4)(4/6) = 1/6\ ,\quad \psi_{x_2} = (0)(2/6) + (1/4)(4/6) = 1/6\ ,$$

$$\psi_{x_3} = (1/2)(2/6) + (2/4)(4/6) = 1/2\ ,\ \psi_{x_4} = (1/3)(3/6) + (1/3)(3/6) = 1/3.$$

Note that $\psi_{x_3} > \psi_{x_4} > \psi_{x_2} = \psi_{x_1}$. Since x_3 does not exist in the Core and ψ_{x_3} is the largest, x_3 is first chosen to check if it is superfluous in C with respect to d. Indeed, attribute x_3 is superfluous, which is then removed from C. The next attribute to be tested is x_4 which is also found to be superfluous in $(C - x_3)$. Since $\theta(x_1x_2) \leq \theta(d)$ and no more superfluous attribute exists in x_1x_2, $R = x_1x_2$ is therefore a Reduct. (Note that $x_1x_3x_4$ is another Reduct in this example.) Now, the attribute from the Reduct with the smallest minimum-overall-risk is chosen to be the root of the decision tree. Since both x_1 and x_2 have the same minimum-overall-risk, x_1 is arbitrarily chosen to be the root and we arrive at the following decision rules :

$$(x_1 = 0) \rightarrow (\ \{e_1,e_3\} = +\ ),$$

$$(x_1 = 1) \wedge (\ x_2 = 0\ ) \rightarrow (\ \{e_2\} = +\ ),$$

$$(x_1 = 1) \wedge (\ x_2 = 1\ ) \rightarrow (\ \{e_4,e_5,e_6\} = -\ ).$$

6. Experiment

The objective of this experiment is to demonstrate the capability of ILS for generating decision rules. The ILS was applied to the diagnosis of soybean diseases. In this experiment, there are 17 different soybean diseases and each soybean disease consists of 17 samples. Each sample disease is described by the values of 50 attributes (These data are similar to those used by Michalski [12] – 15 soybean diseases, 35 attributes, 290 training samples, and 340 test samples.) The experimental results are summarized below :

Core : nil , Reduct : $x_5x_{10}x_{16}x_{21}x_{23}x_{34}x_{36}x_{40}x_{50}$, number of decision rules generated : 86

x_5 = damaged area x_{21} = leaf mildew growth x_{36} = internal discoloration of stem

x_{10} = leaf spot color x_{23} = position of affected leaves x_{40} = fruit spots

x_{16} = leaf spot size x_{34} = external stem discoloration x_{50} = root sclerotia

There are 41 superfluous attributes. Only 9 attributes play a significant role in the classification of soybean diseases. It would be interesting to compare the accuracy of prediction between the decision rules generated from our samples and those derived from AQ11. Unfortunately, we do not have any test samples to do so.

7. Concluding Remarks

The attribute selection criterion for ID3 is based on the concept of entropy which is well founded in information theory. The ID3 provides a simple method for generating decision rules which, however, may still contain superfluous attributes.

The AQ11 can in principle generate more compact decision rules but at a higher cost of computational complexity. ID3 seems to be a simpler method although it may be less powerful.

The ILS provides a simple but effective method in deriving decision rules particularly when compared with the AQ11. In contrast to ID3, the inductive algorithm developed based on the concepts of Core and Reduct guarantees that the decision rules generated do not contain any superfluous attributes. Furthermore, instead of using entropy function, the simpler Bayes decision procedure is adopted as a criterion for selecting attributes in the construction of the decision tree. Such an attribute selection criterion may significantly enhance system performance when the number of attributes is large. This fact is demonstrated by our experiment performed on the diagnosis of soybean diseases.

Acknowledgement : *The authors would like to thank Professor R.S. Michalski for providing the soybean data.*

References

[1] Hunt, E.B., Marin, J., and Stone, P., "Experiment in Induction", New York: Academic Press, (1966).

[2] Michalski, R.S. and Larson, J.B., "Selection of most representative training examples and incremental generation of VL1 hypothesis: the underlying methodology and the description of programs ESEL and AQ11", Report No. 867, Department of Computer Science, University of Illinois, Urbana, Illinois, (1978).

[3] Quinlan, J.R., "Learning efficient classification procedures and their application to chess end games", Chapter 15, Machine Learning: Artificial Intelligence Approach, TIOGA Publishing Company, Palo Alto, R.S. Michalski, J. Carbonell and T. Mitchell (Editors), (1983).

[4] Wong, S.K.M., Ziarko, W., and Ye, R.L., "Remarks on attribute selection criterion in inductive learning based on rough sets", Bulletin of the Polish Academy of Science, Vol. 34, No. 5-6, (1986), pp. 277 - 283.

[5] Pawlak, Z., "Rough set", International Journal of Information and Computer Sciences, Vol. 11, (1982), pp. 341 - 356.

[6] Wong, S.K.M., Ziarko, W., and Ye, R.L., "On learning and evaluation of decision rules in the context of Rough Sets", Proceedings of International Symposium on Methodologies for Intelligent Systems, Knoxville, Tennessee, (1986), pp. 308 - 324.

[7] Wong, S.K.M., Ziarko, W., and Ye, R.L., "Comparison of rough set and statistical methods in inductive learning", International Journal of Man-Machine Studies, Vol. 24, (1986) , pp. 53 - 72.

[8] Wong, J.H., "An Inductive Learning System – ILS ", Thesis, Department of Computer Science, University of Regina, Canada, (1986).

[9] Pawlak, Z., "On superfluous attributes in knowledge representation system", Bulletin of the Polish Academy of Sciences, Vol. 32, No. 3-4, (1984).

[10] Shannon, C.E., "A mathematical theory of communication", Bell System Technical Journal, Vol. 4, (1948), pp. 379 - 423.

[11] Michalski, R.S., "A geometrical model for the synthesis of interval covers", Report No. 461, Department of Computer Science, University of Illinois, Urbana, Illinois, (1971).

[12] Michalski, R.S. and Chilausky, R.L., "Learning by being told and learning from examples: an experimental comparison of the two methods of knowledge acquisition in the context of developing an expert system for soybean disease diagnosis", International Journal of Policy Analysis and Information Systems, Vol. 4, No. 2, (1980), pp. 125 - 161.

[13] Duda, R.O. and Hart, P.E., "Pattern Classification and Scene Analysis", Chapter 2, Wiley Interscience, (1973).

Conceptual Schema Design: A Machine Learning Approach

R. Yasdi, W. Ziarko
Department of Computer Science
University of Regina
Regina, S4S 0A2, Canada

Abstract
In this paper, we first describe a conceptual database model consisting of a semantic model and an event model. Hereafter we present our approach to design knowledge acquisition and representation which is based on inducing schema design rules from examples. We also present relevant aspects of the theory of Rough Sets and the learning method used in our system.[1]

1 Introduction

This research is motivated by the need for an efficient environment to construct a conceptual schema of a database.
Since technology of database has been developed remarkably in recent years, many researchers in various fields (literature, history, economics etc.) have potential wish to construct databases for their studies by themselves. However, constructing a database is an extremely difficult task for such users due to their lack of sufficient knowledge of computers or databases. As a result, they need an expert's help when they build their database. However, with the growing complexity of today's knowledge based-systems this task is becoming more difficult even for database designers themselves particularly because of the lack of knowledge of the specific application. This is the main reason why we have initiated the project of an intelligent assistance system for conceptual design of databases. It is not intended to replace the human expert by providing a black box of useful services but rather an open system which will enable the designer to acquire new knowledge and transfer his expertise through the system to the end user.

Due to the space limitations we have omited here the design specification and design principles of EXIS, an expert system for conceptual schema design for an information system currently under development. The full paper appeared in [YZ86].

Throughout this paper we focus our investigation only on the two main issues:

Firstly, developing a conceptual model which is intended to represent the full extent of the information needs of the enterprise. This means the determination of static and dynamic aspects of an application. Data model like semantic network represents the former, while an event model is developed for representing the later aspects.

Secondly, research on learning is very important in the fields of Artificial Intelligence (AI) since it is one of the most fundamental mechanics of an intelligent system [Mic80]. EXIS has been aimed to apply this technique for generation of general rules based on the principle of inductive learning (learning and generalizing rules from the examples).

Our approach is to use first order predicate logic as formalism for specification of the conceptual schema. This implies that the schema is to be represented by a set of axioms to constitute a theory (first order) which is interpreted according to the model theoretical approach. To remain within a unique declarative specification we use the language Prolog as an implementation language. This language has great expressive power, well defined semantic and operational capabilities, in spite of the lack of the full-clause reasoning.

2 The Representation of Knowledge

The full extent of the information needs of an enterprise is represented in a conceptual schema (or model). The role of conceptual schema in DB technology has much in common with those of knowledge representation in AI. By our definition it covers two aspects of an application, namely static and dynamic aspects. Data models like semantic or relational represent the former, whereas concepts of event and transaction are used for representing the later aspect. In the following sections we specify our conceptual schema [Yas85]. We begin with descriptions of the semantic network and continue with the event model.

[1]This research was partially supported by the National Sciences and Engineering Research Council of Canada.

Methodologies for Intelligent Systems
Z. W. Ras and M. Zemankova, Editors

2.1 Semantic Network Model (SM)

To capture the semantics of the real world with more preciseness and naturalness, many researchers have proposed several data models such as SHM [SS77], SDM[HM81], TAXIS [M*80]. Our semantic network presented hereafter contains most of the concepts of semantic networks like classification, generalization, aggregation. However, we emphasize here on precise definition of schema integrity constraints and their formalization in the first order logic, which are extremely important for design of a conceptual schema.

A Semantic network is a directed graph whose nodes represent individuals and whose arcs represent the relationships between individuals. It is defined as a triple

(NC, AC, IC)

where NC stands for the category of nodes, AC for the category of arcs and IC is the category of constraints. For each element of AC, there exists a function:

$$f = \text{NC} \times \text{NC} \longrightarrow \{\text{true, false}\}$$

such that $f(n_i, n_j)$ is true if there exists an arc of class f between n_i and n_j, and false otherwise.

The semantic network has the following beneficial features:

1. Representation is very close to the natural language.
2. It employs a number of abstract concepts which help to include more meaning about the observed objects.
3. It can be used to obtain more efficient implementation.
4. It can be extended so that it can have the same expressive power as predicate logic [Kow79], [Sch76,Sow86].

2.1.1 Concepts of the Semantic Network

Classification (entities or attributes)

Objects with similar qualities can be grouped into a class. For example, we can create the class of "employee" for an entity-class (ec) and the class "colour" for an attribute-class (ac). Elements of an entity-class are entities and elements of attribute-class are values. For example e_5 is an instance of the employee-class and red is an instance of colour. A class is defined by a predicate; the predicate is satisfied by instances of its arguments
(e.g. employee(x) =true).

Declaration

The arguments of attribute-class are associated with their types or with a domain by the predicate dec. For example, if we consider the predicate

person(P, Name : string, Age : ages, Address : address)

the arguments will be defined by

dec(ages, '[1.... 100]')
dec(address, '[Toronto, Frankfurt, London]').

The elements of different entity-classes are connected to each other by the following categories of arcs.

Association

It accounts for the binary relationship between two entity- classes. For example works-for (person, company), indicates that persons from class person work for companies from class company.
We use the notation $r(ec_1, ec_2)$ to specify the relationship between two classes and formalize it by:

$$\forall x \forall y[\text{works-for}(x, y) \rightarrow \text{person}(x) \wedge \text{company}(y)].$$

Note that relationships are recursive and linked bi-directionally; usually one direction is shown.
Semantic network offers abstraction mechanics. This enables us to discuss an abstract class while temporarily deferring the details of its properties. We introduce some of the abstraction mechanisms.

Generalization

Generalization provides a concise way to express constraints that define some classes as "more general" class of other ones. This relationship is also called the "specialization", when viewed the other way around, i.e. going from the more general to the more specific definition. E.g.

$$\forall x(\text{emp}(x) \lor \text{student}(x) \iff \text{person}(x)).$$

The left to right implication states that the set of employees and the set of students are sub-classes of the set of persons. The right to left implication states that all persons are either students or employees, or both. One can say that the later implication "closes" the set of persons in that it prohibits an entity from being a person without also being an employee or student. Generalization is usually abbreviated by the keyword "is-a" and represented by a "g" arc whereas specialization is represented by an "s" arc.

Let $ec_1, \ldots, ec_n$ be the subclasses of ec and let e and e_i be respectively the elements of ec and ec_i, then $\cup e_i = e$. Class ec is called a completely specialized class in this case; otherwise ec is called a partially specialized class.

Aggregation
Grouping classes into higher level classes is called aggregation. It is a common-sense intersection of sets. In a mathematical sense aggregation corresponds to the Cartesian Product. For example, the fact that author, publisher and title are components of the entity-class book is represented by an arc "a" going from author, publisher and title to book. Thus,

$$\text{book(x)} \rightarrow \exists y \exists z \exists w(author(y) \land publ(z) \land title(w))$$

where the aggregation is defined downwards whereas the "particularization" is defined upwards and shown by an arrow labeled with "p".

Equivalence
Equivalence specifies that two classes are equivalent. This is specially useful when it is important to see the same objects in different ways. Denotation $eq(ec_1, ec_2)$ specifies that two classes are equivalent. For example eq(student, sportsman) or eq(student, pupil) specify that student, sportsman and pupil are equivalent classes if we assume that all students practice one sport. More generally, $eq(x, y)$ is equivalent to the two following assertions $g(x, y)$ and $g(y, x)$.

An example of a semantic network is portrayed in Fig 1.

2.1.2 Schema Constraints

The above description does not characterize the network completely. There are several constraints which are not shown in the diagram. These constraints contribute to a more precise definition of the network. In the following we define some types of these constraints.

Entity-class Constraints
Every entity-class must have a unique name. Thus, a constraint can be expressed in the form:

$$\forall x \forall y(\text{mec}(x) \land \text{mec}(y) \rightarrow \neg(= (x, y))).$$

Where mec is a class of entity-class called *meta entity-class*, x and y are entity-classes.

Cardinality Constraints
We distinguish two categories of cardinality constraints:
a) Cardinalities of nodes (entity-classes)
A cardinality declaration denotes the number of entities of an entity-class and can be of three types, namely: minimum, maximum, and exact cardinality. For example, the constraint "the number of employees is at most two" can be represented as:

$$\forall x \forall y \forall z(\text{emp}(x) \land \text{emp}(y) \land \text{emp}(z)) \rightarrow = (x, y) \lor = (x, z) \lor = (y, z)).$$

Correspondingly, "the number of employees is at least three" can be represented as:

$$\exists x \exists y \exists z(\text{emp}(x) \land \text{emp}(y) \land \text{emp}(z) \rightarrow \neg(= (x, y) \lor = (x, z) \lor = (y, z))).$$

The exact cardinality can be represented by a combination of minimum and maximum cardinality. In general:

$$\forall x \text{emp}(x) \iff \exists n \text{card}(n = \text{min}) \land \exists m \text{card}(m = \text{max}).$$

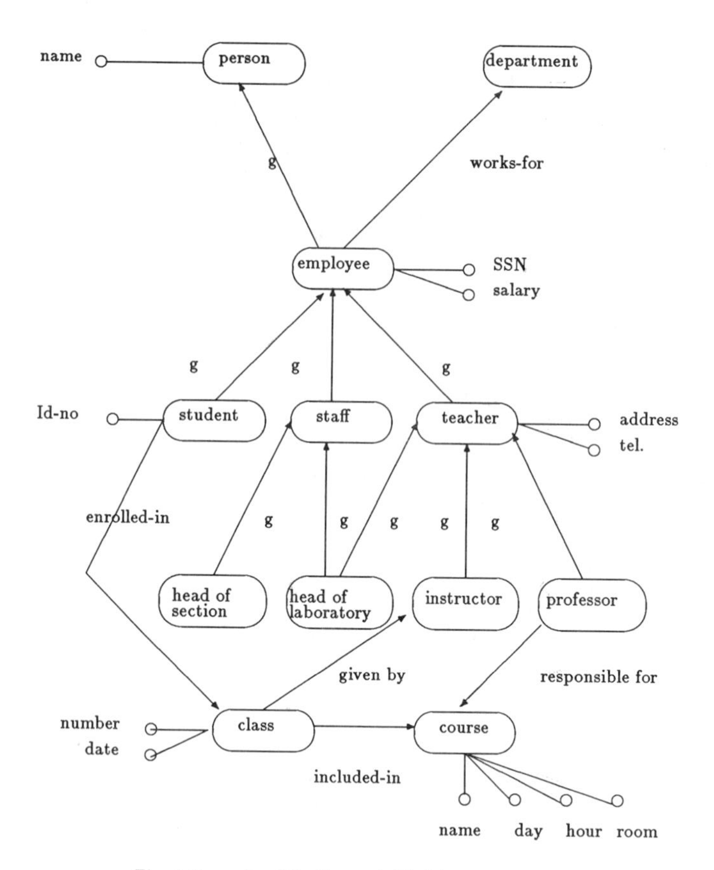

Fig. 1 Example of the Semantic Model

b) Cardinality constraints of arcs (relationship-classes)

Each instance of an entity-class "can" have a relation to another entity-class.
For a given relationship between two entity-classes A and B, cr = (min, max) specifies the minimal and maximal number of entities of class A related to class B. The minimum and maximum cardinality constraints attached to a relationship describe how many times an entity can occur or must occur in the set of relationship. Standard cardinalities are:

(0, 1), (1, 1), (0, *), (1, *), where * means that the value is not restricted.
E.g. for cr(1, 1):

$$\forall x \exists y \exists z (r(x, y) \wedge r(x, z) \rightarrow = (y, z)).$$

For example all persons with an age can be represented as:

$\forall$ x person$(x) \rightarrow \exists y$has-age$(x, y)$.

A partial relationship signifies that some entity-classes does not participate in a relationship-class:
$\exists x \exists y$(person$(x) \wedge$salary(x, y)).
This construction indicates the existence of at least one person who is associated with the relationship.

Attribute Constraints

1. Every attribute-class ac must have an owner entity-class ec. This is defined by a meta attribute-class mac(ac, ec, type, key). The first argument of this predicate is the attribute-class, the second argument represents the owner of the attribute-class, the third argument is the data type and the fourth argument indicates whether this attribute-class is a primary key or a non-primary key. Every ac owned by some ec must have a unique name.

   $\forall x \exists y \exists z (mac(y, x, type, key) \wedge mac(z, x, type, key) \rightarrow \neg(= (y, z))).$

Domain Constraints

The range of attributes can be defined in four ways by:

a. setting explicitly its value; e.g. color: red;

b. listing the values eg: color: 'red, blue, green';

c. defining as basic data types (integer, real, or text) or as declared types using dec predicate; dec(color, '[red, blue, green]');

d. specifying a range eg: high-mark: 85-95.

For an entity-class we have to check that specializations are valid with respect to all hierarchy predecessors. Therefore, we check the limits of ranges and subsets; for example, the range 14 to 18 is a subclass of the range 1 to 20; or 'green blue' is a subset of 'red, green, yellow, brown'. We enforce the additional restriction that the order of the values cannot be changed by specialization.

Every domain D must have a unique name. A meta type-class (mtc) contains the set of all defined types.

$$\forall x \forall y (mtc(x) \wedge mtc(y) \rightarrow \neg(= (x, y))).$$

Attributes can be specializations of their hierarchy. That is, if a *ec*, characterized by an *ac* with the range D is a subclass of an ac_1 whose attribute has the range D_1, then we must verify that D is a specialization of D_1.

For example:

person (age: age-value,....);
child (age: under-18,....);
child is-a person.

Consequently under-18 is an age-value. To avoid ambiguity and to simplify the attribute inheritance, we impose the following restriction: if two classes ec_1 and ec_2 have a sub-class ec_0 in common, they may not both own an attribute with the same name, because otherwise it would not be clear if ec_0 inherits this from ec_1 or ec_2. Thus, the constraint can be expressed in the form:

$$\forall x \forall y [ec_1(x) \wedge ec_2(y) \wedge g(ec_1, ec_0) \wedge g(ec_2, ec_0)] \rightarrow \exists z ec_0(z).$$

Relationship Constraints

1. Every relationship r(ec1, ec2) must have a unique name. Thus, the following relation must hold for a meta relation-class mrc:

   $\forall x \forall y (mrc(x) \wedge mrc(y) \rightarrow \neg(= (x, y))).$

   where x, y are relationship-classes.

2. The transivity of implication $\rightarrow$ is a simple consequence of transitive relations. Thus, the following is provable:

   $\forall x \forall y \forall z (r(x, y) \wedge r(y, z) \rightarrow r(x, z)).$

Generalization Constraints

These constraints are expressed with respect to the generalization hierarchy:

1. Every generalization g must have a unique name. Thus the following restriction must hold for a meta generalization class mgc:

   $\forall x \forall y (mgc(x) \wedge mgc(y) \rightarrow \neg(= (x, y)))$

   where x, y are generalization.

2. No entity-class must be a subclass of itself. This property is reflected in the schema by the requirement that the arguments of the predicate g must be different, e.g.

   $\forall x g(ec_0(x)$,list-of-subset$) \rightarrow \neg$member$(x$,list-of-subset(y))

   $\forall x \forall y s(ec_i(x), ec_0(y)) \rightarrow \neg(ec_i(x), ec_0(y))$ i=1,2,3,....

3. The transitivity of implication $\rightarrow$ is a simple consequence of the transitivity of is-a. Thus the following is provable;

   $\forall x \forall y \forall z (g(x, y) \wedge g(y, z) \rightarrow g(x, z))$

   $\forall x \forall y \forall z (s(y, x) \wedge s(z, y) \rightarrow s(z, x))$.

4. A subclass and its superclass may not both own an attribute with the same name. Otherwise, one cannot distinguish whether it is an attribute of a superclass or subclass. This constraint forces the principle of attribute inheritance:

   $\forall x \forall y [(g(ec_0(x), ec_1(y))] \rightarrow \neg \exists z (ec_0(z) \wedge ec_1(z))$.

5. Two is-a paths having the same starting point must end in the same place i.e.

   $g(ec_{mid1}, ec_{sta}) \wedge g(ec_{mid2}, ec_{sta}) \wedge g(ec_{end1}, ec_{mid1}) \wedge g(ec_{end2}, ec_{mid2})$

   $\rightarrow ec_{end1} = ec_{end2}$.

Aggregation Constraints

1. Aggregation is the concept of disjointness, which means that two entity-classes do not have any entities in common. For example, the set of days is disjoint from the set of years, i.e.

   $\neg \exists x$(day$(x) \wedge$year(x)).

2. Each instance of an aggregate must uniquely determine its components:

   $\forall x a(ec_0(x)) \rightarrow \exists y \exists z (ec_1, (y) \wedge ec_2(z))$.

3. Like generalization, aggregation can be viewed in two directions. Also, inheritance is applicable to aggregation, since knowing that a class is a part of another class allows one to concentrate on the additional information needed to characterize the subclass.

Functional Dependency Constraints

Functional dependency expresses the functional dependencies between attributes of an entity-class. In the representation of dependencies, we do not assume the uniqueness of attribute names of all the attributes of a semantic network, since each attribute can be qualified by the name of its entity. For example:

dep(d, name,...) $\rightarrow$ dep(d, ..., address).

2.2 The Event Model (EM)

The dynamic part of the conceptual schema concerns data manipulation aspects of database and is shown in the event model. An event is intended to indicate that something has happened either in the real world or in the system which requires some action. For example:

$\forall x \forall t$(hiring$(x) \wedge$date$(t =$Oct$) \wedge$person$(x) \rightarrow$hire(x, t))

means that when the event hire has happened at time $t =$ October and x is a person (preconditions), then x has to be hired. We define preconditions as those that must be satisfied for an event to take place and postcondition as those that defines a state transition. This makes our events very similar to the production rules of a rule-based system. In an information system an event takes place if it is initiated from the outside of the event base, either by a user or by an internal events responder. In a rule-based expert system, on the other hand, an event is free to fire any time when all preconditions are satisfied. This constitutes the fundamental difference between an information system and an expert system. A further difference is that arguments of an event represent an input into an information system, whereas an expert system requests this kind of input when it is needed.

An information system consists of data types, events and a monitor. The data types are represented in a model like, hierarchy-, relational-, or semantic-model. The specification of events consists of preconditions, actions and postconditions. Preconditions determine under what circumstances an event may take place. They are used to check the feasibility of input values and embody consistent criteria for the consistency of database of an information system. These constraints are referred to as "integrity constraints"and are checked during the "run time" (in contrast to schema constraints which are tested during the design time). The action part of the event representation indicates the change to the data as a consequence of an event taking place. Post conditions are integrity rules, which must hold after performing the action(s). They are subdivided into check conditions and signal conditions. Check conditions verify the execution of actions and signal conditions send signals to the monitor in the form of raised exceptions.

The monitor processes the internal events either immediately, or at some specific time, eg. 06:30 every morning, or the end of each month. The monitor initiates events on its own accord, prompts the user to initiate events, or reminds the user that some action is to be performed. For example, in a Library application the return date of a book would be sent to the monitor. When the date is due, the monitor would initiate an event that reminds the user to return the book. Events received from or initiated by the monitor are called Internal Events (IEv); all other events are external (EEv). Internal events have no preconditions. All input data associated with such events are assumed to have been already checked. Sometimes, however, the monitor establishes that external events are to be initiated. In such cases, the monitor issues prompts to the user. For example, on receipt of a paper for a conference, referees have to be found for this paper. The monitor deals with it by prompting the user to initiate referee assignment events until the required number of referees has been assigned to the paper [Yas85].
The declaration of an event has the following structure:

```
EEv:    event-name (events, parameters)
        Pre: <Pre-conditions>
        Act: <actions>
        Post: <Post-conditions>,<IEV>
Eend ;
```

For example, when a new employee is to be hired, the hire-employee event is issued to the system with employee data as arguments. The first precondition of hire-employee requires that the new employee must not already be a member of the set of persons, the second requires that the person has not been fired, the third verifies whether there is budget for the salary, etc. The Act part inserts the name of an employee in the person list and the post condition raises an internal event for informing the personnel office about the new employee. This is requested in the following form:

```
EEv         hire-employee (name1, salary1, code,...);

        Pre:        not person (Name = name1, salary = salary,...);
                    not fired-person (Name = name1);
                    not (sum(salary) + salary1 ( Sal-budget)
                    ________________
                    Some other checks
                    ________________
        Act:        insert (name1, person(name1, salary1,...)
                    ________________
                    Some other actions
                    ________________
        Post:       IEV-inform (Personal-office, name1, salary1,...);
Eend;
```

3 Rule generation by learning from examples

Our main objective in this section is to show how the concept of machine learning can be applied during design of an information system. In the following we address some of the problems which can be solved more efficiently by going through the process of inductive learning.

a. Generating the schema rules.

The major problem in the schema design is the construction of schema rules. We have pointed out these difficulties in the previous section.

b. Recognizing the Functional Dependencies

We may ask the user to give some examples of tuples of the relation person(SSN, Name, Address, Tel).

5543	Smith	Toronto	4445885
5543	Smith	London	772532
3500	Smith	Frankfurt	996542
4000	Meier	Toronto	3840785
4000	Meier	New York	426830

From these tuples we may infer the following functional dependencies: Name $\rightarrow$ SSn, Tel $\rightarrow$ Address.
We may also find out that the following functional dependencies do not hold:
Name $\rightarrow$ Address, Address $\rightarrow$ Tel
Address $\rightarrow$ Name, Name $\rightarrow$ Tel
(SSN, Name) $\rightarrow$ Address.

There are a number of approaches to automatic learning or to the generation of decision rules by a machine [Mic83,SD76,For86]. In particular, inductive learning i.e. extraction and generalization of decision rules from examples of decisions attracted a great deal of interest in recent years [DM79,BF78,Paw84,Qui83,Mic80,WZ8
In some domains of application, particularly when the problems were sufficiently well defined and specialized, results were very impressive [Mic80,Qui83].
In any approach to inductive learning we encounter the following two major problems:

1. How to represent the partial knowledge collected in the form of examples;
2. How to generalize this knowledge in the form of decision rules so they could be used in automated reasoning.

Both of these issues can be addressed in the framework of the theory of the Rough Sets and of a formal model of Knowledge Representation System (KRS) introduced by Pawlak. Because of the evident potential of the rough set approach confirmed by a growing number of applications and researchers working in this field we decided to investigate the possibility of applying this method to our system. In particular, the Probabilistic Learning Algorithm (PLA) developed to induce decision rules from examples represented as feature vectors can be adopted here to generate decision rules. This enables us to incorporate the learning component into EXIS by making its inference rules dependent upon the contents of the example base. The example base consists of a number of schema design decisions represented by means of predicates. The algorithm PLA is used to produce generalized design rules which subsequently will be employed in advising the database designer. The system will be extendable and adaptive i.e. correct or incorrect design decision will be used by the system as a new experience to increase the number or to improve the decision rules.

In what follows we give an introduction to the main ideas underlying our approach to learning. We introduce the concept of Knowledge Representation System and explain the way we are going to apply it to represent the design knowledge. Also, we present basics of the idea of approximate classification which are necessary to describe the learning method of EXIS.

3.1 Knowledge Representation System in inductive learning

The basic component of a Knowledge Representation System is a set of objects (entities), for instance, books or human beings. We assume that our knowledge about these objects is expressed through assignment of some features (attributes) and their values (attribute values) to the objects. For example, human beings can be described by sex and age.

The formal definition of a knowledge representation system S [OP84] is given by:

S = < E, C, D, V, f >

where:

- E is a set of objects,
- $At = C \cup D$ is a set of attributes, of which the two disjoint subsets of attributes C and D are referred to as condition and expert decision (conclusion) respectively,
- $V = \cup Va$, for $a \in At$
  is a set of attribute values, where Va is the domain of attribute $a \in At$.
- $f : E \times At \rightarrow V$ is an information function such that
  $f(e, a) \in \forall a$ for every $e \in E$ and $a \in A$
  i.e., the function f assigns attribute values to each object e in E.

A Knowledge Representation System can be conveniently represented by a table. Consider, for example, the following collection of objects [Qui83]:

At	C			D
E	HEIGHT	HAIR	EYES	expert classification
e1	short	dark	blue	-
e2	tall	dark	blue	-
e3	tall	dark	brown	-
e4	tall	red	blue	+
e5	short	blond	blue	+
e6	tall	blond	brown	-
e7	tall	blond	blue	+
e8	short	blond	brown	-

Table 1. An example of a Knowledge Representation System.

In Table 1, the universe of discourse E consists of eight objects:
$E = \{e_1, e_2, \ldots, e_8\}$. Each of the objects is described by the set of attributes
C = HEIGHT, HAIR, EYES.
According to the expert classification, each object belongs to either class "+" or class "-". The set of values Vd = {+, -} of the expert attribute D represents the set of concepts which the system wants to learn based on the attribute values of C.

We extend the above representation by introducing predicates into the table to represent more complex situations. In particular this will allow us to deal effectively with the problem of representing schema design decisions. In this extension the objects will be referred to as "situations". Each situation consists of a number of entity-classes and of a number of predicates $p_1, p_2, \ldots, p_m$, corresponding to some relationships among selected elements. The predicates associated with situations fall into two disjoint categories referred to respectively as recognition predicates and attribute predicates. The recognition predicates are used to recognize that a given situation to be represented in the example base actually occurred. In other words, they all must be satisfied in order to include a representation of a particular situation in the table. The attribute predicates describe some properties of situations. Thus the condition and conclusion predicates of a rule will be constructed from the attribute predicates. They can be viewed as attributes of these situations with attribute values being true or false (T, F). Our knowledge about situations will be represented in KRS by truth values of these predicates.

As an example, let's consider the collection of situations s = $\{ s_1, s_2, s_3, s_4, s_5 \}$ given in the Table 2. Each situation $s \in S$ is a vector S = (X, Y, Z) characterized by the recognition predicates $c_1(X), c_2(Y), c_3(Z)$ and attribute predicates is-a(Y, X), is-a(Z, Y), is-a(Z, X).

Is-a(X, Y) is a generalization predicate which is satisfied whenever entity-class Y is more general than entity class X. The recognition predicates c_1, c_2, c_3 correspond to domain of variables X, Y, Z respectively, that is,

c_1 = {person, employee }, c_2 = {employee, teacher, staff }, c_3 = {teacher, staff, instructor, student, head-of-section}. The predicate is-a(X, Y) can be chosen as a conclusion predicate; all remaining predicates will be referred to as condition predicates.

Our goal is to establish a set of decision rules which would enable us to predict whether the entity class X is a generalization of the class Z based solely on the information encoded in truth values of condition predicates.

situation	X	Y	Z	is-a(Y, X)	is-a(Z, Y)	is-a(Z, X)
s1	person	employee	teacher	T	T	T
s2	person	employee	staff	T	T	T
s3	person	teacher	instructor	F	F	F
s4	person	employee	student	T	F	T
s5	employee	staff	hd-of-sect	T	T	T

Table 2

3.2 Probabilistic Learning Algorithm (PLA)

Before we present the learning method adapted in our system some preliminary introduction to the idea of probabilistic approxiamte classification is needed. Due to space limitation it is rather sketchy. Readers interested in details should refer to [WZ86a].

In general, our approach to learning is based on the probabilistic approach to rough set model [Paw84]. The basic assumption in this approach is that we don't know all possible situations. The set of situations contained in the KRS forms a sample which can be used to draw some conclusions. The conclusions, however, are bound to be uncertain. Therefore, we can look at the universe of all possible situations belonging to a certain homogeneous class characterized by specified recognition predicates from the probabilistic point of view as a space of elementary random events Ω. Each conclusion and condition predicate becomes a random variable in this model.
To explain the idea, assume for simplicity, that there is only one conclusion predicate D representing expert judgement (or concept) regarding the feasibility of decisions, and a number of condition predicates $b_1, b_2, \ldots, b_m$ reflecting the chosen properties of situations. It is known that a set of all possible values of a random variable or combination of them generates a partition of the space of random events into a family of equivalence classes $T_r = \{Z_1, Z_2, \ldots, Z_n\}$. The partition T_r of Ω and the probability measure P on a σ - algebra of subsets of Ω form a basis for a probabilistic approximation space (Ω, Tr, P). In this approximation space we can find a probabilistic characterization of any unknown expert concept $Y \subseteq \Omega$. In other words, we can produce a set of probabilistic decision rules which will permit us to discriminate, with some uncertainty, between concept Y and its complement. Concept Y, for example, might be defined as satisfying the predicate "entity-class X is a generalization of the entity-class Z".

In the extended KRS model, each equivalence class Z_i of the partition Tr is associated with a unique specification Des(Z_i) in terms of the truth values of some condition predicates. This means that all situations in the class Z_i share the same values of some selected condition predicates. The specification assumes the form of a Boolean expression:
Des(Z_i) $= f(e, b_1) \wedge \ldots \wedge f(e, b_k)$ where $e \in Z_i$ and $b_i \in C$. For instance,
is-a(Y, X) := $T \wedge$ is-a(Z, Y) := F
may form a plausible specification for a class in the example shown in the Table 2.

Our objective is to characterize approximately each expert concept Y (in our case T or F) in terms of specifications Des(Z_i) of classes of Tr and conditional probabilities of Y with respect to Z_i. The concept Y represents the expert judgment expressed by assigning the same truth value of the predicate D to all situations in Y, so we would like to learn how to predict the expert judgment (i.e. value of D) based solely on the known values of condition predicates and estimated conditional probabilities. This can be achieved by associating the notion of probabilistic profile with each concept Y.

The profile of the concept of Y is the conditional probability distribution

$$P(Y|Z_i) = P(Y \cap Z_i)/P(Z_i) \qquad for \qquad i = 1, 2, \cdots, n.$$

Each value $P(Y|Z_i)$ can be interpreted as the probability that situation satisfying the specification of the class Z_i also satisfies the specification of the class Y. In this sense $P(Y|Z_i)$ is a measure of uncertainty when predicting the truth value of the predicate D based on the knowledge of truth values of condition predicates. In other words, each situation can be approximately classified into set Y with certainty $P(Y|Z_i)$. Whenever $0 < P(Y|Z_i) < 1$ for $Z_i \in$ Tr, we say that Y is rough (in probabilistic sense) i.e., the classification cannot be done with 100 % accuracy. In this case, probability distribution $P(Y|Z_i)$ may be used to define a set of probabilistic decision rules to predict the truth values of conclusion predicates, based on the values of condition ones. The central problem in this approach to learning is therefore the estimation and maximization of the probabilities $P(Y|Z_i)$ through generation of an appropriate partition Tr of the universe U.

However, all we know about the universe is included in our collection of example situations E. Consequently, the problem of generating a "good" partition of the universe U reduces, due to our lack of knowledge, to the problem of finding a similar partition of the set of examples E. This is the primary task of a learning algorithm. Ideally, the learning algorithm should be able to produce an optimal partition i.e. one which could be used to obtain minimal set of highly generalized decision rules without giving away the accuracy of predictions.

Although finding an optimal partition turned out to be computationally infeasible, a reasonable degree of generalization of knowledge contained in examples can be achieved by employing simple heuristics in the learning process.

In order to describe the algorithm we will assume that our universe is the set of examples E. We will also have to introduce the notions of lower and upper approximations of a set
$Y = \{e \in E | f(e, D) = T\}$ in the approximation space (E, Tr, P) as follows.

(1) The lower approximation or positive region of Y is defined as
$\mathrm{POS}(Y) = \{e \in E | e \in Z_i$ and $P(Y|Z_i) = 1\}$.

(2) The upper approximation of Y is defined as
$\bar{Y} = \{e \in E | e \in Z_i$ and $P(Y|Z_i) > 0.5\}$.

In addition a boundary or doubtful region $\mathrm{BN}(Y)$ of the set Y can be defined as

(3) $\mathrm{BN}(Y) = \{e \in E | \in Z_i$ and $P(Y|Z_i) = 0.5\}$ and the negative region $\mathrm{NEG}(Y)$ is given by

(4) $\mathrm{NEG}(Y) = E - (\bar{Y} \cup \mathrm{BN}(Y))$.

The regions we defined have the following interpretations:

(1) Whenever a situation belongs to $\mathrm{POS}(Y)$ it can be determined with full certainty that this situation also belongs to Y.

(2) The same conclusion as in (1) can be made in this case. However, some statistical uncertainty will be connected with such a decision.

(3) No conclusion at all can be made if an object belongs to the boundary region of a set. Both choices are equally probable in this case.

(4) A decision with some degree of certainty can be made that a situation does not belong to Y if it belongs to $\mathrm{NEG}(Y)$.

Based on the above interpretations we can associate with each class Z_i a decision rule r_i according to the following criteria:

(1) $r_i : \mathrm{Des}(Z_i) \Rightarrow D$ if $Z_i \subseteq \mathrm{POS}(Y)$.

(2) $r_i : \mathrm{Des}(Z_i) \overset{c}{\Rightarrow} D$ if $Z_i \subseteq \bar{Y}$.

The parameter c is the certainty measure associated with this decision rule. The entropy function [Sha48] or simpler formula given below (which is equivalent to entropy in this case) can be used to compute c:

$c = \mathrm{ABS}(P(Y|Z_i) - 0.5)$.

(3) $r : \mathrm{Des}(Z_i) \Rightarrow$ "unknown" if $Z_i \subseteq \mathrm{BN}(Y)$.
The certainty equals zero in this case.

(4) $r : \mathrm{Des}(Z_i) \overset{c}{\Rightarrow} \neg D$ if $Z_i \subseteq \mathrm{NEG}(Y) = (E - \bar{Y})$.

(5) $r : \mathrm{Des}(Z_i) \Rightarrow \neg D$ if $Z_i \subseteq \mathrm{POS}(E - Y)$.

Rules defined by criteria (1) and (5) are referred to as deterministic decision rules. They can be used directly in the reasoning process using standard theorem proving techniques.

Rules (2) and (4) are nondeterministic. The reasoning process which employes these rules should be able to take into account the effect of combined uncertainty. Rules given by (3) are "dead end" rules. The reasoning cannot proceed whenever this kind of rule is encountered.

3.2.1 The Learning Algorithm

To present the algorithm in precise terms let us denote by $Q(B)$ an equivalence relation defined on a set of sample situations E. The relation $Q(B)$ is defined by:

(1) B is a subset of condition predicates i.e. $B \subseteq C$,

(2) $(e_i, e_j) \in Q(B)$ iff $f(e_i, b) = f(e_j, b)$, for all $b \in B$.

Since each such an equivalence relation corresponds to a partition of E we can associate an approximation space, denoted here as $< E, Q(B), P >$, with each subset of condition predicates B.
Additionally, we introduce the notion of predicate discrimination factor of the collection of condition predicates B with respect to the concept Y. The discrimination factor $G(B, Y)$, given by

$$G(B, Y) = P(\mathrm{POS}(Y)) + P(\mathrm{POS}(E - Y)$$

measures the "power" of the set of attributes B in distinguishing two concepts Y and $E - Y$ by combining the sum of probabilities of positive regions of Y and $E - Y$ in the approximation space $< E, Q(B), P >$.
In the learning procedure we use $G(B, Y)$ in a similar way to ID3 [Qui83] using the entropy function for this purpose.
The core issue in learning is generation of the partition Tr of E which has the following features:

(1) The partition is not too fine; fine partition results in an excessive number of narrow decision rules whereas coarse partition corresponds to a low number of general decision rules.

(2) The certainty of conclusions drawn from generalized decision rules is not affected by the generalization process.

The algorithm, which we present below, satisfies the objective (2) and attempts to satisfy (1) by applying the discriminating factor $G(B,Y)$.

Let $Y = \{e \in E | f(e, D) = T\}$.

Algorithm 1: Generation of the partition Tr on E.

Input: A Knowledge Representation System.

Variables: F represents a set of samples, M or N represent a subset of predicates, Tr represents a family of subsets of E.

Procedure:

1. Let $F \leftarrow E$; $M \leftarrow \emptyset$; $N \leftarrow C$; $T \leftarrow \emptyset$,
2. Repeat until either $F = \emptyset$ or $M = C$;

- Let $N \leftarrow N - M$;
- find a condition predicate p in N such that $G(M \cup \{p\}, Y)$ in the approximation space $< F, Q(M \cup \{p\}), P >$ is maximum;
- Let $M \leftarrow M \cup \{p\}$;
- Compute POS(Y)$\cup$ POS($E - Y$) in the approximation space $< F, Q(M), P >$ by identifying those equivalence classes Z_i of $Q(M)$ such that $P(Y|Z_i) = 1$ or $P(E - Y|Z_i) = 1$; Attach all these classes to Tr;
- Let $F \leftarrow F -$ (POS(Y)$\cup$POS($E - Y$));

3. If $F \neq \emptyset$, add all the equivalence classes of the relation $Q(M)$ on F to Tr.

Output: Partition Tr on E induced by the condition predicates.

The algorithm has been implemented in LISP in the form of a small decision tree generating program INFER [WZ86b].

To illustrate the operations of the rule learning system built according to this algorithm let us consider the collection of situations given in Table 2. The predicate is-a(Z, X) has been chosen as a decision predicate. Because the discriminating factor of the condition predicate is-a(Y, X) is maximum (i.e. equals 1) and is greather than the discriminating factor of is-a(Z, Y) we can conclude that is-a(Z, X) can be fully characterized by is-a(Z, Y). In other words the following decision rules would be extracted by Algorithm 1.

is-a(Y, X) := $T \Rightarrow$ is-a(Z, X) := T and is-a(Y, X) := $F \Rightarrow$ is-a(Z, X) := F .

Consequently, one of the possible inference rules induced from Table 2 can be expressed as

is-a(Z, X) $\leftarrow$ is-a(Y, X)

or in words, entity set X is a generalization of the entity set Z if the entity set X is a generalization of the entity set Y.

This rule (and eventually the other rules induced from the table) represent our current state of knowledge about relationships among predicate attributes. Future examples may invalidate this rule and some new rules may appear. In the longer run the system of rules will tend to stabilize to reflect real interrelationships existing among entity sets of sample situations.

4 Conclusions

We have described design of a conceptual schema which is intended to help the end user in designing an information system. We have initiated the project recently, so we cannot report from results, but from goals. Several of the techniques discussed here have been implemented elsewhere [Yas85,WZ86b]. Most of the components are implemented but they are not integrated yet.

The main features of the system are summarized below:

1. The conceptual schema and its associated rules are represented in predicate logic which can be adapted to any other application.
2. The conceptual schema is based on both the semantic model, which is close to natural language, and on the event model, which captures the dynamic behaviour of the system.

3. Database design procedure starts with a naive description of an application and proceeds in the form of a dialogue between the system and the user.
4. We adapt a learning mechanism by which the design knowledge can be acquired from examples; rules can be either generated from examples or new design rules can be explicitely added to the existing ones.
5. We claim that after a certain period of time the experience accumulated in the system will allow us to replace the expert by the system.

References

[BF78] B.G. Buchanan and E.A. Feigenbaum. Denderal and metadenderal, their applications dimension. *Artif. Intell.*, 2(11):5–24, 1978.

[DM79] T.G. Dietterich and R.S. Michalski. Learning and generalization of characteristic descriptions: evaluation criteria and comparable review of selected methods. *Proceedings of the 6th IJCAI*, 1979.

[For86] R. Forsyth. *Machine learning: Applications in Expert Systems and Information Retrieval.* John Wiley and Sons, 1986.

[HM81] N. Hammer and D. McLeod. Database description with sdm: a semantic data model. *ACM-TODS*, 6(3), Sep 1981.

[Kow79] R. Kowalski. Logic and semantic networks. *CACM*, 22(3):184–192, March 1979.

[M*80] J. Mylopoulos et al. A language facility for designing database intensive applications. *ACM TODS*, 15(2), 1980.

[Mic80] R.S. Michalski. Learning by being told and learning from examples: an experimental comparison of the two methods of knowledge acquisition in the context of developing an expert system for soybean disease diagnosis. *Inter. J. Poly. Anal. and Infor. Sys.*, 4(2):125–161, 1980.

[Mic83] R. Michalski. *Machine Learning, An Artificial Intelligence Approach.* Springer Verlag, Berlin, 1983.

[OP84] E. Orlawska and A.Z. Pawlak. Expressive power of knowledge representation systems. *Man-Machine Studies*, 1(20):485–500, 1984.

[Paw84] Z. Pawlak. Rough classification. *Man-Machine Studies*, 20:469–493, 1984.

[Qui83] J.R. Quinlan. *Learning Efficient Classification Procedure and Their Application to Chess and Games.* Springer Verlag, Berlin, 1983.

[Sch76] L.K. Schubert. Extending the expressive power of semantic networks. *Artificial Intelligence*, 7:163–198, 1976.

[SD76] E.H. Shortlifte and R. Davis. *Computer-Based Medical Consultations: MYCIN.* Elsevier, North Holland, New York, 1976.

[Sha48] C.E. Shannon. A mathematical theory of communication. *Bell System Technical Journal*, 4:379–423, 1948.

[Sow86] J.F. Sowa. Semantic networks. *Encyclopedia of Artificial Intelligence*, 1986.

[SS77] J.M. Smith and D.C.P. Smith. Database abstractions, aggregation and generalization. *ACM-TODS*, June 1977.

[WZ86a] S.K.M. Wong and W. Ziarko. Algorithm for inductive learning. *Bulletin of Polish Academy of Science*, 34(5-6):271–276, 1986.

[WZ86b] S.K.M. Wong and W. Ziarko. On learning and evaluation of decision rules in the context of rough sets. *Proceedings of ACM International Symposium on Methodologies For Intelligent Systems , Knoxville*, 1986.

[Yas85] R. Yasdi. A conceptual design aid environment for expert data base systems. *Data and Knowledge Engineering*, 1(1), March 1985.

[YZ86] R. Yasdi and W. Ziarko. An expert system for conceptual schema design: a machine learning approach. In *Technical Report CS-86-18*, University of Regina, 1986.

Update and Conditionals

Charles B. Cross[†] and *Richmond H. Thomason*[‡]
[†]Computer Science and Systems Branch, Naval Research Laboratory, Washington, D.C. 20375, U.S.A.; [‡]Linguistics Department, University of Pittsburgh, Pittsburgh, PA 15260, U.S.A.

IT HAS BEEN SUGGESTED that indicative conditional propositions, such as *if Oswald didn't shoot Kennedy, then Kennedy is still alive,* record dispositions to revise beliefs in the face of new information.[1] Philosophical logicians refer to this suggestion as the *Ramsey rule*, and it can be formulated, in the context of knowledge representation, as follows:

Knowledge base $\mathcal{K}$ contains the information IF P, THEN Q if and only if updating $\mathcal{K}$ with the information P produces a (new) knowledge base that contains the information Q.

It follows from the Ramsey rule that any system of conditional logic can be translated into a set of principles about knowledge update, which in turn implies that conditional logic can provide a theoretical framework for the semantics of knowledge update.[2] For example, in some systems of conditional logic the formulas $(Q > (P > R))$ and $(P > (Q > R))$ are logically equivalent. Under the Ramsey rule this equivalence would translate into the following principle about update: *Updating first with Q and then with P accomplishes the same thing as updating first with P and then with Q.*

In this paper we give some preliminary results of our investigation of conditional logic as a theoretical framework for the semantics of knowledge update. We will examine the system of conditional logic that is generated (by means of the Ramsey rule) from a particular semantics for knowledge update, namely the semantics for inheritance and update in nonmonotonic semantic networks found in [5]. This particular semantics makes an appropriate case study for several reasons. *First of all,* its update mechanism is straightforward—to update a network with a link one merely adds the link to the network; the nonmonotonic inheritance semantics does the work of revising the knowledge contained in the network. *Secondly,* since the inheritance semantics is well-motivated, the system of conditional logic that it generates will be of some interest, for it will embody a well-motivated set of constraints on update in semantic networks. *Thirdly,* one of our ongoing projects is to investigate the possibility that a well-motivated semantics for multiple inheritance with exceptions can be specified in terms of the update behavior of semantic networks. The present study supports this project because we hope eventually to use an extension of the deduction system presented here to reformulate the inheritance semantics of [5] in terms of the update operation. *Fourthly,* this case study teaches us something about conditional logic, for it demonstrates that when one approaches conditionals with knowledge update in mind, the system of logic that emerges may be quite different from systems that exist in the literature. In the case of our system, the differences are both pronounced and interesting. Reflecting on update in semantic networks has led us to a system of conditional logic that avoids a major theoretical problem that has been thought to refute the Ramsey rule principle.[3] In addition, our inheritance-based models for conditional

[0]The research reported here was performed at Carnegie Mellon University and the University of Pittsburgh with support from the National Science Foundation under Grant No. IST-8516313. The first author thanks the Naval Research Laboratory for its support, as well.

[1]See the articles in [4], especially [8].

[2]For a survey of recent work in conditional logic see [7]. A formula of the form $(A > B)$ should be read "If A then B," but do not regard $>$ as standing for the familiar *material* conditional.

[3]See [3]. Our Ramsey rule semantics is nontrivial despite Gärdenfors' trivialization theorem, as we show in a forthcoming technical report.

Methodologies for Intelligent Systems
Z. W. Ras and M. Zemankova, Editors

logic provide a natural class of counterexamples to *modus ponens* of the very same sort as those identified in [6].

1 Multiple inheritance with exceptions

Since our system of conditional logic is based on the nonmonotonic inheritance semantics of [5], we will state that semantics below for reference and explain it very briefly. Limitations of space prevent us from explaining it in detail or offering many examples, and so we refer the reader to [5], where a careful and complete exposition is given.

First, some preliminaries. Primitive vocabulary consists of one set of terms a, b, c, d with and without subscripts to represent *individuals* and a second set of terms p, q, r, s with and without subscripts to represent *kinds*. Where y is a kind term and x is either an individual term or a distinct kind term, the *links* $x \rightarrow y$ and $x \not\rightarrow y$ will represent the statements x *is-a* y and x *is-not-a* y, respectively.[4] If x represents an individual, then we refer to $x \rightarrow y$ and $x \not\rightarrow y$ as *atomic* links; if x refers to a kind, then $x \rightarrow y$ and $x \not\rightarrow y$ are *generic* links. A *net* is defined to be any finite set of links. We use the symbol $\succ$ as a variable ranging over the set $\{\rightarrow, \not\rightarrow\}$, so that $u \succ v$ is a link of the form $u \rightarrow v$ or $u \not\rightarrow v$, and we define $\not\succ$ to be the opposite of $\succ$. We define a *generalized path* from x to y in a net $\mathcal{G}$ to be any sequence $x \succ u_1 \succ \ldots \succ u_m \succ y$, where $x \succ u_1$, $u_m \succ y \in \mathcal{G}$, and for all i such that $1 \leq i < m$, $u_i \succ u_{i+1} \in \mathcal{G}$. A *path* from x to y in a net $\mathcal{G}$ is defined to be a sequence of the form $x \rightarrow u_1 \rightarrow \ldots \rightarrow u_m \succ y$, where $x \rightarrow u_1$, $u_m \succ y \in \mathcal{G}$ and for each i such that $1 \leq i < m$, $u_i \rightarrow u_{i+1} \in \mathcal{G}$. A *basic* path is a path of length 1. We use lower case Greek letters (σ, τ, ξ, etc) with and without subscripts to range over paths. We will use calligraphic capital letters $\mathcal{D}, \mathcal{E}, \mathcal{F}, \mathcal{G}$ with and without subscripts to range over nets.

We restrict our attention to *acyclic* nets, *i.e.* nets in which no there are no generalized paths from x to x. Where $\mathcal{G}$ is an acyclic net, and where σ is a path from x to y in $\mathcal{G}$, the degree of σ in $\mathcal{G}$, denoted by $\deg_{\mathcal{G}}(\sigma)$, is defined to be the length (number of arrows) of the longest generalized path from x to y in $\mathcal{G}$. Since we concern ourselves only with acyclic nets, every path in a given net will have a well-defined degree.

Definition 1 *Let $\mathcal{G}$ be an acyclic net, and let σ be a path in $\mathcal{G}$ from x to y. Inheritance is defined inductively as follows.*

1. *If σ is basic, then $\mathcal{G}$ permits σ; this defines inheritance for all paths of degree 1.*
2. *Suppose that inheritance is settled for all paths in $\mathcal{G}$ of degree less than n, and let $\deg_{\mathcal{G}}(\sigma) = n$. If $\sigma = x \rightarrow \xi \rightarrow u \succ y$, then $\mathcal{G}$ permits σ iff*
   - *(a) $\mathcal{G}$ permits $x \rightarrow \xi \rightarrow u$;*
   - *(b) $u \succ y \in \mathcal{G}$;*
   - *(c) $x \not\succ y \notin \mathcal{G}$;*
   - *(d) If $\mathcal{G}$ permits $x \rightarrow \tau \rightarrow v$ and $v \not\succ y \in \mathcal{G}$, then there exists a z distinct from v such that $\mathcal{G}$ permits $x \rightarrow \tau_1 \rightarrow z \rightarrow \tau_2 \rightarrow v$ and $z \succ y \in \mathcal{G}$.*

We abbreviate "$\mathcal{G}$ permits σ" as follows: $\mathcal{G} \models \sigma$. If $\mathcal{G} \models x \rightarrow \sigma \succ y$, then we say that $\mathcal{G}$ *supports* $x \succ y$, where $x \rightarrow \sigma \succ y$ is thought of as an *argument* and $x \succ y$ as this argument's *conclusion*.

[4] We are talking about inheritance with *exceptions*, so it is important to remember that where x and y are both kind terms, x *is-a* y and x *is-not-a* y carry the qualification "typically" or "as a rule."

This semantics for multiple inheritance with exceptions is driven by three ideas. *First, inheritance reasoning should proceed from the specific to the general.* The intuition is not one of inheritable properties flowing down the net to the individuals that inherit them, but, instead, of paths as *arguments* that are constructed by drawing a series of conclusions about an individual's membership in classes of increasing generality. Consequently, more complex permitted paths are constructed by *appending* (rather than prepending) appropriately chosen links to less complex permitted paths. *Secondly, when two opposing arguments present themselves, a conclusion drawn directly from a more specific reason is to be preferred to a conclusion drawn directly from a less specific reason.* If, for example, I learn that Clyde is an elephant, elephants being gray, and that Clyde is a royal elephant, royal elephants being white, I should conclude that Clyde is white, since *royal elephant* is a more specific class than *elephant.* For our purposes, specificity of reasons goes by specificity of predicates. *Finally, inheritance reasoning with exceptions should be skeptical, in the sense that two arguments with opposing conclusions should cancel each other out unless one of them can be discredited through specificity considerations.* Suppose, for example, that I am presented only with (a) the information that Dick is a Quaker, Quakers being pacifists, and (b) the information that Dick is a Republican, Republicans being non-pacifists. In this case I should refrain from concluding that Dick is a pacifist, or that he is not one, because *Quaker* and *Republican* are incomparable classes and so cannot be ranked according to specificity . (In particular, I should refrain from concluding that he is *both* a pacifist and a non-pacifist. According to the inheritance semantics of [5], a net supports all and only those inconsistencies that it explicitly contains.) However, suppose that I now learn that Dick is a Liberal-Republican, Liberal-Republicans being both Republicans and pacifists. In such a case argument (b) is discredited since *Liberal-Republican* is more specific than *Republican.* If no *other* argument in the knowledge base opposes argument (a), then argument (a) goes through.

This last example illustrates the simple update procedure that can be associated with the inheritance semantics of [5]. To update a network with the information that x *is-a* y, one simply adds the link $x \rightarrow y$ to the net. In the example, learning that Dick is a Liberal-Republican and that Liberal-Republicans are both Republicans and pacifists therefore means adding direct positive links from *Dick* to *Liberal-Republican,* from *Liberal-Republican* to *Republican*, and from *Liberal-Republican* to *Pacifist.*

2 Inheritance-based models for conditional logic

Next we present an inheritance-based semantics for conditional logic and a proof system that is sound but incomplete with respect to this semantics. In future work we hope to extend the proof system to a complete one.

2.1 Update in semantic nets

As we have said, the update mechanism we propose for semantic networks is simple: to update with a given link you just add the link to the network. This update mechanism is fine, as far as it goes, but in order to give a robust semantics for the conditional, we will need to define net-update for logically complex formulas. Our (extended) update operation will be defined for statements containing conjunction, disjunction, and negation ($\wedge$, $\vee$, and $\neg$).

Since [5] allows inconsistent and incomplete semantic nets, it would not do to base our semantics for conditional logic on standard two-valued Boolean logic, for if we did, the resulting logical consequence relation would not be conservative of the original support relation. For example, if we were to use two-valued Boolean connectives, the net $\{a \rightarrow p, a \not\rightarrow p\}$ would then support $a \rightarrow q$, though nothing in the inheritance semantics itself requires this. We therefore follow [9] and use four-valued (paraconsistent) conjunction, disjunction, and negation, as described in [1] and [2].

We will not define the update operation on formulas containing generic links, nor will we allow such formulas as well-formed formulas of our conditional logic. Our aim at this stage is to relate multiple inheritance with exceptions to systems of conditional logic of a more or less familiar sort (such as [8]). In particular, this means looking at systems that have monotonic consequence relations. If we were to include generic links among the well-formed formulas of our conditional logic, the resulting consequence relation would be *non*monotonic.

Nor will we define our update operation on conditional formulas, since these do not correspond semantically to links or to truth-functional combinations of links. We will define disjunctive updates, however, even though semantic networks would be a poor choice of knowledge representation system for an application in which disjunctive updates were needed. Disjunctive updating will involve selecting a *least disruptive* disjunct to use in the update. This will insure that the update-image of a semantic network is always another semantic network, rather than, say, a set of networks.

2.2 Inheritance-based models

We abbreviate atomic links of the form $a \rightarrow p$ as pa and those having the form $a \not\rightarrow p$ as $\neg pa$. We define the set of well-formed formulas to be the smallest set $\mathcal{S}$ meeting the following conditions:

(wff-1) if A is an unnegated atomic link, then $A \in \mathcal{S}$;

(wff-2) if $A, B \in \mathcal{S}$, then $(A \wedge B)$, $(A \vee B)$, $\neg A \in \mathcal{S}$;

(wff-3) if $A, B \in \mathcal{S}$ and A contains no occurrence of $>$, then $(A > B) \in \mathcal{S}$.

Condition **(wff-3)** ensures that antecedents of conditionals do not themselves contain any conditionals, although the consequents of conditionals *are* permitted to contain conditionals.

An *inheritance-based model* is an ordered triple $\langle W, v, f \rangle$, where f is an update function as described below, W is a set of semantic networks closed under f, and v is a four-valued valuation function[5] on unnegated atomic links defined as follows: $\mathrm{T} \in v_{\mathcal{G}}(pa)$ iff $\mathcal{G} \models a \rightarrow p$ and $\mathrm{F} \in v_{\mathcal{G}}(pa)$ iff $\mathcal{G} \models a \not\rightarrow p$. Each $v_{\mathcal{G}}$ is extended to a full valuation $[\![\,]\!]_{\mathcal{G}}$ according to the following rules:

(v-1) If A is atomic, then $[\![A]\!]_{\mathcal{G}} = v_{\mathcal{G}}(A)$;

(v-2) $\mathrm{T} \in [\![\neg A]\!]_{\mathcal{G}}$ iff $\mathrm{F} \in [\![A]\!]_{\mathcal{G}}$; $\mathrm{F} \in [\![\neg A]\!]_{\mathcal{G}}$ iff $\mathrm{T} \in [\![A]\!]\mathcal{G}$;

(v-3) $\mathrm{T} \in [\![A \wedge B]\!]$ iff $\mathrm{T} \in [\![A]\!]$ and $\mathrm{T} \in [\![B]\!]$; $\mathrm{F} \in [\![A \wedge B]\!]$ iff $\mathrm{F} \in [\![A]\!]$ or $\mathrm{F} \in [\![B]\!]$;

(v-4) $\mathrm{T} \in [\![A \vee B]\!]_{\mathcal{G}}$ iff $\mathrm{T} \in [\![A]\!]_{\mathcal{G}}$ or $\mathrm{T} \in [\![B]\!]_{\mathcal{G}}$; $\mathrm{F} \in [\![A \vee B]\!]_{\mathcal{G}}$ iff $\mathrm{F} \in [\![A]\!]_{\mathcal{G}}$ and $\mathrm{F} \in [\![B]\!]_{\mathcal{G}}$.

[5]In four-valued logic, formulas are assigned values from the set $\mathcal{T} = \{\{\mathrm{T}\}, \{\mathrm{F}\}, \emptyset, \{\mathrm{T}, \mathrm{F}\}\}$. The members of $\mathcal{T}$ should be understood not as truth values but as the possible epistemic states of a system with respect to a statement. A statement A is assigned the value $\{\mathrm{T}\}$ provided that the system has been told that A is true but not that A is false. A is assigned the value $\{\mathrm{F}\}$ if the system has been told that A is false but not that A is true. A is assigned the value $\emptyset$ if the system has been told nothing regarding A's truth. A is given the value $\{\mathrm{T}, \mathrm{F}\}$ provided that the system has been told both that A is true and that A is false.

(v-5) $[\![A > B]\!]_{\mathcal{G}} = [\![B]\!]_{f(A,\mathcal{G})}$.

Condition **(v-5)** makes it clear that this is a Ramsey rule semantics for the conditional: $(A > B)$ is true at a network $\mathcal{G}$ iff updating $\mathcal{G}$ with A yields a network at which B is true.

The heart of the model is f, the update function. In general we need to be able to define net update for formulas of the form $((\phi_{1,1} \wedge \ldots \wedge \phi_{1,n}) \vee \ldots \vee (\phi_{m,1} \wedge \ldots \wedge \phi_{m,n}))$. In order to define f we introduce two additional formalisms: $\lhd_{\mathcal{H}}$ and g. Intuitively, given a formula in disjunctive normal form and a semantic network $\mathcal{H}$, $\lhd_{\mathcal{H}}$ orders the disjuncts, g selects the disjunct that comes first in the ordering, and f adds to $\mathcal{H}$ the links whose logical conjunction comprises the selected disjunct. These conjunctions of links are ordered relative to $\mathcal{H}$ in such a way that (1) all the *true-at-$\mathcal{H}$* conjunctions come before all the non-*true-at-$\mathcal{H}$* conjunctions, (2) no conjunction comes before any of its sub-conjunctions, and (3) among non-*true-at-$\mathcal{H}$* conjunctions, non-*false-at-$\mathcal{H}$* conjunctions come before *false-at-$\mathcal{H}$* conjunctions. The idea behind these three restrictions is that when updating a semantic network with a disjunction one should use a disjunct that changes the class of supported links to the smallest degree possible while making the disjunction true.[6]

In order to define f formally we will need some notation. Let $\mathcal{P}_{\mathcal{G}} = \{p_1, \ldots, p_n\}$ be an enumeration of the kind terms appearing in $\mathcal{G}$, and let $\mathcal{A}_{\mathcal{G}} = \{a_1, \ldots, a_m\}$ be an enumeration of the individual terms appearing in $\mathcal{G}$. Let $\mathcal{G}^+ = \{x \rightarrow p : x \in \mathcal{A}_{\mathcal{G}}, p \in \mathcal{P}_{\mathcal{G}}\}$ and let $\mathcal{G}^- = \{x \not\rightarrow p : x \in \mathcal{A}_{\mathcal{G}}, p \in \mathcal{P}_{\mathcal{G}}\}$. Formally, $\lhd_{\mathcal{H}}, g, f$ are as follows: for each $\mathcal{H} \in W$, let $\lhd_{\mathcal{H}}$ be a well-ordering of the nonempty subsets of $\mathcal{H}^+ \cup \mathcal{H}^-$ that meets the following conditions, where $\mathbf{T}(\mathcal{H}) = \{x \rightarrow p : \mathcal{H} \models x \rightarrow p\} \cup \{x \not\rightarrow p : \mathcal{H} \models x \not\rightarrow p\}$ and $\mathbf{F}(\mathcal{H}) = \{x \rightarrow p : \mathcal{H} \models x \not\rightarrow p\} \cup \{x \not\rightarrow p : \mathcal{H} \models x \rightarrow p\}$:

($\lhd$-1) $X \lhd_{\mathcal{H}} Y$ whenever $X \subseteq \mathbf{T}(\mathcal{H})$ but $Y \not\subseteq \mathbf{F}(\mathcal{H})$;

($\lhd$-2) If $X \subseteq Y$, then $Y \not\lhd_{\mathcal{H}} X$;

($\lhd$-3) If $X \not\subseteq \mathbf{T}(\mathcal{H})$, $Y \not\subseteq \mathbf{T}(\mathcal{H})$, $X \cap \mathbf{F}(\mathcal{H}) = \emptyset$, and $Y \cap \mathbf{F}(\mathcal{H}) \neq \emptyset$, then $X \lhd_{\mathcal{H}} Y$.

If A is a conditional-free formula, then a disjunctive normal form A^+ of A is any disjunction of conjunctions of atomic links that is equivalent (under the four-valued semantics for $\wedge$, $\vee$, $\neg$,) to A. We let $\overline{A} = \{X : X$ is the set of all conjuncts of B for some disjunct B of a disjunctive normal form of $A\}$. We define a function g as follows: for each conditional-free formula A and $\mathcal{H} \in W$, $g(A, \mathcal{H})$ is the $\lhd_{\mathcal{H}}$-least element of $\overline{A}$. Finally we define the update function f as follows: $f(A, \mathcal{H}) = \mathcal{H} \cup g(A, \mathcal{H})$.

Finally, we define semantic entailment: If Γ is a set of formulas and A is a formula, then Γ is said to *entail* A iff $\mathrm{T} \in [\![A]\!]_{\mathcal{G}}$ for every model $\langle W, v, f\rangle$ and $\mathcal{G} \in W$ such that every B belonging to Γ satisfies $\mathrm{T} \in [\![B]\!]_{\mathcal{G}}$. Formula A is said to be *valid* iff the empty set entails A.

2.3 An incomplete logic for inheritance-based models

We call the following Gentzen system **INH**4. In the description of the following rules, propositional metavariables range as follows: A, B, C range over arbitrary formulas; P, Q, R range over conditional-free formulas, and U, V, W range over (possibly degenerate) conjunctions of negated and unnegated atomic formulas. Taken by itself, the $\wedge$, $\vee$, $\neg$ fragment of this logic characterizes Relevant Tautological Entailment (see [1] and [2]).

[6]Readers who are not interested in working through the details of the definition of the update function may want to skip the next paragraph.

Structural Rules

$$A \in \Gamma \Rightarrow \Gamma \vdash A \qquad \frac{\Gamma \vdash A}{\Gamma, \Delta \vdash A} \qquad \frac{\Gamma \vdash A \quad \Delta, A \vdash B}{\Gamma, \Delta \vdash B}$$

Logical Rules for Conjunction, Disjunction, and Negation

$$\frac{\Gamma \vdash A \wedge B}{\Gamma \vdash A} \qquad \frac{\Gamma \vdash A \wedge B}{\Gamma \vdash B} \qquad \frac{\Gamma \vdash A \quad \Gamma \vdash B}{\Gamma \vdash A \wedge B} \qquad \frac{\Gamma \vdash \neg B}{\Gamma \vdash \neg(A \wedge B)}$$

$$\frac{\Gamma \vdash \neg(A \wedge B) \quad \Delta_1, \neg A \vdash C \quad \Delta_2, \neg B \vdash C}{\Gamma, \Delta_1, \Delta_2 \vdash C} \qquad \frac{\Gamma \vdash A \vee B \quad \Delta_1, A \vdash C \quad \Delta_2, B \vdash C}{\Gamma, \Delta_1, \Delta_2 \vdash C}$$

$$\frac{\Gamma \vdash \neg A}{\Gamma \vdash \neg(A \wedge B)} \qquad \frac{\Gamma \vdash A}{\Gamma \vdash A \vee B} \qquad \frac{\Gamma \vdash B}{\Gamma \vdash A \vee B} \qquad \frac{\Gamma \vdash \neg(A \vee B)}{\Gamma \vdash \neg A}$$

$$\frac{\Gamma \vdash \neg(A \vee B)}{\Gamma \vdash \neg B} \qquad \frac{\Gamma \vdash \neg A \quad \Gamma \vdash \neg B}{\Gamma \vdash \neg(A \vee B)} \qquad \frac{\Gamma \vdash \neg\neg A}{\Gamma \vdash A} \qquad \frac{\Gamma \vdash A}{\Gamma \vdash \neg\neg A}$$

Logical rules for the conditional

$$\frac{\Gamma \vdash P > B_1 \ \ldots \ \Gamma \vdash P > B_n \quad \{B_1, \ldots, B_n\} \vdash C}{\Gamma \vdash P > C} \qquad \frac{\Gamma \vdash P > (A \vee B)}{\Gamma \vdash (P > A) \vee (P > B)}$$

$$\Gamma \vdash P > P \qquad \frac{\Gamma \vdash P \quad \Gamma \vdash P > Q}{\Gamma \vdash Q} \qquad \frac{\Gamma \vdash P \quad \Gamma \vdash Q}{\Gamma \vdash P > Q}$$

$$\frac{\Gamma \vdash U \wedge \neg U}{\Gamma \vdash P > (U \wedge \neg U)} \qquad \frac{\Gamma \vdash \neg(P > B)}{\Gamma \vdash P > \neg B} \qquad \frac{\Gamma \vdash P > \neg B}{\Gamma \vdash \neg(P > B)}$$

$$\frac{\Gamma \vdash U > (V > C)}{\Gamma \vdash (U \wedge V) > C} \qquad \frac{\Gamma \vdash (U \wedge V) > C}{\Gamma \vdash U > (V > C)} \qquad \frac{\Gamma \vdash P > Q \quad \Gamma \vdash Q > P \quad \Gamma \vdash P > R}{\Gamma \vdash Q > R}$$

The proof of soundness is straightforward, except for the case of the last rule, which requires the following lemma:

Lemma 1 *For any net $\mathcal{G}$ and any sets Δ_1 and Δ_2 of atomic links, if $\mathcal{G} \cup \Delta_1$ supports every member of Δ_2 and $\mathcal{G} \cup \Delta_2$ supports every member of Δ_1, then for any path σ, $\mathcal{G} \cup \Delta_1 \models \sigma$ iff $\mathcal{G} \cup \Delta_2 \models \sigma$.*

Theorem 1 (Soundness) *For any set Γ of formulas and any formula A, if $\Gamma \vdash A$ then Γ entails A.*

As we mentioned above, **INH4** is not complete with respect to inheritance-based models. To prove this we need the following lemma:

Lemma 2 *Suppose that* $\mathcal{G} \not\models a \to p$, *that* $\mathcal{G} \not\models a \not\to p$, *and that* $\sigma = b \to \tau \succ q$, *where* $\sigma \neq a \to \xi \not\to p$. *Then* $\mathcal{G} \cup \{a \not\to p\} \models \sigma$ *iff* $\mathcal{G} \models \sigma$.

Given this lemma it is not difficult to prove:

Lemma 3 *For any connective-free statements A and B, the inference from* $\{(\neg A > \neg B), B\}$ *to* $(A \vee \neg B)$ *is valid in net-models.*

Since the sequent $(\neg A > \neg B), B \vdash (A \vee \neg B)$ is not provable in the logic presented above, we have:

Theorem 2 (Incompleteness) *There is a set* Γ *of formulas and a formula A such that* Γ *entails A but* $\Gamma \not\vdash A$.

Conditionals in **INH**4 are like *singular* default rules in nonmonotonic logic; $pa > qa$, for instance, is like $(pa \wedge \Diamond qa) \supset qa$. As a way of reasoning about defaults, however, our conditional logic is much weaker than nonmonotonic logic, since it has no way of expressing general default rules. On the conditional approach to default rules, a universal conditional such as $\forall x(px > qx)$ should not be regarded as corresponding to a general default such as *Elephants are grey.* The former is false as long as there is an elephant that is not grey, whereas the latter is not. To express general defaults using conditionals, we need to explore logics that treat quantification in a nonstandard way and provide a way of representing the generic plural, rather than universal quantification; roughly, the meaning of $p \to q$ would be that we should conclude qa on learning pa of a new individual a. We are exploring such weak quantificational logics in our current research.

2.4 The invalidity of modus ponens

As we mentioned at the beginning, one interesting property of inheritance-based models is the invalidity of *modus ponens*; if B is a conditional formula, a net may support both A and $(A > B)$ without supporting B. Here we find ourselves in agreement with Vann McGee, who has recently argued in [6] that *modus ponens* is simply not valid for the English indicative conditional.

McGee's counterexamples to *modus ponens* are all of the following form: Q and $(Q > (P > S))$ are true, but $(P > S)$ is not true. Semantic nets, in the context of inheritance-based models, provide a class of counterexamples to *modus ponens* of precisely this form. Consider the net consisting of the following set of links: $\{a \to r, r \to q, q \to s, p \not\to q\}$. This net supports the statements qa and $(qa > (pa > sa))$, but it does not support the statement $(pa > sa)$. We obtain a concrete example by letting s stand for the predicate *malnourished*, q for the predicate *ill-fed*, p for the predicate *wealthy*, and r for the predicate *beggar*. The name a will stand for *Alfred.* The net then tells us this: Alfred is a beggar and can therefore be presumed to be ill-fed (and hence malnourished). Indeed, if it turns out that Alfred is ill-fed, then even if it turns out that he is wealthy, we can still presume that he is malnourished. But it does not follow that if it turns out that Alfred is wealthy, then we can presume that he is malnourished! On the contrary, if, in our present state of knowledge, we learn *only* that Alfred is wealthy, we will be unable to make any presumption about whether he is malnourished, for in that case we will have two pieces of evidence, one for and one against his being ill-fed, without any basis for deciding which evidence to base a presumption on (since *beggar* and *wealthy person* are incomparable classes).

This example highlights the fact that our update operation maps a given net to a new net in which the update proposition is not merely supported but *indefeasibly supported.* The failure of *modus ponens* and the validity of Importation and Exportation (the first and second rules in the last row of logical rules for the conditional) are direct consequences of this. Indeed, Importation and Exportation are exactly the inferences whose joint validity *guarantees* that once an update takes place the update proposition cannot be withdrawn by making further updates.

3 Conditionals and update constraints

The system **INH**4 presented above can be used as a specification criterion for knowledge representation systems implementing an update function—the criterion being that *the system should satisfy all of the principles validated by this logic, when the conditional $>$ is interpreted in the logic using the Ramsey rule.* Thus, for example, since the logic validates the sequent $pa, (pa > qb) \vdash qb$, any inheritance algorithm that supports pa and $(pa > qb)$ should also support qb.

Though this criterion may seem trivial, it is not; in fact, it rules out many of the algorithms that have been proposed for multiple inheritance with exceptions. Touretzky's criticism of shortest-path algorithms in [10], pp. 117-119, discusses an example in which the valid instance of *modus ponens* that we mentioned above fails. By presenting an inheritance algorithm for which the logic is sound, we have also shown that the criterion is not impractically strict.

The fact that we can state update constraints in a relatively tractable logic gives us the opportunity of designing systems that can reason explicitly about update principles by means of the logic. So far, though, we have not taken this step and are employing the logic only as an external criterion for inheritance algorithms.

References

[1] Belnap, N., "How a computer should think." In G. Ryle (ed.), *Contemporary aspects of philosophy,* Oriel Press, 1977, pp. 30–56.

[2] Belnap, N., "A useful four-valued logic." In J.M. Dunn and G. Epstein (eds.), *Modern uses of multiple-valued logic*, D. Reidel, Dordrecht, 1977, pp. 8–37.

[3] Gärdenfors, P., "Belief revisions and the Ramsey test for conditionals." *Philosophical Review* **95**: 81-93, (1986).

[4] Harper, William L., R. C. Stalnaker and G. Pearce (eds.), *Ifs: Conditionals, Beliefs, Decision, Chance, and Time*, D. Reidel, 1981.

[5] Horty, J., Thomason, R., and Touretzky, D., "A skeptical theory of inheritance in nonmonotonic semantic networks," in *AAAI 1987*.

[6] McGee, Vann, "A counterexample to *modus ponens*," *Journal of Philosophy* **82**: 462-471, (1985).

[7] Nute, Donald, "Conditional Logic," in *Handbook of Philosophical Logic*, Volume 2, Gabbay, Dov and Franz Guenthner (eds.), D. Reidel, 1984.

[8] Stalnaker, Robert C. "A theory of conditionals," in N. Rescher (ed.), *Studies in Logical Theory*, (Oxford: Blackwell, APQ Monograph No. 2, 1968). Reprinted in [4], pp. 41-55.

[9] Thomason, R. H., Horty, J. F., and Touretzky, D. S. A calculus for inheritance in monotonic semantic nets. Technical Report CMU-CS-138, Computer Science Department, Carnegie Mellon University, 1986.

[10] Touretzky, David S., *The mathematics of inheritance systems.* Los Altos: Morgan Kaufmann, 1986.

Resolution for Intuitionistic Logic[1]

Melvin Fitting

Department of Mathematics and Computer Science, Herbert H. Lehman College (CUNY), Bronx, New York 10468.
Department of Computer Science, The Graduate School and University Center (CUNY), Graduate Center, 33 West 42 Street, New York, New York 10036.
Bitnet MLFLC@CUNYVM

A resolution style theorem prover is presented for first-order Intuitionistic logic. Soundness and completeness proofs are sketched. Relationships with Classical resolution are considered.

§1 Introduction.

Most automated theorem provers have been built around some version of resolution [4]. But resolution is an inherently Classical logic technique. Attempts to extend the method to other logics have tended to obscure its simplicity. In this paper we present a resolution style theorem prover for Intuitionistic logic that, we believe, retains many of the attractive features of Classical resolution. It is, of course, more complicated, but the complications can be given intuitive motivation. We note that a small change in the system as presented here causes it to collapse back to a Classical resolution system.

We present the system in some detail for the propositional case, including soundness and completeness proofs. For the first order version we are sketchier.

§2 Background.

In Classical logic, X and $\neg X$ are duals. To deny X is to assert $\neg X$, and conversely. Intuitionistic logic does not behave this way though. Loosely speaking, when an Intuitionist says "X is true," what is meant is "I have a proof of X." To deny this is not to assert $\neg X$, that is "I have a *refutation*

[1] Research supported by PSC-CUNY Grants 666396 and 667295.

Methodologies for Intelligent Systems
Z. W. Ras and M. Zemankova, Editors

of X," but only "I don't have a proof of X." This is the source of the failure of the law of excluded middle in Intuitionistic logic. We need formal notation that can capture this proof/no proof distinction. Following [1, 2, 5] we use signed formulas.

Definition. *Let T and F be two new symbols. By a* signed formula *we mean TX or FX, where X is a formula.*

Think of TX as asserting that X is Intuitionistically true (X has been proved), and FX as asserting the opposite (X has not been proved).

In Classical resolution one generally begins by putting formulas into clause form. Some variations of Classical resolution allow resolutions at non-clausal stages, and it is possible to construct Classical systems in which the reduction to clause form is interwoven with resolution applications. This is the approach we adopt here, but with a twist. In Intuitionistic logic, not every formula is equivalent to one in clause form (indeed, all of $\wedge$, $\vee$, $\neg$ and $\supset$ are independent). The effect is that the analog of reduction to clause form used here proceeds by a series of implications, not equivalences. And there may be incompatible reductions possible; consequently backtracking may be necessary. Once the rules have been presented it will be clear that the changes that turn the system into a Classical one also remove the need for this backtracking.

We continue to use the terminology of clause and clause set, but because of the problems mentioned in the previous paragraph we broaden their usual meaning. In particular we do not confine ourselves to the literal level. (*Literal* now means a *signed atomic* formula.) Basically, we retain only the disjunctive interpretation for clauses, and the conjunctive one for clause sets. In the following definition we assume the notion of Kripke Intuitionistic model is known [3].

Definitions. *A* clause, *denoted $[Z_1, \ldots, Z_n]$, is a finite set of signed formulas. A* clause set *is a finite set of clauses, denoted $[C_1, \ldots, C_n]$. Let Γ be a possible world of a Kripke model. The signed formula TX is* true *at Γ if X is forced at Γ; the signed formula FX is* true *at Γ if X is not forced at Γ. A* clause *is true at Γ if one of its members is. A* clause set *is true at Γ if each of its members is. Finaly, a clause set is* satisfiable *if it is true at some possible world of some Kripke model.*

Clauses and clause sets are officially sets, but in practice they will probably be represented by lists. In stating our rules the following notation will be handy. $[X|Y]$ denotes the clause, or clause set, containing X, with Y as the set (list) of remaining members. We assume X does not occur in Y. Likewise, if Y and Z are sets (lists) we use $Y * Z$ to denote the result of appending Y and Z (and removing repetitions).

§3 The propositional system.

The resolution rule itself retains its usual form, after adjusting in the obvious way for the use of signed formulas. The major change is that the formula being resolved on need not be a literal but can be more complex.

Resolution Rule. *A clause set containing clauses* $[TX|A]$ *and* $[FX|B]$ *may be extended by adding the clause* $A * B$.

This rule may be schematically stated as follows.

$$\frac{[TX|A] \qquad [FX|B]}{A * B}$$

The rest of the system consists of rules that are the counterparts of Classical steps reducing to conventional clause form. These rules fall into two categories, which we call *regular* and *special*.

Regular Reduction Rules. *A clause set that contains the clause shown above the line may have the clause(s) below the line added.*

$$\frac{[TX \wedge Y|A]}{[TX|A],\ [TY|A]} \qquad \frac{[FX \wedge Y|A]}{[FX,\ FY|A]}$$

$$\frac{[TX \vee Y|A]}{[TX,\ TY|A]} \qquad \frac{[FX \vee Y|A]}{[FX|A],\ [FY|A]}$$

$$\frac{[T\neg X|A]}{[FX|A]} \qquad \frac{[TX \supset Y|A]}{[FX,\ TY|A]}$$

Some of these rules are, in effect, equivalences. For example, $FX \wedge Y$ is true at a possible world Γ iff $X \wedge Y$ is not forced at Γ iff X is not forced at Γ or Y is not forced at Γ iff FX or FY is true at Γ. Thus it is easy to see $[FX \wedge Y|A]$ and $[FX,\ FY|A]$ are true at the same possible worlds. The $T\neg$ and $T\supset$ rules are implicational in nature however, not equivalences.

Special Reduction Rules. *A clause set* S *that contains the clause shown above the line may have the clause(s) below the line added,* but first *all clauses in* S *that contain any* F*-signed formulas must be removed. (This includes the clauses displayed above the lines as well.)*

$$\frac{[F\neg X|A]}{[TX|A]} \qquad \frac{[FX \supset Y|A]}{[TX|A],\ [FY|A]}$$

Both of these rules represent implications, not equivalences. The intuitive motivation is not difficult, though. Consider the rule for $F\supset$; the other rule is similar.

Informally, for me to assert $FX \supset Y$ is to say that I do not have a proof of $X \supset Y$. From an Intuitionistic point of view this means that, as far as I know, someday someone might present me with a proof of X which I am unable to convert into a proof of Y. Well, imagine this has happened: I am at some hypothetical future time when X has been proved but Y has not been. Thus I have both TX and FY. In passing from today to that future time I am certainly entitled to retain positive knowledge: what has been proved remains proved. But negative knowledge is more problematical. Even if I don't know Z today, I might discover a proof of it tomorrow. Thus in moving to a hypothetical future time I can not retain clauses that contain F-signed formulas: F's may not remain F's.

The motivation above is loose. Nonetheless, a formal version of it is embodied in the soundness argument in the next section.

Definition. *A* derivation *from a clause set S is a sequence of clause sets, beginning with S, each of which comes from the preceeding using one of the rules above (or a rule to be stated below). A* refutation *of a clause set S is a derivation from S of a clause set containing the empty clause. A* proof *of the formula X is a refutation of the clause set $[[FX]]$.*

Example. *The following is a proof of $(X \supset Y) \supset (\neg Y \supset \neg X)$. We omit the reasons for the steps.*

$[[F((X \supset Y) \supset (\neg Y \supset \neg X))]]$
$[[T(X \supset Y)], [F(\neg Y \supset \neg X)]]$
$[[T(X \supset Y)], [T\neg Y], [F\neg X]]$
$[[T(X \supset Y)], [T\neg Y], [TX]]$
$[[T(X \supset Y)], [T\neg Y], [TX], [FX, TY]]$
$[[T(X \supset Y)], [T\neg Y], [TX], [FX, TY], [FY]]$
$[[T(X \supset Y)], [T\neg Y], [TX], [FX, TY], [FY], [TY]]$
$[[T(X \supset Y)], [T\neg Y], [TX], [FX, TY], [FY], [TY], []]$

Unfortunately the rules above, though sound, are not complete. With them alone we are unable to prove the Intuitionistically valid formula $(P \vee Q) \supset (\neg\neg P \vee \neg\neg Q)$ for instance. The following rule completes the system.

Special Case Rule. *Let $[[A|R]|S]$ be a clause set. (Here $[A|R]$ is a clause containing the signed formula A, with R as the list of other signed formulas making up the clause. S is the list consisting of the remaining clauses of the clause set.) If there is a refutation of the clause set $[[A]|S]$ then the clause set $[R|S]$ follows from $[[A|R]|S]$. Schematically,*

$$\frac{[[A|R]|S]}{[R|S]}$$

provided $[[A]|S]$ *has a refutation.*

The following is a proof of $(P \vee Q) \supset (\neg\neg P \vee \neg\neg Q)$ using this rule.
$[[F((P \vee Q) \supset (\neg\neg P \vee \neg\neg Q))]]$
$[[T(P \vee Q)], [F(\neg\neg P \vee \neg\neg Q)]]$
$[[TP, TQ], [F(\neg\neg P \vee \neg\neg Q)]]$
$[[TP, TQ], [F\neg\neg P], [F\neg\neg Q]]$ $(*)$

Now we consider the *case*
$[[TP], [F\neg\neg P], [F\neg\neg Q]]$
$[[TP], [T\neg P]]$
$[[TP], [T\neg P], [FP]]$
$[[TP], [T\neg P], [FP], []]$

Having derived the empty clause in this case, by the Special Case Rule, the following clause set follows from $(*)$:
$[[TQ], [F\neg\neg P], [F\neg\neg Q]]$
$[[TQ], [T\neg Q]]$
$[[TQ], [T\neg Q], [FQ]]$
$[[TQ], [T\neg Q], [FQ], []]$

Remarks. The proof procedure presented above is inherently more complex than the Classical one because there is hidden branching. Suppose we have a situation in which Special Reduction Rules can be applied to more than one clause of a clause set. Then applying a Special Rule to one clause will cause the deletion of the other clause. In a complete implementation, if a proof is not found after making such a choice of Special Reduction Rule application, backtracking to the choice point must occur, and the other choice must be tried. Of course, such choices are independent, and the derivations could be constructed in parallel.

If we modify the Special Reduction Rules into Regular ones by removing the clause deletion requirements, a sound and complete proof procedure for Classical logic results. Indeed, the Special Case Rule now becomes a derivable rule and need not be taken as primitive. Notice too that now rule applications are never destructive, so there is no need for a backtracking mechanism.

All the Regular Reduction Rules are addition rules: clauses get added, not replaced. In fact the system remains complete if the rules for $T\wedge$, $F\wedge$, $T\vee$ and $F\vee$ are modified to read: the clause above the line may be removed and those below the line added. (This is not the case with the $T\neg$ and $T\supset$ rules however.) Demonstrating completeness is more work with this change, and we do not do so.

Finally, in Classical resolution one reduces to the literal level (the usual clause form) before beginning to use the Resolution Rule. This is still possible here in the sense that, if X has a proof, it has one in which all resolutions are on literals. This is not hard to show, but again we do not prove it here.

§4 Soundness and Completeness.

To show soundness it is enough to establish that refutable clause sets are not satisfiable. Then, if X is provable the clause set $[[FX]]$ will be refutable, hence not satisfiable, and so X must be forced at every world of every Kripke model; i.e. X must be Intuitionistically valid.

Proposition. *The Resolution Rule and each of the Regular and Special Reduction Rules turns a satisfiable clause set into another satisfiable clause set.*

Proof. This is straightforward for the Resolution Rule and for the Regular Reduction Rules. We consider one of the Special Reduction Rules in more detail.

Suppose S is a satisfiable clause set containing the clause $[FX \supset Y|A]$, and the corresponding Special Reduction Rule is applied, producing the new clause set S^*, which contains those clauses from S having no F-signed formulas, and also contains $[TX|A]$ and $[FY|A]$. We show S^* is satisfiable.

Say the clauses in S are all true at the world Γ of some Kripke model. In particular, $[FX \supset Y|A]$ is true at Γ. Suppose first that some member of A is true at Γ. That member is still in both $[TX|A]$ and $[FY|A]$, so both clauses are true at Γ. And the remaining members of S^* all were in S, hence were all true at Γ. Thus all members of S^* are true at Γ; S^* is satisfiable in this case.

Next suppose no member of A is true at Γ. Since $[FX \supset Y|A]$ is true at Γ, $FX \supset Y$ must be true at Γ, that is, $X \supset Y$ is not forced at Γ. Then by the definition of Kripke model there must be a possible world Δ, accessible from Γ, at which X is forced but Y is not. That is, both TX and FY are true at Δ, hence both $[TX|A]$ and $[FY|A]$ are true at Δ. Finally, if a formula is forced at a possible world of a Kripke model, it is forced at any world accessible from it. Then any clause set with no F-signed formulas that is true at Γ is also true at Δ. It follows that S^* is satisfiable, but this time at the world Δ.

Proposition. *A clause set that has a refutation is not satisfiable.*

Proof. This is by an induction on the number of applications of the Special Case Rule in the refutation. The initial case of zero applications is taken care of by the preceeding proposition together with the fact that the empty clause is not satisfiable. Details of the induction step are straightforward and are omitted.

The simplest way to establish completeness is to use an Intuitionistic version of the Model Existence Theorem. We do not give details, but refer to [1, 2] for them. In brief, a completeness proof goes as follows. Call a finite set $\{Z_1, \ldots, Z_n\}$ of signed formulas *consistent* if there is no refutation of the clause set $[[Z_1], \ldots, [Z_n]]$. This meets the requirements of being a (propositional) Intuitionistic consistency property. Then by the Model Existence Theorem, every set that is consistent in this sense is satisfiable.

Now, if X is Intuitionistically valid, X must be provable. For if it were not, there would be no refutation of $[[FX]]$, $\{FX\}$ would be consistent, hence satisfiable, and X would not have been valid.

§5 A First Order System.

The lack of an adequate Intuitionistic version of Herbrand's theorem is no real bar to extending the system just presented to a first-order setting. We briefly sketch such an extension.

We use a first-order language with quantifiers $\forall$ and $\exists$, function symbols, but no $=$ relation. Function symbols are interpreted rigidly in the sense that, whatever a closed term is taken to designate in a possible world, it must designate the same thing in all accessible worlds.

We add reduction rules for the four quantifier cases. And once again they fall into Regular and Special groupings.

Regular Reduction Rules. *A clause set that contains the clause shown above the line may have the clause below the line added.*

$$\frac{[T(\forall x)\phi(x)|A]}{[T\phi(y)|A]} \qquad \frac{[F(\exists x)\phi(x)|A]}{[F\phi(y)|A]}$$

where y is a previously unused free variable,

$$\frac{[T(\exists x)\phi(x)|A]}{[T\phi(f(y_1, \ldots, y_n))|A]}$$

where f is a previously unused function symbol and $y_1, \ldots, y_n$ are all the free variables introduced thus far in the proof.

Special Reduction Rule. *A clause set S that contains the clause shown above the line may have the clause below the line added* but first *all clauses in S that contain any F-signed formulas must be removed.*

$$\frac{[F(\forall x)\phi(x)|A]}{[F\phi(f(y_1,\ldots,y_n))|A]}$$

where f is a previously unused function symbol and $y_1,\ldots,y_n$ are *all the free variables introduced thus far in the proof.*

Finally, the Resolution Rule becomes the following.

Resolution Rule. *Suppose S is a clause set containing clauses $[TX|A]$ and $[FY|B]$. Let σ be a most general unifier for X and Y. Then from S we may obtain the clause set $[A * B|S]\sigma$, that is, the result of adding $A * B$ to S and applying σ to every formula. (This tacitly assumes bound variable renaming is carried out when necessary to prevent unintended free variable capture.)*

Soundness may be shown as before, by establishing that all rules preserve satisfiability in a suitable sense. Completeness for a ground level analog of the system above may be shown using the Model Existence Theorem, and completeness of the system with free variables can be derived from that by using a suitable version of the Lifting Lemma.

References.

1. M. C. Fitting, Model existence theorems for modal and intuitionistic logics, *J. Symbolic Logic 38*, 613–627 (1973).
2. M. C. Fitting, *Proof Methods for Modal and Intuitionistic Logics* (D. Reidel, Dordrecht 1983).
3. S. Kripke, Semantical analysis of Intuitionistic logic I, in: *Formal Systems and Recursive Functions, Proc. of the Eighth Logic Colloquium* J. N. Crossley and M. A. E. Dummett, eds., 92–130 (1965).
4. J. A. Robinson, A Machine-oriented logic based on the resolution principle, *J. Assoc. Comput. Mach. 12*, 23–41 (1965).
5. R. M. Smullyan, *First-Order Logic* (Springer-Verlag, Berlin 1968).

STRATIFIED INTERACTIVE KNOWLEDGE BASES

Catherine Lassez, Kenneth McAloon †

IBM T. J. Watson Research Center, P.O.Box 218, Yorktown Heights, New York 10598; † on leave from the Department of Computer Science, Brooklyn College of CUNY.

ABSTRACT

We discuss stratification as a technique for managing an interactive knowledge base system represented in propositional logic. A Boolean algebraic interpretation of stratification is given and results on sequential and parallel algorithms for testing stratifiability are obtained. Problems of robust knowledge base representation are addressed and computational complexity results are given for the dual problems of intended model semantics and querying.

Introduction

We define an interactive knowledge base system as a system that generates models of a knowledge base according to assertions made by the user. We consider the knowledge bases as being propositional formulae expressed as sets of clauses or rules, the assertions made by the user are also to be expressed in clausal or rule form. Each new assertion made by the user is added to the knowledge base and the system responds with some specific logical consequences of this assertion. These logical consequences provide guidance for further assertions. Thus the user and the system cooperatively construct a model (or models) of the knowledge base. The two key problems lie in maintaining a consistent knowledge base at each step of the interaction and in providing sufficient and fast feedback.

The consistency check for a propositional formula is NP-complete. In general, this check would have to be performed after every assertion made by the user. The key requirement for an interactive model-building system is that at each stage of the interaction the knowledge base be consistent and the partial instantiation resulting from previous assertions always be extendable to a model of the full knowledge base. Here we propose a strategy based on the concept of stratification which provides a framework for maintaining the complexity of the interaction to a manageable level. Simply put, a stratification is a reflexive, transitive relation on the propositional variables of the knowledge base which induces a network structure on the rules and assertions. Processing the knowledge base proceeds along the paths of this network. As the knowledge base evolves so can the stratification. It is possible to view this process as static in which case the initial strata are frozen and the interaction proceeds to higher strata when lower ones are completely instantiated by previous as-

Methodologies for Intelligent Systems
Z. W. Ras and M. Zemankova, Editors

sertions, or as dynamic in which case rules may change strata as a result of assertions. As a rule, the dynamic view offers more expressive power but the static view is computationally more feasible.

After a presentation of basic definitions and algorithms for stratification, we give a Boolean algebraic interpretation and discuss two key knowledge base problems: robustness and rapid updating. Then we treat computational complexity issues that arise in connection with intended model semantics and querying.

Stratification

The stratification of a logic program has been investigated as part of the study of the semantics of the Negation as Failure rule [1,3,4]. Recently the notion has been extended to cover Disjunctive Databases [18,22]. The (close) connection with prioritized circumscription is established in [22].

A *rule* is a propositional formula $a_1\wedge...\wedge a_n\wedge \neg b_1\wedge...\wedge \neg b_m\rightarrow c_1\vee...\vee c_k$ where (1) $n,m,k \geq 0$ and (2) either $k \geq 1$ or $m = 0$. Condition (2) excludes headless rules with negations in the body; this causes no loss in generality as we shall remark below but simplifies the discussion. We shall use the term *disjunctive knowledge base* (abbreviated d.k.b.) for sets of rules of this form.

Let $<=$ denote a reflexive relation and $<=*$ its transitive closure. We write $a < b$ if $a <= b$ but not conversely. An element a is *minimal* if there is no element b such that $b < a$. A stratification of a disjunctive knowledge base KB is a transitive, reflexive relation $<=$ on the letters of KB which satisfies

1. for all rules $(a_1\wedge...\wedge a_n\wedge \neg b_1\wedge... \neg b_m\rightarrow c_1\vee...\vee c_k)$, we have: $a_i <= c_j$, $b_i < c_j$, $c_j <= c_i <= c_j$, for all i,j,
2. for all headless rules $(a_1\wedge...\wedge a_n\rightarrow)$, we have: $a_i <= a_j <= a_i$, for all i,j and $c <= a_i$ implies $a_i <= c$ for all c,i.

The *stratum* of a is the set of all b's such that $a <= b <= a$. The strata partition the letters of KB and $<=$ induces a partial order on the strata. A stratum is *minimal* if it is composed of minimal elements.

Condition (1) insures that the letters that form the head of a disjunctive rule all lie in the same stratum; it also insures that all letters in the body precede the letters in the head and that this relation is strict if the letter in the body is negated in the rule. Condition (2) assures that all letters that appear in a headless rule are minimal and appear in the same stratum.

A d.k.b. is *stratifiable* if it has a stratification. Our definition extends that of [1] and of [22] in that the relation on the strata induced by the stratification is not required to be a linear ordering and in that headless clauses are taken into account. Intuitively, incomparable strata are independent of one another and one stratum precedes another if its variables have higher priority.

The following proposition follows easily from the definitions.

Proposition1. The (set theoretic) intersection of two stratifications of a d.k.b KB is again a stratification of KB.

Since d.k.b.'s are finite, it follows that the intersection of all the stratifications of a stratifiable knowledge base is itself a stratification; we call this stratification the *most general stratification*, denoted *m.g.s.*.

We define a *pre-stratification* of a d.k.b. *KB* to be a reflexive relation $<=$ on the letters of *KB* such that its transitive closure $<=^*$ is a stratification and such that for all letters a, b, if $a <=^* b <=^* a$ then $a <= b <= a$. From a computational point of view it is advantageous to work with a pre-stratification rather than with its transitive closure. The requirement that the pre-stratification define the same equivalence classes as the full stratification is an important property that enables one to replace a full stratification with a pre-stratification in the maintenance of a knowledge base. We present two algorithms for testing stratifiability and for constructing a data structure to maintain a prestratification.

Proposition 2. There is a linear time algorithm to test for stratifiability that returns, in the case a d.k.b. *KB* is stratifiable, a data structure for maintaining a pre-stratification of the m.g.s. of *KB*. This data structure maintains the pre-stratification in the sense that (1) it maps each letter a to a distinguished element of its stratum in the m.g.s. and (2) it records the pre-stratification relation among these distinguished elements.

The proof uses depth-first search techniques [16,23]. We also have a parallel algorithm for stratifiability.

Proposition 3. There is an NC algorithm to test for stratifiability that runs in $\log^2(n)$ time using $n^{2.5}$ processors. In the case a knowledge base is stratifiable the algorithm returns a data structure for maintaining a prestratification of the *mgs*.

The proof uses an NC transitive closure algorithm to compute strongly connected components in a directed graph. The number of processors $n^{2.5}$ in the proposition is the number of arithmetic operations required to compute the product of two n by n matrices [2,5]. The stratifiability test problem is closely related to the graph accessibilty problem for directed acyclic graphs. The existence of an efficient NC-algorithm for this latter problem is considered one of the more important open problems in parallel computation [13].

Stratification naturally induces a partition on the rules of the knowledge base. By condition (1) in the definition of stratification, each rule $(a_1\wedge...\wedge a_n \wedge \neg b_1\wedge...\wedge \neg b_m \rightarrow c_1\vee...\vee c_k)$ of a stratified knowledge base can be mapped unambiguously to the stratum of the letters in its head; by condition (2), each headless rule $(a_1\wedge...\wedge a_n\rightarrow)$ can likewise be mapped to the stratum of the a_i's. It is straightforward to show

Proposition 4. A stratified disjunctive knowledge base is consistent if for each minimal stratum the set of rules associated with it is consistent. Moreover a partial model of the minimal strata can be extended to a model of the full knowledge base.

The partial order of the stratification leads to a strategy for model building where lower strata are treated first and the results of this partial model building are propagated throughout higher levels. Suppose α is an assignment which satisfies a minimal stratum KB_{min} of a stratified d.k.b. *KB*. Then we can propagate α through *KB* by means of the Davis-Putnam One Literal Clause Rule: considering rules as clauses, for each literal l assigned TRUE by α, delete clauses where l appears and delete $\neg l$ from clauses in which it appears. Denote the updated d.k.b. by $KB(\alpha)$. Then, by the stratification requirement on negative literals in the body of rules, the restriction of $<=$ to the letters of $KB(\alpha)$ is a stratification of $KB(\alpha)$. At each point in the interactive model building process, a particular minimal stratum called the *base stratum* will be singled out and a model of the rules associated with it will be developed. This is possible because minimal strata are independent of one another. In the experimental system Knowledgewright developed in collaboration with Graeme Port [21], two extreme (and simple) stratification strategies are employed: i) the completely static strategy where there is no migration of rules among strata and ii) a dynamic strategy where the largest possble base stratum is maintained throughout the interaction.

Boolean Algebraic Interpretation

As defined above, the notion of stratification is highly dependent on the syntactic form in which the d.k.b. is presented. Thus when a knowledge base as given is not stratifiable, it may be possible to transform it into a logically equivalent form which is. For instance, the knowledge base consisting of the rules $\{\neg a \wedge b \rightarrow c, \neg c \rightarrow b\}$ is not stratifiable; however, by writing it in clausal form $\{a \vee \neg b \vee c, c \vee b\}$ and simplifying, the equivalent rule form $\{\neg a \rightarrow c, \neg c \rightarrow b\}$ can be found which uses the same priorities as in the initial rules. Intuitively, the problem of finding a stratifiable form for a d.k.b. is akin to the problem of choosing priorities for circumscription. On the other hand, in the following results we show that stratifiability does have intrinsic meaning independently of the particular representation of the knowledge base. First, we have a "Lifting Lemma":

Proposition5. Let F be a finite Boolean algebra, let I be an ideal on F and let A be a subalgebra of F. Then every homomorphism on $A/(I \cap A)$ can be lifted to a homomorphism on F/I.

The proof uses techniques of [24].

Now consider the situation where F is a product algebra $F = A \times B$ and I_A is an ideal on A and where I is an ideal on F such that $I \cap A = I_A$. Then, by the proposition, a homomorphism on A/I_A can be lifted to one on F/I. To relate this to logic, consider further the situation where F is the algebra of sets of truth assignments to the propositional variables $a_1,\ldots, a_n, b_1,\ldots,b_m$ and C is a set of clauses. Let C_A be the clauses of C which involve literals only from $\{a_1,\ldots,a_n\}$. Let A be the subalgebra of F generated by $\{a_1,\ldots,a_n\}$ and let B be the one generated by $\{b_1,\ldots,b_m\}$. Then $F = A \times B$. Let I_A be the ideal of sets of truth-assignments incompatible with C_A and let I be the ideal of sets of assignments incompatible with C. From the above discussion, if $I_A = I \cap A$, then every assignment satisfying C_A can be extended to a satisfying assignment for C. This, of course, is a variant of Proposition 4. The stratification algorithms of Propostions 2 and 3 can be interpreted as determining a decomposition of the Lindenbaum algebra of the d.k.b., firstly as a product of minimal strata and the remaining strata together, secondly for the quotient algebras determined by satisfying assignments to the minimal strata. Thus stratification can be viewed as an iterative "theorem-proving" strategy that isolates "inconsistency cores" in a set of clauses. The relation between this technique and theorem proving strategies such as set of support remains to be worked out. The possible application of stratification to network based default reasoning formalisms, *e.g.* [8], is another line of research. Three further remarks on the Boolean algebra aspects of stratification: First, the restriction to product algebras is natural in a logic setting and in fact does not sacrifice generality in that every subalgebra of a finite algebra can be shown to be a factor algebra on a partition of unity; that is, given A a subalgebra of F, there are disjoint $p_1,...,p_k$ whose sup is 1_F such that $(A \cap p_i) \times B_i = F \cap p_i$ for some B_i, i = 1,...,k. Second, stratification as a model building strategy is quite analogous to iterated forcing in set theory, where models are also constructed by iteration along a directed set of embeddings of Boolean algebras [12]. Third, this analysis points to a connection between stratification and possible world semantics [9,15].

Robustness and Conciseness of the Knowledge Representation

Our setup allows for great flexibility at the base stratum. Rewriting $(\neg a_1 \vee ... \vee \neg a_k \vee b_1 \vee ... \vee b_l)$ as $(a_1 \wedge ... \wedge a_k \rightarrow b_1 \vee ... \vee b_l)$ allows one to write arbitrary formulae in the base stratum, in particular negative clauses. So the check for consistency in the base stratum can be expensive. However this check can be done in isolation from the rest of the knowledge base, since no contradiction can arise in the higher strata. Furthermore the consistency checking required at the base stratum can be exploited to maintain this stratum in a more concise and more usable form. Ideally the base stratum would be maintained in a robust form that allowed for rapid consistency checking and there would be an efficient updating routine. Moreover, the form of the knowledge base would be robust under iteration - the updating routine would have to return a knowledge base of the same form to allow for further efficient consistency checking and updating. We now discuss the form of knowledge base representation and updating mechanism we have used in the experimental system Knowledgewright. Following [11], we recall that a *primitive* of a set of clauses C is a clause which is a logical consequence of C and which is not subsumed by any other clause which is a logical consequence of C (this is the dual of the concept of prime implicant of a formula in disjunctive normal form). A *kernel* of C is defined as an independent subset of the set of primitives of C which is logically equivalent to C. A kernel is a compact and explicit representation of a set of clauses. In particular, it is non-redundant in the sense that no literal can be removed from a clause without loss of information. The computational cost of constructing a kernel from a set of clauses is $O(n \times t)$ where n is the number of distinct occurrences of literals in C and t is the cost of a consistency check. It follows from the definition that a clause $l_1 \vee ... \vee l_n$ is consistent with a kernel K if and only if there exists at least one literal l_i such that $\neg l_i$ is not a unit clause of K. So if the base stratum is in kernel form, testing whether a clause or rule is consistent with the knowledge base is immediate. The rapid updating routine used in Knowledgewright is based on the Davis-Putnam rule discussed above. However, the kernel form is not stable under ths method of updating. In fact, kernels which preserve kernel form under iterated Davis-Putnam updating are characterized in [11] and [16] where it is shown that, among other things, such kernels are deductively shallow in that all resolutions of clauses in the knowledge base must be tautologous! In the Knowledgewrite system, after each update, a full recomputation of the kernel of the current base stratum is made. The problem of whether it is at all possible to have robust representations of knowledge bases, even at the expense of initial preprocessing, is a challenging one. We conjecture, pessimistically, that (modulo $P \neq NP$) for any updating procedure running in time n^k, the inferencing depth of a robust set of clauses is bounded by $n^{O(k)}$

Semantics and Queries

While our basic viewpoint is that of ordinary propositional logic with the ordinary truth-table semantics, it is also of interest to consider situations with alternative semantics - for example situations where the models to be constructed are required to be in an intended class. In working with knowledge bases expressed in logic, computational feasibility is an overriding concern. In the discussion that follows we consider the cost of some model building requirements and remark on the dual situation, that of querying the knowledge base. First, let us make some definitions. A *disjunctive data base* is a knowledge base with no headless rules. A rule $a_1 \wedge \ldots \wedge a_n \wedge \neg b_1 \wedge \ldots \wedge \neg b_m \rightarrow c_1 \vee \ldots \vee c_k$ with $k \geq 2$ is called a *disjunctive rule*; a disjunctive data base with no disjunctive rules is a *logic program*. A disjunctive data base is *elementary* if no rules have negation in the body. Elementary disjuctive data bases always admit the stratification where all variables are assigned the same stratum. Note that a stratifiable disjunctive data base is necessarily consistent since minimal strata can contain no headless rules and no rules with negation in the body. A principal motivation for stratifying knowledge bases is to reduce the exponential time overhead associated with maintaining general structures of this kind. However in the case of Horn clause knowledge bases, the consistency and consequence problems have linear time solutions, even with negative clauses in the knowledge base, [7], and the model building task can be performed in quadratic time. In an interactive situation, a model can be efficiently constructed while allowing the user to introduce Horn clause assertions. Moreover, the system can compute the current minimal model in linear time and kernel in quadratic time.

Complexity results justifying a stratum-by-stratum approach to model building under the usual semantics even in the somewhat simpler cases of propositional logic programs and disjunctive data bases are given in [16]. The upshot of the analysis there is that it is important to limit the number of literals occuring in the heads of disjunctive rules but that with stratification considerably more disjunctive behavior can be tolerated computationally. On the other hand, if the models to be constructed are to fall within intended classes, the situation is more delicate. For example even in the Horn clause case, computing consequence and consistency relative to models where a preassigned number of variables must be assigned TRUE leads to co-NP and NP complete problems [16]. If the intended models are to be minimal models, then other interesting questions arise. In model building, the typical question is whether a literal is consistent relative to the models of the intended class - that is, is the literal true in some model in the class? In querying the situation is dual - is the literal true in all models of the intended class? For example, if a knowledge base is being querried relative to the GCWA [19], the relevant models are the minimal models and a query is answered YES if it is satisfied in all minimal models. In a positive vein, if the knowledge base is a stratified propositional logic program and if the intended model is the perfect model, a unit query q can be answered in time linear in the size of the base. For stratified disjunctive knowledge bases querying is more complex: if the class of intended models is simply all models, then querying has co-NP complexity:

Proposition6. The following problem in co-NP-Complete:

Input: An elementary disjuctive data base D and a propositional variable q

Output: YES if q is satisfied in all models of D

This can be shown by reducing SAT to the complementary problem.

If the GCWA is invoked and if querying is relative to the class of minimal models, then computing the answer to a positive query q is co-NP-Complete and, on the face of it, the negative query $\neg q$ is a Π_2^p question. We conjecture that in fact this problem is Π_2^p complete. As a preliminary step in this direction we have

Proposition7. The following problem is co-NP-Complete:

Input: A set of general propositional clauses G
and an assignment f which satisfies G

Output: YES if f is a minimal model of G

The proof is by reduction of the complement of SAT and the remark that the given problem is in co-NP. We conjecture that restricting the formula G in the above problem to be an elementary disjunctive data base still yields a co-NP complete problem. As a related result we have

Proposition8. The following problem is co-NP-hard:

Input: An elementary disjunctive data base D
and a unit negative clause $\neg p$

Output: YES if $\neg p$ is satisfied in all minimal models of D.

Because of the link between stratification and circumscription this complexity theoretic reseach will also shed light on the difficulty of computing relative to simple abnormality theories and theories with prioritized circumscription [20].

Conclusion

Work is in progress to extend the techniques described above to the function free predicate case. Interesting problems arise in connection with theorem proving techniques and with stratification. For example, while the pre-stratification algorithm is still available, stratification strategies must be reevaluated as in general dynamic stratification is no longer possible.

References

1. Apt, K.R., Blair H. and Walker A., Towards a theory of declarative knowledge, to appear.
2. Chandra, A., Maximal parallelism in matrix multiplication, RC 6193, IBM, 1976
3. Chandra, A. and Harel D., Horn clauses queries and generalizations, The Journal of Logic Programming, vol.1, pp.1-15, 1985.
4. Clark, K.L., Negation as failure, in: Logic and Databases, H. Gallaire and J. Minker (Eds.), Plenum Press, New York, pp. 293-322, 1978.

5. Coppersmith D. and Winograd S., On the asymptotic complexity of matrix multiplication, SIAM J. of Computing, pp. 472-492, 1982.

6. Davis, M. and Putnam, H., A computing procedure for quantification theory, J. ACM 7, pp. 201-215, July 1960.

7. Dowling, W.F. and Gallier J.H., Linear-time algorithms for testing the satisfiability of propositional Horn formulae, The Journal of Logic programming, vol.3, pp.267-284, 1984.

8. Etherington, D., Formalizing non-monotonic reasoning systems, Artificial Intelligence 31, pp. 41-85, 1987.

9. Fagin, R., Halpern, J.Y., Belief, awareness and limited reasoning: preliminary report, Proc. IJCAI 85, pp. 491-501.

10. Garey, M.R. and Johnson, D.S., Computers and intractability, A guide to the theory of NP-Completeness, Freeman, San Francisco, 1979.

11. Helm, A.R., Lassez C. and Yee M.Y., A canonical representation for logic knowledge bases, Proc. First Australian AI Conference, Nov. 1986.

12. Jech, T., Set Theory, Academic Press 1972

13. Kanellakis, P., Logic programming and parallel complexity

14. Kohavi, Z., Switching and Finite Automata Theory. 2nd ed., McGraw-Hill, 1978.

15. Kripke, S., Semantical analysis of modal logic, Zeit. fur Math. Log. u. Grundlagen der Math. 9 (1963), pp. 67-96.

16. Lassez, C. McAloon, K. and Port, G., Stratification and interactive knowledge base management, Proc. Fourth International Conference on Logic Programming, Melbourne May 1987, MIT Press.

17. Lloyd, J.W. and Topor, R.W., A basis for deductive database systems, Journal of Logic Programming, vol.2, pp.93-109, 1985.

18. Lloyd, J.W. and Topor, R.W., A basis for deductive database systems II, Journal of Logic Programming, vol.2, to appear.

19. Minker, J., On indefinite data bases and the closed world assumption, in Lecture Notes in Computer Science 138, pp.292- 308, Springer Verlag 1982.

20. McCarthy, J., Applications of circumscription to formalizing common sense knowledge, Artificial Intelligence 28 (1986), pp. 89-116.

21. Port, G., Lassez, C., McAloon, K., Knowledgewright: an experimental interactive knowledge base system, in preparation.

22. Przymusinski, T.C., On the semantics of stratified disjunctive databases, to appear.

23. Tarjan, R., Depth-first search and linear graph algorithms, SIAM Journal of Computing, vol.1, No.2, pp.146-160, 1972.

24. Sikorski, R., Boolean Algebras, Springer Verlag 1964.

Inferencing on an Arbitrary Set of Links †

Neil V. Murray
Dept. of Computer Science
State Univ. of N.Y. at Albany
Albany, NY 12222
nvm@albany.edu

Erik Rosenthal
Dept. of Computer Science
Wellesley College
Wellesley, MA 02181
erik@wellesley.edu

Abstract

In [8] we introduced ***path dissolution,*** a rule of inference that operates on formulas in negation normal form and that employs a representation that we call ***semantic graphs.*** Path dissolution is an unusual deduction rule in that in the ground case it preserves equivalence and is strongly complete: Any sequence of dissolution steps applied to a semantic graph G will produce an equivalent linkless graph G' .

Path dissolution, unlike path ***resolution,*** does not lift directly into first-order logic. However, dissolution may be employed as a recognition procedure for resolution chains. The key advantage of this is that a useful inference may be made from ***any chain whatsoever,*** even if it is not a resolution chain (i.e., even if its associated subgraph is not spanned).

1. Introduction

In [8] we introduced *path dissolution*, a rule of inference that operates on quantifier-free predicate calculus formulas in negation normal form (NNF). Path dissolution is a somewhat unusual deduction rule in that in the ground case it preserves equivalence and is strongly complete: Any sequence of dissolution steps will produce an equivalent linkless graph. We use techniques first developed in [7,9], employing a representation of formulas that we call *semantic graphs.* Dissolution is a generalization to NNF of the Prawitz matrix reduction rule, which operates on formulas in conjunctive normal form (CNF).

One important distinction between dissolution and most other rules of inference is that one *cannot* restrict attention to CNF: A single application of dissolution generally produces a formula that is not in CNF *even if the original formula is.* Another distinction is that path dissolution, unlike path *resolution,* does not lift directly into first-order logic. However, dissolution can be employed as a recognition procedure for resolution chains.

Testing whether a chain spans its subgraph is obviously expensive. This expense could render impractical a path resolution strategy that favors resolving on large collections of links. By employing dissolution as a resolution chain recognizer, we are able to produce a useful inference from *any chain whatsoever*, even if it is not a resolution chain (i.e., even if its associated subgraph is not spanned). Thus, the effort to locate a set of links and to check whether those links span their subgraph is never wasted.

In [4], Bibel presented several algorithms for determining whether a propositional formula is unsatisfiable. He built on the work of Prawitz [10] and on later work of his own [2,3] and of Andrews [1]. His approach was to search for paths containing links (complementary literals). Path dissolution also employs links, but they are used to *remove* the paths through them.

† This research was supported in part by the National Science Foundation under grant DCR-8600848.

Methodologies for Intelligent Systems
Z. W. Ras and M. Zemankova, Editors

2. Preliminaries

We briefly summarize semantic graphs and path resolution, including only those results necessary to make the paper essentially self-contained. We assume the reader to be familiar with the notions of *atom, literal, formula, resolution,* and *unification.* We consider only quantifier-free formulas in which all negations are at the atomic level.

A *semantic graph* is empty, a single node, or a triple *(N,C,D) of nodes, c-arcs,* and *d-arcs,* respectively, where a node is a literal occurrence, a c-arc is a conjunction of two non-empty semantic graphs, and a d-arc is a disjunction of two non-empty semantic graphs. Each semantic graph used in the construction of a semantic graph will be called an *explicit subgraph.* We use the notation $(G,H)_c$ for the c-arc from G to H and similarly use $(G,H)_d$ for a d-arc. We consider an empty graph to be an empty disjunction, which is a contradiction. If $G = (X,Y)_\alpha$ (α = c or d), then every other arc in G is in X or in Y; we call this arc the *final arc* of G.

As an example, the formula

$$((A \wedge B) \vee C) \;\wedge\; (\sim A \vee (D \wedge C))$$

is the graph

$$\begin{array}{ccc} A \rightarrow B & & \overline{A} \\ \downarrow & \rightarrow & \downarrow \\ C & & D \rightarrow C \end{array}$$

Note that horizontal arrows are c-arcs, and vertical arrows are d-arcs.

The formulas we are considering are in *negation normal form* (NNF) in that all negations are at the atomic level, and the only connectives used are AND and OR.

One of the keys to our analysis is the notion of *path.* A *partial c-path through* a semantic graph G is a set c of nodes such that any two are connected by a c-arc, and a *c-path* is a partial c-path that is not properly contained in any partial c-path. We similarly define d-path using d-arcs instead of c-arcs.

Lemma 1. Let G be a semantic graph. Then an interpretation I satisfies (falsifies) G iff I satisfies (falsifies) every literal on some c-path (d-path) through G.

We will frequently find it useful to consider subgraphs that are not explicit; that is, given any set of nodes, we would like to examine that part of the graph consisting of exactly that set of nodes. The previous example is shown below on the left. The subgraph relative to the set {A, $\overline{A}$, D} is the graph on the right.

$$\begin{array}{ccc} \mathbf{A} \rightarrow B & & \overline{\mathbf{A}} \\ \downarrow & \rightarrow & \downarrow \\ C & & \mathbf{D} \rightarrow C \end{array} \qquad\qquad \begin{array}{ccc} & & \overline{\mathbf{A}} \\ \mathbf{A} & \rightarrow & \downarrow \\ & & \mathbf{D} \end{array}$$

The subgraph of G with respect to a set of nodes N is denoted G_N; see [9] for a precise definition.

The most important subgraphs are the *blocks.* A *c-block* C is a subgraph of a semantic graph with the property that any c-path p that includes at least one node from C must pass through C; that is, the subset of p consisting of the nodes that are in C must be a c-path through C. A *d-block* is similarly defined with d-paths, and a *full block* is a subgraph that is both a c-block and a d-block. We define *a strong c-block* in a semantic graph G to be a subgraph C of G with the property that every c-path through G contains a c-path through C; a *strong d-block* is similarly defined.

The *fundamental subgraphs* of a semantic graph G are defined recursively as follows: If $G = (X,Y)_c$, and if the final arc of X is a d-arc, then X is a fundamental subgraph of G. Otherwise, the fundamental subgraphs of X are fundamental subgraphs of G. (The dual case when the final arc of G is a d-arc is obvious.)

An isomorphism from $G = (N, C, D)$ to $G' = (N', C', D')$ is a bijection f: $N \rightarrow N'$ that preserves c- and d-paths, and such that for each A in N, A=f(A).

Theorem 1. Let G be a semantic graph, and let B be a full block in G. Then B is a union of fundamental subgraphs of some explicit subgraph of G.

Theorem 1′. If G and H are isomorphic semantic graphs, then H can be formed by reassociating and commuting some of the arcs in G.

Theorems 1 and 1′, which are crucial to the analysis that follows, are called the *Isomorphism Theorem.* Because of the frequency with which we use these results, they are implicitly assumed throughout the paper.

Several additional definitions are necessary to define the dissolution operation. From the isomorphism theorem we know that any full block U is a conjunction or a disjunction of fundamental subgraphs of some explicit subgraph H. If the final arc of H is a conjunction, then we define the *c-extension* of U to be H and the *d-extension* of U to be U itself. (The situation is reversed if the final arc of H is a d-arc.) We define the *c-path extension* of an arbitrary subgraph H in a semantic graph G as follows (note that this is different from the c-extension of a full block): Let $F_1, \ldots, F_k$ be the fundamental subgraphs of G that meet H, and let $F_{k+1}, \ldots, F_n$ be those that do not. We write G as $(F_1, \ldots, F_k, F_{k+1}, \ldots, F_n)_\alpha$, where $\alpha = \mathrm{c}$ or $\alpha = \mathrm{d}$. Then

$$\mathrm{CPE}(\phi, G) = \phi \qquad \text{and} \qquad \mathrm{CPE}(G, G) = G.$$

$$\mathrm{CPE}(H, G) = \mathrm{CPE}(H_{F_1}, F_1) \vee \ldots, \vee\, \mathrm{CPE}(H_{F_n}, F_n) \quad \text{if } \alpha = \mathrm{d}$$

$$\mathrm{CPE}(H, G) = \mathrm{CPE}(H_{F_1}, F_1) \wedge \ldots, \wedge\, \mathrm{CPE}(H_{F_k}, F_k) \;\wedge\; F_{k+1} \wedge \ldots, \wedge F_n \quad \text{if } \alpha = \mathrm{c}$$

Lemma 2. The c-paths of CPE(H, G) are precisely the c-paths of G that pass through H.

Using the same notation we define the *strong split graph of H in G*, denoted SS(H,G), as follows:

$$\mathrm{SS}(\phi, G) = G \qquad \text{and} \qquad \mathrm{SS}(G, G) = \phi.$$

$$\mathrm{SS}(H, G) = \mathrm{SS}(H, F_1) \vee \ldots, \vee\, \mathrm{SS}(H, F_n) \quad \text{if } \alpha = \mathrm{d}$$

$$\mathrm{SS}(H, G) = \mathrm{SS}(H, F_1) \vee \ldots, \vee\, \mathrm{SS}(H, F_k) \;\wedge\; F_{k+1} \wedge \ldots, \wedge F_n \quad \text{if } \alpha = \mathrm{c}$$

Lemma 3. If H is a c-block in G, then SS(H, G) is isomorphic to the subgraph of G relative to the nodes that lie on c-paths that miss H.

Define the *auxiliary subgraph* Aux(H, G) of a subgraph H in a semantic graph G to be the subgraph of G relative to the set of all nodes in G that lie on extensions of d-paths through H to d-paths through G.

Lemma 4. If H is a non-empty subgraph of G, then Aux(H, G) is empty iff H is a strong c-block. Moreover, Aux(H, G) cannot contain a d-path through G; if H is a c-block, then so is Aux(H, G).

Lemma 5. If H is a c-block then CPE(H, G) = SS(Aux(H, G), G).

3. Path Dissolution

We define a *chain* in a graph to be a set of pairs of c-connected nodes such that each pair can simultaneously be made complementary by an appropriate substitution. A *link* is an element of a chain, and a chain is *full* if it is not properly contained in any other chain. A graph G is *spanned* by the chain K if every c-path through G contains a link from K; in that case, we call K a *resolution chain* for G.

Intuitively, path dissolution operates on a resolution chain by constructing a semantic graph whose c-paths are exactly those that do not pass through the chain. Not all resolution chains are candidates for dissolution: A special type of chain that we call a *dissolution chain* (what else?) is required. Since single links always form dissolution chains, the class is not too specialized. The construction of the dissolvent from such a chain is straightforward.

A resolution chain H is a *dissolution chain* if it is a single c-block or if it has the following form: If M is the smallest full block containing H, then $M = (X, Y)_\mathrm{c}$, where $H \cap X$ and $H \cap Y$ are each c-blocks.

Given a dissolution chain H, define DV(H, M), the *dissolvent of H in M*, as follows (using the above notation): If H is a single c-block, then DV(H, M) = SS(H, M).

Otherwise (i.e., if H consists of two c-blocks), then

$$\mathrm{DV}(H, M) \quad = \quad \begin{array}{ccc} \mathrm{CPE}(H, X) & \rightarrow & \mathrm{SS}(H, Y) \\ & \downarrow & \\ \mathrm{SS}(H, X) & \rightarrow & \mathrm{CPE}(H, Y) \\ & \downarrow & \\ \mathrm{SS}(H, X) & \rightarrow & \mathrm{SS}(H, Y) \end{array}$$

Intuitively, $\mathrm{DV}(H, M)$ is a semantic graph whose c-paths miss at least one of the c-blocks of the dissolution chain. The only paths left out are those that go through the dissolution chain and hence are unsatisfiable. Notice that we may express $\mathrm{DV}(H, M)$ in either of the two more compact forms shown below (since $\mathrm{CPE}(H, X) \cup \mathrm{SS}(H, X) = X$ and $\mathrm{CPE}(H, Y) \cup \mathrm{SS}(H, Y) = Y$):

$$\begin{array}{ccc} X & \rightarrow & \mathrm{SS}(H, Y) \\ & \downarrow & \\ \mathrm{SS}(H, X) & \rightarrow & \mathrm{CPE}(H, Y) \end{array} \qquad \text{or} \qquad \begin{array}{ccc} \mathrm{SS}(H, X) & \rightarrow & Y \\ & \downarrow & \\ \mathrm{CPE}(H, X) & \rightarrow & \mathrm{SS}(H, Y) \end{array}$$

Note that the three representations are semantically equivalent but are not in general isomorphic; in particular their d-paths need not be the same. The c-paths of all three representations, however, are identical; they consist of exactly those c-paths in M that do not pass through H.

Theorem 2. Let H be a ground dissolution chain in a graph G, and let M be the smallest full block containing H. Then M and $\mathrm{DV}(H, M)$ are equivalent.

We may therefore select an arbitrary dissolution chain H in G and replace the smallest full block containing H by its dissolvent, producing (in the ground case) an equivalent graph. We call the resulting graph the *dissolution of G with respect to H* and denote it $\mathrm{Diss}(G,H)$; links are inherited in the obvious way.

The graph formed by dissolution has strictly fewer c-paths than the old one: All remaining c-paths were present in the old graph, and the two graphs are semantically equivalent. The original graph has only finitely many c-paths, and each dissolution operation preserves its meaning. As a result, finitely many dissolutions (bounded above by the number of c-paths in the original graph) will yield a graph without links. If this graph is empty, then the original graph was spanned; if not, then every (necessarily linkless) c-path characterizes a model of the original graph.

4. A Sample Derivation Using Dissolution

We may always apply dissolution to a ground semantic graph until the graph is without links. The remaining c-paths, if any, characterize exactly the interpretations satisfying the graph.

The graph below is satisfiable. We box the smallest full block containing a dissolution chain about to be activated.

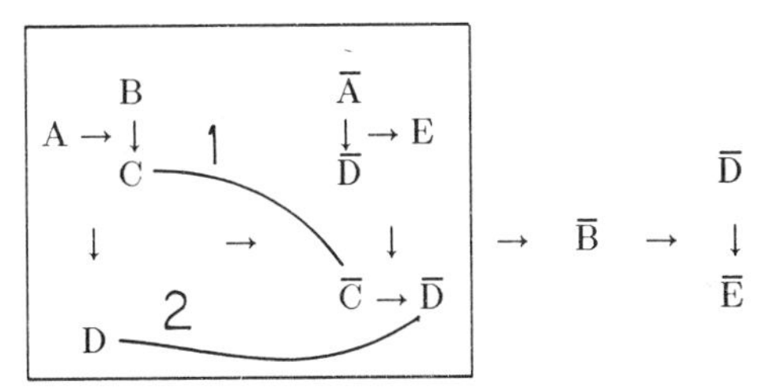

Links 1 and 2 form a dissolution chain and $M = (X, Y)_c$, where X and Y are the two leftmost fundamental subgraphs of the entire graph. (We use the second of the two compact versions of dissolvent throughout this section):

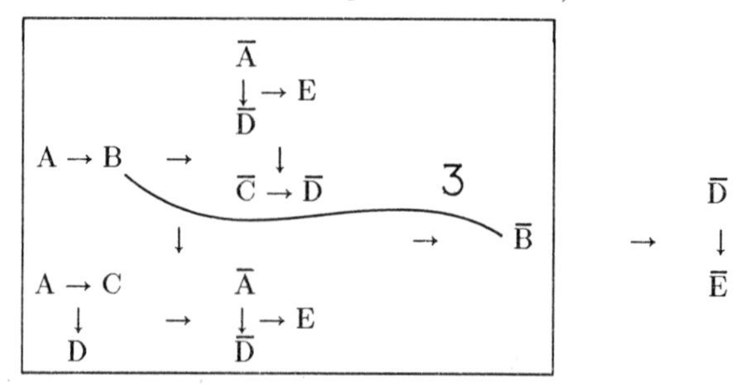

We next dissolve on link 3. The c-block comprised of the node $\bar{B}$ is strong. This is especially desirable since in this case the entire graph grows smaller. In fact, here path dissolution and path resolution yield the same result: The replacement of a full block by its dissolvent is duplicated by the path resolvent subsuming one but not both of its parents.

$$\begin{matrix} A \rightarrow C & & \bar{A} & & & & & & \bar{D} \\ \downarrow & \rightarrow & \downarrow & \rightarrow & E & \rightarrow & \bar{B} & \rightarrow & \downarrow \\ D & & \bar{D} & & & & & & \bar{E} \end{matrix}$$

The graph above has 8 c-paths whereas the original one had 18. If we continue dissolving until the graph is linkless, we are left with the single c-path $\{A, C, \bar{D}, E, \bar{B}, \bar{D}\}$; the details are left to the reader. Note that $\bar{D}$ appears twice because a path is a set of *nodes*, not literals. The associated literal set clearly specifies those interpretations that satisfy the original graph.

5. Dissolution and Path Resolution

Dissolution does not lift in the sense that Theorem 2 cannot hold at the first order level: If it did, we would have a decision procedure for first order logic. In [8], we employed dissolution at the first order level as a rule of inference rather than as a replacement procedure. Here, we combine dissolution and resolution into a single inference rule called *partial path resolution.*

Lemma 6. Let G be a semantic graph with dissolution chain D having mgsu σ. Then Diss(G,D)σ is equivalent to $G\sigma$.

Since G entails $G\sigma$ for any semantic graph G and substitution σ, Theorem 3 below is immediate.

Theorem 3. If σ is the mgsu of a dissolution chain D, and if M is the smallest full block containing D, then DV(D,M)σ is logically entailed by M.

Theorem 3 yields a technique for producing a useful inference at the first order level given an arbitrary set L of links. If H is a subgraph containing L, and if the links in L span H, then H is unsatisfiable and we may infer the path resolvent of H in G. Even if H is satisfiable, we may infer this path resolvent if we disjoin to it the subgraph that results when the links in H are dissolved away. This is the essence of the idea of partial path resolution, which is developed in Section 5.2.

5.1. Path Resolution

We present a brief review of the ideas behind path resolution. Binary resolution operates on a single link in a formula in CNF; path resolution generalizes this to resolution chains of unrestricted size within formulas in NNF. The binary resolvent is the union of literals from the two clauses containing the link. Conceptually, the path resolvent is a subgraph built from literals that lie on d-paths through a resolution chain. It turns out that an appropriate way to compute the path resolvent is the *weak split* of the chain. The weak split graph of H in G, denoted WS(H,G), is defined as follows: Let $F_1, ..., F_k$ be the fundamental subgraphs of G that meet H, and let $F_{k+1}, ..., F_n$

be those that do not. Then

$WS(\phi, G) = G$ and $WS(G, G) = \phi$.

$WS(H, G) = WS(H_{F_1}, F_1) \vee ..., \vee WS(H_{F_n}, F_n)$ if the final arc of G is a d-arc

$WS(H, G) = WS(H_{F_1}, F_1) \vee ..., \vee WS(H_{F_k}, F_k)$ if the final arc of G is a c-arc

Notice that weak split is defined structurally for any subgraph. When H is a resolution chain, $WS(H,G)$ may be soundly inferred and is called the *path resolvent*. The reason that this inference is sound is that any c-path that does not pass through H must pass through $WS(H,G)$. (See [9] for a detailed analysis with examples and proofs of appropriate theorems.)

5.2. Partial path resolution

Suppose that H is a subgraph of a semantic graph G. As we noted above, $WS(H,G)$ may be inferred when H is unsatisfiable. If H is satisfiable, we cannot make this inference since there might be satisfiable c-paths in G that pass through H. However, if we disjoin to $WS(H,G)$ the satisfiable c-paths that go through H, we then have a sound inference. From earlier observations, we now know that all we need do to find the satisfiable c-paths through H is to dissolve in H until a linkless graph results.

To properly define this procedure, we unfortunately need additional definitions and notation. Given any semantic graph H, the *full dissolvent* of H, denoted $FD(H)$, is a graph formed when links are dissolved upon repeatedly until none are left.

We define the partial path resolvent of H in G by

$$PPR(H, G) = \begin{array}{c} WS(H, G)\sigma \\ \downarrow \\ FD(H) \end{array}$$

where σ is the composition of the unifiers of all links used to create $FD(H)$.

Theorem 4. Let H be any subgraph of a semantic graph G. Then $PPR(H,G)$ is logically entailed by G.

Notice that when H is spanned by its links, $FD(H)$ is empty, and $PPR(H,G) = WS(H,G)\sigma$; i.e., the partial path resolvent is a full path resolvent. On the other hand, $WS(H,G)$ might be empty, in which case $PPR(H,G)$ gives us the kind of inference made in [8].

It is interesting to note that even at the ground level, $FD(H)$ need not be unique: In general, the graph obtained is dependent on the order in which links are activated. Observe, however, that both $WS(H,G)$ and the set of c-paths through $FD(H)$ are always unique.

In the first order case, the set of c-paths through $FD(H)$ need not be unique. The reason is that the activation of certain links may preclude the activation of others due to incompatibility. The weak split graph will be structurally unique, but the terms in the predicates depend upon σ.

This lack of uniqueness should not be viewed as a shortcoming. It arises from doing large inferences that are based on a nondeterministic selection of links. There are never more than finitely many such selections.

Observe that there is no restriction whatsoever on the subgraph H; that is, for any H in G, $PPR(H,G)$ may be soundly inferred. This leads to the question, how do we choose H? Consider our purposes in the development of this inference rule. The dissolution operation may be employed to determine whether a collection of links forms a resolution chain. If the chain is not a resolution chain, the work done in testing would be wasted unless we inferred a partial path resolvent. This brings us back to the question: On what subgraph H should the partial path resolvent be computed?

The obvious choice for H is the subgraph corresponding to a set L of links. This is almost but not quite the right choice. The partial path resolvent will be stronger if we account for a subtle point. Let M be the union of those fundamental subgraphs of G that contain H, and let $H' = M - WS_{H,G}$, where $WS_{H,G}$ is the subgraph consisting of the nodes used to form $WS(H,G)$. In general, H' is larger than H, and it is

H' that we want to use to form the partial path resolvent. The reason is that H' is the largest subgraph of G guaranteed to be spanned by L whenever L *is* a resolution chain. In that case, the full dissolvents of both H and H' are empty. However, if L is not a resolution chain, a linkless c-path of H' may contain a c-path of H as a proper subpath; the longer path is the one that ought to be inferred.

5.3. A derivation using PPR

The semantic graph G below is unsatisfiable. Links 1-4 comprise a chain that might be chosen. (It is worth noting that having c-connected nodes in one part of the graph linked, respectively, to d-connected nodes elsewhere is a good heuristic for choosing chains.)

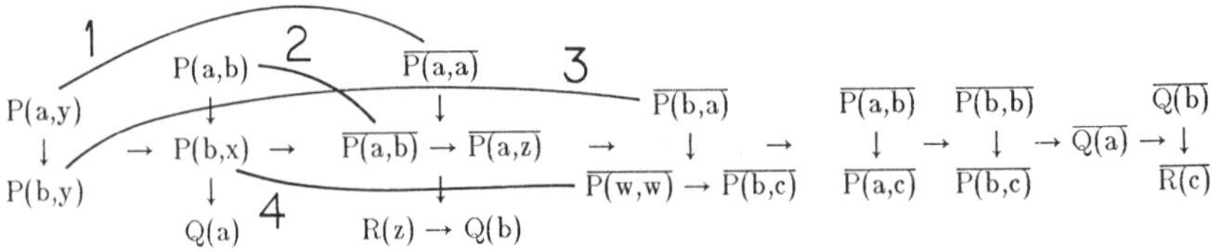

$$\begin{array}{ccccccccccccccc}
 & & P(a,b) & & \overline{P(a,a)} & & & & & & & & & & \\
P(a,y) & & \downarrow & & \downarrow & & \overline{P(b,a)} & & \overline{P(a,b)} & & \overline{P(b,b)} & & & & \overline{Q(b)} \\
\downarrow & \rightarrow & P(b,x) & \rightarrow & \overline{P(a,b)} \rightarrow \overline{P(a,z)} & \rightarrow & \downarrow & \rightarrow & \downarrow & \rightarrow & \downarrow & \rightarrow & \overline{Q(a)} & \rightarrow & \downarrow \\
P(b,y) & & \downarrow & & \downarrow & & \overline{P(w,w)} \rightarrow \overline{P(b,c)} & & \overline{P(a,c)} & & \overline{P(b,c)} & & & & \overline{R(c)} \\
 & & Q(a) & & R(z) \rightarrow Q(b) & & & & & & & & & &
\end{array}$$

(links labelled 1, 2, 3, 4)

The smallest full block M containing these links consists of the four leftmost fundamental subgraphs of G. Below on the left we show L_1, the subgraph corresponding to links 1-4. On the right is $WS(L_1,G)$.

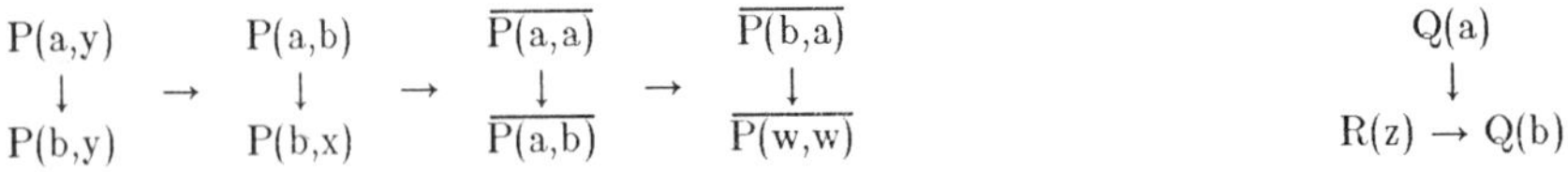

$$\begin{array}{ccccccc}
P(a,y) & & P(a,b) & & \overline{P(a,a)} & & \overline{P(b,a)} \\
\downarrow & \rightarrow & \downarrow & \rightarrow & \downarrow & \rightarrow & \downarrow \\
P(b,y) & & P(b,x) & & \overline{P(a,b)} & & \overline{P(w,w)}
\end{array}
\qquad\qquad
\begin{array}{c}
Q(a) \\
\downarrow \\
R(z) \rightarrow Q(b)
\end{array}$$

Having guessed that links 1-4 *might* be a resolution chain, we compute the partial path resolvent. The subgraph relative to $M - WS_{L_1,G}$ is:

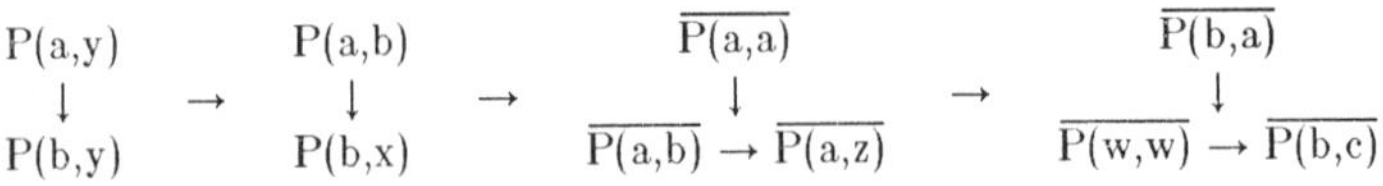

$$\begin{array}{ccccccc}
P(a,y) & & P(a,b) & & \overline{P(a,a)} & & \overline{P(b,a)} \\
\downarrow & \rightarrow & \downarrow & \rightarrow & \downarrow & \rightarrow & \downarrow \\
P(b,y) & & P(b,x) & & \overline{P(a,b)} \rightarrow \overline{P(a,z)} & & \overline{P(w,w)} \rightarrow \overline{P(b,c)}
\end{array}$$

The reader may verify that $FD(M - WS_{H,M})$ consists of two 5-node c-paths, $\sigma = \{a/y,\ b/w,\ b/x\}$, and thus

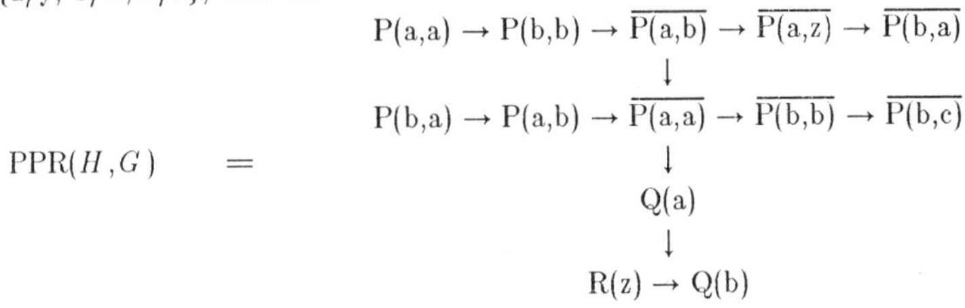

$$PPR(H,G) \quad = \quad \begin{array}{c}
P(a,a) \rightarrow P(b,b) \rightarrow \overline{P(a,b)} \rightarrow \overline{P(a,z)} \rightarrow \overline{P(b,a)} \\
\downarrow \\
P(b,a) \rightarrow P(a,b) \rightarrow \overline{P(a,a)} \rightarrow \overline{P(b,b)} \rightarrow \overline{P(b,c)} \\
\downarrow \\
Q(a) \\
\downarrow \\
R(z) \rightarrow Q(b)
\end{array}$$

Links 5-8 in the original graph with associated subgraph L_2 will yield a similar inference. Note that in this case, $H \;=\; M - WS_{L_2,G} \;=\; L_2$.

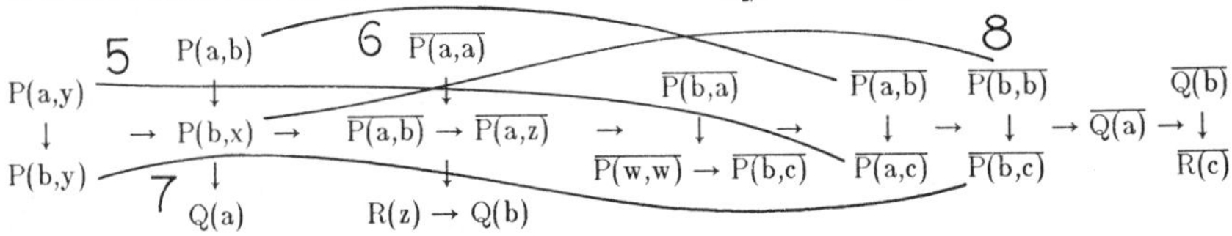

$$\begin{array}{ccccccccccccccc}
 & & P(a,b) & & \overline{P(a,a)} & & & & & & & & & & \\
P(a,y) & & \downarrow & & \downarrow & & \overline{P(b,a)} & & \overline{P(a,b)} & & \overline{P(b,b)} & & & & \overline{Q(b)} \\
\downarrow & \rightarrow & P(b,x) & \rightarrow & \overline{P(a,b)} \rightarrow \overline{P(a,z)} & \rightarrow & \downarrow & \rightarrow & \downarrow & \rightarrow & \downarrow & \rightarrow & \overline{Q(a)} & \rightarrow & \downarrow \\
P(b,y) & & \downarrow & & \downarrow & & \overline{P(w,w)} \rightarrow \overline{P(b,c)} & & \overline{P(a,c)} & & \overline{P(b,c)} & & & & \overline{R(c)} \\
 & & Q(a) & & R(z) \rightarrow Q(b) & & & & & & & & & &
\end{array}$$

(links labelled 5, 6, 7, 8)

The newly computed partial path resolvent is shown below on the right; the earlier one is on the left. Links 9-12 form a resolution chain within these partial path resolvents, and hence the partial resolvent on these links is the standard path resolvent.

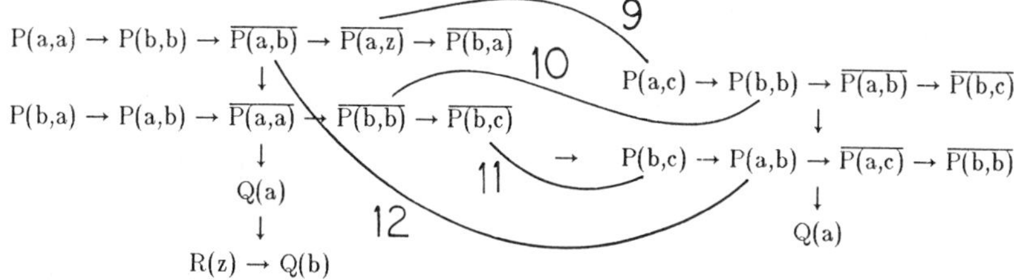

The resolvent of links 9-12 is shown below on the left, and on the right are the rightmost two fundamental subgraphs of the original graph. Because our formulas are not in clause form, we cannot assume that the extra occurrence of Q(a) is factored out. If it were, then the last inference would involve three links instead of four. Resolving on links 13-16 produces the empty graph.

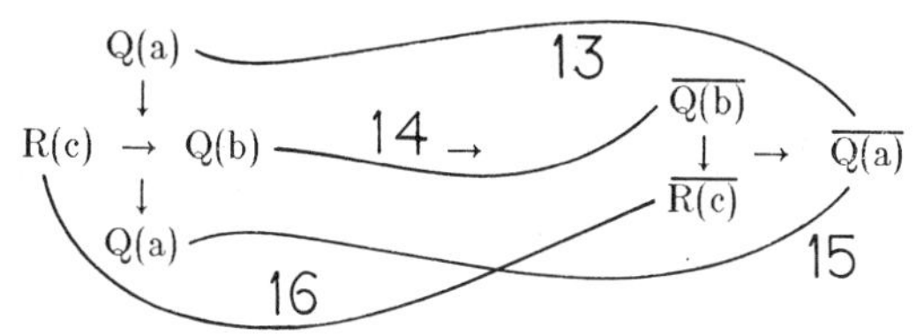

References

1. Andrews, P.B. Theorem proving via general matings. *J.ACM* 28,2 (April 1981), 193-214.
2. Bibel, W. Tautology testing with a generalized matrix reduction method. *Theoretical Computer Science* 8 (1979), 31-44.
3. Bibel, W. On matrices with connections. *J.ACM* 28,4 (Oct. 1981), 633-645.
4. Bibel, W. A comparative study of several proof procedures. *Artificial Intelligence*, 18,3 (1982), 269-293.
5. Chang, C.L., and Slagle, J.R. Using rewriting rules for connection graphs to prove theorems. *Artificial Intelligence* 12 (Aug. 1979), 159-178.
6. Kowalski, R. A proof procedure using connection graphs. *J.ACM* 22,4 (Oct. 1975), 572-595.
7. Murray, N.V. and Rosenthal, E. Path Resolution and Semantic Graphs. Proceedings of *EUROCAL '85*, Linz Austria, April 1-3, 1985. In Lecture Notes in Computer Science, Springer-Verlag, vol. 204, 50-63.
8. Murray, N.V. and Rosenthal, E. Path Dissolution: A Strongly Complete Rule of Inference. To appear in the Proceedings of *AAAI-87*, Seattle, Washington, July 13-17, 1987.
9. Murray, N.V. and Rosenthal, E. Inference With Path Resolution and Semantic Graphs. *J.ACM* 34,2 (April 1987), 225-254.
10. Prawitz, D. A proof procedure with matrix reduction. *Lecture Notes in Mathematics*, Springer-Verlag, Vol. 125, 207-213.
11. Robinson, J.A. A machine oriented logic based on the resolution principle. *J.ACM* 12,1 (Jan. 1965), 23-41.
12. Stickel, M.L. A nonclausal connection-graph resolution theorem-proving program. Proc. AAAI-82 *National Conference on A.I.*, Pittsburgh, Pennsylvania, Aug. 1982, 229-233.

AN EXPERIMENTAL IMPLEMENTATION OF A COMPILER FOR TWO-LEVEL GRAMMARS

Torbjörn Näslund
Department of Computer and Information Science
Linköping University
S - 581 83 Linköping, Sweden

ABSTRACT

This paper introduces a flexible type system for logic programs. The type system in question originates from the notion of two-level grammar, and can be seen as specifying subsets of the Herbrand universe by means of context-free grammar. An interactive system for editing and incremental compilation (into Prolog) of a typed logic programming language, called Two-Level Prolog, based on this idea is presented. The use of type declarations in Two-Level Prolog is optional, taking as default the universal type of the Herbrand universe. Thus, Prolog is a proper subset of our language. Our implementation also shows that the notion of two-level grammar is an extension of the concept of logic program.

INTRODUCTION

Logic programming, and especially Prolog, has proved to be useful in AI applications. However, existing Prolog systems provide too little support in program development. It is often claimed that a type discipline could be very helpful for that purpose [3,9,10,15].

A logic program specifies relations on its Herbrand universe (see e.g. [5]). A concept of type should allow specifications of subsets of this universe on which to define relations. This would contribute to a better understanding of the problem, both by the programmer and by the user. Type declarations would also provide additional redundant information which could be used for compile-time checking of a logic program. On the other hand, it is sometimes argued that typing destroys flexibility and requires additional programming effort.

In this paper we present an interactive system for editing and incremental compilation (into Prolog) of typed logic programs. The type system in question originates from the notion of two-level grammar [17], following the ideas of [6,7]. The idea can be seen as specifying subsets of the Herbrand universe by means of a context-free grammar. However, the terms in question are not the strings of the language specified by this grammar but the parse trees of such strings. This also allows for defining problem-specific user-friendly syntax of terms.

A similar approach is implemented in Turbo-Prolog [1]. In contrast to this work the use of type declarations in our language is optional, taking as default the universal type of the Herbrand universe. Thus Prolog is a proper subset of our language. When working with Prolog the use of the system reduces to syntax-directed editing.

PRELIMINARIES

Two-level grammars

In this section we give a brief description of the notion of two-level grammar upon which our project is based. Two-level grammars were originally introduced for defining languages [17]. However, a two-level grammar can also specify a relation.

A two-level grammar is usually viewed as a context-free grammar with a possibly infinite set of production rules. These production rules are specified by a finite set of parameterized rule schemata, called basic hyperrules. Domains of the parameters are possibly infinite context-free languages specified by context-free grammars called the metagrammars. Formally a two-level grammar is a 5-tuple W = (M, H, T, C, S) where

- M = (N, X, P), the *metagrammar*, consists of a finite set P of context-free production rules over some nonterminal alphabet N and a terminal alphabet X. The nonterminals of the metagrammar are called *metanotions*. There is no distinguished start nonterminal.

Methodologies for Intelligent Systems
Z. W. Ras and M. Zemankova, Editors

- H is a finite set of *basic hypernotions;* it is a subset of $\{ <(V \cup X)^*> \}$ where '<' and '>' are auxiliary symbols and V is the set of *grammatical variables.* A grammatical variable is a metanotion suffixed by a nonnegative integer, the metanotion is called the *type* of the variable.
- T is a terminal alphabet
- C is the finite set of *basic hyperrules;* it is a subset of $\{ H \times (H \cup T)^* \}$
- $S \in H$ is the *start hypernotion*

We adopt here the notation of [7].

Example 1.
Let W be the two-level grammar where
N = {A}
X is the set that consists of all lowercase letters
P consists of the production rules
$A \rightarrow i\ A \mid \varepsilon$
H = { <bit string of length i A1 with value A2 A2>,
<bit string of length i A1 with value i A2 A2>,
<bit string of length A1 with value A2>,
<bit string of length with value> }
T = {0, 1}
C consists of the basic hyperrules
<bit string of length i A1 with value A2 A2> →
<bit string of length A1 with value A2>0
<bit string of length i A_1 with value i A2 A2> →
<bit string of length A1 with value A2>1
<bit string of length with value> → ε
S = <bit string of length A1 with value A2>
(End of example)

A *production rule* of a two-level grammar is an instance of a basic hyperrule where all grammatical variables have been replaced by strings from the terminal alphabet of the metagrammar. The replacement of variables has to be *consistent,* that is, each occurrence of a grammatical variable in each hypernotion is replaced with the same string and this string should be derivable from the type of the variable.

The *start nonterminals* of a two-level grammar are instances of the start hypernotion where the grammatical variables have been consistently replaced with terminal strings.

We are now able to define the language generated by a two-level grammar W, L(W); it is the set of strings from the terminal alphabet T that can be derived from some start nonterminal of W using the production rules of W.

Let $v_1, \ldots, v_n$ be grammatical variables that occur in the start hypernotion. The set of start nonterminals from which it is possible to derive terminal strings defines an n-ary relation, Rel(W), on X*. An n-tuple $(x_1, \ldots, x_n) \in Rel(W)$ iff each v_i can be consistently replaced by x_i and it is possible to derive a terminal string from the obtained start nonterminal.

Example 2.
The string 10 is in the language defined by the two-level grammar W of example 1 because:
1) <bit string of length ii with value ii> is a start nonterminal of W
2) There is a derivation of the string 10 from this start nonterminal, namely
<bit string of length ii with value ii> ⇒
<bit string of length i with value i>0 ⇒
<bit string of length with value>10 ⇒
10

The above also states that $(ii, ii) \in Rel(W)$
(End of example)

Grammatical programs

In this section we present the concept of grammatical program upon which our language is based, and we show how grammatical programs are compiled into logic programs. We derive it at as an extension of the notion of logic program while it can also be seen as a two-level grammar. We also relate the semantics of grammatical programs to the semantics of two-level grammars.

We consider first pure logic programs [4]. A logic program is a finite set of clauses which have predefined form based on the syntax of terms and atoms. The syntax does not explicitly introduce any typing of terms. We now suggest the specification of classes of terms by means of context-free grammars.

Abstractly terms and atoms are trees. A context-free grammar defines classes of derivation trees; with each nonterminal one can associate the class of trees which can be derived from it. In this context, names of the production rules play the role of functors. Let

$$p\colon X \rightarrow a_1\ X_1\ \ldots\ X_n\ a_m$$

be a production rule where $a_1,\ldots,a_m$ are terminal strings and $X_1,\ldots,X_n$ are nonterminals. p can be seen as a typed n-ary operation that transforms n derivation trees of the types, respectively $X_1, \ldots, X_n$, into a tree of type X. Clearly, The Herbrand base of a logic program can be described with a context-free grammar characterizing the structure of each atom by its derivation tree. Since the syntax of atoms is standard there is no need to specify this grammar. We now allow the specification of the structure of non-standard atoms by means of a context-free grammar with start nonterminal ATOM. If the grammar is unambiguous each derivation tree can be represented by a terminal string. If on the other hand, the grammar is ambiguous then a terminal string may represent many trees, in the worst case an infinite number. To avoid this we restrict the grammars allowed.

A grammar G is said to be *left-circular* iff there exists a nonterminal X and a string ω such that $X\omega$ can be derived from X. Clearly, if a grammar is not left-circular no string has an infinite number of derivation trees. In our system the use of left-circular grammars is not allowed. (This condition is only a sufficient one. We have chosen it because our implemented editor uses a top-down parsing-technique).

If we denote an individual variable of a given sort v by v suffixed by a nonnegative integer, we can represent (non-ground) atoms and terms by sentential forms of the grammar with all occurrences of nonterminals subscribed by nonnegative integers. Such an "indexed" string derivable from a nonterminal v of the grammar will be called a *grammatical term of type v*. Grammatical terms of type ATOM will be called *grammatical atoms*.

We now define the notion of grammatical program. By a grammatical program P we mean a pair (G, GC) where

- G = (N, X, R, ATOM) is a non-left-circular context-free grammar, where N is the nonterminal alphabet, X is the terminal alphabet, R is a finite set of production rules and ATOM is the start nonterminal.
- GC is a finite set of grammatical clauses, where a grammatical clause consists of a grammatical atom as head and a (possibly empty) sequence of grammatical atoms as body. We use the auxiliary characters '<' and '>' to enclose grammatical atoms, '←' to separate the head from the body and period to denote the end of a clause.

Example 3.
Consider a world consisting of persons and things with a binary relation *likes*. Clearly things are not in the domain of this relation but may only be in its codomain. We want to model our world by specifying three classes of terms:

Person - a class of terms denoting persons
Thing - a class of terms denoting things, and
PersonThing - their union

and

likes - a subset of Person×PersonThing

We use a context-free grammar to specify the domains and to define a problem-specific syntax of the clauses which describes the relation *likes*. The grammar consists of the following production rules r1-r6:

r1: ATOM → Person likes PersonThing
r2-r3: Person → John | Mary
r4-r5: PersonThing → Person | Thing
r6: Thing → orange

The *likes* relation can now be described with the following grammatical clauses:

<John likes Mary> ← .
<Mary likes orange> ← .
<Person1 likes Person2> ← <Person2 likes Person1>.
<Person1 likes PersonThing1> ← <Person1 likes Person2> <Person2 likes PersonThing1>.

(End of example)

Clearly, a grammatical program is a special case of a two-level grammar where the structure of hypernotions is described by the metagrammar and the language derived is {ε} or Ø .

Let Treesp(X) be the set of derivation trees whose roots are labelled by X and all leaves are labelled by terminal symbols. The base for a grammatical program P is then taken to be Treesp(ATOM) and the declarative semantics can be defined as a subset of this base. This conforms with the usual declarative semantics of logic programs, which is considered a subset of the Herbrand base (see e.g. [5]). To define the declarative semantics we consider a grammatical program P = ((N, X, R, ATOM), GC) as a two-level grammar W where

- (N, X, R) is the metagrammar
- H, the set of basic hypernotions, is the set of grammatical atoms that occur in GC
- T, the set of terminal symbols, is {ε}
- C, the set of basic hyperrules, is the set defined in the following way:
  - i) $a \to \varepsilon \in C$ iff $a \leftarrow . \in GC$
  - ii) $a \to b_1 \ldots b_n \in C$ iff $a \leftarrow b_1 \ldots b_n . \in GC;\ n > 0$
- S, the start hypernotion, is <ATOM1>

Let String(X), where X is a derivation tree, be the yield of X. We now define the declarative semantics, Den(P), of a grammatical program P in the following way:

$$Den(P) = \{ X \in Treesp(ATOM) \mid String(X) \in Rel(W) \}$$

Example 4.
The grammatical program of example 3 can be considered a two-level grammar where we have the following start nonterminals:
<John likes Mary>, <John likes orange>, <Mary likes John>,
<Mary likes orange>, <John likes John>, <Mary likes Mary>
From the first four of these terminal strings (i.e. ε) can be derived. Thus
Rel(W) = { "John likes Mary", "John likes orange",
"Mary likes John", "Mary likes orange" }
The declarative semantics of the grammatical program of example 3 is therefore the set that consists of the following trees:

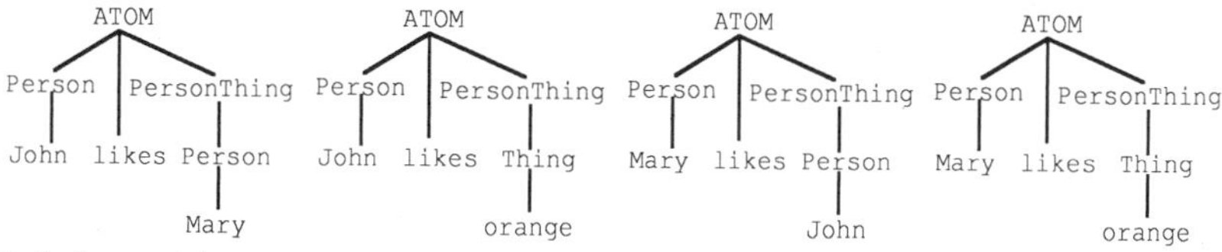

(End of example)

We now give the procedural semantics of grammatical programs by compiling them into Prolog. Thus the procedural meaning of a grammatical program is defined as the corresponding logic program.

Each atom of a grammatical program has a finite number of derivation trees, and each tree can be transformed into a Prolog atom by using the names of the production rules as functors, as illustrated by example 5.

Example 5.
The grammatical atom <John likes Mary> in the grammatical program of example 3 represents the tree.

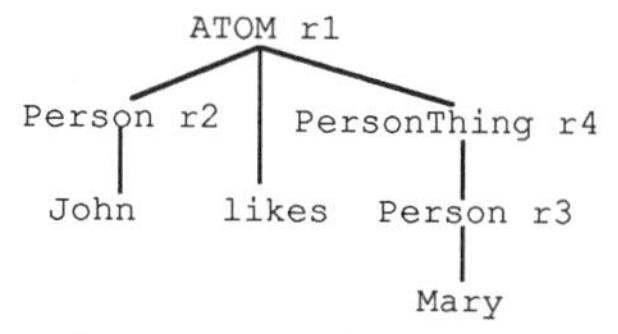

The names of the production rules used to build this tree are marked at each interior node. The tree can thus be characterized by the the Prolog term
r1(r2, r4(r3)).
(End of example)

The grammatical clauses can now be be compiled to Prolog clauses in a straightforward way. A grammatical clause

$a_0 \leftarrow a_1 \ldots a_n$

is compiled into the finite set of Prolog clauses

$t_0 \leftarrow t_1 \ldots t_n$

where each t_i is a Prolog atom representing a derivation tree of a_i. Thus if the grammar is ambiguous, one grammatical atom may be compiled into many Prolog clauses.

We now give an example of a grammatical program with an ambiguous metagrammar.

Example 6.
Consider the problem of determining if a given string is a substring of a string of a's and b's, i.e. we want a relation *is_substring* such that x and y is in this relation iff x is a substring of y. We can model our domains with the following ambiguous grammar:

r1: ATOM → Sub is a substring of String

r2: String → Sub Sub Sub

r3-r5: Sub → ε | a Sub | b Sub

The problem can now be very easily formulated using a single unit grammatical clause:

<Sub2 is a substring of Sub1 Sub2 Sub3> ← .

This grammatical clause is compiled into the clause:

r1(Sub2, r2(Sub1, Sub2, Sub3))

Since the grammar is ambiguous the goal <a is a substring of ab> represents six derivation trees. These can be characterized by the terms:

r1(r4(r3), r2(r4(r5(r3)), r3, r3)),
r1(r4(r3), r2(r4(r3), r5(r3), r3)),
r1(r4(r3), r2(r4(r3), r3, r5(r3))),
r1(r4(r3), r2(r3, r4(r5(r3)), r3)),
r1(r4(r3), r2(r3, r4(r3), r5(r3))) and
r1(r4(r3), r2(r3, r3, r4(r5(r3))))

The fifth of these is unifiable with the unit clause above, hence "a" is a substring of "ab".
(End of example)

By characterizing trees with terms the procedural semantics is not complete. There are cases where the trees of atoms can not be unified, but the atoms can derive the same terminals of the metagrammar. In these cases some elements of Den(P) will not be computed by the procedural semantics.

TWO-LEVEL PROLOG

In this section we present the logic programming language Two-Level Prolog (TLP), which is based on the notion of grammatical program given in the previous section. TLP is an extension of grammatical programs in the sense that

1) terminal symbols are admitted in the bodies of grammatical clauses
2) there is a default structure of atoms and terms

The first extension results in a programming language that comprises language generation and language analyzing facilities similar to those of of Definite Clause Grammars (DCG) [11]. DCG is a formalism which is implemented as an integrated part of most Prolog systems. Actually, a TLP program is compiled into a DCG.

The default structure of atoms and terms in the second extension is that given by Prolog. This means that in a TLP program the universal type of terms is the Herbrand universe. Hence, Prolog programs are a special case of TLP programs.

The notation used to specify the metagrammar for a TLP program is a version of BNF. The left-hand side of a metagrammar rule is separated from the right-hand side by a colon. A semicolon is used to separate alternatives of the right-hand side and a period is used to denote the end of a metagrammar rule.

In TLP there are two predefined nonterminals, FUNCTOR and TERM, of the metagrammar. From the nonterminal FUNCTOR all strings of letters and digits beginning with a lowercase letter are derivable. The nonterminal TERM is interpreted as a nonterminal from which all other nonterminals (except ATOM) are derivable. TERM also specifies the structure of Prolog terms. This means that TERM is associated with the class of all derivation trees whose root are not ATOM. As a result the user need not fully specify the structure of some terms or atoms but may leave parts unspecified. FUNCTOR and TERM may not appear as the left-hand side of any rule specified by the user.

The notation used to specify grammatical clauses is that of the previous section, except that two colons are used to separate the head from the body and apostrophes are used to enclose terminal symbols.

The class of derivation trees associated with an individual variable of a TLP program can either be specified with a variable declaration, or left unspecified. In the latter case, the class of derivation trees associated with the variable is the class associated with any nonterminal of the metagrammar that can consistently replace the variable. A variable declaration is a non-empty sequence of identifiers separated from a nonterminal of the metagrammar by a colon. A comma is used to separate identifiers and a semicolon is used to denote the end of a variable declaration.

AN EDITOR/COMPILER FOR TWO-LEVEL PROLOG

We have implemented an experimental editor/compiler that enforces the syntax and static semantics of Two-Level Prolog. The implementation was made using the Cornell Synthesizer Generator (CSG) [13,14], a tool for implementing language based editors. In this section we describe the use of the editor and how a TLP program is run by means of an example. The example we have chosen is a TLP program that describes the relation between the infix- and prefix form of arithmetic expressions.

The editor can help the user with the syntax by providing code skeletons which the user can fill in, so when the editor is invoked the user is informed that either a metagrammar rule, a variable declaration or a clause can be inserted. We want to start with the specification of the structure of the TLP atom that describes the relation and the specification of the two domains we have in mind, i.e. infix and prefix arithmetic expressions. Hence we command the editor to provide us with a metagrammar skeleton and insert the following rules:

```
ATOM : Infix in prefix form is Prefix .
Infix : Exp .
Exp : Term + Exp .
Prefix : + Prefix Prefix .
```

Now we want to write the first clause that describes the relation, so we command the editor to display a clause skeleton and insert an appropriate TLP atom as head (shown below). The editor's response to this is an error message.

```
<X + Y in prefix form is + Z W> {*<- Can't parse this *} :: {* Body *} .
```

Since the symbol *Term* in the metagrammar does not appear as a left-hand side of any rule it is considered a terminal symbol. Consequently, the symbol *X* in the head of is not interpreted as a variable, which was the intended meaning. We correct this by inserting the metagrammar rule *Term : Prod * Term*. As a result the error message disappears, since now the symbol *X* is interpreted as a variable of type *Term*. The error message depends on whether the editor can parse the atom with the given metagrammar or not. As a consequence, each modification of the metagrammar forces the editor to check each atom to see if it can be parsed with the modified grammar. If there are many atoms to parse this leads to an unacceptable response time. The user can avoid this by commanding the editor not to parse atoms during editing or writing of metagrammar rules.

We continue by trying to give the full specification of our datadomains.

```
ATOM : Infix in prefix form is Prefix .
Infix : Exp .
Exp : Term + Exp ; Term . {*<- The grammar is left-circular *}
Term : Prod * Term ; Prod . {*<- The grammar is left-circular *}
Prod : Const ; Exp. {*<- The grammar is left-circular *}
Const : FUNCTOR .
Prefix : Const ; + Prefix Prefix ; * Prefix Prefix .
```

FUNCTOR is, as mentioned in the previous section, a special nonterminal that specifies the domain of all strings of letters and digits beginning with a lowercase letter. When we inserted the rule *Prod : Exp* an error message concerning the circularity of the metagrammar appeared on all metagrammar rules that could be the cause of the circularity. The parsing of an atom with a left-circular grammar would go into an infinite loop, either due to left-recursion, as in the case above, or by trying to construct infinitely many parse trees. If we insert parentheses around *Exp* the error message disappears.

We complete the program by finishing the clause we started with and by inserting the rest of the clauses needed.

```
<X + Y in prefix form is + Z W> :: <X in prefix form is Z> <Y in prefix form is W>.
<X * Y in prefix form is * Z W> :: <X in prefix form is Z> <Y in prefix form is W>.
<(X) in prefix form is Y> :: <X in prefix form is Y>.
```

c : Const ;
<c in prefix form is c> :: .

The editor is able to compile a TLP program into a Prolog program which can be loaded into a Prolog system and run. Hence, we command the editor to compile our program and load the result into our Prolog system. We can now ask queries about the relationship between infix- and prefix arithmetic expressions.

The interface between the Prolog system and the compiled TLP program is through the Prolog predicate *get_answer*. To *get_answer* we submit a string that will be interpreted as a TLP atom. In the current system all variables that occur in the atom have to be typed. The reason for this is that the Prolog system needs this information to be able to construct a Prolog atom that can be used as a goal. Typing of a variable is done by prefixing the variable with a nonterminal of the metagrammar followed by a colon. *get_answer* is true if there is a string of terminal symbols of the TLP program that can be derived from the atom. Thus the query

*?- get_answer("a + b * c in prefix form is Prefix: X").*

would be answered by

*a + b * c in prefix form is * + a b c =>*

The => indicates that from the TLP atom is was possible to derive the empty string. At this point the Prolog system is waiting for input of either just a carriage return or else a semicolon followed by a carriage return. Simply typing carriage return terminates the query. Typing semicolon causes the system to backtrack, looking for alternative solutions.

CONCLUSION AND RELATED WORK

We have extended and implemented the idea of using two-level grammars as a logic programming language. The idea originates from an early version of [6] and was also put forward in [7] and [8]. The idea appeared later also in [16] with some suggestions concerning its implementation. There are two main differences between that work and ours:

1) Our objective is to introduce a type system for Prolog while [16] is primarily concerned with a parallel execution scheme for two-level grammars.
2) In contrast to our work, the parsing algorithm for metarules in [16] is based on the concept of a non-deterministic automaton, which imposes different restrictions on the metarules and a different way of parsing the grammatical atoms. As a result the structuring aspect of the metagrammar which is essential in our approach (since we want to consider grammatical atoms as trees) is not emphasized in [16].

The idea of defining types in logic programming by means of context-free grammars is present also in Turbo Prolog [1]. However, in contrast to our implementation the type declarations in Turbo Prolog are obligatory and do not allow the use of the universal type TERM. This excludes generic types and, to a certain extent, destroys the flexibility of logic programming. On the other hand, such strong typing makes it possible to achieve efficiency due to the extra information given by type declarations. Clearly, Turbo Prolog-like declarations are also allowed in TLP, but we did not study direct compilation of TLP into machine-code when they could be used to improve executing speed.

The main contributions of our work are the following:

- We introduced a flexible type system for logic programs and created a tool for incremental editing of typed logic programs and their compilation into Prolog. This was greatly facilitated by the use of the Cornell Synthesizer Generator. The logic programming language TLP obtained thus includes Prolog as its proper sublanguage. The version of Prolog used is Quintus Prolog [12].

- We implemented the concept of a two-level grammar as a logic program. Our implementation shows that the notion of a two-level grammar is an extension of the concept of logic program with the following features
  a) it has a type system based on the notion of metagrammar
  b) user-defined syntax of terms and atoms
  c) the notion of language generated by TLP

Our implementation does not enforce the use of these options, which shows that a pure logic program is a two-level grammar of a special kind. Definite Clause Grammars [11] are another special type of two-level grammar. It also shows how close these concepts are to each other, something which makes the implementation rather straightforward.

- We have shown that the use of ambiguous metagrammars makes TLP programs more expressive than logic programs (see example 6). The price we pay for this is incompleteness of the procedural semantics with respect to the declarative one, and combinatory explosion of the object code with the increasing level of ambiguity.

- We extended two-level grammars by combining them with impure features of Prolog in TLP. This opens the way for practical applications of two-level grammars. We claim that the optional use of our type system may be very helpful in program development. This issue is discussed in [3] with a case study illustrating our approach to program development.

Future work includes extending our system with some features for supporting the logic programming methodology discussed in [3]. This will include handling of extended mode declarations, checking of completeness of clauses with respect of type and mode declarations, use of the type declarations to optimize the object Prolog code. We plan to use the extended version of the system as a teaching aid in an undergraduate course in logic programming.

ACKNOWLEDGMENTS

I am indebted to my supervisor, Dr. Jan Maluszynski, who supported and encouraged this work. Many thanks also to Staffan Bonnier, Simin Nadjm-Tehrani and Ulf Nilsson for their help. This work was supported by the National Swedish Board for Technical Development (STU), grants STU-F 85-3166 and STU 86-3372.

REFERENCES

1. Borland, Turbo Prolog - Owner's handbook, Borland (1985).
2. Knuth D.E., Semantics of context-free languages, Math. Syst. Theory 2, 2 (1968).
3. Komorowski H.J., Maluszynski J., Logic programming and rapid prototyping, DCIS, Linköping University, LiTH-IDA-R-86-20, Linköping, (1986).
4. Kowalski R., Predicate logic as a programming language, in Information Processing 74, Rosenfeld J. (ed), North-Holland (1974).
5. Lloyd J.W., Foundations of logic programming, Springer Verlag (1984).
6. Maluszynski J., Towards a programming language based on the notion of two-level grammar, Theoretical Computer Science 28 (1984).
7. Maluszynski J., Nilsson J.F., A comparison of the logic programming language Prolog with two-level grammars, in Proc. of the First International Logic Programming Conference, Van Caneghem M. (ed), Marseille (1982).
8. Maluszynski J., Nilsson J.F., A version of Prolog based on the notion of two-level grammar, in Proc. Prolog Programming Environments, Linköping (1982).
9. Mishra P., Towards a theory of types in Prolog, in Proc. 1984 International Symp. on Logic Programming, Atlantic City, IEEE, (1984).
10. Mycroft A., O'Keefe R.A., A polymorphic type system for Prolog, Artificial Intelligence 23, (1984).
11. Pereira F.C.N., Warren D.H.D, Definite clause grammars for language analysis - a survey of the formalism and a comparison with augmented transition networks, Artificial Intelligence 13 (1980).
12. Quintus, Quintus Prolog user's guide, Quintus Computer Systems, Inc. Mountain View, California (1987).
13. Reps T.W., Generating language based environments, MIT Press, Cambridge, Mass. (1984).
14. Reps T.W., Teitelbaum T., The Synthesizer Generator reference manual, DCS, Cornell University (1985).
15. Sterling L., Shapiro E., The art of Prolog, chapt. 3, MIT Press, Cambridge, Mass., (1986).
16. Turner S.J., W-grammars for logic programming, in Implementations of Prolog, Cambell J.A. (ed), Ellis Harwood (1984).
17. Van Wijngaarden A., et al., Eds., Revised report on the algorithmic language Algol 68, Acta Infomatica 5 (1975).

KNOWLEDGE AND THE PROBLEM OF LOGICAL OMNISCIENCE

Rohit Parikh
Department of Computer Science, Brooklyn College, and
Mathematics Department, CUNY Graduate Center[1]

The notion of knowledge has recently acquired a great deal of importance in Computer Science, partly because of its importance in AI and expert systems, but also because of applications in distributed computing and possible, even likely relevance to cryptography. See [H2] for a representative collection of papers on knowledge.

An important outstanding problem in the logic of knowledge is the problem of logical omniscience, which plagues all the current logics of knowledge that are founded on the notion of a *possible world.* We assume in these logics the notion of a world, or situation which is possible relative to an individual (knower) i. The individual i knows a fact B iff B is true in all the worlds which are possible for i. It follows that if i knows A and also knows $A \rightarrow B$, then both A and $A \rightarrow B$ are true at all worlds possible for i and hence B is true at all the worlds possible for i so that i knows B. In particular, i knows all B which are logically valid. This principle, the principle of logical omniscience, is usually expressed as the formula

$$K_i(A) \wedge K_i(A \rightarrow B) \rightarrow K_i(B)$$

Now my knowledge may itself differ from world to world, and to deal with this fact we need the notion of equivalence of worlds. Two worlds are *equivalent* for me if they create the same evidence for me, and a world w' is *possible* for me at the world w iff w and w' are equivalent for me. Since w is always possible at w, if I know B at w, then B is true at w. In fact we get in this way a logic of knowledge that is sometimes called $S5$.

This kind of model and logic comes in very handy in distributed computing where we consider a bunch of processes connected in a network. At any moment of time, events may take place at zero or more sites, and a global history H is just the complete record of all events that have taken place at all sites. However, the *evidence* of a process is just its *local history* $h = f(i, H)$ and it knows a certain property A of H iff A is true not only of H itself, but also true of all H' such that $f(i, H)$ equals h. See ([PR], [CM]).

Unfortunately, it may well happen that deciding whether i knows a formula A at a history H may be an NP-complete problem, [MT], or even undecidable. Moreover, humans in general do not know the logical consequences of all their knowledge, even when such consequences are not too difficult to compute. Thus, in general, the amount of *actual* knowledge of facts is much less than the $S5$ logic would suggest.

There are, in fact, some proposals in the literature, based on syntactic treatments of knowledge, or more exotically, on the notion of an impossible possible world. See [H3] pages 7-9 for a brief overview of such attempts. However, none of these solutions is very natural and to find a better, more realistic approach, it is worthwhile being quite explicit about the problems that we want to solve. We propose a set of examples that any adequate treatment of knowledge must deal with and then propose one that, in our view, does this.

---

[1]33 West 42nd St., New York, NY, 10036. Research supported by NSF grant DCR 85-04825

Methodologies for Intelligent Systems
Z. W. Ras and M. Zemankova, Editors

1) I point out to you that there is thick smoke coming out of a certain house and you conclude that the house is on fire. Here, if S stands for thick smoke and F stands for fire, then you already knew $S \rightarrow F$, and on learning that S, you also know F. This situation, where knowledge is increased by the increase in evidence, is the only one that the $S5$ logic of knowledge can handle.

2) Nero Wolfe sits in his office and listens to a description of a scene of a murder, given by Archie Goodwin. Afterwards, Wolfe knows who the murderer is, but Archie does not. Wolfe is a fat and lazy man who almost never goes to the scene of crime, and has *no* evidence that Archie does not have. How can he know more than Archie?

3) I know the axioms of Peano arithmetic and also know that if Fermat's theorem is false, then this fact is deducible from the axioms. Hence if F is false, then I know $\neg F$. If, on the other hand, F is true, clearly I cannot know $\neg F$, and hence, by the $S5$ axioms, I know that I do not know $\neg F$. Combining this fact with my previous reasoning, I know F. Hence either I know F or I know $\neg F$. In other words, I know whether F is true. But of course, in fact I do not.

4) I ask someone who knows a little arithmetic but does not know any logic whether it is true that if it is the case that if $3 > 2$ then $3 > 4$, then it is also the case that $3 > 5$. She does not know and suspects me of trying to confuse her. After she learns the propositional calculus and the formalisation of the sentence above as $((P \rightarrow Q) \rightarrow R)$ where P is true and Q and R are false, she sees that the sentence is in fact true.

5) Here is a dialogue between a questioner q and a respondent r:

```
q: Do you  know the factorisation  of 143?
r:  Not off hand.
q: Is 11 a prime?
r: (After thinking  a little) Yes.
q:  Is 13 a prime?
r: Yes,
q: How much is 11 times 13?
r: Let us see; 11 times 10 is  110. 11 times 3 is 33. 110
plus 33 is 143.  Oh, I see.
q: Can you factorise 143 now?
r: Of course, it is 11 times 13.
```

There is nothing mysterious about this dialogue. However, note that q only asked questions. How then could he increase r's knowledge?

6) Do you know the last letter of the string *abracadabra*? Do you know if the number of letters in that string is prime? Notice that the first question was answered immediately, but the second one took a bit of counting. Nonetheless, you did not feel like answering either question with "I don't know", even though that answer was, strictly speaking, correct.

7) Some children having played in mud, have got their foreheads dirty. In fact, k of them have dirty foreheads. Every child can see everyone else's forehead, but not his/her own. The mother arrives on the scene and says "one of you has a dirty forehead." She then asks all the children one by one, if it knows its forehead is dirty. Strange to say, they *all* say, "I don't know."

In the conventional version of this puzzle, (see [HM]) all the children are supposed to be perfect ($S5$) reasoners, and it can be shown that the kth dirty child does know that it has a dirty forehead, but with real children, this is only likely if k is one. If k is two, the child who deduces that his forehead is dirty would be described as clever, and for $k > 2$, the child, unless it had a logician parent, would be described as a prodigy.

Of course, everyone knows that real children will behave differently from idealised children. The problem is to find a theory of real children. To understand the puzzle properly, we should examine the conventional argument that the last dirty child uses to realise that its forehead is dirty. Let k be the number of dirty children. If $k = 1$, then the dirty child sees no one else who is dirty, and realises that it is itself the dirty child. Suppose now that we have justified the case $k = m$ and are considering the case $k = m + 1$. The $(m + 1)$th dirty child sees m dirty faces and knows that $k = m$ if it is itself clean and $k = m + 1$, if it is dirty.

It then reasons: if $k = m$, then the child before me would be the last dirty child and would have realised, using the argument for $k = m$, that its forehead was dirty. However, it said, "I don't know." It follows that $k = m + 1$ and *my* forehead must be dirty.

What happens to this argument in a realistic setting?

Suppose that I am one of the children; all the children that I can see, who have muddy foreheads, have been asked if their foreheads are muddy and have already said "I don't know." I know that if my forehead was clean, then the dirty child before me should have said, "my forehead is dirty." Since that child said "I don't know," then *if* that child was capable of making that inference and did not, then it must be that my forehead is dirty.

However, what if my forehead is in fact clean, and the failure of the child just before me to realise that his forehead is dirty, is merely due to a weak reasoning capacity? In that case I should not assert that my forehead is dirty. Thus my being able to make the right inference about my forehead depends on my trusting the reasoning ability of the child before me, and his depends in turn on his trusting the children before him. Also, perhaps he said "I don't know if my forehead is dirty," not because he lacked the capacity to make the right inference, but doubted the capacity of the child before him.

On the other hand, if the child before me *falsely* believes that all the children before him are perfect reasoners, then I am justified in trusting him *even* if his assertion is due to a false belief. Because I know that he will say "I don't know" iff he sees that my forehead is dirty. If he falsely believes that the children before him are perfect reasoners, then he runs the risk of saying "my forehead is dirty" when in fact it is clean. However, I run no risk.

I claim now that what is crucial here is the actual *behaviour* of the children, and not really their knowledge or even beliefs. Suppose, for example, that I instruct the children: "I am going to put mud on some of your foreheads, and plain water on others. I will put mud on at least one forehead. Then I will point at each of you, one by one. If you do not see any child with mud on his forehead that I have not pointed to, and no one has yet raised his hand, then you must raise your hand."

This procedure can be learned by the children much more easily than learning the $S5$ logic of knowledge. Moreover, if the children follow the instructions properly, then it will *always* be the case that the child who raises its hand will be the last muddy child. The earlier proof that the last dirty child knows that its forehead is dirty can be readily converted into a proof that the child that raises its hand will always be the last dirty child.

Does the child who raises its hand *know* that its forehead is dirty? Not necessarily: it might just think that we are playing some game. What we do have here is the correctness of a concurrent algorithm which depends on external knowledge (or $S5$ knowledge if you like) in the sense to be defined next, rather than a more conventional version of actual knowledge. (See [PR] for a theorem connecting external knowledge with the possibility of safe concurrent procedures.)

Definition: i has *external* knowledge of A if A is true in all situations which are compatible with i's evidence.

Two other notions of knowledge that we can now define are l-knowledge, where l stands for "linguistic" and b-knowledge, where b stands for "behavioral".

i) i l-knows A if i has said "yes" to the question whether A is true and moreover, in all possible situations, i says "yes" to A only if i has external knowledge of A, and says "no" to A only when i has external knowledge that $\neg A$ holds.

ii) i b-knows A if there are three mutually imcompatible actions α, β, γ such that i does α only if A is true, and does β only if A is false, and moreover, i has just done α. (γ has no restrictions.)

Note that l-knowledge is knowledge of the *sentence* whereas b-knowledge is knowledge of the *proposition*. Thus if A and B are equivalent, then b-knowledge of A implies that of B. Not so for l-knowledge.

Thus a pigeon who has been trained to peck at a door with a square painted on it (rather than a circle, say), and has just pecked at a door with a square on it, can be said to b-know that the symbol is a square, though it can hardly respond to the question "is that a square?" Similarly, a thermostat that shows a reading of 70 degrees, b-knows the temperature, if it does not show this reading under other circumstances.

It is easily seen that l-knowledge implies b-knowledge. Just take $\alpha(\beta)$ to be the action of saying "A is true (false)", and γ to be the action of saying "I don't know". However, b-knowledge is more general in that it can be applied also to pigeons and to inanimate objects like thermostats and Turing machines. Thus suppose a Turing machine is programmed to recognise the language L. I.e., when started on a string x as input, it halts and prints a * on the tape only if x is in L. Then for a particular x in L, it has external knowledge that x is in L already when it starts, but it has b-knowledge that x is in L, only when it prints a * on the tape.

In general, b-knowledge should imply external knowledge, for it is presumably impossible to persistently do α only when A is true unless one has some sort of evidence that reveals the presence of A.

We now consider the question of *computing* knowledge, a question which involves resource bound considerations. In general, the goal is to compute external knowledge, but it may be incomputable or intractable and l or b-knowledge of facts that one may succeed in computing will generally be less than external knowledge. But knowledge of other people's knowledge that one may have, could *exceed* what is possible with external knowledge; for example, it is possible for me to have l-knowledge that you do not know Fermat's theorem, but if the theorem is true, then it is impossible for me to have external knowledge that you do not have external knowledge of it.

The dirty children puzzle shows, moreover, that a concurrent algorithm which works if everyone acted according to external knowledge, might not work if l-knowledge is substituted for it.

Let us return to a discussion of the role of resource bounds which, we claim, are implicit in every query about knowledge.

Suppose I ask someone, "do you know what time it is?" He is likely to look at his watch and say "four PM", or whatever his watch shows. At this point it would be silly for me to say, "If you didn't know what time it was, since you had to look at your watch, why didn't you say so?" Presumably he took my inquiry, not really to be an inquiry about his state of knowledge, but about the time. What happens is that he is carrying out an algorithm which terminates with his knowing the value of the time. If I now ask the same question of a person not wearing a watch, she is likely to say, "I don't know". If, however, I say, "Do you know what time it is? I have a plane to catch at six". Then she may suggest calling the special number for time, or remember someone around who is wearing a watch. Thus the algorithm is carried further if the likely benefit from the answer exceeds the cost of carrying out the algorithm. Note also, that unlike a computer, when a person is asked the same question twice, and the question was answered successfully the first time, then the second query is answered quite fast. This clearly points to some database that has been updated in the meanwhile.

Definition: A *knowledge algorithm* consists of a database together with a procedure that takes as input a question (say the truth value of some formula) and some resource bound, and operates on the question and the database upto some point determined by the value of the resource bound. Then either an answer is obtained or the bound is exceeded. In the first case, the answer is given and the database may be updated, even if the answer depended logically on evidence already at hand. In the second case the answer "I don't know" is given[2]. The database may also be updated as a result of information received from the outside.

We illustrate this by describing a possible knowledge algorithm for factorisation. The database in this case consists of a finite sequence of primes, not necessarily in increasing order. A query consists of a pair n, b where n is the number to be factorised and b is a resource bound. The algorithm uses some test for primality, perhaps a probabilistic one. On receiving the query, the number is first tested for divisibility by a number in the database. If the answer is positive, say n is divisible by p, then p is set aside as a factor and n is replaced by n/p. If no prime in the database divides n, then n is tested for primality. If n turns out to be a prime, then the factorisation of n is trivial and *n is added to the database.* If n is not a prime and is not divisible by any prime in the database, then some dreary routine for factorisation is started. If, at any time during this process, the bound b is exceeded then the answer "I don't know" is given.

We now look at the various problems that we have discussed earlier. Problem 1 is also solved by the usual $S5$ logic, but the current framework allows us to see that you *might not* see that there is a fire. Consider number 2. The explanation is that Nero Wolfe uses a more efficient algorithm for answering queries. The possibility that he knows more *initial* facts is discounted by the fact that his explanations can be followed by Archie. Problem 3 is now quite straightforward. Perhaps my algorithm

[2]This answer really should be distinguished from the same answer given when one knows that one lacks external knowledge.

for answering queries about number theoretic questions is merely to enumerate all possible proofs in Peano arithmetic. In that case, if F is false and there is a small (relative to my resource bound) counterexample, then I will find it. However, we know in fact that there is no small counterexample, and thus my ignorance of the truth value of F is easily understood.

Consider problem 4. In this case the person who knows arithmetic has an algorithm for answering inequalities, and perhaps simple truth functional combinations. However, the question asked falls outside the domain of the algorithm. When she learns the propositional calculus, she changes her algorithm and can now answer the question asked.

Problem 5 illustrates the use of a database. At first the person asked only has the possibility of trying all possible factors up to the square root of 143 and does not want to bother. (If money were offered, then this would increase the value of an answer and increase the value of b.) However, the rest of the dialogue puts 11 and 13 in the database, and the same question is now easily answered. Similarly, in public key cryptosystems, the private key is part of the database so that two people with different databases will be in different positions regarding the decoding of some message. It is also clear that if one party knows a fast algorithm for factorisation and the other party does not even know that there is one, then their situation is quite unsymmetric, a fact that the $S5$ logic cannot represent.

Problem 6 illustrates the fact that any query is accompanied by a computation. In those cases where one already "knows" the answer, i.e. the answer is stored in a database, the query can be answered in logarithmic time (in the size of the database), and this will usually be swamped by the linear time (in the size of the query) needed to hear the question. For giving the last letter of the string *abracadabra*, the computation is fast and one notices no hesitation. For deciding whether the number of letters is a prime, more time is needed, and one is conscious of the computation. A similar situation arises with understanding English. In most cases, the parsing can be done in real time, but a complicated sentence may cause one to think a bit.

We finally come to the dirty children puzzle. To understand this puzzle properly, we have to distinguish two different kinds of "I don't know" answers. If I ask you of some large odd number if it is a prime, you will say "I don't know", meaning really that you could find out with enough time, but you don't know the answer offhand and do not want to bother to compute. Suppose, however, that I ask you if Rajiv Gandhi's age is a prime number, your answer "I don't know" probably means that you lack external knowledge of his age. Hence you also lack l-knowledge of the answer, and your ignorance is stable relative to further computation.

Under special circumstances, external knowledge or the lack of it may be decidable relatively cheaply. If a person knows this, then he might respond to a query by carrying out the computation till it terminates in a "yes", "no", or a stable "I don't know". In the dirty children puzzle, there is such an algorithm which works, provided that all the children carry it out faithfully. This is why we have a proof that the kth child "knows" that it is dirty, provided that all children are perfect reasoners. If they are not, then the kth child does not even have external knowledge that he is dirty, because part of his evidence is the answers given by the other children, and there is no way to interpret this if their l-knowledge is properly less than their external knowledge.

We have so far talked only about how inquiries about knowledge may be answered. But what then is *knowledge*? Given that a person has a knowledge algorithm, we may perhaps like to say that A is *knowable* to him if the algorithm with input A will terminate for some large b and give a "yes" answer. The set of all knowable A need not follow any pattern in general, but we can show the following theorem:

Theorem: Given a knowledge algorithm α, there is an algorithm β, extending it, such that the set of β-knowable A obeys the $S4$ logic.

The theorem follows from the fact that the set of knowable A under α is r.e. and hence the closure of it under the $S4$ axioms and rules (in the propositional or first order versions) is also r.e. The theorem will not necessarily hold if $S5$ closure is wanted because of the $S5$ requirement that one knows which facts one does not know.

Conclusion: We have tried in this paper to make a case that real knowledge is not a *set* but a *behaviour* ([R] pp. 26-32 makes a similar point) and that positive answers to questions like "is A true?" are given for A lying between the already known set (A in the database) and the set of externally true statements. Moereover, in response to a particular query even for an *externally knowable* A not in the database, the answer may be "I don't know" or "Yes", depending on the value of the resource bound and whether the algorithm followed is complete relative to the external knowledge. The definitions of knowledge we have proposed may not strike the reader as all that surprising. However, they seem to be new, they handle the verious problems satisfactorily and they are relatively simple.

What about notions like polynomial time knowledge? We feel that "polynomial time" is a theoretical notion whose primary interest is due to the fact that it leads to a nice theory and important mathematical questions. In practice our knowledge does not follow it very much even in areas that have already been thoroughly investigated. For example, matrix multiplication is in polytime while propositional tautologies are not, (so far) and first order logic is even undecidable. Nonetheless most of us know far more valid formulae of the propositional and first order logics, than know products of matrices, nor would we be enthusiastic about multiplying two 100×100 matrices by hand.

Moreover, given any particular sentence A, it belongs to many polytime sets as well as to many sets of much higher complexity classes. Thus complexity of classes can't always tell us much that is meaningful about individual questions. We may like to study complexity theory, but we should not lose sight of the fact that the paradigm situation is where we have a particular question and a particular (perhaps rough) resource bound, and want to know if this question can be answered in this context.

We thank Paul Krasucki for comments and Anil Khullar for help with LaTeX.

References

[CM] M. Chandy and J. Misra, "How Processes Learn", *Proceedings of the 4th PODC* (1985), 204-214.

[H] J. Hintikka, *Knowledge and Belief*, Cornell U. Press, 1962.

[H2] *Reasoning about Knowledge*, Ed. J. Halpern, Morgan Kaufman, 1986.

[H3] J. Halpern, "Reasoning about Knowledge: an Overview", in [H2] above, 1-17.

[HM] J. Halpern and Y. Moses, "Knowledge and Common Knowledge in a distributed Environment", *ACM-PODC 1984*, pp. 50-61.

[MT] Y. Moses and M. Tuttle, "Programming simultaneous actions using common knowledge" *27th IEEE-FOCS* (1986) pp. 208-221.

[Pa] R. Parikh, "Logics of Knowledge, Games and Dynamic Logic", in *FST/TCS 4*, Springer LNCS no. 181, pp. 202-222.

[PR] R. Parikh and R. Ramanujam, "Distributed Processing and the Logic of Knowledge", in *Logics of Programs '85* Springer LNCS no.193, pp. 256-268.

[R] G. Ryle, *The Concept of Mind*, Barnes and Noble, originally published in 1949 by the Hutchinson company.

CIRCUMSCRIPTION AS INTROSPECTION[1]

DONALD PERLIS
Department of Computer Science and Institute for Advanced Computer Studies, University of Maryland, College Park, MD 20742

ABSTRACT

We isolate two key technical features of circumscription (consistency and minimization), and use the first as the basis for a reformulation of the circumscription principle in a way related to self knowledge. The second (minimization) then can be separately expressed on its own. Conceptual clarity and a kind of validity are results of this separation.

INTRODUCTION

McCarthy [4] introduced a powerful and important new technique into artificial intelligence and logic: circumscription. However, the foundational and conceptual status of circumscription, in its various versions, has remained unsettled (see Davis [1], Etherington et al [2], Lifschitz [3]; McCarthy [4,5], Perlis & Minker [10])[2] and also bound up with the equally unsettled status of various theories of default reasoning. Here we focus on one of the key advances provided by McCarthy's original insight, namely a way to finesse consistency proofs (via a technique of Shepherdson). McCarthy exploited the idea that if a true interpretation of certain axioms can be established in such a way that a particular predicate letter P is interpreted via a formula Z, then Z is indeed a possible reading for P, i.e., $P \leftrightarrow Z$ is consistent with those axioms. He observed that this establishing might be possible within the very theory itself having those axioms. In effect, McCarthy has discovered a technique for determining, at least in some cases, when a particular wff is *not* a logical consequence of others.[3] This is a very striking result, for in general the logical consequences of a set of wffs are at best only semi-decidable; thus there is hope now that in many cases of interest to commonsense reasoning, a computationally viable mechanism may be available to determine when a wff is not one of those among what a particular agent knows (can conclude). This is of importance because of the central role that "what I don't know" plays in non-monotonic reasoning in general.

Now, McCarthy and others have studied this from the point of view of asserting $P \leftrightarrow Z$ as the conclusion once Z is established as a viable interpretation of P. This has seemed appropriate to the main goal of modelling minimizing assumptions as in default reasoning. However, formulations to date have made the passage from the viability of Z to $P \leftrightarrow Z$ in one fell swoop, rather than first recording the viability as a result in its own right and then with a further axiom (when desired) basing the minimizing of P via $P \leftrightarrow Z$ on the former.

However, there are at least two advantages to separating the viability (or relative consistency) of $P \leftrightarrow Z$ from the *conclusion* that in fact $P \leftrightarrow Z$ holds:

[1]This research has been supported in part by the U.S. Army Research Office (DAAG29-85-K-0177) and the Martin Marietta Corporation.

[2]At my last count there were at least eight versions of circumscription on the AI market. My apologies for introducing yet another here. I offer the mitigating plea that *this* one is not really circumscription at all, in the sense that it does not aim at minimizing extensions, though it does borrow outright the truly novel portion of McCarthy's original schema.

[3]In effect, circumscription involves a relative consistency proof, that identity of P and Z is consistent with (and relative to) A[P].

Methodologies for Intelligent Systems
Z. W. Ras and M. Zemankova, Editors

1. The semantics of the viability are simpler to study, and in particular the conclusion of viability is *sound*: if there is a true interpretation Z of P for which, say, Zb is false, then Pb *cannot* be provable (unless the original theory is inconsistent).[4]

2. It is not always the case that one wishes to minimize all viable interpretations, yet one might still want to know of the viability; for instance, one might wish to conclude that another agent with a somewhat different belief set S than one's own, will not be able to infer something.

These will be taken up at greater length in a longer paper, although some sample applications will be given in section IV below. Here we aim mainly at discussing some of the choices available for formal mechanisms involved in such an undertaking. What we wish to do, then, is formalize the idea that if there is a true interpretation of a set of axioms, in which P is interpreted as Z, then it is *not* concludable that P and Z are different. Note that this is different from concluding that P and Z are the *same*.

An overview of the theme we are pursuing can be indicated in the following diagram, where *C* stands for some mechanism that sets up conditions under which it may be desirable to conclude non-monotonically that ¬Px.

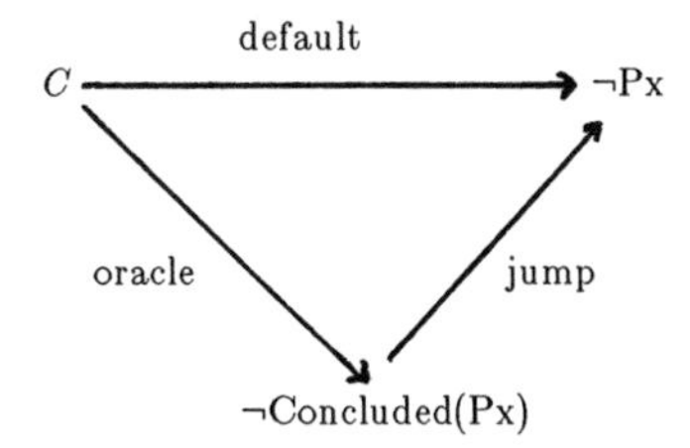

Here *C* could be a portion of McCarthy's circumscription schema (as used below), or appropriate aspects of Reiter's [11] or McDermott & Doyle's [6] forms of non-monotonic reasoning. The point is that the conclusion of the default has been broken into two steps, first recognizing explicitly the fact that the default conclusion is not prevented by anything known, and then the actual passage to the default. In Perlis [8] these steps are called the 'oracle' and the 'jump' respectively. However, here we will be exploring the extent to which a variation on circumscription can actually render the oracle computationally feasible.[5]

AN INTROSPECTIVE TREATMENT

We begin by recalling one standard form of circumscription, the so-called predicate circumscription schema (McCarthy [4]) where Z is an arbitrary wff:

$$A[Z] \; \& \; (\forall x)(Zx \rightarrow Px) \; .\!\rightarrow\!. \; (\forall x)(Px \rightarrow Zx)$$

Here A[P] is given as (a conjoined of) axioms, and A[Z] is this conjunction rewritten by substituting Z for P. It is natural to think of Z as a candidate interpretation for (the underdetermined) P. For instance, suppose A[P] is the conjunction of Pb and $(\forall x)(Qx \rightarrow Px)$; this might formalize the idea that b is winged, and that flyers are winged. However, A[P] really says very little as to what winged things (P-things) are: all we know is that b is one, and flyers (Q-things) are winged. This leaves open what the extent of winged things is. Possibly

[4]There are subtleties here which will be discussed in the longer paper.

[5]The name 'oracle' was chosen before to indicate an intractable (even undecidable) problem -- namely, that of determining non-provability -- so that now it may be inappropriate.

b is the only such, possibly not. The predicate circumscription schema above has as consequence that, after all, the class of winged things is the smallest class Z satisfying A[Z], i.e., the union of the class of flyers and the object b. For we need only choose Z to be the formula Qx v x=b. Then A[Z] and Zx → Px follow from A[P], so the schema yields $(\forall x)(Px \rightarrow Zx)$, i.e., $(\forall x)(Px \rightarrow .\ Qx \vee x{=}b)$.

Now suppose we wish to know that Qx v x=b is a *viable* interpretation of P, i.e., that winged things *may be* precisely b and the flyers, but we are not prepared to conclude, yet, that this is *true*. Then we must avoid the final part of the schema, namely $(\forall x)(Px \rightarrow Zx)$. What can we put in its place? We presumably want something like Viable($(\forall x)(Px \rightarrow Zx)$. However, there is a simpler and more useful formulation, namely we first rewrite the conclusion in contrapositive form

$$(\forall x)(\neg Zx \rightarrow \neg Px)$$

and then instead of the boldness of ¬Px we use ¬Concluded(Px), i.e., rather than assert that Px is *false,* we simply record that it is not concluded that Px:

$$(\forall x)(\neg Zx \rightarrow \neg \mathrm{Concluded}(Px))$$

Thus this amounts to a kind of meta-conclusion about the reasoner's own conclusions: the reasoner is (to be) endowed with the ability to introspect that it has not been able to draw certain conclusions. The advantage to using ¬Concluded(Px) instead of Viable($(\forall x)(Px \rightarrow Zx)$ will emerge below.

TECHNICAL DETAILS

There is one obvious aspect in which a complication arises: the syntax of the underlying first-order language must include names for wffs, so that they can appear as terms in formulas. That is, we must reify wffs as first-order objects. This is not new, however; the reader is referred to (Perlis [7]) for one way to do this. Thus we may employ a predicate symbol Concluded(g,b) where g is an agent and b is the name of a wff, to mean that the wff (named) b is concluded by g. The predicate symbol Concluded can just as well be read as "g knows (or believes) α." We have chosen the more neutral 'Concluded' simply to avoid discussion of the ins and outs of epistemic operators, which are not the point of this paper. Since we assume for now a fixed reasoner g, we will suppress this argument to Concluded, writing simply Concluded('α').

Suppose then that L is a first-order language, with predicate symbol Concluded and term 'α' for each wff α. If α is closed, 'α' will be a constant; otherwise 'α' will be a function-term with free variables identical to those of α[6] Then we can present the following revised schema, in a form we call *auto-circumscription* (for it is designed to isolate the feature of determining what is (not) known to the agent *itself,* rather than what is (not) true in the outer world):

$$\mathrm{AUTO{:}}A[Z]\ \&\ (\forall x)(Zx \rightarrow Px)\ .\!\rightarrow\!.\ (\forall x)(\neg Zx \rightarrow \neg \mathrm{Concluded}(\text{'}Px\text{'}))$$

Now, what is preferable about this version over the one with Viable($(\forall x)(Px \rightarrow Zx)$? Well, the latter would require us to write axioms for Viable, and to be useful these would have to provide ways to break apart $(\forall x)(Px \rightarrow Zx)$ into subformulas so that knowing, say ¬Zc, would allow a conclusion about the viability of ¬Pc. Schema AUTO avoids this by placing Concluded directly where desired.

---

[6]This device is sometimes called 'quasi-quoting.'

Another possibility is to circumscribe the predicate Concluded itself with ordinary circumscription, rather than go to the trouble of inventing a new version. However, this is illusory: to make it useful, axioms relating Concluded to the actual provability conditions of g would be necessary, and this is not at all easy (see Perlis [9]).[7] The present approach, on the other hand, requires no particular axiomatization of Concluded, for it serves via AUTO simply to record when a wff is *not* a theorem of g; positive cases of theorems are left unrecorded, but they are not needed for the applications sketched below.

APPLICATIONS

We briefly sketch three applications of auto-circumscription. The longer paper will give more details.

A. We suggest that auto-circumscription has a natural role in default reasoning, in that it makes more explicit the 'oracle of ignorance' (Perlis [8]). Namely, the fact that a default conclusion is being based on ignorance of something can now be directly stated, even within a default rule. For instance, a general form of default might be as follows:

$$\text{Typically}(\text{'B'},\text{'F'}) \ \&\ \text{Bx} \ \&\ \neg\text{Concluded}(\text{'}\neg\text{Fx'}) \ .\!\rightarrow\!.\ \text{Fx}$$

That is, if typically birds fly, and if x is a bird, and if it is not concluded (known) that x does not fly, then x flies. We will not explore this in detail here. Note that although McDermott & Doyle [6] have a similar axiom, in terms of the expression M(Fx) (it is consistent with all that is known, that Fx), it is not given proof-theoretic teeth with which to derive this intermediate conclusion.

B. As another sample application suppose I have the belief that I am more knowledgeable than Bill about LISP, and in particular that if I don't know some proposition about LISP then neither does he. Suppose further that propositions are constants in our first-order language. Then our situation might be formalized as

$$\text{About-Lisp}(p) \ \&\ \neg\text{Know}(me,p) \ .\!\rightarrow\!.\ \neg\text{Know}(Bill,p)$$

Now, this will allow me to infer that Bill does not know p *if* I can first infer that *I* don't know p. This is where a technical ignorance-prover will be of use. Taking *Know* to be the first-order predicate *Concluded*, where now we reinstate the agent-argument to Concluded, we can derive that Bill does not know p if indeed I do not know p. Now, the auto-circumscription schema will facilitate establishing that I do not know (certain cases of) p, so that useful conclusions (Bill's ignorance of p) can follow.[8]

Note that this example is *not* contingent on, or even significantly related to, the separate issue of whether the proposition p happens to be *true*. My ignorance of p is, in general, quite independent of its truth. In particular, no claim at all is made that p will be false merely on the basis of its being unknown to me. Nonetheless, an interesting conclusion is derivable, namely that it is also unknown to Bill, and not due to any particularly odd brand of inference. Plain unvarnished modus ponens is all that it amounts to.

C. As our final example, we offer one raised by McCarthy [private communication 1984]: How can an agent decide that, on the basis of all it knows, the question as to whether

[7]Nevertheless, provability is likely to provide a key to a sound *semantics* for auto-circumscription; this will be taken up in the longer paper.

[8]For this and other cases, a more ambitious underlying version of circumscription may be needed, such as formula circumscription (McCarthy [5]).

Ronald Reagan is (currently) standing or seated is indeterminate? Here the Concluded predicate together with the auto-circumscription schema, solves this problem. For instance, let g have the following axioms A[Seated]:

$$\begin{gathered} \text{Seated(Bill)} \\ \neg\text{Seated(Sue)} \\ \text{Apple}(x) \rightarrow \text{Red}(x) \end{gathered}$$

Then letting Z(x) be x=Bill, we find A[Z] and also Z(x)→Seated(x). But then AUTO will give us ¬Z(x) → ¬Concluded('Seated(x)'), from which we get

$$\text{Ronald Reagan} \neq \text{Bill} \;.\!\rightarrow\!.\; \neg\text{Concluded('Seated(Ronald Reagan)')}$$

Similarly we can show ¬Concluded('Standing(Ronald Reagan)'), but this will require that the schema AUTO be reformulated as for formula circumscription to allow variable predicates. This is not difficult, but we will leave it for the longer paper.

CONCLUSIONS

In short, auto-circumscription allows an automatic answer to the query "Do you know x?" when in fact x is not known.[9] Of course, this will not work in all cases, due to Gödel's result on undecidability. But perhaps most cases of interest to commonsense reasoning can be so handled.

So, we claim that being able to prove ignorance is an important phenomenon in its own right, and that certain more specialized forms of reasoning such as defaults and auto-epistemic conclusions are best viewed as embellishments of proving ignorance, which in turn seems to lend itself to formalization via auto-circumscription.

REFERENCES

1. Davis, M. [1980] The mathematics of non-monotonic reasoning. *Artificial Intelligence 13*, 73-80.

2. Etherington, D, Mercer, R., and Reiter, R. [1985] On the adequacy of predicate circumscription for closed-world reasoning. *Computational Intelligence 1*, 11-15.

3. Lifschitz, V. [1986] On the satisfiability of circumscription. *Artificial Intelligence 28*, 17-28.

4. McCarthy, J. [1980] Circumscription -- a form of non-monotonic reasoning. *Artificial Intelligence 13*, 27-39.

5. McCarthy, J. [1986] Applications of circumscription to formalizing common-sense knowledge. *Artificial Intelligence, 28*, 89-118.

6. McDermott, D. and Doyle, J. [1980] Non-Monotonic Logic I. *Artificial Intelligence 13*, 41-72.

7. Perlis, D. [1985] Languages with self reference I: foundations. *Artificial Intelligence 25*, 301-322.

8. Perlis, D. [1987] On the consistency of commonsense reasoning. *Computational Intelligence 2*, 180-190.

9. Perlis, D. [to appear] Languages with self reference II: knowledge, belief, and modality. *Artificial Intelligence.*

10. Perlis, D., and Minker, J. [1986] Completeness results for circumscription. *Artificial Intelligence 28*, 29-42.

11. Reiter, R. [1980] A logic for default reasoning. *Artificial Intelligence 13*, 81-132.

---

[9]When x *is* known, i.e., when it is a logical conclusion from g's axioms, then of course no special techniques are needed to determine this -- ignoring questions of efficiency, which is not our concern here in any case.

ON THE RELATIONSHIP BETWEEN AUTOEPISTEMIC LOGIC AND PRIORITIZED CIRCUMSCRIPTION FOR STRATIFIED DEDUCTIVE DATA BASES

HALINA PRZYMUSINSKA
The University of Texas at El Paso
Computer Science Department
El Paso, TX 79968

ABSTRACT

The aim of this paper is to investigate the relationship between two important formalizations of non-monotonic reasoning, McCarthy's prioritized circumscription and Moore's autoepistemic logic. Since these two approaches differ considerably in scope, we will be interested in situations when some common ground can be found, in particular we consider the propositional case only.

We argue that the natural class of theories for which such a relationship should be established is the class of stratified disjunctive databases and prove that for a broad class of stratified databases prioritized circumscription can be interpreted in autoepistemic logic. We also provide a characterization of the class of stratified databases for which prioritized circumscription and autoepistemic logic are equivalent. This class turns out to be the class of stratified logic programs.

It is known that for propositional stratified logic programs suitable forms of prioritized circumscription, default theory and negation as failure rule are equivalent. Our result shows that for stratified databases formalizations of non-monotonic reasoning based on autoepistemic logic coincide with those mentioned above for logic programs only.

1.0 INTRODUCTION

Extending the results obtained by Apt, Blair and Walker [1] and, independently, by Van Gelder [21] and Naqvi [17], T. Przymusinski introduced in [18] the notion of a perfect model of a deductive database and argued that the class of perfect models provides a natural intended semantics for deductive databases and logic programs. He also generalized the notion of stratification from the class of logic programs to the class of deductive databases and showed that every stratified deductive database has at least one perfect model. This result established the importance of the class of stratified databases in the theory of deductive databases.

The investigation of the relationship between different formalizations of commonsense reasoning for stratified databases was initiated by Lifschitz [9] and Przymusinski ([18,19]) who have shown that perfect models of stratified databases coincide with models of suitable forms of McCarthy's circumscription. Gelfond, H. Przymusinska and T. Przymusinski [6] proved that under appropriate assumptions characterizing the name structure of a database, prioritized circumscription is equivalent to a special form of the negation as failure rule called the Iterated Closed World Assumption (ICWA). In [2] Bidoit and Froidevaux showed that for propositional stratified databases a suitable form of Reiter's default logic is equivalent to the perfect model semantics. Consequently, for propositional stratified databases three important formalizations of commonsense reasoning - prioritized

Methodologies for Intelligent Systems
Z. W. Ras and M. Zemankova, Editors

circumscription, default theory and negation as failure, coincide.

Autoepistemic logic (AEL) proposed by Moore [16] as a reconstruction of non-monotonic logics of McDermott and Doyle ([14],[12]) provides the next major approach to the formalization of commonsense reasoning. Moore uses modal logic to formalize agent's reasoning about his knowledge or beliefs. Due to some problems with the meaning of quantifying into the scopt of an autoepistemic operator, he considers the propositional case only.

The aim of this paper is to investigate the relationship between prioritized circumscription and autoepistemic logic for the class of stratified databases and, in particular, logic programs. Since these two concepts differ considerably in scope, we will limit our attention to the propositional case and we will use a suitable mapping I from propositional language into the language of autoepistemic logic with the belief operator.

In this paper, we extend previous results obtained by Gelfond and H. Prsymusinska [5], by proving that for a broad class of stratified databases prioritized circumscription can be interpreted in terms of beliefs. We also show that for a stratified database T, prioritized circumscription is I - equivalent (i.e., is equivalent under the given interpretation I) to autoepistemic logic if and only if T is a logic program. Since prioritized circumscription, default theory and negation as failure are equivalent in the class of propositional stratified logic programs, the above mentioned result implies that only for stratified logic programs autoepistemic logic is I - equivalent to three major formalizations of commonsense reasoning.

This result can be helpful in establishing some underlying principle of non-montonic reasoning on which these formalizations are based. It also implies, as was observed by Gelfond in [4], that SLDNF-resolution - implemented e.g. in Prolog - can be used as a deductive mechanism for a broad class of autoepistemic theories. This is particularly important in view of the fact that autoepistemic logic was presented non-constructively and no procedural mechanism was provided for arriving at the theorems of a given autoepistemic theory.

The paper is organized as follows. In Sections 2 and 3 we discuss the notions of a stratified database and a stratified autoepistemic theory, respectively, and in Section 4 we present our results on the relationship between prioritized circumscription and autoepistemic logic.

2.0 STRATIFIED DATABASES

A disjunctive deductive database T consists of a set of clauses of the form:

$$A1 \ \& \ \ldots \ \& \ Am \ \& \ -B1 \ \& \ \ldots \ \& \ -Bn \rightarrow C1 \ v \ \ldots \ v \ Cp$$

where m, n $\geqslant 0$, p $\geqslant 1$, and Ai, Bj and Ck denote propositional variables. If p = 1 for all clauses, then such a database is called a (general) logic program (see [10]). If n = 0 for all clauses, then T is called a positive disjunctive database (see [18]).

Let M(T) be the class of all models of T. By TRUE(M) we will denote the set of propositional letters which are true in M.

<u>Definition 2.1</u> ([1],[21],[18])

A database T is called stratified if it is possible to decompose the set P of propositional letters in T into disjoint sets P0, P1, ... Pr, called strata, so that for every clause

$$A1 \& \ldots \& Am \& -B1 \& \ldots \& -Bn \rightarrow C1 \vee \ldots \vee Cp$$

in T we have that:

a) all the consequents Ci belong to the same stratum, say Pk;
b) all the positive premises Ai belong to the union of Pj for $j \leq i$;
c) all the negative premises Bi beong to the union of Pj for $j < i$.

Any decomposition P0, P1, ... Pr of P is called a stratification of T.

Example 2.2

Let T consist of a single clause $Q \& -P \rightarrow R$. The database T is a stratified logic program with a stratification $P0 = \{ P \}$ and $P1 = \{ Q,R \}$. Database T' consisting of clauses $-P \rightarrow Q$ and $-Q \rightarrow P$ is not stratified.

The following Theorem establishes the importance of stratified databases in the theory of deductive databases by ensuring the existence of perfect models and thus also the existence of a natural and elegant semantics.

Theorem 2.3 ([18])

Every stratified disjunctive database has at least one perfect model. Moreover, if T is a logic program then T has a unique perfect model, which then coincides with the model introduced by Apt, Blair, Walker [1] and Van Gelder [21].

The semantics of a disjunctive database T based on the class PERF(T) of all perfect models of T is called the perfect model semantics of T. It turns out that the perfect model semantics is equivalent to the appropriate form of prioritized circumscription introduced by McCarthy [11] and further developed by Lifschitz [7]. We recall here its model-theoretic characterization.

Theorem 2.4 ([11],[7])

Suppose that P0, P1, ... Pn, is any decomposition of the set of all propositional letters in a database T into disjoint sets. A model M of T is a model of prioritized circumscription of T with respect to priorities $P0 > P1 \ldots > Pn$ or, briefly, a model of $CIRC(T,P0 > P1 > \ldots > Pn)$, if for every $i \leq n$ the set of propositional letters from Pi that belong to TRUE(M) is minimal among all models of T which coincide with M on all propositional letters from the union of Pj's for $j < i$.

If P0 consists of all propositional letters in T then we have the case of standard (parallel) circumscription and we will denote it by CIRC(T).

Theorem 2.5 ([18])

If T is a stratified database and P0, P1, ... Pn is a stratification of T then a model of T is perfect if and only if it is a model of $CIRC(T,P0 > P1 > \ldots > Pn)$.

3.0 STRATIFIED AUTOEPISTEMIC THEORIES

By an autoepistemic theory T we mean a set of formulae in the language of propositional calculus augmented by a belief operator L where, for any formula F, LF is interpreted as "F is believed". The language of theory T consists of all propositional combinations of propositional formulae and formulae beginning with L.

The central role in Moore's formalization of autoepistemic logic (AEL) is played by the notion of a stable autoepistemic expansion of T which intuitively represents a possible set of beliefs of an ideally rational agent. The agent is ideally rational in the sense that his beliefs are sound with respect to the set of premises T and that he believes in everything that he can conclude from his beliefs and from the knowledge that they are his beliefs. The following definition presents a formalization of the above intuition.

Definition 3.1 ([16])

A set of formulae E(T) is a stable autoepistemic expansion of T if it satisfies the following condition:

$$E(T) = Cn(T + \{LF : F \text{ is in } E(T)\} + \{-LF : F \text{ is not in } E(T)\})$$

where Cn(S) denotes the set of all propositional consequences of S and F is an arbitrary formula in the language of T.

If an autoepistemic theory T has a unique stable expansion then this expansion can be viewed as the set of theorems which follow from T in the autoepistemic logic. Unfortunately, as was observed by Moore, a theory T may have several stable expansions or no consistent stable expansion at all. In such cases there is no clear notion of 'theoremhood' that can be associated with this theory in AEL.

This raises an important question of characterization of autoepistemic theories with unique stable expansions. This question was first addressed by Marek (see [13]) whose results imply the following theorem:

Theorem 3.2 ([13])

Any consistent theory T without the belief operator L has a unique stable expansion E(T).

Gelfond in [4] extended considerably the class of autoepistemic theories with the above uniqueness property. He has introduced the notion of a stratified autoepistemic theory and proved that stratified autoepistemic theories have unique stable expansions. Informally, for a stratified autoepistemic theory T a certain hierarchy of propositions can be defined which allows the use of formulae of the form LF on the level k of this hierarchy if and only if F is fully defined on a lower level. More precisely

Definition 3.3 ([4])

An autoepistemic theory T is called stratified if

a) T consists of clauses of the form $S \rightarrow V$, where V is a disjunction of propositional letters and where S is a conjunction of propositional letters, their negations and formulae of the form LF and -LF, with F not containing the operator L;
b) There is a partition T = T0 + ... + Tn of T such that:
   i) T0 (possibly empty) does not contain the operator L;
   ii) Clauses with the empty heads do not belong to Tk for $k>0$;
   iii) If a propositional letter P belongs to the head of a clause in Tk then literals P and -P do not belong to T0+...+Tk-1, while literals LF and -LF, where F contains P, do not belong to T0+...+Tk.

For stratified autoepistemic theories we have the following result:

Theorem 3.4 ([4])

Any consistent stratified autoepistemic theory has a unique stable expansion.

As mentioned above, this result guarantees a clear notion of 'theremhood' in AEL for stratified autoepistemic theories. It also allows to establish a relationship between AEL and other forms of non-monotonic reasoning.

4.0 RELATIONSHIP BETWEEN AEL AND PRIORITIZED CIRCUMSCRIPTION

Although AEL is based on an intuition quite different from those used for the development of other non-monotonic formalisms, such as negation as fialure rule or circumscription, some relationships between these different concepts can be found. Gelfond and H. Przymusinska [5] showed that a close relationship exists between autoepistemic theories and parallel circumscription. More precisely, for any propositional formula F let I(F) be the formula obtained from F by replacing every occurence of a negative literal -P in F by -L(P).

Then the following theorem holds:

Theorem 4.1 ([5])

For any clause C and any propositional theory T we have:

a) if CIRC(T) $\vdash$-C, then E(T) $\vdash$ I(C)

b) if CIRC(T) $\vdash$ -C, then E(T) $\nvdash$ I(C).

The converse of this result does not hold and hence (in propositional case) query answering in circumscriptive theories can be interpreted in terms of beliefs, but not vice versa. It was also shown (see [5]) that under this interpretation, parallel circumscription is I - equivalent to autoepistemic logic if and only if T is a positive logic program. In view of the equivalence of circumscription and CWA (see [8]), a form of negation as failure rule, we infer that for positive logic programs suitable forms of all three formalizations of non-monotonic reasoning coincide.

The aim of this paper is to modify and extend the above mentioned results in two directions:

(i) we will consider a more general form of circumscription, namely prioritized circumscription;

(ii) we will define an interpretation in terms of beliefs of the entire theory T and not just an interpretation of queries C involving T, as it is done in the Theorem immediately preceeding.

As a result we will establish a relationship between broader classes of circumscriptive and autoepistemic theories. We will restrict ourselves to the class of stratified disjunctive databases. In view of the arguments presented in the Introduction, we believe that this is a natural class of theories for which a common ground for different formalizations should be saught.

First, we will define a class of stratified disjunctive databases for which prioritized circumscription is equivalent to parallel circumscription of some positive database.

Definition 4.2

Let T be a stratified database with stratification P0, P1, ... Pn. We will say that T is a reducible stratified database if for every propositional letter Q that appears as a negated premise of some clause in stratum Pi, we have CIRC(T; P0 > ... > Pi-1) | = Q or CIRC(T; P0 > ... > Pi-1) |= -Q.

It is easy to observe, that every stratified logic program is reducible.

Definition 4.3

Let T be a reducible stratified database with stratification P0, P1, ... Pn. Its positive reduction T* is obtained by removing from T all clauses containing at least one negative premise -Q such that CIRC(T; P0 > ... > Pn) |= Q and by erasing all negative premises from the remaining clauses in T.

Proposition 4.4

If T is reducible stratified database then CIRC(T; P0 > ... > Pn) is equivalent to CIRC(T*).

To establish a relationship between prioritized circumscription and autoepistemic logic we have to define an interpretation of propositional clauses in terms of beliefs.

Definition 4.5

By I(T) we will denote the autoepistemic theory obtained as a result of applying the mapping I to all clauses in T.

Proposition 4.6

If T is a stratified database then I(T) is a stratified autoepistemic theory and in virtue of Theorem 3.4 it has a unique stable expansion E(I(T)).

The relationship between stable autoepistemic expansions of I(T) and T* is established in the following proposition.

Proposition 4.7

If T is a reducible stratified database then E(I(T)) = E(T*).

Propositions 4.4 and 4.7 reduce the problem of establishing a relationship between prioritized circumscription of T and stable expansion of I(T) to the problem of establishing a relationship between parallel circumscription of T* and stable expansion of T*. The second problem has been already solved in [5] and therefore as a consequence we obtain

Theorem 4.8

If T is reducible stratified database then for every propositional formula C in conjunctive normal form

if CIRC(T ; P0 > ... > Pn) |= C, then E(I(T)) |- I(C).

This result extends considerably the class of theories for which circumscription can be interpreted in terms of beliefs. The existence of such an interpretation helps to clarify the intuition behind the idea of circumscription.

The following example shows that reducibility of a stratified database T is an essential assumption.

Example 4.9

Let T consist of clauses P v Q and -P & -Q → R. Database T is stratifiable with P0 = { P,Q } and P1 = { R }. It is easy to verify that CIRC(T; P0 > P1)) |= -R. The theory I(T), which consists of clauses P vQ and -LP & -LQ →R, has a unique stable expansion E(I(T)). Neither P nor Q can be derived in it and thus both -LP and -LQ belong to E(I(T)). Since E(I(T)) is closed with respect to the propositional consequence operation we infer that R is in E(I(T)). By definition this implies that LR also belongs to E(I(T)) and therefore E(I(T)) |/ -LR.

Corollary 4.10 ([4])

If T is a stratified logic program, then autoepistemic logic and prioritized circumscription are I - equivalent. More precisely for every propositional formula C in conjunctive normal form

CIRC(T ; P0 > ... > Pn) |= C iff E(I(T)) |- I(C).

As a consequence for a broad class of stratified autoepistemic theories SLDNF-resolution of Prolog can be used as an inference mechanism.

The next result shows that logic programs are the only stratified databases for which prioritized circumscription and autoepistemic logic are I - equivalent.

Theorem 4.11

Let T be a stratified database and C(T) a consistent extension of T. Then, the autoepistemic logic E(I(T)) is I - equivalent to C(T) iff T is a logic program and C(T) is prioritized circumscription of T.

The above characterization of the class of stratified databases for which prioritized circumscription and autoepistemic logic coincide is an improvement of the corresponding result for positive logic programs from [5]. It provides a characterization of a much broader class of theories for which autoepistemic logic is I - equivalent to the three important formalizations of non-monotonic reasoning.

ACKNOWLEDGEMENTS

The author is grateful to Michael Gelfond and Teodor Przymusinski for discussions and comments which helped to improve this paper.

REFERENCES

1. Apt, K., Blair, H. and Walker, A., "Towards a Theory of Declarative Knowledge", in: Foundations of Deductive Databases and Logic Programming, (ed. J. Minker), to appear.
2. Bidoit, N. and Froidevaux, C., "Minimalism Subsumes Default Logic and Circumscription in Stratified Logic Programming", L.R.I. Research Report, to appear.
3. Bossu, G. and Siegel, P., "Saturation, Nonmonotonic Reasoning and the Closed World Assumption", Artificial Intelligence 25 (1985), 13-63.
4. Gelfond, M., "On Stratified Autoepistemic Theories", preprint.
5. Gelfond, M. and Przymusinska, H., "On the Relationship between Circumscription and Autoepistemic Logic", Proceedings of International Symposium on Methodologies for Intelligent Systems, Knoxville, Tenn., 1986.

6. Gelfond, M., Przymusinska, H. and Przymusinski, T., "The Extended Closed Workd Assumption and its Relationship to Parallel Circumscription", Proceedings ACM SIGACT-SIGMOD Symposium on Principles of Database Systems, Cambridge, Mass., March 1986, 133-139.
7. Lifschitz, V., "Computing Circumscription", Proceedings IJCAI-85, Los Angeles 1985, 121-127.
8. Lifschitz, V., "Closed World Data Bases and Circumscription", Artificial Intelligence 27 (1985), 229-235.
9. Lifschitz, V., "On the Declarative Semantics of Logic Programs with Negation", in: Foundations of Deductive Databases and Logic Programming, (ed. J. Minker), 1986, to appear.
10. Lloyd, J.W., Foundations of Logic Programming, Springer-Verlag 1984.
11. McCarthy, J., "Applications of Circumscription to Formalizing Common Sense Knowledge", AAAI Workshop on Non-Monotonic Reasoning 1984, 295-323.
12. McDermott, D., "Non-Monotonic Logic II: Non-Monotonic Modal Theories", ACM Journal 29 (1) (1982), 33-57.
13. Marek, W., "Stable Theories in Autoepistemic Logic", preprint, 1986.
14. McDermott, D. and Doyle, J., "Non-Monotonic Logic I", Artificial Intelligence 13 (1980), 41-72.
15. Minker, J., "On Indefinite Data Bases and the Closed World Assumption", Proc. 6th Conference on Automated Deduction, Springer Verlag, 292-308.
16. Moore, R.C., "Semantic Considerations on Non-Monotonic Logic", Artificial Intelligence 25 (1985), 75-94.
17. Naqvi, S.A., "A Logic for Negation in Database Systems", preprint 1986.
18. Przymusinski, T., "On the Declarative Semantics of Deductive Databases and Logic Programs", submitted to Foundations of Deductive Databases and Logic Programming (ed. J. Minker).
19. Przymusinski, T., "On the Declarative and Procedural Semantics of Logic Programs", submitted Journal of Logic Programming.
20. Van Emden, M.H. and Kowalski, R.A., "The Semantics of Predicate Logic as a Programming Language", Journ. ACM 3 (4) (1976), 733-742.
21. Van Gelder, A., "Negation as Failure Using Tight Derivations for General Logic Programs", in: Foundations of Deductive Databases and Logic Programming, (ed. J. Minker), to appear.

Forcing versus Closed World Assumption

by
Marek A. Suchenek†
The Wichita State University
KS 67208

Key words: *implicit negative information, model-theoretic forcing, non-monotonic reasoning, proof-theoretic approach to data bases.*
AMS classification : *68G99, 03C25.*

0. Abstract.

In this paper we present a solution of the problem of reasoning under a generalization cwa_S of Reiter's closed world assumption. As a by-product, applying cwa_S to the inequality symbol $\neq$ we obtain a promising alternative to McCarthy's domain circumscription. Our approach is based on the model-theoretic forcing of Robinson, used here in an explicitly syntactic definition of non-monotonic logic, complete with respect to cwa_S, whose simplicity and regular behavior are rare properties in existing systems for non-monotonic reasoning. Moreover, the presented logic meets McDermott and Doyle's postulate of asymptotic decidability (in fact, it is co-r.e.), which seems to be an advantage in comparsion, e.g., with the incredibly high degree of undecidability of circumscription.

1. Introduction.

Reasoning from the absence of evidence to the contrary has been a traditional way of authentication in the process of law, where appeal has been a frequent source of non-monotonicity, i.e. the rejection of previous conclusions exclusively on the basis of the increase in the set of premises. A general inclination toward compacting information eventually brought the institution of presumption into Computer Science under the name of default, a word - *absit omen* - also of litigious origin.

The closed world assumption of Reiter [1978] (in abbreviation cwa_R) seems to be an accepted postulate, which by validating some presumptive allegations concluded from the information represented in a data base enables us to make such a representation considerably shorter. Based on empirically justified ascertainment that the negative information is fairly more frequent than the positive one, cwaR in its original version, which precludes appearances of composed statements in the data base, is equivalent to the assertion that the absence of a positive elementary sentence substitutes for the presence of its negation. Thus, as a matter of fact, it expresses the completeness of the data base with respect to elementary sentences. Such an assertion, however, immediately led to a contradiction when applied to a more general kind of data base admitting composed sentences like $\phi \vee \psi$, since both $\neg\phi$ and $\neg\psi$ that is to say, $\neg(\phi \vee \psi)$ follows from $cwa_R + \phi \vee \psi$. This provided the evidence that cwa_R in its primitive form cannot be simply generalized over non-elementary data bases.

Several attempts have been made to find a proper generalization of cwa_R, which would not cause a paradox. They have usually resulted in adoption of some additional rules of inference, which, justified at least to some extent in classic-like manner semantically, seem strange to classical logic because of their inductive non-monotonicity. Besides some serious problems of semantic interpretation of such rules, they transcend seemingly the evident intention of cwa_R, which has been rather an economic technique of knowledge representation than a rational method of cognition.

† *on leave from Warsaw Technical University, Poland.*

Methodologies for Intelligent Systems
Z. W. Ras and M. Zemankova, Editors

Our approach is different. Instead of *ad hoc* epistemological apologia, we will treat cwa_R using purely syntactic means. Starting from the very same reflection of an actual predominance of the negative information, we will, in fact, design a method for the reconstruction of data bases from their complete positive fragments.

The problem of reasoning under the closed world assumption we pose through generalization of Reiter's cwa_R as a postulate:

> "a sentence ϕ is intended to be implied by (the information contained in) a data base Σ iff it does not enlarge the set of positive consequences of Σ"

to which we will refer as cwa_S. However, for some technical reasons we restrict it to the case of universal or universally negative ϕ, and universal Σ. We will show later, how a slight modification of cwa_S will allow us to resign this limitation.

In this paper we present the syntactic definition of cwa_S logic and discuss its degree of undecidability. As a consequence of properties of the introduced system, we provide the evidence that cwa_S makes no conflict; that is to say, it is impossible to derive both ϕ and $\neg\phi$ from $cwa_S + \Sigma$, unless Σ itself is inconsistent. Our logical system is a result of a certain conservative transformation of Robinson's [1971] model-theoretic forcing, to the syntactic aspect of which we will intentionally restrict ourselves in current considerations. We only mention here that the regular semantical behavior of forcing's logic, in particular, its completeness (in a generalized sense) and its soundness with respect to pragmatic truth, is discussed in detail by Suchenek [1984, 1986a], among others.

2. Preliminaries. We will follow the notation of the Handbook of Mathematical Logic [1977]. Moreover, we will use the following conventions.

Throughout the paper, L denotes a first-order language of finite signature, without the equality symbol = and with the symbol $\mathbf{1}$ of truth; Σ - a first-order consistent theory in L, C - an infinite countable set of constants from outside L, and L_C - the first-order language obtained by adding all elements of C to L. If ϕ is a formula, $\mathbf{x}$ is a sequence of variables, and $\mathbf{t}$ is a sequence of terms of L_C then $[\mathbf{x}\leftarrow\mathbf{t}]\phi$ denotes the result of simultaneous replacement of all free occurences of $\mathbf{x}$ in ϕ by $\mathbf{t}$. Natural numbers we will treat according to von Neuman's definition, i.e. 0 is the empty set, $n+1 = n \cup \{n\} = \{0,\ldots,n\}$, and ω is the smallest set containing 0 and closed under $\cdot\cup\{\cdot\}$ operation. #(A) stands for the cardinality of A. The set of all recursively enumerable subsets of ω we denote by r.e. We identify formulae of L_C with elements of ω (their codings). Moreover, for each finite set Σ of formulae, we will use $\bigwedge\Sigma$ and $\bigvee\Sigma$ as, respectively, the conjunction and disjunction of all elements of Σ. An $\mathbf{A}_{n+1}$-formula (where $n \in \omega$) is a first-order formula of the form $Q_1x_1\ldots Q_kx_k\phi$, where ϕ is quantifier-free, Q_1 is the universal quantifier, and there are exactly n alternations between universal and existential quantifiers in the sequence $Q_1,\ldots,Q_k$. We use $\mathbf{AE}$ instead of $\mathbf{A}_2$, and $\mathbf{A}$ instead of $\mathbf{A}_1$. Each formula of L_C is logically equivalent to an $\mathbf{A}_n$-formula. A positive formula is a first-order formula which does not contain logical symbols other than $\mathbf{1}$, $\mathbf{A}$, $\vee$ and &. A class of positive formulae we denote by Pos. A class Neg of negative formulae we define as $\{\neg\phi \mid \phi \in \text{Pos}\}$. $\mathbf{A}$Neg denotes the class of universal closures of the negative formulae. A first-order formula is in conjunctive normal form iff it is identical with $\bigwedge\{\bigvee\{\phi_{i,j} \mid i \in n_j\} \mid j \in n\}$ for some family $\phi_{i,j}$ of atomic and negated atomic formulae. Each quantifier-free formula is logically equivalent to a formula in conjunctive normal form. We will denote by Open the class of all quantifier-free sentences. By Gen(ϕ) and Ex(ϕ) we will understand, respectively, the universal and existential closure of ϕ. The first-order consequence relation of L is defined by $Cn_L(\Sigma) = \{\phi \in L | \Sigma \vdash \phi\}$. A transformation $\Phi: L \to M$, where L and M are first-order languages, we call conservative, iff $\Sigma \vdash \phi$ is always equivalent to $\Phi(\Sigma) \vdash \Phi(\phi)$. Moreover, we will use the notion of the discriminant first-order model, in which every two nonidentical constant terms have different values. (As an example of the discriminant model one can take the structure for L with Genzen-Herbrand's universe, i.e. whose elements are the terms of L).

3. Forcing. *(This section may be skiped by the reader not interested in the technical details of the proof of our main theorem 4.1. The content of the section is, however, a prerequisite for sections 5 and 6.)* A basic sentence is an atomic or negated atomic sentence of L_C. A condition for Σ is a finite set p of basic sentences, such that $\Sigma \cup p$ is consistent. A set of all conditions for Σ we denote by Cond(Σ), and its elements by p, q,... . The relation $\Vdash$ of *forcing* between conditions for Σ and sentences of L_C ("p $\Vdash \phi$" means: "p forces ϕ") is defined inductively:

if ϕ is atomic then: $p \Vdash \phi$ iff $\phi \in p$
$p \Vdash \neg\phi$ iff for all $q \supseteq p$, q non$\Vdash \phi$
$p \Vdash \phi \vee \psi$ iff $p \Vdash \phi$ or $p \Vdash \psi$
$p \Vdash \boldsymbol{E}x\phi$ iff for certain $c \in C$, $p \Vdash [x \leftarrow c]\phi$

where other connectives and universal quantifiers are interpreted as appropriate abbreviations. We will make use of the operator ^{f} defined by:

$$\Sigma^f = \{\phi \in L | 0 \Vdash \neg\neg\phi\}.$$

The operator ^{f} is the well known companion operator, therefore $\Sigma^f \cap \mathbf{A} = Cn_L(\Sigma) \cap \mathbf{A}$. It is consistent ($\Sigma^f$ is consistent unless Σ is not), closed under Cn_L ($Cn_L(\Sigma^f) = \Sigma^f$), and idempotent ($(\Sigma^f)^f = \Sigma^f$). It moreover has the following characterization (see Henrard [1973] for proof).

Henrard's Theorem. $\Sigma^f \cap \mathbf{A}_{n+1} = \{\phi \in L \cap \mathbf{A}_{n+1} | Cn_L((\Sigma^f \cap \mathbf{A}_n) \cup \{\phi\}) \cap \mathbf{A} = \Sigma^f \cap \mathbf{A}\}$.■

Henrard's Theorem says that $\Sigma^f \cap \mathbf{AE}$ is the set of all **AE**-sentences of L, which do not enlarge the set of **A**-consequences of Σ.

If we want a computer program to decide whether a tuple is in a given relation or not, e.g. whether $\phi \in \Sigma^f$, the recursiveness of the relation is the best case that could happen; however, it may be quite (e.g. exponentially) complex yet. Unfortunately, many interesting relations, such as the provability relation $\vdash$ of first-order predicate calculus, are not recursive. Some authors suggest that there exist relations of practical interest to Artificial Intelligence, which are not even r.e., such as the non-monotonic predicate calculus of McDermott and Doyle [1980]. This observation led them to a property weaker than recursive enumerability (or semidecidability), so called asymptotic decidability, mentioned informally in §11 of McDermott and Doyle [1980]. We use here the precise definition of this notion.

A relation X is said to be asymptotically decidable iff there exists a recursive relation g_X, such that
$(\mathbf{A}x \in X)(\mathbf{E}n \in \omega)(\mathbf{A}m>n)(g_X(m, x))$ and $(\mathbf{A}x \notin X)(\mathbf{E}n \in \omega)(\mathbf{A}m>n)(\neg g_X(m, x))$.
X is said to be asymptotically decidable in A iff g_X is recursive in A.

(**Remark.** The set of all assymptotically decidable subsets of ω coincides with Δ_2 in Kleene's [1943] - Mostowski's [1947] hierarchy of sets. It follows immediately from the definition of Δ_2 that it is a field of sets; it is not, however, according to Mostowski's [1948] theorem 4.4, the least field of sets, which contains all r.e. subsets of ω.)

The degree of undecidability of Σ^f depends on Σ, and on the signature of L. It has been proved in Goldrei et al. [1973], that if Σ contains **AE**-part of Peano Arithmetic then Σ^f is not even arithmetical. Thus for Σ = P.A., Σ^f is not arithmetical in Cond(Σ), since Cond(P.A.) is arithmetical. On the other hand, reasonable fragments of Σ^f are arithmetical in Cond(Σ), e.g. corollary 3.3.2 of Suchenek [1985] says that for $n \in \omega$, $\Sigma^f \cap \mathbf{A}_{n+1}$ is $\Pi_n(\mathrm{Cond}(\Sigma))$, where Π_0 stands for Δ_0. As a special case of the foregoing, $\Sigma^f \cap \mathbf{AE}$, so called Kaiser Hull of Σ, is asymptotically decidable in Cond(Σ).

4. Closed world assumption. We identify a data base Σ with the set of all sentences, whose representations it contains, and assume that it is a subset of $L \cap \mathbf{A}$ for some first-order language L. For simplicity we will consider the case, where the equality symbol does not belong to L. Later, we will resign this restriction.

The closed world assumption we interpret as

(cwa$_S$) $(\mathbf{A}\phi \in L \cap (\mathbf{A} \cup \mathbf{A}\mathrm{Neg}))(Cn_L(\Sigma \cup \{\phi\}) \cap \mathrm{Pos} = Cn_L(\Sigma) \cap \mathrm{Pos} \supset \phi)$

which is a precise articulation of the postulate mentioned in the Introduction.

Example. Let P, Q, R be unary predicate symbols, and a, b, c be constant symbols of L. $cwa_S + 0 \;|\!- (\mathbf{A}x)(\sim P(x))$. If $\Sigma = \{P(a) \vee P(b)\}$ then $cwa_S + \Sigma \;|\!- \sim P(c)$ **(**this shows that reasoning under cwa_S is non-monotonic, since $cwa_S + \Sigma \cup \{P(c)\} \;|\!\not- \sim P(c)$**)**, but $cwa_S + \Sigma \;|\!\not- \sim P(a)$ nor $cwa_S + \Sigma \;|\!\not- \sim P(b)$ **(**thus cwa_S does not imply the paradox of cwa_R**)**. If $\Pi = \Sigma \cup \{P(a) \equiv Q(a), P(b) \equiv R(b)\}$ then $cwa_S + \Pi \;|\!- (\mathbf{A}x)((\sim Q(x) \;\&\; \sim R(x)) \supset \sim P(x))$ **(**so, although we cannot express the formula $(\mathbf{A}x \notin \{a, b\})(\sim P(x))$, we may formulate something essentially equivalent**)**. Moreover, $cwa_S + \Sigma \;|\!- \mathbf{E}xP(x)$ **(**since $\Sigma \;|\!- \mathbf{E}xP(x)$**)**, and $cwa_S + \Sigma \;|\!- \mathbf{E}x{\sim}P(x)$ **(**since $cwa_S + \Sigma \;|\!- \sim P(c)$**)**. ■

It is clear that, in general, cwa_S does not coincide with cwa_R, unless Σ is a complete theory. However, for each quantifier-free sentence ϕ and set Σ of quantifier-free sentences of L, $cwa_S + \Sigma \;|\!- \phi$ and $cwa_R + \Sigma \;|\!- \phi$ are equivalent, provided $cwa_R + \Sigma$ is consistent.

Let ^{S} be the cwa_S-complete consequence operation, defined by

$$\Sigma^S = \{\phi \in L \mid cwa_S + \Sigma \;|\!- \phi\}.$$

From this definition immediately follows that the operation ^{S} is idempotent and closed under $|\!-$. Moreover, ^{S} is non-monotonic. However, it is questionable whether Σ^S has to be consistent relative to Σ. We will prove that it is.

Theorem 4.1. (i) For each consistent theory $\Sigma \subseteq L$, Σ^S is consistent.
(ii) if $\Sigma \subseteq L \cap \mathbf{A}$ then $\Sigma \subseteq \Sigma^S$, and $\Sigma^S = (Cn_L(\Sigma) \cap \mathrm{Pos})^S$.

Proof. We will construct a conservative interpretation Φ of L into a certain other first-order language M in a way which ensures that

(iii) $\Phi(L \cap \mathrm{Pos}) \subseteq \mathbf{A}$,

(iv) $\Phi(L \cap (\mathbf{A} \cup \mathbf{A}\mathrm{Neg})) \subseteq \mathbf{AE}$

and for each $\Sigma \subseteq L \cap (\mathbf{A} \cup \mathbf{A}\mathrm{Neg})$:

(v) $Cn_M(\Phi(\Sigma)) \cap \mathbf{A} = Cn_M(\Phi(Cn_L(\Sigma) \cap \mathrm{Pos})) \cap \mathbf{A}$

(the last one means that the set of **A**-consequences of $\Phi(\Sigma)$ in M is determined by the set of positive consequences of Σ in L). Having such Φ, for each $\phi \in L \cap (\mathbf{A} \cup \mathbf{A}\mathrm{Neg})$ and $\Sigma \subseteq L \cap \mathbf{A}$ we may infer a sequence of equivalent statements:

$\phi \in \Sigma^S$ iff $Cn_L(\Sigma \cup \{\phi\}) \cap \mathrm{Pos} = Cn_L(\Sigma) \cap \mathrm{Pos}$ iff (by the conservativeness of Φ)
$\Phi(Cn_L(\Sigma \cup \{\phi\}) \cap \mathrm{Pos}) = \Phi(Cn_L(\Sigma) \cap \mathrm{Pos})$ iff (again by the conservativeness of Φ)
$Cn_M(\Phi(Cn_L(\Sigma \cup \{\phi\}) \cap \mathrm{Pos})) = Cn_M(\Phi(Cn_L(\Sigma) \cap \mathrm{Pos})$ iff (by(iii))
$Cn_M(\Phi(Cn_L(\Sigma \cup \{\phi\}) \cap \mathrm{Pos})) \cap \mathbf{A} = Cn_M(\Phi(Cn_L(\Sigma) \cap \mathrm{Pos})) \cap \mathbf{A}$ iff (by(v))
$Cn_M(\Phi(\Sigma) \cup \{\Phi(\phi)\}) \cap \mathbf{A} = Cn_M(\Phi(\Sigma)) \cap \mathbf{A}$ iff (by Hernard's Theorem)
$\Phi(\phi) \in \Phi(\Sigma^f)$. From the above we obtain that

(vi) $\Sigma^S = Cn_L(\Phi^{-1}(\Phi(\Sigma)^f \cap \mathbf{AE}))$.

If Σ is consistent then (vi) proves the consistency of Σ^S (by the conservativeness of Φ and consistency of $\Phi(\Sigma)^S$), which gives us (i). If $\Sigma \subseteq L \cap \mathbf{A}$ then (vi) proves that $\Sigma \subseteq \Sigma^S$ (because by (iv), $\Phi(\Sigma) \subseteq \mathbf{AE}$, and hence $\Phi(\Sigma) \subseteq \Phi(\Sigma)^f$) and $\Sigma^S = (Cn_L(\Sigma) \cap \mathrm{Pos})^S$ (because by (iii), $\Phi(Cn_L(\Sigma) \cap \mathrm{Pos}) = \Phi(Cn_L(\Sigma)) \cap \mathbf{A}$, therefore by (v) and Henrard's Theorem $\Phi(Cn_L(\Sigma) \cap \mathrm{Pos})^f = \Phi(Cn_L(\Sigma))^f$, and by the the conservativeness of Φ, $\Phi(Cn_L(\Sigma) \cap \mathrm{Pos})^f = \Phi(\Sigma)^f$). These give us (ii).

We define Φ inductively:

(viii) if P is an n-ary predicate symbol of L then P^Φ is an n+1 - ary predicate symbol of M, with $P^\Phi \neq Q^\Phi$ for $P \neq Q$

(ix) if $P(\mathbf{t})$ is atomic formula of L then $\Phi(P(\mathbf{t})) = (\mathbf{A}\alpha)(P^\Phi(\mathbf{t}, \alpha))$, where α is the first variable which does not appear in $\mathbf{t}$.

(x) Φ is a homomorphism with respect to logical connectives and quantifiers (for example, $\Phi(\mathbf{A}x{\sim}P(x)) = \mathbf{A}x{\sim}\mathbf{A}yP^\Phi(x, y)$).

Φ obviously satisfies (iii) and (iv). Moreover, (x) implies that if $\Sigma \vdash \phi$ then $\Phi(\Sigma) \vdash \Phi(\phi)$. For proof of the converse implication we define the notions of cylindrization and projection of first-order structures.

If $\mathfrak{M}$ is a structure of L, then by its cylindrization $Cyl(\mathfrak{M})$ we mean a structure $\mathfrak{N}$ of M, which differs from $\mathfrak{M}$ only on relations and satisfies

(xi) $(\mathbf{a}, b) \in P^\Phi_{\mathfrak{N}}$ iff $\mathbf{a} \in P_{\mathfrak{M}}$.

If $\mathfrak{N}$ is a structure of M, then by its projection $Proj(\mathfrak{N})$ we mean a structure $\mathfrak{M}$ of L, which differs from $\mathfrak{N}$ only on relations and satisfies

(xii) $\mathbf{a} \in P_{\mathfrak{M}}$ iff for all b in $\mathfrak{N}$, $(\mathbf{a}, b) \in P^\Phi_{\mathfrak{N}}$.

We have $Proj(Cyl(\mathfrak{M})) = \mathfrak{M}$. Moreover, it may be proved by induction, that $\mathfrak{N} \models \Phi(\Sigma)$ iff $Proj(\mathfrak{N}) \models \Sigma$. In particular, $\mathfrak{M} \models \Sigma$ iff $Cyl(\mathfrak{M}) \models \Phi(\Sigma)$. Moreover, if $\mathfrak{M}$ is an infinite structure of L, and $\mathfrak{N} = Cyl(\mathfrak{M})$, and $\mathfrak{A}$ is a result of the addition of a finite number of tuples to the relations in $\mathfrak{N}$, then $Proj(\mathfrak{A}) = Proj(\mathfrak{N}) = \mathfrak{M}$.

Now, suppose that $\Phi(\Sigma) \nvdash \Phi(\phi)$, that is to say, there exists $\mathfrak{N} \models \Phi(\Sigma) \cup \{{\sim}\Phi(\phi)\}$. This implies $Proj(\mathfrak{N}) \models \Sigma \cup \{{\sim}\phi\}$, or $\Sigma \nvdash \phi$. Thus Φ is a conservative interpretation.

For demonstration of (v) let us observe, that $Cn_M(\Phi(Cn_L(\Sigma) \cap \mathrm{Pos})) \cap \mathbf{A} \subseteq Cn_M(\Phi(Cn_L(\Sigma))) \cap \mathbf{A}$, which by the conservativeness of Φ implies $Cn_M(\Phi(Cn_L(\Sigma) \cap \mathrm{Pos})) \cap \mathbf{A} \subseteq Cn_M(\Phi(\Sigma)) \cap \mathbf{A}$. Hence it is sufficient to show, that

(xiii) $Cn_M(\Phi(\Sigma)) \cap \mathbf{A} \subseteq Cn_M(\Phi(Cn_L(\Sigma) \cap \mathrm{Pos})) \cap \mathbf{A}$.

Suppose

(xiv) $\Phi(\Sigma) \vdash Gen(\phi)$

where ϕ is quantifier-free. Without loss of generality, we may assume that ϕ is in normal conjunctive form, that is to say, it is identical with $\bigwedge\{\phi_i \mid i \in n\}$, where the ϕ_i are disjunctions of atomic and/or negated atomic formulae. We will demonstrate, that (xiv) implies the existence of a positive sentence ψ of L such that $\Sigma \vdash \psi$, and $\{\Phi(\psi)\} \vdash Gen(\phi)$, which will provide the evidence of (xiii). Because $\Phi(\Sigma) \vdash Gen(\bigwedge\{\phi_i \mid i \in n\})$ iff for each $i \in n$, $\Phi(\Sigma) \vdash Gen(\phi_i)$, and because a disjunction of positive sentences is a positive sentence, we may reduce the general case of ϕ to the particular case, when $n = 1$. In this case ϕ is identical with $\bigvee\{P_i^\Phi(\mathbf{t}_i, s_i) \mid i \in k\} \vee \bigvee\{{\sim}Q_j^\Phi(\mathbf{u}_j, w_j) \mid i \in m\}$ for some naturals k, m, sequences $\mathbf{t}_i$, $\mathbf{u}_j$ of terms, terms s_i, w_j, and predicate symbols P_i, Q_j, where:

- $i \in k$ and $j \in m$
- $P_i^\Phi(\mathbf{t}_i, s_i)$ is non-identical with $Q_j^\Phi(\mathbf{u}_j, w_j)$ and with $P_h^\Phi(\mathbf{t}_h, s_h)$ for any $h \neq i$, $h \in k$

(otherwise ϕ would be equivalent to $\Phi(\mathbf{1})$, or addend $P_i^\Phi(\mathbf{t}_i, s_i)$ could be eliminated from ϕ).

Let $\sigma = \bigvee\{P_i(\mathbf{t}_i) \mid i \in k\}$. We will show that $\psi = Gen(\sigma)$ is the positive sentence whose existence we are going to prove. Of course, $\{\Phi(\psi)\} \vdash Gen(\phi)$. So let us assume conversely, that

(xv) $\Sigma \nvdash \psi$,

which implies that $\Sigma \cup \{Ex({\sim}\sigma)\}$ has a model. Let $\mathbf{x}$ be a sequence of all variables of ϕ, and let $\mathbf{c}$ be a sequence of the same number of different constants from outside L. Obviously, $\Sigma \cup \{\sim[x\leftarrow c]\sigma\}$ has also a model, say $\mathfrak{A}$. Because the equality symbol = does not belong to L_C, we may consistently require $\mathfrak{A}$ to be infinite and discriminant. Let $\mathfrak{B}$ = Cyl($\mathfrak{A}$). Of course, $\mathfrak{B}$ is infinite and discriminant, as $\mathfrak{A}$ has been. Moreover, $\mathfrak{B} \models (\mathbf{A}y)(\sim P_i^{\Phi}([x\leftarrow c]t_i, y)$ for each $i \in k$, that is to say for all valuations v in $\mathfrak{B}$, $([x\leftarrow c]t_i(v), [x\leftarrow c]s_i(v)) \notin P_i^{\Phi}{}_{\mathfrak{B}}$. Let $\mathfrak{N}$ be the result of the addition of all tuples of the form $([x\leftarrow c]u_j(v), [x\leftarrow c]w_j(v))$ to $Q_j^{\Phi}{}_{\mathfrak{B}}$, for all $j \in m$. Because there are only finitely many such tuples, we have

(xvi) $\quad$ $\mathrm{Proj}(\mathfrak{N}) = \mathrm{Proj}(\mathfrak{B}) = \mathfrak{A}$.

and, by definition, $\mathfrak{N} \models [x\leftarrow c] \bigwedge\{Q_j^{\Phi}(u_j, w_j) | j \in m\}$, so (since $\mathfrak{N}$ is discriminant as $\mathfrak{B}$ has been) for all $i \in k, ([x\leftarrow c]t_i(v), [x\leftarrow c]s_i(v)) \in P_i^{\Phi}{}_{\mathfrak{N}}$, which means that $\mathfrak{N} \models [x\leftarrow c] \bigwedge\{\sim P_i^{\Phi}(t_i, s_i) | i \in k\}$. Finally, we obtain that $\mathfrak{N} \models [x\leftarrow c]\sim\phi$, which implies $\mathfrak{N} \models \sim\mathrm{Gen}(\phi)$. Thus by (xvi), $\mathfrak{N} \models \Phi(\Sigma) \cup \{\sim\mathrm{Gen}(\phi)\}$, hence $\Phi(\Sigma) \not\models \mathrm{Gen}(\phi)$, which contradicts (xiv).

So, our assumption (xv) led to a contradiction, which remark completes the proof. ■

As a simple consequence of theorem 1 we obtain

Corollary 4.1.1. *If* Σ and Π have exactly the same sets of positive consequences then $\Sigma^S = \Pi^S$. ◘

The following testifies that operator ^{S} reconstructs $(\mathbf{A} \cup \mathbf{A}\mathrm{Neg})$-parts of complete theories on the basis of their positive fragments, making thus cwa_S a method of parsimonious representation of such parts.

Corollary 4.1.2. If $\Sigma \subseteq L$ is an $(\mathbf{A} \cup \mathbf{A}\mathrm{Neg})$-complete theory (i.e. for each $\phi \in L \cap (\mathbf{A} \cup \mathbf{A}\mathrm{Neg})$, $\phi \in \Sigma$ or $\sim\phi \in \Sigma$) then $(\Sigma \cap \mathrm{Pos})^S = \Sigma \cap (\mathbf{A} \cup \mathbf{A}\mathrm{Neg})$.

Proof. *By corollary 1.1.*, $(\Sigma \cap (\mathbf{A} \cup \mathbf{A}\mathrm{Neg}))^S = (\Sigma \cap \mathrm{Pos})^S$, which implies $\Sigma \cap (\mathbf{A} \cup \mathbf{A}\mathrm{Neg}) \subseteq (\Sigma \cap \mathrm{Pos})^S$. If $\phi \in (\Sigma \cap \mathrm{Pos})^S$ then $\sim\phi \notin \Sigma$, so by the above completeness, $\phi \in \Sigma$, which proves the converse inclusion. ■

The proof of theorem 1 remains valid if Σ is an arbitrary theory of L, such that $\Phi(\Sigma) \subseteq \mathbf{AE}$. This, as a matter of fact, allows a more general case of Σ, namely $\Sigma \subseteq L \cap (\mathbf{A} \cup \mathbf{A}\mathrm{Neg})$. Corollary 1.1, however, makes all cases other than $\Sigma \subseteq L \cap \mathrm{Pos}$ unnecessary, i.e. instead of Σ^S we may always use $(\mathrm{Cn}(\Sigma) \cap \mathrm{Pos})^S$.

As follows from the proof of theorem 1, the cwa_S-complete consequence operation ^{S} has a nice characterization:

$$\Sigma^S = \mathrm{Cn}_L(\Phi^{-1}(\Phi(\Sigma)^f \cap \mathbf{AE})).$$

We may also think of the stronger operation $^{S+}$, defined by

$$\Sigma^{S+} = \Phi^{-1}(\Phi(\Sigma)^f)$$

satisfying by the conservativeness of Φ

$$\Sigma^S = \Sigma^{S+} \cap \Phi^{-1}(M \cap \mathbf{AE}) = \Sigma^{S+} \cap (\mathbf{A} \cup \mathbf{A}\mathrm{Neg})$$

which is closed under $\vdash$, consistent and idempotent, as ^{f} has been. This by Henrard's Theorem leads to the following, defined by induction generalization cwa_{S+} of cwa_S:

(cwa_{S0}) $\quad$ *1*

$(\mathrm{cwa}_{S(n+1)})$ $\quad$ $(\mathbf{A}\phi \in L \cap (\mathbf{A}_n \cup \mathbf{A}_n\mathrm{Neg}))(\mathrm{Cn}_L(\mathrm{cwa}_{Sn} + \Sigma \cup \{\phi\}) \cap \mathrm{Pos} = \mathrm{Cn}_L(\Sigma) \cap \mathrm{Pos} \supset \phi)$

(cwa_{S+}) $\quad$ $\bigwedge\{\mathrm{cwa}_{Si} | i \in \omega\}$.

One can demonstrate (the proof is analogous to that of theorem 1) that the operation $^{S+}$ is complete with respect to cwa_{S+}.

5. Inequality contra circumscription. Despite the fact that the absence of the equality symbol in L has been used as an argument in the proof of theorem 1, the case of = may be easily included in the presented approach. The essential matter is that = is $\mathbf{A}$-axiomatizable, so we may simply introduce a new binary relation symbol to L, applying to it the appropriate axiomatization Ax. This lead us to the definition of another operator

$$\Sigma^{S=} = \Phi^{-1}(\Phi(\Sigma \cup \mathrm{Ax})^f \cap \mathbf{AE})$$

which will define the corresponding $\mathrm{cwa}_{S=}$-logic with the equality.

There are at least two different ways that we may proceed: it is possible to introduce a formal equality symbol EQ, or a formal inequality symbol NE. In the first case we will have $tEQs \in \Sigma^{S=}$ only if $\Sigma \mid\!- tEQs$, which will assure a different interpretation of different and Σ-nonequivalent terms. In the second case we will obtain $tNEs \in \Sigma^{S=}$ only if $\Sigma \mid\!- tNEs$, which seems to be equivalent in intention to the domain circumscription of McCarthy[1979].

Example. $(\mathbf{A}x)(\sim xNEa \quad \sim xNEb) \quad \{aNEb\}^{S=}$. ■

It should be mentioned, however, that the degree of unsolvability of circumscription exceeds, as Schlipf [1986] recently proved, all reasonable limitations. As we shall see, our approach makes the situation slightly better.

6. Degree of unsolvability. The problem of deciding whether $cwa_S + \Sigma \mid\!- \phi$ is, in general, unsolvable. Even if we assume that Σ is a decidable theory, answering the question: is $Cn(\Sigma)$ equal to $Cn(\Sigma \cup \{\phi\})$ may still be a quite difficult task. It may be observed that in case the decision procedure for $Cn(\Sigma)$ is given, the set $\{\phi \in \Phi^{-1}(\mathbf{AE}) \mid cwa_S + \Sigma \mid\!- \phi\}$ is a complement of a r.e. set, that is to say, the problem of reasoning under the closed world assumption is co-semidecidable relative to the degree of undecidability of $Cn(\Sigma)$.

The above estimation may be improved. As has been demonstrated in Suchenek [1985] (a decision procedure *forces* for operator ^{f}, co-semirecursive in $Cond(\Sigma)$ has been presented there), if the language L does not contain non-constant function symbols then $\Sigma^f \cap \mathbf{AE}$ is co-r.e. in $Cond(\Sigma)$, that is to say, co-r.e. in $Cn(\Sigma) \cap Open$. Using this result we may conclude, that Σ^S is co-r.e. in $Cn_{M_C}(\Phi(\Sigma)) \cap Open$, which may be easily proved to be of the same degree of unsolvability as $Cn_{L_C}(\Sigma) \cap Open$. We may put this observation into the form of

Theorem 6.1. The set Σ^S is co-r.e. in the set of all quantifier-free consequences of Σ in the predicate language L_C. ■

Corollary 6.1.1.. If Σ has a recursive set of quantifier-free consequences in the predicate language L_C then the problem of whether $cwa_S + \Sigma \mid\!- \phi$ is asymptotically decidable.
Proof follows from the fact that each co-r.e. set is asymptotically decidable. ■

7. Concluding remarks. As we have demonstrated, the operation ^{S} defines the consequence operator, which is **A**-complete with respect to the following version of closed world assumption:

"all models satisfy as few positive formulae as possible".

The above is a generalization of cwa_R, since in the case when only atomic sentences are allowed in Σ, Σ^S contains the negations of all atomic sentences which do not appear in Σ. It should be mentioned that there exist other generalizations, such as cwa_{BS} introduced in Bussou and Siegel [1985], of cwa_R over some particular kind of **A**-sentences (so called "groundable clauses"). This leads to the relation]= of subimplication, "groundable clauses" -complete with respect to cwa_{BS}. Although it has been proved in Suchenek [1986b], that]= preserves completeness over arbitrary sets of **A**-sentences, the problem of the relation between our forcing-based reasoning system and]= remains open (our conjecture is, that Σ]= ϕ is equivalent to $\phi \in \Sigma^S$ in all cases allowed in Bussou and Siegel [1985]). However, as has been pointed out in Suchenek [1986b], they left several basic questions concerning]= unanswered; among others, there is no syntactic characterization of]=, the definition of which seems to be fairly complicated. Also the degree of undecidability of]= is still unknown. Moreover, including the equality symbol in the language of]= seems to cause a serious problem.

As Anonymous Referees have suggested, our version of cwa is closely related to generalized cwa (in abbr: GCWA) of Minker [1982], with further modifications (as e.g. of Gelfond and Przymusinska [1986]). In fact, the condition cwa_S is a generalization of GCWA over the sentences of **A** ∪ **A**Neg and **A**-axiomatizable data bases. A similar approach can be found also in Bidoit and Hull [1986]. The relation between these works and ours requires, however, further investigation.

Acknowledgements. The author would like to express his gratitude to Prof. Wiktor Marek, Mrs. Peggy Wright, and Referees for their valuable suggestions.

8. References

1. Bidoit N., Hull R., Positivism vs. minimalism in deductive databases, ***Proc. 5-th ACM SIGACT-SIGMOD Symp. on Principles of Database Systems,*** Silberschatz A. (chr.), A.C.M. (New York 1986), 123-132.
2. Bussou G., Siegel P., Saturation, nonmonotonic reasoning and the closed world assumption, ***AI 25*** (1985), 13-63.
3. Gelfond M., Przymusinska H., Negation as failure: Careful closure procedure, ***AI 30*** (1986) 273-267.
4. Goldrei D.C., Macintyre A., Simons H., The Forcing companions of number theories, ***Israel Journal of Mathematics 14*** (1973), 317-337.
5. ***Handbook of Mathematical Logic***, J.Barwise (ed), North-Holland (Amsterdam 1977).
6. Kleene S. C., Recursive predicates and quantifiers, ***Transactions of the American Mathematical Society 53***, 41-73.
7. Minker J., On indefinite databases and the closed world assumption, Proc. 6th Conf. on Automated Deduction, ***LNCS 138***, Springer-Verlag (Berlin, New York 1982), 292-308.
8. Mostowski A., On definable sets of positive integers, ***Fund. Math. 34*** (1947), 81-112.
9. Mostowski A., On a set of integers not definable by means of one-quantifier predicates, *Ann. Soc. Pol. Math. 21* (1948), 114-119.
10. McDermott D., Doyle J., Non-monotonic logic I, ***AI 13*** (1980), 41-72.
11. Mc Carthy J., Circumscription - a form of non-monotonic reasoning,***AI 13*** (1980), 27-39.
12. Reiter R., On closed world data bases, ***Logic and Data Bases***, Gaillaire H., Minker J. (eds), Plenum Press, (New York 1978), 55-76.
13. Reiter R., A logic for default reasoning, ***AI 13*** (1980), 81-132.
14. Robinson A., Forcing in Model Theory, ***Proc. of Simp. Math. Instituto Nazionale di Alta Matematica 5*** (1971), 64-80.
15. Schlipf J.S., How uncomputable is general circumscription?, ***Proc. IEEE Symposium on Logic in Computer Science*** (Cambridge 1986), 92-95.
16. Suchenek M.A., Forcing treatment of incomplete information in data bases, ***International Symposium on Model Theoretic Methods in Computer Science*** (Budapest 1984).
17. Suchenek M.A., On asymptotic decidability of model-theoretic forcing, ***IV Hungarian Computer Science Conference***, (Gyor 1985).
18. Suchenek M. A., Non-monotonic derivations which preserve pragmatic truth, ***Proc. Int. Symp. on Methodologies for Intelligent Systems, Knoxville 1986***, Colloquia Program, Zemankova M, Emrich M. L. (eds), ORNL-6362 (Oak Ridge National Laboratory 1987), 69-74.
19. Suchenek M.A., review of item 2, ***Zentralblatt fur Mathematik 569*** (1986b), rev. no. 68078, 332-333.

MINIMIZATION AND COMMON-SENSE REASONING

Włodek Zadrożny

IBM T.J.Watson Research Center
P.O. Box 704
Yorktown Heights, NY 10598

Abstract. We examine some difficulties that arise in using circumscription: we present three examples of problems that cannot be solved by certain types of circumscription; we argue that sometimes commonsense arguments require not a minimization, but its dual -- an Open World Assumption; finally, we prove a proposition to the effect that it is always possible to make intended models of a (commonsense) theory precisely the minimal models of its simple, although unnatural, extension.

1. Introduction

We discuss two difficulties that arise in using different kinds of circumscription to formalize common-sense reasoning:

1. common-sense reasoning sometimes requires an **open world assumption** ; and, because minimization is a form of CWA, there may exist classes of problems for which any kind of circumscription will be inadequate.
2. usually, there is no clear match between a natural formalization of a common-sense problem and a circumscription which would produce correct conclusions.

We argue that these are real issues by

- showing a possible conflict between minimization of *abnormality* and maximization of safety (Example 3)
- defining a class of examples for which pointwise circumscription fails (Example 1)
- suggesting that the temporal minimization and similar methods do not solve the problems raised by Hanks and McDermott [1], and presenting an example of conflict between defaults in a static situation (Example 2)
- proving a proposition to the effect that for a given theory T and a finite collection IM of finite models of T it is always possible to find an extension T' of T such that the IM's are precisely the minimal models of T'.

We have then three new and natural examples showing different weaknesses of circumscription. The first example shows that pointwise circumscription may be too weak to handle commonsense reasoning about flying from New York to Europe. The second example proves that the problem of Hanks and McDermott has a formulation not involving time and therefore cannot be solved by temporal minimization. Finally, we show that minimization of abnormality may indirectly cause a minimization of safety of a reasoning agent and hence contradict common sense.

Depending on personal philosophy, these examples can be viewed as either supporting the thesis that circumscription fails as a general method for commonsense reasoning, (cf. Hanks and McDermott [1], McDermott [6], McDermott [7]) or justifying work on identifying classes of situations for which a minimization can give the right class of models (cf. Lifschitz [4]). In the latter case, the examples presented in this paper may help in separating these classes of situations.

Methodologies for Intelligent Systems
Z. W. Ras and M. Zemankova, Editors

Note: We assume that the reader has some familiarity with the notions of (Herbrand) model, minimal model and circumscription. But a detailed knowledge of different circumscription techniques is not necessary for understanding of this paper. The only technical results we will use are the semantic characterizations of circumscriptions :

- the theory obtained by circumscribing abnormality using formula circumscription is the set of all sentences true in all *ab*- minimal models
- the models corresponding to pointwise circumscription of the *ab* -predicate are these for which there is no *ab*- smaller model differing in one point.

2. *Non - adequacy of pointwise circumscription*

V.Lifschitz [3] introduced a new version of minimization - the pointwise circumscription - as a conceptually simpler and more flexible form of circumscription. It turns out however that there is a simple class of examples of common sense reasoning that cannot be handled by pointwise circumscription.

Example 1 : TRAVEL

A person is flying to Europe from New York City [1]. Usually, people fly from the JFK airport. And if they don't, they are *abnormal* with respect to flying to Europe.

These general rules are described by the axioms below; the predicate *flies*(P, A, D) expresses the fact that a person P flies from an airport A to a destination D .

F1. $(\forall X, D)$ [$flies(X, JFK, D) \vee flies(X, LGA, D) \vee flies(X, NWK, D)$]

F2. $(\forall X)$ [$\neg flies(X, JFK, Europe) \rightarrow ab(Europe, X)$]

F3. $(\forall X)$ [$flies(X, JFK, Europe) \rightarrow \neg ab(Europe, X)$]

Clearly, if John flies to Europe from NY, any minimization of abnormality yields the correct conclusion that he flies from JFK.

We will see in a moment that the situation changes if a wife and a husband are flying together to Europe.

M1. $(\forall A, D)$ { [$flies(husband, A, D) \Longleftrightarrow flies(wife, A, D)$] $\vee$
$\vee$ [$ab(Europe, wife)$ & $ab(Europe, husband)$] }

The question is: From where do they fly ?

To answer it, we have to consider a family of Herbrand models for F1-F3 + M1 . Their Herbrand bases consist of : *wife, husband ; JFK, LGA , NWK ; Europe.* And we can assume that variables and constants are typed, e.g. *Europe* cannot be substituted for *husband*

[1] there are three major airports in the New York area : J.F. Kennedy (JFK) , LaGuardia(LGA), and Newark (NWK) .

MODELS OF F1-F3 + M1

Models 0 - 4 : Models where they fly from 2 airports at the same time. (The husband and wife are *abnormal*).

Model 5 : JFK

Model 6 : LGA, ab(husband), ab(wife).

Model 7 : NWK, ab(husband), ab(wife).

Note: We write JFK , for *flies(husband,JFK,Europe) & flies(wife,JFK,Europe)* -- similarly for LGA and NWK.

The minimal models include the models 5, 6 and 7 ; the minimality assures that a person flies from one airport only. One can easily check that there is no model in which only one person is abnormal, and therefore 5, 6 and 7 will be among the models chosen by pointwise circumscription. This is so, because it is impossible to switch from models 6 or 7 to 5 by changing only one value of the abnormality predicate, and varying *flies(P,A,D)* . Thus, by pointwise circumscription, one can conclude only that either the husband and wife fly from JFK, or else they fly from an another airport, and they are both abnormal.

Although, as V.Lifschitz pointed out, we *can* obtain the right model by dropping F3 from the list of axioms and deleting the second disjunct of M1, we do not see any fundamental reason for doing it -- F3 explains the meaning of "abnormality with respect to flying to Europe." Neither can the problem be avoided by allowing changes of abnormality in two points, instead of one, because we can have a family consisting of three, four, or *n* persons flying together.

Conclusion : Pointwise circumscription is weaker than the formula circumscription of J.McCarthy [5]. (Notice that the right model -- 5 -- can be obtained by formula circumscription in this case.) Although this *may* help in avoiding certain paradoxes, like the one of Hanks and McDermott [1], it also makes it possible to find examples in which it is *too weak* to express some commonsense minimizations of abnormality.

In general, in cases where two or more facts expressible by the same predicate (with different parameters) normally occur together, and situations are declared abnormal otherwise, pointwise circumscription will yield different results than formula circumscription. And as we've seen, they may be incorrect.

Also, the above example is not unique -- a group of families planning a picnic together will produce another class of similar examples.

3. Interacting abnormalities

We present an example quite similar to the one presented by Hanks and McDermott [1]. However, it has formulation not involving time and so it cannot be solved by minimization according to a temporal order (cf. e.g. Shoham [8], Kautz [2]) ; although, as in the case of their paradox, it is easy to find a solution by pointwise circumscription.

Example 2 : BOOK

Certain common situations can be axiomatized and reasoned about independently of events that caused them. For instance, buying and reading books. The following rules and their translation into logical formulae seem to be intuitively correct (or at least reasonable) :

1. Usually, if somebody has just bought a book, he reads it.
2. Only one person can enjoy a book (at a given moment).
3. Usually, if one has a book one reads it.
4. Usually, when one buys a book one has it.
5. In a family books are common property.

$B1.$ $book(B)$ & $bought(X,B)$ & $\neg ab(reading(B),X) \rightarrow reads(X,B)$

$B2.$ $reads(X,B)$ & $X \neq Y \rightarrow ab(reading(B),Y)$ & $enjoys(X,B)$,
$ab(reading(B),X) \rightarrow \neg enjoys(X,B)$

$B3.$ $has(Y,B)$ & $\neg ab(reading(B),Y) \rightarrow reads(Y,B)$

$B4.$ $bought(X,B)$ & $\neg ab(buying(B),X) \rightarrow has(X,B)$

$B5.$ $same\_family(X,Y)$ & $has(X,B)$ & $\neg ab(family(X,Y),Y) \rightarrow has(Y,B)$

We want to consider a situation in which

S. John bought a book. He and Susan are a family.

$S1.$ $book(b)$

$S2.$ $bought(john, b)$

$S3.$ $same\_family(john,susan)$

ab - MINIMAL MODELS OF B1-B5 + S1-S3

Model 1. This is the intended model -- John is the only reader of the book b . This means $ab(reading(b),susan)$, $reads(john,b)$, *etc.* hold true in it.

Model 2. John bought a book but he is abnormal with respect to reading (for instance, he has lost his glasses) : $ab(reading(b),john)$, $reads(susan,b)$, *etc.*

There are also other models: in the third one, both John and Susan are abnormal. In the fourth model John bought the book but is abnormal with respect to $bought(b)$ and so we cannot deduce he has the book.

Since both models, Model 1 and Model 2, minimize abnormality we have evidence that (formula) circumscription cannot choose the right extension i.e. the first model. In this case we do not have a problem of temporal projection but the problem of abnormalities/defaults that interact with themselves.

Our example suggests that circumscription may be insufficient to solve the qualification problem, in general. Ambiguous default rules may create situations in which problem dependent knowledge has to suggest how abnormalities are to be minimized.

BOOK can be solved by pointwise circumscription, after a reformulation. But how should we know in advance which circumscription would work and what would be the right formulation of axioms describing general rules and a current situation ?

4. *Common sense and the open world assumption*

Example 3 : HIGHWAY

An intelligent robot is driving a car. He approaches a slow moving pick-up truck in front of him. The robot should decide whether to overtake it. It is intuitively plausible to assume the robot should overtake the truck, unless the truck behaves abnormally.

The rules H1-H3 formally describe this situation : [1]

H1. $\neg ab(truck) \rightarrow overtake$

H2. $ab(truck) \rightarrow danger$

H3. $danger \rightarrow \neg overtake$

Of course, it may happen that the truck in front just swerved to the left. The reason for this sinusoidal driving may be that the truck driver is not sober, and hence the situation is not normal and may be dangerous ; but it is also possible that the driver in the truck is changing radio stations or drinking coffee (which means he isn't a first class driver but the situation is not abnormal) , and therefore there is no real danger.

H4. $swerve(truck) \rightarrow ab(truck) \vee radio \vee coffee$

If the truck in front of the robot drives straight, circumscription proves (correctly) that the robot should *overtake* :

The *ab* - **minimal model** of H1- H4 + $\{ \neg swerve(truck) \}$ is

$\{ \neg swerve(truck) , \neg ab(truck) , \neg danger , overtake \}$.

However, any *ab* - **minimal model** of H1-H4 + $\{ swerve(truck) \}$ contains

$\{ swerve(truck) , \neg ab(truck) , \neg danger , overtake \}$.

This model is not an intended one -- the conclusions $\neg danger$, *overtake* certainly do not contribute to the robot's safety; the minimization of abnormality results in the wrong conclusion: "no danger".

The moral of this example is that sometimes common sense requires not minimization of abnormality, but a maximization of another predicate such as safety. But notice that a direct maximization of *danger* would give wrong conclucion when the truck is driving straight. Circumscription, at least for the most obvious formalization, does not work here because it is a form of Closed World Assumption , while minimization of danger seems to require an **Open World Assumption,** i.e. taking into account all reasonable possibilities.

---

[1] Since the problem is whether to overtake or not, we can for the sake of simplicity ignore the temporal component of the situation.

5. Why is it always possible to reformulate a problem ?

The proposition which follows is very elementary, but it gives some explanation why it is always possible to reformulate a problem, like the problem of Hanks and McDermott, or the problems above, in such a way that a circumscription will work correctly on its new version.

Remark. We formulate this proposition only for the finite case, because we believe that it is the only case which matters for common-sense reasoning. [1]

PROPOSITION.

Assume that intended models $IM(T)$ *of a theory* T *are finite, and there are only finitely many of them. Let* **P** *be any finite set of the predicates of* T. *Then there is an extension* $T' \supset T$ *of the theory* T *such that the intended models of* T *are exactly the* **P** *- minimal models of* T'.

Proof.

The proof is elementary: we introduce a number of redundant predicates $A_m(\bar{x})$ whose purpose is to make all the models $IM(T)$ **P** - minimal.

Let $Pred(T)$ is the set of predicates of T , $Cnst(T)$ denote the set of all its constants. Let $\bar{c}$ be the list of all elements of $Cnst(T)$. Let $IM(T) = \{ \mathcal{M}_1, \ldots \mathcal{M}_n \}$. Without loss of generality, we can assume that all elements of $\mathcal{M}_m$, $1 \leq m \leq n$ are members of $Cnst(T)$.

Then $\mathcal{M}_m = \{ \varepsilon^m_{ij} P_i(c_j) : P_i \in Pred(T) \ \& \ c_j \in Cnst(T) \}$, $1 \leq m \leq n$. And each ε^m_{ij} is either the empty string or the negation sign.

Let $A_m(\bar{x})$, $1 \leq m \leq n$, be predicates which do not appear among P_i's . Let $Q_m(\bar{c})$ denote the definition

$$Q_m(\bar{c}) = (A_m(\bar{c}) \Longleftrightarrow \bigwedge_{i,j} \varepsilon^m_{ij} P_i(c_j))$$

Thus $A_m(\bar{c})$ is a predicate describing the elementary diagram of the m-th model, i.e. what what is true in $\mathcal{M}_m$.

$$\text{Let} \quad T' = \bigvee_m Q_m(\bar{c}) \ \& \ A_m(\bar{c})$$

The models of T' are exactly the models $IM(T)$. Moreover, each of these models is **P** - minimal (in fact, minimal for *any* set of predicates of T) : the truth value of $A_m(\bar{c})$'s is not allowed to change in the process of minimization.

□

The proposition shows that any example pointing to an inadequacy of minimization can be fixed. Namely, if the class of ab - minimal models of a theory T does not coincide with the intended models, one can change the theory and obtain the intended models as the minimal ones for the extension. But this seems to support the validity of the critique of circumscription by Hanks and McDermott [1] :

> (...) it can be very hard to characterize the consequences of the circumscription axioms for a reasonably large and complex theory, and when the consequences are understood they may not be what we intended. The upshot is that no one really wants to know what follows from circumscription axioms; they usually wind up as hopefully harmless decoration to the actual theory. (...)

---

[1] The proposition holds also in certain infinite cases but is false for infinite theories with infinite models, in general.

The problem is that the original idea behind circumscription, that a simple, problem independent extension to a first order theory would minimize predicates in just the right way has been lost along the way.

6. Remarks

We think that in order to deal effectively with McDermott's critique (cf. McDermott [6], [7]; Hanks and McDermott [1]) it is necessary to show that there is a class of examples for which a (fixed type of) circumscription is not a "harmless decoration to the actual theory", but always produces expected conclusions.

Circumscription will not always work. But some types of common-sense reasoning do seem to involve minimization of abnormality. The examples presented in this paper may help in describing classes of problems for which different kinds of circumscription do not work. Lifschitz's work [4] shows promise in identifying classes of situations for which a minimization can give a right class of models.

Finally, certain types of common-sense inferences do not use minimization at all, or even seem to incompatible with it. Hence, other techniques are necessary for dealing with them; the theory of default reasoning introduced by this author ([9], [10]) may be a possible alternative.

Acknowledgements. I want to thank Ken McAloon, Vladimir Lifschitz and an anonymous referee for comments which helped me to improve the paper. Of course, the opinions presented here are mine, and so is responsibility for any possible shortcomings.

REFERENCES.

1. S. Hanks and D. McDermott , *Default Reasoning, Nonmonotonic Logics, and the Frame Problem,* Proc. AAAI-86, 1986, pp. 328 - 333.

2. H. Kautz, *The Logic of Persistence,* Proc. AAAI-86, 1986, pp. 401 - 405.

3. V. Lifschitz , *Pointwise Circumscription: Preliminary Report,* Proc. AAAI-86, 1986, pp. 406 - 410.

4. V. Lifschitz , *Formal theories of action* , manuscript, 1987.

5. J. McCarthy , *Applications of Circumscription to Formalization of Common-Sense Knowledge,* AI Journal, 28 , 1986, pp. 89 - 116 .

6. D. McDermott , *AI, Logic, and the Frame Problem,* undated manuscript , 1986?.

7. D. McDermott , *A Critique of Pure Reason,* manuscript , June 24, 1986.

8. Y. Shoham, *Chronological Ignorance: Time,Nonmonotonicity, Necessity and Causal Theories,* Proc. AAAI-86, 1986, pp. 389 - 393.

9. W.Zadrożny, *Intended models, circumscription and commonsense reasoning,* Proc. IJCAI-87, 1987.

10. W.Zadrożny, *A theory of default reasoning,* Proc. AAAI-87, 1987.

Inferring Causality and Cyclic Behavior through Data Flow Analysis

Paul A. Fishwick
University of Florida
Department of Computer and Information Science
Bldg. CSE
Gainesville, FL 32611
CSNET: fishwick@ufl.edu

June 29, 1987

Abstract

Studying the behavior of a process entails utilizing some sort of analytic procedure so that certain facets of the process can be better understood. These facets include oscillation, damping, cyclic behavior, and causal links. In this paper we propose a method predicated on static analysis to determine cyclic and causal attributes for processes defined using production rules. This method is in contrast to the "aggregation" approach which relies on partial simulation to determine such attributes. The proposed analytic method produces information about cyclic and causal behavior by analyzing the structure of the model; control flow is present within the model and becomes "visible" after applying specific data flow methods.

1 Introduction

There has been much recent interest in algorithms which allow for the study and simulation of qualitative behavior. The general area of qualitative physics[5] and qualitative simulation[15] are examples of such work in AI literature. Recently, Weld[19] has discussed his theory of aggregation which has been proposed as a method of reasoning about cyclic behavior. Presumably, such a method can be useful as a part of a qualitative simulation system. We have found certain problems, though, with Weld's approach which we will elucidate in this paper. We will consider another approach which seems more appropriate in many cases but admittedly involves certain tradeoffs with respect to the complexity of analysis.

Recent aggregation research in artificial intelligence is primarily concerned with recognizing and verifying cycles (possibly nested) from sequences of events. Aggregation was mentioned by Rieger and Grinberg[17] and Goldin and Klahr[12] who discuss a method for creating abstractions for low level event graphs. Unfortunately, neither of these approaches was described in sufficient detail. Zeigler[22,21] provides a formalism of aggregation based on morphisms (although cyclic behavior is not specifically addressed). There is also some related work in creating continuous process descriptions from positive examples[2], however, this relates more to matching and learning. Also, there has been a great deal of study in aggregation theory[13] outside of AI. Fishwick[7] discusses model

Methodologies for Intelligent Systems
Z. W. Ras and M. Zemankova, Editors

abstraction which is related, although, the emphasis is on abstraction level traversal (especially during scene animation[9]) rather than the automatic creation of new models or continuous processes. Recently a general theory of process abstraction in simulation modeling has been proposed[8]. Weld[19] has recently espoused his theory of aggregation which involves the creation of a continuous process description from a sequence of events. This event sequence is created by *partially simulating* a model while continually checking for cycles. If we split possible methods for inferring cyclic behavior into three types 1) Complete Simulation, 2) Partial Simulation, and 3) Static Analysis, then Weld's approach is of the second type. These types assume the prior knowledge of a model. This is important to note since the study of attributes such as cyclic behavior involves other distinct possibilities when the underlying behavioral model is either unknown or not considered during analysis. Let's consider some problems with Weld's method and some solutions to be given by our static approach:

- If one has a model and one uses simulation in conjunction with cyclic recognition facilities to determine continuous behavior then a logical question arises: "Why partially simulate the model to determine cyclic behavior when the essence of the cyclic behavior is visible within the model in the first place?" An alternate approach would be to operate directly on the process model to infer such behavior without resorting to simulation. This is the approach taken in this paper.

- Weld has pointed out some inherent problems in aggregation. Many of these problems, such as the inability in recognizing interacting, parallel cycles are rooted in his approach to aggregation. That is, if one already knows the parallel process models then cyclic behavior is best determined through a static analytic method rather than analyzing strictly the results of simulation. The "thorny problem" discussed by Weld that relates to "anticipating interference from other processes" is not really a problem if we assume two conditions: 1) A "closed-world assumption" stating that all processes and methods of interrupts are coded within the model (which includes all assumed endogenous and exogenous variables), and 2) The model is consistent. The assumptions of completeness and consistency in a simulation model are essential to perform analysis and to obtain accurate results. If, indeed, the model is unknown then issues such as "process interference" and process identification do rise to the surface, however, neither aggregation nor the proposed method describe this scenario.

- The choice of the language used to define the model is critical when considering cyclic behavior patterns. Weld uses production systems (subsequently denoted "PS") to define all example models; visibility of control flow is therefore obscured, requiring an analytic method to determine cyclic behavior. In many cases, a model is best designed with control flow made explicit, thereby nullifying proposed extended analytic approaches (such as simulation) since "the answer is already within the design." This point is also germane to studying causal behavior: in many instances, a model should explicitly reflect causal behavior so that further analysis to determine this behavior becomes unnecessary. Causal networks such as the one proposed by Rieger and Grinberg[17] and those defined by Forrester[10,11] are examples of such an approach.

Throughout the paper we will concentrate primarily on the problem of inferring cyclic and continuous behavior for processes. The notion of "causal" inference will be briefly discussed in section 3.

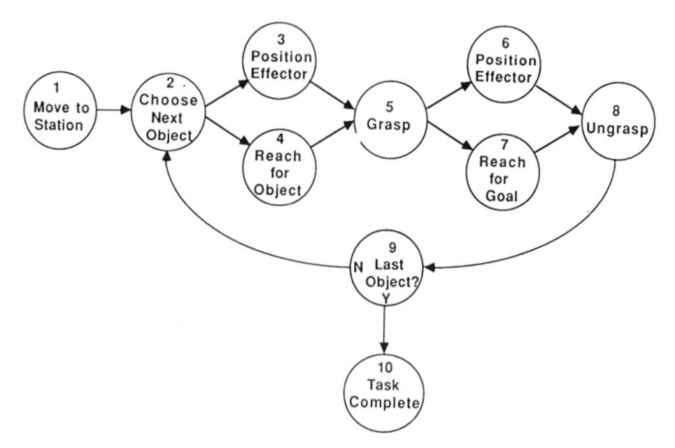

Figure 1: Robot Arm Movement

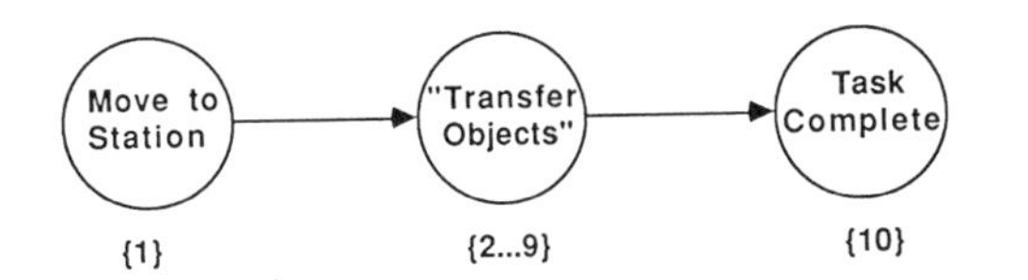

Figure 2: G^2 after Interval Analysis

2 Interval Analysis

We propose using a type of data flow analysis to infer cyclic and causal components of a process. Just as in simulation, we must create different analysis methods depending on the model language used. Let us first examine the situation with a robot arm where we have a model of the robot moving a set of objects from one station to another (see figure 1). The model language is represented by a directed graph. This graph model shows us that the robot achieves its task by positioning the end effector and reaching for the object to be moved (note the partial ordering denoting simultaneity), grasping the object, then re-positioning the effector (for correct placement) and reaching for the goal. The robot then ungrasps the object and continues while other objects exist. We can infer cyclic behavior using many graph techniques, but we choose *interval analysis* (which has been widely used during code optimization[1]) since this type of analysis provides us with an abstraction of the robot behavior in addition to locating cycles. Interval analysis yields maximal, single entry subgraphs. For figure 1 we obtain three intervals, $I(1) = \{1\}, I(2) = \{2..9\}$, and $I(3) = \{10\}$. This new graph, denoted G^2 is shown in figure 2. In general, one can use the interval method for deriving multiple abstractions $(G^2, G^3, ..., G^i)$ for any process representable as a simple, directed graph (G^1). It is also straightforward to modify the algorithm to create more abstractions based on partial ordering or some other graph feature. A cursory examination of this approach yields the following information:

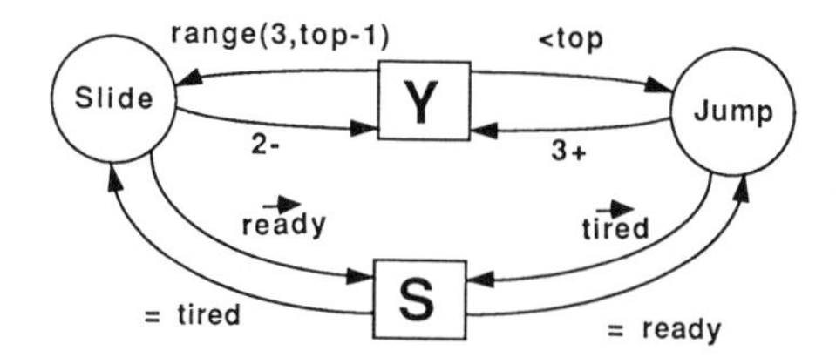

Figure 3: Initial Graph for "Frog" System

- Advantage: the approach permits a machine to reason-about or infer cyclic behavior. In addition, abstractions, which are amenable to describing qualitative behavior, are easily derived using traditional graph methods.
- Disadvantage: the model language is too simple. In most cases, we will want to build highly complex models that require more complicated model languages. The problem of inferring cyclic behavior becomes more difficult as we start adding more semantics (variable assignments, functions) to the model.

3 A Method for Analyzing PS's

PS's[16] can be quite complex since they have the computational expressiveness of a Turing machine, however, it is possible to develop methods for analyzing PS behavior (in specific, cyclic behavior) by using some basic steps which will be outlined in this section. Davis and King[6] give an overall survey of PS's and discuss the "opacity" associated with the visibility of control flow. Let us consider an example PS (similar to Weld's[19]) given as follows:

Discrete Process: **Jump**
Preconditions: $frog.height < top \wedge frog.state = ready.$
Changes: Increment $frog.height$ by 3 $\wedge$ set $frog.state = tired.$

Discrete Process: **Slide**
Preconditions: $2 < frog.height < top \wedge frog.state = tired.$
Changes: Decrement $frog.height$ by 2 $\wedge$ set $frog.state = ready.$

The example is simple, yet descriptive enough to illustrate the inference of cyclic behavior. Imagine that we have a frog which is climbing up a slippery well. The frog jumps forward in an effort to escape the well but then slides back down. For purposes of brevity, we will denote the variables $frog.height$ and $frog.state$ as Y and S, respectively. We note that any PS consisting of variable assignments, functions, and predicates can be represented as a bipartite graph as displayed in figure 3. Arcs from variables to rules represent predicates (i.e. preconditions) and arcs from rules to variables represent

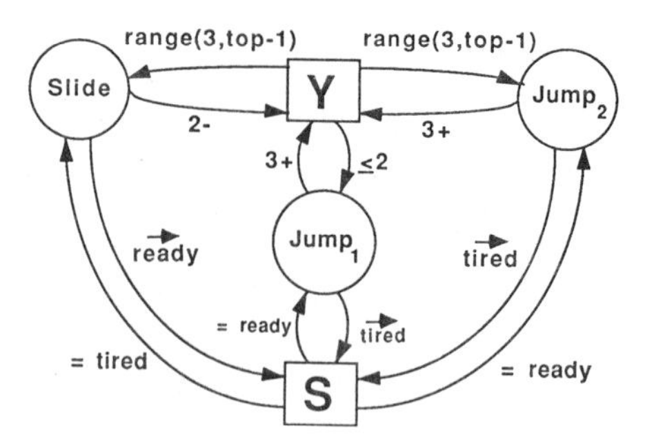

Figure 4: Graph after Predicate Partitioning

functions. The "predicates" are actually sets that are created when applying predicate definitions to the variable. For example the forms $Y < 2$ and $Y \in \{-\infty..1\}$ are identical. Functions are represented in postfix form if they involve simple algebraic manipulation. For example, $2-$ on an arc pointing to Y means $Y \leftarrow Y - 2$. "$\rightarrow$ *tired*" means to set the corresponding variable to *tired*. We will start with this graph and proceed to describe the analysis procedure informally as the example is explained. In the next section, we formalize the algorithm for general PS's. The first item to note in figure 3 is the dependence of the two rules, *Slide* and *Jump*, on the two variables, Y and S. The graph representation visually illustrates this dependency whereas the set of production rules, due to its emphasis on modularity, hides this dependency. We choose to partition the predicates on each variable by adding new production rules where appropriate. Partitioning is based on creating new rules where ranges overlap. In the example, $Y < top$ and $2 < Y < top$ overlap. We can create two partitions, $Y \leq 2$ and $2 < Y < top$ (denoted $range(3, top - 1)$ in the graph). The reason for partitioning is that we can better understand the control flow within the PS if all of the production rules contain non-overlapping predicates within the preconditions. This process will cause in increase in the number of productions some of which have ranges either exactly equal to or distinct from other productions. We now have two productions $Jump_1$ and $Jump_2$ that replace *Jump*. This process yields a new graph as seen in figure 4.

A loop between a given rule and variable forms a basis for studying and representing continuous behavior in the form of a *while loop*. For instance, if we note the loop between Y and $Jump_1$, this can be represented by the expression *while* $Y \leq 2$ *do* $Y \leftarrow Y + 3$. A *while* is reduced to a simple *if* when the predicate is "equals." We are still unsure of the synchronization and ordering associated with executing these loops. This will soon be discussed. Still considering the graph in figure 4, we note the interesting arc connections to variable S. We see that rule *Slide* "enables" rules $Jump_1$ and $Jump_2$ since *Slide* asserts as a postcondition the exact preconditions needed by $Jump_1$ and $Jump_2$ to fire. A rule can also "disable" another rule if the first rule assigns a value to the variable that can never be satisfied as a precondition to the second rule. In addition $Jump_1$ and $Jump_2$ enable *Slide*. When two rules such as *Slide* and $Jump_1$ enable each other then we call this a *synchronization ring* of size 2. This type of synchronization is extremely common

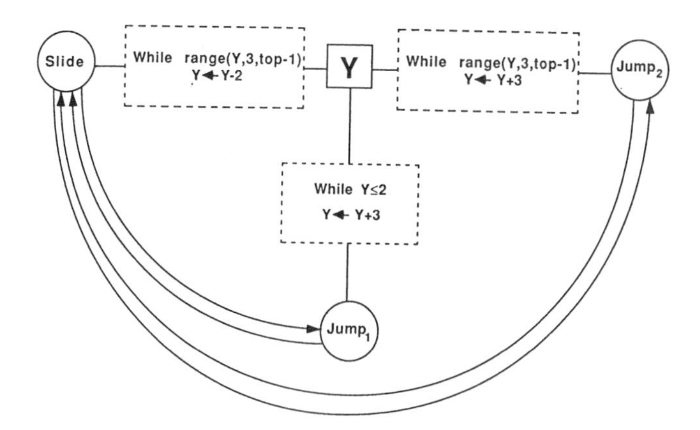

Figure 5: After Applying $\mathcal{G}$

in PS's and serves to orchestrate rule firings using a specified order. Rings of arbitrary sizes involving several rules are also possible. As a direct result of abstracting while loops and denoting "enables" (which are represented as arcs from one rule to another), we arrive at figure 5. In essence, the abstraction of loops can be described using a graph grammar $\mathcal{G}$ (which will be discussed).

We can view "$Rule_1$ enables $Rule_2$" to mean either "$Rule_1$ causes $Rule_2$" or "$Rule_1$ occurs before $Rule_2$." Rule disabling can have a similar meaning with respect to a kind of "negative causation/sequencing" (or "$Rule_1$ causes $Rule_2$ not to happen"). The exact meaning of "causality" has been widely presented in the literature[20,18,4] and discussions of causal graphs with feedback have prompted debates within AI literature[14]. It seems reasonable to eventually be able to infer connections such as "jump causes slide" and "slide causes jump." Given a set of productions and little additional semantic information, it is difficult to assign the correct meaning to "enable" — should it be interpreted as as a sequence link or causal link? Production rules by their very notation suggest directional associations (i.e. forward chaining) during simulation and so causal interpretation is somewhat easier than if our model language was a system of equations or constraints. We can often use a causal interpretation unless specific variables forcing time sequencing are used; the enable links used in the two examples within this paper can be interpreted as causal. An example of a non-causal link would usually involve a variable called $TIME$, for instance, which would be used by rules to enforce synchronicity. At this point; however, with figure 5 we need to continue with analysis before we can infer causality or the exact nature of the cyclic behavior in the PS.

At this point, we use the synchronization and behavioral information within figure 5 and use two more procedures: 1) grouping according to synchronization and, 2) predicate ordering. In the graph, we consider a given variable and look to see whether that variable is connected to synchronized rules. If this is the case then we compound looping constructs together between the rules. Then we order the compounds with respect to the predicates. If these two items are performed then we arrive at figure 6. Note that $Jump_1$ is on top of the graph due to the ordering ($Y \leq 2$ comes first). When predicates are equal (within the while loop), then we combine the bodies of the loops together to form a single while loop. We can perform this operation since the while loops within the

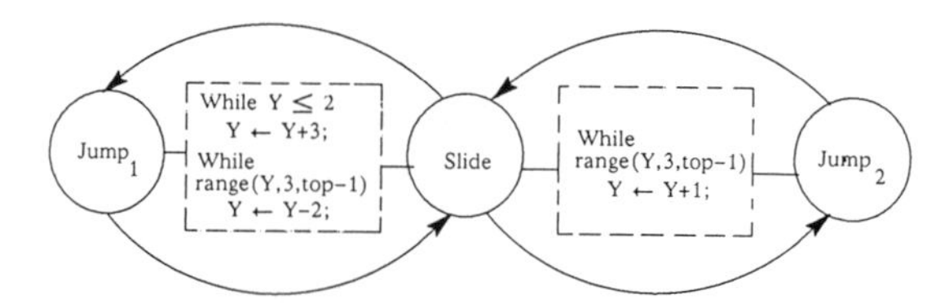

Figure 6: After Ordering and Compounding

compound expression contain loops which execute alternately (since they are synchronized). This means that the compound between rules *Slide* and $Jump_2$ can be reduced to *while* $range(Y, 3, top - 1)$ *do begin* $Y \leftarrow Y - 2$; $Y \leftarrow Y + 3$ *end* which can further be reduced by substitution to *while* $range(Y, 3, top - 1)$ *do* $Y \leftarrow (Y + 3) - 2$ and finally *while* $range(Y, 3, top - 1)$ *do* $Y \leftarrow Y + 1$. If we assume that $Y = 0$ initially (i.e. the frog is at the base of the well) then we see either through analysis or via simulation of the two synchronized rules ($Jump_1$ and *Slide*) that $Jump_1$ will occur exactly three times (for $Y \in \{0, 1, 2\}$). A compound is active only as long as preconditions are satisfied during the rule synchronization. When $Y = 5$, Y takes on the value 3 after executing $Y \leftarrow Y - 2$. But then $Y = 3$ does not satisfy the precondition $Y \leq 2$ causing the compound to become inactive. Control is subsequently passed to *Slide* which will cycle with $Jump_2$ until $Y = top$. $Y \leftarrow Y + 1$ is a linear difference equation whose general form is $y_k = Ay_{k-1} + B$. Substituting 1 for A and B yields the simple equation whose solution is N where N is the number of loop iterations (note: without a termination the solution would clearly diverge to $+\infty$). We were able to reason that $Jump_1$ was never re-activated since Y is monotonically increasing (in fact, linear) after *Slide* is enabled.

4 PS Analysis

We will outline the algorithm used in the previous section and then discuss some its features.

1. *Begin with PS model of behavior. Call it P.*

2. *Create P' from P by adding new productions whenever predicates in precondition slots overlap in range. For instance, the predicates* $0 < X < 6$ *and* $3 < X < 12$ *overlap. We would create new rules using* $0 < X \leq 3$, $3 < X < 6$, *and* $6 \leq X < 12$ *as new precondition elements since they define X using partitions. This procedure produces a total ordering of predicates (with the exception of those predicate ranges that are identical).*

3. *Use graph grammar* $\mathcal{G}$ *to infer "enables," "disables," and continuous behavior. The grammar is defined by the rules in figure 7.*

4. *Perform Limit and Ordering Analysis.*

   (a) *If a synchronization ring exists consisting of the rules* $R_1, R_2, ..., R_n$ *then compound continuous expressions together to form a single behavior for each variable.*

Enable Rule

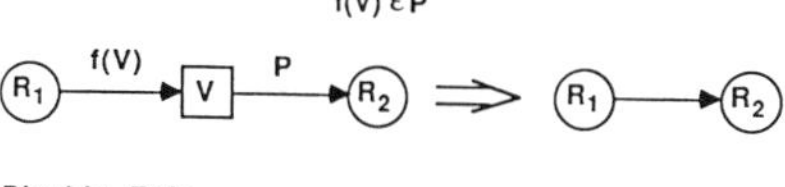

Disable Rule

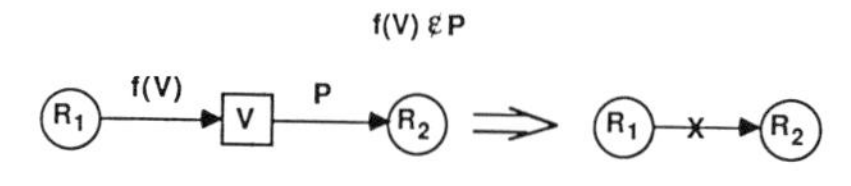

Compound Rule

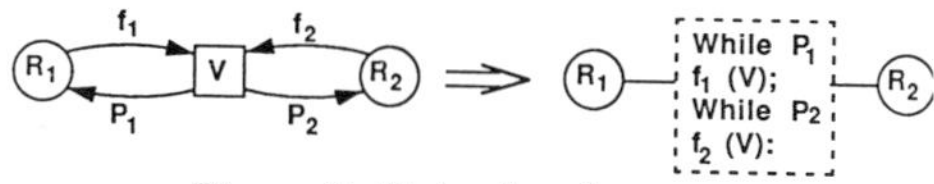

Figure 7: Rules for $\mathcal{G}$

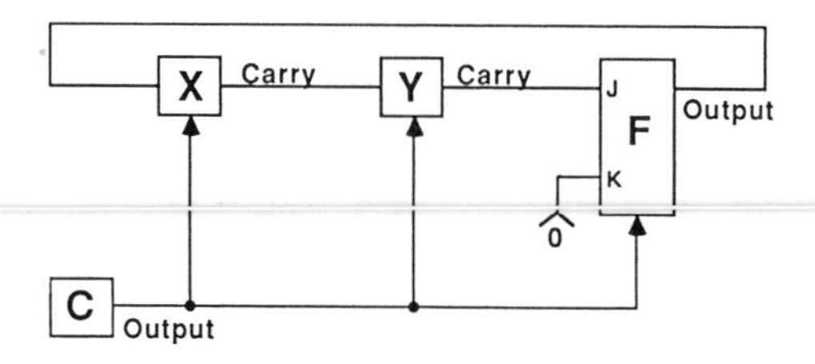

Figure 8: Decade Counters

(b) *Order compound expressions (developed in part 4a) by predicate. Limit Analysis is done using difference calculus and traditional concepts in limit theory. Ordering can use a sorting procedure for each variable's range endpoints since the predicates are totally ordered.*

5 Decade Counters: A Second Example

To illustrate the capability of inferring *nested* cyclic behavior, we choose another of Weld's examples[19]. The system is composed of two decade counters connected in sequence. The design is depicted in figure 8. The effect of the system is to count from 0 to 99. Note that the variables *X.mem* and *Y.mem* contain the single digit values for registers X and Y respectively. Figure 9 shows the bipartite graph representing the PS. Figure 10 shows the graph after the loops have been compounded. Limit analysis demonstrates that the loops between rules $Count_x$ — $Carry_x$ and $Count_y$ — $Carry_y$ count from 0 to 9. The important feature is the group of "nested" cycles inherent within the graph in figure 10. We can see the three individual loops clearly: 1) the clock loop, 2) the $Count_x$ — $Carry_x$ loop, and 3) the $Count_y$ — $Carry_y$ loop. The disable arcs provide the nested synchronization; otherwise loops 2 and 3 would execute concurrently. Because $Count_x$

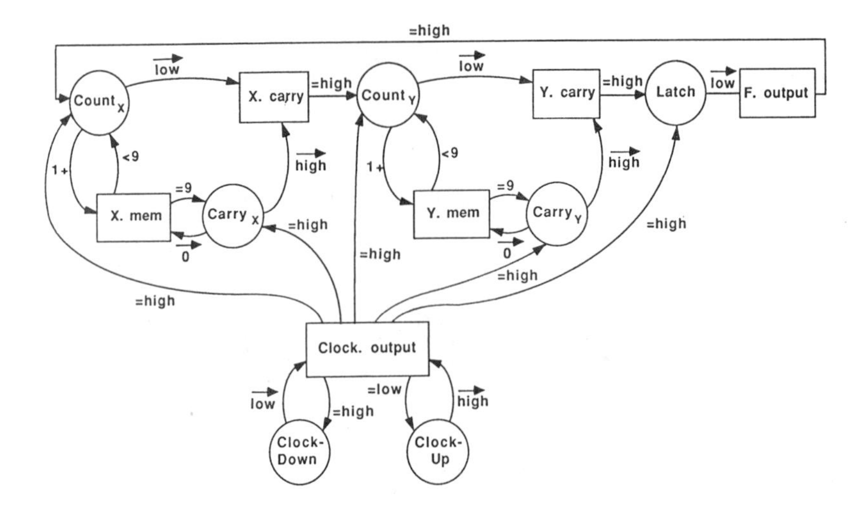

Figure 9: Initial Graph for Decade Counters

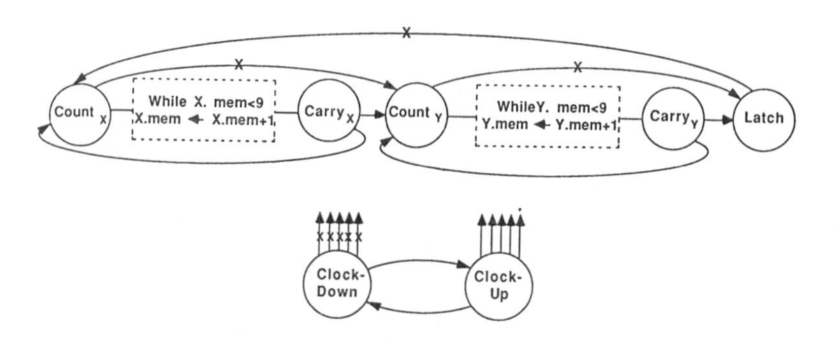

Figure 10: Final Graph after Analysis

disables $Count_y$ and then $Count_y$ is re-enabled only after $Carry_x$, we see that loop 2 counts from 0 to 9 for every single iteration of loop 3. The arcs from the clock loop have not been drawn so as not to overcomplicate the picture. $Clock - Up$ enables the five rules ($Count_x$,$Carry_x$,$Count_y$,$Carry_y$, and *Latch*) and $Clock - Down$ disables the rules. This knowledge could have easily allowed us to eliminate the clock from the final graph (or "abstract it away") since 1) $Clock - Up$ enables all rules, and 2) $Clock - Up$ is in a closed loop. This information could be added to $\mathcal{G}$ in figure 7.

6 Discussion of the Static Approach

It could be argued that the introduction of this more complex example causes problems for the analytic method in the form of odd graph searching techniques. We should note, however, that the "form" of the nested cycle will be the same for all PS's: parallel cycles synchronized with disable arcs. The clock has added some complexity to the situation. There are two ways of dealing with this: 1) allow the analysis procedure to contain domain dependent knowledge about special cycles such as "clocks," and 2) add new graph grammar rules to reduce complexity and form an abstraction.

An essential question with this example is "Is a PS the most appropriate model language for designs?" With the frog PS, the modular PS approach seems to make sense since we might wish to add separate behaviors for each object in the system (the frog being one such object). On the other hand, the cascaded decade counters example is more of a design situation — we know exactly how we want the system to behave in terms of nested loops; we aren't constructing a model to study some unknown behavior. It is most likely that a circuit designer would start with a model which explicitly specifies the nested cyclic behavior. So, why are we trying to infer this knowledge?

Some of the problems with the approach in this paper can be compared with analog problems between analytic and numerical approaches in differential and integral calculus. An additional analogy can be used when considering differences between dialectic and algorithmic approaches in mathematics. The approach in this paper is fundamentally analytic. Analytic approaches for integration problems, for instance, necessarily involve specifying many rules — one must constantly carry around a bag of tricks ("by parts", substitution, transforms, etc.) whereas numerical methods can be far more generally applicable (requiring less specialized rules and procedures). Likewise, the use of simulation can be widely applicable based on a wide variety of models. Each model type may require some slight modifications to the simulation methodology adopted. It appears that simple models, in general, are more amenable to basic analytic methods and that complex models are better suited to extended analysis (such as simulation). Since there are so many methods of analysis available it is often difficult to decide on which to choose. We feel that the best procedure when solving a problem (in which it is desired to infer or induct cycles) is to start with the specific application domain and only then, through optimization, decide on the most appropriate analysis procedure(s). If we consider a model based on a set of equations (instead of a PS) we might, for instance, choose the analytic method of *comparative statics* discussed by Iwasaki and Simon[14].

7 Conclusions

Clearly, the method described for inferring causal and cyclic behavior in a PS falls short of providing a complete solution to the general problem of inferring these behaviors given any PS model. If the model is inordinately complex then it is probable that the analytic method described in the paper will not be appropriate. With extremely complex models it may be best to perform traditional discrete or continuous simulation so that the behavior of the overall system can be better comprehended. The PS examples that we have considered have dealt with linear behavior in terms of a variable's value change over time; non-linear behavior would be very difficult to analyze without resorting to complete simulation.

It is possible that Weld's aggregation approach may succeed where the static analytic approach will fail although we have some reservations about this postulation. Specifically, aggregation has the potential to succeed in cases where an extremely complex model exhibits relatively simple patterns of nested cycles. This is not often the case in real life models, though, since very complex models usually exhibit complex behavior patterns[1]. Models involving stochastic inputs and other forms of non-determinism are best analyzed using full-fledged continuous or discrete simulation. Then the standard analytic methods can be carried out after the model is simulated for a specified time duration. Certain problems with aggregation, such as the inability to work with interfering processes and parallel processes (in general) are a direct result of not using all of the information already provided in the model — this is a benefit of using static analysis.

It is important to note that the general study of cyclic behavior has been long studied, especially where there is no underlying model. Some example methodologies are *inductive inference*[3], time series analysis, and Fourier analysis in particular. Most real world phenomena can only be modelled with the more traditional analytic techniques such as the Fourier transform especially when noise is considered. Other methods such as the one described in this paper or the aggregation method are still useful when analyzing discrete (or qualitative) modeling methods, however, we should recognize their limitations when applying them to complex domains. It may be useful to mix techniques where appropriate to solve a specific problem.

The analytic method contributed within this paper is appropriate for PS's. Since the PS model is widely used within control mechanisms indicative of many AI implementations, we feel that this method is important for the automatic analysis of PS-based models. The method is to be viewed, not as a replacement to traditional simulation, but rather as an auxiliary tool which can be used on PS's that incorporate arithmetic rules (such as those that define dynamic systems). Similar static methods for detecting cyclic behavior should be studied for other knowledge representation techniques (aside from the PS model). We should also keep in mind, as discussed at the beginning of the paper, that one should consider the appropriate model representation language carefully prior to actual analysis. The right model language can make analysis much easier — in terms of detecting cyclic behavior, graph based models tend to make the cycles more "visible" to the analysis. An implementation of the defined graph analysis method is under consideration and we hope to learn more about ways in which to effectively combine analytic and simulation techniques in the study of PS-based models.

References

[1] F. E. Allen and J. Cocke. A program data flow analysis. *Communications of the ACM*, 19(3):137 - 147, 1976.

[1]Although the converse of this statement is not true — consider some behaviors generated through recursive enumeration

[2] Peter M. Andreae. Constraint limited generalization: acquiring procedures from examples. In *Fourth National Conference on Artificial Intelligence*, pages 6–10, AAAI, 1984.

[3] Dana Angluin and Carl H. Smith. Inductive inference: theory and methods. *Computing Surveys*, 15(3):237 – 269, September 1983.

[4] H. M. Blalock. *Causal Models in the Social Sciences.* Aldine Publishing Co., 1971.

[5] Daniel G. Bobrow. *Qualitative Reasoning about Physical Systems.* MIT Press, 1985.

[6] R. Davis and J. King. An overview of production systems. *Machine Intelligence*, 8, 1977.

[7] Paul A. Fishwick. *Hierarchical Reasoning: Simulating Complex Processes over Multiple Levels of Abstraction.* Technical Report, University of Pennsylvania, 1986. Ph.D. Dissertation.

[8] Paul A. Fishwick. The role of process abstraction in simulation. IEEE Transactions on Systems, Man and Cybernetics. (status: submitted revised draft).

[9] Paul A. Fishwick and Norman I. Badler. Animation using multi-level process abstraction. IEEE Computer Graphics and Applications. (in preparation).

[10] J. W. Forrester. *Industrial Dynamics.* MIT Press, 1961.

[11] J. W. Forrester. *World Dynamics.* Wright-Allen Press, 1971.

[12] Sarah E. Goldin and Philip Klahr. Learning and abstraction in simulation. In *Seventh International Joint Conference on Artificial Intelligence*, pages 212 – 214, IJCAI, August 1981.

[13] Yuji Ijiri. Fundamental queries in aggregation theory. *Journal of the American Statistical Association*, 66(336), December 1971.

[14] Yumi Iwasaki and Herbert A. Simon. Causality in device behavior. *Artificial Intelligence*, 29(1):3 – 32, July 1986.

[15] Benjamin Kuipers. Qualitative simulation. *Artificial Intelligence*, 29(3):289 – 338, September 1986.

[16] E. Post. Formal reductions of the general combinatorial problem. *American Journal of Mathematics*, 65:197 – 268, 1943.

[17] Chuck Rieger and Milt Grinberg. The declarative representation and procedural simulation of causality in physical mechanisms. In *Fifth International Joint Conference on Artificial Intelligence*, pages 250 – 256, IJCAI, August 1977.

[18] Herbert A. Simon. On the definition of the causal relation. *Journal of Philosophy*, 44(16):517 – 528, 1952.

[19] Daniel S. Weld. The use of aggregation in causal simulation. *Artificial Intelligence*, 30(1):1 – 34, October 1986.

[20] Sewall Wright. Correlation and causation. *Journal of Agricultural Research*, 20(7), 1921.

[21] Bernard P. Zeigler. *Multi-Facetted Modelling and Discrete Event Simulation*. Academic Press, 1984.

[22] Bernard P. Zeigler. *Theory of Modelling and Simulation*. John Wiley and Sons, 1976.

HUMAN-COMPUTER INTERACTION IN THE GAME OF GO

ANDERS KIERULF
Dept. of Computer Science,
University of North Carolina, Chapel Hill, NC 27514

ABSTRACT

The conventional goal in designing an intelligent system is to let it perform a complex task by itself. If this task is not well understood, the following interactive approach may be advantageous:

1. Design a tool to support human experts in those subtasks suited for computers.
2. Analyze the task by investigating the interaction between human and computer.
3. Iterate these steps by letting the computer take over more and more functions.

The endgame phase in the game of Go is presented as a case-study for this approach.

GAMES OF STRATEGY AND ARTIFICIAL INTELLIGENCE

Games of strategy are good proving grounds for artificial intelligence (AI) techniques: they are simple enough to be completely formalized, complex enough to provide good models for AI problems, and expert knowledge is readily available. An important advantage over real-world problems is that progress can be measured accurately by exhibiting and comparing playing skill.

Research in computer chess has brought us insights that are relevant to other areas of computer science:

- The history of overly optimistic and pessimistic predictions about the strength of chess programs shows that the only way to find out what can really be done in an unexplored field is to do it.
- The unexpected success of programs using brute-force search and special-purpose hardware, as opposed to domain-specific knowledge, is a guideline for other applications.

In view of these results, the effort invested in computer chess has not been wasted. These spin-offs are more important than direct results, such as commercially available chess computers.

Chess is often described as the "drosophila" of artificial intelligence. This assessment may be exaggerated: chess has advanced the state of the art in heuristic search, but has had little direct effect on other parts of AI. I think the oriental game of Go [1] has a chance to make a broader contribution. Goals, plans, patterns, search, coordination, and perception are both important aspects of Go strategy and important topics in AI.

Methodologies for Intelligent Systems
Z. W. Ras and M. Zemankova, Editors

COMPUTER GO

In marked contrast to chess, where programs have achieved expert and master ratings, the best Go programs play only slightly better than human beginners. I see two reasons why brute-force search, which worked so well in chess, cannot by itself lead to a strong Go-playing program:

- Branching factor: Due to the large board (19*19), there is an average of two hundred legal moves each turn, which makes it impossible to examine all legal moves for more than a few plies ahead. Compared to about forty legal moves in chess, this seriously reduces the depth of the search tree. This cannot lead to good play, because experienced Go players look about equally far ahead as experienced chess players.
- Evaluation function: Material is a dominating factor in chess evaluation functions, and is easy to compute. In Go, possession of territory is the closest equivalent to material possession in chess, but its evaluation is much more subtle: except at the very end of the game, a player's claim to territory can always be challenged.

On the other hand, the Go board can be divided into tactically independent scenes of action, where many moves have only local consequences and no global side effects. But this division is a difficult strategic problem not amenable to brute force.

The era of computer Go started with the dissertations of Zobrist [2, 3] and Ryder [4, 5]. Both programs played the whole game, but at a level worse than beginners play after just a few games. Zobrist relied on pattern recognition, Ryder on tree search. Both approaches captured part of what Go is about, but were bound to fail. Human players use pattern recognition to a large extent, but their patterns are more complex and abstract than those used by Zobrist. Neither is pure tree search good enough: without a goal to focus the search, the branching factor is far too high. A combination of the two approaches is necessary: patterns may suggest good moves, but look-ahead is necessary to verify the consequences.

The Reitman-Wilcox program was a large step forward [6]. It was based on an internal representation of the Go board that reflected the way good human players perceive the board. They concentrated on strategy; some tactical analysis was included late in the project. Their approach to model human perception is promising, but even so the program has only reached the level of a novice player. Bruce Wilcox analyzed the strong and weak points of his first program, then rewrote it from scratch [7].

A strong Go-playing program was one goal of the Japanese "Fifth Generation" project; this was later dropped as too hard.

My conclusion is that we don't know enough yet to write a good Go-playing program. When the goal is to play the whole game, effort is spread to thinly: as yet there is not a single aspect of the game where computers can claim to be experts. This is understandable for strategy, which requires an overview of the whole board, but tactical calculation seems to be more suited to computers: it should be possible to solve many tactical problems with selective search, or with brute-force search limited to some small area of the board.

Strategy and tactics depend on each other: long-range strategic plans often depend on tactical details - tactical look-ahead depends on strategic information to determine boundary conditions and to decide which goals are important. For example, to escape with a stone is only a good idea if that stone has an important function, such as cutting apart two weak groups that can be attacked later. Go-playing programs tend to mix up the issue of choosing a worthy goal, a strategic problem, with the task of solving a well-defined tactical problem.

Strategy in the game of Go might be a good research paradigm for AI, but as yet the foundation (tactics) is missing. Strategic plans are worthless when they rely on tactical blunders. To be able to invest effort where AI research is profitable, it is important first to identify the tasks that can be solved by well-known "dumb" methods.

INTERACTIVE APPROACH

The Smart Go Board [8] is designed to explore isolated tasks in the game of Go. Instead of letting the computer play the whole game, we use it to support a human player much the same way a pocket calculator supports an engineer: the engineer knows what he wants to compute, but leaves the actual calculation to the calculator - the Go player knows what he wants to achieve, but leaves the actual lookahead to the Go calculator.

This interactive approach allows us to leave strategy to the human player, and fully concentrate on solving independent tactical problems. Our results should be a useful foundation for a later implementation of a full Go-playing program.

For example, the program knows how capture stones in ladders and loose ladders; it has no idea whether it would make sense to capture those stones. But given a specific block of stones to capture and a method of how to capture them, selective search works well. The Smart Go Board solves some difficult loose ladders by looking 25 moves ahead, generating only two hundred nodes.

We believe this approach can be fruitfully applied to other problems that are not well understood. It is akin to prototyping in that the system built so far is used to find out more about the problem:

- Design a framework to support human experts (e.g. an electronic Go board to play, replay, and document game trees), and program the tasks that are easy for computers (keep track of the score, opening library).
- Analyze the remaining problems and find something the computer can do by using well-known methods. Program that task so well that using this tool improves the performance of the expert. Treat the expert as an important resource, e.g. to handle exceptions, and to supply boundary conditions which may help the program.
- Investigate the interaction between human expert and program. Find out what parameters are relevant, under what circumstances the tool is used, and how its results are applied.
- Iterate these steps, and integrate the tools into larger units.

The tasks which after a while are still left to the human expert are exactly those tasks where human expertise plays an important role, and for which knowledge-based methods will probably be most appropriate.

This method is not new, but is is seldom chosen deliberately. For example, automatic translation seems to have gone that way after first attempts failed.

ADVANTAGES

If the specification of a program is known in advance, it is obviously simpler to write a batch program than an interactive program: a good user interface takes a substantial amount of work. However, for new problems, finding out what the program can and should do is the hardest part. My experience is that the small-grained interactive method outlined above is effective in identifying goals that are worthwhile and achievable.

The interactive approach has other advantages:

- At each stage of the project there is a useful product. (In fact, a tool to support Go players may prove to be more useful than an eventual Go-playing program.)
- Dependent tasks can be attacked independently. The user decides which results to use as input for other tools. (In a Go-tool, the expert selects the goal and defines boundary conditions, the computer solves a limited, well-defined problem. In a Go-playing program, both tasks must be programmed and coordinated.)
- The tool is useful for debugging, because the state of the computation must be shown to the expert.

THE ENDGAME IN GO

I have used the above approach to investigate the endgame in Go. The endgame starts when the black and white territories are defined in outline, but the boundaries are still flexible. Depending on who gets to play first in a local area, the boundaries can be moved a few points to either side. Under some assumptions, moves have only local consequences, and the territory in each local area can be counted precisely.

Despite all these nice properties, computer programs play a horrible endgame. Two factors make the endgame difficult:

- Coordination: Local move sequences in different parts of the board must be coordinated. The local areas form a partially ordered set, which means that some elements cannot be compared: it is often not possible to say whether it is worth more to play in area A than in area B without taking all other local areas into account. In addition, the optimal local move need not be optimal in the overall game.
- Tactics: Correct endgame play depends on the solution of other tactical problems. For example, it is important to know whether a stone can be captured or not: protecting a stone costs a move, and the opponent gets to play first in some other local area. Also, forcing moves that threaten the life of a group of stones are important to recognize.

The partial endgame below illustrates these problems [9]. There are three places where there are still points to be made, at 'a', 'b', and 'c'. The optimal sequence starts with Black 'c', which forces White to play 'd', followed by Black 'b'.

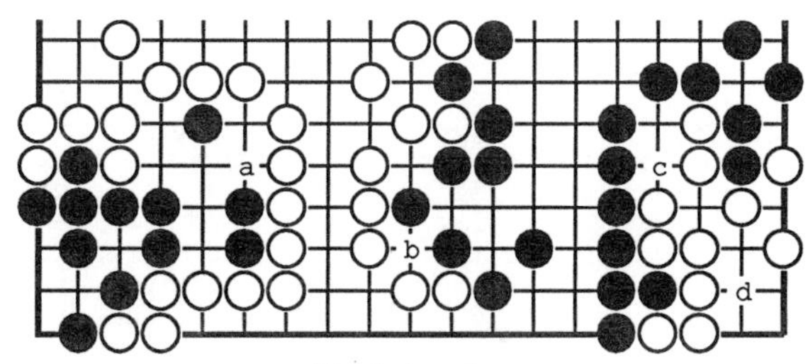

Black to play

Each of the areas illustrates a different aspect:

Brute force: The area around 'a' is completely surrounded by stable black and white stones, which means that brute-force search limited to that area is a simple way to find all possible moves. This tree can be reduced by throwing out the sequences that cannot be optimal in the overall game.

Standard pattern: Assuming White got to play 'b', we get a standard position with one open line along the edge of the board. If Black plays first, Black can push a bit into White's territory with 1, White protects and threatens to capture Black's stone with 2, and Black connects with 3. If White plays first, White gets to push a bit into Black's territory. In the first case, Black has control over (enclosed or occupied) eleven points, in the second only nine - a difference of two points depending on who plays first.

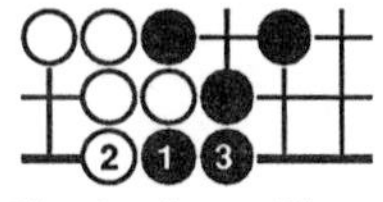

Black plays first

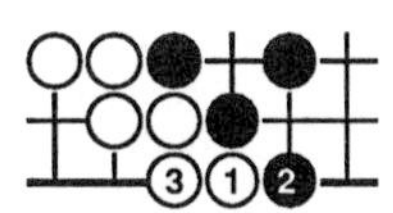

White plays first

In some situations, it is too dangerous to answer White 1 with Black 2. Thus either the pattern must be defined very precisely, or it must be augmented by look-ahead.

Forcing moves: The situation in the corner is such that Black 'c' forces White to defend at 'd' in order to save his corner. However, this is forcing only because White doesn't have an equally threatening move - if he had, he might gain a few points by playing it before coming back to defend, and settle on an exchange if Black decides to capture the corner.

COMPUTERIZING THE ENDGAME

Finding out which moves to consider in the endgame is a difficult problem: as shown above, different methods can be used to generate the moves, and one has to know the black and white territories, a problem which requires look-ahead to decide the life-and-death status of groups. Thus I decided to leave this task to the human player, and let him specify the local area involved and a small move tree with all relevant moves for both players.

With these messy problems out of the way, it proved relatively easy to count local areas exactly, and assign a value to each terminal node in the local move trees (assuming there are no more points to be contested in the local area, so each point is controlled by either Black or White).

Human players use various heuristics to find out in which area to play next. Because my goal is to create a tool and not to mimic human play, I don't want to use those inaccurate heuristics to tell the players something they already know. Instead, I take advantage of the strength of computers (fast and accurate calculation) to calculate precisely as far back to the midgame as possible: brute force is a simple method to coordinate local areas in an optimal way. It is computationally less expensive than I expected: for the problem above with three areas and local move trees with a total of 100 nodes, finding the overall optimal sequence takes 5900 nodes. Techniques such as forward pruning when one local area completely dominates another (that is, even in the worst case there is more to gain in one area than in the best case in another area), and hashing to detect repeated positions, reduce the tree to 970 nodes. Note that this method assumes that the local move trees are small and contain only reasonable moves, otherwise the combinatorial explosion would be much too fast.

Solving this central task of finding the optimal overall move sequence has given me a framework in which future research and solutions to other tactical problems can be integrated:

- Trade-offs: Once the limit of brute force is explored, I can use heuristics to gain speed at the expense of precision.
- Find endgame moves: Both pattern recognition and brute force can be used to generate the local move trees now supplied by the expert.
- Relax assumptions: Local areas are currently assumed to be independent. This is not always the case: playing in one area may affect whether a block of stones in another area can be captured.
- Forcing moves: A life-and-death calculator will help the human player find out whether groups of stones are alive or can be captured. This tool will help him most in the midgame, but results from those calculations can be used to find forcing moves in the endgame.

Like in chess, the endgame of Go offers many of the same problems as other phases of the game, but in a simplified setting. For example, coordinating different scenes of action is important throughout the game, and the method of first finding a tree of moves for each scene and then using brute force to combine them may prove useful, albeit with approximate rather than exact counting.

Ko fights are another problem that is best explored in an endgame context, and which Go programs don't know how to handle. Ko is a local situation where a stone can be taken endlessly back and forth. Because the rules of Go forbid repetition of the same overall position, if both players think it's important to gain that stone (e.g. to connect a group out to safety), there will be a ko fight: a player makes a threat elsewhere, and if the opponent answers, he is allowed to take back the ko. Deciding when to stop playing the ko depends one how much there is to gain or lose, and the size and number of ko threats of both players. The advantage of exploring ko fights in the endgame is that a precise numerical value can be assigned to each threat.

CONCLUSIONS

The approach of initially leaving some tasks to the expert in order to investigate them has given me valuable insights and led to an interesting program. The Smart Go Board, running on the Apple Macintosh™, helps human players with tactical analysis: it solves some problems quite well by itself (e.g. loose ladder captures) or with some human input (e.g. endgame); for other tactical problems it supports manual lookahead by doing the bookkeeping.

In contrast, Go-playing programs have to solve both strategic and tactical problems before getting a result, and most likely this will lead to compromise: the program does a bit of all, but nothing really well.

Acknowledgments. Many thanks to Jay Nievergelt for his comments on this paper.

REFERENCES

1. K. Baker, The Way to Go. American Go Association (*), 1986.
2. A.L. Zobrist, Feature Extraction and Representation for Pattern Recognition and the Game of Go. Ph.D. Thesis, Univ. of Wisconsin (1970), 1-152 (Microfilm 71-03, 162).
3. B. Wilcox, Zobrist's Program. American Go Journal (*) 13, 4/6 (1978), 48-51.
4. J.L. Ryder, Heuristic Analysis of Large Trees as Generated in the Game of Go. Ph.D. Thesis, Stanford Univ. (1971), 1-298 (Microfilm 72-11, 654).
5. B. Wilcox, Ryder's Program. American Go Journal (*) 14, 1 (1979), 23-28.
6. W. Reitman and B. Wilcox, The Structure and Performance of the Interim.2 Go Program. Proc. IJCAI-6 (Tokyo, August 20-23, 1979), 711-719.
7. B. Wilcox, Reflections on Building Two Go Programs. SIGART Newsletter, 94 (Oct. 1985), 29-43.
8. A. Kierulf and J. Nievergelt, Computer Go: A Smart Board and its Applications. Go World (Ishi Press, Tokyo), 42 (Winter 1985/86), 62-64 & 53-54.
9. T. Ogawa and J. Davies, The Endgame. Ishi Press, Tokyo, 1976.
10. A. Kierulf, Computer Go Bibliography. Computer Go (*), 1 (Winter 1986/87), 17-19 (part 1); 3 (Summer 1987) (part 2).

(*) American Go Association, P.O. Box 397, Old Chelsea Station, New York, NY 10113.

A METHODOLOGY FOR DYNAMIC TASK ALLOCATION IN A MAN-MACHINE SYSTEM*

LYNNE E. PARKER and FRANCOIS G. PIN
Oak Ridge National Laboratory, Center for Engineering Systems Advanced Research, P.O. Box X, Oak Ridge, TN 37831-6364.

ABSTRACT

This paper presents a methodological approach to the dynamic allocation of tasks in a man-machine symbiotic system in the context of dexterous manipulation and teleoperation. This paper addresses symbiosis containing two symbiotic partners which work toward controlling a single manipulator arm for the execution of a series of sequential manipulation tasks. The proposed automated task allocator uses knowledge about the allocation policies of the problem, the available resources and the tasks to be performed to dynamically allocate tasks to the man and the machine.

INTRODUCTION

During the last few decades, there has been a growing awareness and belief that automation-related technologies and intelligent machines will play an increasing role in improving the development and operation of complex and advanced systems. In this context, research and development has taken place on a broad range of technologies aimed at achieving automated systems varying from fully remotely-controlled systems such as advanced teleoperators and servomanipulators to fully autonomous intelligent robots involving artificial intelligence, super-computing, machine vision, and advanced control. Within this large spectrum of technological research, work has recently been initiated on what is proposed to be a new class of automated systems which appear promising for improving the productivity, quality, and safety of operation of advanced systems. This new type of automated system is referred to as "Man-Machine Symbiosis" and would utilize the concepts of machine intelligence and remote-control technology to achieve full man-machine cooperative control and intelligence[1],[5].

The ultimate function of such symbiotic systems would be to dynamically optimize the division of work between the man and the machine and to facilitate their cooperation through shared knowledge, skills, and experiences. The optimization of the man-machine partnership in both the electromotive and intellectual domain would be realized by coupling a dynamic allocation of tasks between the human and the machine with an embedded system learning capability to allow the machine, an intelligent robotic system, to learn new tasks through assimilation of experience and observation of the human[2],[3],[4].

This paper presents a methodological approach to the dynamic allocation of tasks for a man-machine symbiotic system in a simplified case of dexterous manipulation and teleoperation. In this formulation, two symbiotic partners are considered: a human teleoperator and an intelligent robotic system. Both partners work toward controlling a single manipulator arm for

---

*Research sponsored by the Engineering Research Program of the Office of Basic Energy Sciences, of the U.S. Department of Energy, under contract No. DE-AC05-840R21400 with Martin Marietta Energy Systems, Inc.

Methodologies for Intelligent Systems
Z. W. Ras and M. Zemankova, Editors

the execution of a series of sequential manipulation tasks. The following sections outline the characteristics of the specific man-robot symbiot being considered, followed by a description of the required knowledge areas and the generalized task allocation procedure. Refer to Ref. 6 for an example illustrating the results of the task allocation methodology in the context of remote manipulation.

CHARACTERISTICS OF A MAN-MACHINE SYMBIOTIC SYSTEM

The man-machine system addressed in this paper consists of two symbiotic partners, a human teleoperator and an intelligent robot system with its controller, which cooperate to perform a series of sequential manipulation tasks involving a single manipulator arm. To facilitate the division of work between the man and the robot, several automated modules are proposed to be incorporated into the system to perform responsibilities such as task subdivision, analysis, and allocation. Such a scenario can be depicted as shown in Fig. 1.

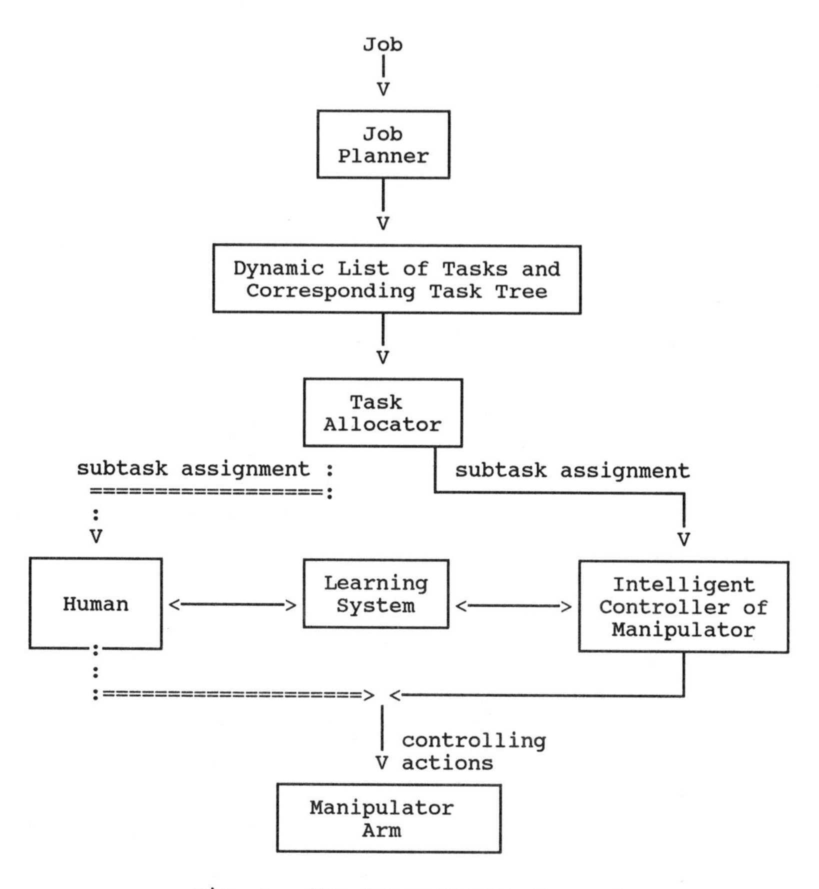

Fig. 1. Man-Robot System Scenario.

A job planner is responsible for decomposing the overall job to be performed (such as INSTALL ELECTRICAL EQUIPMENT) into its component lower-level subtasks (such as FIND WRENCH or GRASP WRENCH), indicating the order in which the subtasks must be performed. The resulting task decomposition tree (discussed in a later section), is passed to the task allocator, which assigns a subtask either to the human or to the intelligent robot controller of the manipulator. The human or the intelligent robot controller then sends controlling actions to the manipulator arm for execution of the subtask. To improve its performance and to increase its range of capabilities, the intelligent robot controller of the manipulator arm must ultimately use an embedded learning system to learn new tasks through assimilation of experience, observation of the human, and direct instruction[2],[3],[4]. In this context, this paper is concerned only with the task allocator and the methodology for allocating tasks in the man-machine symbiotic system. This paper assumes that a complete description of the tasks to be performed is provided to the task allocator by either the human or an automated system.

To determine the necessary characteristics of the task allocator in this symbiotic system, one can first observe that both intelligent resources (the human and the intelligent controller of the manipulator arm) are using the same medium (the manipulator arm) to execute the subtasks. The manipulator arm actuator can receive and respond to commands from a single source at any instant in time. Consequently, the human and the intelligent robot controller cannot command the arm simultaneously or independently. Therefore, the task allocator must deal with the allocation of sequential manipulation tasks, rather than concurrent tasks. However, it is likely that while the human or the machine is performing a subtask with the manipulator arm, other actions are occurring in the background, such as monitoring of the task execution, world modeling, planning, and learning. This aspect is necessary in order for the symbiotic system to function effectively. Nevertheless, as a first step, this work will focus on the sequential task problem of allocating a series of sequential manipulation subtasks to the man and the machine.

Another essential requirement of the task allocator in this man-machine system is its ability to be event-driven, responding to changes in the work constraints, physical environment, or unexpected events by altering the task allocation to adjust to new conditions. This dynamic nature of the task allocator allows the man-machine symbiont to cope with a changing environment, causing the resource most appropriate for performing a subtask to be assigned the subtask[7].

The remainder of this paper will address a task allocation methodology having these characteristics.

DYNAMIC TASK ALLOCATION METHODOLOGY

The purpose of the task allocator in man-machine symbiosis is to attempt to dynamically optimize the division of work between the man and the machine. Since the exact interpretation of "optimal division of work" must be allowed to vary according to the requirements of each individual problem scenario, the task allocator must know what allocation policies are placed on the task allocation, what the requirements of the subtasks are, and information concerning the characteristics of the environment in which the problem is to be solved. The task allocator must also have information about the capabilities of the human and the intelligent robot controller to determine the resource which is most appropriate for performing a subtask in a given scenario. The knowledge about these areas can be categorized into separate knowledge bases which are described in the following sections.

Allocation Policies

The allocation policies are determined by a source external to the task allocator and place performance measures, limitations, restrictions, and/or regulations on the task allocation problem solution. The intent of the allocation policies is to alter the task allocation strategy to adapt to differing problem contexts. The task allocator must adhere to these policies in determining the task allocation. These limitations may prevent the use of certain resources for some subtasks, or may mandate the use of certain resources for other subtasks.

Examples of possible allocation policies are as follows:

- — minimize time of job completion
- — maximize quality of result

The task allocator must know how to handle any allocation policy that is placed on the solution. For example, if the policy is to minimize the time of task completion, the task allocator must compute the estimated time each resource will take to complete a subtask and then assign the subtask to the resource requiring the lesser time. For each application of the task allocator, certain allocation policies are initially in effect while others are ignored. Although this paper only deals with situations having one allocation policy in effect at a time, this methodology has the potential for being extended to handle combinations of several policies for the optimization of the solution.

Resources

In this paper, resources are defined to be intelligent entities (such as humans or computers) which are available for performing subtasks to solve a problem, or to achieve a goal. In this paper, only two resources are considered: a human and an intelligent robot controller. In order to begin the job of task allocation, the task allocator must have information concerning the capabilities of each of the resources. The capabilities of the resources are defined in this paper to be either the abilities the resources have to perform certain physical actions, or the knowledge the resources have of certain objects. The capabilities can be defined as needed for particular applications, and could include physical abilities such as MANIPULATION or VISION, or knowledge of objects, such as WRENCH or BOLT.

The knowledge about the capabilities of the resources is initially given to the task allocator as input. The actual information stored about the capabilities of the resources is directly related to the allocation policies which might at some time be present in the problem scenario. For example, the policy "minimize time of task completion" requires that "timeliness of achievement" factors be provided, while the policy "maximize quality of result" requires that "level of achievement" factors be provided. Additional policies placed on the problem may require the storage of further information on the capabilities of the resources. As explained later, this knowledge of the resources may change in time as tasks are performed, reflecting the acquisition of new knowledge and experience.

Although the knowledge about the capabilities is quantified differently depending upon whether the capability refers to a physical ability or to a knowledge about an object, one evaluation number is obtained for each factor (such as level of achievement or timeliness of achievement) for each capability. The evaluation numbers are then used in determining the appropriate task allocation. If the capability refers to a physical ability, the evaluation number indicates the skill with which the ability is performed, perhaps on a scale from 0 to 10, or from "unacceptable" to "superior". If perhaps on a scale from 0 to 10, or from "unacceptable" to "superior". If the capability refers to a knowledge about an object, the evaluation number indicates how complete the knowledge of that object is, perhaps on a scale from 0 to 10, or from "unknown" to "always known". The lowest value on the scale is reserved to indicate that the resource does not possess the capability. The evaluation number characterizing the effective allocation policy p for capability i of resource x is denoted θ^{x}_{pi}. Thus, if the effective allocation policy p is "maximize the quality of the result", θ^{x}_{pi} gives the level of achievement factor associated with capability i of resource x.

Tasks

A job planner must analyze and decompose the job to be performed into its component tasks, subtasks, and sub-subtasks. The role of the job planner can be fulfilled by either the human or an automated job planning system. This paper assumes that the task breakdown is available as input to the task allocator.

A typical task breakdown tree is shown in Fig. 2.

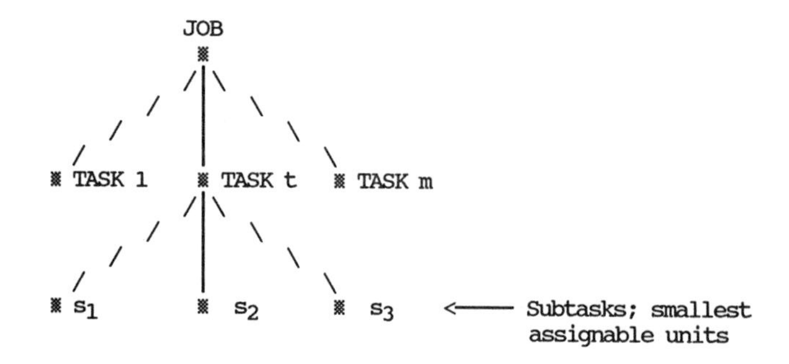

Fig. 2. Typical Task Breakdown Tree.

The job is the highest-level description of a series of related tasks to be performed, such as ASSEMBLE MODULE. The job is decomposed into several tasks, such as INSERT ROD, which must be successfully completed by the resources in order to solve a problem, or to achieve a goal. Each task can be performed entirely by the human, entirely by the robot, or by the human and robot in cooperation. Each task t is subdivided as much as needed into a set Z_t which consists of the smallest assignable units, or subtasks, of that task. These subtasks are the smallest units that can be feasibly assigned to a single resource. The definitions of smallest assignable units, resources, and capabilities are, in general, system and task domain dependent.

In order to allocate the subtasks, the task allocator must know what capabilities are required for the resources to perform the subtasks and any merit factors associated with each capability. Due to the considerable differences between the intelligent robot controller and the human, the capabilities required for one of these resources to perform a subtask may be very different from those required by the other resource. Because of this, the subtasks must be further subdivided for each resource down to the elemental sub-subtasks (ESSTs) which can be characterized by one or more capabilities and merit factors which are independent of the environment and the context of the problem. The concept of an "elemental sub-subtask" is very important since it represents the smallest subdivision of the elements of a task which correlate with the physical mechanics of the actual operation of the symbiotic resources. Figure 3 shows a typical subtask subdivision.

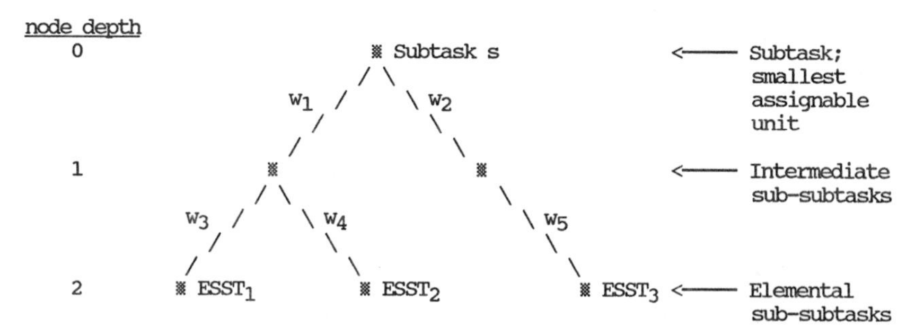

Fig. 3. Typical Subtask Breakdown Trees.

The set C^{sx} is the set of capabilities required for resource x to perform subtask s. This set is obtained by including all of the capabilities required for the lowest-level nodes, or elemental sub-subtasks, in the subtask breakdown tree for resource x. Associated with each capability i in this set is an importance factor f derived as follows:

$$f^{sx}{}_i = \sum_{j=1}^{b^{sx}} \left[\left(\prod_{h=1}^{r^{sx}{}_j} w^{sx}{}_{jh} \right) (m^{sx}{}_{ij}) \right] \quad , \quad \begin{array}{l} 0 \le w^{sx}{}_{jh} \le 1 \\ 0 \le m^{sx}{}_{ij} \le 1 \end{array} \qquad (1)$$

where:

b^{sx} = number of ESSTs in the subtask tree for subtask s of resource x

$r^{sx}{}_j$ = the depth of the jth ESST in the subtask tree s for resource x

$w^{sx}{}_{jh}$ = weight associated with the branch into the node at depth h of the path from the root to the jth ESST of the subtask tree s for resource x

$m^{sx}{}_{ij}$ = the merit factor associated with the ith capability required by the jth ESST of subtask s for resource x

The weight value associated with each branch emanating from a node in the subtask breakdown tree indicate the importance of that branch in the successful performance of the subtask or sub-subtask represented by that node. The merit factor associated with each capability indicates the importance of that capability in the successful performance of the elemental sub-subtask, relative to the other capabilities required by that elemental sub-subtask. At the beginning of the problem execution, these weight values and merit factors have initial values; however, as the subtasks are performed, the job planner can alter the weights or merit factors as necessary after each subtask completion to reflect new knowledge about the tasks. The task allocator would then derive a new allocation based on the adjusted weight values and merit factors.

Determining Task Allocation Recommendation

To derive the task allocation recommendation, the task allocator seeks to determine, for all resources x, the membership of the set T^x_t, which is the set of subtasks of task t which should be performed by resource x. This is done by comprising T^x_t such that, for all subtasks $s \in Z_t$, x gives:

for a maximization allocation policy p:

$$\text{MAX} \left[\sum_{i \in C^{sx}} ({}^{x}{}_{pi})(f^{sx}{}_{i}) \right] \quad , \quad 1 \le x \le n, \quad x_{pi} \ne 0 \tag{2}$$

for a minimization allocation policy p:

$$\text{MIN} \left[\sum_{i \in C^{sx}} ({}^{x}{}_{pi})(f^{sx}{}_{i}) \right] \quad , \quad 1 \le x \le n, \quad x_{pi} \ne 0 \tag{3}$$

where n is the number of resources.

Dynamics of the System

One of the key features of this task allocation methodology is its ability to be event-driven, responding to changes in the information about the allocation policies, resources, or tasks by altering the task allocation. Such a dynamic nature of the task allocation is essential to allow the man-machine symbiont to cope with a changing work context. The dynamic nature of the task allocator is directly related to the information in the knowledge bases. If the information in the knowledge bases never changed, the task allocation would never change. However, in a real-world problem, the information in each of the knowledge bases will be undergoing continual changes to reflect the true state of the problem and the accumulation of experience.

First of all, although the allocation policy is initially set for a particular application, dynamic changes in the work context or environment may cause the allocation policy to be changed. Secondly, as the resources execute the subtasks, the level of achievement factors and the timeliness-of-achievement factors for their capabilities may change, reflecting new knowledge about the resources. Such changes could take place in two ways: through a learning scheme and through monitoring of the resources. The learning scheme would allow the robot to learn and improve its capabilities by observing the human, whereas the monitor of the resources would observe and quantify the resource's performance to determine if there is a proper correlation between the resource and the knowledge about the resource. If not, the resource knowledge base would be corrected. The information in the third knowledge base, the task information, is subject to change during the execution of the subtasks when environmental changes, unexpected events, or human requests or controls occur which require the job planner to update the list of subtasks to be performed. The task allocator will recognize these changes and be able to replan the task allocation appropriately.

CONCLUSIONS AND FUTURE WORK

A methodological approach for dynamically allocating tasks to a human and an intelligent machine involved in a man-machine symbiotic system has been presented. The necessary knowledge areas have been outlined, and the proposed methodology has been shown to allow dynamic reallocation due to changes in the allocation policy or in the capabilities of the human or the robot, as well as to unanticipated events and human requests or controls. Although this methodology was designed in the context of a control of a single manipulator arm to accomplish a series of sequential tasks, the methodology has the potential for being extended to systems including more than two partners, multitasking operations, or multi-policy situations. Future work will include the addition of automated monitoring, automated learning, and automated job planning techniques to the current system.

REFERENCES

1. W. R. Hamel, C. C. Jorgensen, C. R. Weisbin, "Man-Robot Symbiosis: Schemes for the Evolution of Autonomous Systems," ORNL/TM-10396 (in process).
2. C. C. Jorgensen, "Neural Network Recognition of Robot Sensor Graphs using Hypercube Computers," Second Conference on Hypercube Multiprocessors, Sept. 29-Oct. 1, 1986, Knoxville, TN.
3. C. C. Jorgensen, "Neural Network Representation of Sensor Graphs for Autonomous Robot Navigation," Presented at IEEE International Conference on Neural Networks, June 21-24, 1987, San Diego, CA.
4. C. C. Jorgensen, C. Matheus, "Catching Knowledge in Neural Nets", AI Expert, 1 (1986).
5. J. C. R. Licklider, "Man-Computer Symbiosis," IRE Trans. on Human Factors in Electronics, HFE-1, 4-11 (1960).
6. L. E. Parker, F. G. Pin, "Dynamic Task Allocation for a Man-Machine Symbiosis System," ORNL/TM-10397.
7. W. B. Rouse, "Human-Computer Interaction in the Control of Dynamic Systems," Computing Surveys, 13, 1, 71-99 (1979).

KNOWLEDGE STRUCTURES FOR INTELLIGENT INTERACTION

Brian R. Gaines

Knowledge Science Institute, University of Calgary
Calgary, Alberta, CANADA T2N 1N4

ABSTRACT

This paper presents systemic foundations for complex systems of computers and people operating together to pursue common goals. A general systems analysis is developed based on the knowledge structures underlying the distinctions between technology and people, and between computers and non-programmed technology. This is used to show how various forms of analogy and abstraction may be used to derive design principles for person-computer interaction. The systemic analysis is extended to include relations between system structure and behavior, and used to develop a hierarchical model of the protocols in complex person-computer systems.

INTRODUCTION

We are now in the fifth generation computing era with its emphasis on complex, knowledge-based systems involving close person-computer interaction [13,21].The multi-task, multi-user, multi-modal systems of the fourth and fifth generations go beyond human factors knowledge based on the textual display and keyboard technology of yesterday. If we continue to rely on empirical knowledge based on studies of the past we shall never be equipped to deal with the systems of the present let alone those of the future.

New technologies create new problems but they also often provide new means to solve them. The development of knowledge-based systems has focused attention on techniques for *knowledge engineering*, the acquisition of knowledge from human experts and its transfer to expert systems [14]. Effective techniques for knowledge engineering are based on the observation that there are common patterns in the way in which we model the world, explain phenomena, anticipate events and communicate knowledge. These patterns are part of the process of human understanding and may be termed general systems principles [16]. Their significance is that, since they underlie physical laws and social conventions, their identification in particular modeling schema enables us to analyze those schema in a universal framework.

The extraction of these systemic principles is straightforward if we examine the systems of *distinctions* being used in the evaluation and protocol methodologies. As Brown has noted, by analyzing the distinctions made in any discipline, "we can begin to reconstruct, with an accuracy and coverage that appear almost uncanny, the basic forms underlying linguistic, mathematical, physical and biological science, and can begin to see how the familiar laws of our own experience follow inexorably from the original act of severance" [3].

ABSTRACTION AND ANALOGY

When people face new situations where empirical data and models are lacking, there are various patterns of reasoning that they use. One is argument by analogy based on relating the new situation to known situations of different types but similar structures. Another is argument by abstraction based on discarding specific features of the situation and analyzing in terms of basic laws and systemic principles. As Lakoff and Johnson have noted the linguistic metaphors resulting from these analogies and abstractions can become so much a part of our thinking and vocabulary that we are no longer aware of their metaphorical nature [20]. The terminology of computing abounds with words that were originally specific to human knowledge processes but are now used for equipment. We forget the origins of these words and the metaphorical thinking from which they derive.

Analogy and abstraction and both be misleading if, for example, similarity in partial structure does not extend to further structure or key elements of the situation are lost through abstraction. In analyzing person-computer interaction it is important to establish what are the

Methodologies for Intelligent Systems
Z. W. Ras and M. Zemankova, Editors

critical characteristics of a person and what are those of a computer. How are the differentiated from one another and from other forms of system? Habermas has emphasized the essential differences between the dynamics of society and that of physical systems [18].

The "laws" that govern human behavior are largely conventions embedded in our society and propagated through our culture. They do not have the necessity of the laws underlying physical systems and their analysis differs in many ways from those of physical systems. Human beings create their future through acts of choice that are constrained by their forward-looking intentions. Physical systems unroll their future through acts of necessity that are determined by their previous states.

In person-computer interaction we are dealing with phenomena of the life-world [25] which are essentially different from those of the physical world and cannot be encompassed by causal models [28]. We are also dealing with phenomena of computing which have a physical, causal basis. However, we have to remember that the computing was programmed by people and hence also involves human choice within the framework of the life-world. We need a systemic model that accounts for these essential distinctions, differentiating people from technology and computing from non-programmed physical systems, while supporting the analogies and abstractions that we use in analyzing and designing person-computer systems.

Popper's *3 worlds theory* [22] can be used to provide basic systemic foundations for the distinctions underlying the physical processes, human activities, and information technologies. He bases his theory on Bolzano's notion of "truths in themselves" in contradistinction to "those thought processes by which a man may grasp truths", proposing that "thoughts in the sense of contents or statements in themselves and thoughts in the sense of thought processes belong to two entirely different worlds" [24], and making the three-fold distinction: "If we call the world of things—of physical objects—the first world and the world of subjective experience the second world we may call the world of statements in themselves the third world (world 3)." These concepts capture the differences between physical systems and people, and the role of abstraction in moving the distinctions into a third realm regardless of source.

Figure 1 shows the existential hypotheses underlying Popper's 3 worlds as a knowledge structure based on very general distinctions made about distinctions. It introduces a 'World 0' of distinctions in their own right before Popper's criteria are applied. This world is one where distinctions are made without reference to any criteria except that they are useful. It captures the notions of value and of the underlying anarchy that Feyerabend sees in the scientific process [6]. Gaines has argued that this any distinction generates a system and hence that World 0 as defined here is that of general systems [10].

- World 0 arises from the hypothesis that there exist distinctions
  - —this defines a world of *systems*
  - —a key concept is that of *anarchy*, that distinctions may be made freely
  - —the conceptual framework involved is that of *axiology*, that distinctions have value
  - —truth in this world is *utilitarian*, that distinctions made are useful
  - —inference is *pragmatic*, based on chains of reasoning that appear to work
- World 1 arises from the hypothesis that there exist *necessary* distinctions
  - —this defines a world of *physical systems*
  - —a key concept is that of *actuality*, that the distinctions made are actual
  - —the conceptual framework involved is that of *epistemology*, that the distinctions have to be drawn from the actual world
  - —truth in this world is by *correspondence*, that the distinctions made correspond to the properties of physical systems
  - —inference is *causal*, based on chains of physical cause and effect
- World 2 arises from the hypothesis that there exist *chosen* distinctions
  - —this defines a world of *mental systems*
  - —a key concept is that of *agency*, that distinctions have a maker
  - —the conceptual frameworks involved are those of *psychology and sociology*, that distinctions exist in the mental worlds of individuals and groups
  - —truth in this world is *performative,* that the distinctions chosen will be continue to be chosen
  - —inference is *conventionalist*, based on accepted chains of reasoning that are chosen within a culture

• World 3 arises from the hypothesis that there exist distinctions *independent* of their source
  —this defines a world of *coherent systems*
  —a key concept is that of *abstraction*, that systems of distinctions have their own existence
  —the conceptual framework involved is that of *ontology*, that some distinctions are made independent of any criteria other than intrinsic structure
  —truth in this world is by *coherence*, that the systems of distinctions have an acceptable intrinsic structure
  —inference is *structuralist*, based on chains of reasoning that conform to the structure

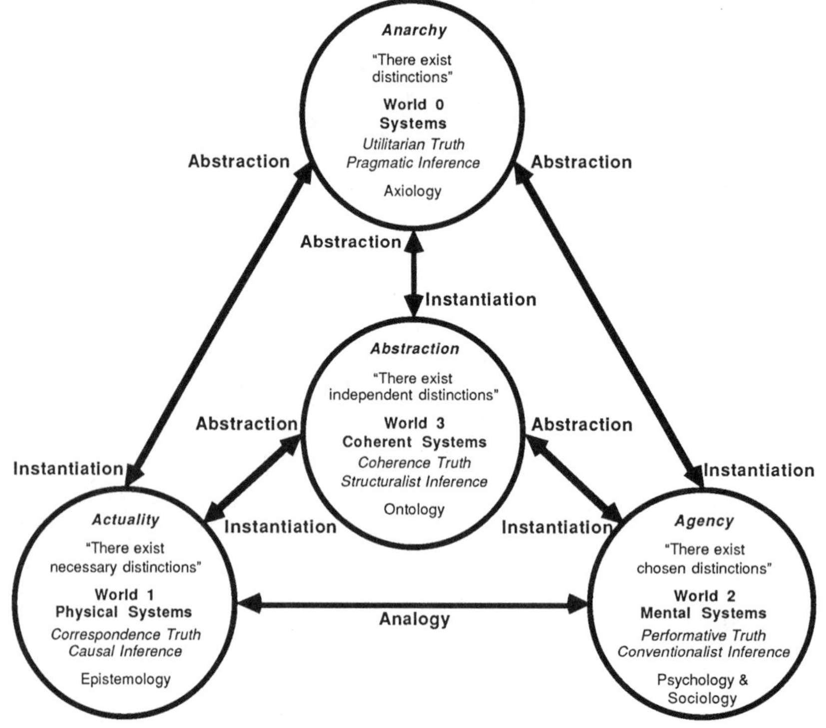

Fig.1 Anarchy, abstraction, actuality, and agency as systemic distinctions

The knowledge structure of Figure 1 shows how the the worlds relate through *abstraction* and *instantiation*. It also shows the *analogy* between worlds 1 and 2 when we attribute agency to the causal dynamics of physical objects or necessity to the social conventions of human activity.

Figure 2 extends the knowledge structure to show equipment as an instance of a physical system, people as an instance of mental systems, and computers as an instance of both physical and mental systems, inheriting properties through both paths. The peculiar property of electronic digital computers is that they are the archetype of deterministic causal systems, modeled in their behavior as finite-state automata whose next state and output are precisely determined by their current states and inputs.

However, they are also programmed devices where the transition tables of the automaton are completely under the control of people—what computers do is what we chose them to do. Hence, they are also the archetype of performative, conventional systems, modeled in their behavior as the intentional artefacts of people, and whose next state and output are in major part determined by open choices made in programming.

This dual nature of computing systems underlies many of the problems and controversies in person-computer interaction. The computer is a technological system and it may be advisable to present it to its users as such, avoiding animistic considerations. However, the behavior of

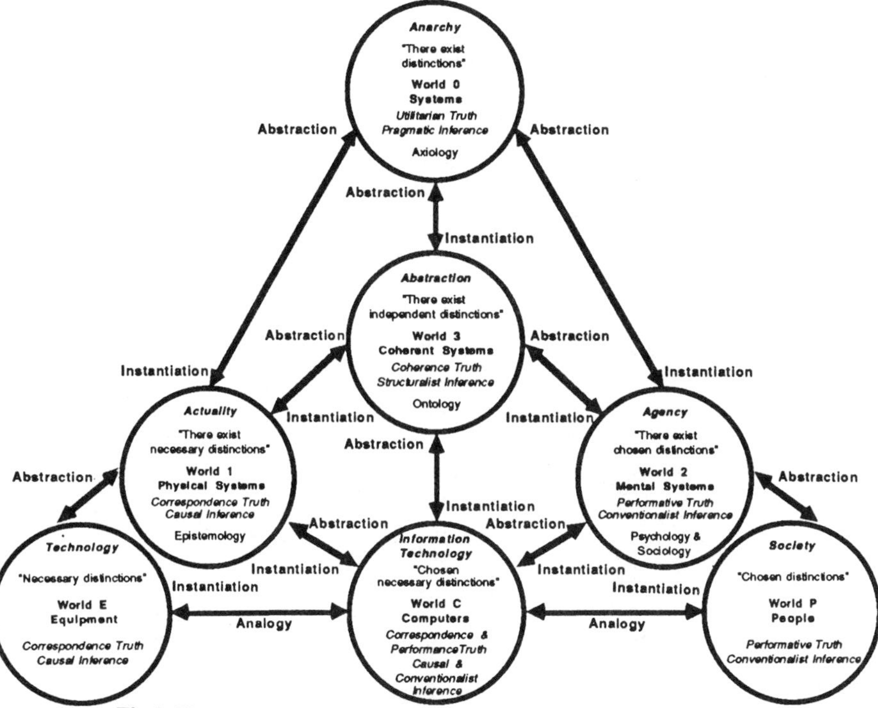

Fig.2 Knowledge structures for human-computer interaction

the computer is prescribed by people and this underlying prescription may also be evident to the user. The value systems and inter-personal attitudes of the system designer and programmer may have become embedded in the system behavior, making an animistic perspective unavoidable.

The performative truth and conventionalist inference aspect of computers is very evident in rules for programming effective person-computer dialog. For example, "The system should be consistent in operation—the commands should always do the same thing throughout—the information presentation should always mean the same thing throughout" and "The system should be uniform in operation—the facilities which users have learned to use in one part of the package should be available to them in other parts if they might reasonably expect this" [15], are both example of performative truths allowing inference from reasonable conventions.

The analogies between computers, people and equipment shown in Figure 2 are particularly interesting. If the conventions of the life-world become widely accepted in a culture then they assume the same status as the necessary distinctions of the physical world and the behavior of people within a culture may appear as completely causal. In informal terms, one may be just as hurt attempting to break a moral convention as attempting to walk through a brick wall. In person-computer interaction the skilled operator may have highly practiced patterns of behavior that may be modeled through causal dynamics. He is no longer making choices at the lower levels of functioning. This is the basis for "transfer of training" phenomena when automatic functioning developed for one system is carried over to another where it may result in inappropriate choices. It should also be noted that all technology has some aspects of human choice embodied in it so that the distinction between technology in general and information technology shown in Figure 2 is not a hard boundary.

The computer is also shown in Figure 2 as an instance of a World 3 system, that is an abstract entity defined in terms of its coherent structure. Category-theoretic models of software systems exemplify the possibility for a high degree of abstraction while still capturing essential features of computing systems [17]. Such models also gives foundations for analogical relations between computing systems, and also for the person-computer analogy [7].

KNOWLEDGE STRUCTURES FOR EQUIPMENT, COMPUTERS & PEOPLE

The bases for the analogies between computers and people and between computers and other technical equipment show up clearly in Figure 2. The bases of the abstractions that treat both computers and people as general systems are also apparent. Figure 3 illustrates how these analogies and abstractions give rise to a variety of models of person-computer interaction which have been previously noted as major sources of information about, and insight into, the analysis and design of person-computer systems.

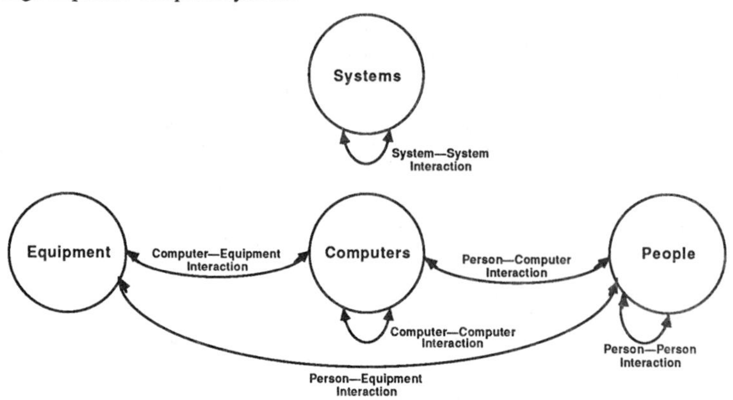

Fig.3 Abstraction and analogies in the analysis of person-computer interaction

System-System Interaction

At the abstract level of system-system interaction there are many system-theoretic principles that are instantiated in the situation where one system is a person and the other a computer. Wiener emphasized this in his development of cybernetics as the study of "communication and control in men and machines" [29], and many principles of communication theory and control theory apply directly to person-computer interaction. For example, the dialog rule that "the user should dominate the computer" [11] derives from a stability-theoretic result in control theory, that two coupled systems with similar time constants may oscillate unstably around their intended equilibrium state: the person modeling a computer and adapting to it while the computer is modeling the person and adapting to him is a potential source of mutual instability. General systemic principles at the abstraction level interact with more specific considerations at the instantiation level. For example, the dialog rule "avoid acausality" [11] has a system-theoretic foundation in that causal modeling systems generate meaningless models of systems with even slight acausalities. However, to apply this principle we have to know that people are causal modelers [8], and we would not regard the rule as significant unless we knew that time-sharing system generate apparently random delay distributions.

Computer-Equipment Interaction

The analogy from people to physical systems enables person-computer interaction to be seen to be analogous to interfacing a computer to another system such as a piece of equipment. The design principles applicable to computer-equipment interfaces are well known and carry over to person-computer dialog. Problems arise because the system to which the computer is to be interfaced already exists and is not another programmable computer. We may to take it as it is and design an interface that copes with its peculiarities. The dialog rule "use the user's model" [11] derives from this, that the dialog engineer should identify the existing interface and attempt to emulate it rather than change it. Problems also commonly arise through noise at the interface and the designer attempts both to provide a low-noise channel and to provide error-detection and correction for unavoidable noise. In person-computer interaction such noise may arise through lack of clarity in information presentation giving rise to perceptual errors in one direction, mis-keying giving rise to errors in the other direction, and so on. The dialog rule "validate data on entry" [11] is a principle of communication over a noisy channel.

Computer-Computer Interaction

The analogy from people to computers enables person-computer interaction to be seen to be analogous to computer-computer interaction. It is then possible to define protocols that it is reasonable to expect any programmable system to be able to implement. The Open System Interconnection standard [4] is particularly interesting because it hierarchically structures computer-computer protocols for networks in a way that may have relevance for person-computer protocols. For example, dialog engineering rules may be seen as defining a "human protocol" [26]. The concept of an open system is itself relevant because it expresses objectives for computer networks that are equally applicable to people using those networks. The aim is to allow integrated systems to be formed from multiple components not all from one vendor and not all installed at the same time [12]. The OSI concept is that the network is open to all systems that conform in their communications with certain well-defined protocols. In human terms the protocols may be seen as social norms for the behavior of members of a club; anyone may join provide they agree to conform to these norms. Taylor has applied such protocol concepts to the analysis of person-computer dialog as a hierarchical communications system [27].

Person-Equipment Interaction

The analogy from computers to physical systems enables person-computer interaction to be seen to be analogous to the classic case of man-machine interaction. Consideration of people interacting with equipment has been treated as a branch of applied psychology termed ergonomics that arose, under the same pressures as computer technology, out of World War II studies of pilots, gunners and so on. There is a wealth of results on general problems of human skills, training, its transfer between different learning situations, the effects of fatigue, and so on, that is immediately applicable to person-computer interaction. While interactive computers were used primarily as programming and data entry systems these effects were not major considerations. However, as computer-based interfaces became increasingly the norm for a wide variety of human activities the classic results of applied psychology and ergonomics have become increasingly important. The novelty of the computer should not blind us to commonality with much earlier equipment. We do not have the time and effort to waste on rediscovering what is already known.

Person-Person Interaction

The analogy from computers to people, enables person-computer interaction to be seen to be analogous to person-person interaction, that is normal linguistic interaction from which the terms human-computer "conversation" and "dialog" in computing terminology have been generalized. Modern linguistic theory has become increasingly concerned with the interaction between participants in a dialog, rather than a view of linguistic output as a predefined stream to be decoded [1]. This provides a rich source of models for person-computer interaction, particularly as artificial intelligence techniques take us closer to emulating people and their language behavior. There are also useful analogies of casual users in transactional analysis of the behavior of strangers meeting, for example "What do you say after you say hello?" [2]. Taylor notes that many of the principles of language such as scoping and pronomial reference are general principles of communication that occur in graphic/gesture dialog with computers that involves no textual interaction [27].

SYSTEM ORIGINS AND ACTIVITY

The principles underlying Figure 3 provide systemic foundations for the forms of reasoning by analogy and abstraction that are commonly used in the analysis and design of person-computer systems. To develop these concepts more formally and provide a framework for the overall dynamics of participant systems, we need to introduce a further distinction, that between the activity and the origins of a system, between its behavior and its structure. In abstract terms the behavior of a system provides a description of what the system does, and the structure of a system provides a description of what the system is. One of the most important problems of system theory is the analysis of the relations between behavior and structure—in one direction, given the structure of a system, to derive its behavior—in the other direction, given the behavior of a system, to derive its structure. In the study of physical systems, mathematical techniques have been developed for moving in both directions with causal models [9,19], that is interrelating the necessities of World 1 behavior and structure. However, as already noted, integrated computing systems involve the choice behavior of people and hence show phenomena of the life-world which are essentially different from those of the physical world and cannot be encompassed by causal models.

The dynamics of human behavior are best modelled as those of an *anticipatory system* [23], enhancing its survival by modeling the world, both passively and actively, in order to better anticipate the future. This corresponds to the choice component of World 2 phenomena, that agents are not bound by rigid necessity but can plan and chose certain aspects of their behavior. Figure 4 shows an analysis of the relations between a system, its origins and its activities, when the *actuality—agency* distinction of Figure 1 is also taken into account. The origins of a system have two components: its *causal structure* relating to how it was created; and its *anticipatory structure* relating to why it was created. The activities of a system also have two components: its *causal behavior* relating to how it carries out its activity; and its *anticipatory behavior* relating to why it carries out its activity.

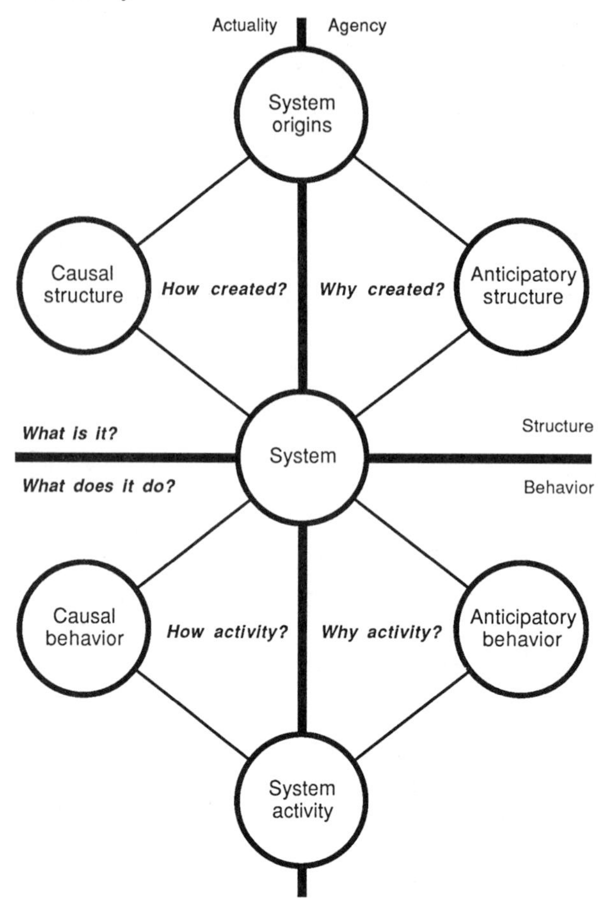

Fig.4 System origins and activity in terms of actuality and agency

The basic distinctions of *actuality—agency* and *structure—behavior* are sufficient to define the virtual machine hierarchy fundamental to computing, and to account for its technical and human components and their relations. Figure 5 fills in Figure 4 to show how the levels of virtual machine arise from the basic distinctions.

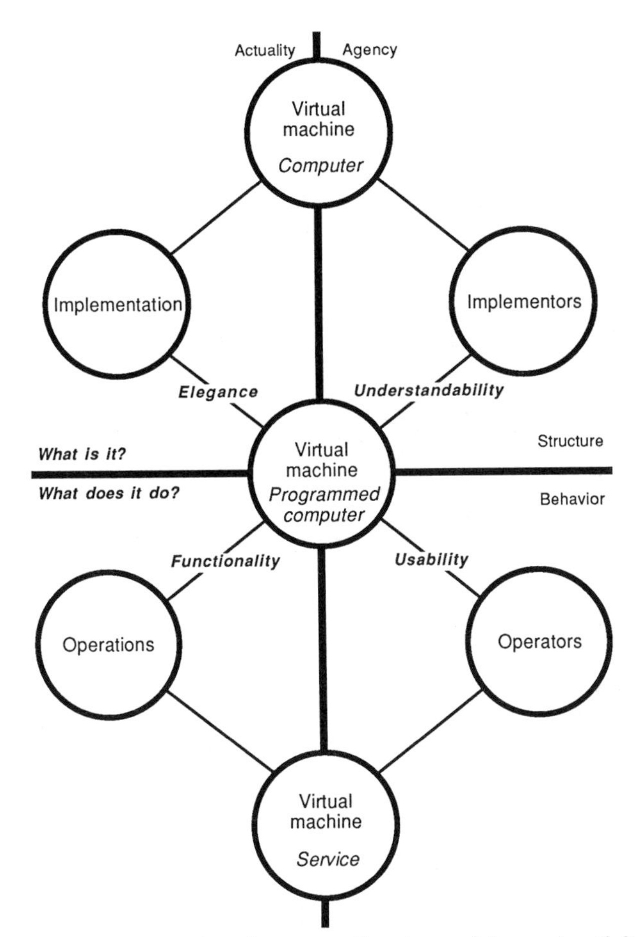

Fig.5 Virtual machines in terms of system origins and activity

The origins of any computer-based service are that a *virtual machine*, a computing system, has been programmed by agents, the *implementors*, to create an actuality, the *implementation*. This results in a second virtual machine, the programmed computing system. The activities of the computer-based service are that a *virtual machine*, a programmed computing system, is being operated by agents, the *operators*, to create an actuality, the *operations*. This results in a third virtual machine, the service itself. The relations between the central virtual machine and its structural and behavioral components represent fundamental concepts in system implementation and operation [5]:

- *elegance* considerations, capturing the notion of efficiency in design, concern the relation between the system virtual machine and the underlying resource with which it is implemented—this is another virtual machine capturing the characteristics of the high-level language, operating system, and so on, used in implementation;
- *understandability* considerations, capturing the notion of comprehensibility in design, concern the relation between the system virtual machine and the implementors who created it;
- *functionality* considerations, capturing the notion of capabilities provided, concern the relation between the system virtual machine and the tasks for with which it is being implemented.
- *usability* considerations, capturing the notion of capabilities suitably interfaced, concern the relation between the system virtual machine and the operators who use it.

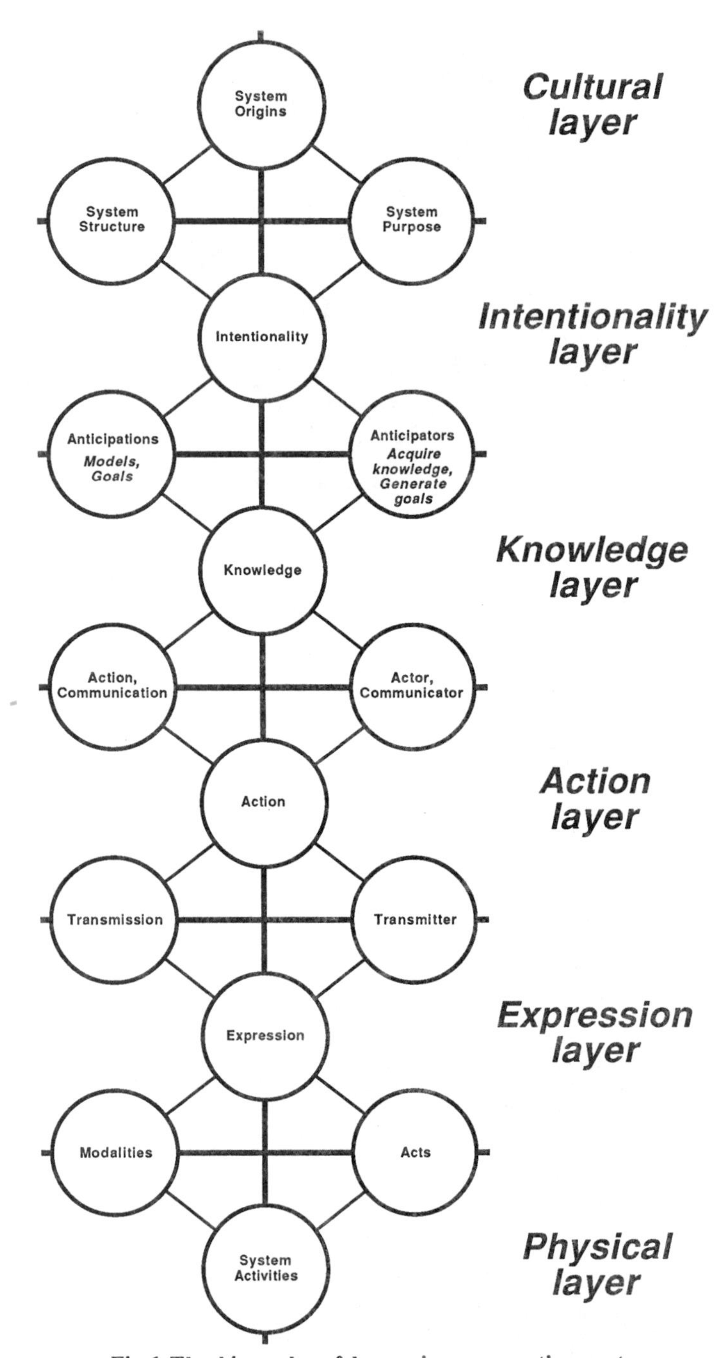

Fig.6 The hierarchy of layers in a computing system

The logic underlying Figures 4 and 5 may be iterated to interpolate as much detail as required between the upper and lower levels—what is "activity" at one level becomes "structure" for the lower level. Figure 6 shows an analysis of the key features of a computer system in terms of six layers:

- At the top level the overall computer system originates in terms of purpose and structure as part of the culture within which it embedded. This *cultural layer* captures the milieu within which the system has been generated and can itself be subject to detailed analysis.
- At the next level the activities generated through this structure and purpose lead to a system of intentionality in which anticipatory activity leads to the acquisition of knowledge, or models of the world, and the generation of goals. This *intentionality* layer captures the anticipatory nature of an intelligent system in supporting its survival through prediction and action.
- At the next level the activities generated through anticipation lead to actions and communications—a linguistic distinction between activities directed to World 1 effects and World 2 effects, respectively. This *knowledge* layer captures the internal processes supporting the modeling and control activities of an anticipatory system.
- At the next level the activities generated through action and communication have to be transmitted to some external medium. This *action* layer captures the internal processes supporting the interfacing of an anticipatory system to the world.
- At the next level the activities generated through transmission have to be expressed in such a way as to have the desired effect in the world. This *expression* layer captures the internal processes supporting the encoding of actions and communications.
- At the lowest level the activities generated through expression exist physically in the external world. This *physical* layer captures the external effects of the activities of an anticipatory system.

It is interesting to relate the iterated levels of Figure 6 back to the terminology of Figure 5:

- First, consider Figure 6 as a model of a person. Systemically, the culture is the 'implementor' of the person, taking the genetic 'virtual machine' and socializing it to have intentions and knowledge that conform with the purpose of a particular society. The intentions of the person are carried out by the formation of anticipatory systems that acquire knowledge and generate goals. These in turn implement goal-directed actors or communicators, which themselves implement processes to transmit the activities of the actors to the world, ultimately as sequences of acts that are directly expressed in the physical world.
- Second, consider Figure 6 as a model of a computer system, an intelligent integrated system. The diagram from bottom up represents the evolution of computer technology, from the physical device technology to carry out acts, through the programmed control of action, through the knowledge-based derivation of action in fifth-generation systems, through the goal-creating activities of intentionally-specified systems in future-generation computing, to the origins of information technology in our culture at the top level.

Figure 7 extends Figure 6 to multiple systems showing the virtual circuits in, and between, two people communicating through a computer system. What is particularly interesting about this diagram is that the same distinctions, terminology and model are being applied to the people, their interactions with each other, their interface to the information technology, and its interface to other information technology. The same systems principles apply to the psychology, sociology, human-computer interaction, and computer-computer interaction because computing systems have the dual identity shown in Figure 6. They are both technological and humanistic systems and it is human component, the choice available in programming, that determines their roles and behavior in interacting with people.

CONCLUSIONS

Complex interactive systems are being built and, despite many problems, they will be made to work because they are needed to deal with some of the very complex activities necessary to our society. Conventional empirical studies of human-computer interaction based on single users operating at standard workstations do not, and cannot, give adequate foundations for the design and analysis of participant systems. We have to go back to the systemic foundations of people, computing and person-computer interaction and develop new models that can encompass the problems and design considerations of complex interactive systems. The analysis developed in this paper is foundational and yet does provide an adequate framework within which to analyze the structure and operation of experimental participant systems developed to date.

Establishing knowledge structures for the computer and human components of complex systems provides an operational framework within which to express specifications, designs, implementations and evaluations. The knowledge structures can be simply and naturally expressed within an object-orientated expert system shell and then applied to design, decision-making and simulation. Specific systems become represented as particular instantiations of the general knowledge structure and analogical relations between systems can be formally expressed as inheritance rules in the knowledge hierarchy. The knowledge structures are available in overt form, yet they are not frozen but can be simply updated. The consequences of changes in the structures can be immediately evaluated in terms of their impact of past case histories and future designs. The development of complex intelligent integrated systems requires the use of intelligent tools with the maximum power available. Well-founded knowledge structures for human-computer interaction provide us with computer-aided design and computer-aided manufacturing tools for complex systems.

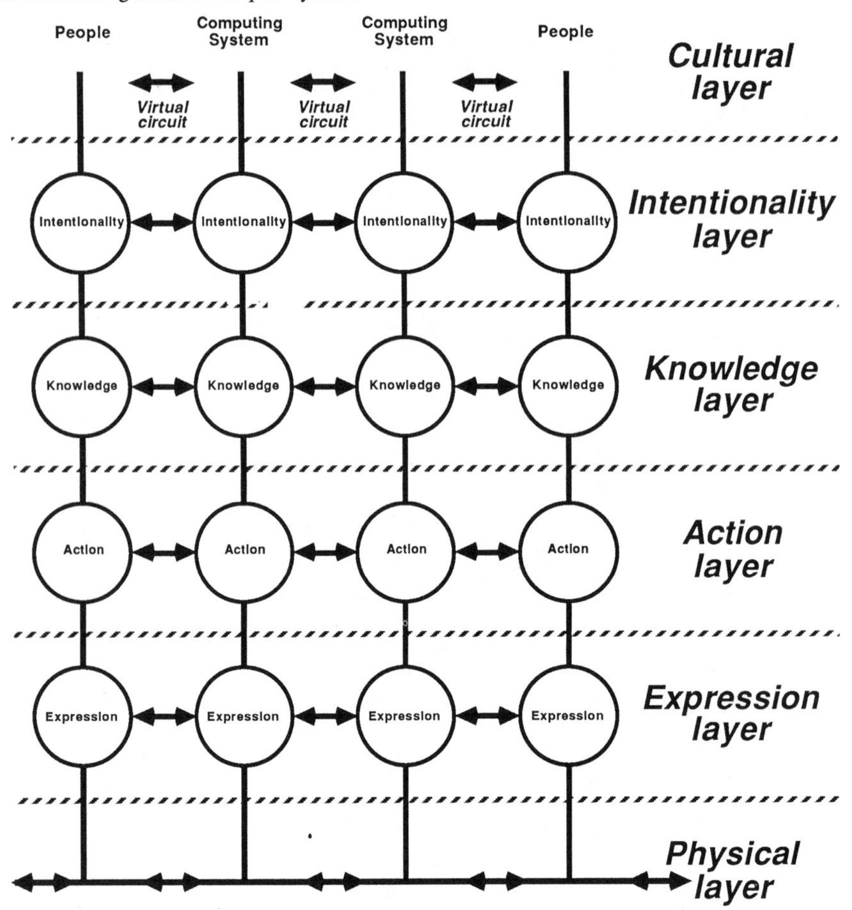

Fig.7 Virtual circuits between layers in computing systems

ACKNOWLEDGEMENTS

Financial assistance for the studies on which it is based has been made available by the National Sciences and Engineering Research Council of Canada.

REFERENCES

1. Bennett, J. **Linguistic Behaviour**. Cambridge, (Cambridge University Press 1976).
2. Berne, E. **What Do You Do After You Say Hello?**. (Andre Deutsch, London 1974).
3. Brown, G.S. **Laws of Form**. (George Allen & Unwin, London 1969).
4. Day, J.D. & Zimmerman, H. The OSI reference model. **Proceedings IEEE, 71**(12), 1334-1340 (1983).
5. Edwards, J.L. & Mason, J.A. Evaluating the intelligence in dialogue systems. **International Journal of Man-Machine Studies, 27** (1986).
6. Feyerabend, P. **Against Method**. NLB, London 1975).
7. Gaines, B.R. Analogy categories, virtual machines and structured programming. Goos, G. & Hartmanis, J., Eds. **GI—5.Jahrestagung. Lecture Notes in Computer Science, 34**, 691-699. (Springer Verlag, Berlin 1975).
8. Gaines, B.R. On the complexity of causal models. **IEEE Transactions on Systems, Man & Cybernetics, SMC-6**(1), 56-59 (1976).
9. Gaines, B.R. System identification, approximation and complexity. **International Journal of General Systems, 3**, 145-174 (1977).
10. Gaines, B.R. General systems research: quo vadis? Gaines, B.R., Ed. **General Systems 1979**. Vol. 24, pp. 1-9. (Society for General Systems Research, Kentucky 1980).
11. Gaines, B.R. The technology of interaction—dialogue programming rules. **International Journal of Man-Machine Studies, 14**(1), 133-150 (1981).
12. Gaines, B.R. From word processing to image processing in office systems. **Proceedings of International Electrical, Electronics Conference and Exposition, IEEE 83CH1955-4**, 622-625 (1983).
13. Gaines, B.R. Perspectives on fifth generation computing. **Oxford Surveys in Information Technology, 1**, 1-53 (1984).
14. Gaines, B.R. Foundations of knowledge engineering. Bramer, M.A., Ed. **Research and Development in Expert Systems III**. pp.13-24. (Cambridge University Press, 1986).
15. Gaines, B.R. & Shaw, M.L.G. (1984). **The Art of Computer Conversation: A New Medium for Communication**. (Prentice Hall, New Jersey 1984).
16. Gaines, B.R. & Shaw, M.L.G. Hierarchies of distinctions as generators of system theories. Smith, A.W., Ed. **Proceedings of the Society for General Systems Research International Conference**. pp. 559-566. (Intersystems, California 1985).
17. Goguen, J.A. & Meseguer, J. Programming with parametrized abstract objects in OBJ. **Theory and Practice of Programming Technology**. (North-Holland, Amsterdam, 1983).
18. Habermas, J. **The Theory of Communicative Action: Reason and the Rationalization of Society**. (Beacon Press, Boston 1981).
19. Klir, G.J. **Architecture of Systems Problem Solving**, (Plenum Press, New York 1985).
20. Lakoff, G. & Johnson, M. **Metaphors We Live By**. (Chicago University Press 1980).
21. Moto-oka, T., Ed. **Fifth Generation Computer Systems**. (North-Holland, Amsterdam 1982).
22. Popper, K.R. Epistemology without a knowing subject. Van Rootselaar, B., Ed. **Logic, Methodology and Philosophy of Science III**. pp. 333-373. (North-Holland, Amsterdam, 1968).
23. Rosen, R. **Anticipatory Systems**. (Pergamon, Oxford, 1985).
24. Schilpp, P.A., Ed. **The Philosophy of Karl Popper**. (Open Court, Illinois 1974).
25. Schutz, A. & Luckmann, T. **The Structures of the Life-World**. (Heinemann, London 1973).
26. Shaw, M.L.G. & Gaines, B.R. Does the human component in a network have a protocol?. **Proceedings of International Electrical, Electronics Conference and Exposition, IEEE 83CH1955-4**, 546-549 (1983).
27. Taylor, M.M. Layered protocols for computer-human dialogue: I Principles. **International Journal of Man-Machine Studies, 27** (1987).
28. Ulrich, W. **Critical Heuristics of Social Planning**. (Haupt, Bern 1983).
29. Wiener, N. **Cybernetics**. (MIT Press, Cambridge, Massachusetts 1948).

INDEX